The Best Bed & Breakfast in England, Scotland & Wales

2001–2002

Sigourney Welles

Jill Darbey

Joanna Mortimer

The finest Bed & Breakfast accommodations in the British Isles

from the Scottish Hebrides to

London's Belgravia

Country Houses, Town Houses, City Apartments, Manor Houses, Village Cottages, Farmhouses, Castles

U.K.H.M. Publishing, London, U.K.

The Globe Pequot Press, Guilford, Connecticut, U.S.A.

Library of Congress Catalog Card Number: 91-074158

U.S. ISBN 0-7627-0879-4

Typeset by U.K.H.M. Publishing Ltd., London.
Printed and bound in China.
Produced by Phoenix Offset Ltd.

U.K.H.M. Publishing Ltd. P.O. Box 2070, London W12 8QW, England. U.K.

Contents

Foreword

Bed & Breakfast has suddenly become the fashionable way to travel. The secret has escaped & thousands of people are discovering for themselves that it is possible to combine high quality accommodation with friendly, personal attention at very reasonable prices. The New York Times said about us that "...after an unannounced inspection of rooms booked through The Worldwide Bed & Breakfast Association it is clear that the standards of comfort & cleanliness are exemplary ...at least as good as in a five star hotel & in most cases, better, reflecting the difference between sensitive hosts taking pride in their homes & itinerant hotel staff doing as little as they can get away with..."

Discerning travellers are turning away from the impersonal hotels with the expensive little refridgerators & microwave breakfasts in each room. How much nicer to have a real English breakfast to begin the day, enough to keep you going until evening. Many of our houses will provide dinner too - often the hostess will be a Cordon Bleu cook & the price will be within your range. We try to provide the best accommodation possible within a wide range of prices, some as little as £15.00 per person per night, whilst others will be up to £60.00 per person per night. The choice is yours, but you can be certain that each will be the best available in that particular area of the country at that price.

Our inspectors are out & about visiting our homes to ensure that standards are maintained. We encourage everyone to use the recommendations & complaints page at the back of the book. Let us know your opinion of the accommodation or inform us of any delightful homes you may have come across & would like to recommend for future inclusion.

In order to avoid the classification trap, which we feel is invidious, we encourage you to read about each home, what they offer & their respective price range, so that you find the one that best suits your expectations. Our hosts in turn offer hospitality in their own unique style, so each home naturally retains its individuality & interest. We have found this to be a very successful recipe which often leads to lasting friendships.

Bed & Breakfast really is a marvellous way to travel, meeting a delightful cross section of fellow travellers with whom to exchange information & maybe the address of ...that lovely little place which was discovered by chance and which serves the most delicious dinner or... the best route to take to a particular farmhouse but make sure you get there by 5 o'clock so that you're in time to watch the evening milking...

This is the fun & real pleasure that is part of Bed & Breakfasting. Once you've tried it you will be a dedicated Best Bed & Breakfaster.

How to use this Guide

To get the full benefits of staying at our Bed & Breakfast homes it is important to appreciate how they differ from hotels, so both hosts & guests know what to expect.

Arrival & Departure

These times are more important to a family than to hotel desk clerks, so your time of arrival (E.T.A.) is vital information when making a reservation either with the home directly or with one of our agencies. This becomes even more important to your reception if you intend travelling overnight & will be arriving in the early morning. So please have this information & your flight number ready when you book your rooms. **At most B & Bs the usual check-in time is 6 P.M. & you will be expected to check out by 10 A.M. on the morning of departure.** These arrangements do vary from home to home. The secret to an enjoyable visit is to let your hosts know as much about your plans as possible & they will do their best to meet your requirements.

Other personal requests

There are a few other details that you should let your hosts know when planning your Bed & Breakfast trip that will make everyone much happier during your visit. Do you smoke? Would you prefer to be in a non-smoking home? Do you suffer from any allergies? Some families have cats, dogs, birds & other pets in the house....Can you make it up a flight of stairs? Would you prefer the ground floor? Do you have any special dietary requirements? Will you be staying for dinner?
Do you prefer a private bathroom or are you prepared to share facilities? Do you prefer a shower instead of a bath? The ages of any children travelling.
In all these cases let your host know what you need & the details can be arranged before you arrive rather than presenting a problem when you are shown to your rooms.

Prices

The prices quoted throughout the guide are the *minimum* per person per night for two sharing. Single occupancy usually attracts a supplement. Prices will increase during busy seasons. You should always confirm the prevailing rate when you make a reservation.

Facilities

The bathroom & toilet facilities affect the prices. Sharing is the cheapest, private is a little more costly & en-suite carries a premium.

Descriptions

Rooms are described as follows:
Single: 1 bed (often quite small).
Double: 1 large bed (sometimes King or Queensize).
Twin: 2 separate single beds.
Four-poster: a King or Queen size bed with a canopy above supported by four corner posts.
Bathrooms and toilets are described as follows;
Shared: these facilities are shared with some other guests or perhaps the hosts.
Private: for your use only, however they may occasionally be in an adjacent room.
En-suite: private facilities within your bedroom suite.

Making a Reservation

Once you have chosen where you want to stay, have all the following information ready & your reservation will go smoothly without having to run & find more travel documents or ask someone else what they think you should do. Here is a brief check list of what you will probably be asked & examples to illustrate answers:

Dates & number of nights...August 14-19(6 nights).

Estimated time of arrival at the home ...7 P.M.(evening) & flight number.

Type & number of rooms...1 Double & 2 Single.

Toilet & Bathroom facilities...1 Double en-suite) & 2 singles (shared)

Smoking or Non-smoking?

Any allergies?

Special dietary requests?

Children in the party & their ages?

Any other preferences... Is a shower preferred to a bath?

Maximum budget per person per night based on all the above details.

The London Reservation Agency

There is a minimum two night consecutive stay at our London homes.

Reservations for London homes can only be made through one of our Worldwide Bed & Breakfast Agencies. They can be contacted by 'phone, fax, e-mail or on-line from our website at http://www.bestbandb.co.uk.

All reservations must be confirmed with advance payments which are non-refundable in the event of cancellation. You simply pay the balance due after you arrive at the home. The advance payment can be made with major credit & charge cards or by cheque. Cash is the preferred method of paying the balance & always in pounds sterling.

The advance payments confirm each night of your visit, **not just the first one**. When arriving at a later date or departing at an earlier date than those confirmed, the guest will be liable to pay only the appropriate proportion of the stated balance that is due. For example, staying three nights out of four booked means paying 3/4 of the stated balance due. The advance payment is non-refundable. A minimum of 2 nights will always apply.

Outside London

We encourage you to make use of the information in this guide & contact the homes directly. The hosts may require varying amounts of advance payments & may or may not accept credit & charge cards. Remember, many B&Bs are small, family-run establishments and are unable to accept payment by credit card. The confirmed prices shall be those prevailing on the dates required... as previously mentioned, *the prices shown in this guide are the **minimum** & will increase during the busy seasons.*

Alterations

If you wish to alter or change a previously confirmed booking through one of the agencies there will be a further fee of £15 per alteration.

Cancellations

All advance payments for London are non-refundable.

All booking fees outside London are non-refundable.

Notice of cancellation must be given as soon as possible & the following suggested rates shall apply outside London only;

30 - 49 days notice - 80% refund.

10-29 days notice -50% refund.

0 - 9 days notice - No refund.

The Worldwide Bed & Breakfast Agencies reserve the right to alter your accommodation should it be necessary & will inform you of any alteration as soon as possible

London Reservation Agency

Website:http://www.bestbandb.co.uk

We offer an outstanding selection of accommodation in London. As with all our accommodation each one has been personally inspected so you can be sure of the highest standards. We offer an immensely wide range of accommodation. We have a type, style and location to suit everyone. From city apartments close to shops, museums and galleries to spacious homes in leafy residential suburbs near the river, parks and restaurants. No matter what your reason for visiting London we can accommodate you. Whether on business or vacation the Best Bed & Breakfast provides great accommodation together with a fast, efficient reservation service. Our helpful staff are always happy to advise you on all your accommodation requirements. We are located in London, we know the city and all our hosts. We know how to provide an enjoyable, affordable, hassle free trip. There are plenty of ways to contact us. To make a reservation simply do one of the following;

Worldwide call Tel: +44 (0)20 8742 9123 (24Hrs.)

North America call Toll Free: 011 800 852 26320

Australia call Toll Free: 0011 800 852 26320

E-mail: bestbandb@atlas.co.uk

Fax: +44 (0)20 8749 7084

The Discount Offer

This offer is made to people who have bought this book & wish to make reservations for Bed & Breakfast in London through our London Reservation Agency. The offer only applies to a minimum stay of three consecutive nights at one of our London homes between the following dates; January 7. 2001& April 1. 2001 then from September 15. 2001 to December 1. 2001. Only one discount per booking is allowed. Call the reservation office to make your booking in the normal way & tell the clerk that you have bought the book & wish to have the discount. After a couple of questions the discount will be deducted from the advance payment required to confirm the reservation.

Regions

To assist tourists with information during their travels, counties have been grouped together under Regional Tourist Boards that co-ordinate the various efforts of each county.

The British Tourist Authority has designated these areas in consultation with the English, Scottish & Wales Tourist Boards & we have largely adopted these areas for use in this guide

Counties are listed alphabetically throughout our guide & then have a sub-heading indicating which Tourist Region they belong to.

ENGLAND

Cumbria
County of Cumbria

Northumbria.
Counties of Cleveland, Durham, Northumberland, Tyne & Wear.

North West
Counties of Cheshire, Greater Manchester, Lancashire, Merseyside, High Peaks of Derbyshire.

Yorkshire & Humberside
Counties of North Yorkshire, South Yorkshire, West Yorkshire, Humberside.

Heart of England
Counties of Gloucestershire, Herefordshire & Worcestershire, Shropshire, Staffordshire, Warwickshire, West Midlands.

East Midlands
Counties of Derbyshire, Leicestershire, Nottinghamshire, Rutland, Lincolnshire & Northamptonshire,

East Anglia
Counties of Cambridgeshire, Essex, Norfolk, Suffolk.

West Country
Counties of Cornwall, Devon, Dorset (parts of), Somerset, Wiltshire, Isles of Scilly.

Southern
Counties of Hampshire, Dorset (East & North), Isle of Wight.

South East
Counties of East Sussex,Kent, Surrey, West Sussex.

SCOTLAND

The subdivisions of Scottish Regions in this guide differ slightly from the current Marketing Regions of the Scottish Tourist Board.

The Borders, Dumfries & Galloway
Districts & counties of Scottish Borders, Dumfries & Galloway.

Lothian & Strathclyde
City of Edinburgh, Forth Valley, East Lothian, Kirkaldy, St. Andrews & North-East Fife, Greater Glasgow, Clyde Valley, Ayrshire & Clyde Coast, Burns Country.

Argyll & The Isles
Districts & counties of Oban & Mull, Mid Argyll, Kintyre & Islay, Dunoon, Cowal, Rothesay & Isle of Bute, Isle of Arran.

Perthshire, Loch Lommond & The Trossachs.
Districts & counties of Perthshire, Loch Lomond, Stirling & Trossachs.

The Grampians
Districts & counties of Banff & Buchan, Moray, Gordon, Angus, City of Aberdeen, Kincardine & Deeside, City of Dundee.

The Highlands & Islands
Districts & counties of Shetland, Orkney, Caithness, Sutherland, Ross & Cromarty, Western Isles, South West Ross & Isle of Skye, Inverness, Loch Ness & Nairn, Aviemore & Spey Valley, Fort William & Lochaber.

WALES

The regions are defined as follows:

North Wales
Counties of Anglesey, Conwy, Denbighshire, Flintshire & Gwynedd.

Mid Wales
Counties of Ceredigion & Powys.

South Wales
Counties of Carmarthenshire,Glamorgan, Monmouthshire, Newport, Pembrokeshire & Swansea.

The photographs appearing in the Introductions & Gazeteers are by courtesy of the appropriate Tourist Board for each county or W.W.B.B.A.

Counties map

Each county has been assigned a page number where a more detailed map can be found. These maps include principal towns, major roads & the location of each Bed & Breakfast establishment.

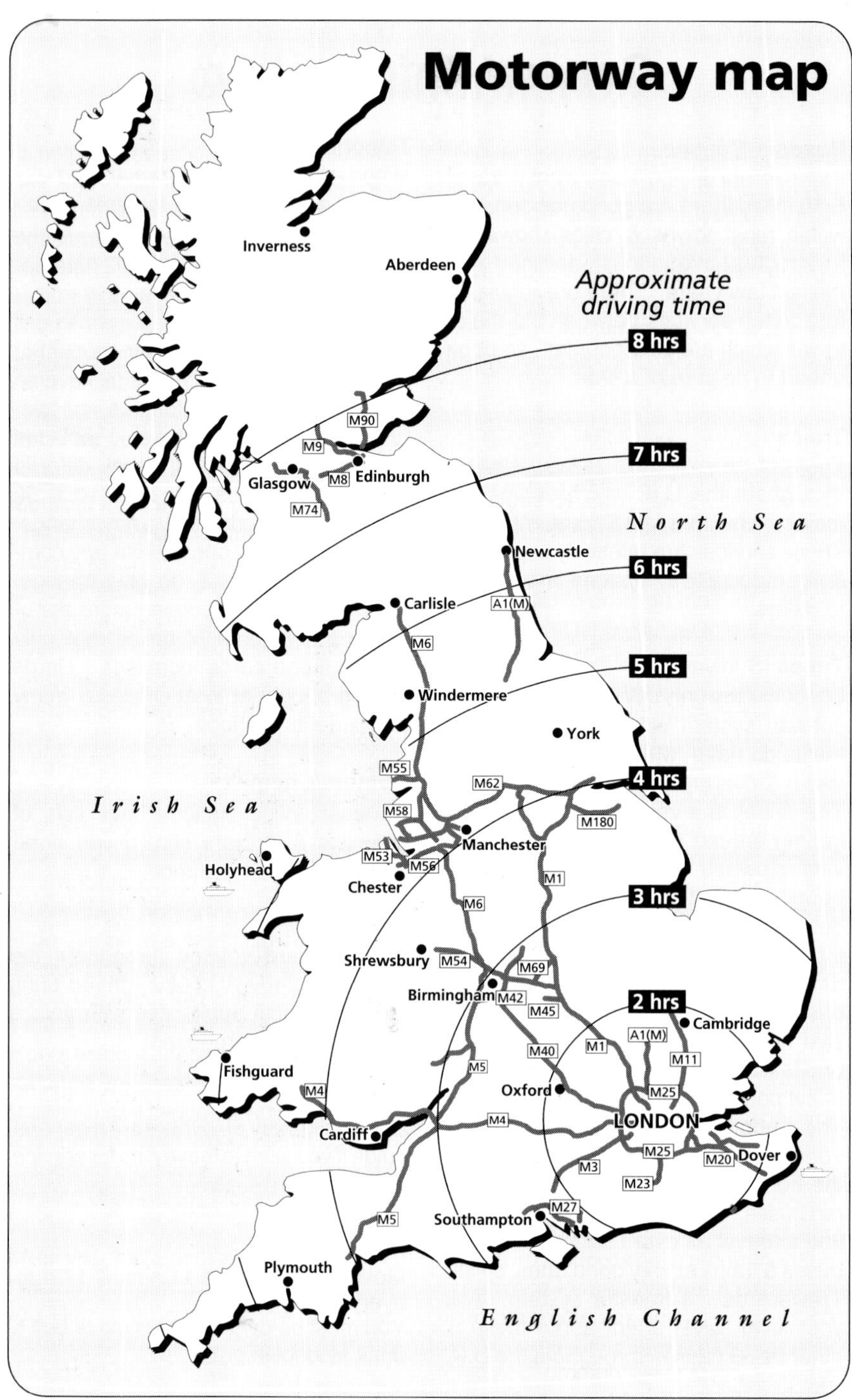
Motorway map
Approximate driving time
8 hrs
7 hrs
6 hrs
5 hrs
4 hrs
3 hrs
2 hrs
Inverness
Aberdeen
M90
M9
Edinburgh
Glasgow
M8
M74
North Sea
Newcastle
Carlisle
A1(M)
M6
Windermere
York
M55
M62
Irish Sea
M58
M180
Manchester
M53
M56
Holyhead
Chester
M1
M6
Shrewsbury
M54
M69
Birmingham
M42
M45
Cambridge
A1(M)
M1
M11
M40
M5
Fishguard
M4
Oxford
M25
LONDON
Cardiff
M4
M25
M20
Dover
M3
M23
M27
M5
Southampton
Plymouth
English Channel

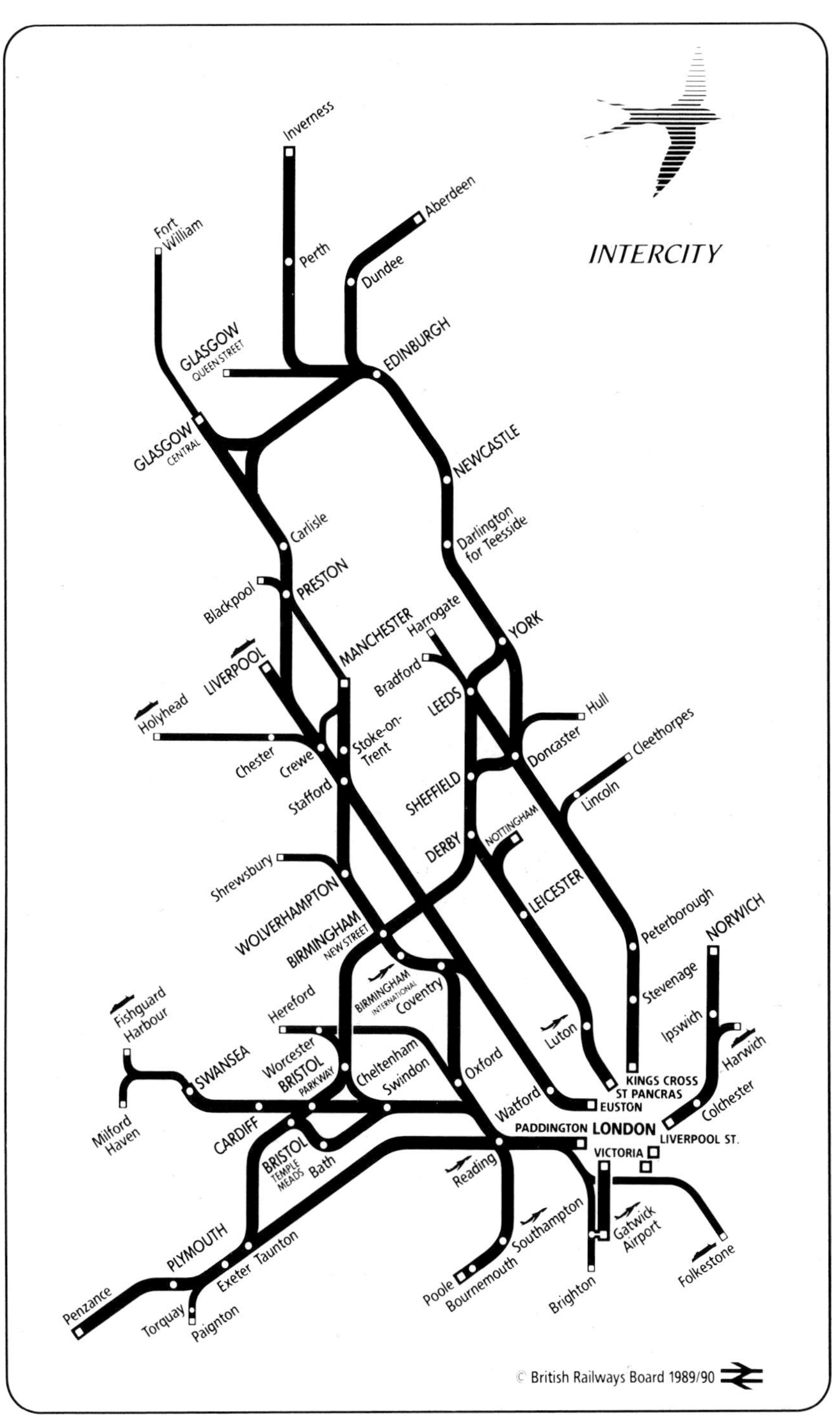
INTERCITY
Inverness
Aberdeen
Fort William
Perth
Dundee
GLASGOW QUEEN STREET
EDINBURGH
GLASGOW CENTRAL
NEWCASTLE
Carlisle
Darlington for Teesside
PRESTON
Blackpool
MANCHESTER
Harrogate
YORK
LIVERPOOL
Bradford
LEEDS
Holyhead
Hull
Chester
Crewe
Stoke-on-Trent
Doncaster
Cleethorpes
Stafford
SHEFFIELD
Lincoln
DERBY
NOTTINGHAM
Shrewsbury
LEICESTER
WOLVERHAMPTON
BIRMINGHAM NEW STREET
Peterborough
NORWICH
BIRMINGHAM INTERNATIONAL
Coventry
Stevenage
Fishguard Harbour
Hereford
Ipswich
Luton
Worcester
Harwich
SWANSEA
Cheltenham
Oxford
BRISTOL PARKWAY
Swindon
KINGS CROSS
ST PANCRAS
Colchester
EUSTON
Milford Haven
Watford
CARDIFF
PADDINGTON
LONDON
LIVERPOOL ST.
VICTORIA
BRISTOL TEMPLE MEADS
Bath
Reading
Southampton
Gatwick Airport
PLYMOUTH
Taunton
Exeter
Penzance
Torquay
Paignton
Poole
Bournemouth
Brighton
Folkestone
© British Railways Board 1989/90

TLB/90/1008

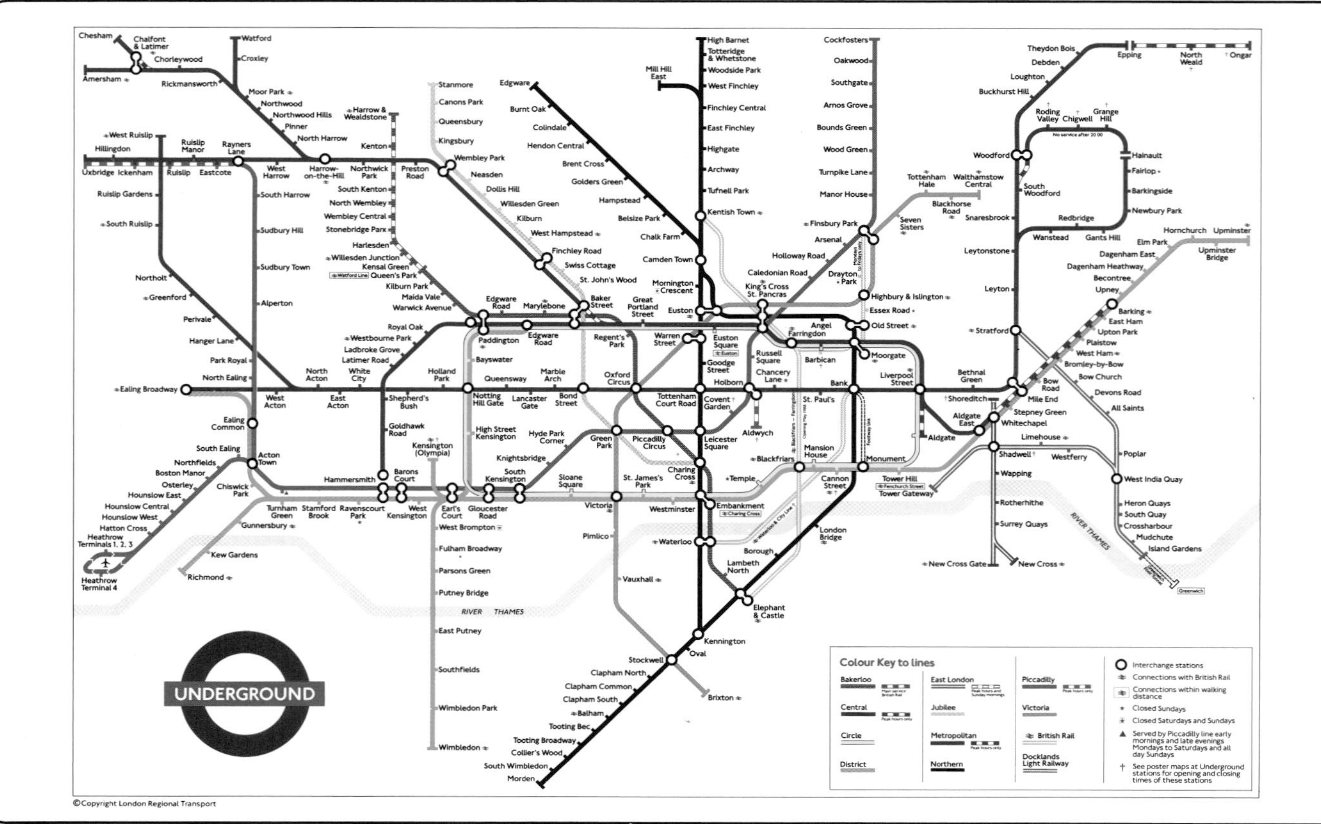
UNDERGROUND
Colour Key to lines
Bakerloo
Central
Circle
District
East London
Jubilee
Metropolitan
Northern
Piccadilly
Victoria
British Rail
Docklands Light Railway
Interchange stations
Connections with British Rail
Connections within walking distance
Closed Sundays
Closed Saturdays and Sundays
Served by Piccadilly line early mornings and late evenings Mondays to Saturdays and all day Sundays
See poster maps at Underground stations for opening and closing times of these stations
RIVER THAMES
©Copyright London Regional Transport

91/1258

LONDON MAP

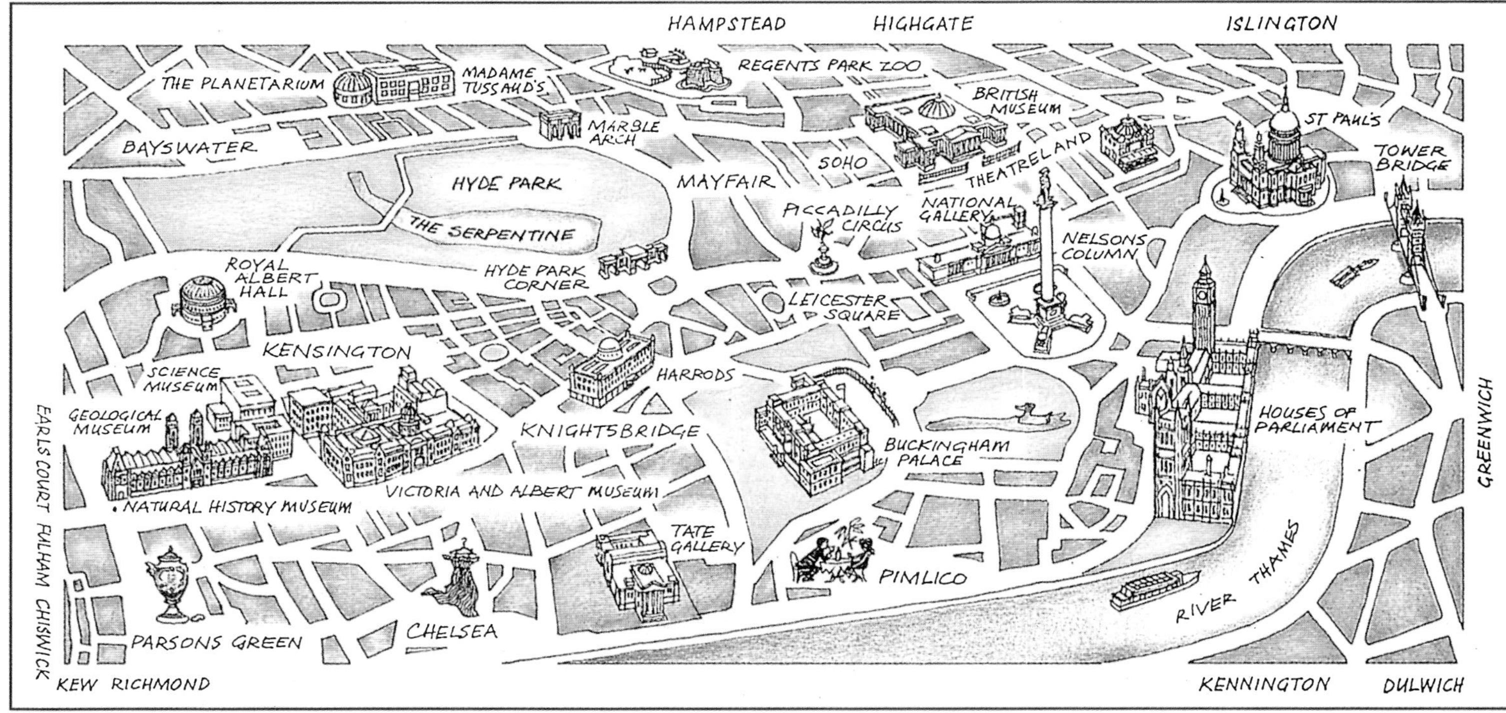

HAMPSTEAD
HIGHGATE
ISLINGTON
THE PLANETARIUM
MADAME TUSSAUD'S
REGENTS PARK ZOO
BRITISH MUSEUM
ST PAUL'S
TOWER BRIDGE
MARBLE ARCH
BAYSWATER
SOHO
THEATRELAND
HYDE PARK
MAYFAIR
NATIONAL GALLERY
PICCADILLY CIRCUS
THE SERPENTINE
NELSONS COLUMN
ROYAL ALBERT HALL
HYDE PARK CORNER
LEICESTER SQUARE
KENSINGTON
SCIENCE MUSEUM
HARRODS
GEOLOGICAL MUSEUM
KNIGHTSBRIDGE
HOUSES OF PARLIAMENT
BUCKINGHAM PALACE
GREENWICH
VICTORIA AND ALBERT MUSEUM
NATURAL HISTORY MUSEUM
TATE GALLERY
PIMLICO
RIVER THAMES
PARSONS GREEN
CHELSEA
EARLS COURT FULHAM CHISWICK
KEW RICHMOND
KENNINGTON
DULWICH

London

Visit our website: www.bestbandb.co.uk

Home	Description	rate £ from - to per person	children taken	evening meals	animals taken
Home No. 01. London. **Tel: +44 (0)20-8742-9123** **Fax: +44 (0)20-8749-7084** **U.S.A, Canada call:** **Toll Free 011-800-852-26320** **Australia call:** **Toll Free 0011-800-852-26320** **E-mail:bestbandb@atlas.co.uk**	Nearest Tube: Putney Bridge An attractive Victorian terraced house, situated in a quiet residential street, yet only 3 mins' walk from the station. 1 spacious double-bedded room with an en-suite bathroom & a twin-bedded room with a private bathroom. Each room is tastefully furnished & has tea/coffee-making facilities. (T.V. available.) Breakfast is served in the very pleasant kitchen/dining room. Good pubs, restaurants & shops locally. An excellent location from which to explore London. Parking. Children over 12.	**£29.00 to £50.00**	Y	N	N
Home No. 06. London. **Tel: +44 (0)20-8742-9123** **Fax: +44 (0)20-8749-7084** **U.S.A, Canada call:** **Toll Free 011-800-852-26320** **Australia call:** **Toll Free 0011-800-852-26320** **E-mail: bestbandb@atlas.co.uk**	Nearest Tube: East Putney A Victorian terraced house with a traditional family atmosphere & set in a quiet residential street. The friendly hosts offer 1 comfortable twin-bedded room with T.V., overlooking the rear garden, & with an adjacent private bathroom. A large Continental or Full English breakfast is served. Putney is a lovely area with good shops & restaurants. Transport facilities are excellent & provide easy access to central London & the sights.	**£26.00 to £40.00**	Y	N	N
Home No. 07. London. **Tel: +44 (0)20-8742-9123** **Fax +44 (0)20-8749-7084** **U.S.A, Canada call:** **Toll Free 011-800-852-26320** **Australia call:** **Toll Free 0011-800-852-26320** **E-mail: bestbandb@atlas.co.uk**	Nearest Tube: Fulham Broadway Set in the heart of Fulham, this is an attractive Victorian maisonette which is elegantly furnished throughout with antiques. The charming host, who has an in-depth knowledge of London, offers 2 beautifully furnished double-bedded rooms. Each is attractively decorated & has tea/coffee-making facilities & an en-suite or private bathroom. In summer, breakfast can be taken in the delightful garden. Only 8 mins' walk from the tube this is an ideal base for exploring London. Many good restaurants & antique shops close by.	**£33.00 to £50.00**	N	N	N
Home No. 08. London. **Tel: +44 (0)20-8742-9123** **Fax: +44 (0)20-8749-7084** **U.S.A, Canada call:** **Toll Free 011-800-852-26320** **Australia call:** **Toll Free 0011-800-852-26320** **E-mail: bestbandb@atlas.co.uk**	Nearest Tube: Maida Vale An attractive Victorian maisonette very well situated only 3 mins' walk from the tube. Offering 1 spacious & comfortably furnished twin-bedded room with T.V. & an en-suite shower room. Breakfast is served in the dining area looking out onto the pretty garden. Good local pubs & restaurants. An excellent central location providing easy access to many attractions; with a direct tube line to Piccadilly Circus & the Embankment. Also, Paddington Station for the Heathrow Express.	**£35.00 to £52.00**	N	N	N
Home No. 12. London. **Tel: +44 (0)20-8742-9123** **Fax: +44 (0)20-8749-7084** **U.S.A, Canada call:** **Toll Free 011-800-852-26320** **Australia call:** **Toll Free 0011-800-852-26320** **E-mail: bestbandb@atlas.co.uk**	Nearest Tube: Parsons Green Set in a quiet residential street, yet only 5 mins' walk from the station, this is a delightful Victorian terraced house. It has been beautifully decorated & is furnished throughout with antiques. The charming hosts offer 1 attractive King-size double/twin-bedded room with T.V., tea/coffee-making facilities & an en-suite shower room. Breakfast is taken in the elegant dining room which overlooks the garden. There are many interesting antique shops & good restaurants just a short walk away. Easy access to central London & the sights.	**£40.00 to £78.00**	N	N	N

Home No. 17. London.

Home No. 39. London.

London

Visit our website: www.bestbandb.co.uk

		rate £ from - to per person	children taken	evening meals	animals taken
Home No. 42. London. **Tel: +44 (0)20-8742-9123** **Fax: +44 (0)20-8749-7084** **U.S.A., Canada call:** **Toll Free 011-800-852-26320** **Australia call:** **Toll Free 0011-800-852-26320** **E-mail: bestbandb@atlas.co.uk**	Nearest Tube: Hammersmith An imposing 4-storey Victorian terraced house situated in a quiet residential street approx. 8-10 mins' walk from the tube. The charming hosts have furnished their home with artistic flair & imagination & offer 2 attractive (Gothic inspired) double bedrooms each with an en-suite or private bathroom. There is easy access to central London & the sights by both bus & tube. Many good local restaurants offer a fine selection of international cuisine. An elegant home.	**£32.00 to £52.00**	Y	N	N
Home No. 44. London. **Tel: +44 (0)20-8742-9123** **Fax: +44 (0)20-8749-7084** **U.S.A., Canada call:** **Toll Free 011-800-852-26320** **Australia call:** **Toll Free 0011-800-852-26320** **E-mail: bestbandb@atlas.co.uk**	Nearest Tube: Richmond Situated in the heart of delightful Richmond this really is the perfect location for a relaxing break in London. The charming host, who is an interior designer has refurbished this Victorian home & offers 1 double-bedded room with a private bathroom. Delicious Continental breakfasts are served in the lovely kitchen/diner which overlooks a pretty plantsmans garden. Richmond abounds with fashionable shops & restaurants. Within easy reach of several stately homes. Central London is only 25 mins. Easy access to Heathrow Airport.	**£32.00 to £50.00**	N	N	N
Home No. 48. London. **Tel: +44 (0)20-8742-9123** **Fax: +44 (0)20-8749-7084** **U.S.A., Canada call:** **Toll Free 011-800-852-26320** **Australia call:** **Toll Free 0011-800-852-26320** **E-mail: bestbandb@atlas.co.uk**	Nearest Tube: Parsons Green A beautifully decorated, very stylish late Victorian house, situated in Parsons Green & only 20 mins. from Harrods by tube. Offering 2 double/twin-bedded rooms & 1 single room, all are en-suite & have T.V. & tea/coffee-making facilities. Each room is furnished to the highest standards of comfort. Guests are welcomed with a glass of sherry. A country house breakfast is served. This is a no smoking house.	**£41.00 to £60.00**	N	N	N
Home No. 50. London. **Tel: +44 (0)20-8742-9123** **Fax: +44 (0)20-8749-7084** **U.S.A., Canada call:** **Toll Free 011-800-852-26320** **Australia call:** **Toll Free 0011-800-852-26320** **E-mail: bestbandb@atlas.co.uk**	Nearest Tube: Parsons Green This is a delightful Victorian terraced house which has been beautifully decorated & furnished throughout. The lovely hosts offer 1 very comfortable king-size double-bedded room & 1 attractive single-bedded room. Each room has a T.V. & bottled water etc. & an excellent private bathroom. There are a variety of good bars, bistros & restaurants nearby. Located only 5 mins' walk from the tube station, this is a perfect spot from which to explore London. A charming home.	**£34.00 to £50.00**	N	N	N
Home No. 51. London. **Tel: +44 (0)20-8742-9123** **Fax: +44 (0)20-8749-7084** **U.S.A., Canada call:** **Toll Free 011-800-852-26320** **Australia call:** **Toll Free 0011-800-852-26320** **E-mail: bestbandb@atlas.co.uk**	Nearest Tube: Holland Park Set in a quiet, secluded street, this is a modern mews house with an original brick kiln which has been converted into an elegant dining room. Only a few minutes walk from fashionable restaurants, antique shops, Portobello Market & beautiful Holland Park. It has been attractively furnished throughout by the host who is an interior designer. 1 delightful & spacious en-suite double-bedded room with T.V. etc. & a dressing room. Easy access to many of London's attractions.	**£37.00 to £60.00**	N	N	N

Beds:Berks:Bucks:Herts.

Hertfordshire

Gazeteer

Areas of outstanding natural beauty.
Parts of the Chilterns.

Historic Houses & Castles

Hatfield House - Hatfield
Home of the Marquess of Salisbury. Jacobean House & Tudor Palace - childhood home of Queen Elizabeth I.

Knebworth House - Knebworth
Family home of the Lyttons. 16th century house transformed into Victorian High Gothic. Furniture, portraits. Formal gardens & unique Gertrude Jekyll herb garden.

Shaw's Corner - Ayot St. Lawrence
Home of George Bernard Shaw.

Cathedrals & Churches

St. Albans Cathedral - St. Albans
9th century foundation, murals, painted roof over choir, 15th century reredos, stone rood screen.

Stanstead St. Abbots (St. James)12th century nave, 13th century chancel, 15th century tower & porch, 16th century North chapel, 18th century box pews & 3-decker pulpit.

Watford (St. Mary)
13 - 15th century. Essex chapel. Tuscan arcade. Morryson tombs.

Museums

Rhodes Memorial Museum & Commonwealth Centre - at Bishop Stortford

Zoological Museum - Tring Gardens

Gardens of the Rose - Chiswell Green Nr. St Albans
Showgrounds of the Royal National Rose Society

Capel Manor
Extensive grounds of horticultural college.
Many fine trees, including the largest copper beech in the country.

Bledlow Village; Bucks.

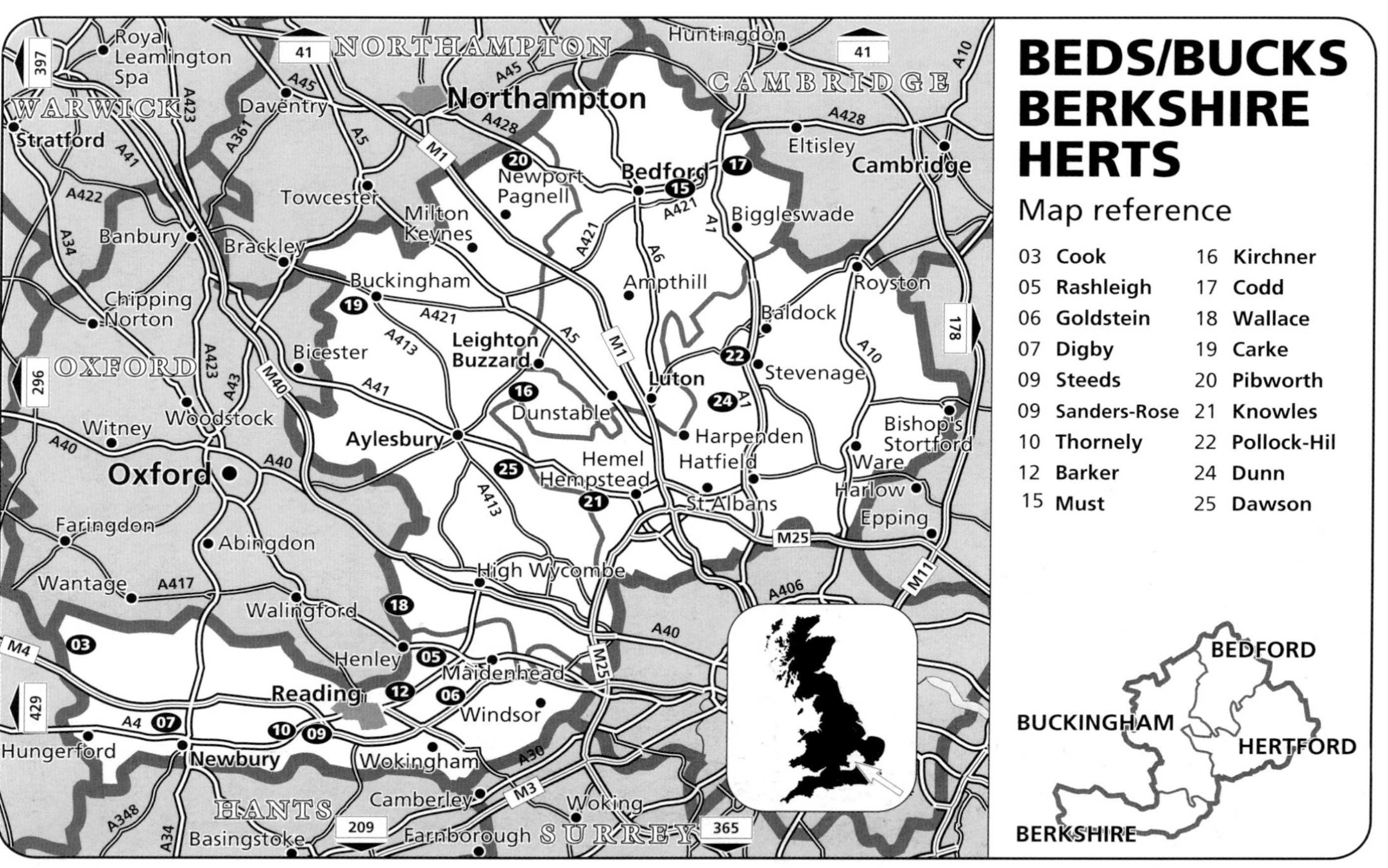

BEDS/BUCKS BERKSHIRE HERTS

Map reference

03	**Cook**	16	**Kirchner**
05	**Rashleigh**	17	**Codd**
06	**Goldstein**	18	**Wallace**
07	**Digby**	19	**Carke**
09	**Steeds**	20	**Pibworth**
09	**Sanders-Rose**	21	**Knowles**
10	**Thornely**	22	**Pollock-Hil**
12	**Barker**	24	**Dunn**
15	**Must**	25	**Dawson**

Bedfordshire & Berkshire

	rate £ from - to per person	children taken	evening meals	animals taken
Church Farm	£25.00 to £30.00	N	N	Y
The Old Vicarage	£27.50 to £32.50	Y	Y	N
Highfield Farm	£25.00 to £30.00	Y	N	Y
Lodge Down	£30.00 to £50.00	N	N	N

Church Farm

Nearest Road: A.421

Church Farm is a Grade II listed, 17th-century part-timber framed house. It is a perfect base for those wanting somewhere a little special & a comfortable place to stay. Accommodation is in 3 delightful bedrooms (all en-suite) each with a colour T.V. & a welcome tray. (In the twin room, there is the 'Coat of Arms' of the Stuart Kings.) A guest lounge with open fire is available for relaxation. Breakfast is served in the attractive beamed 17th-century dining room. There are walks around the village & countryside, & inns for evening meals.

Janet Must Church Farm High Street Roxton Bedford MK44 3EB Bedfordshire
Tel: (01234) 870234 Fax 01234 870234 Open: ALL YEAR Map Ref No. 15

The Old Vicarage

Nearest Road: A.418

Only 45 mins from central London, this imposing Gothic house is set in mature gardens in a picturesque Rothschild estate village. Mentmore boasts a good pub in addition to architectural interest & a fine setting. It is very much a family home with plenty of activity. The guest rooms are spacious with en-suite bathrooms, enjoying uninterrupted views over rolling countryside. Meals are served in the 'William Morris' dining room using garden produce when available.

E-mail: susie.kirchner@tesco.net

Charles & Susie Kirchner The Old Vicarage Mentmore Leighton Buzzard LU7 0QG Bedfordshire
Tel: (01296) 661243 Fax 01296 661243 Open: ALL YEAR Map Ref No. 16

Highfield Farm

Nearest Road: A.1

A tranquil & very welcoming house with comfort, warmth & a friendly atmosphere in a lovely setting on an arable farm. Accommodation is in 6 attractive bedrooms, 4 en-suite, including 3 ground-floor rooms in tastefully converted stables. Highfield Farm is set back off the A.1, giving peaceful seclusion & yet easy access to London, Cambridge, Bedford, the Shuttleworth Collection, the R.S.P.B. & the east-coast ports. Ample parking. Most guests return to this lovely home.

VISA: M'CARD:

Mrs M. Codd Highfield Farm Great North Road Sandy SG19 2AQ Bedfordshire
Tel: (01767) 682332 Fax 01767 692503 Open: ALL YEAR Map Ref No. 17

Lodge Down

Nearest Road: A.338

A warm welcome is assured at Lodge Down, a country house with superb accommodation & en-suite bathrooms, set in lovely grounds. Excellent & varied dining in surrounding villages. Easy access to the M.4 motorway at Jts 14 & 15. 1 hr or less for Heathrow (60 miles), Bath (43 miles) & Oxford (26 miles). This location provides a central base for excursions to Stonehenge, Salisbury & the Cotswolds, etc., or an easy drive to Heathrow & London. A charming home.

E-mail: lodgedown@hotmail.com

see PHOTO over p. 33

Sally Cook Lodge Down Lambourn Hungerford RG17 7BJ Berkshire
Tel: (01672) 540304 Fax 01672 540304 Open: ALL YEAR Map Ref No. 03

Lodge Down. Lambourn.

Berkshire

Dumbledore

rate £ from - to per person	children taken	evening meals	animals taken
£28.00 to £35.00	Y	N	N

Nearest Road: A.4

A charming (part-16th-century) Tudor country house, located in the pretty village of Warren Row, close to the picturesque town of Henley-on-Thames. Accommodation is in 2 elegantly furnished bedrooms, 1 en-suite & each with T.V. & tea/coffee-making facilities. Breakfast is served in the attractive dining room. A residents' lounge is available throughout the day in which guests may choose to relax. Easy access to Windsor, Marlow & Heathrow & Gatwick Airports. Children over 12.

Lavinia Rashleigh Dumbledore Warren Row Nr. Maidenhead RG10 8QS Berkshire
Tel: (01628) 822723 Fax 01628 822723 Open: ALL YEAR Map Ref No. 05

Beehive Manor

rate £ from - to per person	children taken	evening meals	animals taken
£30.00 to £45.00	Y	N	N

VISA: M'CARD:

Nearest Road: A.404 (M.)

Beehive Manor offers all the charm & country house atmosphere of a Tudor home set in a traditional English garden. Yet, amongst the massive oak beams, latticed windows & linenfold panelling are also all the comforts of the 20th century. Within its wisteria-clad walls, 3 superb bedrooms are available to guests, as well as a sunny drawing & a delightful dining room. London is just 35 mins away by train. Children over 12.
E-mail: beehivemanor@cs.com

Lesley & Stanley Goldstein Beehive Manor Cox Green Lane Maidenhead SL6 3ET Berkshire
Tel: (01628) 620980 Fax 01628 621840 Open: ALL YEAR (Excl. Xmas & New Year) Map Ref No.06

Rookwood Farmhouse

rate £ from - to per person	children taken	evening meals	animals taken
£35.00 to £45.00	Y	N	N

VISA: M'CARD:

Nearest Road: A.4

This charming & comfortable former farmhouse combines ease of access with rural views & a large garden. The lovely guest bedrooms are in a newly converted coach house which is traditionally furnished & yet affords all modern facilities. In winter, there is a welcoming log fire in the guests' sitting room, while in summer, breakfast is served in the attractive conservatory overlooking the swimming pool. Rookwood Farmhouse is an ideal base for touring & is a perfect spot for a relaxing break.

Mrs C. F. Digby Rookwood Farmhouse Stockcross Newbury RG20 8JX Berkshire
Tel: (01488) 608676 Open: ALL YEAR Map Ref No. 07

Highwoods

rate £ from - to per person	children taken	evening meals	animals taken
£24.00 to £30.00	Y	N	N

Nearest Road: A.4, M.4

A friendly & relaxing atmosphere at this fine Victorian country house set in 4 acres of attractive grounds, with unspoilt, far-reaching views. 3 spacious, comfortable, attractively furnished rooms (1 en-suite) all with T.V. etc. Guests are welcome to use the garden & hard tennis court. Also, a gallery specialising in English watercolours & prints. Easy access to London, Heathrow Airport, Windsor, Oxford & Bath. Non-smokers preferred.
E-mail: janesteeds@aol.com

Mrs Jane Steeds Highwoods Hermits Hill Burghfield Common Reading RG7 3BG Berkshire
Tel: (0118) 9832320 Fax 0118 9831070 Open: ALL YEAR (Excl. Xmas & New Year) Map Ref No. 09

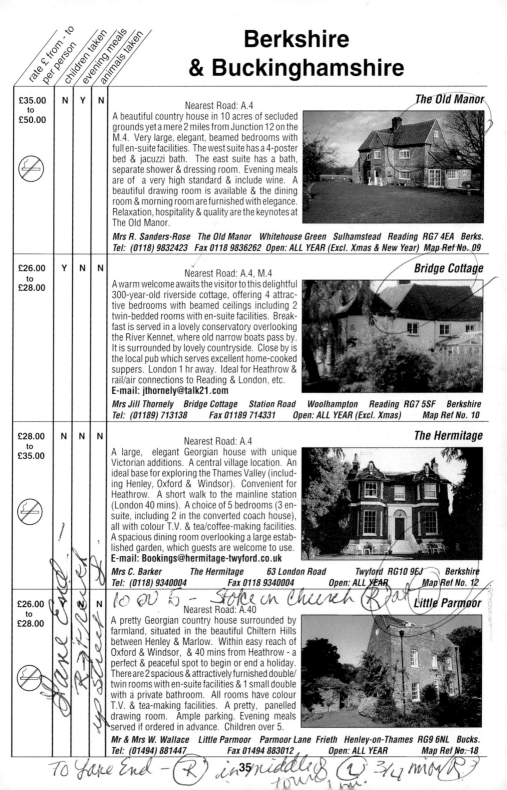

Berkshire & Buckinghamshire

rate £ from - to per person	children taken	evening meals	animals taken	
£35.00 to £50.00	N	Y	N	The Old Manor
£26.00 to £28.00	Y	N	N	Bridge Cottage
£28.00 to £35.00	N	N	N	The Hermitage
£26.00 to £28.00	Y	N	N	Little Parmoor

The Old Manor

£35.00 to £50.00 — N — Y — N

Nearest Road: A.4

A beautiful country house in 10 acres of secluded grounds yet a mere 2 miles from Junction 12 on the M.4. Very large, elegant, beamed bedrooms with full en-suite facilities. The west suite has a 4-poster bed & jacuzzi bath. The east suite has a bath, separate shower & dressing room. Evening meals are of a very high standard & include wine. A beautiful drawing room is available & the dining room & morning room are furnished with elegance. Relaxation, hospitality & quality are the keynotes at The Old Manor.

Mrs R. Sanders-Rose The Old Manor Whitehouse Green Sulhamstead Reading RG7 4EA Berks.
Tel: (0118) 9832423 Fax 0118 9836262 Open: ALL YEAR (Excl. Xmas & New Year) Map Ref No. 09

Bridge Cottage

£26.00 to £28.00 — Y — N — N

Nearest Road: A.4, M.4

A warm welcome awaits the visitor to this delightful 300-year-old riverside cottage, offering 4 attractive bedrooms with beamed ceilings including 2 twin-bedded rooms with en-suite facilities. Breakfast is served in a lovely conservatory overlooking the River Kennet, where old narrow boats pass by. It is surrounded by lovely countryside. Close by is the local pub which serves excellent home-cooked suppers. London 1 hr away. Ideal for Heathrow & rail/air connections to Reading & London, etc.

E-mail: jthornely@talk21.com

Mrs Jill Thornely Bridge Cottage Station Road Woolhampton Reading RG7 5SF Berkshire
Tel: (01189) 713138 Fax 01189 714331 Open: ALL YEAR (Excl. Xmas) Map Ref No. 10

The Hermitage

£28.00 to £35.00 — N — N — N

Nearest Road: A.4

A large, elegant Georgian house with unique Victorian additions. A central village location. An ideal base for exploring the Thames Valley (including Henley, Oxford & Windsor). Convenient for Heathrow. A short walk to the mainline station (London 40 mins). A choice of 5 bedrooms (3 en-suite, including 2 in the converted coach house), all with colour T.V. & tea/coffee-making facilities. A spacious dining room overlooking a large established garden, which guests are welcome to use.

E-mail: Bookings@hermitage-twyford.co.uk

Mrs C. Barker The Hermitage 63 London Road Twyford RG10 9EJ Berkshire
Tel: (0118) 9340004 Fax 0118 9340004 Open: ALL YEAR Map Ref No. 12

Little Parmoor

£26.00 to £28.00 — Y — N — N

Nearest Road: A.40

A pretty Georgian country house surrounded by farmland, situated in the beautiful Chiltern Hills between Henley & Marlow. Within easy reach of Oxford & Windsor, & 40 mins from Heathrow - a perfect & peaceful spot to begin or end a holiday. There are 2 spacious & attractively furnished double/twin rooms with en-suite facilities & 1 small double with a private bathroom. All rooms have colour T.V. & tea-making facilities. A pretty, panelled drawing room. Ample parking. Evening meals served if ordered in advance. Children over 5.

Mr & Mrs W. Wallace Little Parmoor Parmoor Lane Frieth Henley-on-Thames RG9 6NL Bucks.
Tel: (01494) 881447 Fax 01494 883012 Open: ALL YEAR Map Ref No. 18

Buckinghamshire & Hertfordshire

rate £ from - to per person	children taken	evening meals	animals taken

Field Cottage

Nearest Road: A.413

Field Cottage is a 17th-century thatched & stone farmhouse which is set in 4 acres in a small hamlet with stunning views. The house retains many original features including beams & old fireplaces, yet offers guests every modern day comfort. Guest rooms include 1 double bedroom with an en-suite bathroom & a twin-bedded room & a single room which share a bathroom. Waddesdon Manor, Claydon House, Stowe Gardens, Silverstone, Oxford & the Cotswolds are within easy reach.

E-mail: martin.tessa@virgin.net

£25.00 to £35.00	Y	N	Y

Martin & Tessa Clarke *Field Cottage* *Hillesden Hamlet MK18 4BX* *Buckinghamshire*
Tel: (01280) 815360 *Fax 01280 815360* *Open: ALL YEAR* *Map Ref No. 19*

Home Farm

Nearest Road: A.509, A.428

The Pibworths' offer a warm welcome to their stone farmhouse. 3 individually decorated en-suite rooms offer colour T.V., mini-fridge & tea/coffee facilities. Guests have their own lounge & a traditional breakfast is served in the dining room. A kitchen is also available. Summer use of outdoor heated pool & gardens. Home Farm is an arable farm 1 1/2 miles north of Olney. 10 miles from Bedford, Northampton & Milton Keynes. Central for Cotswolds, Oxford, Cambridge, Stratford-upon-Avon & London.

E-mail: ruth@oldstonebarn.co.uk

£27.50 to £35.00	Y	N	N

VISA: M'CARD:

Mrs Ruth Pibworth *Home Farm* *Warrington* *Olney MK46 4HN* *Buckinghamshire*
Tel: (01234) 711655 *Fax 01234 711855* *Open: ALL YEAR* *Map Ref No. 20*

Broadway Farm

Nearest Road: A.4251

A warm welcome is guaranteed at Broadway, a working arable farm with its own fishing lake. There are 3 comfortable en-suite rooms in a recently converted building adjacent to the farmhouse. Each has tea/coffee-making facilities & colour T.V.. Everything for the leisure or business guest: the relaxation of farm life in an attractive rural setting, yet easy access to London, airports, motorways & mainline rail services.

E-mail: a.knowles@broadway.nildram.co.uk

£25.00 to £35.00	Y	N	N

Mrs Alison Knowles *Broadway Farm* *Berkhamsted HP4 2RR* *Hertfordshire*
Tel: (01442) 866541 *Fax 01442 866541* *Open: ALL YEAR (Excl. Xmas)* *Map Ref No. 21*

Homewood

Nearest Road: A.1 M

Homewood is a classic blend of comfort & style: an Edwardian country house which is also a well-equipped family home. It has been used as a location for period drama by the B.B.C., & is often sought out by admirers of its designer, the distinguished architect Edwin Lutyens. You will be treated as a member of the family, or your privacy will be respected - whichever you prefer. Additional meals can be arranged, including dinner. 2 lovely bedrooms, each with an en-suite/private bathroom.

£45.00 to £45.00	Y	Y	Y

see PHOTO over p. 37

Samantha Pollock-Hill *Homewood* *Knebworth SG3 6PP* *Hertfordshire*
Tel: (01438) 812105 *Open: ALL YEAR (Excl. Xmas)* *Map Ref No. 22*

Homewood. Knebworth.

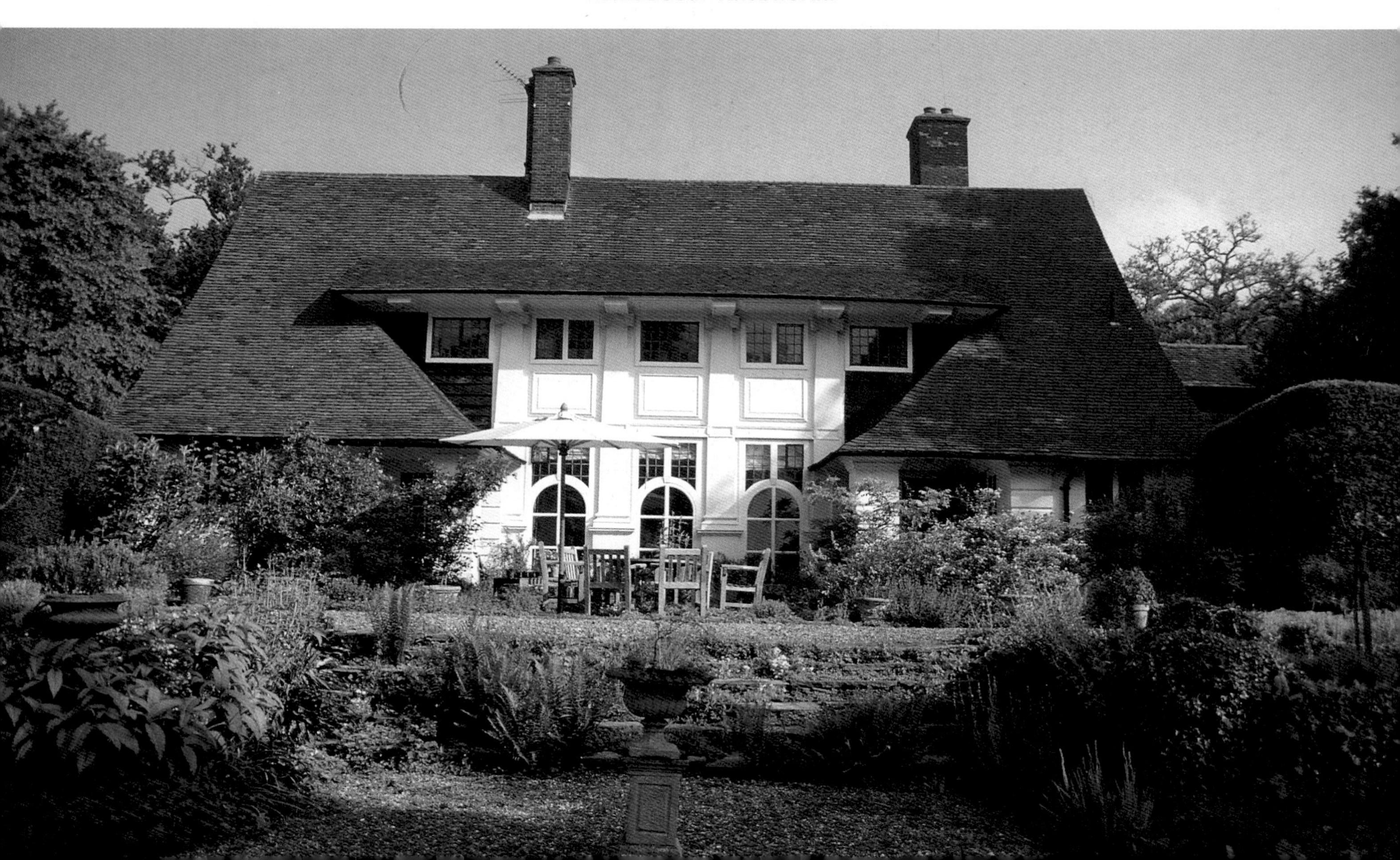

Hertfordshire

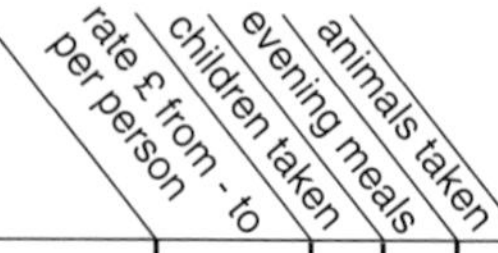

The Old Rectory

Nearest Road: A.1

A Grade II listed rectory built around 1680, surrounded by open countryside yet at the heart of a most beautiful conservation village. Ayot was the home of George Bernard Shaw & his house is now owned by the N. T. & open Apr - Oct. Breakfast is served on the terrace or in the 17th-century dining room (light supper trays available). Dinner is on request. There are 3 charming bedrooms. Squash court. London is 30 mins' away. Easy access to Stansted, Luton & Heathrow Airports.

E-mail: AyotBandB@aol.com

Helen & Dick Dunn *The Old Rectory* *Ayot St. Lawrence* *Welwyn AL6 9BT* *Hertfordshire*
Tel: (01438) 820429 *Fax 01438 821844* *Open: ALL YEAR* *Map Ref No. 24*

rate £ from - to per person	children taken	evening meals	animals taken
£25.00 to £40.00	Y	N	N

Rangers Cottage

Nearest Road: A.41

Built by the Rothschild family in 1880, Rangers Cottage has lovely views over open countryside & Woodland Trust forest, & is set in an Area of Outstanding Natural Beauty. The Ridgeway Path is 200 metres away. All rooms are situated on the ground floor & are attractively furnished. Each bedroom is well-equipped & has an en-suite bathroom with power shower. Tring station (London 35 mins') & the M.25 are 10 mins' away. Heathrow & Luton Airports 30 mins'. Single supplement.

E-mail: rangerscottage@aol.com

Sally Dawson *Rangers Cottage* *Tring Park* *Wigginton HP23 6EB* *Hertfordshire*
Tel: (01442) 890155 *Fax 01442 827814* *Open: ALL YEAR (Excl. Xmas)* *Map Ref No. 25*

rate £ from - to per person	children taken	evening meals	animals taken
£27.00 to £29.00	Y	N	N

VISA: M'CARD:

All the establishments mentioned in this guide are members of The Worldwide Bed & Breakfast Association

When booking your accommodation please mention The Best Bed & Breakfast

Cambridge & Northants

Cambridgeshire

(East Anglia)

A county very different from any other, this is flat, mysterious, low-lying Fenland crisscrossed by a network of waterways both natural & man-made.

The Fens were once waterlogged, misty marshes but today the rich black peat is drained & grows carrots, sugar beet, celery & the best asparagus in the world.

Drive north across the Fens & slowly you become aware of a great presence dominating the horizon. Ely cathedral, the "ship of the Fens", sails closer. The cathedral is a masterpiece with its graceful form & delicate tracery towers. Begun before the Domesday Book was written, it took the work of a full century before it was ready to have the timbered roof raised up. Norman stonemasons worked with great skill & the majestic nave is glorious in its simplicity. Their work was crowned by the addition of the Octagon in the 14th century. Despite the ravages of the Reformation, the lovely Lady Chapel survives as one of the finest examples of decorated architecture in Britain with its exquisitely fine stone carving.

To the south, the Fens give way to rolling chalk hills & fields of barley, wheat & rye, & Cambridge. Punts gliding through the broad river, between smooth, lawned banks, under willow trees, past college buildings as extravagant as wedding cakes. The names of the colleges resound through the ages - Peterhouse, Corpus Christi, Kings, Queens, Trinity, Emmanuel. A city of learning & progress, & a city of great tradition where cows graze in open spaces, just 500 yards from the market square.

Northamptonshire

(East Midlands)

Northamptonshire has many features to attract & interest the visitor, from the town of Brackley in the south with its charming buildings of mellow stone, to ancient Rockingham Forest in the north. There are lovely churches, splendid historic houses & peaceful waterways.

The Waterways Museum at Stoke Bruerne makes a popular outing, with boat trips available on the Grand Union Canal beside the museum. Horse-racing at Towcester & motor-racing at Silverstone draws the crowds, but there are quieter pleasures in visits to Canons Ashby, or to Sulgrave Manor, home of George Washington's ancestors.

In the pleasantly wooded Rockingham Forest area are delightful villages, one of which is Ashton with its thatched cottages, the scene of the World Conker Championships each October. Mary Queen of Scots was executed at Fotheringay, in the castle of which only the mound remains.

Rockingham Castle has a solid Norman gateway & an Elizabethan hall; Deene Park has family connections with the Earl of Cardigan who led the Charge of the Light Brigade & Kirby Hall is a dramatic Elizabethan ruin.

The county is noted for its parish churches, with fine Saxon examples at Brixworth & at Earl's Barton, as well as the round Church of the Holy Sepulchre in the county town itself.

Northampton has a fine tradition of shoemaking, so it is hardly surprising that boots & shoes & other leather-goods take pride of place in the town';s museums. The town has one of the country's biggest market squares, an historic Royal Theatre & a mighty Wurlitzer Organ to dance to at Turner's Musical Merry-go-round ! !

Cambridge & Northants

Cambridgeshire

Gazeteer

Areas of outstanding natural beauty
The Nene Valley

Historic Houses & Castles

Anglesy Abbey - Nr. Cambridge
Origins in the reign of Henry I. Was redesigned into Elizabethan Manor by Fokes family. Houses the Fairhaven collection of Art treasures - stands in 100 acres of Ground.

Hinchingbrooke House - Huntingdon
13th century nunnery converted mid-16th century into Tudor house. Later additions in 17th & 19th centuries.

King's School - Ely
12th & 14th centuries - original stonework & vaulting in the undercroft, original timbering 14th century gateway & monastic barn.

Kimbolton Castle - Kimbolton
Tudor Manor house - has associations with Katherine of Aragon. Remodelled by Vanbrugh 1700's - gatehouse by Robert Adam.

Longthorphe Tower - Nr. Peterborough
13th & 14th century fortification - rare wall paintings.

Peckover House - Wisbech
18th century domestic architecture - charming Victorian garden.

University of Cambridge Colleges

Peterhouse - ----------------- 1284
Clare - ------------------------ 1326
Pembroke -------------------- 1347
Gonville & Caius-------------1348
Trinity Hall - ------------------ 1350
Corpus Christi - ------------- 1352
King's --------------------------1441
Queen's - -------------------- 1448
St. Catherine's ----------------1473
Jesus ------------------------- 1496
Christ's - ----------------------1505
St. John's----------------------1511
Magadalene -----------------1542
Trinity- ----------------------- 1546
Emmanuel------------------- 1584
Sidney Sussex -------------- 1596
Downing----------------------- 1800

Wimpole Hall - Nr. Cambridge
18th & 19th century - beautiful staterooms - aristocratic house.

Cathedrals & Churches

Alconbury (St. Peter & St. Paul)
13th century chancel & 15th century roof. Broach spire.

Babraham (St. Peter)
13th century tower - 17th century monument.

Ely Cathedral
Rich arcading - west front incomplete. Remarkable interior with Octagon - unique in Gothic architecture.

Great Paxton (Holy Trinity)
12th century.

Harlton (Blessed Virgin Mary)
Perpendicular - decorated transition. 17th century monuments

Hildersham (Holy Trinity)
13th century - effigies, brasses & glass.

Lanwade (St. Nicholas)
15th century - mediaeval fittings

Peterborough Cathedral
Great Norman church fine example - little altered. Painted wooden roof to nave - remarkable west front - Galilee Porch & spires later additions.

Ramsey (St. Thomas of Canterbury)
12th century arcades - perpendicular nave. Late Norman chancel with Angevin vault.

St. Neots (St. Mary)
15th century

Sutton (St. Andrew)
14th century

Trumpington (St. Mary & St. Nicholas)
14th century. Framed brass of 1289 of Sir Roger de Trumpington.

Westley Waterless (St. Mary the Less)
Decorated. 14th century brass of Sir John & Lady Creke.

Wimpole (St. Andrew)
14th century rebuilt 1749 - splendid heraldic glass.

Yaxley (St. Peter)
15th century chancel screen, wall paintings, fine steeple.

Museums & Galleries

Cromwell Museum - Huntingdon
Exhibiting portraits, documents, etc. of the Cromwellian period.

Fitzwilliam Museum - Cambridge
Gallery of masters, old & modern, ceramics, applied arts, prints & drawing, mediaeval manuscripts, music & art library.

Cambridge & Northants

Scott Polar Research Institute - Cambridge
Relics of expeditions & the equipment used. Current scientific work in Arctic & Antarctic.
University Archives - Cambridge
13th century manuscripts, Charters, Statutes, Royal letters & mandates. Wide variety of records of the University.
University Museum of Archaeology & Anthropology - Cambridge
Collections illustrative of Stone Age in Europe, Africa & Asia.
Britain prehistoric to mediaeval times.
Prehistoric America.
Ethnographic material from South-east Asia, Africa & America.
University Museum of Classical Archaeology - Cambridge
Casts of Greek & Roman Sculpture - representative collection.
Whipple Museum of the History of Science - Cambridge**16th, 17th & 18th century scientific instruments - historic collection.**

Other Things to see & do

Nene Valley Railway
Steam railway with locomotives & carriages from many countries.

Caius College; Cambridge.

Cambridge & Northants

Northamptonshire

Gazeteer

Historic Houses & Castles

Althorp - Nr. Northampton
Family home of the Princess of Wales, with fine pictures & porcelain.

Boughton House - Nr. Kettering
Furniture, tapestries & pictures in late 17th century building modelled on Versailles, in beautiful parkland.

Canons Ashby House - Nr. Daventry
Small 16th century manor house with gardens & church.

Deene Park - Nr. Corby
Family home for over 4 centuries, surrounded by park, extensive gardens & lake.

Holdenby House - Nr. Northampton
Gardens include part of Elizabethan garden, with original entrance arches, terraces & ponds. Falconry centre. Rare breeds.

Kirby Hall - Nr. Corby
Large Elizabethan mansion with fine gardens.

Lamport Hall - Nr. Northampton
17th & 18th century house with paintings, furniture & china. One of the first garden rockeries in Britain. Programme of concerts & other special events.

Rockingham Castle - Rockingham, Nr. Market Harborough
Norman gateway & walls surrounding mainly Elizabethan house, with pictures & Rockingham china. Extensive gardens with 16th century yew hedge.

Rushton Triangular Lodge - Nr. Kettering
Symbolic of the Trinity, with 3 sides, 3 floors, trefoil windows.

Sulgrave Manor - Nr. Banbury
Early English Manor, home of George Washington's ancestors.

Museums

Abington Museum - Northampton
Domestic & social life collections in former manor house.

Museum of Leathercraft - Northampton
History of leather use, with Queen Victoria's saddle, & Samuel Pepys' wallet.

Waterways Museum - Stoke Bruerne Nr. Towcester
200 years of canal & waterway life, displayed beside the Grand Union Canal.

Cathedrals & Churches

Brixworth Church - Nr. Northampton
One of the finest Anglo-Saxon churches in the country, mostly 7th century.

Earls Barton Church - Nr. Northampton
Fine Anglo-Saxon tower & Norman arch & arcading.

Church of the Holy Sepulchre - Northampton
Largest & best preserved of four remaining round churches in England, dating from 1100.

Other Things to see & do

Billing Aquadrome - Nr. Northampton
Boating, fishing, swimming & amusements.

Wicksteed Park - Kettering
Large playground & variety of amusements for families.

Lilford Park - Nr. Oundle
Birds & farm animals in parkland setting where many special events are held.

Rushton Triangular Lodge.

CAMBRIDGESHIRE & NORTHAMPTONSHIRE

Map reference

01 **Percival**
02 **Hindley**
03 **Scott**
05 **Myburgh**
06 **Nix**
08 **Roper**
09 **Elbourn**
10 **Barlow**
11 **Clarke**

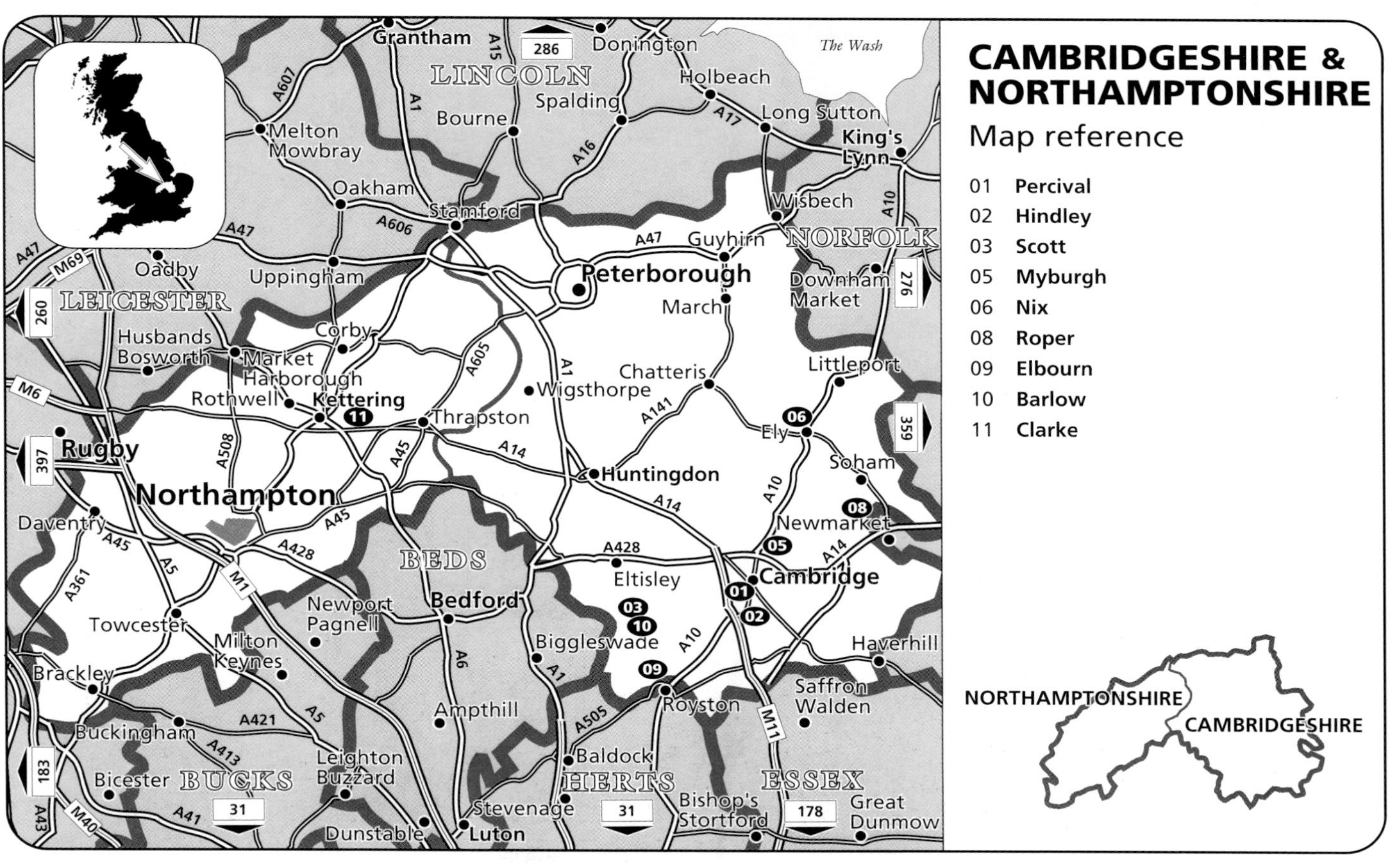

	rate £ from - to per person	children taken	evening meals	animals taken
46 Panton Street	£33.00 to £35.00	Y	N	N
Purlins	£23.00 to £29.00	Y	N	N
Church Farm	£35.00 to £45.00	Y	Y	N
Berry House	£30.00 to £50.00	Y	Y	N

46 Panton Street

Nearest Road: M.11

A 19th-century cottage situated in the historic centre of Cambridge with the great advantage of private car parking. An excellent location near the Botanical Gardens & Fitzwilliam Museum, & only 10 mins' walk from the station, Kings College Chapel & the many beautiful colleges. 2 comfortable bedrooms are provided with a tea tray & T.V.. A full English breakfast is served. (A self-contained flat is also available for short stays.) A charming home & the perfect location from which to explore Cambridge. Children over 12. Single supplement.

VISA: M'CARD:

Mrs Alice Percival 46 Panton Street Cambridge CB2 1HS Cambridgeshire
Tel: (01223) 365285 Fax 01223 461142 Open: ALL YEAR Map Ref No. 01

Purlins

Nearest Road: A.10

Lovely, individually designed family home, with 2 acres of parkland, situated in a quiet, pretty village on the Cam, 4 miles south of Cambridge. An ideal centre for Colleges, Audley End House, the Imperial War Museum & bird watching. There are 3 well-appointed double bedrooms (2 ground-floor), all with en-suite bathrooms, colour T.V. & tea/coffee-making facilities. Varied breakfasts (special diets by arrangement). Restaurants nearby. Children over 8 welcome. Single supplement.

E-mail: dgallh@ndirect.co.uk

Olga & David Hindley Purlins 12 High Street Little Shelford Cambridge CB2 5ES Cambridgeshire
Tel: (01223) 842643 Fax (01223) 842643 Open: FEB - Mid DEC Map Ref No. 02

Church Farm

Nearest Road: A.1198

This elegant & spacious listed farmhouse, which retains original 16th- & 17th-century features with 19th-century additions, is set in over 3 acres of rural peace. A wealth of oak beams, antiques, English watercolours, open log fires, comfortable beds & imaginative country-house cooking make for a relaxing stay. Ely Cathedral, Wimpole Hall, Kings College Chapel, Audley End & the Fitzwilliam Museum are all within easy reach. A delightful home. Children over 8, by arrangement.

E-mail: Churchfarm@aol.com

VISA: M'CARD:

Peter & Maggie Scott Church Farm Gransden Road Caxton Cambridge CB3 8PL Cambridgeshire
Tel: (01954) 719543 Fax 01954 718999 Open: ALL YEAR Map Ref No. 03

Berry House

Nearest Road: A.14

Berry House is a Grade II listed building built around 1820. The garden still contains a number of fruit trees from the original orchards. The elegant bedrooms have mahogany double beds, Edwardian & Georgian furniture & modern en-suite facilities, including powerful Victorian-style showers. Tea/coffee-making facilities & radio/alarms, etc. are provided. A beautiful home, perfect for visiting Cambridge & Ely, or for exploring this delightful county. Children & evening meals by arrangement.

E-mail: sal@BERRYHOUSE.DEMON.CO.UK

Phil & Sally Myburgh Berry House High Street Waterbeach\ Cambridge CB5 9JU Cambridgeshire
Tel: (01223) 860702 Fax 01223 570588 Open: ALL YEAR Map Ref No. 05

Cambridgeshire

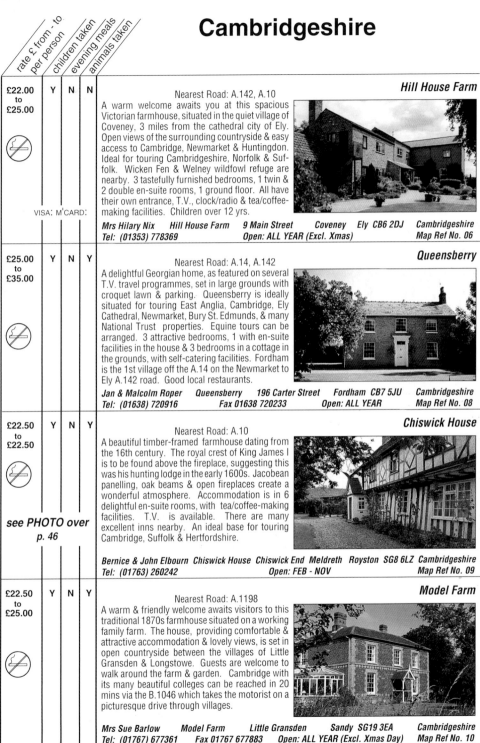

rate £ from - to per person	children taken	evening meals	animals taken	
£22.00 to £25.00	Y	N	N	**Hill House Farm**
VISA: M'CARD:				
£25.00 to £35.00	Y	N	Y	**Queensberry**
£22.50 to £22.50	Y	N	Y	**Chiswick House**
£22.50 to £25.00	Y	N	Y	**Model Farm**

Hill House Farm

Nearest Road: A.142, A.10

A warm welcome awaits you at this spacious Victorian farmhouse, situated in the quiet village of Coveney, 3 miles from the cathedral city of Ely. Open views of the surrounding countryside & easy access to Cambridge, Newmarket & Huntingdon. Ideal for touring Cambridgeshire, Norfolk & Suffolk. Wicken Fen & Welney wildfowl refuge are nearby. 3 tastefully furnished bedrooms, 1 twin & 2 double en-suite rooms, 1 ground floor. All have their own entrance, T.V., clock/radio & tea/coffee-making facilities. Children over 12 yrs.

Mrs Hilary Nix Hill House Farm 9 Main Street Coveney Ely CB6 2DJ Cambridgeshire
Tel: (01353) 778369 Open: ALL YEAR (Excl. Xmas) Map Ref No. 06

Queensberry

Nearest Road: A.14, A.142

A delightful Georgian home, as featured on several T.V. travel programmes, set in large grounds with croquet lawn & parking. Queensberry is ideally situated for touring East Anglia, Cambridge, Ely Cathedral, Newmarket, Bury St. Edmunds, & many National Trust properties. Equine tours can be arranged. 3 attractive bedrooms, 1 with en-suite facilities in the house & 3 bedrooms in a cottage in the grounds, with self-catering facilities. Fordham is the 1st village off the A.14 on the Newmarket to Ely A.142 road. Good local restaurants.

Jan & Malcolm Roper Queensberry 196 Carter Street Fordham CB7 5JU Cambridgeshire
Tel: (01638) 720916 Fax 01638 720233 Open: ALL YEAR Map Ref No. 08

Chiswick House

see PHOTO over p. 46

Nearest Road: A.10

A beautiful timber-framed farmhouse dating from the 16th century. The royal crest of King James I is to be found above the fireplace, suggesting this was his hunting lodge in the early 1600s. Jacobean panelling, oak beams & open fireplaces create a wonderful atmosphere. Accommodation is in 6 delightful en-suite rooms, with tea/coffee-making facilities. T.V. is available. There are many excellent inns nearby. An ideal base for touring Cambridge, Suffolk & Hertfordshire.

Bernice & John Elbourn Chiswick House Chiswick End Meldreth Royston SG8 6LZ Cambridgeshire
Tel: (01763) 260242 Open: FEB - NOV Map Ref No. 09

Model Farm

Nearest Road: A.1198

A warm & friendly welcome awaits visitors to this traditional 1870s farmhouse situated on a working family farm. The house, providing comfortable & attractive accommodation & lovely views, is set in open countryside between the villages of Little Gransden & Longstowe. Guests are welcome to walk around the farm & garden. Cambridge with its many beautiful colleges can be reached in 20 mins via the B.1046 which takes the motorist on a picturesque drive through villages.

Mrs Sue Barlow Model Farm Little Gransden Sandy SG19 3EA Cambridgeshire
Tel: (01767) 677361 Fax 01767 677883 Open: ALL YEAR (Excl. Xmas Day) Map Ref No. 10

Chiswick House. Royston

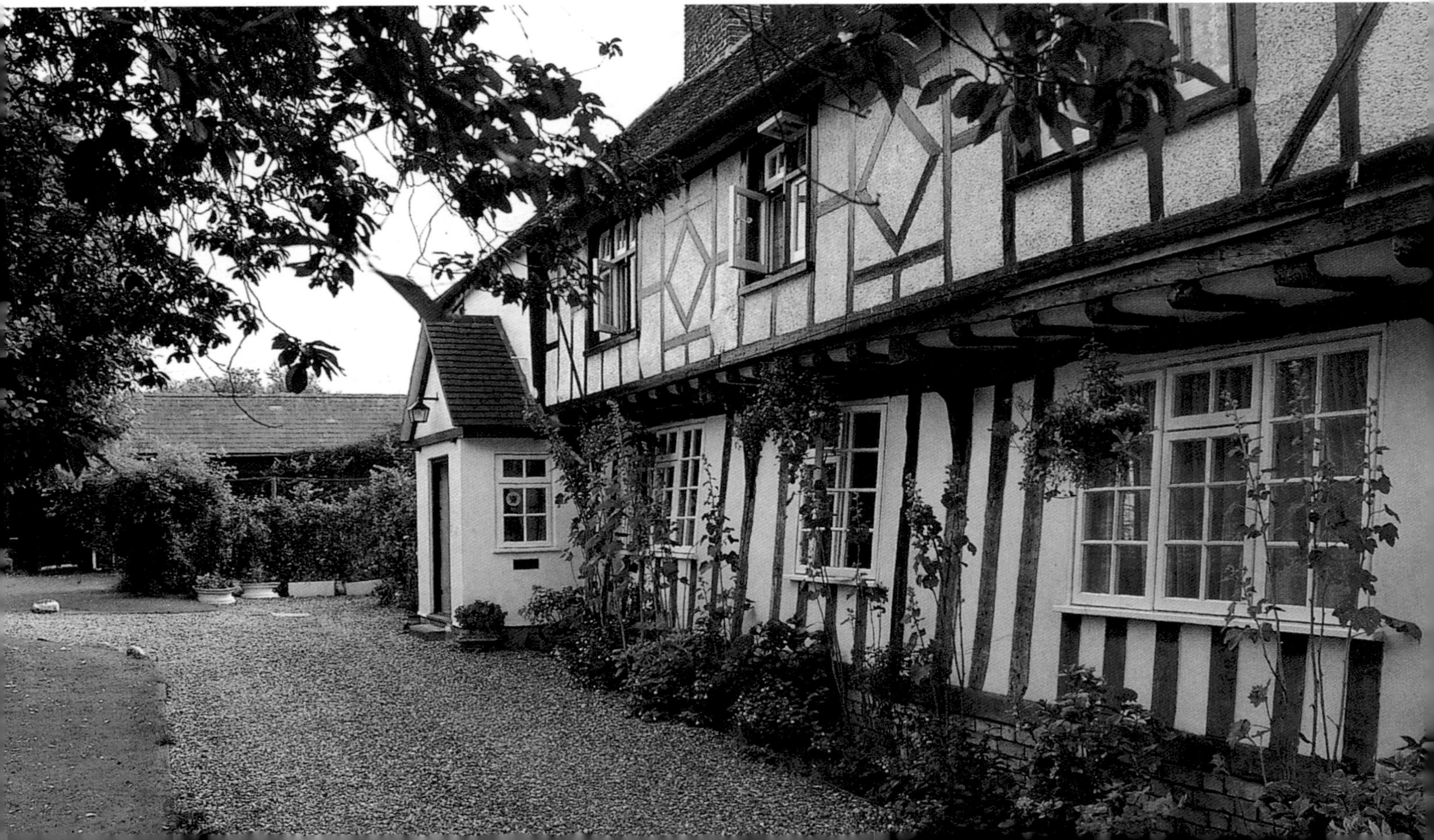

Northamptonshire

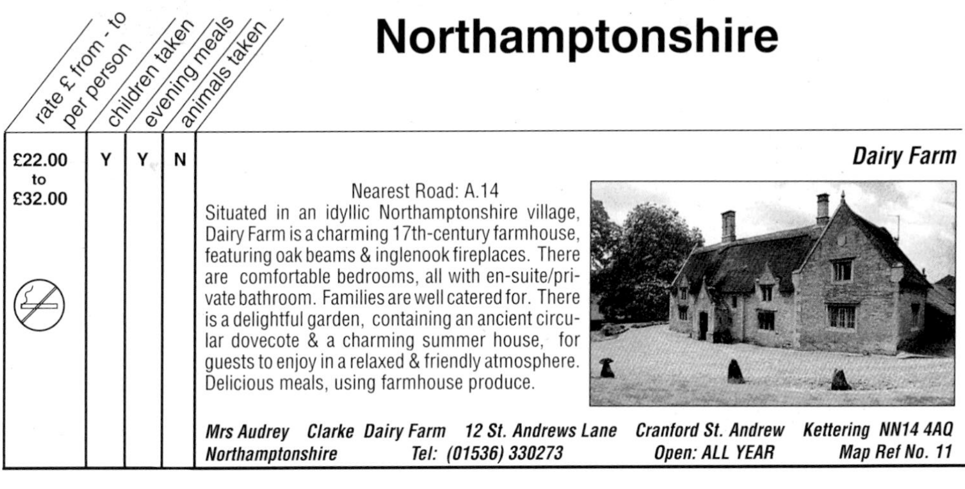

rate £ from - to per person	children taken	evening meals	animals taken	
£22.00 to £32.00	Y	Y	N	***Dairy Farm*** Nearest Road: A.14 Situated in an idyllic Northamptonshire village, Dairy Farm is a charming 17th-century farmhouse, featuring oak beams & inglenook fireplaces. There are comfortable bedrooms, all with en-suite/private bathroom. Families are well catered for. There is a delightful garden, containing an ancient circular dovecote & a charming summer house, for guests to enjoy in a relaxed & friendly atmosphere. Delicious meals, using farmhouse produce. *Mrs Audrey Clarke Dairy Farm 12 St. Andrews Lane Cranford St. Andrew Kettering NN14 4AQ Northamptonshire Tel: (01536) 330273 Open: ALL YEAR Map Ref No. 11*

All the establishments mentioned in this guide are members of The Worldwide Bed & Breakfast Association

When booking your accommodation please mention The Best Bed & Breakfast

Cheshire & Lancashire

Cheshire (North West)

Cheshire is located between the Peak District & the mountains of North Wales & is easily accessible from three major motorways. It has much to attract long visits but is also an ideal stopping-off point for travellers to the Lake District & Scotland, or to North Wales or Ireland. There is good access eastwards to York & the east coast & to the south to Stratford-upon-Avon & to London.

Cheshire can boast seven magnificent stately homes, the most visited zoo outside London, four of Europe's largest garden centres & many popular venues which feature distinctive Cheshire themes such as silk, salt, cheese, antiques & country crafts.

The Cheshire plain with Chester, its fine county town, & its pretty villages, rises up to Alderley Edge in the east from where there are panoramic views, & then climbs dramatically to meet the heights of the Peaks.

To the west is the coastline of the Wirral Peninsula with miles of sandy beaches & dunes &, of course, Liverpool.

The countryside shelters very beautiful houses. Little Moreton Hall near Congleton, is one of the most perfect imaginable. It is a black & white "magpie" house & not one of its walls is perpendicular, yet it has withstood time & weather for nearly four centuries, standing on the waterside gazing at its own reflection.

Tatton Hall is large & imposing & is splendidly furnished with many fine objects on display. The park & gardens are a delight & especially renowned for the azaleas & rhododendrons. In complete contrast is the enormous radio telescope at Jodrell Bank where visitors can be introduced to planetary astronomy in the planetarium.

Chester is a joy; a walk through its streets is like walking through living history. The old city is encircled by city walls enclosing arcaded streets with handsome black & white galleried buildings that blend well with modern life. There are many excellent shops along these "Rows". Chester Cathedral is a fine building of monastic foundation,with a peaceful cloister & outstanding wood carving in the choir stalls. Boat rides can be taken along the River Dee which flows through the city.

Manchester has first rate shopping, restaurants, sporting facilities, theatres & many museums ranging from an excellent costume museum to the fascinating Museum of Science & Industry.

Little Moreton Hall.

Liverpool grew from a tiny fishing village on the northern shores of the Mersey River, receiving its charter from King John in 1207. Commercial & slave trading with the West Indies led to massive expansion in the 17th & 18th centuries. The Liverpool of today owes much to the introduction of the steam ship in the mid 1900s, which enabled thousands of Irish to emigrate when the potatoe famine was at its height in Ireland. This is a city with a reputation for patronage of art, music & sport.

Cheshire & Lancashire

Lancashire (North West)

Lancashire can prove a surprisingly beautiful county. Despite its industrial history of cotton production, there is magnificent scenery & there are many fine towns & villages. Connections with the Crown & the clashes of the Houses of Lancaster & York have left a rich heritage of buildings with a variety of architecture. There are old stone cottages & farmhouses, as well as manor houses from many centuries.

For lovers of the countryside, Lancashire has the sweeping hills of Bowland, the lovely Ribble Valley, the moors of Rossendale & one mountain, mysterious Pendle Hill.

The Royal Forest of Bowland is a forest without trees, which has provided rich hunting grounds over the centuries. An old windswept pass runs over the heights of Salter Fell & High Cross Fell from Slaidburn, where the Inn, the "Hark to Bounty", was named after the noisiest hound in the squire's pack & used to be the courtroom where strict forest laws were enforced.

Further south, the Trough of Bowland provides an easier route through the hills, & here is the beautiful village of Abbeystead in Wynesdale where monks once farmed the land. The church has stained glass windows portraying shepherds & their flocks & there are pegs in the porch where shepherds hung their crooks.

Below the dramatic hills of Bowland, the green valley of the Ribble climbs from Preston to the Yorkshire Dales. Hangridge Fell, where the tales of witches are almost as numerous as those of Pendle Hill, lies at the beginning of the valley.

Pendle Hill can be reached from the pretty village of Downham which has Tudor, Jacobean & Georgian houses, village stocks & an old inn. Old Pendle rises abruptly to 1831 feet & is a strange land formation. It is shrouded in legend & stories of witchcraft.

Between Pendle Hill & the moors of Rossendale are the textile towns of Nelson, Colne, Burnley, Accrington & Blackburn. The textile industry was well established in Tudor times & the towns grew up as markets for the trading of the cloth woven in the Piece Halls.

The moors which descend to the very edges of the textile towns are wild & beautiful & have many prehistoric tumuli & earthworks. Through the towns & the countryside, winds the Liverpool & Leeds canal, providing an excellent towpath route to see the area.

Lancaster is an historic city boasting the largest castle in England, dating back to Norman times.

Lancashire's coastal resorts are legendary, & Blackpool is Queen of them all with her miles of illuminations & millions of visitors.

Downham Village.

Cheshire & Lancashire

Lancashire Gazeteer

Areas of outstanding natural beauty.
The Forest of Bowland, Parts of Arnside & Silverdale.

Historic Houses & Castles

Rufford Old Hall - Rufford
15th century screen in half-timbered hall of note. Collection of relics of Lancashire life.
Chingle Hall - Nr. Preston
13th century - small manor house with moat. Rose gardens. Haunted!
Astley Hall - Chorley
Elizabethan house reconstructed in 17th century. Houses pictures, tapestries, pottery & furniture.
Gawthorpe Hall - Padiham
17th century manor house with 19th century restoration. Moulded ceilings & some fine panelling. A collection of lace & embroidery.
Bramall Hall - Bramall
Fine example of half-timbered (black & white) manor house built in 14th century & added to in Elizabethan times. .
Lancaster Castle - Lancaster
Largest of English castles - dates back to Norman era.
Astley Hall - Chorley
16th century half-timbered grouped around central court. Rebuilt in the Jacobean manner with long gallery. Unique furniture.
Hoghton Tower - Nr. Preston
16th century - fortified hill-top mansion - magnificent banquet hall. Dramatic building - walled gardens & rose gardens.
Thurnham Hall - Lancaster
13th century origins. 16th century additions & 19th century facade. Beautiful plasterwork of Elizabethan period. Jacobean staircase.

Cathedrals & Churches

Lancaster (St. Mary)
15th century with 18th century tower. Restored chapel - fine stalls.
Whalley (St. Mary)
13th century with 15th century tower, clerestory & aisle windows. Fine wood carving of 15th century canopied stalls.
Halsall (St. Cuthbert)
14th century chancel, 15th century perpendicular spire. 14th century tomb. Original doors, brasses & effigies. 19th century restoration.
Tarleton (St. Mary)
18th century, part 19th century.
Great Mitton (All Hallows)
15th century rood screen, 16th century font cover, 17th century pulpit.

Museums & Galleries

Blackburn Museum - Blackburn
Extensive collections relating to local history archeology, ceramics, geology & natural history. One of the finest collection of coins & fine collection of mediaeval illuminated manuscripts & early printed books.
Bury Museum & Art Gallery - Bury
Houses fine Victorian oil & watercolours. Turner, Constable, Landseer, de Wint.
City Gallery - Manchester
Pre-Raphaelites, Old Masters, Impressionists, modern painters all represented in this fine gallery; also silver & pottery collections.
Higher Mill Museum - Helmshaw
One of the oldest wool textile finishing mills left in Lancashire. Spinning wheels, Hargreave's Spinning Jenny, several of Arkwrights machines, 20 foot water wheel.
Townley Hall Art Gallery & Museum, & Museum of Local Crafts & Industries - Burnley.

Cheshire Gazeteer

Area of outstanding natural beauty
Part of the Peaks National Park
Addington Hall - Macclesfield
15th century Elizabethan Black & White half timbered house.
Bishop Lloyd's House - Chester
17th century half timbered house (restored). Fine carvings. Has associations with Yale University & New Haven, USA.
Chorley Old Hall - Alderley Edge
14th century hall with 16th century Elizabethan wing.
Forfold Hall - Nantwich
17th century Jacobean country house, with fine panelling.

Cheshire & Lancashire

Gawsworth Hall - Macclesfield
Fine Tudor Half timbered Manor House. Tilting ground. Pictures, furniture, sculptures, etc.
Lyme Park - Disley
Elizabethan with Palladian exterior by Leoni. Gibbons carvings. Beautiful park with herd of red deer.
Peover Hall - Over Peover, Knutsford
16th century- stables of Tudor period; has the famous magpie ceiling.
Tatton Park - Knutsford
Beautifully decorated & furnished Georgian House with a fine collection of glass, china & paintings including Van Dyke & Canaletto. Landscaping by Humphrey Repton.
Little Moreton Hall - Nr. Congleton
15th century timbered, moated house with 16th century wall-paintings.

Cathedrals & Churches

Acton (St. Mary)
13th century with stone seating around walls. 17th century effigies.
Bunbury (St. Boniface)
14th century collegiate church - alabaster effigy.
Congleton (St. Peter)
18th century - box pews, brass candelabrum, 18th century glass.
Chester Cathedral - Chester
Subjected to restoration by Victorians - 14th century choir stalls.
Malpas (St. Oswalds)
15th century - fine screens, some old stalls, two family chapels.
Mobberley (St. Wilfred)
Mediaeval - 15th century rood screen, wall paintings, very old glass.
Shotwick (St. Michael)
Twin nave - box pews, 14th century quatre - foil lights, 3 deck pulpit.
Winwick (St. Oswald)
14th century - splendid roof. Pugin chancel.
Wrenbury (St. Margaret)
16th century - west gallery, monuments & hatchments. Box pews.
Liverpool Cathedral - the Anglican Cathedral was completed in 1980 after 76 years of work. It is of massive proportions, the largest in the U.K. with much delicate detailed work.

Museums & Galleries

Grosvenor Museum - Chester
Art, folk history, natural history, Roman antiquities including a special display of information about the Roman army.
Chester Heritage Centre - Chester
Interesting exhibition of the architectural heritage of Chester.
Cheshire Military Museum - Chester
The three local Regiments are commemorated here.
King Charles Tower - Chester
Chester at the time of the Civil War illustrated by dioramas.
Museum & Art Gallery - Warrington
Anthropology, geology, ethnology, botany & natural history. Pottery, porcelain, glass, collection of early English watercolours.
West Park Museum & Art Gallery - Macclesfield
Egyptian collection, oil paintings, watercolours, sketches by Landseer & Tunnicliffe.
Norton Priory Museum - Runcorn
Remains of excavated mediaeval priory. Also wildlife display.
Quarry Bank Mill - Styal
The Mill is a fine example of industrial building & houses an exhibition of the cotton industry: the various offices retain their original furnishing, & the turbine room has the transmission systems & two turbines of 1903.
Nether Alderley Mill - Nether Alderley
15th century corn mill which was still used in 1929. Now restored.
The Albert Dock & Maritime Museum - Liverpool
Housing the Liverpool Tate Gallery, the Tate of the North.
Walker Art Gallery - Liverpool
Jodrell Bank - radio telescope & planetarium.

Historic Monuments

Chester Castle - Chester
Huge square tower remaining.
Roman Amphitheatre - Chester
12th legion site - half excavated.
Beeston Castle - Beeston
Remains of a 13th century fort.
Sandbach Crosses - Sandbach
Carved stone crosses date from the 9th C.

CHESHIRE & LANCASHIRE

Map reference

01	**D.Taylor**	07	**Sutcliffe**	14	**Townend**
02	**Ikin**	08	**I. Taylor**	14	**M. Smith**
03	**West**	11	**Butler**	15	**G. Smith**
04	**Read**	12	**Rothwell**		

Longview Hotel. Knutsford.

Cheshire

rate £ from - to per person	children taken	evening meals	animals taken

Ash Farm

Nearest Road: A.56

Set in beautiful National Trust countryside. David & Janice have renovated this 18th-century farmhouse to a very high standard. Bedrooms are en-suite & have many features to delight the discerning traveller. The residents' lounge & dining area is furnished with an antique oak dining suite & open log fire & is the setting for excellent farmhouse food. Only 5 mins' walk to Dunham Deer Park; 2 miles M.56, M.6 less than 6 miles. Manchester Airport 10 mins. Easy access to Manchester & Chester. Single supplement.

rate £ from - to per person	children taken	evening meals	animals taken
£28.50 to £33.50	N	N	N

VISA: M'CARD: AMEX:

David Taylor Ash Farm Park Lane Little Bollington Altrincham WA14 4TJ Cheshire
Tel: (0161) 9299290 Fax 0161 9285002 Open: ALL YEAR (Excl. Xmas) Map Ref No. 01

Golborne Manor

Nearest Road: A.41

Golborne Manor is an elegant 19th-century country residence with glorious views, renovated to a high standard & set in 3 1/2 acres of gardens & grounds. It is beautifully decorated with spacious en-suite bedrooms. Delicious farmhouse breakfasts are served. Evening meals by arrangement. Piano & croquet set available for guests' use. Large car park. Easy access for motorways. 10 mins' drive south from Chester on the A.41, turning right a few yards after D.P. Motors (on the left).
E-mail: ann.ikin@golbornemanor.co.uk

rate £ from - to per person	children taken	evening meals	animals taken
£30.00 to £35.00	Y	N	N

Ann Ikin Golborne Manor Platts Lane Hatton Heath Chester CH3 9AN Cheshire
Tel: (01829) 770310 Fax 01829 770370 Open: ALL YEAR Map Ref No. 02

Longview Hotel & Restaurant

Nearest Road: A.50

Set in this pleasant Cheshire market town overlooking the common is this lovely, friendly hotel, furnished with many antiques that reflect the elegance of this Victorian building. Care has been taken to retain its character, while also providing all required comforts for the discerning traveller. All of the 26 en-suite bedrooms are prettily decorated, giving them that cared-for feeling which is echoed throughout the hotel. You are assured of a warm welcome as soon as you step into reception.
E-mail: longview_hotel@compuserve.com

rate £ from - to per person	children taken	evening meals	animals taken
£33.25 to £65.00	Y	Y	Y

see PHOTO over p. 53

VISA: M'CARD: AMEX:

Mr & Mrs S. West Longview Hotel & Restaurant 51+55 Manchester Rd Knutsford WA16 0LX Cheshire
Tel: (01565) 632119 Fax 01565 652402 Open: ALL YEAR Map Ref No. 03

Hardingland Farm

Nearest Road: A.537

Enjoy yourself in this early Georgian farmhouse, lovingly restored & furnished with antiques. In a beautiful position in the Peak National Park, with superb views over the Cheshire Plain. Relax in the delightful lounge, & enjoy delicious meals prepared by Anne, who is renowned for her cooking. Accommodation is in 3 bedrooms, 2 en-suite & all individually decorated. Hardingland Farm is ideally situated for the Peak District & Cheshire.
E-mail: AnneBandB@aol.com

rate £ from - to per person	children taken	evening meals	animals taken
£20.00 to £25.00	N	Y	N

Mrs Anne Read Hardingland Farm Macclesfield Forest Macclesfield SK11 0ND Cheshire
Tel: (01625) 425759 Fax 01625 615011 Open: MAR - NOV Map Ref No. 04

Roughlow Farm. Willington.

The Manor. Worthenbury.

rate £ from - to per person	children taken	evening meals	animals taken

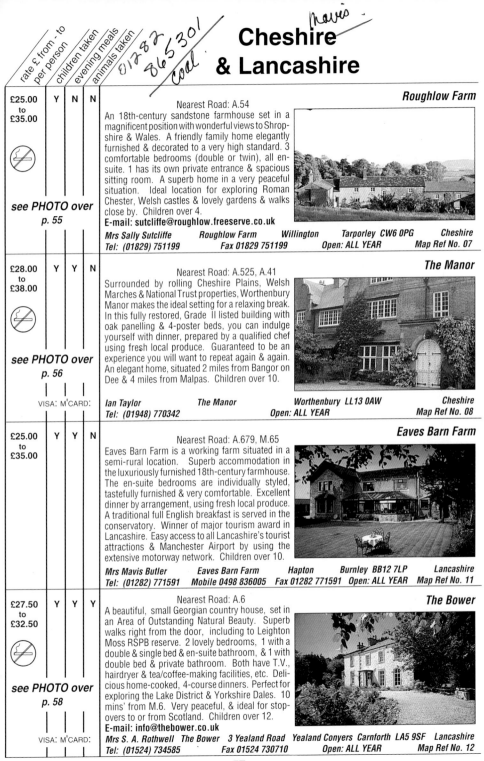

01282 865301 Coal Mavis

Roughlow Farm

£25.00 to £35.00	Y	N	N

see PHOTO over p. 55

Nearest Road: A.54

An 18th-century sandstone farmhouse set in a magnificent position with wonderful views to Shropshire & Wales. A friendly family home elegantly furnished & decorated to a very high standard. 3 comfortable bedrooms (double or twin), all en-suite. 1 has its own private entrance & spacious sitting room. A superb home in a very peaceful situation. Ideal location for exploring Roman Chester, Welsh castles & lovely gardens & walks close by. Children over 4.

E-mail: sutcliffe@roughlow.freeserve.co.uk

Mrs Sally Sutcliffe *Roughlow Farm* *Willington* *Tarporley CW6 0PG* *Cheshire*
Tel: (01829) 751199 *Fax 01829 751199* *Open: ALL YEAR* *Map Ref No. 07*

The Manor

£28.00 to £38.00	Y	Y	N

see PHOTO over p. 56

VISA: M'CARD:

Nearest Road: A.525, A.41

Surrounded by rolling Cheshire Plains, Welsh Marches & National Trust properties, Worthenbury Manor makes the ideal setting for a relaxing break. In this fully restored, Grade II listed building with oak panelling & 4-poster beds, you can indulge yourself with dinner, prepared by a qualified chef using fresh local produce. Guaranteed to be an experience you will want to repeat again & again. An elegant home, situated 2 miles from Bangor on Dee & 4 miles from Malpas. Children over 10.

Ian Taylor *The Manor* *Worthenbury LL13 0AW* *Cheshire*
Tel: (01948) 770342 *Open: ALL YEAR* *Map Ref No. 08*

Eaves Barn Farm

£25.00 to £35.00	Y	Y	N

Nearest Road: A.679, M.65

Eaves Barn Farm is a working farm situated in a semi-rural location. Superb accommodation in the luxuriously furnished 18th-century farmhouse. The en-suite bedrooms are individually styled, tastefully furnished & very comfortable. Excellent dinner by arrangement, using fresh local produce. A traditional full English breakfast is served in the conservatory. Winner of major tourism award in Lancashire. Easy access to all Lancashire's tourist attractions & Manchester Airport by using the extensive motorway network. Children over 10.

Mrs Mavis Butler *Eaves Barn Farm* *Hapton* *Burnley BB12 7LP* *Lancashire*
Tel: (01282) 771591 *Mobile 0498 836005* *Fax 01282 771591* *Open: ALL YEAR* *Map Ref No. 11*

The Bower

£27.50 to £32.50	Y	Y	Y

see PHOTO over p. 58

VISA: M'CARD:

Nearest Road: A.6

A beautiful, small Georgian country house, set in an Area of Outstanding Natural Beauty. Superb walks right from the door, including to Leighton Moss RSPB reserve. 2 lovely bedrooms, 1 with a double & single bed & en-suite bathroom, & 1 with double bed & private bathroom. Both have T.V., hairdryer & tea/coffee-making facilities, etc. Delicious home-cooked, 4-course dinners. Perfect for exploring the Lake District & Yorkshire Dales. 10 mins' from M.6. Very peaceful, & ideal for stop-overs to or from Scotland. Children over 12.

E-mail: info@thebower.co.uk

Mrs S. A. Rothwell *The Bower* *3 Yealand Road* *Yealand Conyers* *Carnforth LA5 9SF* *Lancashire*
Tel: (01524) 734585 *Fax 01524 730710* *Open: ALL YEAR* *Map Ref No. 12*

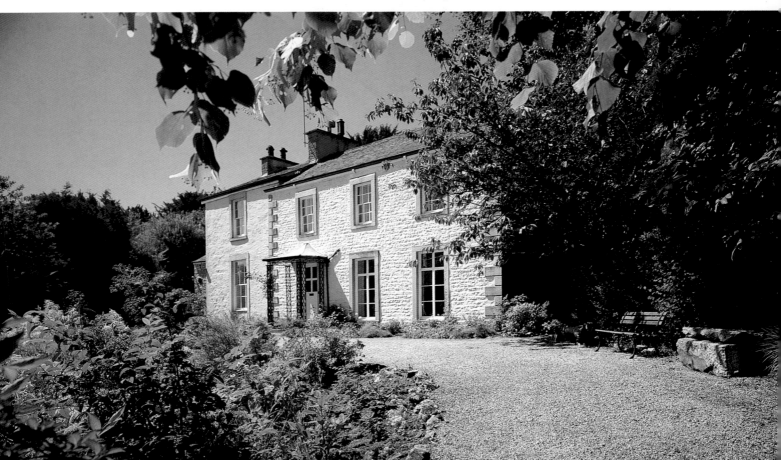

The Bower. Yealand Conyers.

Lancashire

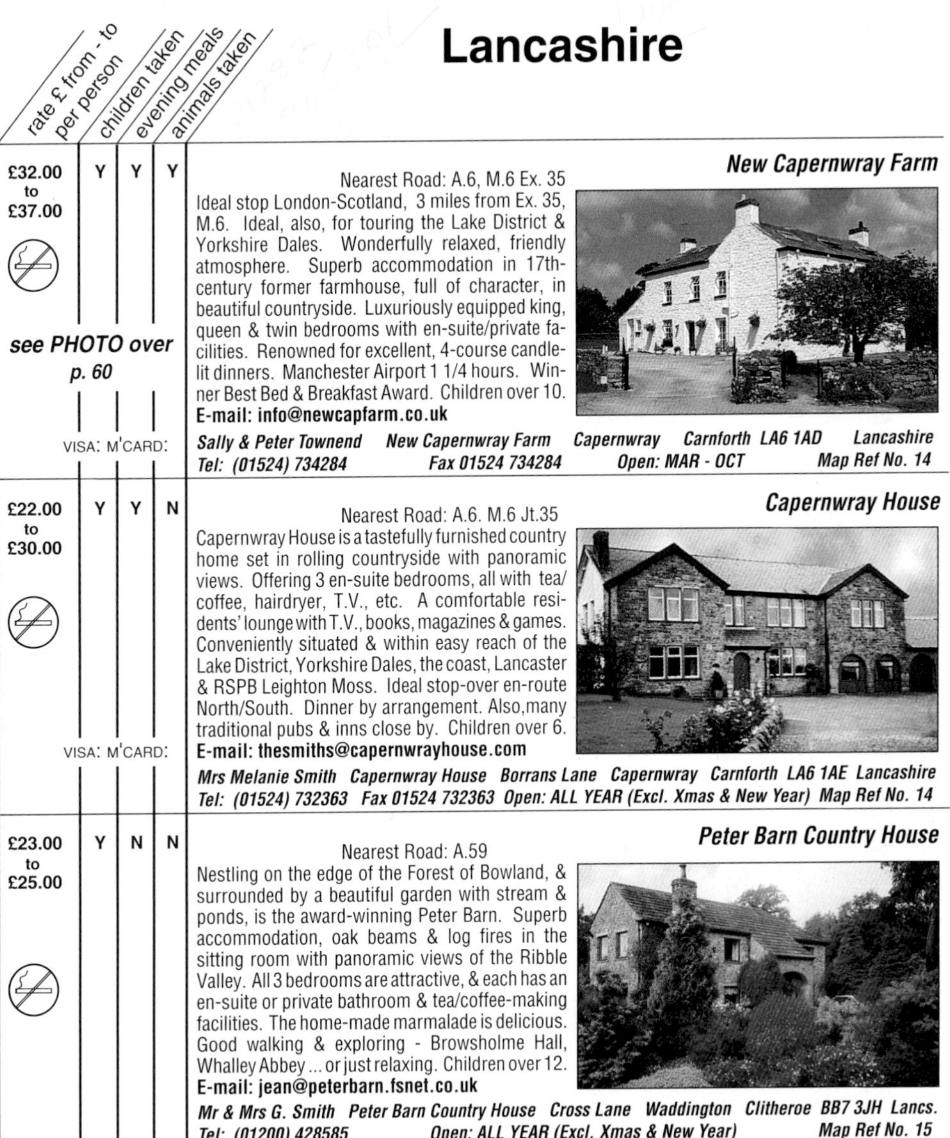

rate £ from - to per person	children taken	evening meals	animals taken	
£32.00 to £37.00	Y	Y	Y	New Capernwray Farm
£22.00 to £30.00	Y	Y	N	Capernwray House
£23.00 to £25.00	Y	N	N	Peter Barn Country House

New Capernwray Farm

£32.00 to £37.00 — Y Y Y

see PHOTO over p. 60

VISA: M'CARD:

Nearest Road: A.6, M.6 Ex. 35

Ideal stop London-Scotland, 3 miles from Ex. 35, M.6. Ideal, also, for touring the Lake District & Yorkshire Dales. Wonderfully relaxed, friendly atmosphere. Superb accommodation in 17th-century former farmhouse, full of character, in beautiful countryside. Luxuriously equipped king, queen & twin bedrooms with en-suite/private facilities. Renowned for excellent, 4-course candle-lit dinners. Manchester Airport 1 1/4 hours. Winner Best Bed & Breakfast Award. Children over 10.

E-mail: info@newcapfarm.co.uk

Sally & Peter Townend New Capernwray Farm Capernwray Carnforth LA6 1AD Lancashire
Tel: (01524) 734284 Fax 01524 734284 Open: MAR - OCT Map Ref No. 14

Capernwray House

£22.00 to £30.00 — Y Y N

VISA: M'CARD:

Nearest Road: A.6. M.6 Jt.35

Capernwray House is a tastefully furnished country home set in rolling countryside with panoramic views. Offering 3 en-suite bedrooms, all with tea/coffee, hairdryer, T.V., etc. A comfortable residents' lounge with T.V., books, magazines & games. Conveniently situated & within easy reach of the Lake District, Yorkshire Dales, the coast, Lancaster & RSPB Leighton Moss. Ideal stop-over en-route North/South. Dinner by arrangement. Also,many traditional pubs & inns close by. Children over 6.

E-mail: thesmiths@capernwrayhouse.com

Mrs Melanie Smith Capernwray House Borrans Lane Capernwray Carnforth LA6 1AE Lancashire
Tel: (01524) 732363 Fax 01524 732363 Open: ALL YEAR (Excl. Xmas & New Year) Map Ref No. 14

Peter Barn Country House

£23.00 to £25.00 — Y N N

Nearest Road: A.59

Nestling on the edge of the Forest of Bowland, & surrounded by a beautiful garden with stream & ponds, is the award-winning Peter Barn. Superb accommodation, oak beams & log fires in the sitting room with panoramic views of the Ribble Valley. All 3 bedrooms are attractive, & each has an en-suite or private bathroom & tea/coffee-making facilities. The home-made marmalade is delicious. Good walking & exploring - Browsholme Hall, Whalley Abbey ... or just relaxing. Children over 12.

E-mail: jean@peterbarn.fsnet.co.uk

Mr & Mrs G. Smith Peter Barn Country House Cross Lane Waddington Clitheroe BB7 3JH Lancs.
Tel: (01200) 428585 Open: ALL YEAR (Excl. Xmas & New Year) Map Ref No. 15

Visit our website at:
http://www.bestbandb.co.uk

New Capernwray Farm. Carnforth.

Cornwall

Cornwall

(West Country)

Cornwall is an ancient Celtic land, a narrow granite peninsula with a magnificent coastline of over 300 miles & wild stretches of moorland.

The north coast, washed by Atlantic breakers, has firm golden sands & soaring cliffs. The magnificent beaches at Bude offer excellent surfing & a few miles to the south you can visit the picturesque harbour at Boscastle & the cliff-top castle at Tintagel with its legends of King Arthur. Newquay, with its beaches stretching for over seven miles, sheltered coves & modern hotels & shops, is the premier resort on Cornwall's Atlantic coast. St. Ives, another surfing resort, has great charm which has attracted artists for so long & is an ideal place from which to explore the Land's End peninsula.

The south coast is a complete contrast - wooded estuaries, sheltered coves, little fishing ports, & popular resorts. Penzance, with its warmth & vivid colours, is an all-the-year-round resort & has wonderful views across the bay to St. Michael's Mount. Here are excellent facilities for sailing & deep-sea fishing, as there are at Falmouth & Fowey with their superb harbours. Mevagissey, Polperro & Looe are fine examples of traditional Cornish fishing villages.

In the far west of Cornwall, you can hear about a fascinating legend: the lost land of Lyonesse - a whole country that was drowned by the sea. The legend goes that the waters cover a rich & fertile country, which had 140 parish churches. The Anglo-Saxon Chronicle records two great storms within a hundred years, which drowned many towns & innumerate people. Submerged forests are known to lie around these coasts - & in Mount's Bay beech trees have been found with the nuts still hanging on the branches, so suddenly were they swamped.

Today, St Michael's Mount & the Isles of Scilly are said to be all that remains of the vanished land. St. Michael's Mount, with its tiny fishing village & dramatic castle, can be visited on foot at low tide or by boat at high water. The Isles of Scilly, 28 miles beyond Land's End, have five inhabited islands, including Tresco with its sub-tropical gardens. Day trips to the numerous uninhabited islands are a special feature of a Scilly holiday.

Inland Cornwall also has its attractions. To the east of Bodmin, the county town, are the open uplands of Bodmin Moor, with the county's highest peaks at Rough Tor & Brown Willy. "Jamaica Inn", immortalised in the novel by Daphne du Maurier, stands on the lonely road across the moor, & "Frenchman's Creek" is on a hidden inlet of the Helford River.

There is a seemingly endless number & variety of Cornish villages in estuaries, wooded, pastoral or moorland settings, & here customs & traditions are maintained. In Helston the famous "Fleury Dance" is still performed, & at the ancient port of Padstow, May Day celebrating involves decorating the houses with green boughs & parading the Hobby Horse through the street to the tune of St. George's Song.

Helford Creek

Cornwall

Cornwall Gazeteer

Areas of outstanding natural beauty.
Almost the entire county.

Historic Houses & Castles

Anthony House - Torpoint
18th century - beautiful & quite unspoiled Queen Anne house, excellent panelling & fine period furnishings.
Cotehele House - Calstock
15th & 16th century house, still contains the original furniture, tapestry, armour, etc.
Ebbingford Manor - Bude
12th century Cornish manor house, with walled garden.
Godolphin House - Helston
Tudor - 17th century colonnaded front.
Lanhydrock - Bodmin
17th century - splendid plaster ceilings, picture gallery with family portraits 17th/ 20th centuries.
Mount Edgcumbe House - Plymouth
Tudor style mansion - restored after destruction in 1949. Hepplewhite furniture & portrait by Joshua Reynolds.
St. Michael's Mount - Penzance
Mediaeval castle & 17th century with 18th & 19th century additions.
Pencarrow House & Gardens - Bodmin
18th century Georgian Mansion - collection of paintings, china & furniture - mile long drive through fine woodlands & gardens.
Old Post Office - Tintagel
14th century manor house in miniature - large hall used as Post Office for a period, hence the name.
Trewithen - Probus Nr. Truro
Early Georgian house with lovely gardens.
Trerice - St. Newlyn East
16th century Elizabethan house, small with elaborate facade. Excellent fireplaces, plaster ceilings, miniature gallery & minstrels' gallery.

Cathedral & Churches

Altarnun (St. Nonna)
15th century, Norman font, 16th century bench ends, fine rood screen.
Bisland (St. Protus & St. Hyacinth)
15th century granite tower - carved wagon roofs, slate floor. Georgian wine - glass pulpit, fine screen.
Kilkhampton (St. James)
16th century with fine Norman doorway, arcades & wagon roofs.
Laneast (St. Michael or St. Sedwell)
13th century, 15th century enlargement, 16th century pulpit, some painted glass.
Lanteglos-by-Fowley (St. Willow)
14th century, refashioned 15th century, 13th century font, 15th century brasses & altar tomb, 16th century bench ends.
Launcells (St. Andrew)
Interior unrestored - old plaster & ancient roofs remaining, fine Norman font with 17th century cover, box pews, pulpit, reredos, 3 sided alter rails.
Probus (St. Probus & St. Gren)
16th century tower, splendid arcades, three great East windows.
St. Keverne (St. Keverne)
Fine tower & spire. Wall painting in 15th century interior.
St. Neot (St. Neot)
Decorated tower - 16th century exterior, buttressed & double-aisled. Many windows of mediaeval glass renewed in 19th century.

Museums & Galleries

Museum of Witchcraft - Boscastle
Relating to witches, implements & customs.
Military Museum - Bodmin
History of Duke of Cornwall's Light Infantry.
Public Library & Museum - Cambourne
Collections of mineralogy, archaeology, local antiquities & history.
Cornish Museum - East Looe
Collection of relics relating to witchcraft customs & superstitions. Folk life & culture of district.
Helston Borough Museum - Helston
Folk life & culture of area around Lizard.
Museum of Nautical Art - Penzance
Exhibition of salvaged gold & silver treasures from underwater wreck of 1700's.
Museum of Smuggling - Polperro
Activities of smugglers, past & present.

Cornwall

Penlee House Museum - Penlee, Penzance
Archaeology & local history & tin mining exhibits.
Barbara Hepworth Museum - St. Ives
Sculpture, letters, documents, photographs, etc., exhibited in house where Barbara Hepworth lived.
Old Mariners Church - St. Ives
St. Ives Society of Artists hold exhibitions here.
County Museum & Art Gallery - Truro
Ceramics, art local history & antiquities, Cornish mineralogy.

Historic Monuments

Cromwell's Castle - Tresco (Scilly Isles)
17th century castle.
King Charles' Fort - Tresco (Scilly Isles)
16th century fort.
Old Blockhouse - Tresco (Scilly Isles)
16th century coastal battery.
Harry's Wall - St. Mary's (Scilly Isles)
Tudor Coastal battery
Ballowall Barrow - St. Just
Prehistoric barrow.
Pendennis Castle - Falmouth
Fort from time of Henry VII.
Restormel Castle - Lostwithiel
13th century ruins.
St. Mawes Castle - St. Mawes
16th century fortified castle.
Tintagel Castle - Tintagel
Mediaeval ruin on wild coast, King Arthur's legendary castle.

Things to see & do

Camel trail - Padstow to Bodmin
12 miles of recreation path along scenic route, suitable for walkers, cyclists & horse-riders.
Tresco Abbey Gardens - Tresco
Collection of sub-tropical flora
Trethorne Leisure Farm - Launceston
Visitors are encouraged to feed & stroke the farm animals
Seal sanctuary - Gweek Nr. Helston
Seals, exhibition hall, nature walk, aquarium, seal hospital, donkey paddock.
Dobwalls Theme Park - Nr. Liskeard
2 miles of scenically dramatic miniature railway based on the American railroad.
Padstow tropical bird gardens - Padstow
Mynack Theatre - Porthcurno

Lands End.

CORNWALL

Map reference

02	**Purslow**	44	**Studley**
06	**Knight**	46	**Epperson**
08	**Tremayne**	48	**Dodds**
10	**Leith**	50	**Nancarrow**
12	**Griffin**	52	**Martin**
14	**Rowe**	54	**Sykes**
16	**Stanley**	56	**Semmens**
18	**Eades**	58	**Bryant**
20	**Mackenzie**	58	**Devlin**
22	**Woodley**	60	**Fry**
30	**Smith**	64	**Poole**
32	**Richards**	66	**Heasman**
34	**Wilson**	68	**Vichniakov**
36	**Taylor**	70	**Barstow**
38	**Wooldridge**	72	**A. Tremayne**
40	**Tuckett**	74	**Dymond**
42	**Rowe**	76	**Walker**

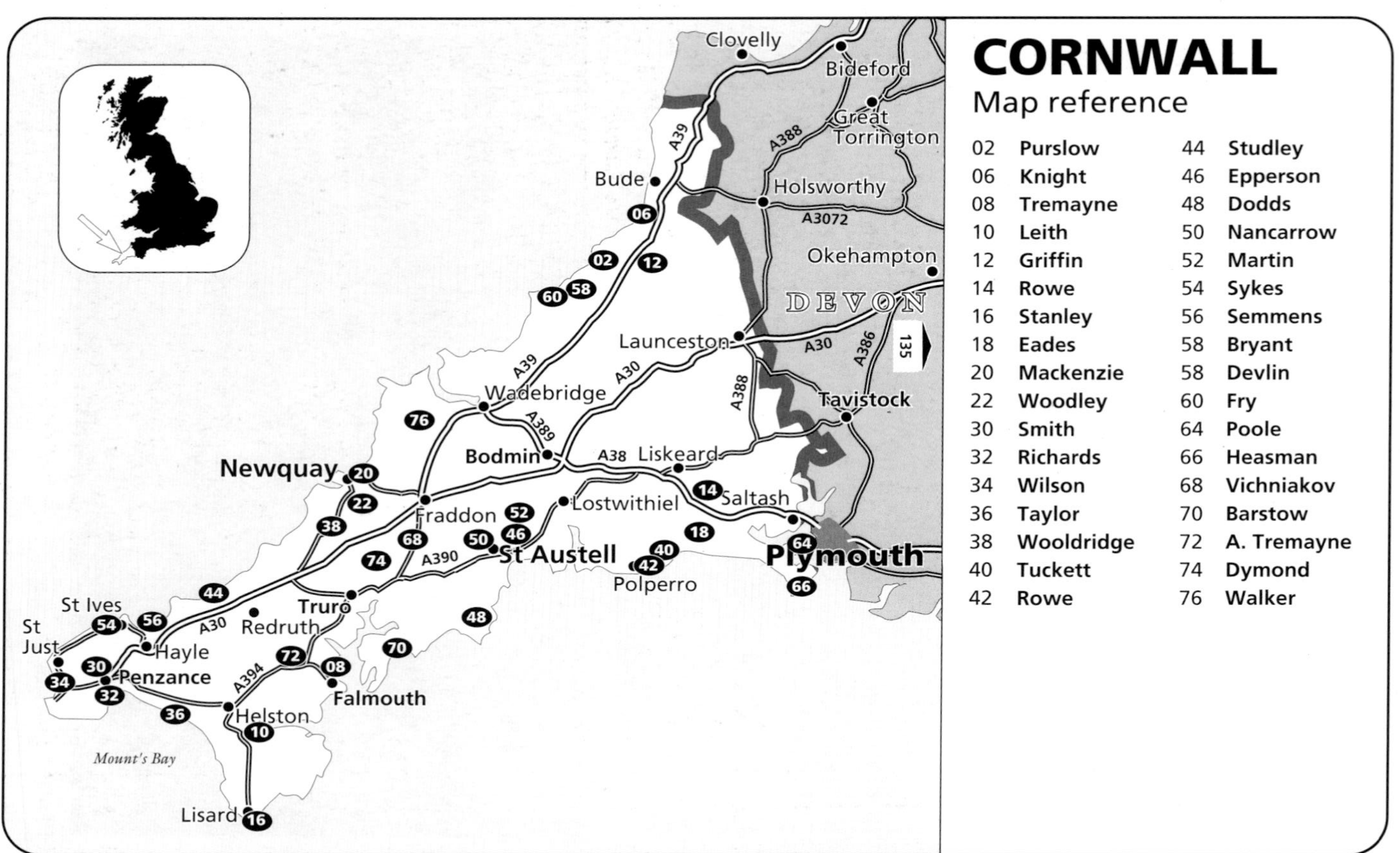

Cornwall

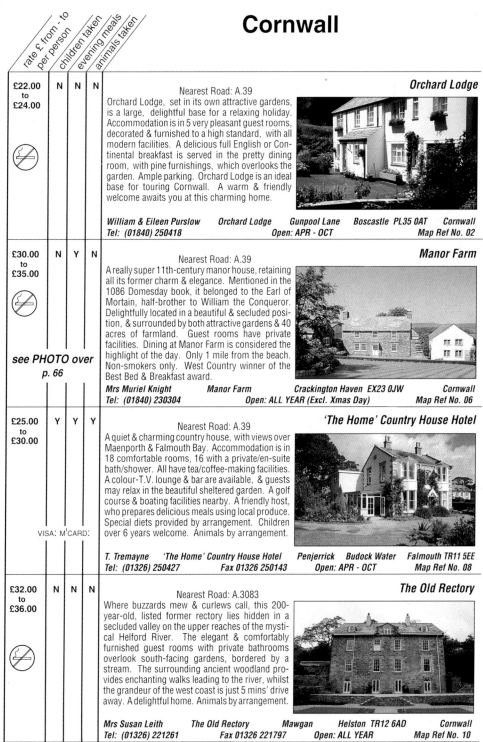

rate £ from - to per person	children taken	evening meals	animals taken	
£22.00 to £24.00	N	N	N	**Orchard Lodge** Nearest Road: A.39 Orchard Lodge, set in its own attractive gardens, is a large, delightful base for a relaxing holiday. Accommodation is in 5 very pleasant guest rooms, decorated & furnished to a high standard, with all modern facilities. A delicious full English or Continental breakfast is served in the pretty dining room, with pine furnishings, which overlooks the garden. Ample parking. Orchard Lodge is an ideal base for touring Cornwall. A warm & friendly welcome awaits you at this charming home. *William & Eileen Purslow Orchard Lodge Gunpool Lane Boscastle PL35 0AT Cornwall* *Tel: (01840) 250418 Open: APR - OCT Map Ref No. 02*
£30.00 to £35.00 *see PHOTO over p. 66*	N	Y	N	**Manor Farm** Nearest Road: A.39 A really super 11th-century manor house, retaining all its former charm & elegance. Mentioned in the 1086 Domesday book, it belonged to the Earl of Mortain, half-brother to William the Conqueror. Delightfully located in a beautiful & secluded position, & surrounded by both attractive gardens & 40 acres of farmland. Guest rooms have private facilities. Dining at Manor Farm is considered the highlight of the day. Only 1 mile from the beach. Non-smokers only. West Country winner of the Best Bed & Breakfast award. *Mrs Muriel Knight Manor Farm Crackington Haven EX23 0JW Cornwall* *Tel: (01840) 230304 Open: ALL YEAR (Excl. Xmas Day) Map Ref No. 06*
£25.00 to £30.00 VISA: M'CARD:	Y	Y	Y	**'The Home' Country House Hotel** Nearest Road: A.39 A quiet & charming country house, with views over Maenporth & Falmouth Bay. Accommodation is in 18 comfortable rooms, 16 with a private/en-suite bath/shower. All have tea/coffee-making facilities. A colour-T.V. lounge & bar are available, & guests may relax in the beautiful sheltered garden. A golf course & boating facilities nearby. A friendly host, who prepares delicious meals using local produce. Special diets provided by arrangement. Children over 6 years welcome. Animals by arrangement. *T. Tremayne 'The Home' Country House Hotel Penjerrick Budock Water Falmouth TR11 5EE* *Tel: (01326) 250427 Fax 01326 250143 Open: APR - OCT Map Ref No. 08*
£32.00 to £36.00	N	N	N	**The Old Rectory** Nearest Road: A.3083 Where buzzards mew & curlews call, this 200-year-old, listed former rectory lies hidden in a secluded valley on the upper reaches of the mystical Helford River. The elegant & comfortably furnished guest rooms with private bathrooms overlook south-facing gardens, bordered by a stream. The surrounding ancient woodland provides enchanting walks leading to the river, whilst the grandeur of the west coast is just 5 mins' drive away. A delightful home. Animals by arrangement. *Mrs Susan Leith The Old Rectory Mawgan Helston TR12 6AD Cornwall* *Tel: (01326) 221261 Fax 01326 221797 Open: ALL YEAR Map Ref No. 10*

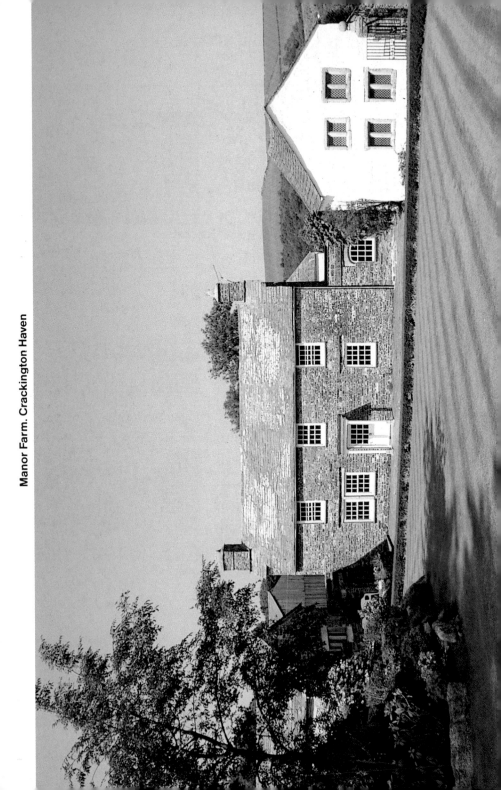

Manor Farm. Crackington Haven

Cornwall

rate £ from - to per person	children taken	evening meals	animals taken
£19.00 to £23.00	Y	Y	N

Wheatley Farm

Nearest Road: A.39

You will be made very welcome at Wheatley, a spacious farmhouse, built by the Duke of Bedford in 1871, which stands in landscaped gardens on a working family farm in the peaceful Cornish countryside. Excellent touring base for exploring Cornwall/Devon. Spectacular coastline nearby. Beautiful en-suite bedrooms, 1 with romantic 4-poster; each with T.V. & tea/coffee-making facilities. Splendid food using local produce. Log fires. Special breaks April, May, Sept. Children over 8.

E-mail: wheatley@farming.co.uk

VISA: M'CARD:

Valerie Griffin   Wheatley Farm   Maxworthy   Launceston PL15 8LY   Cornwall
Tel: (01566) 781232   Fax 01566 781232   *Open: FEB - NOV   Map Ref No. 12*

rate £ from - to per person	children taken	evening meals	animals taken
£21.50 to £23.00	Y	Y	N

Tregondale Farm

Nearest Road: A.390, A.38

Feeling like a break? Relax in style in this charming, elegant farmhouse, beautifully set in an original walled garden. 3 delightful bedrooms, 2 en-suite & 1 with private bathroom, all with T.V., radio & tea/coffee. Log fires. Home produce a speciality. Play tennis, explore the woodland trail with its abundance of wild flowers & birds, through a 200-acre mixed farm. Find award-winning pedigree cattle, lambs in spring. Cycling, fishing from the pond. Plenty of information for walkers. A warm welcome awaits you. Children over 3 years.

Stephanie Rowe   Tregondale Farm   Menheniot   Liskeard PL14 3RG   Cornwall
Tel: (01579) 342407   Fax 01579 342407   *Open: ALL YEAR (Excl. Xmas)   Map Ref No. 14*

rate £ from - to per person	children taken	evening meals	animals taken
£40.00 to £46.00	N	Y	N

Landewednack House

Nearest Road: A.3083

An elegant, Grade II listed, restored Georgian country house, idyllically positioned overlooking the sea, offering absolute peace & comfort. Delightful sea-view bedrooms, furnished with antiques; 4-poster & half-tester beds with private bathrooms (1 with jacuzzi). Relax in front of log fires, laze in the secluded walled garden by the swimming pool, play croquet or just step onto the Heritage coastal footpath of the beautiful Lizard Peninsula. A delightful home at England's most southerly point.

E-mail: landewednack.house@virgin.net

VISA: M'CARD:

Mr & Mrs Peter Stanley   Landewednack House   Church Cove   The Lizard TR12 7PQ   Cornwall
Tel: (01326) 290909   Fax 01326 290192   *Open: ALL YEAR   Map Ref No. 16*

rate £ from - to per person	children taken	evening meals	animals taken
£30.00 to £36.00	Y	Y	Y

Coombe Farm

Nearest Road: A.374

A lovely country house, beautifully furnished with antiques, set in 10 acres of lawns, meadows, woods, streams & ponds, with superb views down a wooded valley to the sea. The atmosphere is delightful, with open log fires, a candlelit dining room (in which to enjoy delicious home-cooking) & an informal licensed bar. An old barn has been converted for indoor games. Croquet lawn, a swimming pool & many birds & animals, including peacocks & horses. All bedrooms are en-suite.

E-mail: coombe_farm@hotmail.com

see PHOTO over p. 68

VISA: M'CARD: AMEX:

Sylvia & Martin Eades   Coombe Farm   Widegates   Looe PL13 1QN   Cornwall
Tel: (01503) 240223   Fax 01503 240895   *Open: APR - OCT   Map Ref No. 18*

Coombe Farm. Widegates.

rate £ from - to per person	children taken	evening meals	animals taken	
£25.00 to £35.00	N	Y	N	***Trenance Lodge Restaurant/Hotel*** Nearest Road: A.3075 An attractive house standing in its own grounds, overlooking the lakes & gardens of Trenance Valley, leading to the Gannel Estuary. The restaurant has a reputation for serving the finest fresh local food in elegant surroundings. Adjoining the restaurant is a spacious, relaxing bar lounge. Accommodation is in 5 comfortable en-suite bedrooms, with colour T.V., radio & tea/coffee-making facilities. An excellent base for touring Cornwall, with a warm welcome assured. **E-mail: info@trenance-lodge.co.uk** *Mr & Mrs Mackenzie Trenance Lodge Restaurant/Hotel 83 Trenance Road Newquay TR7 2HW Cornwall* *Tel: (01637) 876702 Fax 01637 878772 Open: ALL YEAR Map Ref No. 20*
see PHOTO over p. 70 VISA: M'CARD:				
£22.00 to £25.00	Y	Y	N	***Degembris Farmhouse*** Nearest Road: A.3058 The original manor house of Degembris was built in the 16th century & is now used as a barn. The present-day house, surrounded by attractive gardens, was built 200 years ago, & its slate-hung exterior blends well with the rolling countryside. 5 bedrooms, 3 en-suite, each prettily decorated, with dried flowers enhancing the country atmosphere. Hearty breakfasts & traditional 4-course evening meals. Centrally situated in superb countryside, yet close to the sea, this is the perfect holiday base. **E-mail: kathy@tally-connect.co.uk** *Kathy Woodley Degembris Farmhouse St. Newlyn East Newquay TR8 5HY Cornwall* *Tel: (01872) 510555 Fax 01872 510230 Open: ALL YEAR Map Ref No. 22*
VISA: M'CARD:				
£14.00 to £21.00	Y	N	Y	***Con Amore*** Nearest Road: A.30 A warm, friendly welcome awaits you at Con Amore. All bedrooms are tastefully decorated, some en-suite & all to a high standard. All of the rooms are well-equipped & have colour T.V. & tea-making facilities. An elegant T.V. lounge just for your relaxation. Breakfast of your choice available throughout the year. Con Amore is ideally situated for visiting the 'island kingdom' of west Cornwall that is among the finest in Europe. **E-mail: krich30327@aol.com** *Carol Richards Con Amore 38 Morrab Road Penzance TR18 4EX Cornwall* *Tel: (01736) 363423 Fax 01736 363423 Open: ALL YEAR Map Ref No. 32*
VISA: M'CARD:				
£22.00 to £22.00	Y	Y	N	***Boscean Country Hotel*** Nearest Road: A.3071 The Boscean Country Hotel is set in 3 acres of walled gardens in an Area of Outstanding Natural Beauty overlooking the sea & countryside. There are a wealth of oak beams in the downstairs rooms & a grand staircase. (Much of the wood is from HMS Camperdown.) All 12 en-suite bedrooms are attractively furnished & have tea/coffee-making facilities. A comfortable T.V. lounge, a well-stocked bar & a residents dining room. The Boscean has a reputation for excellent home-cooking. **E-mail: boscean@aol.com** *Mr & Mrs Wilson Boscean Country Hotel Boswedden Road St. Just Penzance TR19 7QP Cornwall* *Tel: (01736) 788748 Fax 01736 788748 Open: ALL YEAR Map Ref No. 34*
VISA: M'CARD:				

Trenance Lodge. Newquay.

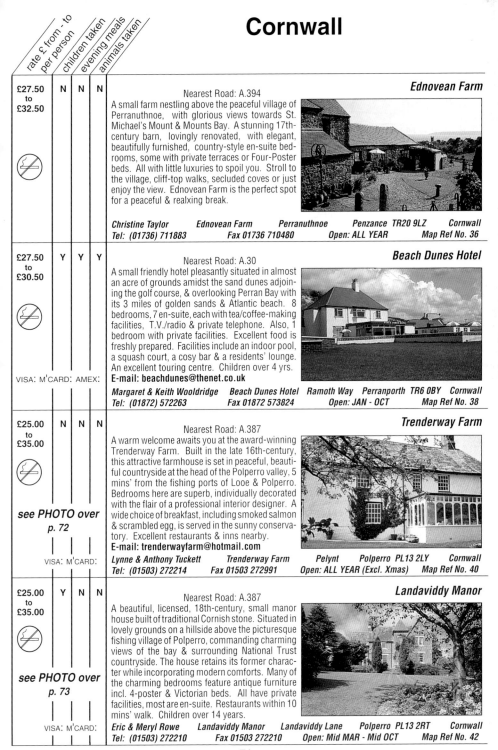

rate £ from - to per person	children taken	evening meals	animals taken
£27.50 to £32.50	N	N	N

Ednovean Farm

Nearest Road: A.394

A small farm nestling above the peaceful village of Perranuthnoe, with glorious views towards St. Michael's Mount & Mounts Bay. A stunning 17th-century barn, lovingly renovated, with elegant, beautifully furnished, country-style en-suite bedrooms, some with private terraces or Four-Poster beds. All with little luxuries to spoil you. Stroll to the village, cliff-top walks, secluded coves or just enjoy the view. Ednovean Farm is the perfect spot for a peaceful & realxing break.

Christine Taylor   Ednovean Farm   Perranuthnoe   Penzance TR20 9LZ   Cornwall
Tel: (01736) 711883   Fax 01736 710480   Open: ALL YEAR   Map Ref No. 36

rate £ from - to per person	children taken	evening meals	animals taken
£27.50 to £30.50	Y	Y	Y

VISA: M'CARD: AMEX:

Beach Dunes Hotel

Nearest Road: A.30

A small friendly hotel pleasantly situated in almost an acre of grounds amidst the sand dunes adjoining the golf course, & overlooking Perran Bay with its 3 miles of golden sands & Atlantic beach. 8 bedrooms, 7 en-suite, each with tea/coffee-making facilities, T.V./radio & private telephone. Also, 1 bedroom with private facilities. Excellent food is freshly prepared. Facilities include an indoor pool, a squash court, a cosy bar & a residents' lounge. An excellent touring centre. Children over 4 yrs.

E-mail: beachdunes@thenet.co.uk

Margaret & Keith Wooldridge   Beach Dunes Hotel   Ramoth Way   Perranporth TR6 0BY   Cornwall
Tel: (01872) 572263   Fax 01872 573824   Open: JAN - OCT   Map Ref No. 38

rate £ from - to per person	children taken	evening meals	animals taken
£25.00 to £35.00	N	N	N

see PHOTO over p. 72

VISA: M'CARD:

Trenderway Farm

Nearest Road: A.387

A warm welcome awaits you at the award-winning Trenderway Farm. Built in the late 16th-century, this attractive farmhouse is set in peaceful, beautiful countryside at the head of the Polperro valley, 5 mins' from the fishing ports of Looe & Polperro. Bedrooms here are superb, individually decorated with the flair of a professional interior designer. A wide choice of breakfast, including smoked salmon & scrambled egg, is served in the sunny conservatory. Excellent restaurants & inns nearby.

E-mail: trenderwayfarm@hotmail.com

Lynne & Anthony Tuckett   Trenderway Farm   Pelynt   Polperro PL13 2LY   Cornwall
Tel: (01503) 272214   Fax 01503 272991   Open: ALL YEAR (Excl. Xmas)   Map Ref No. 40

rate £ from - to per person	children taken	evening meals	animals taken
£25.00 to £35.00	Y	N	N

see PHOTO over p. 73

VISA: M'CARD:

Landaviddy Manor

Nearest Road: A.387

A beautiful, licensed, 18th-century, small manor house built of traditional Cornish stone. Situated in lovely grounds on a hillside above the picturesque fishing village of Polperro, commanding charming views of the bay & surrounding National Trust countryside. The house retains its former character while incorporating modern comforts. Many of the charming bedrooms feature antique furniture incl. 4-poster & Victorian beds. All have private facilities, most are en-suite. Restaurants within 10 mins' walk. Children over 14 years.

Eric & Meryl Rowe   Landaviddy Manor   Landaviddy Lane   Polperro PL13 2RT   Cornwall
Tel: (01503) 272210   Fax 01503 272210   Open: Mid MAR - Mid OCT   Map Ref No. 42

Trenderway Farm. Pelynt.

Landaviddy Manor. Polperro.

Cornwall

	rate £ from - to per person	children taken	evening meals	animals taken
Aviary Court	£31.00 to £31.00	Y	Y	N
Anchorage House Guest Lodge	£27.00 to £34.00	N	Y	N
Mevagissey House	£20.00 to £25.00	Y	N	Y
Poltarrow Farm	£23.00 to £25.00	Y	N	N

Aviary Court

Nearest Road: A.30

Aviary Court stands in 2 1/2 acres of grounds on the edge of Illogan Woods. This part-300-year-old house offers guests a choice of 6 comfortable bedrooms, all with en-suite facilities, overlooking the gardens. Each has radio, colour T.V., tea/coffee-making facilities & 'phone. The comfortable lounge has a bar &, in winter, a log fire. The restaurant serves delicious food with a selection of wine. Tennis court available. Children over 3.

E-mail: aviarycourt@connexions.co.uk

VISA: M'CARD:

The Studley Family Aviary Court Mary's Well Illogan Redruth TR16 4QZ Cornwall
Tel: (01209) 842256 Fax 01209 843744 Open: ALL YEAR Map Ref No. 44

Anchorage House Guest Lodge

Nearest Road: A.390

Every attention has been paid to the smallest detail in this impressive antique-filled house featured in a national magazine. Guests are treated to a heated pool, jacuzzi, T.V., large beds, conservatory & luxurious, en-suite rooms with everything to make you very comfortable. Breakfast is worth getting up for. Dine by arrangement. Steven (American) & Jane (English) combine wonderful hospitality & pleasing informality for a special stay. Perfect for visiting historic houses, gardens, Heligan & Eden.

E-mail: stay@anchoragehouse.co.uk

see PHOTO over p. 75

VISA: M'CARD:

Mr & Mrs Epperson Anchorage House Nettles Corner Tregrehan Mills St. Austell PL25 3RH
Tel: (01726) 814071 Open: ALL YEAR Map Ref No. 46

Mevagissey House

Nearest Road: A.390

Mevagissey House is an elegant Georgian rectory standing in 3 acres of woodland with exceptional views of the valley & harbour to the sea beyond. Guests can relax in peaceful surroundings but are only 10 minutes walk from the pretty, ancient fishing village of Mevagissey. There are 3 attractively furnished bedrooms, all with en-suite showers, T.V. & tea/coffee-making facilities. Also, 2 self-catering cottages. A full English breakfast is served. Mevagissey House is an excellent base from which to explore glorious Cornwall.

Mrs G. Dodds Mevagissey House Vicarage Hill Mevagissey St. Austell PL26 6SZ Cornwall
Tel: (01726) 842427 Fax 01726 844327 Open: MAR - OCT Map Ref No. 48

Poltarrow Farm

Nearest Road: A.390

Set in 45 acres of pastoral farmland, this wisteria-clad farmhouse holds a commanding position, with views across rolling pastures. 5 individually decorated & attractively furnished bedrooms with en-suite/private bathroom, T.V. & tea/coffee facilities. The dining room offers traditional farmhouse fare, with a full English breakfast made using fresh local produce & served in generous Cornish portions. Sitting room. Log fire. Indoor heated swimming pool. Close to the south coast of Cornwall, yet centrally situated between Plymouth & Penzance.

VISA: M'CARD:

Judith Nancarrow Poltarrow Farm St. Mewan St. Austell PL26 7DR Cornwall
Tel: (01726) 67111 Fax 01726 67111 Open: ALL YEAR Map Ref No. 50

Anchorage House Guest Lodge. Tregrehan.

Nanscawen House. St. Blazey.

Cornwall

rate £ from - to per person	children taken	evening meals	animals taken	
£25.00 to £42.00	Y	N	N	Nanscawen Manor House
£22.00 to £27.00	Y	N	Y	Old Vicarage Hotel
£22.50 to £27.50	Y	N	N	Beckside Cottage
£25.00 to £40.00	Y	Y	N	The Old Borough House

Nanscawen Manor House

see PHOTO over p. 76

VISA: M'CARD:

Nearest Road: A.390

A beautiful 15th-century manor house with an elegant, stately Georgian wing, set in 5 acres of grounds with stunning views across a romantic valley. Keith & Fiona offer you a relaxed welcome & friendly hospitality. You can enjoy the heated outdoor swimming pool, & the luxurious bedrooms are all en-suite, with spa baths. Breakfasts are a treat to the eye & the palette. Ideally situated for visiting the Heligan Gardens, Fowey, Lanhydrock & the future Eden Project. Children over 12.

E-mail: keith@nanscawen.co.uk

Mr & Mrs Martin Nanscawen Manor House Prideaux Road Luxulyan Valley St. Blazey PL24 2SR Cornwall Tel: (01726) 814488 Fax 01726 814488 Open: ALL YEAR Map Ref No. 52

Old Vicarage Hotel

VISA: M'CARD:

Nearest Road: A.30

The Old Vicarage Hotel, set in its own wooded grounds on the edge of the moorlands to the west of St. Ives, is secluded & peaceful. Offering 5 bedrooms, 4 with an en-suite or private bath/shower, all with colour T.V. All rooms have tea/coffee-making facilities. Families well catered for. A delightful large garden for guests to relax in, & a safe recreation area for children. Convenient for beach & places of interest.

E-mail: holidays@oldvicaragehotel.freeserve.co.uk

Mr J. & Miss D. Sykes Old Vicarage Hotel Parc-an-Creet St. Ives TR26 2ES Cornwall Tel: (01736) 796124 Fax 01736 796343 Open: APR - OCT Map Ref No. 54

Beckside Cottage

see PHOTO over p. 78

Nearest Road: A.30

'Beck' means stream in Celtic, so naturally there's one in the garden of Beckside Cottage, where butterflies visit from the adjacent nature reserve. Nearby, 400 acres of sand dunes nudge the Atlantic coast. Cornish gardens, charming St. Ives, the National Trust beach which inspired Virginia Woolf, helicopters for the Isles of Scilly ... all are accesible from this 200-year-old cottage with its 2 delightful en-suite bedrooms, guests' lounge & genuine friendly feel. Children over 12 welcome.

E-mail: enquiry@becksidecottage.demon.co.uk

Suzanne Semmens Beckside Cottage Treeve Lane Connor Downs St. Ives TR27 5BN Cornwall Tel: (01736) 756751 Open: ALL YEAR Map Ref No. 56

The Old Borough House

VISA: M'CARD:

Nearest Road: A.39

An historic listed 16th-century house formerly the home of J.B. Priestley & the Mayors of Bossiney, now beautifully furnished with country antiques. Close to the coastal path & Bossiney Cove, a sandy sea-washed beach. Accommodation includes 4 delightful rooms with large comfortable beds & en-suite or private facilities, guests' lounge & cosy dining room. Freshly prepared meals, cooked on the Aga from the highest quality local ingredients. (Dinner is by arrangement.) Children over 12.

Suzanne Bryant The Old Borough House Bossiney Tintagel PL34 0AY Cornwall Tel: (01840) 770475 Fax 01840 770475 Open: ALL YEAR (Excl. Xmas & New Year) Map Ref No. 58

Beckside Cottage. Connor Down.

Trebrea Lodge. Trenale.

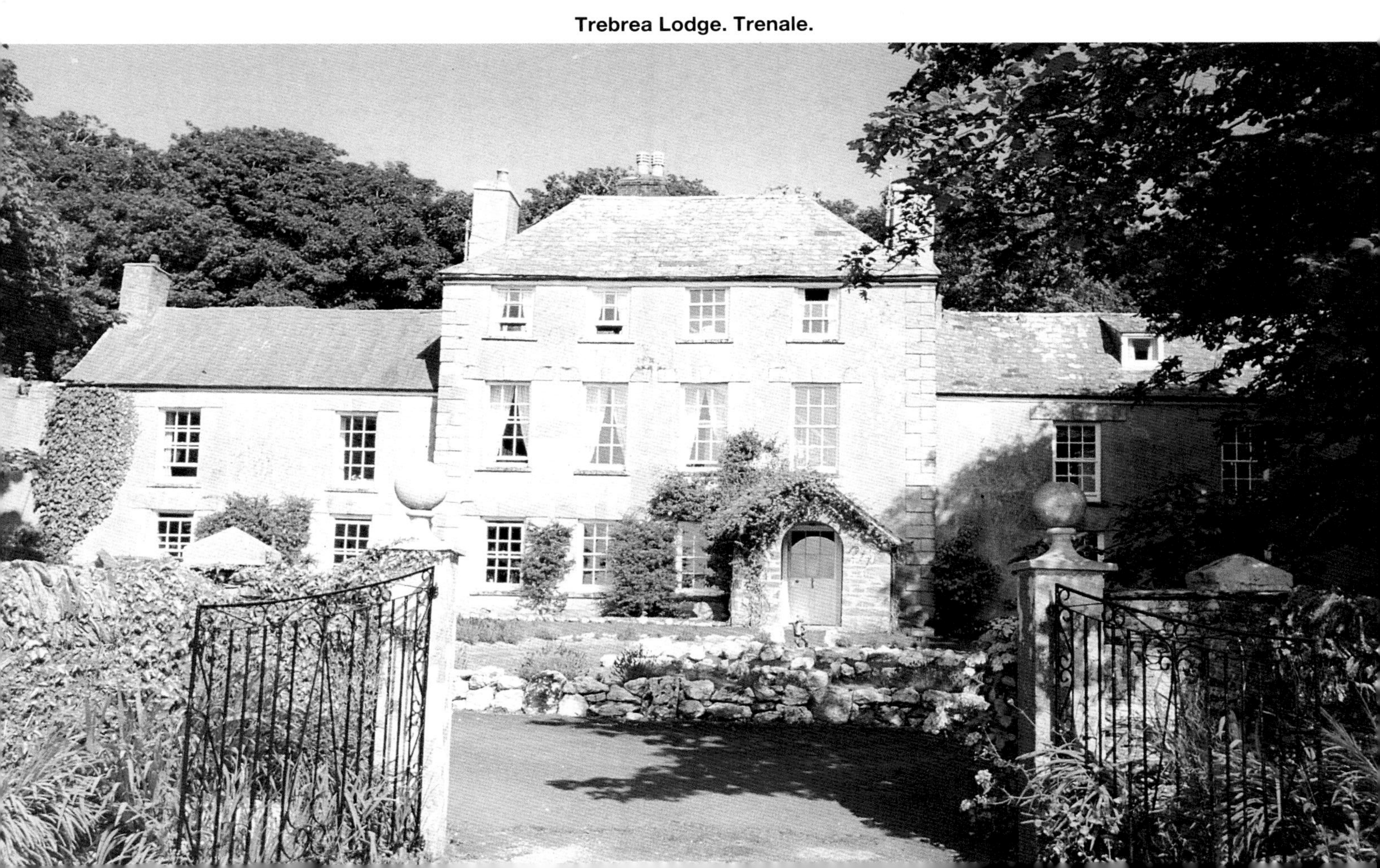

Cornwall

Polkerr Guest House

Nearest Road: A.39

Polkerr has been converted from a farmhouse to a refurbished guest house of a very high standard. All rooms have an en-suite or private bathroom, T.V. & tea-making facilities. A recent addition has been a beautifully appointed sun lounge where guests can relax after viewing some of the most impressive coastal views of north Cornwall. Within easy reach of Tintagel village is the King Arthur Castle & other amenities such as golf, gardens, horse riding & much more. A charming home.

Mrs J. A. Fry   Polkerr Guest House   Molesworth Street   Tintagel PL34 0BY   Cornwall
Tel: (01840) 770382/770132   Open: ALL YEAR (Excl. Xmas Day)   Map Ref No. 60

rate £ from - to per person	children taken	evening meals	animals taken
£20.00 to £26.00	Y	N	N

Trebrea Lodge

Nearest Road: A.39

This lovely Grade II listed Georgian house, set in 4 1/2 acres of wooded hillside, has outstanding views of the glorious north Cornish coast. The land was originally granted by the Black Prince to the Bray family, who lived here for 600 years. The beautiful & attractive bedrooms are individually decorated with antique furniture, & all have en-suite bathrooms. Award-winning, high-quality cooking, log fires & a relaxed atmosphere. Trebrea Lodge is a truly delightful home.

John Charlick & Sean Devlin   Trebrea Lodge   Trenale   Tintagel PL34 0HR   Cornwall
Tel: (01840) 770410   Fax 01840 770092   Open: FEB - DEC   Map Ref No. 58

rate £ from - to per person	children taken	evening meals	animals taken
£43.00 to £48.00	N	Y	Y

see PHOTO over p. 79

VISA: M'CARD: AMEX:

The Old Rectory

Nearest Road: A.374

Regency-period, Grade II listed country house with subtropical garden & millpond located by tidal creek in this 'forgotten corner of Cornwall'. This home, full of interest, allows guests time to reflect; to enjoy its understated elegance with its beautifully appointed & romantic bedrooms, imaginative breakfasts & relaxing drawing room. Coastal path walks, beaches, moors, golf, sailing & National Trust properties close by. 4 miles from chain ferry.
E-mail: oldrectory@free4all.co.uk

Clive & Button Poole   The Old Rectory   St. John-in-Cornwall   Nr. Torpoint PL11 3AW   Cornwall
Tel: (01752) 822275   Fax 01752 823322   Open: ALL YEAR   Map Ref No. 64

rate £ from - to per person	children taken	evening meals	animals taken
£32.50 to £47.50	Y	N	Y

see PHOTO over p. 81

Cliff House

Nearest Road: A.374

Cliff House is a Grade II listed, 17th-century building, converted from 2 cottages into 1 house around 150 years ago. Although modernised to include en-suite facilities, it still retains many of its original features. A drawing room, with wonderful views, log fires, T.V. etc. is available for guests' use. It has a large balcony through French windows overlooking Plymouth Sound, Cawsand Bay & the village. Ann is an enthusiastic wholefood cook, & meals (by arrangement) include soups & freshly baked bread.
E-mail: info@cliffhse.abel.co.uk

Ann Heasman   Cliff House   Kingsand   Torpoint PL10 1NJ   Cornwall
Tel: (01752) 823110   Fax 01752 822595   Open: ALL YEAR   Map Ref No. 66

rate £ from - to per person	children taken	evening meals	animals taken
£18.00 to £27.50	Y	Y	N

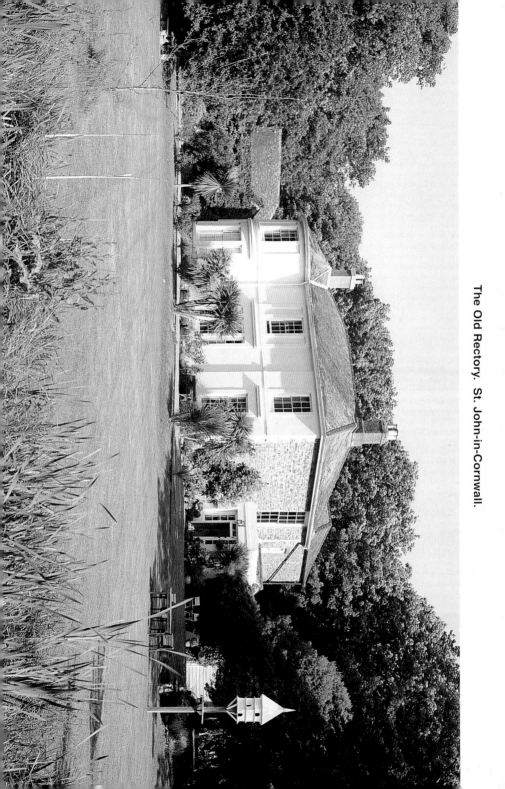

The Old Rectory. St. John-in-Cornwall.

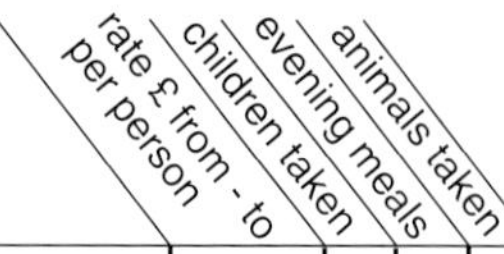

Bissick Old Mill

Nearest Road: A.30, A.390

Bissick Old Mill, formerly a working corn mill, is conveniently situated in the village of Ladock (10 mins' drive from Truro), & provides exceptional standards of comfort, cuisine & hospitality. Its central position makes it an ideal base from which to visit all areas of Cornwall, whether it be on business or purely for pleasure. A chef proprietor (mostly English/French dishes). A residential licence. Children over 10 years welcome. The perfect spot for a relaxing break.

Mikhail & Sonia Vichniakov Bissick Old Mill Ladock Nr. Truro TR2 4PG Cornwall
Tel: (01726) 882557 Fax 01726 884057 Open: ALL YEAR Map Ref No. 68

rate £ from - to per person	children taken	evening meals	animals taken
£27.20 to £39.95	Y	Y	N

VISA: M'CARD:

Crugsillick Manor

Nearest Road: A.3078

A hidden treasure of the Roseland Peninsula, one of Cornwall's loveliest areas - meandering lanes, unspoilt fishing villages & sheltered coves. Find Crugsillick, a beautiful Grade II listed Queen Anne manor house, offering peace & comfort. Stroll down the smugglers' path below the house to glorious beaches & spectacular coastline, visit the historic houses & famous gardens - returning to dine, if you wish, on freshly caught seafood & home-grown vegetables. Children over 12.

E-mail: barstow@adtel.co.uk

Mr & Mrs O. Barstow Crugsillick Manor Ruan High Lanes St. Mawes Truro TR2 5LJ Cornwall
Tel: (01872) 501214 Fax 01872 501228 Open: ALL YEAR Map Ref No. 70

rate £ from - to per person	children taken	evening meals	animals taken
£35.00 to £48.00	Y	Y	Y

VISA: M'CARD:

Apple Tree Cottage

Nearest Road: A.39

Apple Tree Cottage, set amid rolling countryside with delightful gardens & river, is furnished with country antiques & has a warm, welcoming atmosphere. The large lounge has a log fire, & traditional farmhouse breakfasts, cooked on the Aga, are taken in the sunlit dining room. The attractive bedrooms have pine double beds, tea/coffee facilities, washbasins & lovely views. Many N.T. gardens & the famous Trebah Gardens on the Helford River are only 15 mins' away. Children over 10.

E-mail: raistlin@dial.pipex.com

D. Ann Tremayne Apple Tree Cottage Laity Moor Ponsanooth Truro TR3 7HR Cornwall
Tel: (01872) 865047 Open: ALL YEAR (Excl. Xmas) Map Ref No. 72

rate £ from - to per person	children taken	evening meals	animals taken
£22.50 to £25.00	Y	N	Y

Trevispian-Vean Farm Guest House

Nearest Road: A.39

A delightful farmhouse, dating back over 300 years, offering a very warm welcome & good accommodation in 9 pleasant & comfortably furnished en-suite guest rooms. Only 7 miles from the coast, & surrounded by beautiful countryside, it is a perfect base for everyone. Families will particularly enjoy it here, as children can look around the farm, & there are plenty of places to visit & things to do. There's even a donkey for the children. Trevispian-Vean Farm is a charming home.

Ernie & Bridget Dymond Trevispian-Vean Farm Guest House St. Erme Truro TR4 9AT Cornwall
Tel: (01872) 279514 Fax 01872 263730 Open: JAN - NOV Map Ref No. 74

rate £ from - to per person	children taken	evening meals	animals taken
£21.00 to £24.00	Y	Y	N

Cornwall

rate £ from - to per person	children taken	evening meals	animals taken	
£24.00 to £30.00	N	N	N	**The Old Mill Country House**

Nearest Road: A.389

This delightful, 16th-century, converted corn mill, complete with water wheel, stands in its own grounds at the head of Little Petherick Creek. The house & bedrooms are furnished with antiques & collections of genuine artifacts, & each bedroom has an en-suite/private bathroom & tea/coffee-making facilities. Licensed, with a colour T.V. available for the guests' use. Also, a terraced sun garden. Light supper available on request. Children over 14 years welcome.

E-mail: <dwalker@oldmillbandb.demon.co.uk>

see PHOTO over p. 84

VISA: M'CARD:

Mr & Mrs D. Walker The Old Mill Country House Little Petherick Wadebridge PL27 7QT Cornwall

Tel: (01841) 540388 Fax 0870 0569360 Open: APR - OCT Map Ref No. 76

All the establishments mentioned in this guide are members of The Worldwide Bed & Breakfast Association

When booking your accommodation please mention The Best Bed & Breakfast

The Old Mill. Little Petherick.

Cumbria

Cumbria

The Lake District National Park is deservedly famous for its magnificent scenery. Here, England's highest mountains & rugged fells surround shimmering lakes & green valleys. But there is more to Cumbria than the beauty of the Lake District. It also has a splendid coastline, easily accessible from the main lakeland centres, as well as a border region where the Pennines, the backbone of England, reach their highest point, towering over the Eden valley.

Formation of the dramatic Lakeland scenery began in the Caledonian period when earth movements raised & folded the already ancient rocks, submerging the whole mass underseas & covering it with limestone. During the ice age great glaciers ground out the lake beds & dales of todays landscape. There is tremendous variety, from the craggy outcrops of the Borrowdale Volcanics with Skiddaw at 3054 feet, to the gentle dales, the open moorlands & the lakes themselves. Each lake is distinctive, some with steep mountain sides sliding straight to the water's edge, others more open with sloping wooded hillsides. Ellerwater, the enchanting "lake of swans" is surrounded by reed & willows at the foot of Langdale. The charm of Ullswater inspired Wordsworth's famous poem "Daffodils". Whilst many lakes are deliberately left undisturbed for those seeking peace, there are others - notably Windermere - where a variety of water sports can be enjoyed. The changeable weather of the mountainous region can produce a sudden transformation in the character of a tranquil lake, raising choppy waves across the darkened surface to break along the shoreline. It is all part of the fascination of Lakeland.

Fell walking is the best way to appreciate the full beauty of the area. There are gentle walks along the dales, & the tops of the ridges are accessible to walkers with suitable footwear & an eye to the weather.

Ponytrekking is another popular way to explore the countryside & there are many centres catering even for inexperienced riders.

There are steamboats on lakes such as Coniston & Ullswater, where you can appreciate the scenery. On Windermere there are a variety of boats for hire, & facilities for water-skiing.

Traditional crafts & skills are on display widely. Craft centres at Keswick, Ambleside & Grasmere, & the annual exhibition of the Guild of Lakeland Craftsmen held in Windermere from mid-July to early September represent the widest variety of craft artistry.

Fairs & festivals flourish in Lakeland. The famous Appleby Horse Fair, held in June is the largest fair of its kind in the world & attracts a huge gypsy gathering. Traditional agriculture shows, sheep dog trials & local sporting events abound. The Grasmere Sports, held each August include gruelling fell races, Cumberland & Westmoreland wrestling, hound trails & pole-leaping.

The traditional custom of "Rushbearing" when the earth floors of the churches were strewn with rushes still survives as a procession in Ambleside & Grasmere & many other villages in the summer months

The coast of Cumbria stretches from the estuaries of Grange-over-Sands & Burrow-in-Furness by way of the beautiful beaches between Bootle & Cardurnock, to the mouth of the Solway Firth. The coastal areas, especially the estuaries, are excellent for bird-watching. The sand dunes north of the Esk are famous for the colony of black-headed gulls which can be visited by arrangement, & the colony of seabirds at St. Bees Head is the largest in Britain.

Cumbria

Cumbria

Gazeteer

Area of outstanding natural beauty.
The Lake District National Park.

House & Castles

Carlisle Castle - Carlisle
12th century. Massive Norman keep - half-moon battery - ramparts, portcullis & gatehouse.
Brough Castle - Kirby Stephen
13th century - on site of Roman Station between York & Carlisle.
Dacre Castle - Penrith
14th century - massive pele tower.
Sizergh Castle - Kendal
14th century - pele tower - 15th century great hall. English & French furniture, silver & china - Jacobean relics. 18th century gardens.
Belle Island - Boweness-on-Windermere
18th century - interior by Adams Brothers, portraits by Romney.
Swarthmoor Hall - Ulverston
Elizabethan house, mullioned windows, oak staircase, panelled rooms. Home of George Fox - birthplace of Quakerism - belongs to Society of Friends.
Lorton Hall - Cockermouth
15th century pele tower, priest holes, oak panelling, Jacobean furniture.
Muncaster Castle - Ravenglass
14th century with 15th & 19th century additions - site of Roman tower.
Rusland Hall - Ulveston
Georgian mansion with period panelling, sculpture, furniture, paintings.
Levens Hall - Kendal
Elizabethan - very fine panelling & plasterwork - famous topiary garden.
Hill Top - Sawrey
17th century farmhouse home of Beatrix Potter - contains her furniture, china & some of original drawings for her children's books.
Dove Cottage - Town End, Grasmere
William Wordsworth's cottage - still contains his furnishing & his personal effects as in his lifetime.
Brantwood
The Coniston home of John Ruskin, said to be the most beautifully situated house in the Lake District. Exhibition, gardens, bookshops & tearooms.

Cathedrals & Churches

Carlisle Cathedral - Carlisle
1130. 15th century choir stalls with painted backs - carved misericords, 16th century screen, painted roof.
Cartmel Priory (St. Mary Virgin)
15th century stalls, 17th century screen, large east window, curious central tower.
Lanercost Priory (St. Mary Magdalene)
12th century - Augustinian - north aisle now forms Parish church.
Greystoke (St. Andrew)
14th/15th century. 19th century misericords. Lovely glass in chancel.
Brougham (St. Wilfred)
15th century carved altarpiece.
Furness Abbey
12th century monastery beautiful setting.
Shap Abbey
12th century with 16th century tower.

Museums & Galleries

Abbot Hall - Kendal
18th century, Georgian house with period furniture, porcelain, silver, pictures, etc. Also contains modern galleries with contemporary paintings, sculptures & ceramics. Changing exhibitions on show.
Carlisle Museum & Art Gallery - Carlisle
Archaeological & natural history collections. National centre of studies of Roman Britain. Art gallery principally exhibiting paintings & porcelain.
Hawkshead Courthouse - Kendal
Exhibition of domestic & working life housed in mediaeval building.
Helena Thompson Museum - Workington
displays Victorian family life & objects of the period.
Lakeland Motor Museum - Holker Hall - Grange-over-Sands
Exhibits cars, bicycles, tricycles, motor cycles, etc., & model cars.
Millom Folk Museum - St. George's Road, Millom
Reconstructions of drift in iron ore mine, miner's cottage kitchen, blacksmith's forge & agricultural relics.
Ravenglass Railway Museum - Ravenglass
History of railways
relics, models, etc.

Cumbria

Wordsworth Museum - Town End, Grasmere
Personal effects, first editions, manuscripts, & general exhibits from the time of William Wordsworth.
Border Regiment Museum - The Castle, Carlisle.
Collection of uniforms, weapons, trophies, documents, medals from 1702, to the present time.
Whitehaven Museum - Whitehaven
History & development of area show in geology, paleontology, archaeology, natural history, etc. Interesting maritime past.
Fitz Park Museum & Art Gallery - Keswick.
Collection of manuscripts - Wordsworth, Walpole, Coleridge, Southey.
The Beatrix Potter Gallery - Hawkshead

Things to see & do

Fell Walking - there is good walking throughout Cumbria, but check weather reports, clothing & footwear before tackling the heights.
Pony-trekking - opportunities for novice & experienced riders.
Watersports - Windermere is the ideal centre for sailing, waterskiing, windsurfing, scuba-diving.
Golf - championship course to the north at Silloth.

Grasmere.

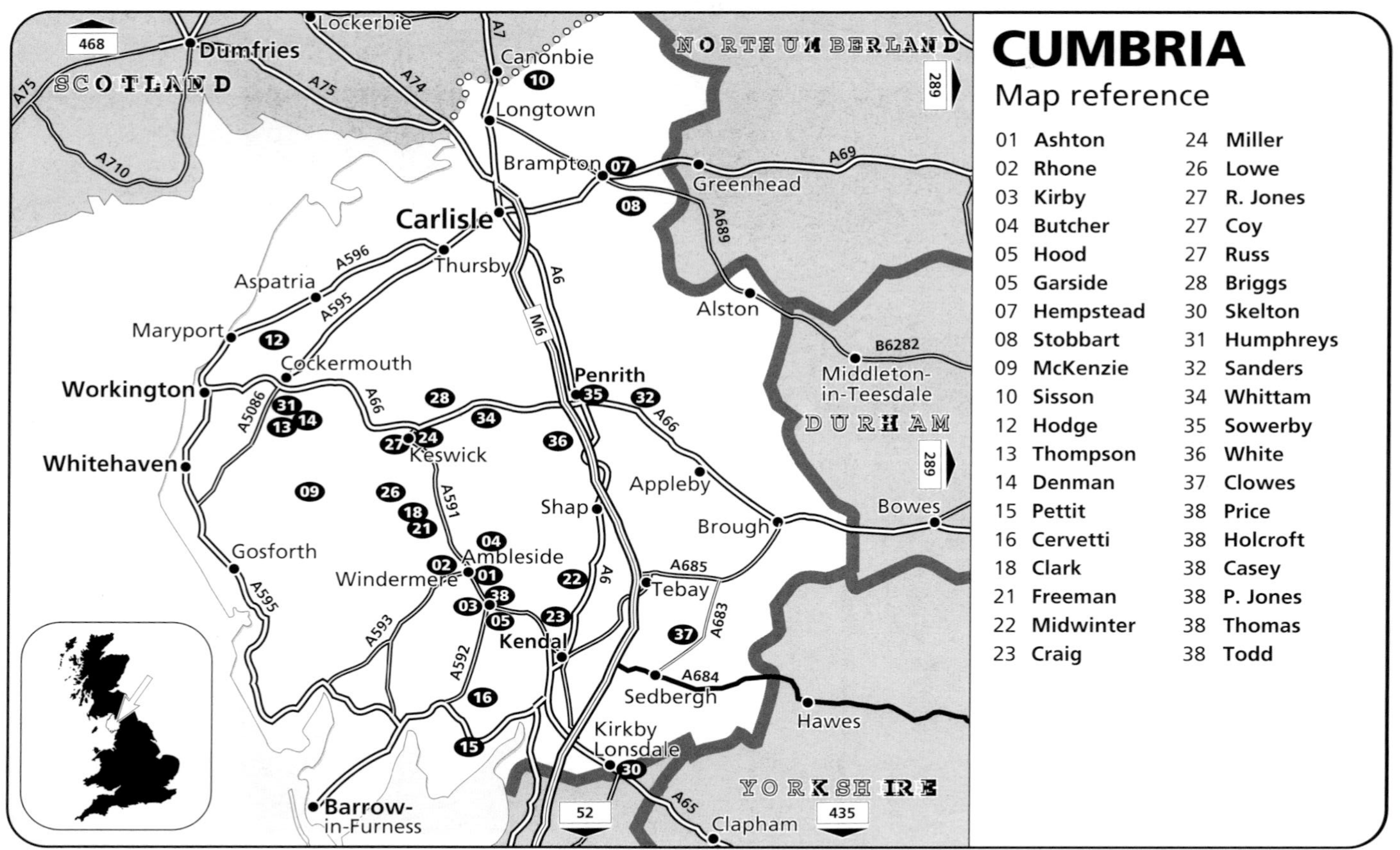

CUMBRIA

Map reference

01	**Ashton**	24	**Miller**
02	**Rhone**	26	**Lowe**
03	**Kirby**	27	**R. Jones**
04	**Butcher**	27	**Coy**
05	**Hood**	27	**Russ**
05	**Garside**	28	**Briggs**
07	**Hempstead**	30	**Skelton**
08	**Stobbart**	31	**Humphreys**
09	**McKenzie**	32	**Sanders**
10	**Sisson**	34	**Whittam**
12	**Hodge**	35	**Sowerby**
13	**Thompson**	36	**White**
14	**Denman**	37	**Clowes**
15	**Pettit**	38	**Price**
16	**Cervetti**	38	**Holcroft**
18	**Clark**	38	**Casey**
21	**Freeman**	38	**P. Jones**
22	**Midwinter**	38	**Thomas**
23	**Craig**	38	**Todd**

Laurel Villa. Ambleside.

Riverside Lodge Country House. Rothay Bridge.

Cumbria

rate £ from - to per person	children taken	evening meals	animals taken
£22.50 to £35.00	Y	N	Y

Laurel Villa

Nearest Road: A.591

Visited by Beatrix Potter, this charming Victorian residence, now sympathetically restored & refurbished to a very high standard, offers 9 comfortable en-suite bedrooms; 2 of which boast 4-poster beds whilst some at the rear have splendid views over the village & surrounding fells. A residents' lounge in which to relax & an attractive dining room. All major outdoor activities are catered for nearby, including watersports, pony trekking &, of course, fell walking. Car park. Children over 5.

E-mail: laurelvilla@hotel.ambleside.co.uk

see PHOTO over p. 89

Guy Ashton — Laurel Villa — Lake Road — Ambleside LA22 0DB — Cumbria
Tel: (015394) 33240 — Fax 015394 33240 — Open: ALL YEAR — Map Ref No. 01

rate £ from - to per person	children taken	evening meals	animals taken
£26.50 to £35.00	N	N	N

Riverside Lodge

Nearest Road: A.593

Riverside Lodge is a house of immense charm & character, superbly situated in a unique riverside setting, just a few mins' walk from the centre of Ambleside & Lake Windermere. The house has been refurbished throughout in keeping with its beamed ceilings & stone-flagged floors. Guests have access to the house without any restrictions in a very relaxed & informal atmosphere. There are 5 beautifully furnished en-suite bedrooms.

E-mail: alanrhone@riversidelodge.co.uk

see PHOTO over p. 90

VISA: M'CARD:

Alan & Gillian Rhone — Riverside Lodge — Rothay Bridge — Ambleside LA22 0EH — Cumbria
Tel: (015394) 34208 — Fax 015394 31884 — Open: ALL YEAR — Map Ref No. 02

rate £ from - to per person	children taken	evening meals	animals taken
£25.00 to £28.00	Y	N	Y

Buckle Yeat

Nearest Road: B.5285, A.590

Buckle Yeat is famous for its connections with Beatrix Potter. Although over 200 years old, it has been sympathetically & tastefully refurbished. There is a large lounge with log fire & an attractive dining room which also serves morning coffee & afternoon teas. There are 6 comfortable en-suite bedrooms. Many good local pubs & restaurants offer excellent meals. Buckle Yeat is in an ideal position for touring Lakeland, with walks, fishing & birdwatching all nearby. Animals by arrangement.

E-mail: info@buckle-yeat.co.uk

VISA: M'CARD: AMEX:

Robert & Helen Kirby — Buckle Yeat — Nr. Sawrey — Hawkshead — Ambleside LA22 0LF — Cumbria
Tel: (015394) 36538/36446 — Fax 015394 36446 — Open: ALL YEAR — Map Ref No. 03

rate £ from - to per person	children taken	evening meals	animals taken
£31.00 to £45.00	Y	Y	N

Rowanfield Country House

Nearest Road: A.591

Set in quiet countryside 3/4 of a mile outside Ambleside, Rowanfield enjoys breathtaking lake & mountain views. Superbly situated for exploring the whole Lake District area. A beautiful period house with Laura Ashley style decor. All bedrooms are en-suite with power showers, some have baths, queen & king-size beds. Certain weeks of the year chef/patron, Philip Butcher performs wizardry in the kitchen. His dinners are superb. Unlicensed but own wine welcome. Children over 8. Parking.

E-mail: email@rowanfield.com

see PHOTO over p. 92

VISA:

Philip & Jane Butcher — Rowanfield Country House — Kirkstone Road — Ambleside LA22 9ET — Cumbria
Tel: (015394) 33686 — Fax 015394 31569 — Open: MAR - DEC — Map Ref No. 04

Rowanfield Country House. Ambleside.

The Fairfield. Bowness-on-Windermere.

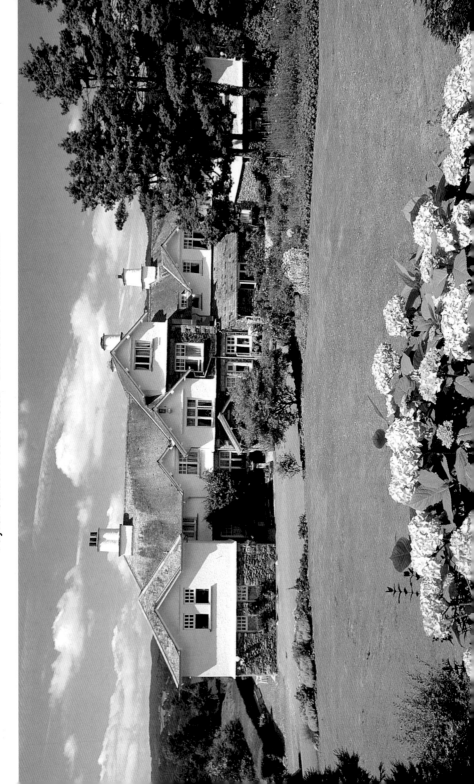

Fayrer Garden House Hotel.   Bowness on Windermere.

Cumbria

The Fairfield

rate £ from - to per person	children taken	evening meals	animals taken
£25.00 to £32.00	Y	N	N

(No smoking symbol)

see PHOTO over p. 93

VISA: M'CARD:

Nearest Road: A.591

Fairfield is a small, friendly, 200-year-old Lakeland hotel found in a peaceful garden setting, 200 metres from Bowness village, 400 metres from the shores of Lake Windermere & at the end of the Dales Way (an 81-mile walk from Ilkley to Bowness). The Beatrix Potter Exhibition is within easy walking distance. 9 well-appointed & tastefully furnished bedrooms with T.V., welcome tray & private showers/bathrooms. Breakfasts are a speciality. Leisure facilities available.

E-mail: Ray&barb@the-fairfield.co.uk

Ray & Barbara Hood The Fairfield Brantfell Road Bowness-on-Windermere LA23 3AE Cumbria
Tel: (015394) 46565 Fax 015394 46565 Open: FEB - NOV Map Ref No. 05

Fayrer Garden House Hotel

rate £ from - to per person	children taken	evening meals	animals taken
£35.00 to £75.00	Y	Y	N

see PHOTO over p. 94

VISA: M'CARD: AMEX:

Nearest Road: A.5074

Beautiful country house hotel, in 5 acres of grounds overlooking Lake Windermere. Award-winning cuisine served in the air-conditioned conservatory restaurant. All of the delightful bedrooms are en-suite with T.V., hairdryers etc. Some have 4-poster beds, whirlpool baths & lake views at a supplement. Special breaks, interest weekends & free use of local leisure centre. An ideal spot for a relaxing break. Colour brochure available on request.

E-mail: lakescene@fayrergarden.com

Mr & Mrs I. Garside Fayrer Garden House Hotel Lyth Valley Rd Bowness-on-Windermere LA23 3JP Cumbria Tel: (015394) 88195 Fax 015394 45986 Open: ALL YEAR Map Ref No. 05

Courtyard Cottages

rate £ from - to per person	children taken	evening meals	animals taken
£25.00 to £30.00	N	N	N

see PHOTO over p. 96

Nearest Road: A.69

You won't be staying in someone else's home but in a comfortable double-bedded en-suite bedroom in the lovely, but tiny, courtyard cottage of a Victorian mansion with stone steps leading to the upper accommodation, providing total independence & privacy. Breakfast is served in your room. Enjoy Hadrian's Wall, the lakes & Scottish borders, or just stay as a stop-over & be pampered as you travel north or south. (M.6 10 mins.)

E-mail: janethempstead@warrenbank.demon.co.uk

Janet Hempstead Courtyard Cottages Warren Bank Station Road Brampton CA8 1EX Cumbria
Tel: (016977) 41818 Fax 016977 41398 Open: ALL YEAR (Excl. Xmas & New Year) Map Ref No. 07

Hullerbank

rate £ from - to per person	children taken	evening meals	animals taken
£22.50 to £23.00	Y	N	N

(No smoking symbol)

VISA: M'CARD:

Nearest Road: A.69

Attractive pink-washed Georgian style farmhouse dated 1635-1751 standing in its own grounds, near the picturesque village of Talkin, 2 1/2 miles from Brampton. Superb walking country & central for visiting Hadrian's Wall, the Lake District & the Borders. A warm, friendly & relaxed atmosphere awaits. 3 comfortable bedrooms with private facilities & tea trays. A T.V. lounge with open fire in chilly weather & comfortable dining room where excellent breakfasts are served. 2 inns with restaurant facilities in nearby Talkin. Children over 12.

E-mail: info@hullerbank.freeserve.co.uk

Sheila Stobbart Hullerbank Talkin Brampton CA8 1LB Cumbria
Tel: (016977) 46668 Fax 016977 46668 Open: FEB - DEC Map Ref No. 08

Courtyard Cottages. Brampton.

Wood House. Buttermere.

Cumbria

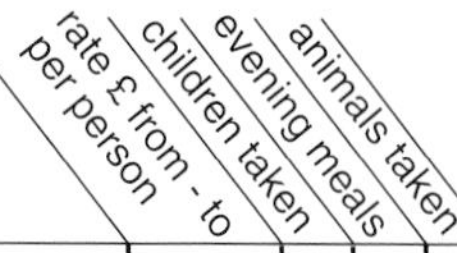

Wood House

Nearest Road: A.66

The view overlooking Wood House was chosen by J.M.W. Turner for his famous painting of Buttermere in 1798. A visitor describing the interior has written, "The furnishings & decor are serene & beautiful though completely unpretentious. The bedrooms reach similarly high standards & enjoy lovely views." Food is freshly prepared from carefully selected ingredients. Woodalls (Royal Warranty) are nearby & supply the house with their renowned meat products. Judy's home-baked bread is highly recommended.

rate £ from - to per person	children taken	evening meals	animals taken
£29.00 to £35.00	N	Y	N

see PHOTO over p. 97

Michael & Judy McKenzie · *Wood House* · *Buttermere CA13 9XA* · *Cumbria*
Tel: (017687) 70208 · *Fax 017687 70241* · *Open: FEB - NOV* · *Map Ref No. 09*

Bessiestown

Nearest Road: A.7

An award-winning farm guest house, overlooking the Scottish borders, where a friendly, relaxing atmosphere is assured. 6 pretty, en-suite rooms with radio, T.V. & tea/coffee-making facilities. Delightfully decorated public rooms & conservatory. Also, ground-floor accommodation in extremely comfortable courtyard cottages. Delicious home-cooking. Residential drinks licence. Guests may use the indoor heated swimming pool (May-Sept). Stop-off to/from Scotland & N. Ireland.
E-mail: Bestbb2000@cs.com

rate £ from - to per person	children taken	evening meals	animals taken
£23.50 to £30.00	Y	Y	N

VISA: M'CARD:

Margaret Sisson · *Bessiestown* · *Catlowdy* · *Longtown* · *Carlisle CA6 5QP* · *Cumbria*
Tel: (01228) 577219 · *Fax 01228 577219* · *Open: ALL YEAR* · *Map Ref No. 10*

Sundawn

Nearest Road: A.595

Bob & Pauline offer you a warm & friendly welcome. The emphasis here is on comfort, relaxation, personal service & imaginative home cooking. From the sun lounge, view the panorama of the Lakeland Fells & the historic market town of Cockermouth, birthplace of William Wordsworth. Accommodation is in 3 tastefully decorated rooms, 2 en-suite, all with modern amenities & tea/coffee makers. A charming home.
E-mail: robert.hodge1@virgin.net

rate £ from - to per person	children taken	evening meals	animals taken
£17.50 to £20.00	Y	N	N

Pauline & Bob Hodge · *Sundawn* · *Bridekirk* · *Cockermouth CA13 0PA* · *Cumbria*
Tel: (01900) 822384 · *Fax 01900 822885* · *Open: ALL YEAR (Excl. Xmas & New Year)* · *Map Ref No. 12*

New House Farm

Nearest Road: B.5289

New House Farm is set superbly in the Lorton Vale, has its own 15 acres of fields, ponds, stream & woods & easy access to nearby fells & lakes. All bedrooms are tastefully furnished & en-suite, & there is a comfortable sitting room with open fire & a cosy dining room. Lots of personal attention is offered by the hosts. The cooking is fine traditional fare with a Cumbrian flavour. Children over 8. Animals by arrangement.
E-mail: hazel@newhouse-farm.co.uk

rate £ from - to per person	children taken	evening meals	animals taken
£38.00 to £42.00	Y	Y	Y

see PHOTO over p. 99

Hazel Thompson · *New House Farm* · *Lorton* · *Cockermouth CA13 9UU* · *Cumbria*
Tel: (01900) 85404 · *Fax 01900 85404* · *Open: ALL YEAR* · *Map Ref No. 13*

New House Farm. Lorton.

Winder Hall. Low Lorton.

Cumbria

rate £ from - to per person	children taken	evening meals	animals taken	
£30.00 to £37.00	Y	Y	N	**Winder Hall Country House** Nearest Road: A.66 This historic manor house has grounds to the River Cocker in possibly the most peaceful valley in the National Park, ideal for the Northern & Western Lakes. Mary & Derek provide 6 luxurious rooms with superb views, 2 with special 4-posters. Guests appreciate the attentive service, the wide breakfast choice & the 4-course dinner featuring local produce. Residential licence. Short breaks available. Children over 8. **E-mail: winderhall@lowlorton.freeserve.co.uk** *Mary & Derek Denman Winder Hall Country House Lorton Nr. Cockermouth CA13 9UP Cumbria* *Tel: (01900) 85107 Fax 01900 85107 Open: ALL YEAR Map Ref No. 14*
see PHOTO over p. 100 VISA: M'CARD:				
£25.00 to £32.00	Y	Y	N	**Greenacres Country Guest House** Nearest Road: A.590 Greenacres is a charming 19th-century cottage ideally located for exploring the lakes & dales. Situated in the National Park, in the small village of Lindale at the foot of the beautiful Winster Valley, where you can walk in unspoilt countryside. All of the 5 bedrooms are luxury en-suite. There is a lovely lounge & conservatory, & cosy dining room where excellent home-cooking is served. A friendly & relaxed atmosphere awaits you. Greenacres is an ideal base for a relaxing break. *Mrs Barbara Pettit Greenacres Country Guest House Lindale Grange-over-Sands LA11 6LP Cumbria* *Tel: (015395) 34578 Fax 015395 34578 Open: ALL YEAR Map Ref No. 15*
VISA: M'CARD:				
£25.00 to £28.00	Y	Y	N	**Lightwood Country Guest House** Nearest Road: A.592 Lightwood is a 17th-century farmhouse built in approx. 1650. It possesses all modern amenities whilst retaining the charm of original oak beams & staircase. 2 acres of lovely gardens, with streams running through. Individually decorated rooms, with countryside views. The 6 comfortable bedrooms have en-suite bathrooms. A cosy lounge with T.V. & log fire. A charming dining room facing the early morning sun. Only 2 miles from the southern end of Lake Windermere. Good English breakfast, with free-range eggs. *Mrs E. Cervetti Lightwood Country Guest House Cartmell Fell Grange-over-Sands LA11 6NP Cumbria* *Tel: (015395) 31454 Fax 015395 31454 Open: FEB - NOV Map Ref No. 16*
VISA: M'CARD:				
£21.00 to £27.00	Y	N	N	**Banerigg Guest House** Nearest Road: A.591 Delightfully situated overlooking Grasmere Lake is this small, friendly guest house. The informal hospitality & relaxing atmosphere make this a super base for a holiday. All 6 comfortable rooms have modern amenities. A pleasant lounge with a cosy log fire. A delicious & plentiful breakfast is served. Ideally located for fell walking, sailing, canoeing & fishing. Angela & Martin ensure that guests have a memorable Lakeland holiday. **E-mail: banerigg@aol.com** *Martin & Angela Clark Banerigg Guest House Lake Road Grasmere LA22 9PW Cumbria* *Tel: (015394) 35204 Open: ALL YEAR Map Ref No. 18*
see PHOTO over p. 102				

Banerigg House. Grasmere.

Cumbria

rate £ from - to per person | children taken | evening meals | animals taken

Oak Bank Hotel

rate £ from - to per person	children taken	evening meals	animals taken
£30.00 to £50.00	Y	Y	Y

VISA: M'CARD:

Nearest Road: A.591

The Oak Bank Hotel is a little gem one stumbles upon all too rarely, with a new conservatory dining room overlooking the garden, by which the river Rothay flows. An award-winning hotel for cordon-bleu cuisine, hospitality & comfort. Log fires in the lounge/bar & delightful Victorian-style bedrooms complete this restful, owner-run hotel. The Oak Bank Hotel is the perfect spot for a relaxing break or for touring the Lake District.

E-mail: grasmereoakbank@btinternet.com

Mrs Carol Freeman Oak Bank Hotel Broadgate Grasmere LA22 9TA Cumbria
Tel: (015394) 35217 Fax 015394 35685 Open: FEB - DEC Map Ref No. 21

Low Jock Scar

rate £ from - to per person	children taken	evening meals	animals taken
£23.50 to £29.00	N	Y	Y

VISA: M'CARD:

Nearest Road: A.6

A charming country guest house. A relaxing & friendly atmosphere with genuine warmth. In an idyllic setting with 6 acres of garden & woodland, it is a peaceful base from which to explore the Lakes & Yorkshire Dales. There are 5 comfortable bedrooms (3 en-suite, 2 on the ground floor) & a lounge well-stocked with books & maps. Excellent freshly prepared dinners - vegetarians catered for. Residential licence. Single supplement.

E-mail: philip@low-jock-scar.freeserve.co.uk

Philip & Alison Midwinter Low Jock Scar Selside Kendal LA8 9LE Cumbria
Tel: (01539) 831259 Fax 01539 831259 Open: MAR - OCT Map Ref No. 22

Burrow Hall

rate £ from - to per person	children taken	evening meals	animals taken
£22.50 to £25.00	N	N	N

VISA: M'CARD:

Nearest Road: A.591

Although built in 1648, this delightful guest house offers modern-day comforts. It is situated amidst open countryside, midway between Kendal & Windermere on the A.591, yet only 10 miles from M.6 Jt. 36. All 4 en-suite bedrooms are centrally heated, have colour T.V., tea/coffee-making facilities, radio/alarms & hairdryer & are all tastefully decorated. A well-furnished guest lounge. A warm & friendly welcome is assured.

E-mail: burrowhall@supanet.com

Maureen & Jack Craig Burrow Hall Plantation Bridge Nr. Kendal LA8 9JR Cumbria
Tel: (01539) 821711 Open: JAN - NOV Map Ref No. 23

The Grange Country House

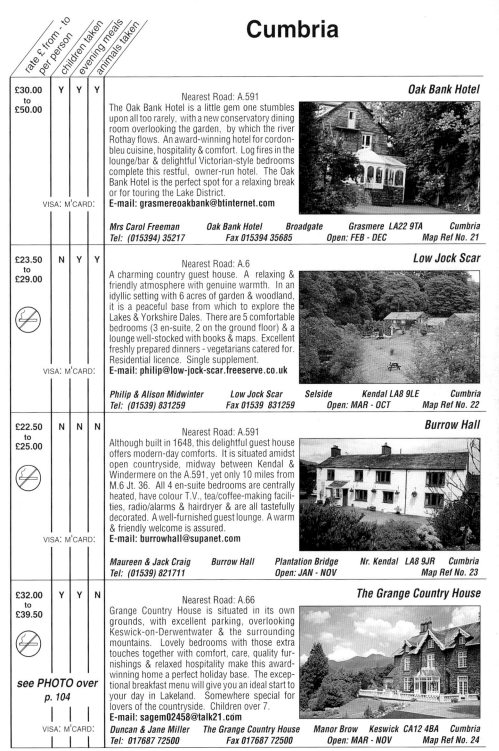

rate £ from - to per person	children taken	evening meals	animals taken
£32.00 to £39.50	Y	Y	N

see PHOTO over p. 104

VISA: M'CARD:

Nearest Road: A.66

Grange Country House is situated in its own grounds, with excellent parking, overlooking Keswick-on-Derwentwater & the surrounding mountains. Lovely bedrooms with those extra touches together with comfort, care, quality furnishings & relaxed hospitality make this award-winning home a perfect holiday base. The exceptional breakfast menu will give you an ideal start to your day in Lakeland. Somewhere special for lovers of the countryside. Children over 7.

E-mail: sagem02458@talk21.com

Duncan & Jane Miller The Grange Country House Manor Brow Keswick CA12 4BA Cumbria
Tel: 017687 72500 Fax 017687 72500 Open: MAR - NOV Map Ref No. 24

The Grange Country House Hotel. Manor Brow.

Greystones. Keswick.

Cumbria

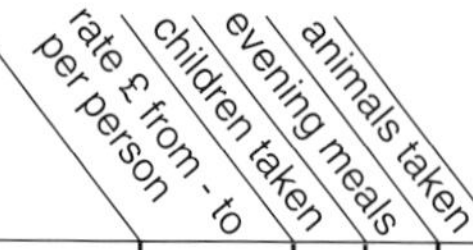

Greystones

Nearest Road: A.66

Greystones enjoys an enviable position overlooking the grounds of St. John's Church, & has excellent fell views. It is just a short walk to the market square & Lake Derwentwater. Accommodation is in 8 delightful & attractively furnished en-suite rooms, each with T.V., hot drinks tray & a folder of suggested walks & tours. Private parking available. Greystones is an excellent base for a relaxing break. Children over 10 years.

E-mail: greystones@keslakes.freeserve.co.uk

Robert & Janet Jones Greystones Ambleside Road Keswick CA12 4DP Cumbria
Tel: (017687) 73108 Open: JAN - NOV Map Ref No. 27

rate £ from - to per person	children taken	evening meals	animals taken
£23.00 to £26.00	Y	N	N

see PHOTO over p. 105

VISA: M'CARD:

Dale Head Hall Lakeside Hotel

Nearest Road: A.591

Lose yourself in the ancient woodlands & mature gardens of an Elizabethan country manor, set serenely on the shores of Lake Thirlmere. Delicious dinners prepared by mother & daughter, using fresh produce from the Victorian kitchen garden, served with fine wines in the oak-beamed dining room. 9 individually decorated bedrooms, some with 4-posters, each with bath/shower rooms. Together with the lounge & bar, there are unspoilt views across lawns, lakes & fells.

E-mail: onthelakeside@dale-head-hall.co.uk

Alan & Shirley Lowe Dale Head Hall Lakeside Hotel Lake Thirlmere Keswick CA12 4TN Cumbria
Tel: (017687) 72478 Fax 017687 71070 Open: FEB - DEC Map Ref No. 26

rate £ from - to per person	children taken	evening meals	animals taken
£33.50 to £50.00	Y	Y	N

see PHOTO over p. 107

VISA: M'CARD: AMEX:

The Ravensworth Hotel

Nearest Road: A.66

Ravensworth Hotel is ideally situated near the town centre & all its amenities. The lake & lower fells are just a short walk away. All rooms are tastefully furnished & all are en-suite with T.V. & beverage tray. Starting with a wholesome breakfast you may enjoy the lakes by day & then relax in the splendid lounge or enjoy a drink in the Herdwick Bar. (Evening meals by arrangement.) Personally run by proprietors Tony & Tina, the Ravensworth ranks amongst the top small hotels in Keswick. Children over 6.

E-mail: info@ravensworth-hotel.co.uk

A. Russ The Ravensworth Hotel 29 Station Street Keswick CA12 5HH Cumbria
Tel: (017687) 72476 Fax 017687 75287 Open: ALL YEAR Map Ref No. 27

rate £ from - to per person	children taken	evening meals	animals taken
£20.00 to £27.50	Y	N	N

VISA: M'CARD:

Lairbeck Hotel

Nearest Road: A.66

On the outskirts of Keswick, yet less than 10 mins' walk from the centre, Lairbeck is a delightful, family-run hotel built in 1875 of Lakeland stone, within a secluded garden setting. All 14 bedrooms are en-suite, non-smoking, each with its own individual character. The atmosphere is welcoming & informal. Featured on a national T.V. programme, Lairbeck offers excellent home-cooking. Log fires, spacious car parking. Children over 5.

E-mail: info@lairbeck.demon.co.uk

Roger & Irene Coy Lairbeck Hotel Vicarage Hill Keswick CA12 5QB Cumbria
Tel: (017687) 73373 Fax 017687 73144 Open: MAR - DEC Map Ref No. 27

rate £ from - to per person	children taken	evening meals	animals taken
£30.00 to £38.00	Y	Y	N

see PHOTO over p. 108

VISA: M'CARD:

Dale Head Hall. Lake Thirlmere

Lairbeck Hotel. Keswick.

Hipping Hall. Kirkby Lonsdale

Cumbria

rate £ from - to per person	children taken	evening meals	animals taken

Scales Farm Country Guest House

Nearest Road: A.66

Stunning open views & a warm friendly welcome await you at Scales Farm, a traditional 17th-century fells farmhouse sensitively modernised to provide accommodation of the highest standard. All bedrooms are en-suite, centrally heated, with tea/coffee-making facilities, colour T.V. & fridges. A separate entrance from the private car park allows guests access to rooms & traditional lounge. Lakeland Inn/Restaurant next door. Scales Farm is a lovely base for touring or walking.

E-mail: scales@scalesfarm.com

Chris & Caroline Briggs Scales Farm Country Guest House Threlkeld Nr. Keswick CA12 4SY Cumbria
Tel: (017687) 79660 Fax 017687 79660 Open: ALL YEAR (Excl. Xmas) Map Ref No. 28

rate £ from - to per person	children taken	evening meals	animals taken
£26.00 to £31.00	Y	N	Y

VISA: M'CARD: AMEX:

Hipping Hall

Nearest Road: A.65

Hipping Hall is a 17th-century country house set in 3 acres of walled gardens on the edge of the Yorkshire Dales National Park, 2 miles from pretty Kirkby Lonsdale & only 30 mins' from Windermere. The 4 bedrooms are all en-suite & for non-smokers & the 2 cottages are attractively furnished & fully equipped. Guests may dine in the Great Hall or in the separate dining room. All dishes are freshly prepared from home & local produce. Reduced rates for 3 nights or more. Single supplement.

E-mail: hippinghal@aol.com

Richard & Jean Skelton Hipping Hall Cowan Bridge Kirkby Lonsdale LA6 2JJ Cumbria
Tel: (015242) 71187 Fax 015242 72452 Open: ALL YEAR (Excl. Xmas) Map Ref No. 30

rate £ from - to per person	children taken	evening meals	animals taken
£46.00 to £55.00	Y	Y	N

see PHOTO over p. 109

VISA: M'CARD: AMEX:

The Old Vicarage

Nearest Road: A.66

The Old Vicarage is a small, family-run, licensed country guest house in an unspoilt part of the National Park. Elegant property which has stunning views, wooded grounds, log fires & historic charm. Accommodation is in 8 attractive en-suite bedrooms including 4-poster & family suite, each with T.V. & tea/coffee-making facilities. An excellent 4-course dinner is served & there is a good wine list. Local pub 5 mins' walk.

E-mail: enquiries@oldvicarage.co.uk

Roger & Helen Humphreys The Old Vicarage Church Lane Lorton CA13 9UN Cumbria
Tel: (01900) 85656 Fax 01900 85656 Open: ALL YEAR Map Ref No. 31

rate £ from - to per person	children taken	evening meals	animals taken
£26.00 to £32.00	Y	Y	N

see PHOTO over p. 111

VISA: M'CARD:

Hornby Hall

Nearest Road: A.66

Hornby Hall is a 16th-century farmhouse situated in quiet countryside near the River Eamont. There are 7 tastefully furnished & comfortable guest rooms, with beverage facilities. 2 are en-suite. Dinner is served in the original sandstone-floored dining hall. Advance bookings are essential, as only the freshest local ingredients are used. Special diets catered for. Licensed. An ideal base for touring the Lake District, Dales, North Pennines & Hadrian's Wall. Animals by arrangement.

Ros Sanders Hornby Hall Brougham Penrith CA10 2AR Cumbria
Tel: (01768) 891114 Fax 01768 891114 Open: ALL YEAR Map Ref No. 32

rate £ from - to per person	children taken	evening meals	animals taken
£28.00 to £35.00	Y	Y	Y

VISA: M'CARD:

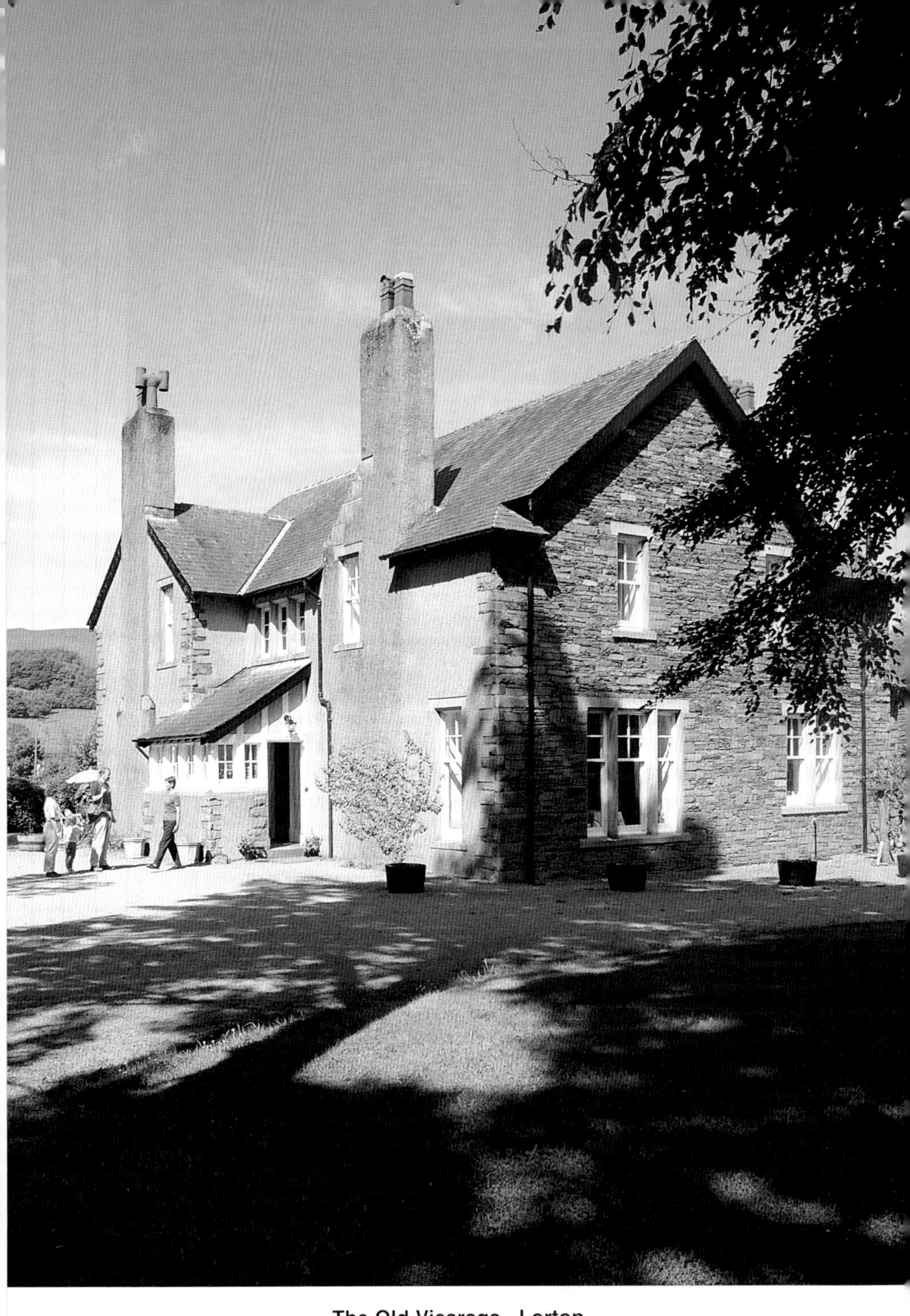

The Old Vicarage. Lorton.

Fir Trees. Windermere.

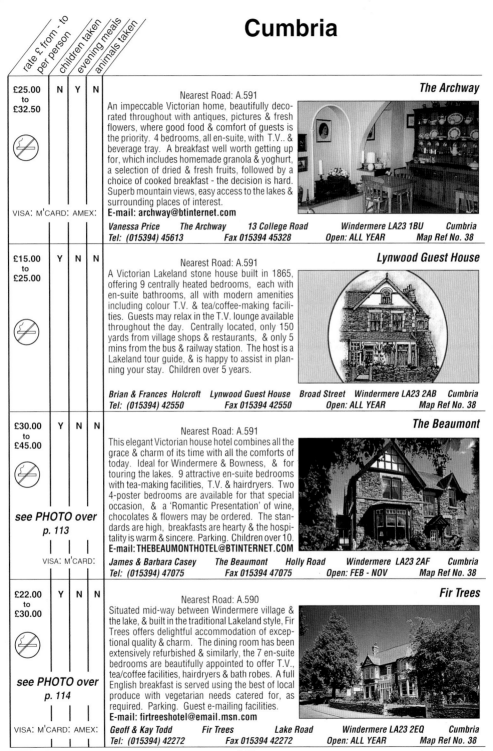

rate £ from - to per person	children taken	evening meals	animals taken
£25.00 to £32.50	N	Y	N

VISA: M'CARD: AMEX:

The Archway

Nearest Road: A.591

An impeccable Victorian home, beautifully decorated throughout with antiques, pictures & fresh flowers, where good food & comfort of guests is the priority. 4 bedrooms, all en-suite, with T.V.. & beverage tray. A breakfast well worth getting up for, which includes homemade granola & yoghurt, a selection of dried & fresh fruits, followed by a choice of cooked breakfast - the decision is hard. Superb mountain views, easy access to the lakes & surrounding places of interest.

E-mail: archway@btinternet.com

Vanessa Price The Archway 13 College Road Windermere LA23 1BU Cumbria
Tel: (015394) 45613 Fax 015394 45328 Open: ALL YEAR Map Ref No. 38

rate £ from - to per person	children taken	evening meals	animals taken
£15.00 to £25.00	Y	N	N

Lynwood Guest House

Nearest Road: A.591

A Victorian Lakeland stone house built in 1865, offering 9 centrally heated bedrooms, each with en-suite bathrooms, all with modern amenities including colour T.V. & tea/coffee-making facilities. Guests may relax in the T.V. lounge available throughout the day. Centrally located, only 150 yards from village shops & restaurants, & only 5 mins from the bus & railway station. The host is a Lakeland tour guide, & is happy to assist in planning your stay. Children over 5 years.

Brian & Frances Holcroft Lynwood Guest House Broad Street Windermere LA23 2AB Cumbria
Tel: (015394) 42550 Fax 015394 42550 Open: ALL YEAR Map Ref No. 38

rate £ from - to per person	children taken	evening meals	animals taken
£30.00 to £45.00	Y	N	N

see PHOTO over p. 113

VISA: M'CARD:

The Beaumont

Nearest Road: A.591

This elegant Victorian house hotel combines all the grace & charm of its time with all the comforts of today. Ideal for Windermere & Bowness, & for touring the lakes. 9 attractive en-suite bedrooms with tea-making facilities, T.V. & hairdryers. Two 4-poster bedrooms are available for that special occasion, & a 'Romantic Presentation' of wine, chocolates & flowers may be ordered. The standards are high, breakfasts are hearty & the hospitality is warm & sincere. Parking. Children over 10.

E-mail: THEBEAUMONTHOTEL@BTINTERNET.COM

James & Barbara Casey The Beaumont Holly Road Windermere LA23 2AF Cumbria
Tel: (015394) 47075 Fax 015394 47075 Open: FEB - NOV Map Ref No. 38

rate £ from - to per person	children taken	evening meals	animals taken
£22.00 to £30.00	Y	N	N

see PHOTO over p. 114

VISA: M'CARD: AMEX:

Fir Trees

Nearest Road: A.590

Situated mid-way between Windermere village & the lake, & built in the traditional Lakeland style, Fir Trees offers delightful accommodation of exceptional quality & charm. The dining room has been extensively refurbished & similarly, the 7 en-suite bedrooms are beautifully appointed to offer T.V., tea/coffee facilities, hairdryers & bath robes. A full English breakfast is served using the best of local produce with vegetarian needs catered for, as required. Parking. Guest e-mailing facilities.

E-mail: firtreeshotel@email.msn.com

Geoff & Kay Todd Fir Trees Lake Road Windermere LA23 2EQ Cumbria
Tel: (015394) 42272 Fax 015394 42272 Open: ALL YEAR Map Ref No. 38

Hawksmoor Guest House. Windermere.

Cumbria

rate £ from - to per person	children taken	evening meals	animals taken
£25.00 to £33.00	Y	N	N

see PHOTO over p. 116

VISA: M'CARD:

Hawksmoor Guest House

Nearest Road: A.591

Hawksmoor is situated halfway between the centres of Windermere & Bowness, just 10 mins' walk from the lake. Standing in lovely grounds, this creeper-clad house has 10 charming rooms, all en-suite & with garden views; some also with 4-poster beds, & some strictly no smoking. A comfortable lounge with T.V., & a garden for guests' enjoyment. Licensed. Boating, golf, tennis, swimming, fishing & pony trekking all nearby. Phone for availability before booking. Children over 6.

E-mail: tyson@hawksmoor.net1.co.uk

Angela & Peter Jones   Hawksmoor Guest House   Lake Road   Windermere LA23 2EQ   Cumbria
Tel: (015394) 42110   Fax 015394 42110   Open: ALL YEAR   Map Ref No. 38

rate £ from - to per person	children taken	evening meals	animals taken
£20.00 to £30.00	Y	N	N

see PHOTO over p. 118

VISA: M'CARD: AMEX:

Rosemount

Nearest Road: A.591

Rosemount is an attractive Victorian house halfway between Windermere & the lake. Accommodation is in 17 comfortable & attractively furnished bedrooms (including 3 singles & 3 spacious family rooms), each with an en-suite or private bathroom, colour T.V. & tea/coffee-making facilities. An excellent breakfast is served. Rosemount is the perfect base for a relaxing break or for touring this lovely region & affords first-class accommodation.

E-mail: ROSEMT3739@AOL.COM

Steve Thomas & Family   Rosemount   Lake Road   Windermere LA23 2EQ   Cumbria
Tel: (015394) 43739   Fax 015394 48978   Open: ALL YEAR   Map Ref No. 38

All the establishments mentioned in this guide are members of The Worldwide Bed & Breakfast Association

When booking your accommodation please mention The Best Bed & Breakfast

Rosemount.Windermere.

Derbyshire & Staffordshire

Derbyshire

(East Midlands)

A county with everything but the sea, this was Lord Byron's opinion of Derbyshire, & the special beauty of the Peak District was recognised by its designation as Britain's first National Park.

Purple heather moors surround craggy limestone outcrops & green hills drop to sheltered meadows or to deep gorges & tumbling rivers.

Derbyshire's lovely dales have delightful names too - Dove Dale, Monk's Dale, Raven's Dale, Water-cum-Jolly-Dale, & they are perfect for walking. The more adventurous can take up the challenge of the Pennine Way, a 270 mile pathway from Edale to the Scottish border.

The grit rock faces offer good climbing, particularly at High Tor above the River Derwent, & underground there are extensive & spectacular caverns. There are show caves at the Heights of Abraham, which you reach by cable-car, & at Castleton, source of the rare Blue John mineral, & at Pole's Cavern in Buxton where there are remarkable stalactites & stalagmites.

Buxton's splendid Crescent reflects the town's spa heritage, & the Opera House is host to an International Festival each summer.

The waters at Matlock too were prized for their curative properties & a great Hydro was built there in the last century, to give treatment to the hundreds of people who came to "take the waters".

Bakewell is a lovely small town with a fascinating market, some fine buildings & the genuine Bakewell Pudding, (known elsewhere as Bakewell tart).

Well-dressing is a custom carried on throughout the summer in the villages & towns. It is a thanksgiving for the water, that predates the arrival of Christianity in Britain. Flower-petals, leaves, moss & bark are pressed in

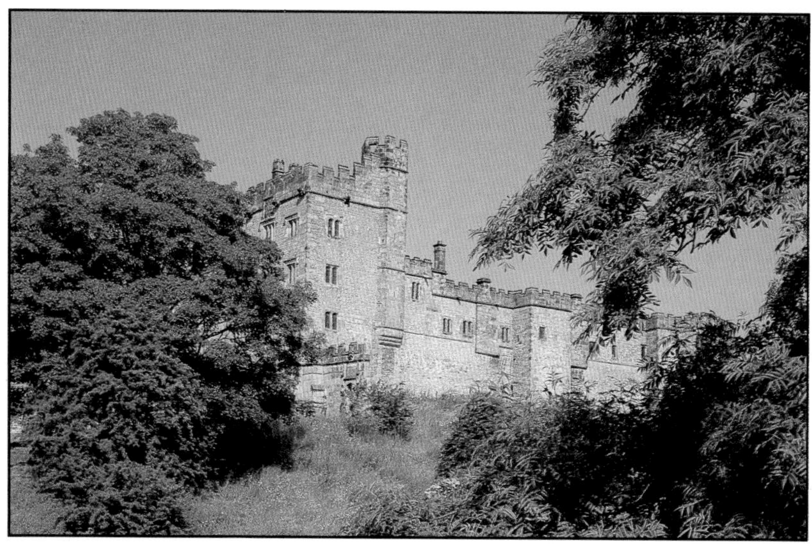

Haddon Hall; Derby.

intricate designs into frames of wet clay & erected over the wells, where they stay damp & fresh for days.

The mining of lead & the prosperity of the farms brought great wealth to the landowning families who were able to employ the finest of architects & craftsmen to design & build their great houses. Haddon Hall is a perfectly preserved 12th century manor house with with terraced gardens of roses & old-fashioned flowers. 17th century Chatsworth, the "Palace of the Peak", houses a splendid collection of paintings, drawings, furniture & books, & stands in gardens with elaborate fountains.

Staffordshire
(Heart of England)

Staffordshire is a contrast of town & county. Miles of moorland & dramatic landscapes lie to the north of the country, & to the south is the Vale of Trent & the greenery of Cannock Chase. But the name of Staffordshire invokes that of the Potteries, the area around Stoke-on-Trent where the world-renowned ceramics are made.

The factories that produce the Royal Doulton, Minton, Spode & Coalport china will arrange tours for visitors, & there is a purpose-built visitor centre at Barlaston displaying the famous Wedgwood tradition.

The Gladstone Pottery Museum is set in a huge Victorian potbank, & the award-winning City museum in Stoke-on-Trent has a remarkable ceramics collection.

There is lovely scenery to be found where the moorlands of Staffordshire meet the crags & valleys of the Peak District National Park. From the wild & windy valleys of The Roaches (from the French 'roche') you can look across the county to Cheshire & Wales. Drivers can take high moorland roads that are marked out as scenic routes.

The valleys of the Dove & Manifold are beautiful limestone dales & ideal for walking or for cycling. Sir Izzak Walton, author of 'The Compleat Angler', drew his inspiration, & his trout, from the waters here.

The valley of the River Churnet is both pretty & peaceful, being largely inaccessible to cars. The Caldon Canal, with its colourful narrowboats, follows the course of the river & there are canal-side pubs, picnic areas, boat rides & woodland trails to enjoy. The river runs through the grounds of mock-Gothic Alton Towers, now a leisure park.

The Vale of Trent is largely rural with small market towns, villages, river & canals.

Cannock Chase covers 20 square miles of heath & woodland & is the home of the largest herd of fallow deer in England. Shugborough Hall stands in the Chase. The ancestral home of Lord Lichfeld, it also houses the Stafforshire County Museum & a farm for rare breeds including the famous Tamworth Pig.

Burton-on-Trent is known as the home of the British brewery industry & there are two museums in the town devoted to the history of beer.

Lichfield is a small & picturesque city with a cathedral which dates from the 12th century & has three graceful spires known as the 'Ladies of the Vale'. Dr. Samuel Johnson was born in the city & his house is now a museum dedicated to his life & work.

One of the Vale's villages retains its mediaeval tradition by performing the Abbot's Bromley Horn Dance every September.

Derbyshire & Staffordshire

Derbyshire

Gazeteer

Areas of outstanding natural beauty.
Peak National Park. The Dales.

Houses & Castles

Chatsworth - Bakewell
17th century, built for 1st. Duke of Devonshire. Furniture, paintings & drawings, books, etc. Fine gardens & parklands.
Haddon Hall - Bakewell
Mediaeval manor house - complete. Terraced rose gardens.
Hardwick Hall - Nr. Chesterfield
16th century - said to be more glass than wall. Fine furniture, tapestries & furnishings. Herb garden.
Kedlestone Hall - Derby
18th century - built on site of 12th century Manor house. Work of Robert Adam - has world famous marble hall. Old Master paintings. 11th century church nearby.
Melbourne Hall - Nr. Derby
12th century origins - restored by Sir John Coke. Fine collection of pictures & works of art. Magnificent gardens & famous wrought iron pagoda
Sudbury Hall - Sudbury
Has examples of work of the greatest craftsmen of the period-Grinling Gibbons,Pierce and Laguerre.
Winster Market House Nr. Matlock
17th century stone built market house.

Cathedrals & Churches

Chesterfield (St. Mary & All Saints)
13th & 14th centuries.
4 chapels, polygonal apse, mediaeval screens, Jacobean pulpit.
Derby (All Saints)
Perpendicular tower - classical style - 17th century plate, 18th century screen.
Melbourne (St. Michael & St. Mary)
Norman with two west towers & crossing tower.
Splendid plate, 18th century screen.
Normbury (St. Mary & St. Barloke)
14th century - perpendicular tower.
Wood carving & brasses.
Wirksworth (St. Mary)
13th century, restored & enlarged.

Staffordshire

Gazeteer

Houses & Castles

Ancient High House - Stafford
16th century - largest timber-framed town house in England.
Shugborough - Nr. Stafford
Ancestral home of the Earl of Lichfield. Mansion house, paintings, silver, ceramics, furniture. County Museum. Rare Breeds Farm.
Moseley Old Hall - Nr. Wolverhampton
Elizabethan house formerly half-timbered.
Stafford Castle
Large & well-preserved Norman castle in grounds with castle trail.
Tamworth Castle
Norman motte & bailey castle with later additions. Museum.

Cathedrals & Churches

Croxden Abbey
12th century foundation Cistercian abbey. Ruins of 13th century church.
Ingestre (St. Mary the Virgin)
A rare Wren church built in1676.
Lichfield Cathedral
Unique triple-spired 12th century cathedral.
Tamworth (St. Editha's)
Founded 963, rebuilt 14th century. Unusual double spiral staircase.
Tutbury (St. Mary's)
Norman church with impressive West front.

Museums & Galleries

City Museum & Art Gallery - Stoke-on-Trent
Modern award-winning museum. Ceramics, decorative arts, etc.
Dr. Johnson Birthplace Museum - Lichfield
Gladstone Pottery Museum - Longton
Izaak Walton Cottage & Museum - Shallowfield, Nr. Stafford
National Brewery Museum & the Bass Museum of Brewing-both in Stoke-on-Trent
Stafford Art Gallery & Craft Shop - Stafford
Major gallery for the visual arts & centre for quality craftsmanship.

DERBYSHIRE & STAFFORDSHIRE

Map reference

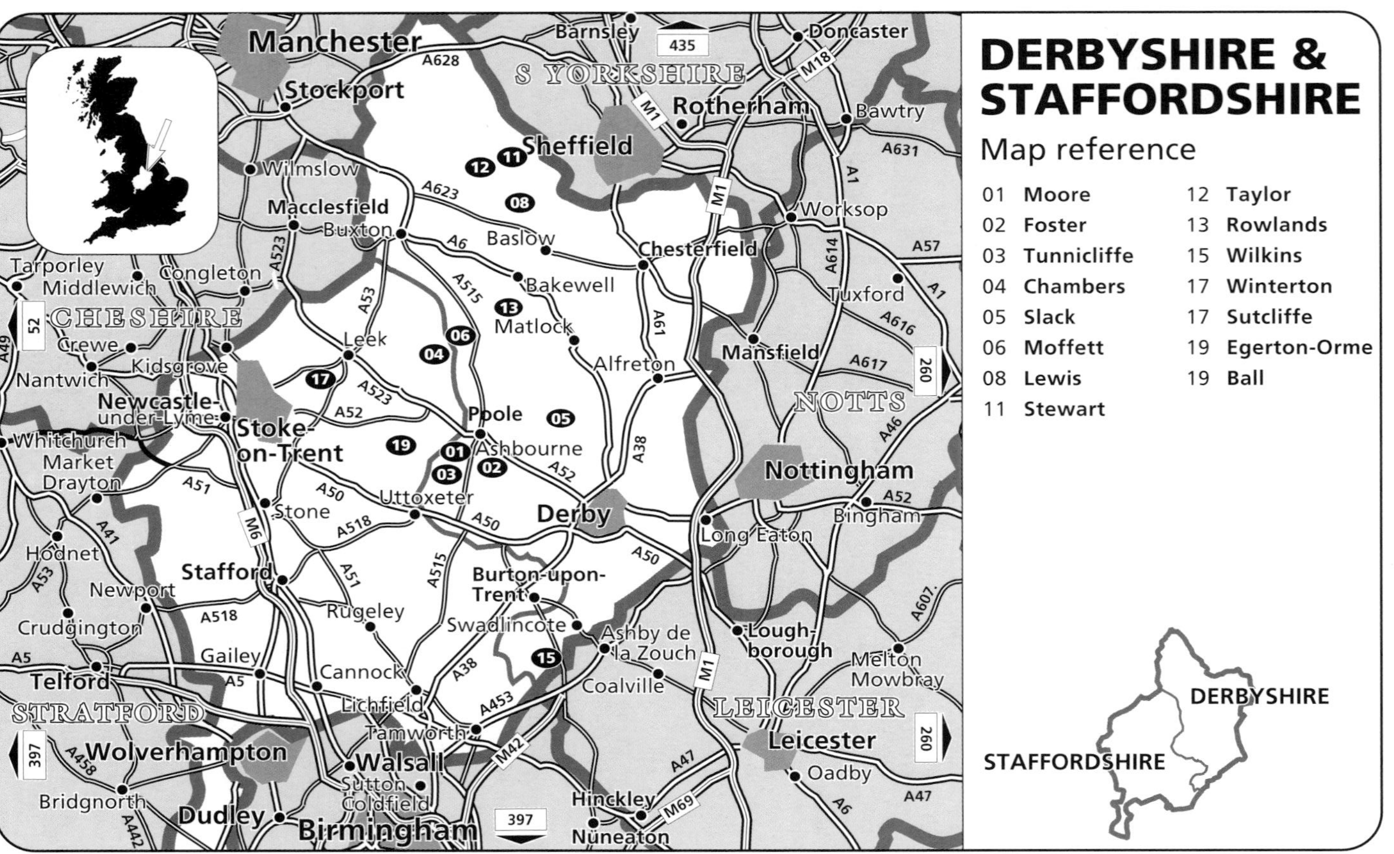

01	**Moore**	12	**Taylor**
02	**Foster**	13	**Rowlands**
03	**Tunnicliffe**	15	**Wilkins**
04	**Chambers**	17	**Winterton**
05	**Slack**	17	**Sutcliffe**
06	**Moffett**	19	**Egerton-Orme**
08	**Lewis**	19	**Ball**
11	**Stewart**		

Beeches Farmhouse. Waldley.

Derbyshire

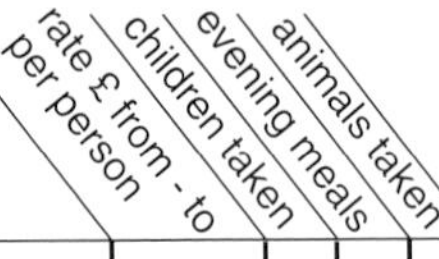

Rose Cottage

Nearest Road: A.515

A mid-Victorian house in 6 acres, Rose Cottage is a family home in quiet, unspoilt, beautiful & peaceful countryside. Bedrooms have panoramic views over Dove Valley towards Weaver Hills (George Eliot's 'Adam Bede' country). Ideal for visiting Dales, walking, country houses (Chatsworth, Haddon Hall etc.), potteries & Alton Towers (9 miles). Comfortable double rooms, private bathrooms, 1 en-suite, T.V., tea-making facilities in rooms. Children over 12.

Mrs Cynthia Moore Rose Cottage Snelston Ashbourne DE6 2DL Derbyshire
Tel: (01335) 324230 Fax 01335 324651 Open: ALL YEAR Map Ref No. 01

rate £ from - to per person	children taken	evening meals	animals taken
£24.00 to £30.00	Y	N	N

Shirley Hall

Nearest Road: A.52

Shirley Hall is a lovely, peaceful old farmhouse, just to the south of Ashbourne, close to the village of Shirley. In the centre of rolling pastureland enjoy the tranquillity of this part-moated, timbered farmhouse, surrounded by a lawned garden. 3 attractive bedrooms with en-suite/private bathrooms, T.V. & tea/coffee facilities. The full English breakfast with homemade bread & preserves is renowned. The village pub is excellent for evening meals. Coarse-fishing available. Woodland walks nearby.
E-mail: sylviafoster@shirleyhallfarm.com

Mrs Sylvia Foster Shirley Hall Shirley Ashbourne DE6 3AS Derbyshire
Tel: (01335) 360346 Fax 01335 360346 Open: ALL YEAR Map Ref No. 02

rate £ from - to per person	children taken	evening meals	animals taken
£22.00 to £26.00	N	N	N

Beeches Restaurant

Nearest Road: A.50

Relax & unwind in this rural farm retreat after exploring the Derbyshire Dales or the thrills of Alton Towers. Offering 10 tastefully furnished en-suite bedrooms. Dine in the award-winning 18th-century licensed farmhouse restaurant on fresh English food & home-made desserts. Guests are invited to meet the Shetland pony, pigs, dogs, rabbits & kittens, whilst enjoying the freedom of the gardens, fields & the beautiful countryside.
E-mail: BEECHESFA@AOL.COM

Paul & Barbara Tunnicliffe Beeches Restaurant Waldley Doveridge Ashbourne DE6 5LR Derbys.
Tel: (01889) 590288 Fax 01889 590559 Open: ALL YEAR (Excl. Xmas) Map Ref No. 03

rate £ from - to per person	children taken	evening meals	animals taken
£32.00 to £48.00	Y	Y	N

see PHOTO over p. 123

VISA: M'CARD: AMEX:

Stanshope Hall

Nearest Road: A.515

Stanshope Hall, with its informal feel but with every comfort, stands in splendid isolation among the dry stone walls of the southern Peak District. Walks from the door lead to verdant Dovedale or the undiscovered seclusion of the Manifold Valley. The en-suite rooms have hand-painted walls & frescos in the bathrooms. Candle-lit dinners (by arrangement) are prepared using uncomplicated but imaginative recipes with local & garden produce.
E-mail: naomi@stanshope.demon.co.uk

Naomi Chambers & Nick Lourie Stanshope Hall Stanshope Nr. Ashbourne DE6 2AD Derbyshire
Tel: (01335) 310278 Fax 01335 310470 Open: ALL YEAR (Excl. Xmas) Map Ref No. 04

rate £ from - to per person	children taken	evening meals	animals taken
£25.00 to £40.00	Y	Y	N

VISA: M'CARD:

Dannah Farm Country House. Shottle.

rate £ from - to per person	children taken	evening meals	animals taken

Dannah Farm Country House

Nearest Road: A.517

Superb Georgian farmhouse set on the Chatsworth Estates at Shottle, beautifully furnished with antiques & old pine. En-suite bedrooms, some with private sitting rooms & 4-poster beds, open fires, whirlpool baths & wonderful views. Award-winning, oak beamed, licensed dining room where guests can enjoy fresh food imaginatively cooked, homemade bread & breakfasts that will 'set you up for the day'. A perfect escape.

E-mail: reservations@dannah.demon.co.uk

Mr & Mrs M. Slack Dannah Farm Country House Bowmans Lane Shottle Belper DE56 2DR Derbys.
Tel: (01773) 550273 Fax 01773 550590 Open: ALL YEAR (Excl. Xmas Day) Map Ref No. 05

rate £ from - to per person	children taken	evening meals	animals taken
£37.50 to £55.00	Y	Y	N

see PHOTO over p. 125

VISA: M'CARD:

Biggin Hall

Nearest Road: A.515

A delightful 17th-century stone house, completely restored & keeping all the character of its origins, with massive oak beams. 17 comfortable rooms, all charmingly furnished, 1 with a 4-poster bed, all with en-suite facilities & modern amenities. Guests have the choice of 2 sitting rooms, 1 with a log fire, 1 with colour T.V. & library, & there is a lovely garden. The house is beautifully furnished, with many antiques. Non-smoking areas. Children over 12. Animals by arrangement.

E-mail: bigginhall@compuserve.com

James Moffett Biggin Hall Biggin-by-Hartington Buxton SK17 0DH Derbyshire
Tel: (01298) 84451 Fax 01298 84681 Open: ALL YEAR Map Ref No. 06

rate £ from - to per person	children taken	evening meals	animals taken
£24.50 to £45.00	Y	Y	Y

see PHOTO over p. 127

VISA: M'CARD: AMEX:

Delf View House

Nearest Road: A.623

Beautiful & tranquil accommodation in an elegant listed Georgian country house in historic Eyam village in the magnificent Peak National Park. Guests are warmly welcomed in the drawing room, delightfully furnished with antiques, pictures & books. 3 bedrooms, 1 en-suite, include a Sheraton 4-poster & 18th-century French twin beds. Sumptuous breakfasts served in the oak-beamed dining room. Restaurants nearby. Ideal for visiting Chatsworth, Haddon & Eyam Hall. Children over 12.

E-mail: lewis@delfview.demon.co.uk

Mrs Meirlys Lewis Delf View House Church Street Eyam S32 5QH Derbyshire
Tel: (01433) 631533 Fax 01433 631972 Open: ALL YEAR Map Ref No. 08

rate £ from - to per person	children taken	evening meals	animals taken
£27.00 to £35.00	Y	N	N

The Old Barn

Nearest Road: A.6187

The Old Barn, believed to be of 16th-century origin, has been sympathetically restored to retain much of its original character, including exposed beams & flagstone floors. 3 beautifully furnished en-suite bedrooms, 1 being a 4-poster. All have T.V. & tea/coffee-making facilities. Also, a residents lounge which is very comfortable. One of the main features of this accommodation is the magnificent view across Hope Valley towards the Pennines. 1 mile from Hathersage & easy access to Bakewell, Chatsworth & Sheffield. Children over 12.

Mrs K. H. Stewart The Old Barn Booths Farm Sheffield Road Hathersage Hope Valley S32 1DA
Tel: (01433) 650667 Fax 01433 650667 Open: APR - OCT Map Ref No. 11

rate £ from - to per person	children taken	evening meals	animals taken
£25.00 to £32.50	Y	N	N

VISA: M'CARD:

Biggin Hall. Biggin by Hartington.

Derbyshire & Staffordshire

Underleigh House

rate £ from - to per person	children taken	evening meals	animals taken
£33.00 to £46.00	N	N	N

Nearest Road: A.6187

Set in an idyllic & peaceful location amidst glorious scenery, this extended cottage & barn conversion (dating from 1873) is the perfect base for exploring the Peak District. Underleigh is in the heart of magnificent walking country & offers 6 en-suite rooms, furnished to a high standard with many thoughtful extras included. Delicious breakfasts in the flagstoned dining hall feature local & home-made specialities. The beamed lounge with log fire is the perfect place to relax. Children over 12.

E-mail: underleigh.house@btinternet.com

see PHOTO over p. 129

VISA: M'CARD:

Philip & Vivienne Taylor Underleigh House Off Edale Road Hope Hope Valley S33 6RF Derbyshire
Tel: (01433) 621372 Fax 01433 621324 Open: ALL YEAR (Excl. Xmas & New Year) Map Ref No. 12

Uppertown Farmhouse

rate £ from - to per person	children taken	evening meals	animals taken
£30.00 to £40.00	Y	N	N

Nearest Road: A.6

Uppertown Farmhouse, formerly a 17th-century coaching inn, is a Grade II listed farmhouse with its own walled courtyard & village stocks. Set in the heart of Derbyshire's National Peak Park it commands a panoramic view over the Dales. It is furnished with antiques & retains many original features. Bedrooms are en-suite. Good pubs, restaurants & antique shops in the area together with historic houses & castles, including Chatsworth House. Children welcome by arrangement.

E-mail: jonliz@hudrow.enterprise-plc.com

VISA: M'CARD:

Mr & Mrs J. Rowlands Uppertown Farmhouse Uppertown Lane Birchover Matlock DE4 2BH Derbys.
Tel: (01629) 650112 Fax 01629 650112 Open: ALL YEAR Map Ref No. 13

The Old Hall

rate £ from - to per person	children taken	evening meals	animals taken
£25.00 to £35.00	Y	Y	N

Nearest Road: A.444

A particularly peaceful Grade II listed manor house set in 18 acres of gardens & woodland, overlooking a lake. The house, dating from 1644, incorporates part of a medieval monastery & despite all modern conveniences retains its unique character, original features & panelling. 3 bedrooms with en-suite/private bathrooms & T.V., etc. Traditional English food is served by arrangement. Convenient for Lichfield, Shugborough, Calke Abbey, Kedleston, Castle Donington & the N.E.C.. Children over 14.

E-mail: clemencywilkins@hotmail.com

Mrs Clemency Wilkins The Old Hall Netherseal Swadlincote DE12 8DF Derbyshire
Tel: (01283) 760258 Fax 01283 762991 Open: ALL YEAR Map Ref No. 15

Brook House Farm

rate £ from - to per person	children taken	evening meals	animals taken
£19.00 to £21.00	Y	N	N

Nearest Road: A.520

Brook House is a dairy farm in a picturesque valley 1/2 a mile from the A.520, down a private lane. Many pleasant walks locally; convenient for the Peak District, pottery museums and Alton Towers. Comfortable rooms in the farmhouse, and 2 spacious family rooms with patio doors in a tastefully converted annex. All en-suite & centrally heated, with tea/coffee facilities. Good farmhouse breakfast served in a conservatory with magnificent views. A warm welcome assured.

Elizabeth Winterton Brook House Farm Brook House Lane Cheddleton Leek ST13 7DF Staffordshire
Tel: (01538) 360296 Open: ALL YEAR Map Ref No. 17

Underleigh House. Hope.

...ffordshire

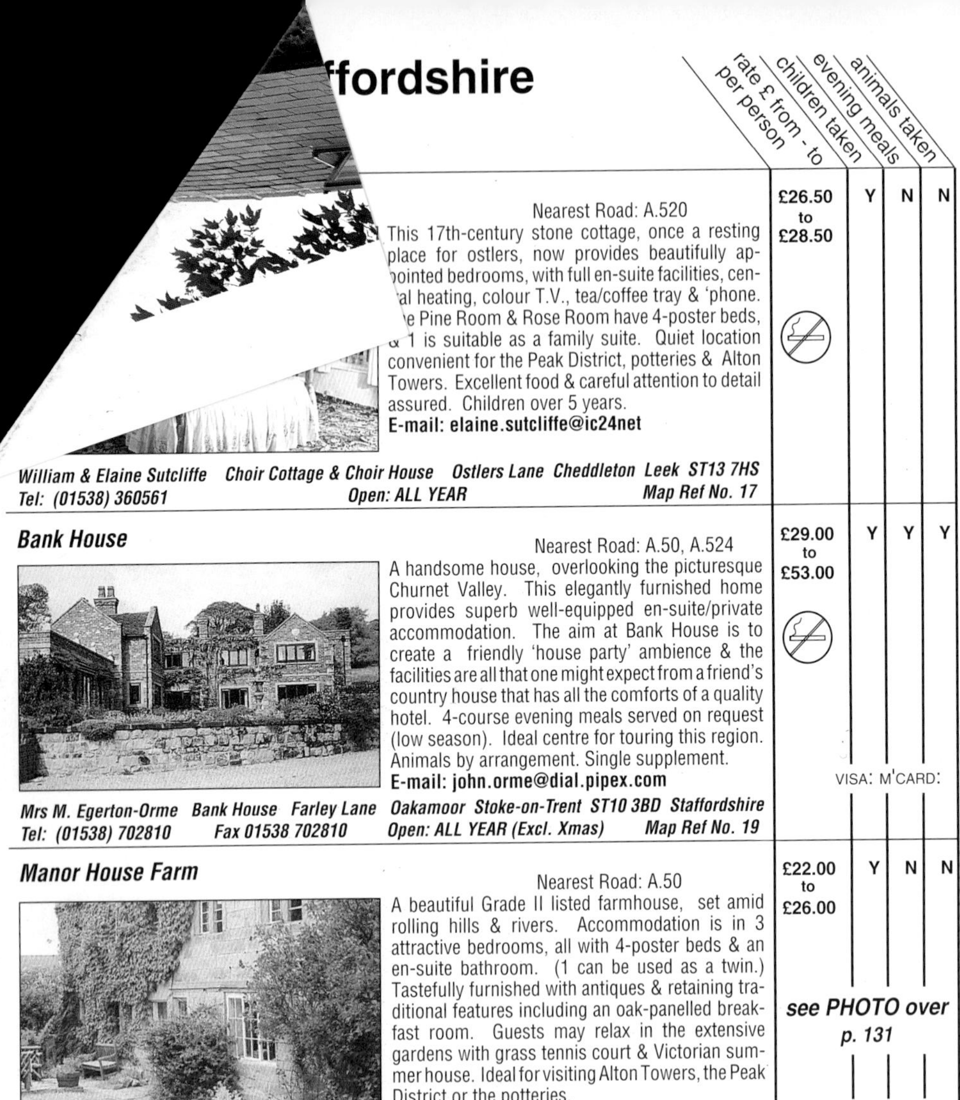

	rate £ from - to per person	children taken	evening meals	animals taken
Choir Cottage & Choir House	£26.50 to £28.50	Y	N	N
Bank House	£29.00 to £53.00	Y	Y	Y
Manor House Farm	£22.00 to £26.00	Y	N	N

Nearest Road: A.520

This 17th-century stone cottage, once a resting place for ostlers, now provides beautifully ap-
)ointed bedrooms, with full en-suite facilities, cen-
ral heating, colour T.V., tea/coffee tray & 'phone. ...e Pine Room & Rose Room have 4-poster beds, ... 1 is suitable as a family suite. Quiet location convenient for the Peak District, potteries & Alton Towers. Excellent food & careful attention to detail assured. Children over 5 years.

E-mail: elaine.sutcliffe@ic24net

William & Elaine Sutcliffe   Choir Cottage & Choir House   Ostlers Lane   Cheddleton   Leek   ST13 7HS
Tel: (01538) 360561   Open: ALL YEAR   Map Ref No. 17

Bank House

Nearest Road: A.50, A.524

A handsome house, overlooking the picturesque Churnet Valley. This elegantly furnished home provides superb well-equipped en-suite/private accommodation. The aim at Bank House is to create a friendly 'house party' ambience & the facilities are all that one might expect from a friend's country house that has all the comforts of a quality hotel. 4-course evening meals served on request (low season). Ideal centre for touring this region. Animals by arrangement. Single supplement.

E-mail: john.orme@dial.pipex.com

VISA: M'CARD:

Mrs M. Egerton-Orme   Bank House   Farley Lane   Oakamoor   Stoke-on-Trent   ST10 3BD   Staffordshire
Tel: (01538) 702810   Fax 01538 702810   Open: ALL YEAR (Excl. Xmas)   Map Ref No. 19

Manor House Farm

Nearest Road: A.50

A beautiful Grade II listed farmhouse, set amid rolling hills & rivers. Accommodation is in 3 attractive bedrooms, all with 4-poster beds & an en-suite bathroom. (1 can be used as a twin.) Tastefully furnished with antiques & retaining traditional features including an oak-panelled breakfast room. Guests may relax in the extensive gardens with grass tennis court & Victorian summer house. Ideal for visiting Alton Towers, the Peak District or the potteries.

E-mail: cm_ball@yahoo.co.uk

see PHOTO over p. 131

VISA: M'CARD:

C. M. Ball   Manor House Farm   Quixhill Lane   Prestwood   Denstone   Uttoxeter   ST14 5DD   Staffs.
Tel: (01889) 590415   Fax 01335 342198   Open: ALL YEAR   Map Ref No. 19

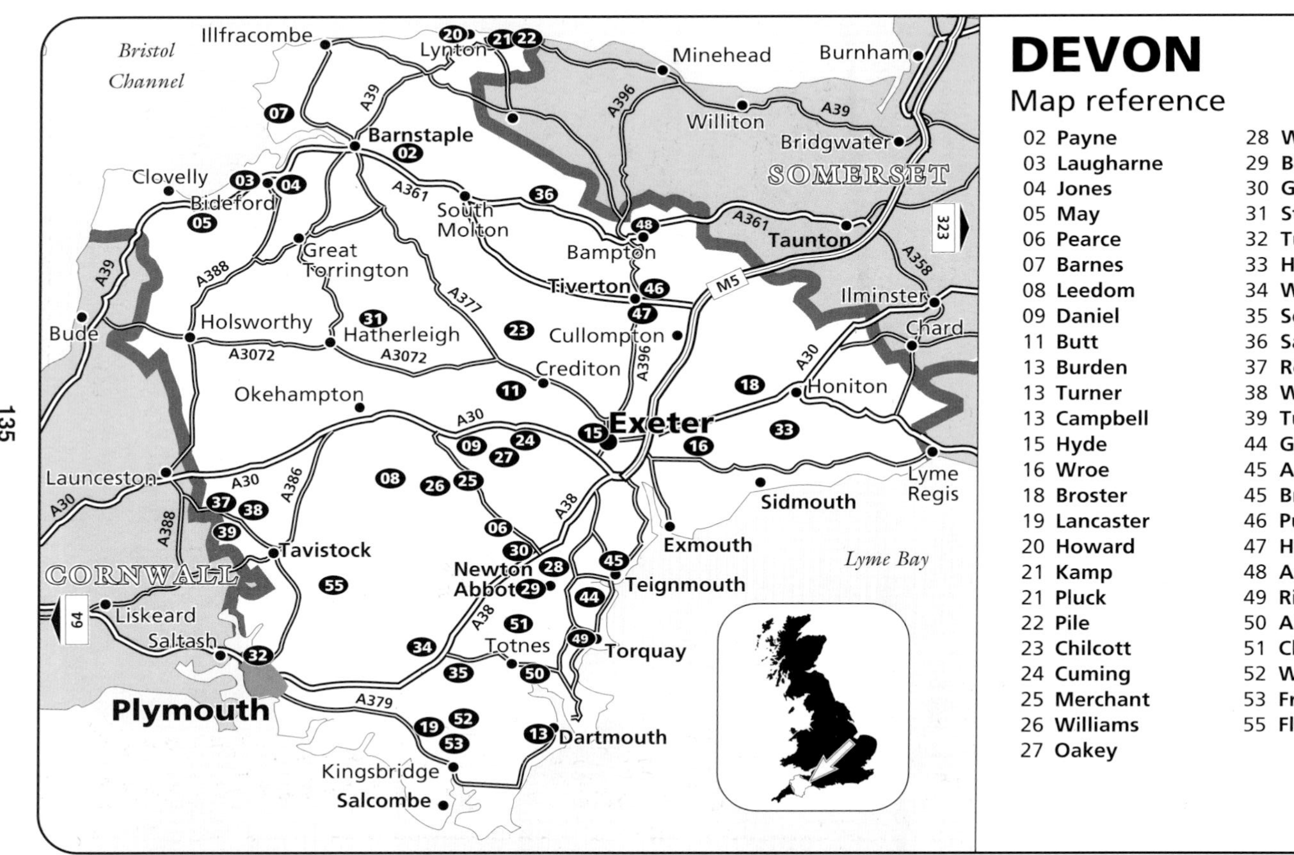

DEVON

Map reference

02 **Payne**
03 **Laugharne**
04 **Jones**
05 **May**
06 **Pearce**
07 **Barnes**
08 **Leedom**
09 **Daniel**
11 **Butt**
13 **Burden**
13 **Turner**
13 **Campbell**
15 **Hyde**
16 **Wroe**
18 **Broster**
19 **Lancaster**
20 **Howard**
21 **Kamp**
21 **Pluck**
22 **Pile**
23 **Chilcott**
24 **Cuming**
25 **Merchant**
26 **Williams**
27 **Oakey**
28 **Wiemeyer**
29 **Bell**
30 **Gregson**
31 **Steele-M.**
32 **Turner**
33 **Hopkinson**
34 **Willey**
35 **Scharenguivel**
36 **Sampson**
37 **Rowlatt**
38 **Wright**
39 **Tucker**
44 **Graeme**
45 **Allan**
45 **Brown**
46 **Pugsley**
47 **Hill-King**
48 **Ayres**
49 **Richards**
50 **Allnut**
51 **Clapp**
52 **Worth**
53 **Frost**
55 **Flint**

Devon

	rate £ from - to per person	children taken	evening meals	animals taken
Huxtable Farm	£24.00 to £25.00	Y	Y	N
The Mount	£23.00 to £27.00	Y	N	N
The Pines at Eastleigh	£35.00 to £45.00	Y	Y	Y
Lower Waytown	£26.00 to £29.50	Y	N	N

Huxtable Farm

Nearest Road: A.361

Enjoy a memorable candlelit dinner of farm/local produce with complimentary home-made wine in this wonderful medieval longhouse with original oak panelling, beams & bread ovens. This secluded sheep farm with abundant wildlife & panoramic views is ideally situated on the Tarka Trail for exploring Exmoor & N. Devon's coastline. Tennis court, sauna, fitness & games room. Log fires in winter. 5 en-suite bedrooms & 1 with a private bathroom, each with T.V. & tea/coffee facilities.

E-mail: jpayne@huxhilton.enterprise-plc.com

VISA: M'CARD:

Jackie & Antony Payne *Huxtable Farm* *West Buckland* *Barnstaple EX32 0SR* *Devon*
Tel: (01598) 760254 *Fax 01598 760254* *Open: FEB - NOV & New Year* *Map Ref No. 02*

The Mount

Nearest Road: A.361

The Mount is a small interesting Georgian house which is full of character & charm. It is set in a pretty garden with large handsome trees. A peaceful haven yet, only 5 minutes walk from the town centre with its quay, narrow streets & medieval bridge. The 6 bedrooms are tastefully furnished & have en-suite facilities & T.V.. (1 ground-floor room.) Conveniently situated for Exmoor, Dartmoor, Clovelly, Lundy & the beautiful North Devon coastline with its sandy beaches & rugged cliffs.

E-mail: alex@laugharnel.freeserve.co.uk

VISA: M'CARD:

Heather & Andrew Laugharne *The Mount* *Northdown Road* *Bideford EX39 3LP* *Devon*
Tel: (01237) 473748 *Fax 01271 373813* *Open: ALL YEAR* *Map Ref No. 03*

The Pines at Eastleigh

Nearest Road: A.39

Rediscover peace & relaxation at this Grade II listed Georgian home. Set in 7 acres of gardens & paddocks with views of Bideford, Lundy & Hartland Point. Licensed. Books & maps to borrow & an audio system for guest use. Generous farmhouse-style cooking featuring fresh local produce by arrangement. Special diets catered for. 5 attractive bedrooms, en-suite facilities. Colour T.V., 'phones, tea/coffee, hairdryers. Ground-floor courtyard rooms & king-size beds.

E-mail: barry@thepinesateastleigh.co.uk

VISA: M'CARD:

Jenny & Barry Jones *The Pines at Eastleigh* *Eastleigh* *Bideford EX39 4PA* *Devon*
Tel: (01271) 860561 *Fax 01271 861248* *Open: ALL YEAR* *Map Ref No. 04*

Lower Waytown

Nearest Road: A.39

This beautifully converted barn & roundhouse provides a delightful, spacious & comfortable home offering superb accommodation. Extensive grounds with ponds & ornamental waterfowl, & a coastal footpath nearby. The en-suite bedrooms, 2 double (1 ground-floor) & 1 twin-bedded, are tastefully furnished, & each has T.V., hairdryers & tea/coffee-making facilities. The unique, round, beamed sitting room adjoins the spacious dining room, where breakfast is served. Children over 12.

Mrs Caroline May *Lower Waytown* *Horns Cross* *Bideford EX39 5DN* *Devon*
Tel: (01237) 451787 Fax 01237 451787 Open: ALL YEAR (Excl. Xmas & New Year) Map Ref No. 05

Devon

Devon

Gazeteer

Areas of outstanding natural beauty.
North, South, East Devon.

Houses & Castles

Arlington Court - Barnstaple
Regency house, collection of shell, pewter & model ships.

Bickleigh Castle - Nr. Tiverton
Thatched Jacobean wing. Great Hall & armoury. Early Norman chapel, gardens & moat.

Buckland Abbey - Nr. Plymouth
13th century Cistercian monastery - 16th century alterations. Home of Drake - contains his relics & folk gallery.

Bradley Manor - Newton Abbot
15th century Manor house with perpendicular chapel.

Cadhay - Ottery St. Mary
16th century Elizabethan Manor house.

Castle Drogo - Nr.Chagford
Designed by Lutyens - built of granite, standing over 900 feet above the gorge of the Teign river.

Chambercombe Manor - Illfracombe
14th-15th century Manor house.

Castle Hill - Nr. Barnstaple
18th century Palladian mansion - fine furniture of period, pictures, porcelain & tapestries.

Hayes Barton - Nr. Otterton
16th century plaster & thatch house. Birthplace of Walter Raleigh.

Oldway - Paignton
19th century house having rooms designed to be replicas of rooms at the Palace of Versailles.

Powederham Castle - Nr. Exeter
14th century mediaeval castle much damaged in Civil War. Altered in 18th & 19th centuries. Fine music room by Wyatt.

Saltram House - Plymouth
Some remnants of Tudor house built into George II house, with two rooms by Robert Adam. Excellent plasterwork & woodwork.

Shute Barton - Nr. Axminster
14th century battlemented Manor house with Tudor & Elizabethan additions.

Tiverton Castle - Nr. Tiverton
Fortress of Henry I. Chapel of St. Francis. Gallery of Joan of Arc.

Torre Abbey Mansion - Torquay
Abbey ruins, tithe barn. Mansion house with paintings & furniture.

Cathedrals & Churches

Atherington (St. Mary)
Perpendicular style - mediaeval effigies & glass, original rood loft. Fine screens, 15th century bench ends.

Ashton (St. John the Baptist)
15th century - mediaeval screens, glass & wall paintings. Elizabethan pulpit with canopy, 17th century altar railing.

Bere Ferrers (St. Andrew)
14th century rebuilding - 14th century glass, 16th century benches, Norman font.

Bridford (St. Thomas a Becket)
Perpendicular style - mediaeval glass & woodwork. Excellent rood screen c.1530.

Cullompton (St. Andrew)
15th century perpendicular - Jacobean west gallery - fan tracery in roof, exterior carvings.

Exeter Cathedral
13th century decorated - Norman towers. Interior tierceron ribbed vault (Gothic) carved corbets & bosses, moulded piers & arches. Original pulpitum c.1320. Choir stalls with earliest misericords in England c.1260.

Haccombe (St. Blaize)
13th century effigies, 14th century glass, 17th century brasses, 19th century screen, pulpit & reredos.

Kentisbeare (St. Mary)
Perpendicular style - checkered tower. 16th century rood screen.

Ottery St. Mary (St. Mary)
13th century, 14th century clock, fan vaulted roof, tomb with canopy, minstrel's gallery, gilded wooded eagle. 18th century pulpit.

Parracombe (St. Petrock)
Unrestored Georgian - 16th century benches, mostly perpendicular, early English chancel.

Sutcombe (St. Andrew)
15th century - some part Norman. 16th century bench ends, restored rood screen, mediaeval glass & floor tiles.

Swimbrige (St. James)
14th century tower & spire - mediaeval stone pulpit, 15th century rood screen, font cover of Renaissance period.

Devon

Tawstock (St. Peter)
14th century, Italian plasterwork ceiling, mediaeval glass, Renaissance memorial pew, Bath monument.
Buckfast Abbey
Living Benedictine monastery, built on mediaeval foundation. Famous for works of art in church, modern stained glass, tonic wine & bee-keeping.

Museums & Galleries

Bideford Museum - Bideford
Geology, maps, prints, shipwright's tools, North Devon pottery.
Burton Art Gallery - Bideford
Hubert Coop collection of paintings etc.
Butterwalk Museum - Dartmouth
17th century row of half timbered buildings, nautical museum. 140 model ships.
Newcomen Engine House - Nr. Butterwalk Museum
Original Newcomen atmospheric/pressure steam engine c.1725.
Royal Albert Memorial Museum Art Gallery - Exeter
Collections of English watercolours, paintings, glass & ceramics, local silver, natural history & anthropology.
Rougemont House Museum - Exeter
Collections of archaeology & local history. Costume & lace collection
Guildhall - Exeter
Mediaeval structure with Tudor frontage - City regalia & silver.
Exeter Maritime Museum - Exeter
Largest collection in the world of working boats, afloat, ashore & under cover.
The Steam & Countryside Museum - Exmouth
Very large working layout - hundreds of exhibits.
Including Victorian farmhouse - farmyard pets for children.
Shebbear - North Devon
Alcott Farm Museum with unique collections of agricultural implements & photographs, etc.
The Elizabethan House - Totnes
Period costumes & furnishings, tools, toys, domestic articles, etc.
The Elizabethan House - Plymouth
16th century house with period furnishings.
City Museum & Art Gallery - Plymouth
Collections of pictures & porcelain, English & Italian drawing. Reynolds' family portraits, early printed books, ship models.
Cookworthy Museum - Kingsbridge
Story of china clay. Local history, shipbuilding tools, rural life.
Honiton & Allhallows Public Museum - Honiton
Collection of Honiton lace, implements etc. Complete Devon Kitchen.
Lyn & Exmoor Museum - Lynton
Life & history of Exmoor.
Torquay & Natural History Society Museum - Torquay
Collection illustrating Kent's Cavern & other caves - natural history & folkculture.

Historic Monuments

Okehampton Castle - Okehampton
11th -14th century chapel, keep & hall.
Totnes Castle - Totnes
13th - 14th century ruins of Castle.
Blackbury Castle - Southleigh
Hill fort - well preserved.
Dartmouth Castle - Dartmouth
15th century castle - coastal defence.
Lydford Castle - Lydford
12th century stone keep built upon site of Saxon fortress town.
Hound Tor - Manaton
Ruins of mediaeval hamlet.

Other things to see & do

The Big Sheep - Abbotsham
Sheep-milking parlour, with gallery, dairy & production rooms. Exhibition & play area.
Dartington Crystal - Torrington
Watch skilled craftworkers make lead crystalware. Glass centre & exhibition.
Dartmoor Wildlife Park - Sparkwell Nr. Plymouth
Over 100 species, including tigers, lions, bears, deer, birds of prey & waterfowl.
The Devon Guild of Craftsmen - Riverside Mill, Bovey Tracey
Series of quality exhibitions throughout the year.
Paignton Zoological & Botanical Gardens - Paignton
Third largest zoo in England. Botanical gardens, tropical house, "The Ark" family activity centre.

Manor House Farm. Prestwood.

O Turn (L) Denston - Church (R) Alliston Ashborne Bridge - (L) crestwood not gates Lane 1 mi - Ranch

A50 - Stoke - Derby Uttoxeter - O McDonald Little chef O Turn (L) Ultox Jws - 4.5 mi JCB FACT on left

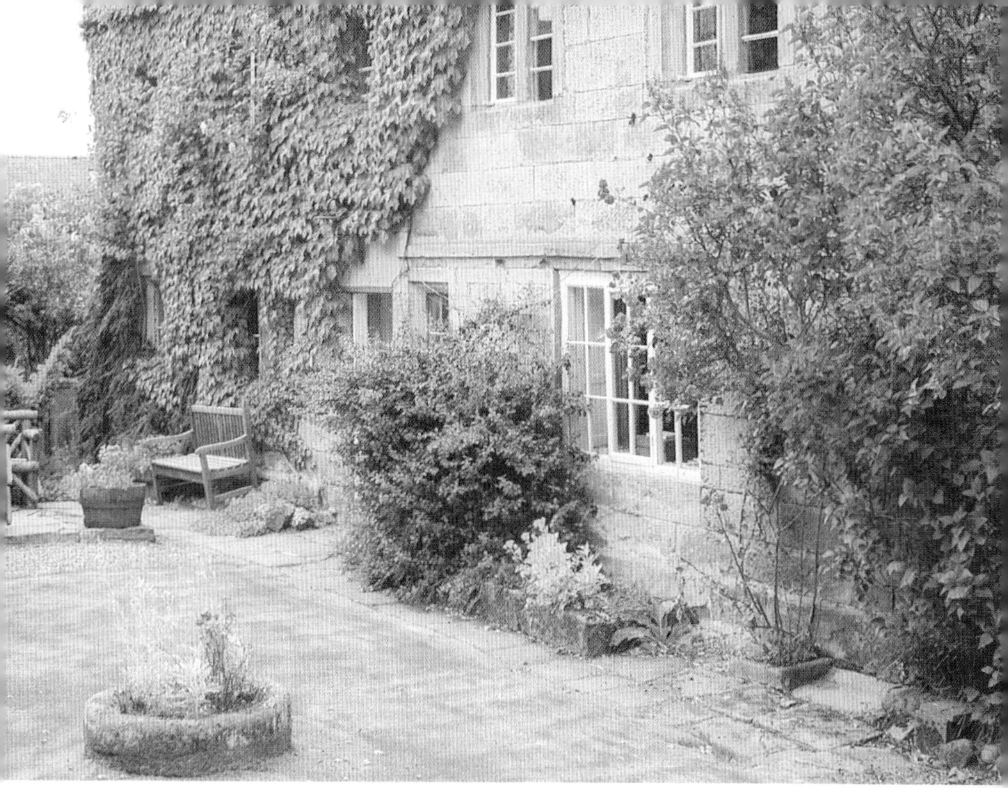

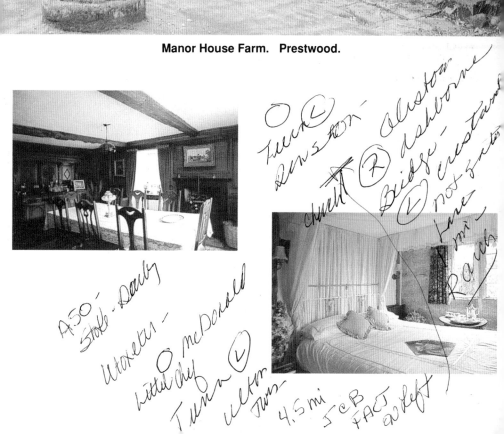

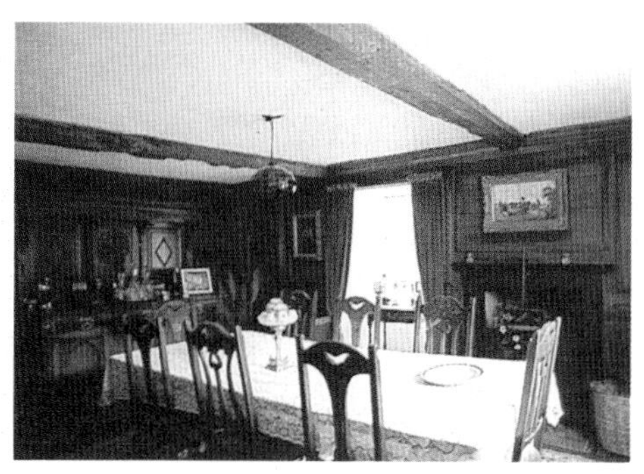

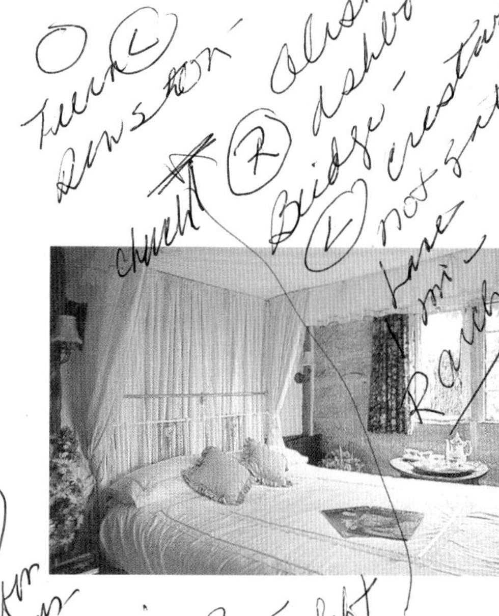

Devon

Devon

(West Country)

Here is a county of tremendous variety. Two glorious & contrasting coastlines with miles of sandy beaches, sheltered coves & rugged cliffs. There are friendly resorts & quiet villages of cob & thatch, two historic cities, & a host of country towns & tiny hamlets as well as the wild open spaces of two national parks.

From the grandeur of Hartland Point east to Foreland Point where Exmoor reaches the sea, the north Devon coast is incomparable. At Westward Ho!, Croyde & Woolacombe the rolling surf washes the golden beaches & out to sea stands beautiful Lundy Island, ideal for bird watching, climbing & walking. The tiny village of Clovelly with its cobbled street tumbles down the cliffside to the sea. Ilfracombe is a friendly resort town & the twin towns of Lynton & Lynmouth are joined by a cliff railway.

The south coast is a colourful mixture of soaring red sandstone cliffs dropping to sheltered sandy coves & the palm trees of the English Riviera. This is one of England's great holiday coasts with a string of popular resorts; Seaton, Sidmouth, Budleigh Salterton, Exmouth, Dawlish, Teignmouth & the trio of Torquay, Paignton & Brixham that make up Torbay. To the south, beyond Berry Head are Dartmouth, rich in navy tradition, & Salcombe, a premiere sailing centre in the deep inlet of the Kingsbridge estuary. Plymouth is a happy blend of holiday resort, tourist centre, historic & modern city, & the meeting-point for the wonderful old sailing vessels for the Tall Ships Race.

Inland the magnificent wilderness of Dartmoor National Park offers miles of sweeping moorland, granite tors, clear streams & wooded valleys, ancient stone circles & clapper bridges. The tors, as the Dartmoor peaks, are called are easily climbed & the views from the tops are superb. Widecombe-in-the-Moor, with its imposing church tower, & much photographed Buckland-in-the-Moor are only two of Dartmoor's lovely villages.

The Exmoor National Park straddles the Devon/Somerset border. It is a land of wild heather moorland above deep wooded valleys & sparkling streams, the home of red deer, soaring buzzards & of legendary Lorna Doone from R.D. Blackmore's novel. The south west peninsula coastal path follows the whole of the Exmoor coastline affording dramatic scenery & spectacular views, notably from Countisbury Hill.

The seafaring traditions of Devon are well-known. Sir Walter Raleigh set sail from Plymouth to Carolina in 1584; Sir Francis Drake began his circumnavigation of the world at Plymouth in the "Golden Hind" & fought the Spanish Armada off Plymouth Sound. The Pilgrim Fathers sailed from here & it was to here that Sir Francis Chichester returned having sailed around the world in 1967.

Exeter's maritime tradition is commemorated in an excellent museum located in converted riverside warehouses but the city's chief glory is the magnificent 13th century cathedral of St. Mary & St. Peter, built in an unusual decorated Gothic style, with its west front covered in statues.

The River Dart near Dittisham.

Devon

rate £ from - to per person	children taken	evening meals	animals taken
£25.00 to £32.00	Y	Y	N

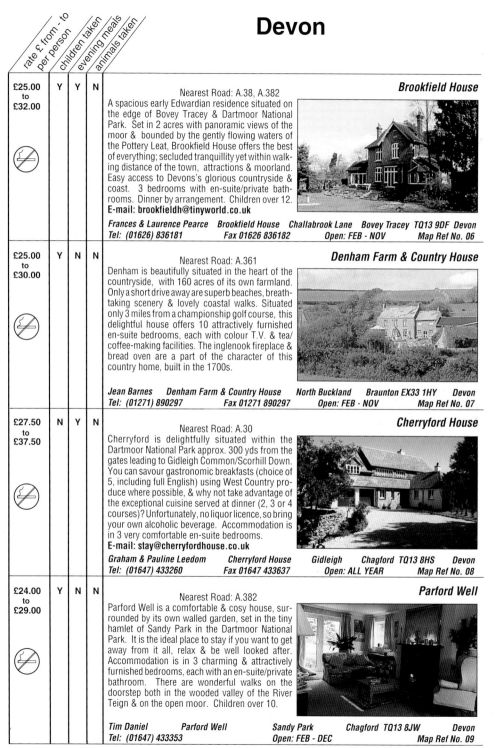

Brookfield House

Nearest Road: A.38, A.382

A spacious early Edwardian residence situated on the edge of Bovey Tracey & Dartmoor National Park. Set in 2 acres with panoramic views of the moor & bounded by the gently flowing waters of the Pottery Leat, Brookfield House offers the best of everything; secluded tranquillity yet within walking distance of the town, attractions & moorland. Easy access to Devons's glorious countryside & coast. 3 bedrooms with en-suite/private bathrooms. Dinner by arrangement. Children over 12.
E-mail: brookfieldh@tinyworld.co.uk

Frances & Laurence Pearce Brookfield House Challabrook Lane Bovey Tracey TQ13 9DF Devon
Tel: (01626) 836181 Fax 01626 836182 Open: FEB - NOV Map Ref No. 06

rate £ from - to per person	children taken	evening meals	animals taken
£25.00 to £30.00	Y	N	N

Denham Farm & Country House

Nearest Road: A.361

Denham is beautifully situated in the heart of the countryside, with 160 acres of its own farmland. Only a short drive away are superb beaches, breathtaking scenery & lovely coastal walks. Situated only 3 miles from a championship golf course, this delightful house offers 10 attractively furnished en-suite bedrooms, each with colour T.V. & tea/coffee-making facilities. The inglenook fireplace & bread oven are a part of the character of this country home, built in the 1700s.

Jean Barnes Denham Farm & Country House North Buckland Braunton EX33 1HY Devon
Tel: (01271) 890297 Fax 01271 890297 Open: FEB - NOV Map Ref No. 07

rate £ from - to per person	children taken	evening meals	animals taken
£27.50 to £37.50	N	Y	N

Cherryford House

Nearest Road: A.30

Cherryford is delightfully situated within the Dartmoor National Park approx. 300 yds from the gates leading to Gidleigh Common/Scorhill Down. You can savour gastronomic breakfasts (choice of 5, including full English) using West Country produce where possible, & why not take advantage of the exceptional cuisine served at dinner (2, 3 or 4 courses)? Unfortunately, no liquor licence, so bring your own alcoholic beverage. Accommodation is in 3 very comfortable en-suite bedrooms.
E-mail: stay@cherryfordhouse.co.uk

Graham & Pauline Leedom Cherryford House Gidleigh Chagford TQ13 8HS Devon
Tel: (01647) 433260 Fax 01647 433637 Open: ALL YEAR Map Ref No. 08

rate £ from - to per person	children taken	evening meals	animals taken
£24.00 to £29.00	Y	N	N

Parford Well

Nearest Road: A.382

Parford Well is a comfortable & cosy house, surrounded by its own walled garden, set in the tiny hamlet of Sandy Park in the Dartmoor National Park. It is the ideal place to stay if you want to get away from it all, relax & be well looked after. Accommodation is in 3 charming & attractively furnished bedrooms, each with an en-suite/private bathroom. There are wonderful walks on the doorstep both in the wooded valley of the River Teign & on the open moor. Children over 10.

Tim Daniel Parford Well Sandy Park Chagford TQ13 8JW Devon
Tel: (01647) 433353 Open: FEB - DEC Map Ref No. 09

Devon

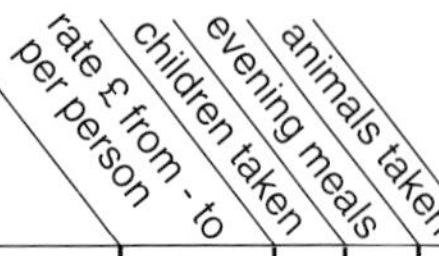

The New Inn

Nearest Road: A.377

The New Inn is a 13th-century thatched inn nestling in a quiet valley by the side of a brook. Accommodation in this attractive property includes 6 en-suite bedrooms with 'phone, T.V. & tea/coffee-making facilities. There is also an extensive menu, using fresh local produce whenever possible. Local amenities include several golf courses, fishing, horse riding & sport & leisure facilities. Easy access to Dartmoor, Exmoor & the north & south Devon coasts.

E-mail: NEW-INN@reallyreal-group.com

Paul & Irene Butt *The New Inn* *Coleford* *Crediton EX17 5BZ* *Devon*
Tel: 01363 84242 *Fax 01363 85044* *Open: ALL YEAR* *Map Ref No. 11*

rate £ from - to per person	children taken	evening meals	animals taken
£34.00 to £39.00	Y	Y	N

see PHOTO over p. 139

VISA: M'CARD: AMEX:

Hedley House

Nearest Road: A.379

Hedley House is a Grade II listed Georgian house overlooking the River Dart. Offering 3 charming en-suite bedrooms which are elegantly furnished throughout with antiques & feature T.V., tea/coffee-making facilities, etc. Each of the bedrooms has superb views of the river & beyond to the sea. Breakfast is served in the attractive dining room & there is a guest lounge leading onto a delightful courtyard. Only a few minutes walk from the town centre, shops, restaurants & pubs. A perfect spot from which to explore beautiful Devon.

Mr Anthony Burden *Hedley House* *37 Newcomen Road* *Dartmouth TQ6 9BN* *Devon*
Tel: (01803) 832885 *Open: ALL YEAR* *Map Ref No. 13*

rate £ from - to per person	children taken	evening meals	animals taken
£25.00 to £32.50	N	N	N

Ford House

Nearest Road: A.3122

Ford House is an attractive Grade II listed Regency house, situated within walking distance of the many shops, restaurants & pubs of Dartmouth. The en-suite, individually decorated bedrooms are equipped with either king- or queen-size double beds or twin beds. Each room has a fridge, hairdryer, T.V. etc. Breakfast is served from 8 a.m. until 12 noon, & ranges from traditional full English to scrambled eggs & smoked salmon. Parking. Special 'dinner party' weekends can be arranged.

E-mail: richard@ford-house.freeserve.co.uk

Richard Turner *Ford House* *44 Victoria Road* *Dartmouth TQ6 9DX* *Devon*
Tel: (01803) 834047 *Fax 01803 834047* *Open: MAR - OCT* *Map Ref No. 13*

rate £ from - to per person	children taken	evening meals	animals taken
£27.50 to £37.50	Y	Y	Y

VISA: M'CARD: AMEX:

Campbells

Nearest Road: A.3122

Set in a quiet location with a lovely garden, Campbells is only a few minutes walk from the centre of Dartmouth. Both bedrooms have stunning panoramic views; they are beautifully furnished with comfortable double beds, colour T.V. & are fully en-suite. The accent at Campbells is on friendliness & comfort with many added extras. Flexible breakfasts, with delicious West Country food & home-baking. Off-road parking. A delightful home & the perfect spot for a relaxing break.

Mrs Angela Campbell *Campbells* *5 Mount Boone* *Dartmouth TQ6 9PB* *Devon*
Tel: (01803) 833438 *Fax 01803 833438* *Open: ALL YEAR* *Map Ref No. 13*

rate £ from - to per person	children taken	evening meals	animals taken
£27.50 to £55.00	N	N	N

The New Inn. Coleford.

Devon

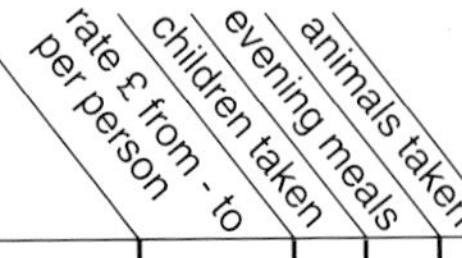

Raffles

Nearest Road: M.5

Imagine a large Victorian town house, furnished with antiques, tastefully decorated, a delightful walled garden yet minutes from the town centre, then come to Raffles the home of Richard & Sue. Their aim is to offer high-quality accommodation with friendly personal service. All bedrooms are en-suite with tea/coffee-making facilities, colour T.V. & central heating. Lock-up garages are also available on request. Raffles is an excellent base from which to explore Devon.

E-mail: raffleshtl@btinternet.com

rate £ from - to per person	children taken	evening meals	animals taken
£25.00 to £50.00	Y	Y	Y

VISA: M'CARD: AMEX:

Richard & Susan Hyde *Raffles* *11 Blackall Road* *Exeter EX4 4HD* *Devon*
Tel: (01392) 270200 *Fax 01392 270200* *Open: ALL YEAR* *Map Ref No. 15*

Lower Marsh Farm

Nearest Road: A.30

Charming 17th-century Grade II listed farmhouse set in 5 acres of gardens & paddocks with orchard, pond, stream & stable courtyard on the edge of a pretty east Devon hamlet. Easy access to Exeter, coast, Exmoor & Dartmoor. This is a beautiful family home, tastefully furnished with antiques. There are 3 comfortable guest bedrooms (2 en-suite, 1 with private bathroom), each with colour T.V. & hospitality tray. Guest sitting room with log fire. Excellent country pubs nearby.

rate £ from - to per person	children taken	evening meals	animals taken
£21.00 to £25.00	Y	N	Y

see PHOTO over p. 141

Mrs Sian Wroe *Lower Marsh Farm* *Marsh Green* *Exeter EX5 2EX* *Devon*
Tel: (01404) 822432 *Open: ALL YEAR* *Map Ref No. 16*

Colestocks Country House

Nearest Road: A.30

Colestocks is an elegant pink-washed thatched, 16th-century Grade II listed country house set in its own grounds. The friendly hosts offer 8 beautifully appointed en-suite bedrooms, each with T.V. & tea/coffee-making facilities. The house is elegantly furnished throughout with period furniture & antiques. Delicious home-cooked dinners available on request. Licensed. Set in a tranquil, rural situation, Colestocks is perfect for a relaxing break & is also well-placed for touring the glorious West Country. Children over 10 years welcome.

rate £ from - to per person	children taken	evening meals	animals taken
£27.50 to £30.00	N	Y	N

VISA: M'CARD:

Gordon Broster *Colestocks Country House* *Payhembury* *Honiton EX14 3JR* *Devon*
Tel: (01404) 850633 *Fax 01404 850633* *Open: APR - OCT* *Map Ref No. 18*

Helliers Farm

Nearest Road: A.379

Set in the heart of the South Hams countryside, this recently modernised farmhouse offers accommdation in 5 pleasant & comfortably furnished bedrooms with tea/coffee-making facilities. Also. a spacious dining room where good farmhouse breakfasts are served, a comfortable lounge with T.V. & a games room. Situated close to the beaches, moors, golf courses, National Trust walks & the city of Plymouth.

E-mail: helliersfarm@ukonline.co.uk

rate £ from - to per person	children taken	evening meals	animals taken
£22.00 to £25.00	Y	N	N

Mrs C. M. Lancaster *Helliers Farm* *Ashford* *Aveton Gifford* *Kingsbridge TQ7 4ND* *Devon*
Tel: (01548) 550689 *Fax 01548 550689* *Open: All Year Excl. Xmas* *Map Ref No. 19*

Lower Marsh Farm. Rockbeare.

Devon

rate £ from - to per person	children taken	evening meals	animals taken

Highcliffe House Hotel

Nearest Road: A.39

Highcliffe House Hotel is a superb, warm & friendly Victorian house with everything provided for your comfort. Situated in an elevated position, only 5 minutes walk from Lynton & commanding stunning woodland & sea views over Lynmouth Bay to south Wales; which can be enjoyed from the bedrooms, lounge & candlelit conservatory restaurant. The hotel offers 6 spacious & attractively furnished, en-suite bedrooms. Excellent walks from the front door. An ideal base for touring picturesque Devon.
E-mail: HIGHCLIFFE.hotel@excite.co.uk

Mr & Mrs B. E. Howard *Highcliffe House Hotel* *Sinai Hill* *Lynton EX35 6AR* *Devon*
Tel: (01598) 752235 *Fax 01598 752235* *Open: FEB - DEC* *Map Ref No. 20*

rate £ from - to per person	children taken	evening meals	animals taken
£20.00 to £35.00	N	Y	N

VISA: M'CARD:

Southcliffe

Nearest Road: A.39

A Listed Victorian gentleman's residence with characteristic pitch-pine staircase & doors & Swiss-style balconies. Beautifully appointed, comfortable bedrooms, all with private bathrooms, colour T.V. & tea/coffee-making facilities. June & Adrian Kamp have been at Southcliffe since 1978, & have a reputation for good food, comfort, cleanliness & value for money. Evening meals are available Thursday-Sunday. Children over 10 years welcome. Animals by arrangement.

June & Adrian Kamp *Southcliffe* *Lee Road* *Lynton EX35 6BS* *Devon*
Tel: (01598) 753328 *Fax 01598 753328* *Open: MAR - OCT* *Map Ref No. 21*

rate £ from - to per person	children taken	evening meals	animals taken
£22.00 to £26.00	Y	Y	Y

VISA: M'CARD:

Longmead House

Nearest Road: A.39

A haven for good home-cooking, with that little extra flair which makes many guests return. John & Carol offer a warm welcome to their home, & encourage a relaxed, friendly atmosphere. The 7 bedrooms are all individually decorated, comfortable & attractively furnished; 6 are en-suite. Set in a large garden with parking, & close to the Valley of Rocks, Longmead provides an ideal base from which to discover Exmoor.
E-mail: info@longmeadhouse.co.uk

John & Carol Pluck *Longmead House* *9 Longmead* *Lynton EX35 6DQ* *Devon*
Tel: (01598) 752523 *Fax 01598 752523* *Open: MAR - OCT* *Map Ref No. 21*

rate £ from - to per person	children taken	evening meals	animals taken
£20.00 to £22.00	Y	Y	N

VISA: M'CARD:

Coombe Farm

Nearest Road: A.39

Coombe is a 365-acre, hill-sheep farm, with an early-17th-century farmhouse set betwixt Lynmouth & the legendary Doone Valley. The coast path runs through the farm at Desolate. All within the spectacular Exmoor National Park. The bedrooms include 2 doubles, en-suite, 1 twin & 2 family rooms. All have hot-drink facilities, shaver points, & bath & hand towels & are comfortably furnished. Central heating. A lounge with woodburner fire & colour T.V. in which to relax.

Susan Pile *Coombe Farm* *Countisbury* *Lynton EX35 6NF* *Devon*
Tel: (01598) 741236 *Fax 01598 741236* *Open: MAR - NOV* *Map Ref No. 22*

rate £ from - to per person	children taken	evening meals	animals taken
£19.50 to £25.00	Y	N	N

VISA: M'CARD:

Wigham. Morchard Bishop.

Devon

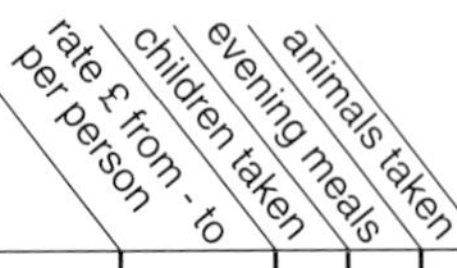

Wigham Organic Farm & Guesthouse

Nearest Road: A.377

Wigham is a 16th-century Devon longhouse, with a 30-acre farm which provides fresh fruit, vegetables & dairy produce for imaginative meals. There are 5 double rooms, including a 4-poster suite. All with T.V. & video & en-suite bathroom. There are 2 sitting rooms in which guests may relax, & a snooker lounge & outdoor heated pool. Licensed. Full S.A. organic symbol Sept. 1999. (Kitchen certified organic Jan. 2000.) Children over 8. (Please note rates printed include dinner).
E-mail: info@wigham.co.uk

Stephen & Dawn Chilcott Wigham Organic Farm & Guesthouse Morchard Bishop EX17 6RJ Devon
Tel: (01363) 877350 Fax 01363 877350 Open: ALL YEAR Map Ref No. 23

rate £ from - to per person	children taken	evening meals	animals taken
£59.00 to £87.50	Y	Y	N

see PHOTO over p. 143

VISA: M'CARD: AMEX:

Great Wooston Farm

Nearest Road: B.3212, A.30

Great Wooston Farm, once part of the Manor House Estate owned by Lord Hambledon. Situated high above the Teign Valley in the Dartmoor National Park, with views across the moors. Plenty of walks, golf, fishing & riding nearby. The farmhouse is surrounded by a delightful garden of 1/2 an acre, also barbeque & picnic area. 3 bedrooms, 2 en-suite, 1 with 4-poster bed, 1 with private bathroom, with every facility. Excellent breakfasts are served. Also, a guests' lounge for your relaxation after a day exploring the magical Dartmoor. Children over 8.

Mrs Mary Cuming Great Wooston Farm Moretonhampstead TQ13 8QA Devon
Tel/Fax: (01647) 440367 Mobile 0498 670590 Open: ALL YEAR Map Ref No. 24

rate £ from - to per person	children taken	evening meals	animals taken
£20.00 to £23.00	Y	N	N

VISA: M'CARD:

Great Sloncombe Farm

Nearest Road: A.382

Great Sloncombe Farm is a listed, granite-&-cob-built, 13th-century farmhouse. Set in a peaceful Dartmoor valley, the rambling house has a magical atmosphere, & is furnished with oak & pine, antique china & interesting old photographs. The 3 warm & pleasant bedrooms are all en-suite, with every facility included. Delicious breakfasts, with home-made bread & plentiful Devonshire suppers, are served. Children over 8 yrs.
E-mail: hmerchant@sloncombe.freeserve.co.uk

Mrs Trudie Merchant Great Sloncombe Farm Moretonhampstead TQ13 8QF Devon
Tel: (01647) 440595 Fax 01647 440595 Open: ALL YEAR Map Ref No. 25

rate £ from - to per person	children taken	evening meals	animals taken
£23.00 to £24.00	Y	Y	Y

Gate House

Nearest Road: A.30, A.38

North Bovey is an historic village set within the Dartmoor National Park. Gate House, near the village green, is a listed 500-year-old thatched medieval longhouse with beamed ceilings, old granite fireplaces & bread oven. An acre of gardens with a swimming pool. The charming bedrooms combine country-style elegance with en-suite/private bathrooms. Lovely walks amidst breathtaking scenery, & N.T. properties within easy reach. Animals by arrangement. Children over 15.
E-mail: gatehouseondartmoor@talk21.com

John & Sheila Williams Gate House North Bovey Moretonhampstead TQ13 8RB Devon
Tel: (01647) 440479 Fax 01647 440479 Open: ALL YEAR Map Ref No. 26

rate £ from - to per person	children taken	evening meals	animals taken
£28.00 to £28.00	N	Y	Y

see PHOTO over p. 145

Gate House. North Bovey.

Devon

rate £ from - to per person	children taken	evening meals	animals taken

Great Doccombe Farm

£18.00 to £20.00	Y	N	N

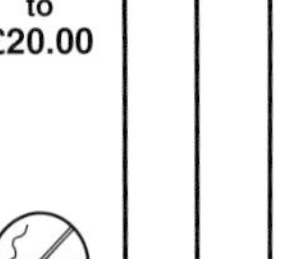

Nearest Road: A.30

Great Doccombe Farm is situated in the pretty hamlet of Doccombe, within the Dartmoor National Park, on the B.3212 from Exeter. An ideal base for walking in the Teign Valley & nearby moors, with golf, riding & fishing nearby. This lovely 16th-century granite farmhouse is surrounded by gardens & fields. The bedrooms (1 ground-floor) are all en-suite, & have shower, T.V. & tea/coffee facilities. A traditional English breakfast is served. Great Doccombe Farm is a perfect place to relax.

Gill & David Oakey   Great Doccombe Farm   Doccombe   Moretonhampstead TQ13 8SS   Devon
Tel: (01647) 440694   Open: ALL YEAR   Map Ref No. 27

The Thatched Cottage Restaurant

£25.00 to £25.00	Y	Y	N

Nearest Road: A.380

A beautiful 400-year-old, Grade II listed, thatched longhouse where old oak beams & a large open fireplace lend a cosy & welcoming atmosphere. There are 2 en-suite bedrooms, all with colour T.V. & tea/coffee-making facilities. A full English breakfast is served. Character bar & restaurant, where table d'hote & a la carte menus are available each evening. A pretty garden for guests' use. An ideal base for touring, with a warm welcome.
E-mail: thatched@globalnet.co.uk

VISA: M'CARD: AMEX:

Mr & Mrs Wiemeyer   The Thatched Cottage Restaurant   9 Crossley Moor Road   Kingsteignton
Newton Abbot TQ12 3LE   Tel: (01626) 365650   Open: ALL YEAR   Map Ref No. 28

Sampsons Farm Restaurant/Accomm.

£22.50 to £50.00	Y	Y	Y

Nearest Road: A.38, A.380

A super, relaxed, family atmosphere is found at this traditional thatched Devon longhouse. This Grade II listed building, of historical importance, retains much of its original charm & character, with oak beams, panelling & inglenook fireplaces. All rooms have modern amenities, 4-poster & en-suite rooms available. (Category 1 for accommodation with disabled access.) An a la carte & table d'hote menu is offered in the evening. A view of Dartmoor from the windows. A short distance from the coast.
E-mail: nigel@sampsonsfarm.com

see PHOTO over p. 147

VISA: M'CARD:

Nigel Bell   Sampsons Farm Restaurant/Accomm.   Preston   Newton Abbot TQ12 3PP   Devon
Tel: (01626) 354913   Fax 01626 354913   Open: ALL YEAR   Map Ref No. 29

Penpark

£25.00 to £28.00	Y	N	N

Nearest Road: A.38

In the Dartmoor National Park, with secluded, beautiful woodland gardens, tennis court & glorious panoramic views, Penpark is an elegant country house, a gem of its period, designed by Clough Williams Ellis of Portmeirion fame. 3 charming rooms: a spacious double/twin with balcony; a single next door & a further double - all with wonderful views; private facilities; tea/coffee & T.V.. The Gregsons offer you a truly relaxed stay in beautiful & friendly surroundings.
E-mail: gregson.penpark@ukgateway.net

Mrs Madeleine Gregson   Penpark   Bickington   Newton Abbot TQ12 6LH   Devon
Tel: (01626) 821314   Fax 01626 821101   Open: ALL YEAR   Map Ref No. 30

Sampsons Farm Restaurant. Newton Abbot

Devon

	rate £ from - to per person	children taken	evening meals	animals taken
Holme Down	£31.00 to £36.00	Y	Y	N
Westways	£22.00 to £££	N	N	N
Bovett's Farm	£20.00 to £22.00	Y	N	N
The Granary	£23.00 to £30.00	N	N	N

Holme Down

Nearest Road: A.30

Situated in 100 acres of private pasture & woodland, Holme Down, a Victorian manor house, offers a tranquil & secluded hide-a-way. The spacious rooms have stunning views over Dartmoor & are attractively furnished throughout. All guests are made to feel very welcome by Peter, Sarah & their young family. Private fishing available on a mile stretch of river plus a stocked lake. Modern equestrian facilities are also available. Children over 12.

E-mail: sarah@holmedown.co.uk

see PHOTO over p. 149

VISA: M'CARD:

Peter & Sarah Steele-Mortimer Holme Down Exbourne Okehampton EX20 3QY Devon
Tel: (01837) 851485 Fax 01837 851585 Open: ALL YEAR Map Ref No. 31

Westways

Nearest Road: A.38

Situated approx. 3 1/2 miles from Plymouth city centre, this attractive detached house offers pleasant accommodation in 3 well-furnished rooms, with tea/coffee-making facilities. Excellent breakfasts are served in the elegant dining room. Guests may choose to relax & plan their excursions in the comfortable sitting room. Also, a small T.V. room. A homely & friendly base both for visitors wishing to make the most of the many attractions in the area, & for touring Devon. Children over 12.

E-mail: westways@cwcom.net

VISA: M'CARD:

John & Daphne Turner Westways 706 Budshead Road Crownhill Plymouth PL6 5DY Devon
Tel: (01752) 776617 Fax 01752 776617 Open: ALL YEAR Map Ref No. 32

Bovett's Farm

Nearest Road: A.375

A tastefully modernised Devon farmhouse, nestling amid the rolling hills of the breathtaking Roncombe valley, only 5 miles from Sidmouth. The attractively furnished en-suite bedrooms overlook the valley & each is well-equipped. A lounge with wood-burning stove. Bovett's is no longer a working farm but there are 12 acres of flower-filled meadows & a garden for guests to enjoy. Many clean, safe beaches within easy reach. A haven of peace & tranquillity. Children over 10.

E-mail: bridget@bovetts.demon.co.uk

Bridget & Brian Hopkinson Bovett's Farm Roncombe Lane Sidbury Sidmouth EX10 0QN Devon
Tel: (01395) 597456 Open: ALL YEAR Map Ref No. 33

The Granary

Nearest Road: A.38

The Granary has a warm relaxed atmosphere where it is easy for guests to feel at ease. It is ideally situated in a peaceful south Dartmoor hamlet & yet, is within easy reach of the South Hams coast. The 3 en-suite bedrooms have been invitingly decorated with great emphasis on comfort & style. All have T.V. & tea/coffee-making facilities. Breakfast may be a leisurely affair with a traditional English or vegetarian meal, complemented with fresh fruits & home-made muffins. Children over 14.

E-mail: twixt.sea.and.moor@ic24.net

Brenda Willey The Granary Harbourneford South Brent TQ10 9DT Devon
Tel: (01364) 73930 Fax 01364 73930 Open: ALL YEAR Map Ref No. 34

Holme Down. Exbourne.

Coombe House. North Huish.

rate £ from - to per person	children taken	evening meals	animals taken
£25.00 to £40.00	Y	Y	N

see PHOTO over p. 150

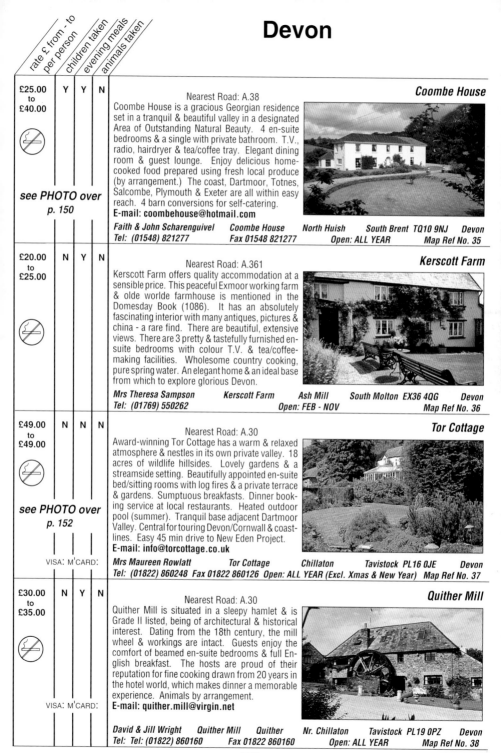

Coombe House

Nearest Road: A.38

Coombe House is a gracious Georgian residence set in a tranquil & beautiful valley in a designated Area of Outstanding Natural Beauty. 4 en-suite bedrooms & a single with private bathroom. T.V., radio, hairdryer & tea/coffee tray. Elegant dining room & guest lounge. Enjoy delicious home-cooked food prepared using fresh local produce (by arrangement.) The coast, Dartmoor, Totnes, Salcombe, Plymouth & Exeter are all within easy reach. 4 barn conversions for self-catering.

E-mail: coombehouse@hotmail.com

Faith & John Scharenguivel Coombe House North Huish South Brent TQ10 9NJ Devon
Tel: (01548) 821277 Fax 01548 821277 Open: ALL YEAR Map Ref No. 35

rate £ from - to per person	children taken	evening meals	animals taken
£20.00 to £25.00	N	Y	N

Kerscott Farm

Nearest Road: A.361

Kerscott Farm offers quality accommodation at a sensible price. This peaceful Exmoor working farm & olde worlde farmhouse is mentioned in the Domesday Book (1086). It has an absolutely fascinating interior with many antiques, pictures & china - a rare find. There are beautiful, extensive views. There are 3 pretty & tastefully furnished en-suite bedrooms with colour T.V. & tea/coffee-making facilities. Wholesome country cooking, pure spring water. An elegant home & an ideal base from which to explore glorious Devon.

Mrs Theresa Sampson Kerscott Farm Ash Mill South Molton EX36 4QG Devon
Tel: (01769) 550262 Open: FEB - NOV Map Ref No. 36

rate £ from - to per person	children taken	evening meals	animals taken
£49.00 to £49.00	N	N	N

see PHOTO over p. 152

VISA: M'CARD:

Tor Cottage

Nearest Road: A.30

Award-winning Tor Cottage has a warm & relaxed atmosphere & nestles in its own private valley. 18 acres of wildlife hillsides. Lovely gardens & a streamside setting. Beautifully appointed en-suite bed/sitting rooms with log fires & a private terrace & gardens. Sumptuous breakfasts. Dinner booking service at local restaurants. Heated outdoor pool (summer). Tranquil base adjacent Dartmoor Valley. Central for touring Devon/Cornwall & coastlines. Easy 45 min drive to New Eden Project.

E-mail: info@torcottage.co.uk

Mrs Maureen Rowlatt Tor Cottage Chillaton Tavistock PL16 0JE Devon
Tel: (01822) 860248 Fax 01822 860126 Open: ALL YEAR (Excl. Xmas & New Year) Map Ref No. 37

rate £ from - to per person	children taken	evening meals	animals taken
£30.00 to £35.00	N	Y	N

VISA: M'CARD:

Quither Mill

Nearest Road: A.30

Quither Mill is situated in a sleepy hamlet & is Grade II listed, being of architectural & historical interest. Dating from the 18th century, the mill wheel & workings are intact. Guests enjoy the comfort of beamed en-suite bedrooms & full English breakfast. The hosts are proud of their reputation for fine cooking drawn from 20 years in the hotel world, which makes dinner a memorable experience. Animals by arrangement.

E-mail: quither.mill@virgin.net

David & Jill Wright Quither Mill Quither Nr. Chillaton Tavistock PL19 0PZ Devon
Tel: Tel: (01822) 860160 Fax 01822 860160 Open: ALL YEAR Map Ref No. 38

Tor Cottage. Chillaton.

Thomas Luny House. Teignmouth.

Devon

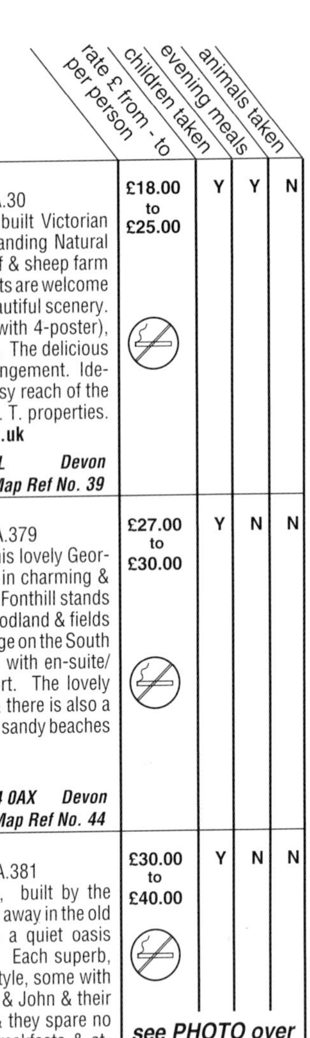

	rate £ from - to per person	children taken	evening meals	animals taken
Beera Farmhouse	£18.00 to £25.00	Y	Y	N
Fonthill	£27.00 to £30.00	Y	N	N
Thomas Luny House	£30.00 to £40.00	Y	N	N
Wytchwood	£25.50 to £32.50	Y	N	N

Beera Farmhouse

Nearest Road: A.30

Beera is a large, traditional stone built Victorian farmhouse set in an Area of Outstanding Natural Beauty. The farm is a 160-acre beef & sheep farm on the bank of the river Tamar. Guests are welcome to walk on the farm & take in the beautiful scenery. 3 attractive en-suite bedrooms (1 with 4-poster), each has T.V. & tea/coffee facilities. The delicious evening meals are provided by arrangement. Ideally situated for touring & within easy reach of the coast, Dartmoor National Park & N. T. properties.

E-mail: robert.tucker@farming.co.uk

Hilary Tucker   Beera Farmhouse   Milton Abbot   Tavistock PL19 8PL   Devon
Tel: (01822) 870216   Fax 01822 870216   Open: ALL YEAR   Map Ref No. 39

Fonthill

Nearest Road: A.379

Visitors are warmly welcomed to this lovely Georgian house, for a peaceful holiday in charming & very comfortable accommodation. Fonthill stands in 20 acres of beautiful gardens, woodland & fields on the edge of Shaldon, a pretty village on the South Devon coast. 2 delightful rooms, with en-suite/private bathrooms & every comfort. The lovely garden is for guests' enjoyment, & there is also a tennis court in the grounds. Several sandy beaches nearby & an 18-hole golf course.

E-mail: swanphoto2@aol.com

Mrs Jennifer Graeme   Fonthill   Torquay Road   Shaldon   Teignmouth TQ14 0AX   Devon
Tel: (01626) 872344   Fax 01626 872344   Open: MAR - NOV   Map Ref No. 44

Thomas Luny House

Nearest Road: A.381

A Grade II listed Georgian house, built by the marine artist Thomas Luny. Tucked away in the old quarter of Teignmouth, it forms a quiet oasis surrounded by its own high walls. Each superb, en-suite bedroom is individual in style, some with views over the River Teign. Alison & John & their family love to share their home, & they spare no effort in preparing the delicious breakfasts & attending to their guests' general well-being. Licensed. Children over 12 yrs.

E-mail: alisonandjohn@thomas-luny-house.co.uk

see PHOTO over p. 153

VISA: M'CARD:

Alison & John Allan   Thomas Luny House   Teign Street   Teignmouth TQ14 8EG   Devon
Tel: (01626) 772976   Open: ALL YEAR   Map Ref No. 45

Wytchwood

Nearest Road: A.381

Award-winning Wytchwood has an outstanding reputation for lavish hospitality & traditional home-cooking. To stay here is to be truly pampered! Panoramic views, beautiful garden, stylish interior design & the prettiest en-suite bedrooms, all combine to fulfil every expectation. Home-made bread, jams, preserves, orchard honey & garden produce. Delicious Devonshire cream teas, sponges & cakes. Many culinary awards. A warm welcome always.

E-mail: wytchwood@yahoo.com

see PHOTO over p. 155

Jenny Richardson Brown   Wytchwood   West Buckeridge   Teignmouth TQ14 8NF   Devon
Tel: (01626) 773482   Open: ALL YEAR   Map Ref No. 45

Wytchwood. West Buckeridge.

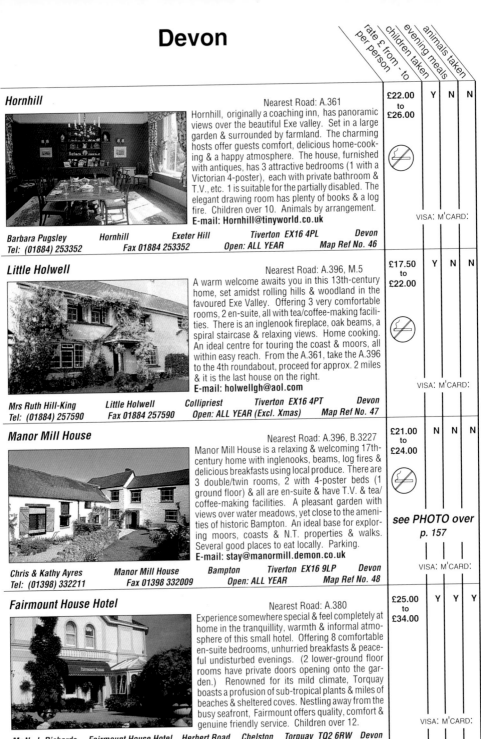

Devon

Hornhill

rate £ from - to per person	children taken	evening meals	animals taken
£22.00 to £26.00	Y	N	N

Nearest Road: A.361

Hornhill, originally a coaching inn, has panoramic views over the beautiful Exe valley. Set in a large garden & surrounded by farmland. The charming hosts offer guests comfort, delicious home-cooking & a happy atmosphere. The house, furnished with antiques, has 3 attractive bedrooms (1 with a Victorian 4-poster), each with private bathroom & T.V., etc. 1 is suitable for the partially disabled. The elegant drawing room has plenty of books & a log fire. Children over 10. Animals by arrangement.

E-mail: Hornhill@tinyworld.co.uk

VISA: M'CARD:

Barbara Pugsley *Hornhill* *Exeter Hill* *Tiverton EX16 4PL* *Devon*
Tel: (01884) 253352 *Fax 01884 253352* *Open: ALL YEAR* *Map Ref No. 46*

Little Holwell

rate £ from - to per person	children taken	evening meals	animals taken
£17.50 to £22.00	Y	N	N

Nearest Road: A.396, M.5

A warm welcome awaits you in this 13th-century home, set amidst rolling hills & woodland in the favoured Exe Valley. Offering 3 very comfortable rooms, 2 en-suite, all with tea/coffee-making facilities. There is an inglenook fireplace, oak beams, a spiral staircase & relaxing views. Home cooking. An ideal centre for touring the coast & moors, all within easy reach. From the A.361, take the A.396 to the 4th roundabout, proceed for approx. 2 miles & it is the last house on the right.

E-mail: holwellgh@aol.com

VISA: M'CARD:

Mrs Ruth Hill-King *Little Holwell* *Collipriest* *Tiverton EX16 4PT* *Devon*
Tel: (01884) 257590 *Fax 01884 257590* *Open: ALL YEAR (Excl. Xmas)* *Map Ref No. 47*

Manor Mill House

rate £ from - to per person	children taken	evening meals	animals taken
£21.00 to £24.00	N	N	N

Nearest Road: A.396, B.3227

Manor Mill House is a relaxing & welcoming 17th-century home with inglenooks, beams, log fires & delicious breakfasts using local produce. There are 3 double/twin rooms, 2 with 4-poster beds (1 ground floor) & all are en-suite & have T.V. & tea/coffee-making facilities. A pleasant garden with views over water meadows, yet close to the amenities of historic Bampton. An ideal base for exploring moors, coasts & N.T. properties & walks. Several good places to eat locally. Parking.

E-mail: stay@manormill.demon.co.uk

see PHOTO over *p. 157*

VISA: M'CARD:

Chris & Kathy Ayres *Manor Mill House* *Bampton* *Tiverton EX16 9LP* *Devon*
Tel: (01398) 332211 *Fax 01398 332009* *Open: ALL YEAR* *Map Ref No. 48*

Fairmount House Hotel

rate £ from - to per person	children taken	evening meals	animals taken
£25.00 to £34.00	Y	Y	Y

Nearest Road: A.380

Experience somewhere special & feel completely at home in the tranquillity, warmth & informal atmosphere of this small hotel. Offering 8 comfortable en-suite bedrooms, unhurried breakfasts & peaceful undisturbed evenings. (2 lower-ground floor rooms have private doors opening onto the garden.) Renowned for its mild climate, Torquay boasts a profusion of sub-tropical plants & miles of beaches & sheltered coves. Nestling away from the busy seafront, Fairmount offers quality, comfort & genuine friendly service. Children over 12.

VISA: M'CARD:

Mr N. J. Richards *Fairmount House Hotel* *Herbert Road* *Chelston* *Torquay TQ2 6RW* *Devon*
Tel: (01803) 605446 *Fax 01803 605446* *Open: ALL YEAR (Excl. Xmas & New Year)* *Map Ref No. 49*

Manor Mill House. Bampton.

The Old Forge at Totnes.   Totnes.

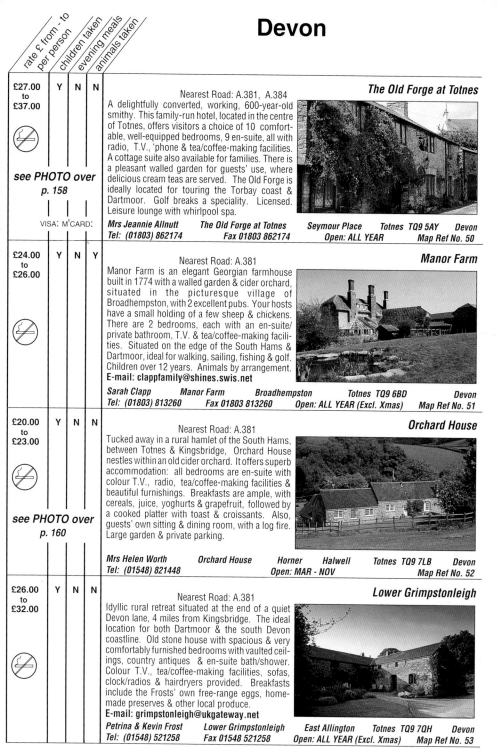

rate £ from - to per person	children taken	evening meals	animals taken
£27.00 to £37.00	Y	N	N

see PHOTO over p. 158

VISA: M'CARD:

The Old Forge at Totnes

Nearest Road: A.381, A.384

A delightfully converted, working, 600-year-old smithy. This family-run hotel, located in the centre of Totnes, offers visitors a choice of 10 comfortable, well-equipped bedrooms, 9 en-suite, all with radio, T.V., 'phone & tea/coffee-making facilities. A cottage suite also available for families. There is a pleasant walled garden for guests' use, where delicious cream teas are served. The Old Forge is ideally located for touring the Torbay coast & Dartmoor. Golf breaks a speciality. Licensed. Leisure lounge with whirlpool spa.

Mrs Jeannie Allnutt *The Old Forge at Totnes* *Seymour Place* *Totnes TQ9 5AY* *Devon*
Tel: (01803) 862174 *Fax 01803 862174* *Open: ALL YEAR* *Map Ref No. 50*

rate £ from - to per person	children taken	evening meals	animals taken
£24.00 to £26.00	Y	N	Y

Manor Farm

Nearest Road: A.381

Manor Farm is an elegant Georgian farmhouse built in 1774 with a walled garden & cider orchard, situated in the picturesque village of Broadhempston, with 2 excellent pubs. Your hosts have a small holding of a few sheep & chickens. There are 2 bedrooms, each with an en-suite/private bathroom, T.V. & tea/coffee-making facilities. Situated on the edge of the South Hams & Dartmoor, ideal for walking, sailing, fishing & golf. Children over 12 years. Animals by arrangement.
E-mail: clappfamily@shines.swis.net

Sarah Clapp *Manor Farm* *Broadhempston* *Totnes TQ9 6BD* *Devon*
Tel: (01803) 813260 *Fax 01803 813260* *Open: ALL YEAR (Excl. Xmas)* *Map Ref No. 51*

rate £ from - to per person	children taken	evening meals	animals taken
£20.00 to £23.00	Y	N	N

see PHOTO over p. 160

Orchard House

Nearest Road: A.381

Tucked away in a rural hamlet of the South Hams, between Totnes & Kingsbridge, Orchard House nestles within an old cider orchard. It offers superb accommodation: all bedrooms are en-suite with colour T.V., radio, tea/coffee-making facilities & beautiful furnishings. Breakfasts are ample, with cereals, juice, yoghurts & grapefruit, followed by a cooked platter with toast & croissants. Also, guests' own sitting & dining room, with a log fire. Large garden & private parking.

Mrs Helen Worth *Orchard House* *Horner* *Halwell* *Totnes TQ9 7LB* *Devon*
Tel: (01548) 821448 *Open: MAR - NOV* *Map Ref No. 52*

rate £ from - to per person	children taken	evening meals	animals taken
£26.00 to £32.00	Y	N	N

Lower Grimpstonleigh

Nearest Road: A.381

Idyllic rural retreat situated at the end of a quiet Devon lane, 4 miles from Kingsbridge. The ideal location for both Dartmoor & the south Devon coastline. Old stone house with spacious & very comfortably furnished bedrooms with vaulted ceilings, country antiques & en-suite bath/shower. Colour T.V., tea/coffee-making facilities, sofas, clock/radios & hairdryers provided. Breakfasts include the Frosts' own free-range eggs, home-made preserves & other local produce.
E-mail: grimpstonleigh@ukgateway.net

Petrina & Kevin Frost *Lower Grimpstonleigh* *East Allington* *Totnes TQ9 7QH* *Devon*
Tel: (01548) 521258 *Fax 01548 521258* *Open: ALL YEAR (Excl. Xmas)* *Map Ref No. 53*

Orchard House. Horner.

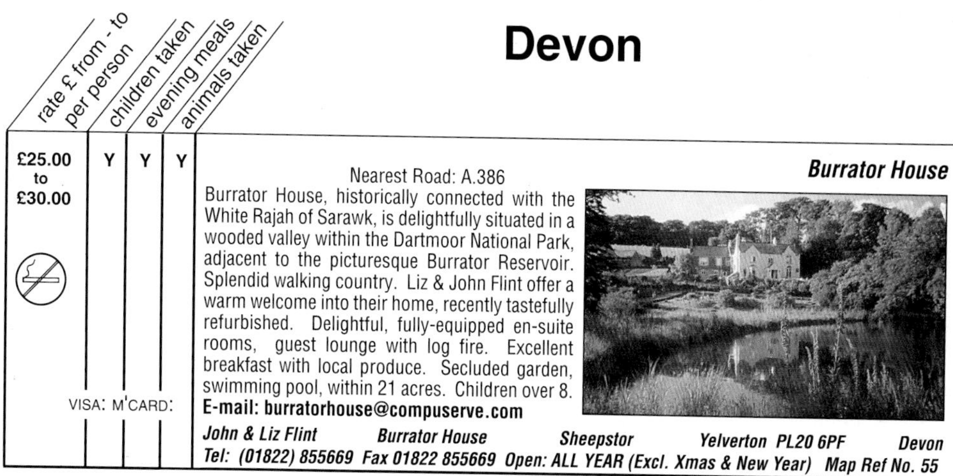

rate £ from - to per person	children taken	evening meals	animals taken	
£25.00 to £30.00	Y	Y	Y	***Burrator House*** Nearest Road: A.386 Burrator House, historically connected with the White Rajah of Sarawk, is delightfully situated in a wooded valley within the Dartmoor National Park, adjacent to the picturesque Burrator Reservoir. Splendid walking country. Liz & John Flint offer a warm welcome into their home, recently tastefully refurbished. Delightful, fully-equipped en-suite rooms, guest lounge with log fire. Excellent breakfast with local produce. Secluded garden, swimming pool, within 21 acres. Children over 8. **E-mail: burratorhouse@compuserve.com**
VISA: M'CARD:				*John & Liz Flint* *Burrator House* *Sheepstor* *Yelverton PL20 6PF* *Devon* *Tel: (01822) 855669 Fax 01822 855669 Open: ALL YEAR (Excl. Xmas & New Year) Map Ref No. 55*

All the establishments mentioned in this guide are members of The Worldwide Bed & Breakfast Association

When booking your accommodation please mention The Best Bed & Breakfast

Dorset

Dorset (West Country)

The unspoilt nature of this gem of a county is emphasised by the designation of virtually all of the coast & much of the inland country as an Area of Outstanding Natural Beauty. Along the coast from Christchurch to Lyme Regis there are a fascinating variety of sandy beaches, towering cliffs & single banks, whilst inland is a rich mixture of downland, lonely heaths, fertile valleys, historic houses & lovely villages of thatch & mellow stone buildings.

Thomas Hardy was born here & took the Dorset countryside as a background for many of his novels. Few writers can have stamped their identity on a county more than Hardy on Dorset, forever to be known as the "Hardy Country". Fortunately most of the area that he so lovingly described remains unchanged, including Egdon Heath & the county town of Dorchester, famous as Casterbridge.

In the midst of the rolling chalk hills which stretch along the Storr Valley lies picturesque Cerne Abbas, with its late mediaeval houses & cottages & the ruins of a Benedictine Abbey. At Godmanstone is the tiny thatched "Smiths Arms" claiming to be the smallest pub in England.

The north of the county is pastoral with lovely views over broad Blackmoor Vale. Here is the ancient hilltop town of Shaftesbury, with cobbled Gold Hill, one of the most photographed streets in the country.

Coastal Dorset is spectacular. Poole harbour is an enormous, almost circular bay, an exciting mixture of 20th century activity, ships of many nations & beautiful building of the 15th, 18th & early 19th centuries.

Westwards lies the popular resort of Swanage, where the sandy beach & sheltered bay are excellent for swimming. From here to Weymouth is a marvellous stretch of coast with scenic wonders like Lulworth Cove & the arch of Durdle Door.

Chesil Beach is an extraordinary bank of graded pebbles, as perilous to shipping today as it was 1,000 years ago. It is separated from the mainland by a sheltered lagoon known as the Fleet. From here a range of giant cliffs rises to 617 feet at Golden Gap & stretches westwards to Lyme Regis, beloved by Jane Austen who wrote "Persuasion" whilst living here.

Dorset has many interesting archaeological features. Near Dorchester is Maiden Castle, huge earthwork fortifications on a site first inhabited 6,000 years ago. The Badbury rings wind round a wooded hilltop near Wimborne Minster; legend has it that King Arthur's soul, in the form of a raven, inhabited this "dread" wood. The giant of Cerne Abbas is a figure of a man 180 feet high carved into the chalk hillside. Long associated with fertility there is still speculation about the figures' origins, one theory suggesting it is a Romano-British depiction of Hercules. A Roman amphitheatre can be seen at Dorchester, & today's road still follows the Roman route to Weymouth.

Corfe Castle.

Dorset

Dorset

Gazeteer

Areas of outstanding natural beauty.
The Entire County.

Houses & Castles

Athelthampton
Mediaeval house - one of the finest in all England. Formal gardens.

Barneston Manor - Nr. Church Knowle
13th - 16th century stone built manor house.

Forde Abbey - Nr. Chard
12th century Cistercian monastery - noted Mortlake tapestries.

Manor House - Sandford Orcas
Mansion of Tudor period, furnished with period furniture, antiques, silver, china, glass, paintings.

Hardy's Cottage - Higher Bockampton
Birthplace of Thomas Hardy, author (1840-1928).

Milton Abbey - Nr. Blandford
18th century Georgian house built on original site of 15th century abbey.

Purse Caundle Manor - Purse Caundle
Mediaeval Manor - furnished in style of period.

Parnham House - Beaminster
Tudor Manor - some later work by Nash. Leaded windows & heraldic plasterwork. Home of John Makepeace & the International School for Craftsmen in Wood. House, gardens & workshops.

Sherborne Castle - Sherborne
16th century mansion - continuously occupied by Digby family.

No. 3 Trinity Street - Weymouth
Tudor cottages now converted into one house, furnished 17th century.

Smedmore - Kimmeridge
18th century manor.

Wolfeton House - Dorchester
Mediaeval & Elizabethan Manor. Fine stone work, great stair. 17th century furniture - Jacobean ceilings & fireplaces.

Cathedrals & Churches

Bere Regis (St. John the Baptist)
12th century foundation - enlarged in 13th & 15th centuries.
Timber roof & nave, fine arcades.
16th century seating.

Blandford (St. Peter & St. Paul)
18th century - ashlar - Georgian design. Galleries, pulpit, box pews, font & mayoral seat.

Bradford Abbas (St. Mary)
14th century - parapets & pinnacled tower, panelled roof. 15th century bench ends, stone rood screen. 17th century pulpit.

Cerne Abbas (St. Mary)
13th century - rebuilt 15th & 16th centuries, 14th century wall paintings, 15th century tower, stone screen, pulpit possibly 11th century.

Chalbury (dedication unknown)
13th century origin - 14th century east windows, timber bellcote. Plastered walls, box pews, 3-decker pulpit, west gallery.

Christchurch (Christ Church)
Norman nave - ribbed plaster vaulting - perpendicular spire. Tudor renaissance Salisbury chantry - screen with Tree of Jesse: notable misericord seats.

Milton Abbey (Sts. Mary, Michael, Sampson & Branwaleder)
14th century pulpitum & sedilla, 15th century reredos & canopy, 16th century monument, Milton effigies 1775.

Sherborne (St. Mary)
Largely Norman but some Saxon remains - excellent fan vaulting, of nave & choir. 12th & 13th century effigies - 15th century painted glass.

Studland (St. Nicholas)
12th century - best Norman church in the country. 12th century font, 13th century east windows.

Whitchurch Canonicorum (St. Candida & Holy Cross)
12th & 13th century. 12th century font, relics of patroness in 13th century shrine, 15th century painted glass, 15th century tower.

Wimbourne Minster (St. Cuthberga)
12th century central tower & arcade, otherwise 13th-15th century. Former collegiate church. Georgian glass, some Jacobean stalls & screen. Monuments & famed clock of 14th century.

Yetminster (St. Andrew)
13th century chancel - 15th century rebuilt with embattled parapets. 16th century brasses & seating.

Dorset

Museums & Galleries

Abbey Ruins - Shaftesbury
Relics excavated from Benedictine Nunnery founded by Alfred the Great.

Russell-Cotes Art Gallery & Museum - Bournemouth
17th-20th century oil paintings, watercolours, sculptures, ceramics, miniatures, etc.

Rothesay Museum - Bournemouth
English porcelain, 17th century furniture, collection of early Italian paintings, arms & armour, ethnography, etc.

Bournemouth Natural Science Society's Museum
Archaeology & local natural history.

Brewery Farm Museum - Milton Abbas
Brewing & village bygones from Dorset.

Dorset County Museum - Dorchester
Geology, natural history, pre-history. Thomas Hardy memorabilia

Philpot Museum - Lyme Regis
Old documents & prints, fossils, lace & old fire engine.

Guildhall Museum - Poole
Social & civic life of Poole during 18th & 19th centuries displayed in two-storey Georgian market house.

Scapolen's Court - Poole
14th century house of local merchant exhibiting local & archaeological history of town, also industrial archaeology.

Sherborne Museum - Sherborne
Local history & geology - abbey of AD 705, Sherborne missal AD 1400, 18th century local silk industry.

Gallery 24 - Shaftesbury
Art exhibitions - paintings, pottery, etc.

Red House Museum & Art Gallery - Christchurch
Natural history & antiques of the region. Georgian house with herb garden.

Priest's House Museum - Wimbourne Minster
Tudor building in garden exhibiting local archaeology & history.

Other things to see & do

Abbotsbury Swannery - Abbotsbury
Unique colony of Swans established by monks in the 14th century. 16th century duck decoy, reed walk, information centre.

Dorset Rare Breeds Centre - Park Farm, Gillingham

Poole Potteries - the Quay, Poole

Sea Life Centre - Weymouth
Variety of displays, including Ocean Tunnel, sharks, living "touch" pools.

West Bay.

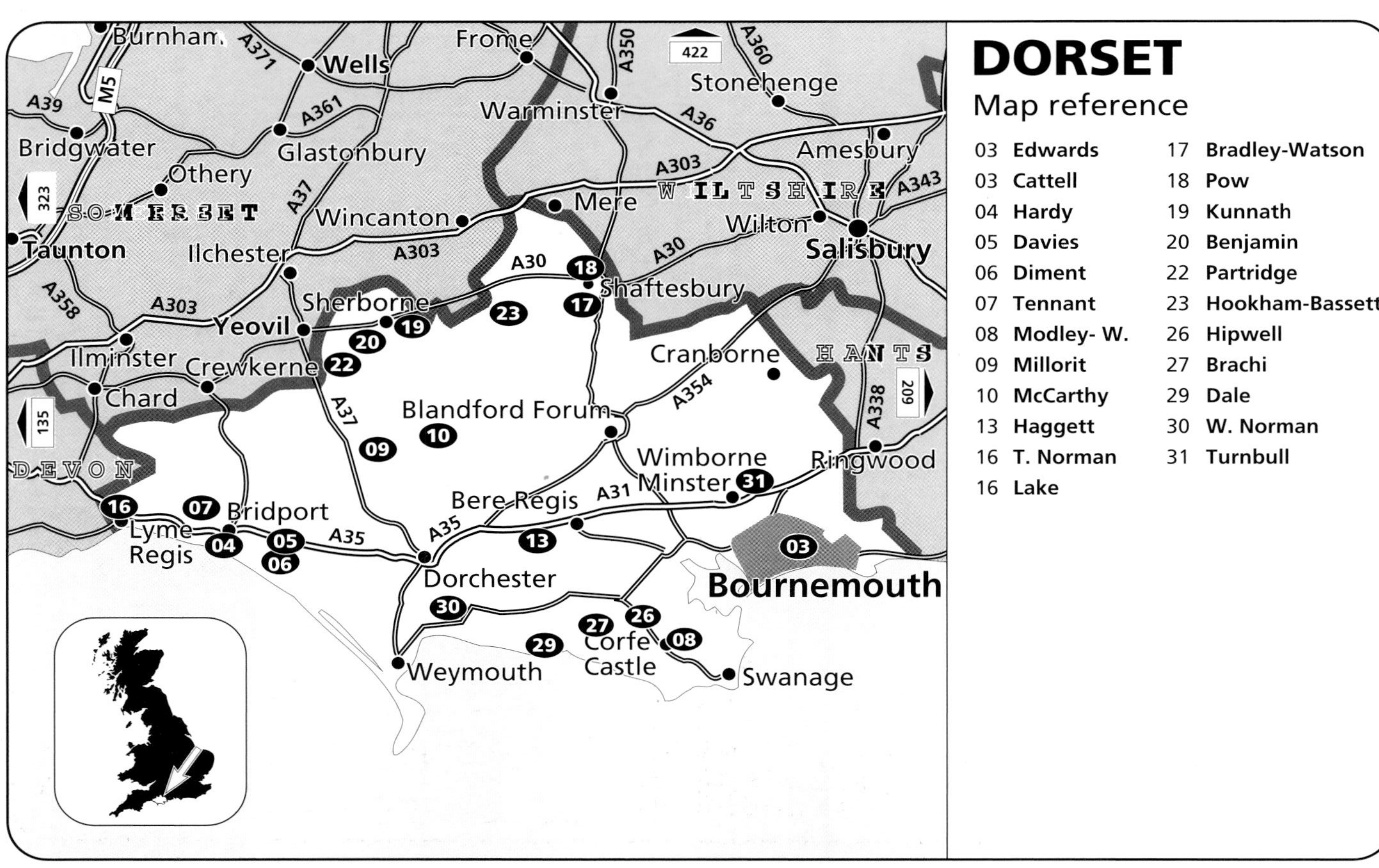

DORSET

Map reference

03	**Edwards**	17	**Bradley-Watson**
03	**Cattell**	18	**Pow**
04	**Hardy**	19	**Kunnath**
05	**Davies**	20	**Benjamin**
06	**Diment**	22	**Partridge**
07	**Tennant**	23	**Hookham-Bassett**
08	**Modley- W.**	26	**Hipwell**
09	**Millorit**	27	**Brachi**
10	**McCarthy**	29	**Dale**
13	**Haggett**	30	**W. Norman**
16	**T. Norman**	31	**Turnbull**
16	**Lake**		

Dorset

	rate £ from - to per person	children taken	evening meals	animals taken
Gervis Court Hotel	£20.00 to £30.00	Y	N	N
Sandhurst	£22.00 to £25.00	Y	Y	N
Britmead House	£21.00 to £31.00	Y	Y	Y
Innsacre Farmhouse	£32.50 to £45.00	Y	Y	Y

Gervis Court Hotel

Nearest Road: A.38

Gervis Court is a charming detached Victorian villa, set in its own grounds amongst the pine trees. Centrally located for all amenities. It is just a very short walk to the beach, shops, theatres, clubs & Conference Centre. Bedrooms are en-suite, tastefully furnished with comfort in mind & all have T.V. & coffee/tea-making facilities. Many rooms are on the ground floor. It is ideally located for visiting the beautiful Dorset coast & the New Forest.

E-mail: enquiries@gerviscourthotel.co.uk

£20.00 to £30.00 — Y N N — VISA: M'CARD:

Alan & Jackie Edwards Gervis Court Hotel 38 Gervis Road Bournemouth BH1 3DH Dorset
Tel: (01202) 556871 Fax 01202 556871 Open: ALL YEAR Map Ref No. 03

Sandhurst

Nearest Road: A.35, A.3060

Guests' comfort is a priority at this friendly, welcoming hotel. There's a choice of 5 comfortable rooms (incl. a ground-floor one), each with en-suite facilities. All have T.V. & tea/coffee makers. Good home-cooked breakfasts, & evening meals available. Situated 2 mins' from the beach in a quiet suburb of Bournemouth. An ideal centre for touring, with Christchurch, Beaulieu, the New Forest, Salisbury & Dorchester a short drive. Parking.

E-mail: sandhursthotel@lineone.net

£22.00 to £25.00 — Y Y N

Brian & Jane Cattell Sandhurst 16 Southern Road Southbourne Bournemouth BH6 3SR Dorset
Tel: (01202) 423748 Open: APR - OCT Map Ref No. 03

Britmead House

Nearest Road: A.35

A friendly welcome in a relaxed & comfortable atmosphere. Renowned for good food, a high standard of facilities & personal service. Situated between Bridport, the fishing harbour of West Bay, Chesil Beach & the Dorset Coastal Path. 7 en-suite bedrooms, 1 on the ground floor, all with T.V., etc. The lounge & dining room overlook the garden & open countryside beyond. Dinner, incorporates local fish & produce. Licensed. Parking.

E-mail: britmead@talk21.com

£21.00 to £31.00 — Y Y Y — VISA: M'CARD:

Alan & Louisa Hardy Britmead House West Bay Road Bridport DT6 4EG Dorset
Tel: (01308) 422941 Fax 01308 422516 Open: JAN - NOV Map Ref No. 04

Innsacre Farmhouse

Nearest Road: A.35

17th-century farmhouse & barn in a magical & peaceful setting. Hidden midway between Lyme Regis & Dorchester, 3 miles from the sea & National Trust coastal path. South-facing, 10 acres of spinneys, steep hillsides, orchard & lawns in a beautiful setting. A mix of French rustic style, English comfort & a genuine, warm welcome. All rooms en-suite (with T.V. & tea tray). Large, cosy sitting-room, log fires, beams & delicious breakfasts. Private parking. Licensed. Children over 9.

£32.50 to £45.00 — Y Y Y — VISA: M'CARD:

Sydney Davies Innsacre Farmhouse Shipton Gorge Bridport DT6 4LJ Dorset
Tel: (01308) 456137 Fax 01308 456137 Open: ALL YEAR (Excl. Xmas & New Year) Map Ref No. 05

rate £ from - to per person	children taken	evening meals	animals taken
£25.00 to £27.00	Y	N	N

VISA: M'CARD:

Rudge Farm

Nearest Road: A.35

Rudge Farm is peacefully situated on a gentle south-facing slope overlooking the beautiful Bride Valley, just over 2 miles from the sea. After a day spent exploring the lovely West Dorset countryside, relax in this comfortable Victorian farmhouse before trying one of the excellent local pubs or restaurants for dinner. The large, attractively furnished rooms are all en-suite, with T.V., tea tray & far-reaching views. A charming home.

E-mail: sue@rudgefarm.co.uk

Sue Diment Rudge Farm Chilcombe Bridport DT6 4NF Dorset
Tel: (01308) 482630 Fax 01308 482635 Open: ALL YEAR (Excl. Xmas) Map Ref No. 06

rate £ from - to per person	children taken	evening meals	animals taken
£25.00 to £35.00	Y	N	Y

Champ's Land

Nearest Road: A.35

Champ's Land is a pretty 17th-century former farmhouse. It is in a beautiful, rural setting, with an attractive walled garden & orchard leading to a stream. It is tastefully decorated throughout with antiques & offers 2 comfortable guest rooms with tea/coffee-making facilities. A delicious breakfast is served. Several good pubs & restaurants locally for dinner. A number of gardens & historic houses within easy reach & some wonderful walks. Children over 12 years. Single supplement.

Mrs Miranda Tennant Champ's Land North Chideock Bridport DT6 6JZ Dorset
Tel: (01297) 489314 Open: ALL YEAR (Excl. Xmas & New Year) Map Ref No. 07

rate £ from - to per person	children taken	evening meals	animals taken
£20.00 to £20.00	Y	N	N

Springbrook Cottage

Nearest Road: A.351

Springbrook Cottage is a beautiful house which is set in an acre of garden, lawn & shrubs including mature trees. There is an attractive conservatory in which guests may choose to relax, which boasts lovely views down to the valley beyond. Traditionally furnished with antiques, the property offers attractive accommodation in 2 charming bedrooms. The light & airy rooms are very comfortable. A delicious breakfast is served. A lovely base from which to explore the Dorset countryside.

Mrs Modley-Wingfield Springbrook Cottage Springbrook Close Corfe Castle BH20 5HS Dorset
Tel: (01929) 480509 Open: ALL YEAR Map Ref No. 08

rate £ from - to per person	children taken	evening meals	animals taken
£18.00 to £25.00	Y	Y	N

see PHOTO over p. 168

Brambles

Nearest Road: A.37

Set in beautiful, tranquil countryside, Brambles is a pretty thatched cottage offering every comfort, superb views & a friendly welcome. There is a choice of en-suite twin, double or single rooms, all very comfortable & with colour T.V. & tea/coffee-making facilities. Pretty garden available for relaxing. A full English or Continental breakfast is served. Evening meals available by prior arrangement. There are many interesting places to visit & wonderful walks for enthusiasts.

Anita & Andre Millorit Brambles Woolcombe Melbury Bubb Dorchester DT2 0NJ Dorset
Tel: (01935) 83672 Fax 01935 83003 Open: ALL YEAR (Excl. Xmas) Map Ref No. 09

Brambles. Woolcombe.

Dorset

rate £ from - to per person	children taken	evening meals	animals taken

Rew Cottage

£21.00 to £26.00	Y	N	Y

Nearest Road: A.35, A.37

A warm welcome awaits you in a peaceful cottage in the heart of Hardy's Dorset. Surrounded by green farmland with lovely views on all sides. An ideal centre for walking or touring & within easy reach of Sherborne, Dorchester & the sea. Bedrooms are comfortably furnished; double, twin & single rooms (with tea/coffee-making facilities & T.V.). 2 private bathrooms adjacent. Attractive pubs within easy reach for evening meals. Children & animals by arrangement.

Annette & Rupert McCarthy   Rew Cottage   Buckland Newton   Dorchester DT2 7DN   Dorset
Tel: (01300) 345467   Fax 01300 345467   Open: Mid JAN - Mid DEC   Map Ref No. 10

Vartrees House

£18.00 to £25.00	Y	N	Y

Nearest Road: A.35

Peaceful & secluded character country house set in 3 acres of picturesque woodland gardens. Built by Hermann Lea, friend of Thomas Hardy. Accommodation throughout is spacious & comfortable. Tea/coffee makers in all 4 rooms, 2 with private bathrooms. T.V. lounge. Situated near the pretty village of Moreton, with its renowned church & burial place of Lawrence of Arabia. Coast 4 miles. Station 1/4 of mile. Excellent local pubs. Children over 10 years welcome.

Mrs D. M. Haggett   Vartrees House   Moreton   Nr. Dorchester DT2 8BE   Dorset
Tel: (01305) 852704   Open: ALL YEAR   Map Ref No. 13

The Red House

£22.00 to £27.00	Y	N	N

Nearest Road: A.3052

This distinguished house, set in mature grounds, enjoys spectacular coastal views, & yet is only a short walk to the centre of Lyme Regis. The 3 en-suite bedrooms (1 for family use; 2 are especially spacious) are furnished with every comfort, including tea/coffee makers, T.V., clock-radio, desk, armchairs, a drink refrigerator, central heating & electric heaters. Fresh flowers & magazines are among the little extras. Breakfast can be taken on the garden balcony. Parking. Children over 8.

E-mail: red.house@virgin.net

VISA: M'CARD:

Tony & Vicky Norman   The Red House   Sidmouth Road   Lyme Regis DT7 3ES   Dorset
Tel: (01297) 442055   Fax 01297 442055   Open: Mid MAR - Early NOV   Map Ref No. 16

Rashwood Lodge

£22.00 to £26.00	Y	N	N

Nearest Road: A.3052, A.35

Rashwood Lodge is an unusual octagonal house, located on the western hillside with views over Lyme Bay. Just a short walk away is the coastal footpath & Ware Cliff, famed for its part in 'The French Lieutenant's Woman'. The lovely bedrooms have their own facilities & benefit from their south-facing aspect overlooking a large & colourful garden set in peaceful surroundings. Golf course only 1 mile. Rashwood Lodge is a charming home. Children over 4 years welcome.

Mrs Diana Lake   Rashwood Lodge   Clappentail Lane   Lyme Regis DT7 3LZ   Dorset
Tel: (01297) 445700   Open: FEB - NOV   Map Ref No. 16

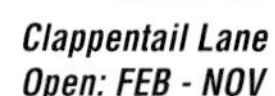

Dorset

Melbury Mill

Nearest Road: A.350

Mr & Mrs Bradley-Watson offer a warm welcome at this old working mill, set in 9 acres of meadows & overlooking a mill pond abounding with waterfowl. All bedrooms are large & have en-suite facilities. Located just south of Shaftesbury, famous for its Gold Hill, it is in picturesque Thomas Hardy countryside. Ideal for walkers, with National Trust downland & the properties of Stourhead & Kingston Lacy close by. An ideal base for a short-break.
E-mail: richardbradleywatson@hotmail.com

Richard & Tavy Bradley-Watson   Melbury Mill   Melbury Abbas   Shaftesbury SP7 0DB   Dorset
Tel: (01747) 852163   Open: ALL YEAR   Map Ref No. 17

rate £ from - to per person	children taken	evening meals	animals taken
£25.00 to £27.50	Y	N	N

see PHOTO over p. 171

Cliff House

Nearest Road: A.350

A fine example of a spacious Grade II listed period property with quiet rooms. Within walking distance of the ancient Saxon hilltop town which is one of the oldest & highest in southern England, and has magnificent views & the famous Gold Hill. An ideal position for visiting the surrounding countryside which abounds with historic country houses, cathedrals & abbeys. Good pubs & restaurants locally. 2 en-suite bedrooms. Children over 5.
E-mail: dianaepow@aol.com

Mrs Diana Pow   Cliff House   Breach Lane   Shaftesbury SP7 8LF   Dorset
Tel: (01747) 852548   Fax 01747 852548   Open: ALL YEAR   Map Ref No. 18

rate £ from - to per person	children taken	evening meals	animals taken
£26.00 to £30.00	Y	N	N

The Old Vicarage

Nearest Road: A.30

The Old Vicarage is a gothic Victorian building, set in 3 1/2 acres of grounds on the edge of a charming village. It is 2 miles from the historic town of Sherborne & affords magnificent views of open country. All of the 7 bedrooms are stylishly decorated & have en-suite facilities. The large lounge is beautifully furnished with antiques. On Friday & Saturday evenings, one of the owners, a highly acclaimed chef, prepares dinner. All inclusive weekend breaks are available. Children over 5.

J. Kunnath & A. Ma   The Old Vicarage   Sherborne Road   Milborne Port Sherborne   DT9 5AT   Dorset
Tel: (01963) 251117   Fax 01963 251515   Open: FEB - DEC   Map Ref No. 19

rate £ from - to per person	children taken	evening meals	animals taken
£25.00 to £45.00	Y	Y	Y

VISA: M'CARD: AMEX:

Munden House

Nearest Road: A.3030

A warm welcome awaits you at Munden House. 6 attractively decorated & tastefully furnished bedrooms & a studio annex. Each room has its own bathroom, T.V., tea/coffee-making facilities, etc. It is located in the picturesque Blackmore Vale on the outskirts of Sherborne with its historic castle, Abbey & Almshouses. Golf & tennis closeby. Horse-riding a short drive away. Excellent pubs & restaurants. Reflexology & aromatherapy massage available from visiting therapists.
E-mail: sylvia@mundenhouse.demon.co.uk

Sylvia & Joe Benjamin   Munden House   Munden Lane   Alweston   Sherborne   DT9 5HU   Dorset
Tel: (01963) 23150   Fax 01963 23153   Open: ALL YEAR   Map Ref No. 20

rate £ from - to per person	children taken	evening meals	animals taken
£27.50 to £42.50	Y	N	N

VISA: M'CARD:

Melbury Mill. Melbury Abbas.

Manor Farmhouse. Yetminster.

Dorset

Columns: rate £ from - to per person | children taken | evening meals | animals taken

---

rate £ from - to per person	children taken	evening meals	animals taken
£35.00 to £35.00	N	Y	N

see PHOTO over p. 172

VISA: M'CARD:

Manor Farmhouse

Nearest Road: A.37

This 17th-century farmhouse, with oak panelling, beams & inglenook fireplaces, offers every comfort to the discerning visitor. 4 bedrooms, all with en-suite facilities & modern amenities, including T.V. & tea/coffee. Delicious meals served, made from traditional recipes & using fresh local produce. The village is described as the best 17th-century stone-built village in the south of England. An excellent centre for visiting Sherborne, Glastonbury, New Forest & Hardy's Dorset.

Mrs Ann C. Partridge Manor Farmhouse High Street Yetminster Sherborne DT9 6LF Dorset
Tel: (01935) 872247 Fax 01935 872247 Open: ALL YEAR Map Ref No. 22

---

rate £ from - to per person	children taken	evening meals	animals taken
£30.00 to £37.00	Y	Y	N

see PHOTO over p. 174

VISA: M'CARD:

Stourcastle Lodge

Nearest Road: A.357

Stourcastle Lodge is a family-run business, offering a very high standard of accommodation, with personal service & excellent cuisine. A superb breakfast is served in the attractive dining room. All the elegant bedrooms are south-facing & overlook the delightful garden, which is stocked full of herbaceous & perennial borders. Stourcastle Lodge is a beautiful home, & an ideal base for exploring Dorset & its many attractions.

E-mail: enquiries@stourcastle-lodge.co.uk

Mr & Mrs Hookham-Bassett Stourcastle Lodge Gough's Close Sturminster Newton DT10 1BU Dorset
Tel: (01258) 472320 Fax 01258 473381 Open: ALL YEAR Map Ref No. 23

---

rate £ from - to per person	children taken	evening meals	animals taken
£22.50 to £35.00	Y	N	N

Gold Court House

Nearest Road: A.351

Gold Court House is a charming Georgian house with walled garden on a small square on the south-side of Wareham. 3 light & airy double or twin rooms with private bathrooms & all facilities at hand, at your request. Wareham is ideally situated for exploring the magnificent coastline of South Dorset & the Isle of Purbeck. Your hosts are pleased to help & advise on the many places of interest, sporting activities & where to dine. (Dinner available winter only.) Children over 10.

Anthea & Michael Hipwell Gold Court House St. John's Hill Wareham BH20 4LZ Dorset
Tel/Fax: (01929) 553320 Open: ALL YEAR (Excl. Xmas & New Year) Map Ref No. 26

---

rate £ from - to per person	children taken	evening meals	animals taken
£20.00 to £30.00	Y	N	N

West Coombe Farmhouse

Nearest Road: A.352

Discover a peaceful way of life when you stay at this restored Georgian farmhouse in the delightful village of Coombe Keynes. In summer, unwind in the beautiful garden & in winter linger by the open fire in the private sitting room. There are 3 attractive guest bedrooms. Lulworth is only 3 miles away & many traditional outdoor activities can be found locally, or explore the glorious countryside on your hosts' mountain bikes. Children over 12.

E-mail: west.coombe.farmhouse@barclays.net

Rachel & Peter Brachi West Coombe Farmhouse Coombe Keynes Wareham BH20 5PS Dorset
Tel: (01929) 462889 Fax 01929 405863 Open: ALL YEAR (Excl. Xmas) Map Ref No. 27

Stourcastle Lodge. Sturminster Newton.

Dorset

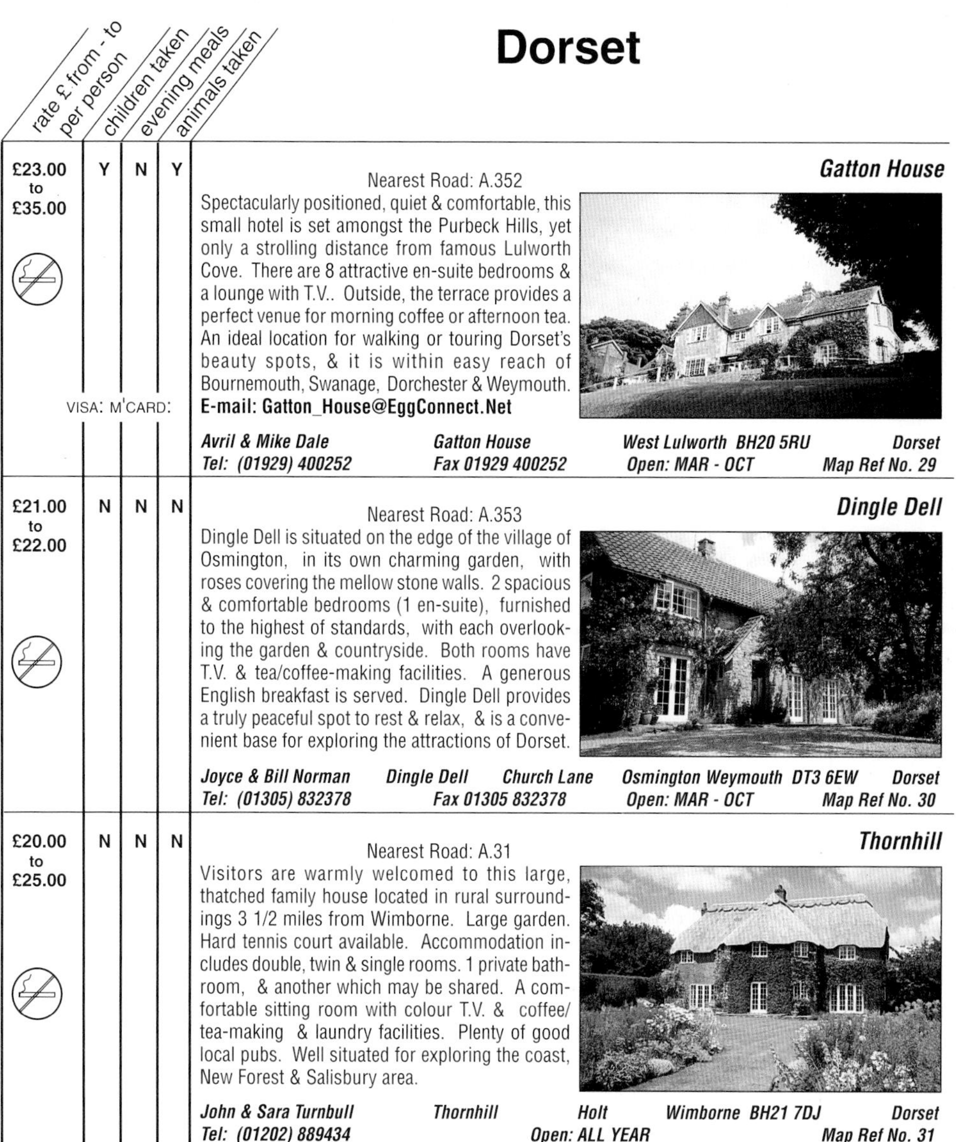

rate £ from - to per person	children taken	evening meals	animals taken
£23.00 to £35.00	Y	N	Y

VISA: M'CARD:

Gatton House

Nearest Road: A.352

Spectacularly positioned, quiet & comfortable, this small hotel is set amongst the Purbeck Hills, yet only a strolling distance from famous Lulworth Cove. There are 8 attractive en-suite bedrooms & a lounge with T.V.. Outside, the terrace provides a perfect venue for morning coffee or afternoon tea. An ideal location for walking or touring Dorset's beauty spots, & it is within easy reach of Bournemouth, Swanage, Dorchester & Weymouth.

E-mail: Gatton_House@EggConnect.Net

Avril & Mike Dale *Gatton House* *West Lulworth BH20 5RU* *Dorset*
Tel: (01929) 400252 *Fax 01929 400252* *Open: MAR - OCT* *Map Ref No. 29*

rate £ from - to per person	children taken	evening meals	animals taken
£21.00 to £22.00	N	N	N

Dingle Dell

Nearest Road: A.353

Dingle Dell is situated on the edge of the village of Osmington, in its own charming garden, with roses covering the mellow stone walls. 2 spacious & comfortable bedrooms (1 en-suite), furnished to the highest of standards, with each overlooking the garden & countryside. Both rooms have T.V. & tea/coffee-making facilities. A generous English breakfast is served. Dingle Dell provides a truly peaceful spot to rest & relax, & is a convenient base for exploring the attractions of Dorset.

Joyce & Bill Norman *Dingle Dell* *Church Lane* *Osmington Weymouth DT3 6EW* *Dorset*
Tel: (01305) 832378 *Fax 01305 832378* *Open: MAR - OCT* *Map Ref No. 30*

rate £ from - to per person	children taken	evening meals	animals taken
£20.00 to £25.00	N	N	N

Thornhill

Nearest Road: A.31

Visitors are warmly welcomed to this large, thatched family house located in rural surroundings 3 1/2 miles from Wimborne. Large garden. Hard tennis court available. Accommodation includes double, twin & single rooms. 1 private bathroom, & another which may be shared. A comfortable sitting room with colour T.V. & coffee/tea-making & laundry facilities. Plenty of good local pubs. Well situated for exploring the coast, New Forest & Salisbury area.

John & Sara Turnbull *Thornhill* *Holt* *Wimborne BH21 7DJ* *Dorset*
Tel: (01202) 889434 *Open: ALL YEAR* *Map Ref No. 31*

Visit our website at: http://www.bestbandb.co.uk

Essex

Essex (East Anglia)

Essex is a county of commerce, busy roads & busier towns, container ports & motorways, yet it is also a landscape of mudflats & marshes, of meadows & leafy lanes, villages & duckponds. Half timbered buildings & thatched & clapboard cottages stand among rolling hills topped by orange brick windmills.

The coast on the east, now the haunt of wildfowl, sea-birds, sailors & fishermen has seen the arrival of Saxons, Romans, Danes, Vikings & Normans. The names of their settlements remain - Wivenhoe, Layer-de-la-Haye, Colchester & Saffron Walden - the original Saxon name was Walden, but the Saffron was added when the crocus used for dyes & flavouring was grown here in the 15th century.

The seaside resorts of Southend & Clacton are bright & cheery, much-loved by families for safe beaches. Harbours here are great favourites with anglers & yachtsmen.

Inland lie the watermeadows & windmills, willows & cool green water which shaped the life & work of John Constable, one of the greatest landscape painters. Scenes are instantly recognisable today as you walk to Dedham along the banks of the swiftly flowing River Stour.

Colchester is England's oldest recorded town, once the Roman capital of Britain trading in corn & cattle, slaves & pearls. Roman remains are still to be seen & their original street plan is the basis of much of modern Colchester. A great feast is held here annually to celebrate the famous oyster - the "Colchester native".

South Essex, though sliced through by the M.25 motorway is still a place of woodland & little rivers. The ancient trees of Epping Forest, hunting ground for generations of monarchs, spread 6,000 acres of leafy glades & heathland into the London suburbs.

Audley End. Saffron Walden.

Essex

Essex

Gazeteer

Areas of outstanding natural beauty.
Dedham Vale (part), Epping Forest.

Houses & Castles

Audley End House - Saffron Walden
1603 - Jacobean mansion on site of Benedictine Abbey. State rooms & Hall.
Castle House - Dedham
Home of the late Sir A. Munnings. President R.A. Paintings & other works.
Hedingham Castle - Castle Hedingham
Norman keep & Tudor bridge.
Layer Marney Tower - Nr. Colchester
1520 Tudor brick house. 8 storey gate tower. Formal yew hedges & lawns.
Payecock's - Coggeshall
1500 - richly ornamented - merchant's house - National Trust.
St. Osyth's Priory - St. Osyth
Was Augustinian Abbey for 400 years until dissolution in 1537, 13th-18th century buildings. 13th century chapel. Wonderful gatehouse containing works of art including ceramics & Chinese Jade.
Spains Hall - Finchingfield
Elizabethan Manor incorporating parts of earlier timber structure. Paintings, furniture & tapestries.

Cathedrals & Churches

Brightlingsea (All Saints)
15th century tower - some mediaeval painting fragments. Brasses.
Castle Hedingham (St. Nicholas)
12th century doorways, 14th century rood screen, 15th century stalls, 16th century hammer beams, altar tomb.
Copford (St. Michael & All Angels)
12th century wall paints. Continuous vaulted nave & chancel
.**Finchingfield** (St. John the Baptist)
Norman workmanship. 16th century tomb -18th centuary tower & cupola.
Layer Marney (St. Mary)
Tudor brickwork, Renaissance monuments, mediaeval screens, wall paintings.
Little Maplestead (St. John the Baptist)
14th century, one of the five round churches in England, having hexagonal nave, circular aisle, 14th century arcade.
Newport (St. Mary the Virgin)
13th century. Interesting 13th century altar (portable) with top which becomes reredos when opened. 15th century chancel screen. Pre-Reformation Lectern. Some old glass.

Museums & Galleries

Dutch Cottage Museum - Canvey Island
17th century thatched cottage of octagonal Dutch design. Exhibition of models of shipping used on the Thames through the ages.
Ingatestone Hall - Ingatestone
Documents & pictures of Essex.
The Castle - Colchester
Norman Keep now exhibiting archeological material from Essex & especially Roman Colchester.
Southchurch Hall - Southend-on-Sea
14th century moated & timber framed manor house - Tudor wing, furnished as meiaeval manor.
Thurrock - Grays
Prehistoric, Romano-British & pagan Saxon archaeology.

Other things to see & do

Colchester Oyster Fishery - Colchester
Tour showing cultivating, harvesting, grading & packing of oysters. Talk, tour & sample.

Burnham on Crouch.

ESSEX

Map reference

01 **Hodge**
02 **Perry**
03 **Larcom**
04 **Westerhuis**

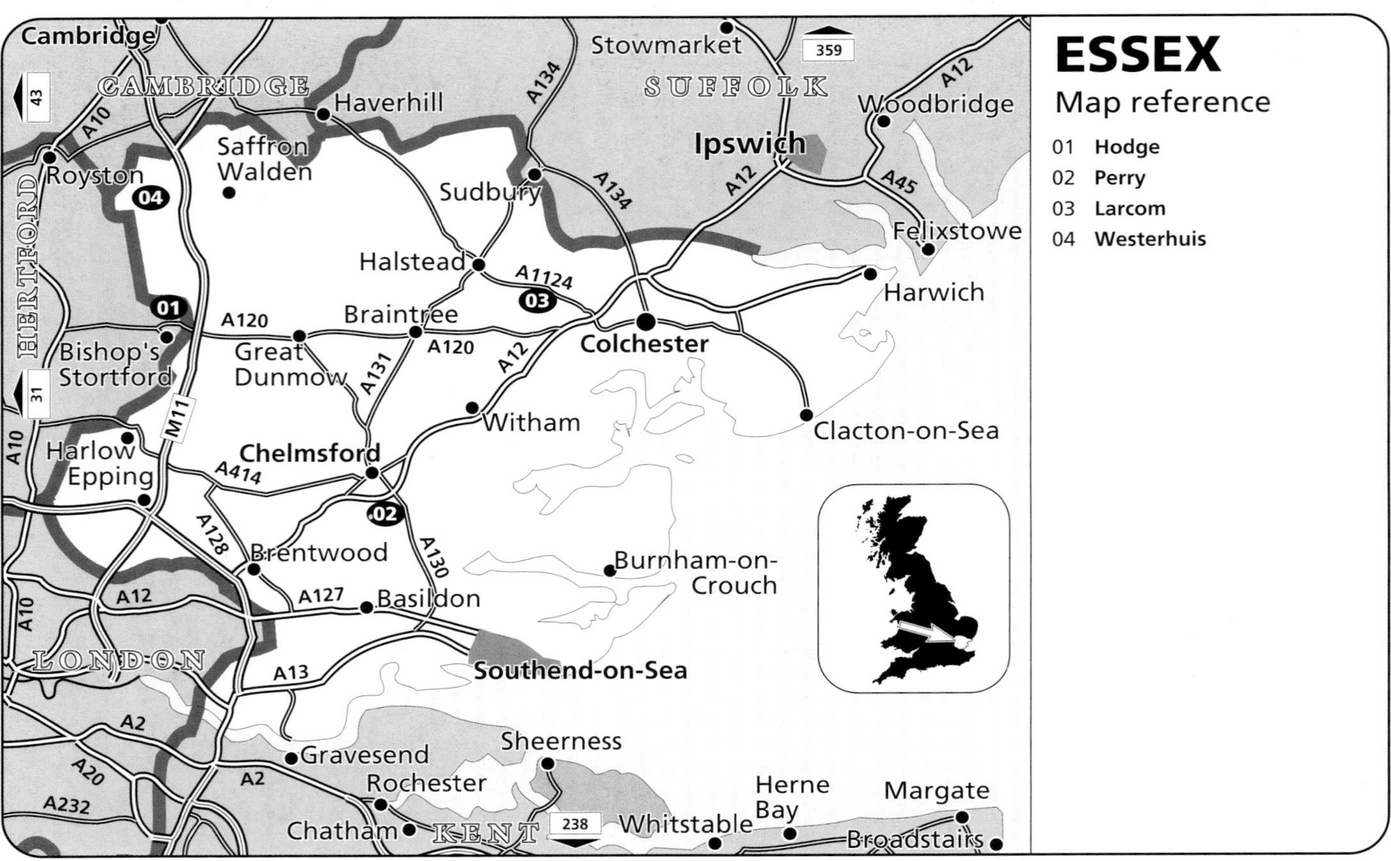

Essex

rate £ from - to per person	children taken	evening meals	animals taken
£32.00 to £50.00	Y	N	N

VISA: M'CARD:

The Cottage

Nearest Road: A.120, M.11

Situated within a quiet village, this charming 17th-century listed house offers 15 comfortable en-suite bedrooms, all with colour T.V. & tea/coffee makers. Oak-panelled reception rooms with log burners, & a conservatory/dining room looking onto mature gardens. A convenient base for trips to Cambridge, London & East Anglia, & within easy reach of Stansted Airport & Bishops Stortford. Private parking available. A delightful home, ideal for a relaxing short break.

John & Angela Hodge   The Cottage   71 Birchanger Lane   Birchanger   Bishop's Stortford   CM23 5QA
Tel: (01279) 812349   Fax 01279 815045   Open: ALL YEAR (Excl. Xmas & New Year)   Map Ref No. 01

rate £ from - to per person	children taken	evening meals	animals taken
£28.50 to £50.00	Y	N	N

Little Sir Hughes

Nearest Road: A.1114, A.12

Little Sir Hughes is a 300-year-old Grade II listed country house set in a 2 1/2 acre formal garden. Set in a very peaceful location, yet only 5 mins from A.12, 10 mins from Chelmsford & 35 mins by rail from London. All rooms are beautifully furnished & decorated. 2 double bedrooms & 1 twin, all en-suite & each with hairdryer, T.V., radio & tea/coffee facilities. Delightful guests' drawing room with T.V. & log fire. Superb breakfasts with home-made preserves a speciality. Parking. Children over 10.
E-mail: accom@englishlive.co.uk

David & Glen Perry   Little Sir Hughes West Hanningfield Road   Great Baddow   Chelmsford   CM2 7SZ
Tel: (01245) 471701   Fax 01245 472722   Open: ALL YEAR   Map Ref No. 03

rate £ from - to per person	children taken	evening meals	animals taken
£19.00 to £25.00	Y	N	Y

Elm House

Nearest Road: A.1124

A comfortable & welcoming 18th-century family home in a village of great architectural interest, & with a delightful, secluded garden. Accommodation is in 3 charming & elegantly furnished bedrooms, 2 with en-suite/private bathroom. A delicious breakfast is served. Elm House is within easy reach of Colchester (Roman walls, Norman castle), Dedham Vale (immortalised by Constable's paintings), Cambridge, Long Melford & Beth Chatto's gardens. Single supplement.

Lady Larcom   Elm House   14 Upper Holt Street   Earls Colne   Colchester   CO6 2PG   Essex
Tel: (01787) 222197   Open: ALL YEAR (Excl. Xmas & Easter)   Map Ref No. 06

rate £ from - to per person	children taken	evening meals	animals taken
£20.00 to £25.00	Y	N	N

Rockells Farm

Nearest Road: A.11, A.505

Rockells is an arable farm in a beautiful corner of Essex. The Georgian house has a large garden with a 3-acre lake for coarse fishing. All of the 3 attractive bedrooms have en-suite facilities. 1 bedroom is located on the ground floor. On the farm are several footpaths. There are many beautiful villages in the area. Within easy reach are Audley End House, Duxford Air Museum & Cambridge. London is approx. 1 hour by car or train. Stansted Airport 30 mins by car.

Mrs Tineke Westerhuis   Rockells Farm   Duddenhoe End   Saffron Walden   CB11 4UY   Essex
Tel: (01763) 838053   Fax 01763 837001   Open: ALL YEAR   Map Ref No. 10

Gloucestershire

Gloucestershire (Heart of England)

The landscape is so varied the people speak not of one Gloucestershire but of three - Cotswold, Vale & Forest. The rounded hills of the Cotswolds sweep & fold in graceful compositions to form a soft & beautiful landscape in which nestle many pretty villages. To the east there are wonderful views of the Vale of Berkeley & Severn, & across to the dark wooded slopes of the Forest of Dean on the Welsh borders.

Hill Forts, ancient trackways & long barrows of neolithic peoples can be explored, & remains of many villas from late Roman times can be seen. A local saying "Scratch Gloucester & find Rome" reveals the lasting influence of the Roman presence. Three major roads mark the path of invasion & settlement. Akeman street leads to London, Ermine street & the Fosse Way to the north east. A stretch of Roman road with its original surface can be seen at Blackpool Bridge in the Forest of Dean, & Cirencester's museum reflects its status as the second most important Roman city in the country.

Offa's Dyke, 80 miles of bank & ditch on the Welsh border was the work of the Anglo-Saxons of Mercia who invaded in the wake of the Romans. Cotswold means "hills of the sheepcotes" in the Anglo-Saxon tongue, & much of the heritage of the area has its roots in the wealth created by the wool industry here.

Fine Norman churches such as those at Tewkesbury & Bishops Cleeve were overshadowed by the development of the perpendicular style of building made possible by the growing prosperity. Handsome 15th century church towers crown many wool towns & villages as at Northleach, Chipping Camden & Cirencester, & Gloucester has a splendid 14th century cathedral. Detailing on church buildings gives recognition to the source of the wealth-cloth-workers shears are depicted on the north west buttresses of Grantham church tower & couchant rams decorate church buttresses at Compton Bedale.

Wool & cloth weaving dominated life here in the 14th & 15th centuries with most families dependent on the industry. The cottage craft of weaving was gradually overtaken by larger looms & water power. A water mill can be seen in the beautiful village of Lower Slaughter & the cottages of Arlington Row in Bibury were a weaving factory.

The Cotswold weaving industry gave way to the growing force of the Lancashire mills but a few centres survive. At Witney you can still buy the locally made blankets for which the town is famous.

From the 16th century the wealthy gentry built parks & mansions. Amongst the most notable are the Jacobean Manor house at Stanway & the contrasting Palladian style mansion at Barnsley Park. Elizabethan timber frame buildings can be seen at Didbrook, Dymock & Deerhurst but houses in the local mellow golden limestone are more common, with Chipping Camden providing excellent examples.

Cheltenham was only a village when, in 1716 a local farmer noticed a flock of pigeons pecking at grains of salt around a saline spring in his fields. He began to bottle & sell the water & in 1784 his son-in-law, Henry Skillicorne, built a pump room & the place received the name of Cheltenham Spa. Physicians published treatises on the healing qualities of the waters, visitors began to flock there & Cheltenham grew in style & elegance.

Gloucestershire

Gloucestershire

Gazeteer

Areas of outstanding natural beauty
The Cotswolds, Malvern Hills & the Wye Valley.

Houses & Castles

Ashleworth Court - Ashleworth
15th century limestone Manor house.
Badminton House - Badminton
Built in the reign of Charles II. Stone newel staircase.
Berkeley Castle - Berkeley
12th century castle - still occupied by the Berkeley family. Magnificent collections of furniture, paintings, tapestries & carved timber work. Lovely terraced gardens & deer park.
Chavenage - Tetbury
Elizabethan Cotswold Manor house, Cromwellian associations.
Clearwell Castle - Nr. Coleford
A Georgian neo-Gothic house said to be oldest in Britain, recently restored.
Court House - Painswick
Cotswold Manor house - has original court room & bedchamber of Charles I. Splendid panelling & antique furniture.
Dodington House - Chipping Sodbury
Perfect 18th century house with superb staircase. Landscape by Capability Brown.
Horton Court - Horton
Cotswold manor house altered & restored in 19th century.
Kelmscott Manor - Nr. Lechlade
16th century country house - 17th century additions. Examples of work of William Morris, Rosetti & Burne-Jones.
Owlpen Manor - Nr. Dursley
Historic group of traditional Cotswold stone buildings. Tudor Manor house with church, barn, court house & a grist mill. Holds a rare set of 17th century painted cloth wall hangings.
Snowshill Manor - Broadway
Tudor house with 17th century facade. Unique collection of musical instruments & clocks, toys, etc. Formal garden.
Sudeley Castle - Winchcombe
12th century - home of Katherine Parr, is rich in historical associations, contains art treasures & relics of bygone days.

Cathedrals & Churches

Bishops Cleeve (St. Michael & All Saints)
12th century with 17th century gallery. Magnificent Norman west front & south porch. Decorated chancel. Fine window.
Bledington (St.Leonards)
15th century glass in this perpendicular church, Norman bellcote. Early English east window.
Buckland (St. Michael)
13th century nave arcades. 17th century oak panelling, 15th century glass.
Cirencester (St. John the Baptist)
A magnificent church - remarkable exterior, 3 storey porch, 2 storey oriel windows, traceries & pinnacles. Wine-glass pulpit c.1450. 15th century glass in east window, monuments in Lady chapel.
Gloucester Cathedral
Birthplace of Perpendicular style in 14th century. Fan vaulting, east windows commemorate Battle of Crecy - Norman Chapter House.
Hailes Abbey - Winchcombe
14th century wall paintings, 15th century tiles, glass & screen, 17th century pulpit. Elizabethan benches.
Iron Acton (St. James the Less)
Perpendicular - 15th century memorial cross. 19th century mosaic floors, Laudian alter rails, Jacobean pulpit, effigies.
Newland (All Saints)
13th century, restored 18th century. Pinnacled west tower, effigies.
Prinknash Abbey - Gloucester
14th & 16th century - Benedictine Abbey.
Tewkesbury Abbey - Tewkesbury
Dates back to Norman times, contains Romanesque & Gothic styles. 14th century monuments.
Yate (St. Mary)
Splendid perpendicular tower.

Museums & Galleries

Bishop Hooper's Lodgings - Gloucester
3 Tudor timber frame buildings - museum of domestic life & agriculture in Gloucester since 1500.
Bourton Motor Museum - Bourton-on-the-Water
Collection of cars & motor cycles.
Cheltenham Art Gallery - Cheltenham.

Gloucestershire

Lower Slaughter.

Gallery of Dutch paintings, collection of oils, watercolours, pottery, porcelain, English & Chinese; furniture.
City Wall & Bastion - Gloucester
Roman & mediaeval city defences in an underground exhibition room.
Stroud Museum - Cirencester
Depicts earlier settlements in the area & has a very fine collection of Roman antiquities.

Historic Monuments

Chedworth Roman Villa - Yanworth
Remains of Romano-British villa.
Belas Knap Long Barrow - Charlton Abbots
Neolithic burial ground - three burial chambers with external entrances.
Hailes Abbey - Stanway
Ruins of beautiful mediaeval abbey built by son of King John, 1246.
Witcombe Roman Villa - Nr. Birdlip
Large Roman villa - Hypocaust & mosaic pavements preserved.
Ashleworth Tithe Barn - Ashleworth
15th century tithe barn - 120 feet long - stone built, interesting roof timbering.
Odda's Chapel - Deerhurst
Rare Saxon chapel dating back to 1056.
Hetty Pegler's Tump - UleLong Barrow- fairly complete, chamber is 120 feet long.

Other things to see & do

Cheltenham International Festival of Music & Literature - Annual event.
Cotswolds Farm Park - dozens of rare breeds of farm animals.
The Three Choirs Festival - music festival staged in alternating years at Gloucester, Hereford & Worcester Cathedrals.
Slimbridge - Peter Scott's Wildfowl Trust.

GLOUCESTERSHIRE

Map reference

01	**Nesbitt**	20	**Parsons**
01	**Bolton**	21	**Sayers**
01	**Wright**	22	**Annis**
02	**Thornely**	23	**Franklin**
03	**Moodie**	24	**Parkes**
04	**Paz**	25	**Helm**
06	**Hazell**	27	**Anderson**
09	**Gamez**	28	**Dean**
09	**Cittadino**	30	**Peacock**
09	**Berg**	31	**Digby**
10	**Gisby**	32	**Walsh**
11	**Minchin**	33	**Brunsdon**
13	**Whent**	34	**Tremellen**
16	**Holdsworth-H.**	35	**Wilson**
18	**Keyser**	36	**Brown**

Church House. Clapton on the Hill.

Gloucestershire

rate £ from - to per person	children taken	evening meals	animals taken
£30.00 to £35.00	Y	N	N

see PHOTO over p. 184

Church House

Nearest Road: A.429, A.40

This completely restored 17th-century family house offers seclusion & privacy to its guests in elegant surroundings. The attractively decorated bedrooms are very comfortable with sloping ceilings, beams, a private bathroom & T.V., etc. The drawing room is available for guests' use & breakfast is served in a galleried dining room. Wonderful views over the church & the Windrush Valley complete the recipe for a delightful relaxing stay in Church House. A charming home.

Mrs Caroline Nesbitt Church House Clapton-on-the-Hill Bourton-on-the-Water GL54 2LG
Tel: (01451) 822532 Fax 01451 822472 Open: ALL YEAR Map Ref No. 01

rate £ from - to per person	children taken	evening meals	animals taken
£30.00 to £35.00	Y	N	N

see PHOTO over p. 186

VISA: M'CARD:

Clapton Manor

Nearest Road: A.40, A.429

Clapton Manor is an impressive 17th-century stone house standing at the top of a quiet village with stunning views across the Windrush Valley. The garden is planted with peonies, old-fashioned shrub roses & many unusual plants. The house is an elegant & informal family home. There is a private sitting room for the guests' use & 2 delightful en-suite bedrooms with comfortable beds. Recently featured in 'The English Garden' magazine. Ideal for visiting the well-known local gardens, Warwick, Stratford, Oxford & Blenheim Palace.

Mrs Karin Bolton Clapton Manor Clapton-on-the-Hill Bourton-on-the-Water GL54 2LG
Tel: (01451) 810202 Fax 01451 821804 Open: ALL YEAR (Excl. Xmas & New Year) Map Ref No. 01

rate £ from - to per person	children taken	evening meals	animals taken
£20.00 to £24.00	N	N	N

Farncombe

Nearest Road: A.429, A.40

Come & share the peace, tranquillity & superb views of Farncombe, & eat, drink & sleep - smoke-free - 700ft above sea level & only 2 miles from Bourton-on-the-Water. 2 attractive doubles with showers, & 1 twin en-suite. A spacious dining room, with tea/coffee-making facilities, & a comfortable T.V. lounge. Tourist information, maps & books, & current menus for your choice when eating out. Numerous walks & drives, with easy access to all attractions & places of interest.

E-mail: jwrightbb@aol.com

Julia Wright Farncombe Clapton-on-the-Hill Bourton-on-the-Water GL54 2LG Gloucestershire
Tel/Fax: (01451) 820120 Mobile 07714 703142 Open: ALL YEAR Map Ref No. 01

rate £ from - to per person	children taken	evening meals	animals taken
£24.00 to £26.00	Y	N	N

Eastcote Cottage

Nearest Road: A.38

Eastcote is a charming 200-year-old stone house located in a lovely rural setting, with splendid views across open countryside. Guests have a choice of 2 comfortable bedrooms with modern amenities. A colour-T.V. lounge is available for guests' use. Eastcote Cottageis an ideal base for touring being conveniently situated for the M.4/ M.5 interchange for the Cotswolds, with Bristol, Bath, Cheltenham & the Wye Valley easily accessible. Private parking available.

Mrs Ann Thornely Eastcote Cottage Knapp Road East Thornbury Bristol BS35 2HJ Gloucestershire
Tel: (01454) 413106 Fax 01454 281812 Open: ALL YEAR (Excl. Xmas) Map Ref No. 02

Clapton Manor. Clapton on the Hill.

The Elms. Olveston.

Gloucestershire

	rate £ from - to per person	children taken	evening meals	animals taken

The Elms

Nearest Road: A.38

The Elms is a Georgian house in a rural area, yet convenient for Bristol (Aztec Business Park) & M.4/ M.5 interchange. Great emphasis is placed on immaculate standards & green issues. Breakfasts are organic when possible. Allergy sufferers are welcome & the environment is kept as pollutant free as possible. Guests are respectfully requested not to use scented products. The owners are great animal & garden lovers & keep cats, dogs, hens, ornamental ducks, geese & doves.

E-mail: b&b@theelmsmoodie.co.uk

Mr & Mrs David Moodie The Elms Olveston Bristol BS35 4DR Gloucestershire
Tel: (01454) 614559 Fax 01454 618607 Open: ALL YEAR Map Ref No. 03

rate £ from - to per person	children taken	evening meals	animals taken
£35.00 to £40.00	N	N	N

see PHOTO over p. 187

Dornden Guest House

Nearest Road: A.432

Dornden, built of local Cotswold stone, stands in a beautiful garden enjoying the peace of the countryside & magnificent views to the west. 9 attractive rooms, 6 en-suite, overlooking the garden and the open country beyond. Delicious meals are prepared, using home-grown produce (where possible) and free-range eggs. There is also a grass tennis court available to guests. A delightful home, with a warm, friendly atmosphere, ideal for exploring the beautiful West Country. (The guest house is also closed end of September & early October.)

John & Daphne Paz Dornden Guest House 15 Church Lane Old Sodbury Bristol BS37 6NB
Tel: (01454) 313325 Fax 01454 312263 Open: ALL YEAR (Excl. Xmas & New Year) Map Ref No. 04

rate £ from - to per person	children taken	evening meals	animals taken
£29.00 to £40.00	Y	Y	Y

Laverton Meadow House

Nearest Road: A.44

Laverton Meadows is a beautiful Cotswold house & stables set in 22 acres with stunning views & lovely gardens. Romantic rooms with canopied beds, antiques & spacious bathrooms make this luxury accommodation. A delicious full English breakfast served in the farmhouse kitchen warmed by the Aga. Superb candlelit dinners in sumptuous private dining room. A log fire in the delightful sitting room offers you the perfect retreat.

E-mail: andrea@lavertonmeadows.demon.co.uk

Andrea Hazell Laverton Meadow House Nr. Broadway WR12 7NA Gloucestershire
Tel: (01386) 584200 Fax 01386 584612 Open: ALL YEAR Map Ref No. 06

rate £ from - to per person	children taken	evening meals	animals taken
£38.75 to £50.00	Y	Y	N

see PHOTO over p. 189

Georgian House

Nearest Road: A.40

Take 3 beautiful bedrooms in an elegant Georgian home, set them among the charming terraces of Montpellier, only 5 mins' from the Promenade, add a warm welcome from your hosts, Penny & Alex, & there you have Georgian House. Each en-suite room has T.V. with satellite, 'phone with modem socket, ironing facilities, trouser press & fridge. The delicious English breakfasts include fresh fruit - the perfect combination! Parking available.

E-mail: georgian_house@yahoo.com

Penny & Alex Gamez Georgian House 77 Montpellier Terrace Cheltenham GL50 1XA
Tel: (01242) 515577 Fax 01242 545929 Open: ALL YEAR (Excl. Xmas & New Year) Map Ref No. 09

rate £ from - to per person	children taken	evening meals	animals taken
£27.50 to £37.50	N	N	N

VISA: M'CARD: AMEX:

Laverton Meadow House. Broadway.

Milton House. Cheltenham.

Gloucestershire

rate £ from - to per person	children taken	evening meals	animals taken
£34.00 to £42.50	Y	N	N

see PHOTO over p. 190

VISA: M'CARD: AMEX:

Milton House Hotel

Nearest Road: A.40

Milton House stands in a quiet tree-lined avenue of elegant Regency homes. Situated a 4 min' stroll from the promenade, restaurants & the Imperial Gardens. 8 tastefully furnished en-suite bedrooms providing all the comforts & amenities. Elegant drawing room, dining room & inviting conservatory facing an attractive garden. Light meals are available from the bar. Staying at Milton House is the perfect way to enjoy the many attractions of Cheltenham & the Cotswolds. Children over 6.

E-mail: info@miltonhousehotel.co.uk

Claude Cittadino Milton House Hotel 12 Bayshill Road Cheltenham GL50 3AY Gloucestershire
Tel: (01242) 582601 Fax 01242 222326 Open: ALL YEAR Map Ref No. 09

rate £ from - to per person	children taken	evening meals	animals taken
£25.00 to £35.00	Y	Y	N

VISA: M'CARD: AMEX:

Hollington House Hotel

Nearest Road: A.40, M.5

An elegant Victorian house, easy to find off the London Road/A.40, with a large garden, croquet lawn & ample parking. Spacious bedrooms, with en-suite/private facilities, tea/coffee trays & T.V.. Good food for breakfast & dinner, with a choice of menu. (Evening meals by arrangement.) A pleasant, relaxed atmosphere, with proprietors' personal attention, & a lounge with a bar. Within easy driving distance of Oxford, Bath, Stratford-upon-Avon & the Cotswolds. Children over 3.

E-mail: hollingtonhscheltenham@lineone.net

Juergen & Annette Berg Hollington House Hotel 115 Hales Road Cheltenham GL52 6ST Glos.
Tel: (01242) 256652 Fax 01242 570280 Open: ALL YEAR Map Ref No. 09

rate £ from - to per person	children taken	evening meals	animals taken
£36.00 to £40.00	N	N	N

see PHOTO over p. 192

Rectory Farmhouse

Nearest Road: A.429

Rectory Farmhouse is an historic 17th-century traditional Cotswold farmhouse located in the quiet hamlet of Lower Swell, which lies about 1 mile to the west of the well-known market town of Stow-on-the-Wold. It is elegantly furnished throughout & boasts superb double bedrooms, enjoying stunning views over open countryside. All bedrooms are have luxurious en-suite bathrooms. Chipping Campden & Bourton-on-the-Water are just a short drive away. Cheltenham, Oxford & Stratford-upon-Avon are all easily accessible.

Sybil Gisby Rectory Farmhouse Lower Swell Nr. Stow-on-the-Wold Cheltenham GL54 1LH Glos.
Tel: (01451) 832351 Open: ALL YEAR Map Ref No. 10

rate £ from - to per person	children taken	evening meals	animals taken
£22.50 to £25.00	Y	N	N

The Ridge

Nearest Road: A.429

The Ridge stands in 2 acres of beautiful secluded grounds just 1 mile from the centre of Bourton-on-the-Water. A large country house with 4 individually decorated, centrally heated bedrooms, most with en-suite facilities. 1 is on the ground floor. This house provides an extremely pleasant & comfortable base for touring the Cotswolds. A delicious full English breakfast is served. Good restaurants & pubs nearby serve excellent evening meals. Children over 6 years welcome.

E-mail: mikeminchin@aol.com

Mr & Mrs M. Minchin The Ridge Whiteshoots Hill Bourton-on-the-Water Cheltenham GL54 2LE
Tel: (01451) 820660 Fax 01451 822448 Open: ALL YEAR Map Ref No. 11

Rectory Farmhouse. Lower Swell.

Lady Lamb Farm. Meysey Hampton.

Gloucestershire

Cotteswold House

rate £ from - to per person	children taken	evening meals	animals taken
£22.50 to £35.00	N	Y	N

Nearest Road: A.40, A.429

Relax in this 400-year-old Cotswold-stone wealthy wool merchant's home with beamed ceilings, original panelling & Tudor archway. It offers the choice of a luxury private suite or en-suite double or twin rooms - all spacious, elegant & well-equipped. Enjoy traditional English food & a friendly welcome. (Evening meals are available by prior arrangement.) Cotteswold House is in the centre of this ancient market town of Northleach in the centre of the Cotswolds - an ideal touring base.

E-mail: cotteswoldhouse@talk21.com

VISA: M'CARD:

Graham & Elaine Whent Cotteswold House Market Place Northleach Cheltenham GL54 3EG Glos.
Tel: (01451) 860493 Fax 01451 860493 Open: ALL YEAR (Excl. Xmas & New Year) Map Ref No. 13

The Kettle House

rate £ from - to per person	children taken	evening meals	animals taken
£27.50 to £30.00	Y	N	Y

Nearest Road: A.44

A Grade II listed building of great historical importance. The Kettle House, which was built in 1640, offers exclusive & original accommodation which includes 2 double bedrooms with en-suite bathrooms, & 2 twin-bedded rooms with a shared bathroom. Guests have their own sitting room with T.V. & refreshment bar, together with paved courtyard & sun balcony approached from their own private entrance. A delightful home. Children over 12. Animals by arrangement.

E-mail: charles@kettlehouse.co.uk

VISA: M'CARD: AMEX:

Susie & Charles Holdsworth Hunt The Kettle House Leysbourne Chipping Campden GL55 6HN
Tel: (01386) 840328 Fax 01386 841740 Open: ALL YEAR Map Ref No. 16

Lady Lamb Farm

rate £ from - to per person	children taken	evening meals	animals taken
£30.00 to £35.00	Y	N	Y

Nearest Road: A.417

Lady Lamb Farm is a Cotswold-stone farmhouse, surrounded by countryside & situated less than a mile from the small market town of Fairford. 2 attractively furnished bedrooms, with T.V. & tea/coffee facilities. (1 is en-suite.) A swimming pool & tennis court are available. Set on the edge of the Cotswolds, Bath, Oxford & Cotswold towns & lovely gardens are within easy reach. Cotswold Water Park offers a range of watersports, & golf, riding & fishing are nearby. Animals by arrangement.

E-mail: jekeyser1@aol.com

see PHOTO over p. 193

VISA: M'CARD:

Mrs J. Keyser Lady Lamb Farm Meysey Hampton Cirencester GL7 5LH Gloucestershire
Tel: (01285) 712206 Fax 01285 712206 Open: ALL YEAR Map Ref No. 18

Winstone Glebe

rate £ from - to per person	children taken	evening meals	animals taken
£30.00 to £36.00	Y	Y	Y

Nearest Road: A.417

A small Georgian rectory overlooking a Saxon church in a Domesday-listed village, & enjoying spectacular rural views. Ideally situated for exploring Cotswold market towns, with their medieval churches, antique shops & rich local history. 3 charming rooms, with private/en-suite bathrooms. Being an Area of Outstanding Natural Beauty, there are well-signposted walks. The more energetic can borrow a bicycle & explore, or just enjoy warm hospitality & delicious food. Single supplement.

E-mail: sparsons@cableinet.co.uk

see PHOTO over p. 195

VISA: M'CARD:

Shaun & Susanna Parsons Winstone Glebe Winstone Cirencester GL7 7JU Gloucestershire
Tel: (01285) 821451 Fax 01285 821451 Open: ALL YEAR (Excl. Xmas) Map Ref No. 20

Winstone Glebe. Winstone.

Gloucestershire

The Old Rectory

Nearest Road: A.433

The Old Rectory (Grade II listed) is a charming home, where a happy & relaxed atmosphere prevails. The friendly hosts offer very comfortable accommodation in 3 attractively furnished bedrooms, each with an en-suite/private bathroom & T.V.. Also, a cosy lounge with T.V. & a pretty garden in which guests may choose to relax. A delicious breakfast is served. The Old Rectory is an ideal base from which to explore this beautiful region & its many attractions.

Mrs Marie-Teresa Sayers *The Old Rectory* *Didmarton GL9 1DS* *Gloucestershire*
Tel: (01454) 238233 Fax 01454 238909 Open: ALL YEAR (Excl. Xmas & New Year) *Map Ref No. 21*

rate £ from - to per person	children taken	evening meals	animals taken
£24.00 to £24.00	N	N	N

Evington Hill Farm

Nearest Road: A.38

Crown your Gloucestershire visit at this lovely 16th-century house. Take tea & homemade cake in the sunny conservatory, stay in the antique pine furnished bedrooms with their beautiful new spacious bathrooms. 1 has a 4-poster bed, all have T.V. & hostess tray. The old beamed sitting room with log burning fire is perfect for a relaxing drink. Set in 4 acres with ample parking. Licensed bar. Games room. Evening meals by arrangement. 2 holiday cottages available for extended stays.

Keith & Joyce Annis *Evington Hill Farm* *Tewkesbury Road* *The Leigh GL19 4AQ* *Gloucestershire*
Tel: (01242) 680255 *Open: ALL YEAR* *Map Ref No. 22*

rate £ from - to per person	children taken	evening meals	animals taken
£30.00 to £36.00 (no smoking)	Y	N	N

New House Farm Guest House

Nearest Road: A.40

New House Farm is a 60 acre farm with sheep, cattle & woodland. The Georgian farmhouse, with a cellar dating back to the 16th century, offers 3 bedrooms, all fully en-suite, with tea/coffee-making facilities, T.V. & clock/radio. There is a guest lounge & licensed bar. Evening meals available by arrangement. The house is set in a commanding position on the hillside of a quiet valley with far reaching views towards the Malvern Hills, yet is within easy reach of both the A.40 & M.50.
E-mail: scaldbrain@aol.com

N. Franklin & R. Smith *New House Farm Guest House* *Barrel Lane* *Aston Ingham* *Longhope GL17 0LS*
Tel: (01452) 830484 *Fax 01452 830484* *Open: ALL YEAR* *Map Ref No. 23*

rate £ from - to per person	children taken	evening meals	animals taken
£20.00 to £30.00	Y	Y	Y

VISA: M'CARD:

Edale House

Nearest Road: A.48

Edale House is a fine Georgian residence facing the cricket green in the village of Parkend at the heart of the Royal Forest of Dean. Once the home of local G.P. Bill Tandy, author of 'A Doctor in the Forest', the house has been tastefully restored to provide comfortable en-suite accommodation with every facility for guests. Enjoy delicious & imaginative cuisine prepared by your hosts. Edale House is fully licensed. Animals by arrangement.
E-mail: edale@lineone.net

Alan & Christine Parkes *Edale House* *Folly Road* *Parkend* *Lydney* *GL15 4JF* *Gloucestershire*
Tel: (01594) 562835 *Fax 01594 564488* *Open: ALL YEAR* *Map Ref No. 24*

rate £ from - to per person	children taken	evening meals	animals taken
£22.00 to £27.00	N	Y	Y

VISA: M'CARD:

Hunters Lodge. Minchinhampton.

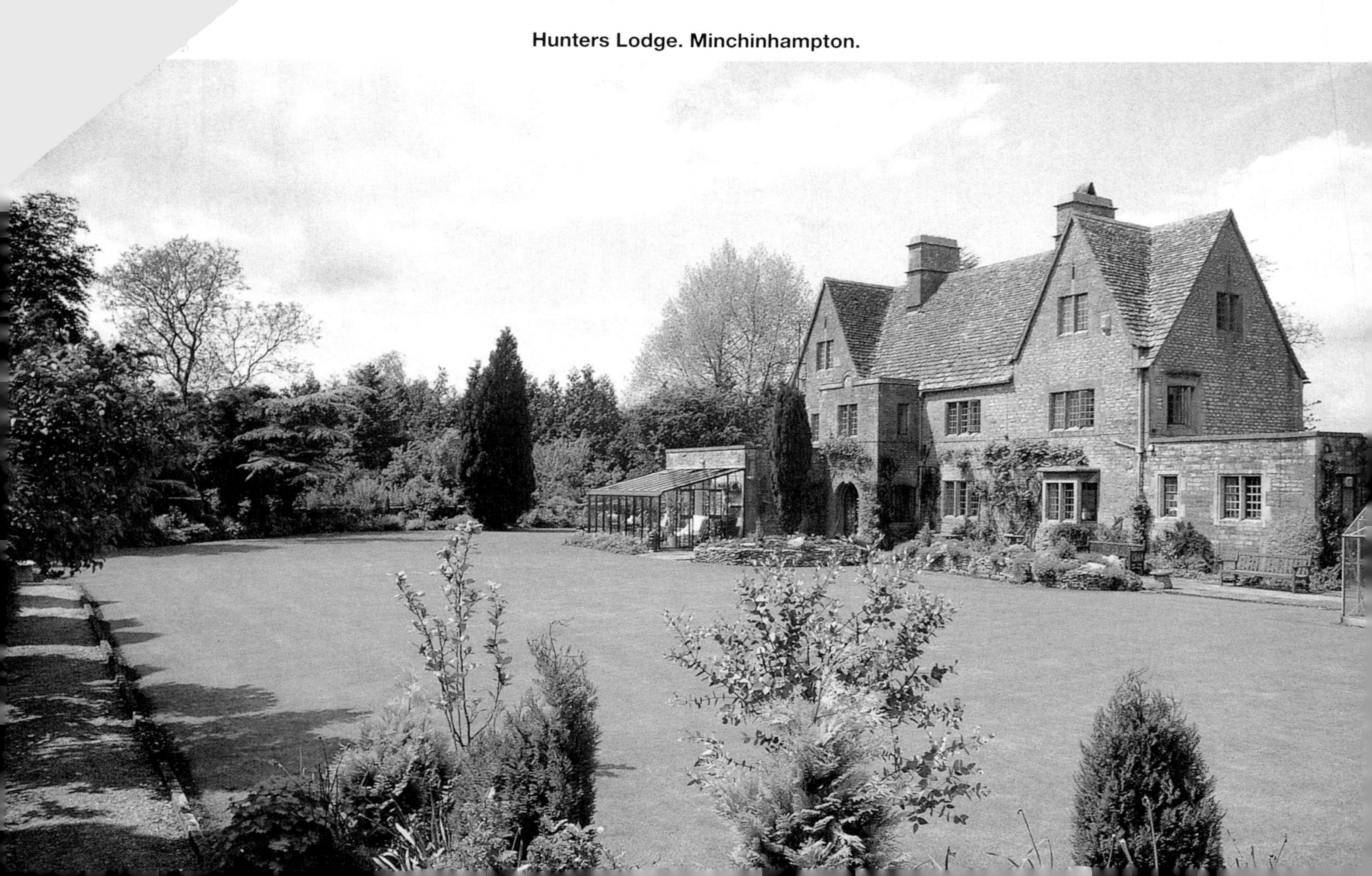

Gloucestershire

	rate £ from - to per person	children taken	evening meals	animals taken
Hunters Lodge	£21.00 to £25.00	Y	N	N
Gunn Mill House	£22.50 to £35.00	Y	Y	Y
Treetops	£22.00 to £24.00	Y	N	N
Cinderhill House	£31.00 to £38.00	Y	Y	N

Nearest Road: A.46, A.419

A friendly and helpful welcome is assured for guests at this beautifully furnished Cotswold stone country house situated adjoining 600 acres of National Trust common land and a golf course. Central heating throughout. All bedrooms have T.V., tea/coffee-making facilities & en-suite/private bathrooms. A visitors' lounge, with colour T.V., adjoins a delightful conservatory overlooking a large garden. An ideal centre for Bath, Cheltenham, Cirencester & the Cotswolds. Peter is a registered tourist guide. Children over 10.

see PHOTO over p. 197

Margaret & Peter Helm Hunters Lodge Dr. Browns Road Minchinhampton GL6 9BT Gloucestershire
Tel: (01453) 883588 Fax 01453 731449 Open: ALL YEAR (Excl. Xmas) Map Ref No. 25

Gunn Mill House

Nearest Road: A.48

Bounded by its mill stream & the Royal Forest of Dean, the Andersons' Georgian home stands in 5 acres of gardens & meadows. Refurbished to a high standard, the galleried sitting room & 8 large en-suite bedrooms & suites (4-poster, doubles, twins, family) are filled with antiques & collectables from around the world. Share your hosts' love of good food, home-made breads & preserves. Vegetarians catered for. Liquor licence. Overseas visitors especially welcomed.

E-mail: info@gunnmillhouse.co.uk

see PHOTO over p. 199

VISA: M'CARD: AMEX:

David & Caroline Anderson Gunn Mill House Lower Spout Lane Mitcheldean GL17 0EA Glos.
Tel: (01594) 827577 Fax 01594 827577 Open: ALL YEAR Map Ref No. 27

Treetops

Nearest Road: A.44

A beautiful family home offering traditional bed & breakfast. There are 6 attractive bedrooms, all with a bathroom en-suite, & 2 of which are on the ground floor and thus suitable for disabled persons or wheelchair users. All rooms have T.V., radio and tea/coffee-making facilities. Cots and high chairs available. Delightful secluded gardens to relax in. Ideally situated for exploring the Cotswolds. A warm and homely atmosphere awaits you here.

E-mail: treetops1@talk21.com

VISA: M'CARD:

Mrs E. M. Dean Treetops London Road Moreton-in-Marsh GL56 0HE Gloucestershire
Tel: (01608) 651036 Fax 01608 651036 Open: ALL YEAR Map Ref No. 28

Cinderhill House

Nearest Road: A.466

A pretty, 14th-century house tucked into the hill below the castle in St. Briavels, with magnificent views across the Wye Valley to the Brecon Beacons & Black Mountains. A lovingly restored & tastefully furnished house with 5 beautiful bedrooms (& 2 four-posters), each with a private or en-suite bathroom. Gillie is a professional cook, & takes delight in ensuring that all meals are well cooked using local produce. 3 self-catering cottages, 1 for the disabled. Licensed.

E-mail: cinderhill.house@virgin.net

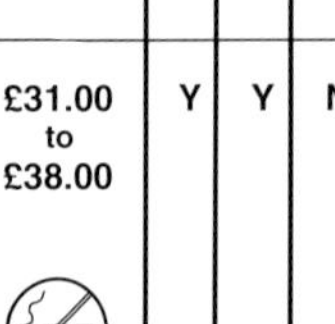

see PHOTO over p. 200

Gillie Peacock Cinderhill House Cinder Hill St. Briavels GL15 6RH Gloucestershire
Tel: (01594) 530393 Fax 01594 530098 Open: ALL YEAR Map Ref No. 30

Gunn Mill House. Mitcheldean.

Cinderhill House. St. Briavels.

Hope Cottage Guest House. Box.

Gloucestershire

	rate £ from - to per person	children taken	evening meals	animals taken

South Hill Lodge

Nearest Road: A.429

South Hill Lodge was built in 1880 as the gate-lodge to the local manor, & is just 4 minutes level walk from Stow centre with its restaurants, cafes, art & antique galleries. There is ample private parking & the garden enjoys wonderful views over the surrounding Cotswold Hills. Elegantly furnished & decorated & serving superb full English breakfasts, South Hill Lodge is a most relaxing base for touring this Area of Outstanding Natural Beauty.
E-mail: digby@southilllodge.freeserve.co.uk

Linda & Barry Digby South Hill Lodge Fosseway Stow-on-the-Wold GL54 1JU Gloucestershire
Tel: (01451) 831083 Fax 01451 870694 Open: ALL YEAR Map Ref No. 31

£25.00 to £30.00 | N | N | N

The Firs

Nearest Road: A.46

The Firs is set in a quiet village location. A fine Georgian house with many period features & panoramic views over the Cotswold escarpment. Within walking distance of several pubs & restaurants. Ideally situated for exploring the north Cotswolds, Bath, Cheltenham, Westonbirt Arboretum, Gatcomb, Badminton, Cirencester, Gloucester Docks & Bristol. There are 2 attractive en-suite rooms. Your hosts put great emphasis on guest comfort & strive to make each guest's stay memorable.
E-mail: CWalsh3088@aol.com

Carol & Gerry Walsh The Firs Selsley Road Woodchester Stroud GL5 5NQ Gloucestershire
Tel: (01453) 873088 Fax 01453 873053 Open: ALL YEAR (Excl. Xmas) Map Ref No. 32

£21.00 to £25.00 | Y | N | N

Hope Cottage

Nearest Road: A.46, A.419

For peace & tranquillity, this charming, undiscovered village 10 miles from Cirencester is unrivalled. Box is in an Area of Outstanding Natural Beauty enjoying glorious Cotswold views. Here, you can savour the charm of this delightful country house, set in 3 acres of landscaped gardens & with a heated pool. Lovely en-suite rooms all with king-size bed, settee, T.V. & hospitality tray. Sumptuous traditional English breakfasts. Good local restaurants & pubs. Strategic base for walking & touring.
E-mail: garth.brunsdon@virgin.net

Sheila & Garth Brunsdon Hope Cottage Box Nr. Stroud GL6 9HD Gloucestershire
Tel: (01453) 832076 Open: FEB - NOV Map Ref No. 33

£22.50 to £30.00 | Y | N | N

see PHOTO over p. 201

Tavern House

Nearest Road: A.433

A Grade II listed, part-17th-century, former staging post that has been sympathetically refurbished to provide an exceptionally high standard of accommodation. All rooms have bath/shower en-suite, direct-dial telephones, T.V., etc. Delightful, secluded, walled gardens in which to relax. Ideally situated for Westonbirt Arboretum, & convenient for Bath, Cheltenham & Gloucester. A genuine country-house atmosphere, & an excellent base from which to explore the Cotswolds. Charming inns offering dinner close by. Children over 10.

Janet & Tim Tremellen Tavern House Willesley Tetbury GL8 8QU Gloucestershire
Tel: (01666) 880444 Fax 01666 880254 Open: ALL YEAR Map Ref No. 34

£32.50 to £36.00 | Y | N | N

see PHOTO over p. 203

VISA: M'CARD:

Tavern House. Willesley.

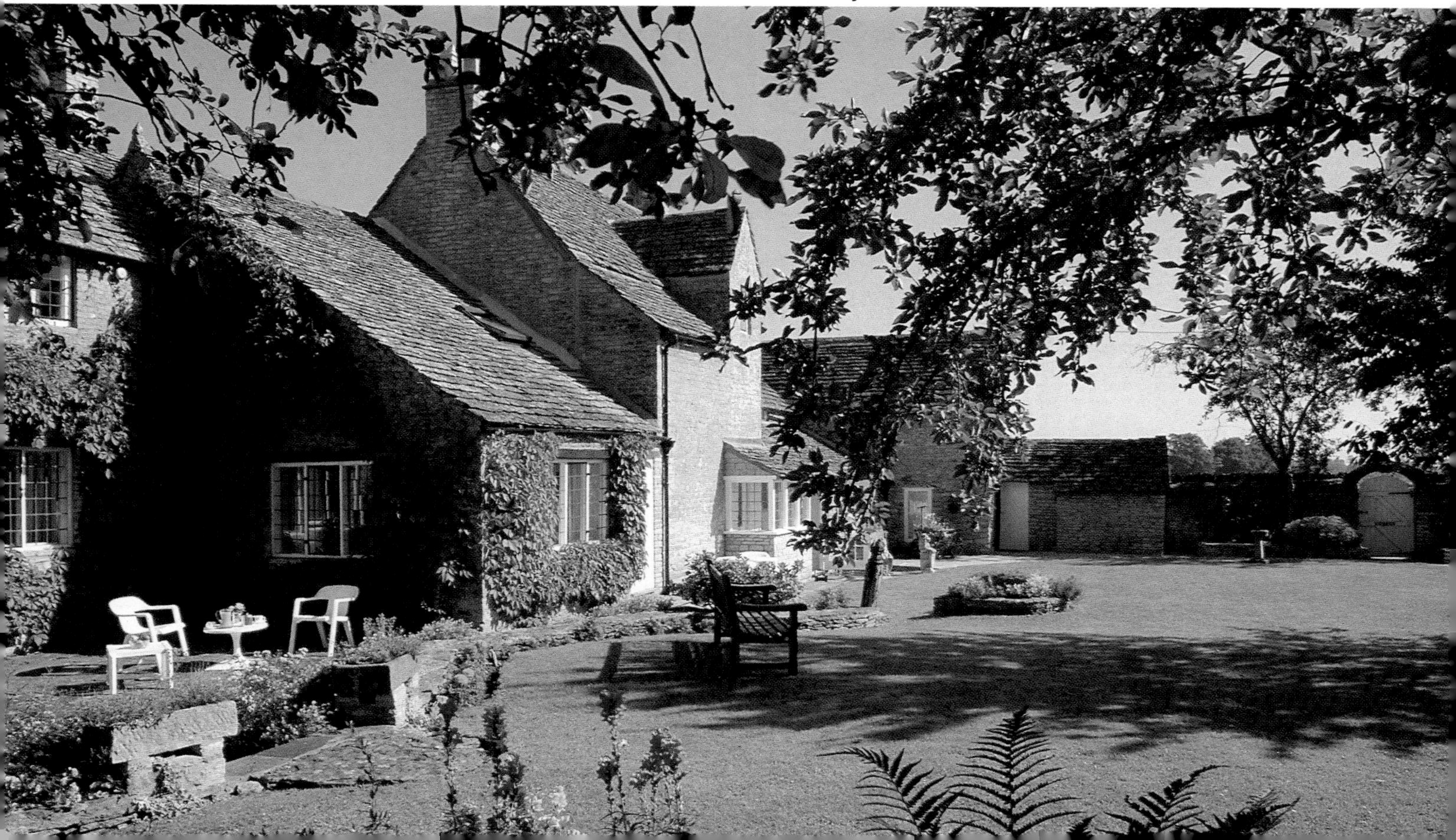

Westward. Sudeley.

Gloucestershire

rate £ from - to per person	children taken	evening meals	animals taken	
£35.00 to £42.50	N	Y	Y	**Westward**
£35.00 to £40.00	Y	Y	N	**Wesley House**

Westward

£35.00 to £42.50 — children taken: N — evening meals: Y — animals taken: Y

see PHOTO over p. 204

VISA: M'CARD:

Nearest Road: A.40

The Wilson families share this beautiful Grade II listed Georgian house on the scarp of the Cotswolds above Sudeley Castle, sitting within its own 600-acre estate with spectacular views to the Malverns. The heart of the Cotswolds is very close, with Broadway, Oxford & Stratford within easy reach. The Wilsons combine good food - Susie trained at Prue Leith's - with elegance & comfort in a relaxed family home. 3 delightful en-suite rooms available. Children over 12 years welcome.

E-mail: westwardww@aol.com

Mrs S. H. Wilson — Westward — Sudeley — Winchcombe GL54 5JB — Gloucestershire
Tel: (01242) 604372 — Fax 01242 604372 — Open: ALL YEAR (Excl. Xmas) — Map Ref No. 35

Wesley House

£35.00 to £40.00 — children taken: Y — evening meals: Y — animals taken: N

see PHOTO over p. 206

VISA: M'CARD: AMEX:

Nearest Road: A.4

Wesley House is a delightful medieval half-timbered house dating from c.1435. John Wesley, the Methodist, is believed to have stayed here in 1779. 5 cosy individually designed en-suite bedrooms. An elegant lounge with log fire which conveys a sense of old world intimacy. Jonathan Lewis has acquired an excellent reputation for fine cuisine at Wesley House. A perfect spot from which to explore the Cotswolds; Cheltenham, Oxford & Stratford are also within easy reach by car.

E-mail: reservations@wesleyhouse.co.uk

Matthew Brown — Wesley House — High Street — Winchcombe GL54 5LJ — Gloucestershire
Tel: (01242) 602366 — Fax 01242 609046 — Open: ALL YEAR — Map Ref No. 36

All the establishments mentioned in this guide are members of The Worldwide Bed & Breakfast Association

When booking your accommodation please mention The Best Bed & Breakfast

Wesley House. Winchcombe.

Hampshire & Isle of Wight

Hampshire (Southern)

Hampshire is located in the centre of the south coast of England & is blessed with much beautiful & unspoilt countryside. Wide open vistas of rich downland contrast with deep woodlands. Rivers & sparkling streams run through tranquil valleys passing nestling villages. There is a splendid coastline with seaside resorts & harbours, the cathedral city of Winchester & the "jewel" of Hampshire, the Isle of Wight.

The north of the county is known as the Hampshire Borders. Part of this countryside was immortalised by Richard Adams & the rabbits of 'Watership Down'. Beacon Hill is a notable hill-top landmark. From its slopes some of the earliest aeroplane flights were made by De Haviland in 1909. Pleasure trips & tow-path walks can be taken along the restored Basingstoke Canal.

The New Forest is probably the area most frequented by visitors. It is a landscape of great character with thatched cottages, glades & streams & a romantic beauty. There are herds of deer & the New Forest ponies wander at will. To the N.W. of Beaulieu are some of the most idyllic parts of the old forest, with fewer villages & many little streams that flow into the Avon. Lyndhurst, the "capital" of the New Forest offers a range of shops & has a contentious 19th century church constructed in scarlet brickwork banded with yellow, unusual ornamental decoration, & stained glass windows by William Morris.

The Roman city of Winchester became the capital city of Saxon Wessex & is today the capital of Hampshire. It is famous for its beautiful mediaeval cathedral, built during the reign of William the Conquerer & his notorious son Rufus. It contains the great Winchester Bible.

William completed the famous Domesday Book in the city, & Richard Coeur de Lion was crowned in the cathedral in 1194.

Portsmouth & Southampton are major ports & historic maritime cities with a wealth of castles, forts & Naval attractions from battleships to museums.

The channel of the Solent guarded by Martello towers, holds not only Southampton but numerous yachting centres, such as Hamble, Lymington & Bucklers Hard where the ships for Admiral Lord Nelson's fleet were built.

The River Test.

The Isle of Wight

The Isle of Wight lies across the sheltered waters of the Solent, & is easily reached by car or passenger ferry. The chalk stacks of the Needles & the multi-coloured sand at Alum Bay are among the best known of the island's natural attractions & there are many excellent beaches & other bays to enjoy. Cowes is a famous international sailing centre with a large number of yachting events throughout the summer. Ventnor, the most southerly resort is known as the "Madeira of England" & has an exotic botanic garden. Inland is an excellent network of footpaths & trails & many castles, manors & stately homes.

Hampshire & Isle of Wight

Hampshire

Gazeteer

Areas of outstanding natural beauty.
East & South Hampshire, North Wessex Downs & Chichester Harbour.

Houses & Castles

Avington Park - Winchester
16th century red brick house, enlarged in 17th century by the addition of two wings & a classical portico. Stateroom, ballroom with wonderful ceiling. Red drawing room, library, etc.
Beaulieu Abbey & Palace House - Beaulieu
12th century Cistercian abbey - the original gatehouse of abbey converted to palace house 1538. Houses historic car museum.
Breamore House - Breamore
16th century Elizabethan Manor House, tapestries, furniture, paintings. Also museum.
Jane Austen's Home - Chawston
Personal effects of the famous writer.
Broadlands - Romsey
16th century - park & garden created by Capability Brown. Home of the Earl Mountbatten of Burma.
Mottisfont Abbey - Nr. Romsey
12th century Augustinian Priory until Dissolution. Painting by Rex Whistler trompe l'oeil in Gothic manner.
Stratfield Saye House - Reading
17th century house presented to the Duke of Wellington 1817. Now contains his possessions - also wild fowl sanctuary.
Sandham Memorial Chapel - Sandham, Nr. Newbury
Paintings by Stanley Spencer cover the walls.
The Vyne - Sherbourne St. John
16th century red brick chapel with Renaissance glass & rare linenfold panelling. Alterations made in 1654 - classical portico. Palladian staircase dates form 1760.
West Green House - Hartley Wintney
18th century red brick house set in a walled garden.
Appuldurcombe House - Wroxall, Isle of Wight
The only house in the 'Grand Manner' on the island. Beautiful English baroque east facade. House now an empty shell standing in fine park.
Osbourne House - East Cowes, Isle of Wight
Queen Victoria's seaside residence.
Carisbrooke Castle - Isle of Wight
Oldest parts 12th century, but there was a wooden castle on the mound before that. Museum in castle.

Cathedrals & Churches

Winchester Cathedral
Largest Gothic church in Europe. Norman & perpendicular styles, three sets of mediaeval paintings, marble font c.1180. Stalls c.1320 with 60 misericords. Extensive mediaeval tiled floor.
Breamore (St. Mary) - Breamore
10th century Saxon. Double splayed windows, stone rood.
East Meon (All Saints)
15th century rebuilding of Norman fabric. Tournai marble front.
Idsworth (St. Hubert)
16th century chapel - 18th century bell turret. 14th century paintings in chancel.
Pamber (dedication unknown)
Early English - Norman central tower, 15th central pews, wooden effigy of knight c.1270.
Romsey (St. Mary & St. Ethelfleda)
Norman - 13th century effigy of a lady - Saxon rood & carving of crucifixion, 16th century painted reredos.
Silchester (St. Mary)
Norman, perpendicular, 14th century effigy of a lady, 15th century screen, Early English chancel with painted patterns on south window splays, Jacobean pulpit with domed canopy.
Winchester (St. Cross)
12th century. Original chapel to Hospital. Style changing from Norman at east to decorated at west. Tiles, glass, wall painting.

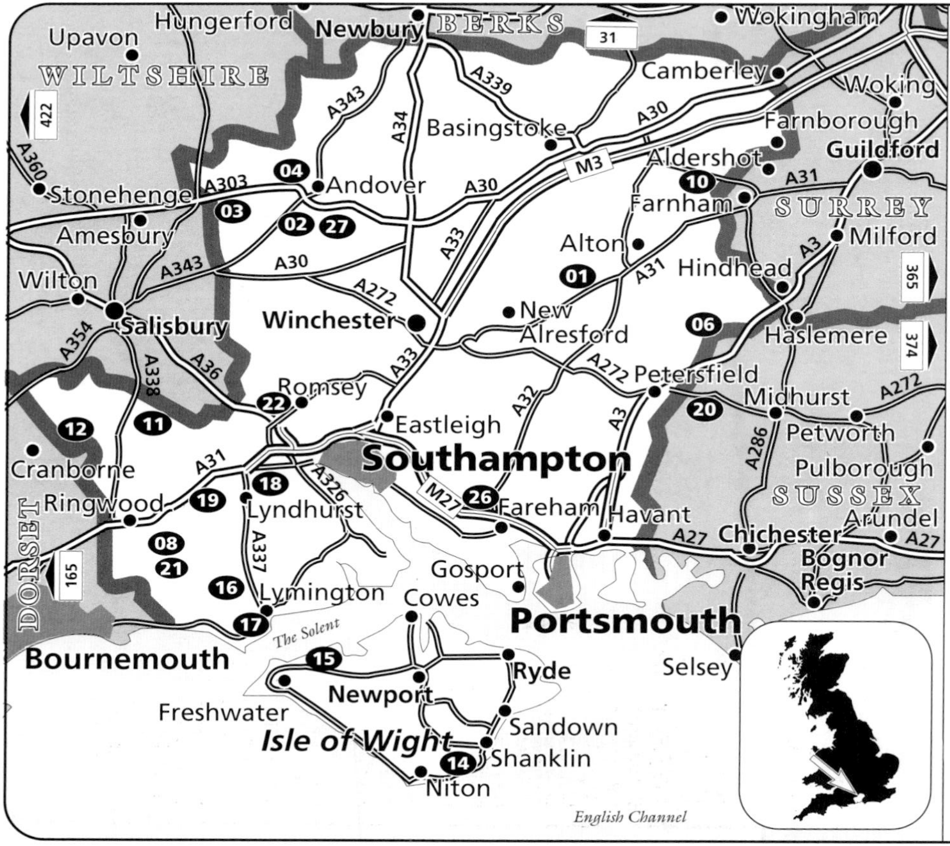

HAMPSHIRE

Map reference

01	**Humphryes**	16	**Barnfield**
02	**Mason**	17	**Cutmore**
03	**Mallam**	17	**Gallagher**
04	**Biddolph**	18	**Ames**
06	**Whitaker**	19	**Hayles**
08	**Buckley**	20	**Baigent**
10	**Tose**	21	**Ford**
11	**Cadman**	22	**Hughes**
12	**Ratcliffe**	26	**Chivers**
14	**Pritchett**	27	**Talbot**
15	**Poulter**		

May Cottage. Thruxton.

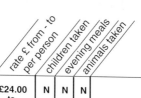

rate £ from - to per person	children taken	evening meals	animals taken
£24.00 to £26.00	N	N	N

Belmont House

Nearest Road: A.31

Belmont House is an attractive Georgian house dating back to the 18th century, set in a pretty acre of garden with rural views. Offering 1 comfortably furnished twin-bedded room with tea/coffee-making facilities & use of study with colour T.V.. A short walk to the village, ancient church, shop, 2 pubs & the famous Watercress Steam Railway. Situated within easy reach of Winchester, Salisbury & 1 hour (approx.) from London airports, this is an ideal base from which to explore Hampshire.

Mr & Mrs A. Humphryes Belmont House Gilbert Street Ropley Alresford SO24 0BY Hampshire
Tel: (01962) 772344 *Open: ALL YEAR* *Map Ref No. 01*

rate £ from - to per person	children taken	evening meals	animals taken
£30.00 to £45.00	Y	Y	N

see PHOTO over p. 212

Malt Cottage

Nearest Road: A.303

Walk around the beautiful 6-acre garden with chalk stream & lakes, or sit by the fire in the charming beamed sitting room. Malt Cottage, an ideal stop en-route from London Heathrow to the West Country, is situated in a picturesque village with many thatched cottages & offers 3 attractively furnished bedrooms with en-suite/private facilities. During the summer, evening barbecues are held. Places to visit include Stonehenge, Salisbury & Winchester. Fly fishing & airport collection can be arranged.
E-mail: info@maltcottage.co.uk

Richard & Patricia Mason Malt Cottage Upper Clatford Andover SP11 7QL Hampshire
Tel: (01264) 323469 Fax 01264 334100 Open: ALL YEAR (Excl. Xmas) Map Ref No. 02

rate £ from - to per person	children taken	evening meals	animals taken
£25.00 to £35.00	Y	N	N

VISA: M'CARD:

Broadwater

Nearest Road: A.303

Broadwater is a 17th-century, listed, thatched cottage situated in a peaceful unspoilt village just off the A.303. It is an ideal base for sightseeing in Hampshire, with easy access to the West Country & London. The cottage offers 2 delightful, double/twin-bedded rooms, both with en-suite facilities. Guests have a private & very comfortable sitting/dining room with a traditional open log fire & a very pretty garden to enjoy. Homemade bread. T.V..
E-mail: carolyn@dmac.co.uk

Mrs Carolyn Mallam Broadwater Amport Andover SP11 8AY Hampshire
Tel: (01264) 772240 Fax 01264 772240 Open: ALL YEAR Map Ref No. 03

rate £ from - to per person	children taken	evening meals	animals taken
£25.00 to £35.00	Y	N	N

see PHOTO over p. 210

May Cottage

Nearest Road: A.303

May Cottage dates back to 1740 & is situated in the heart of this picturesque tranquil village with Post Office & old inn. A most comfortable home with 1 double & 2 twin rooms with en-suite/private bathrooms, 1 on the ground floor. All with colour T.V. & tea trays. Guests' own sitting/dining room with T.V.. An ideal base for visiting ancient cities, stately homes & gardens, yet within easy reach of ports & airports. Excellent home-cooking & dinner by prior arrangement. Parking. Children over 6. (Hosts can be contacted on mobile 07768 242166).

Tom & Fiona Biddolph May Cottage Thruxton Andover SP11 8LZ Hampshire
Tel: (01264) 771241 Fax 01264 771770 Open: ALL YEAR (Excl. Xmas) Map Ref No. 04

Malt Cottage. Upper Clatford.

Land of Nod. Headley.

Hampshire

Land of Nod

Nearest Road: A.3

A large neo-Georgian house set in 7 acres of garden in the centre of 100 acres of a private woodland estate. This attractive home has 3 twin-bedded rooms with private or en-suite bathroom, T.V. & tea/coffee-making facilities. Situated just 1 hour from London, Heathrow, Gatwick & Portsmouth, & within easy reach of many fine gardens & historic houses, the Land of Nod is the perfect spot for a relaxing break. A car, though, is essential for maximum enjoyment. Children over 12.

E-mail: pwhitaker100@hotmail.com

Jeremy & Philippa Whitaker Land of Nod Headley Bordon GU35 8SJ Hampshire
Tel: (01428) 713609 Fax 01428 717698 Open: ALL YEAR (Excl. Xmas) Map Ref No. 06

rate £ from - to per person	children taken	evening meals	animals taken
£30.00 to £37.50	Y	Y	N

see PHOTO over p. 213

Tothill House

Nearest Road: A.35

An Edwardian country house set in 12 acres of woodland. An Area of Outstanding Natural Beauty noted for its flora & fauna. 5 mins' from Burley village, a popular New Forest tourist attraction. Offering good food & 3 attractive rooms, 2 with en-suite facilities & 1 with a private bathroom. Each individually decorated, with T.V. & tea-making facilities. Very secluded, with peace & tranquillity. Local sporting & recreational activities, & a variety of places to visit. Children over 16.

E-mail: tothill@abc-123.co.uk

Mrs Wendy Buckley Tothill House Black Lane Thorney Hill Bransgore Christchurch BH23 8DZ
Tel: (01425) 674414 Fax 01425 672235 Open: JAN - NOV Map Ref No. 08

rate £ from - to per person	children taken	evening meals	animals taken
£30.00 to £35.00	Y	N	N

Rudge House

Nearest Road: A.287

Elegant, spacious family home, dating from the 1850s, featuring a 4-acre garden with tennis court & croquet lawn. Edging an historic village, the house is quiet & secluded, bordering farmland, yet within 45 mins' of Heathrow, Gatwick & London. Windsor, Ascot, Winchester & Oxford highly accessible. Extremely comfortable accommodation, offering en-suite/private facilities & pump showers, plus T.V. lounge & tea/coffee. Evening meal & packed lunches by arrangement. Children over 12.

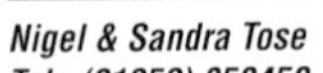

Nigel & Sandra Tose Rudge House Itchel Lane Crondall Farnham GU10 5PR Hampshire
Tel: (01252) 850450 Fax 01252 850829 Open: ALL YEAR (Excl. Xmas) Map Ref No. 10

rate £ from - to per person	children taken	evening meals	animals taken
£32.00 to £38.00	N	N	N

see PHOTO over p. 215

Cottage Crest

Nearest Road: A.338

Woodgreen is a typical New Forest village, with cottages surrounded by thick hedges to keep out the cattle & ponies. Cottage Crest is a Victorian drover's cottage set high in its own 4 acres, & enjoying superb views of the River Avon & valley below. The guest bedrooms are spacious & attractively decorated to a very high standard. All have an en-suite bathroom/shower & W.C.. Children over 8 years are welcome. Cottage Crest is an ideal base from which to explore Hampshire.

Mrs G. Cadman Cottage Crest Castle Hill Woodgreen Fordingbridge SP6 2AX Hampshire
Tel: (01725) 512009 Open: ALL YEAR Map Ref No. 11

rate £ from - to per person	children taken	evening meals	animals taken
£23.00 to £23.00	Y	N	N

Rudge House. Crondall.

Hampshire & Isle of Wight

Hendley House

rate £ from - to per person	children taken	evening meals	animals taken
£25.00 to £££	Y	N	N

Nearest Road: A.338, A.354

Overlooking water meadows, a beautiful, south-facing, 16th-century house with a wealth of beams, elegantly decorated & a relaxed family atmosphere. So much to visit & do in surrounding countryside & south coast. Walking & cycling in New Forest, returning to relax by log fires in winter or swimming pool in spacious garden in summer. Riding, fishing, golf & racing nearby. Discounts for 3 nights or more. 2 charming bedrooms with en-suite shower or private bathroom. Children over 10.

Mrs P. A. Ratcliffe Hendley House Rockbourne Fordingbridge SP6 3NA Hampshire
Tel: (01725) 518303 Fax 01725 518546 Open: APR - OCT Map Ref No. 12

Under Rock Country House B & B

rate £ from - to per person	children taken	evening meals	animals taken
£21.00 to £26.00	N	N	N

Nearest Road: A.3055

Historical Georgian house set in large secluded gardens near Horseshoe Bay & southern coastal paths, with isolated coves, narrow ravines or chines, soaring cliffs & high chalk downland, & country walks. 3 rooms - single/double, double & twin. T.V., tea/coffee trays. Most have their own bath/shower & W.C.. Guest lounge & terrace, a peaceful, relaxed setting. Picturesque Bonchurch village has literary associations including Thackeray, Dickens & Swinburne.

E-mail: underock@btinternet.com

J. Pritchett Under Rock Country House B & B Shore Road Bonchurch Ventnor Isle of Wight PO38 1RF
Tel: (01983) 855274 Open: FEB - NOV Map Ref No. 14

Quinces

rate £ from - to per person	children taken	evening meals	animals taken
£20.00 to £25.00	Y	N	Y

Nearest Road: A.3054

An attractive cedar house, centrally heated throughout, peacefully set between a vineyard & a dairy farm on a private road 2 miles from Yarmouth. 2 delightful bedrooms, with tea/coffee-making facilities. Also available to guests is a comfortable living room with colour T.V. & log fires in season. The Poulters offer an ideal base for exploring the lovely & varied countryside & coastline of the West Wight, as well as the option of wildlife holidays tailored to your interests. Children over 6 yrs.

Mrs Sylvia Poulter Quinces Cranmore Avenue Cranmore Yarmouth Isle of Wight PO41 OXS
Tel: (01983) 760080 Open: ALL YEAR Map Ref No. 15

The Nurse's Cottage

rate £ from - to per person	children taken	evening meals	animals taken
£47.50 to £65.00	Y	Y	Y

Nearest Road: A.337

Renowned for warmth of hospitality & first-class cuisine, this former District Nurse's cottage on the edge of the New Forest is an ideal touring centre. Lovingly refurbished Tony Barnfield, this award-winning restaurant & guest accommodation offers reduced-price short breaks for stays of 2+ nights, with over 60 wines to accompany your selection from the 3-course dinner menu. 3 en-suite ground-floor bedrooms feature T.V., refrigerator, 'phone & many little extras. Children over 10.

E-mail: nurses.cottage@lineone.net

see PHOTO over p. 217

VISA: M'CARD: AMEX:

R. A. Barnfield The Nurse's Cottage Station Road Sway Lymington SO41 6BA Hampshire
Tel: (01590) 683402 Fax 01590 683402 Open: ALL YEAR Map Ref No. 16

The Nurse's Cottage. Sway.

	rate £ from - to per person	children taken	evening meals	animals taken
Wheatsheaf House	£30.00 to £45.00	N	N	N
Albany House	£28.50 to £39.50	Y	Y	Y
Ormonde House Hotel	£23.00 to £44.00	Y	Y	Y
Burbush Farm	£28.00 to £35.00	N	N	N

Wheatsheaf House

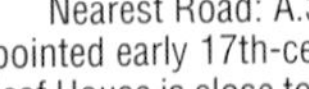

Nearest Road: A.337

A beautifully appointed early 17th-century former tavern, Wheatsheaf House is close to the centre of this charming Georgian market town, & only 3 mins' walk from the historic town quay. Offering 2 large, comfortable, en-suite rooms with tea/coffee-making facilities & there is an attractive drawing room with T.V.. The house is ideally placed for sailing, the New Forest & for touring the whole region, with many excellent restaurants within walking distance. You are assured of a warm welcome.

E-mail: Wheatsheaf@Cutmore.com

Peter & Jennifer Cutmore Wheatsheaf House Gosport Street Lymington SO41 9BG Hampshire
Tel: (01590) 679208 Open: APR - OCT Map Ref No. 17

Albany House

Nearest Road: A.337

This fine Regency house, built in 1842, provides a warm, welcoming atmosphere in a traditionally furnished home. There are views over the town of Solent & the Isle of Wight. There are 3 very comfortably furnished bedrooms, each with en-suite facilities, colour T.V. & tea/coffee makers. Delicious meals are served in the elegant dining room using freshly prepared ingredients. In season, shellfish & New Forest game will be provided. Evening meals, children & animals by arrangement. (Supplement for Saturday night bookings.)

Wendy M. Gallagher Albany House 3 Highfield Lymington SO41 9GB Hampshire
Tel: (01590) 671900 Open: ALL YEAR (Excl. Xmas) Map Ref No. 17

Ormonde House Hotel

Nearest Road: A.35

Ormonde House is set back from the main road opposite the open forest; easy for an early morning walk. Lyndhurst village is just 5 mins' walk & Exbury Gardens & the National Motor Museum, Beaulieu 20 mins' drive. The popular licensed restaurant offers freshly prepared dishes. Accommodation is in 19 pretty en-suite bedrooms, all with satellite T.V., 'phone & tea-making facilities. Delightful rooms with huge king-size beds & whirlpool baths for that special treat.

E-mail: info@ormondehouse.co.uk

see PHOTO over p. 219

VISA: M'CARD: AMEX:

Mr. Paul Ames Ormonde House Hotel Southampton Road Lyndhurst SO43 7BT Hampshire
Tel: (023) 8028 2806 Fax 023 8028 2004 Open: ALL YEAR Map Ref No. 18

Burbush Farm

Nearest Road: A.31

Burbush Farm is an impressive country house set in 12 acres of beautiful gardens & pastures in the heart of the New Forest, offering the finest quality accommodation. Luxury en-suite bedrooms are appointed & decorated to the highest standards, with the spacious lounge ensuring every comfort. Delicious breakfasts (traditional English, Continental, or mouthwatering alternatives) are served in the dining room overlooking the gardens. Guests are well-cared for in a serene & homely atmosphere.

E-mail: burbush-farm@excite.com

VISA: M'CARD:

David & Carole Hayles Burbush Farm Pound Lane Burley New Forest BH24 4EF Hampshire
Tel: (01425) 403238 Fax 01425 403238 Open: ALL YEAR Map Ref No. 19

Ormonde House Hotel. Lyndhurst.

Hampshire

rate £ from - to per person	children taken	evening meals	animals taken

Trotton Farm

Nearest Road: A.272

This charming home, set in 200 acres of farmland, offers comfortable accommodation in 2 twin-bedded rooms & 1 double-bedded room each with an en-suite shower & modern amenities, including tea/coffee-making facilities. Residents' lounge is available throughout the day. Games room & pretty garden for guests' relaxation. Ideally situated for visiting many local, historical & sporting attractions, & 1 hour from Gatwick & Heathrow Airports. Single supplement.

rate £ from - to per person	children taken	evening meals	animals taken
£17.50 to £30.00	Y	N	Y

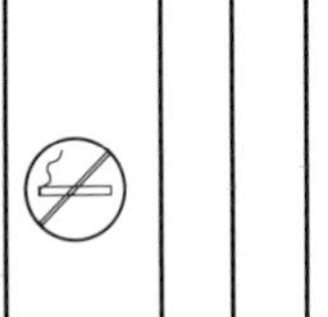

Mrs J. E. Baigent Trotton Farm Trotton Petersfield GU31 5EN Hampshire
Tel: (01730) 813618 Fax 01730 816093 Open: ALL YEAR Map Ref No. 20

Holmans

Nearest Road: A.35, A.31

Holmans is a charming country house in the heart of the New Forest, set in 4 acres with stabling available for guests' own horses. Superb walking, horse riding & carriage driving, with a golf course nearby. A warm, friendly welcome is assured at this elegant home which is ideal for a relaxing break. All bedrooms are tastefully furnished & en-suite with tea/coffee-making facilities, radio & hairdryers. There is a colour T.V. in the guests' lounge with adjoining orangery & log fires in winter.

rate £ from - to per person	children taken	evening meals	animals taken
£27.50 to £30.00	Y	N	Y

Robin & Mary Ford Holmans Bisterne Close Burley Nr. Ringwood BH24 4AZ Hampshire
Tel: (01425) 402307 Fax 01425 402307 Open: ALL YEAR Map Ref No. 21

Ranvilles Farm House

Nearest Road: A.3090

Ranvilles Farm House dates from the 13th century when Richard De Ranville came from Normandy & settled with his family. Now this Grade II listed house provides a peaceful setting surrounded by 5 acres of gardens & paddock. All rooms, with extra large beds, are attractively decorated & furnished with antiques, & each room has its own en-suite bathroom/shower room. Ranvilles Farm House is only 3 miles from the New Forest & just over a mile from Romsey, a small town equidistant from the 2 cathedral cities of Winchester & Salisbury.

rate £ from - to per person	children taken	evening meals	animals taken
£25.00 to £35.00	Y	N	Y

Anthea F. Hughes Ranvilles Farm House Ower Romsey SO51 6DJ Hampshire
Tel: (023) 80814481 Fax 023 80814481 Open: ALL YEAR Map Ref No. 22

Montrose

Nearest Road: A.32

Montrose offers accommodation of a high standard in tasteful surroundings. There are 3 delightful bedrooms, 1 is en-suite. Comfort & personal attention has helped to build a superb reputation. Situated in the Meon Valley between the historical villages of Wickham & Bishops Waltham, & yet close to the M.27, M.3 & continental ferry ports, thus providing an ideal base for exploring the towns of Winchester, Portsmouth & Southampton, & the lovely Hampshire countryside & coastline.

E-mail: bb@montrose78.fsnet.co.uk

rate £ from - to per person	children taken	evening meals	animals taken
£26.00 to £31.00	N	N	N

VISA: M'CARD:

Mrs Y. M. Chivers Montrose Solomons Lane Shirrell Heath Nr. Southampton SO3 2HU Hampshire
Tel: (01329) 833345 Fax 01329 833345 Open: ALL YEAR Map Ref No. 26

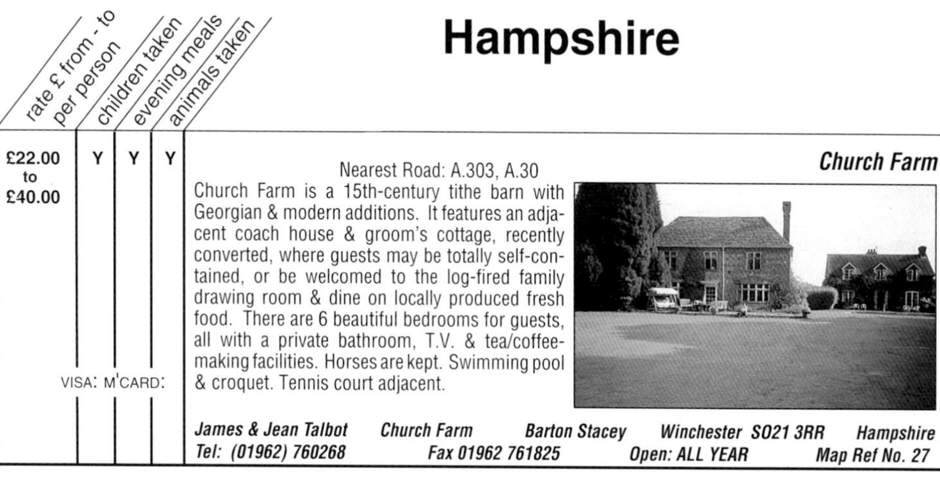

rate £ from - to per person	children taken	evening meals	animals taken	
£22.00 to £40.00	Y	Y	Y	**_Church Farm_** Nearest Road: A.303, A.30 Church Farm is a 15th-century tithe barn with Georgian & modern additions. It features an adjacent coach house & groom's cottage, recently converted, where guests may be totally self-contained, or be welcomed to the log-fired family drawing room & dine on locally produced fresh food. There are 6 beautiful bedrooms for guests, all with a private bathroom, T.V. & tea/coffee-making facilities. Horses are kept. Swimming pool & croquet. Tennis court adjacent. _James & Jean Talbot Church Farm Barton Stacey Winchester SO21 3RR Hampshire_ _Tel: (01962) 760268 Fax 01962 761825 Open: ALL YEAR Map Ref No. 27_
VISA: M'CARD:				

All the establishments mentioned in this guide are members of The Worldwide Bed & Breakfast Association

When booking your accommodation please mention The Best Bed & Breakfast

Hereford & Worcester

Hereford & Worcester (Heart of England)

Hereford is a beautiful ancient city standing on the banks of the River Wye, almost a crossing point between England & Wales. It is a market centre for the Marches, the border area which has a very particular history of its own.

Hereford Cathedral has a massive sandstone tower & is a fitting venue for the Three Choirs festival which dates from 1727, taking place yearly in one or the other of the three great cathedrals of Hereford, Worcester & Gloucester.

The county is fortunate in having many well preserved historic buildings. Charming "black & white" villages abound here, romantically set in a soft green landscape.

The Royal Forest of Dean spreads its oak & beech trees over 22,000 acres. When people first made their homes in the woodlands it was vaster still. There are rich deposits of coal & iron mined for centuries by the foresters, & the trees have always been felled for charcoal. Ancient courts still exist where forest dwellers can & do claim their rights to use the forest's resources.

The landscape alters dramatically as the land rises to merge with the great Black Mountain range at heights of over 2,600 feet. It is not possible to take cars everywhere but a narrow mountain road, Gospel Pass, takes traffic from Hay-on-Wye to Llanthony with superb views of the upper Wye Valley.

The Pre-Cambrian Malvern Hills form a natural boundary between Herefordshire & Worcestershire & from the highest view points you can see over 14 counties. At their feet nestle pretty little villages such as Eastonor with its 19th century castle in revived Norman style that looks quite mediaeval amongst the parklands & gardens.

There are, in fact, five Malverns. The largest predictably known as Great Malvern was a fashionable 19th century spa & is noted for the purity of the water which is bottled & sold countrywide.

The Priory at Malvern is rich in 15th century stained glass & has a fine collection of mediaeval tiles made locally. William Langland, the 14th century author of "Piers Ploughman", was educated at the Priory & is said to have been sleeping on the Malvern Hills when he had the visionary experience which led to the creation of the poem. Sir Edward Elgar was born, lived & worked here & his "Dream of Gerontius" had its first performance in Hereford Cathedral in 1902.

In Worcestershire another glorious cathedral, with what remains of its monastic buildings, founded in the 11th century, stands beside the River Severn. College Close in Worcester is a lovely group of buildings carefully preserved & very English in character.

The Severn appears to be a very lazy waterway but flood waters can reach astonshing heights, & the "Severn Bore" is a famous phenomenon.

A cruise along the river is a pleasant way to spend a day seeing villages & churches from a different perspective, possibly visiting a riverside inn. To the south of the county lie the undulating Vales of Evesham & Broadway - described as the show village of England.

The Malvern Hills.

Hereford & Worcester

Hereford & Worcester Gazeteer

Areas of outstanding natural beauty.
The Malvern Hills, The Cotswolds, The Wye Valley.

Historic Houses & Castles

Berrington Hall - Leominster
18th century - painted & plastered ceilings. Landscape by Capability Brown.
Brilley - Cwmmau Farmhouse - Whitney-on-Wye
17th century timber-framed & stone tiled farmhouse.
Burton Court - Eardisland
14th century great hall. Exhibition of European & Oriental costume & curios. Model fairground.
Croft Castle - Nr. Leominster
Castle on the Welsh border - inhabited by Croft family for 900 years.
Dinmore Manor - Nr. Hereford
14th century chapel & cloister.
Eastnor Castle - Nr. Ledbury
19th century - Castellated, containing pictures & armour. Arboretum.
Eye Manor - Leominster
17th century Carolean Manor house - excellent plasterwork, paintings, costumes, books, secret passage. Collection of dolls.
Hanbury Hall - Nr. Droitwich
18th century red brick house - only two rooms & painted ceilings on exhibition.
Harvington Hall - Kidderminster
Tudor Manor house with moat, priest's hiding places.
The Greyfriars - Worcester
15th century timber-framed building adjoins Franciscan Priory.
Hellen's - Much Marcle
13th century manorial house of brick & stone. Contains the Great hall with stone table - bedroom of Queen Mary. Much of the original furnishings remain.
Kentchurch Court - Hereford
14th century fortified border Manor house. Paintings & Carvings by Grinling Gibbons.
Moccas Court - Moccas
18th century - designed by Adam - Parklands by Capability Brown - under restoration.
Pembridge Castle - Welsh Newton
17th century moated castle.
Sutton Court - Mordiford
Palladian mansion by Wyatt, watercolours, embroideries, china.

Cathedrals & Churches

Amestry (St. John the Baptist & St.Alkmund)
16th century rood screen.
Abbey Dore (St. Mary & Holy Trinity)
17th century glass & great oak screen - early English architecture.
Brinsop (St. George)
14th century, screen & glass, alabaster reredos, windows in memory of Wordsworth, carved Norman tympanum.
Bredon (St. Giles)
12th century - central tower & spire. Mediaeval heraldic tiles, tombs & early glass.
Brockhampton (St. Eadburgh)
1902. Central tower & thatched roof.
Castle Frome (St. Michael & All Angles)
12th century carved font, 17th century effigies in alabaster.
Chaddesley Corbett (St. Cassian)
14th century monuments, 12th century font.
Elmley (St. Mary)
12th century & 15th century font, tower, gargoyles, mediaeval.
Great Witley (St. Michael)
Baroque - Plasterwork, painted ceiling, painted glass, very fine example.
Hereford (All Saints)
13th-14th centuries, spire, splendid choir stalls, chained library.
Hereford Cathedral
Small cathedral.
Fine central tower c.1325,
splendid porch, brasses, early English Lady Chapel with lancet windows. Red sandstone.
Kilpeck (St. Mary & St. David)
Romanesque style - mediaeval windows - fine carvings.
Leominster (St. Peter & St. Paul)
12th century doorway, fine Norman arches, decorated windows.
Much Marcle (St. Bartholomew)
13th century. 14th & 17th century monuments.

Hereford & Worcester

Worcester Cathedral
11th -16th centry. Fine cloisters & crypt.
Tomb of King John
Worcester (St. Swithun)
18th century - furnishings untouched.
Ceiling vaulted in plaster.

Museums& Galleries

Hereford City Museum & Art Gallery
Collections of natural history & archeology, costumes, textiles embroideries, toys, agricultural I bygones.
Paintings by local artists, examples of applied art, silver, pottery & porcelain.
The Old House - Hereford
Jacobean period museum with furnishings of time.
Churchill Gardens Museum - Hereford
Extensive costume collection, fine furniture, work by local artists.
Almonry Museum - Evesham
Anglo-British. Roman-British, mediaeval - monastic remains.
Avoncroft Museum of Buildings - Stoke Heath.
Open air museum showing buildings of reconstructed iron-age dwellings to 15th century merchants homes.
City Museum & Art Gallery
Local History, archaeology, natural history, environmental studies.
Dyson Perins Museums of Worcester
Porcelain - Worcester
Most comprehensive collection of old Worcester in the world.
The Commandery - Sidbury
15th century timber-framed building, was originally a hospital. Royalist H.Q. during battle of Worcester 1651.

Other things to see & do

Three choirs Festival - an annual event, held in the cathedrals of Hereford, Worcester & Gloucestershire, alternately.

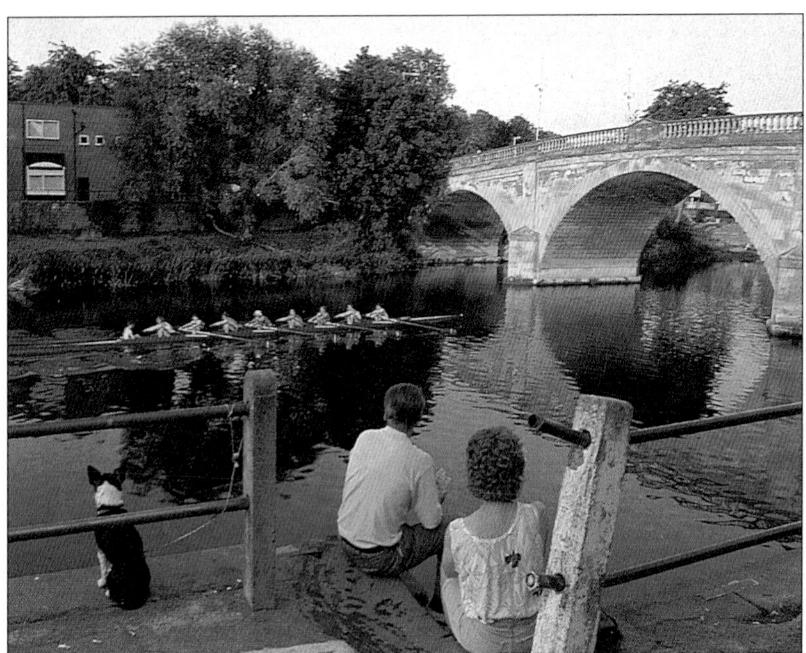

The River Severn at Bewdley.

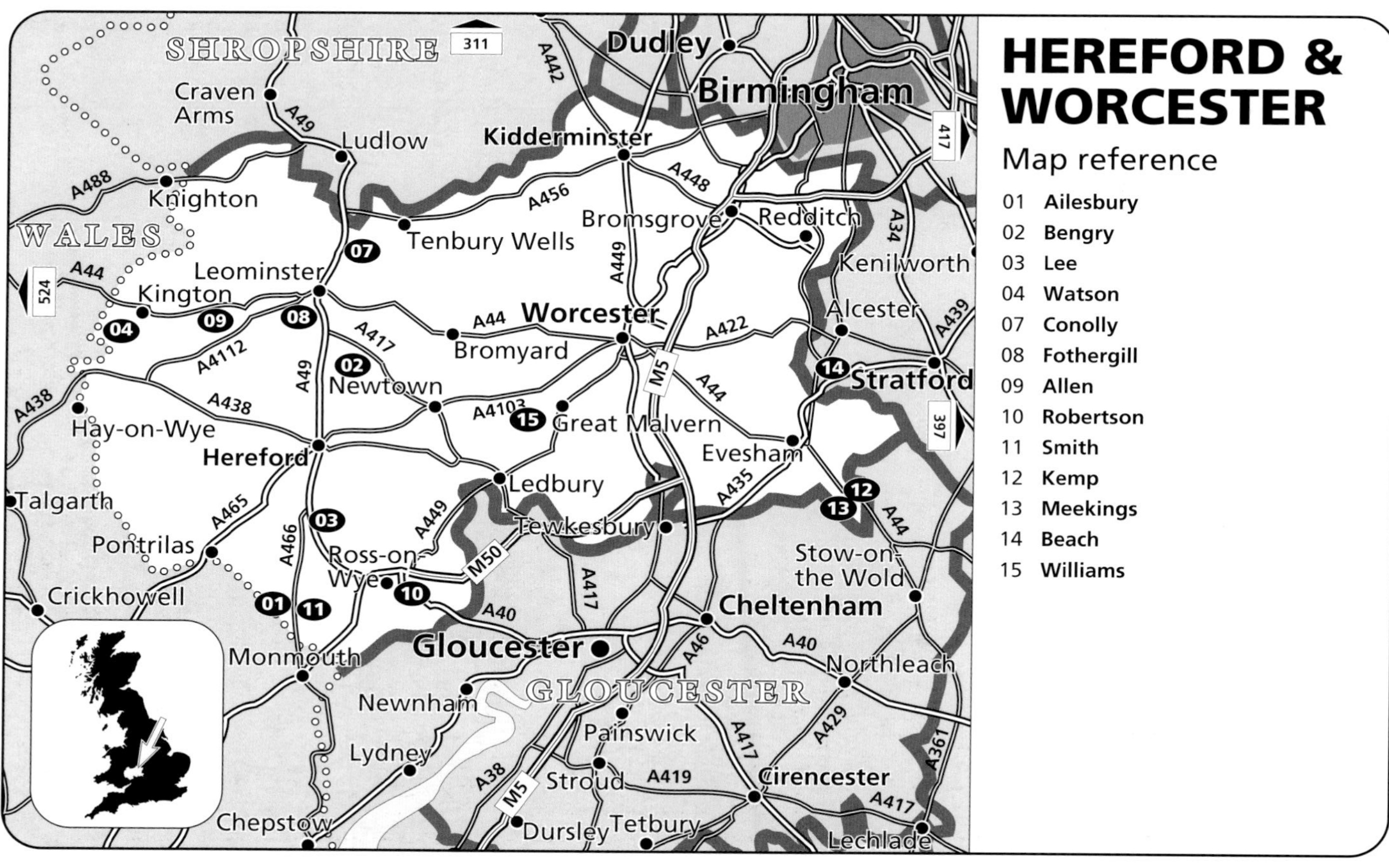

HEREFORD & WORCESTER

Map reference

01 **Ailesbury**
02 **Bengry**
03 **Lee**
04 **Watson**
07 **Conolly**
08 **Fothergill**
09 **Allen**
10 **Robertson**
11 **Smith**
12 **Kemp**
13 **Meekings**
14 **Beach**
15 **Williams**

rate £ from - to per person	children taken	evening meals	animals taken

The Old Rectory

Nearest Road: A.466

Flowers, ticking clocks, log fires & Aga cooking all make you feel very welcome here. Beautiful views towards the Black Mountains & Brecon Beacons. The Blue Bedroom with 4-poster, & the Pink Room with twin beds, have handbasins & T.V.s & share a bathroom. Also a shower room & separate W.C.s. Dinner by arrangement. A full English breakfast sets you up for the day. Hereford Cathedral with Mappa Mundi & Chained Library, Ross, Monmouth or Hay-on-Wye are within easy reach. Children over 8. Single supplement.

Caroline Ailesbury *The Old Rectory* *Garway HR2 8RH* *Herefordshire*
Tel: (01600) 750363 *Fax 01600 750364* *Open: ALL YEAR* *Map Ref No. 01*

£20.00 to £25.00	Y	Y	N

VISA: M'CARD:

The Vauld Farm

Nearest Road: A.49

The Vauld Farm is a delightful 16th-century black-&-white former farmhouse, set in a beautiful garden. It retains many period features throughout & affords attractive accommodation. There are 4 charming & elegantly furnished bedrooms, each with an en-suite bathroom, T.V. & tea/coffee-making facilities. (1 with 4-poster.) Hearty breakfasts & delicious evening meals are served in the tastefully decorated dining room. A beautiful home & the perfect location for a relaxing break.

Mr & Mrs J. Bengry *The Vauld Farm* *The Vauld* *Marden* *Hereford HR1 3HA* *Herefordshire*
Tel: (01568) 797898 *Open: ALL YEAR* *Map Ref No. 02*

£25.00 to £30.00	N	Y	N

Cwm Craig Farm

Nearest Road: A.49

Spacious Georgian farmhouse, surrounded by superb unspoilt countryside. Situated between the cathedral city of Hereford & Ross-on-Wye, & just a few mins' drive from the Wye Valley. Ideal base for touring the Forest of Dean. All 3 bedrooms are comfortably furnished & have modern amenities, shaver points, tea/coffee-making facilities & an en-suite bathroom. There is a lounge & separated dining room, both with colour T.V.. A delicious full English breakfast is served.

Mrs G. W. Lee *Cwm Craig Farm* *Little Dewchurch* *Hereford HR2 6PS* *Herefordshire*
Tel: (01432) 840250 *Fax 01432 840250* *Open: ALL YEAR* *Map Ref No. 03*

£18.00 to £18.00	Y	N	N

Hall's Mill House

Nearest Road: A.438, A.44

Hall's Mill House has recently been restored & is situated in peaceful, idyllic countryside overlooking the River Arrow. Offering 3 attractively furnished rooms with en-suite/private bathrooms available. A comfortable lounge in which guests may choose to relax. An excellent base from which to explore the area. Easy access to Offa's Dyke, the Black Mountains, Hay-on-Wye, black-&-white villages, Welsh border country, churches & castles. Many excellent pubs & restaurants locally. Evening meals by prior arrangement. Children over 4.

Grace Watson *Hall's Mill House* *Huntington* *Kington HR5 3QA* *Herefordshire*
Tel: (01497) 831409 *Open: ALL YEAR (Excl. Xmas)* *Map Ref No. 04*

£18.00 to £22.00	Y	Y	N

The Hills Farm. Leystors.

	rate £ from - to per person	children taken	evening meals	animals taken
The Hills Farm	£26.00 to £30.00	N	Y	Y
Highfield	£18.50 to £23.00			
Broxwood Court	£33.00 to £50.00	Y	Y	N
Sunnymount Hotel	£22.00 to £28.00	Y	Y	N

The Hills Farm

Nearest Road: A.4112

Magnificent views & a splendid welcome await you at this 15th-century farmhouse on the edge of the village of Leysters betwixt Ludlow & Leominster. Delightful en-suite bedrooms have T.V. & beverage-making facilities. 3 are in charming barn conversions offering complete seclusion. Scrumptious dinners, traditional or vegetarian, are available in the individually tabled dining room - the dairy in days gone by - which is unlicensed, so bring your own wine. A wonderful escape.

E-mail: conolly@bigwig.net

Peter & Jane Conolly The Hills Farm Leysters Leominster HR6 0HP Herefordshire
Tel: (01568) 750205 Fax 01568 750306 Open: MAR - OCT Map Ref No. 07

£26.00 to £30.00 — N Y Y

see PHOTO over p. 227

VISA: M'CARD:

Highfield

Nearest Road: A.44, A.49

Twins Catherine & Marguerite are eager to make you feel welcome & at home in their elegant Edwardian house, set in a rural, tranquil location. You will be very comfortable in any of the 3 attractive bedrooms, all with a bathroom (1 being en-suite) & tea/coffee-making facilities. There is a large garden & a T.V. lounge with a crackling fire in which guests may relax, & the home-made food is absolutely delicious. Residential licence.

E-mail: highfieldgh@talk21.com

Catherine & Marguerite Fothergill Highfield Newtown Ivington Road Leominster HR6 8QD
Tel: (01568) 613216 Open: ALL YEAR Map Ref No. 08

£18.50 to £23.00

Broxwood Court

Nearest Road: A.4112

Elegant manor house with superb views & stunning 30-acre garden; sweeping lawns, specimen trees & trout lake with numerous white & coloured peacocks who roam the grounds. For the energetic there is a 40ft heated swimming pool in the rose garden & an all-weather tennis court. The delightful bedrooms all have en-suite bathrooms. Anne is an excellent cook whose delicious dinners include fruit & vegetables from the organic kitchen garden. A really warm welcome awaits you.

E-mail: mikeanne@broxwood.kc3.co.uk

Mike & Anne Allen Broxwood Court Broxwood Leominster HR6 9JJ Herefordshire
Tel: (01544) 340245 Fax 01544 340573 Open: ALL YEAR (Excl. Xmas & New Year) Map Ref No. 09

£33.00 to £50.00 — Y Y N

see PHOTO over p. 229

VISA: M'CARD:

Sunnymount Hotel

Nearest Road: A.40

Quietly situated on the edge of the town, this attractive Edwardian house is warm & inviting. Offering 6 well-appointed bedrooms, with en-suite bathrooms & tea/coffee-making facilities. The sitting rooms (1 with colour T.V.) & dining room overlook the pretty garden. A wide choice of breakfasts using home & local produce freshly prepared for each meal. English/French cooking. Licensed. Ample private parking. An ideal base from which to explore this fascinating area.

E-mail: sunnymount@tinyworld.co.uk

Mr & Mrs R. Robertson Sunnymount Hotel Ryefield Road Ross-on-Wye HR9 5LU Herefordshire
Tel: (01989) 563880 Fax 01989 566251 Open: ALL YEAR Map Ref No. 10

£22.00 to £28.00 — Y Y N

VISA: M'CARD:

Broxwood Court. Broxwood.

Cowley House. Broadway.

S42-
A3400- Stratford-upon-Avon
A46-R Evesham-Bypass-
3rd Roundabout (L) A44
Oxford Broadway
O-Brdwy Village Ctr.

main rd into Brdwy
S B46 32
2 mi (R) - Wormington Dumbleton.
1 mi - 1st R

Herefordshire & Worcestershire

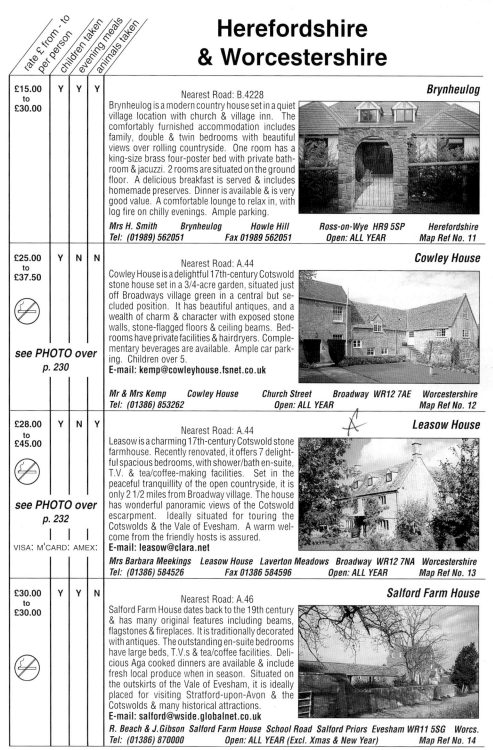

rate £ from - to per person	children taken	evening meals	animals taken	
£15.00 to £30.00	Y	Y	Y	***Brynheulog*** Nearest Road: B.4228 Brynheulog is a modern country house set in a quiet village location with church & village inn. The comfortably furnished accommodation includes family, double & twin bedrooms with beautiful views over rolling countryside. One room has a king-size brass four-poster bed with private bathroom & jacuzzi. 2 rooms are situated on the ground floor. A delicious breakfast is served & includes homemade preserves. Dinner is available & is very good value. A comfortable lounge to relax in, with log fire on chilly evenings. Ample parking. ***Mrs H. Smith Brynheulog Howle Hill Ross-on-Wye HR9 5SP Herefordshire Tel: (01989) 562051 Fax 01989 562051 Open: ALL YEAR Map Ref No. 11***
£25.00 to £37.50 ***see PHOTO over p. 230***	Y	N	N	***Cowley House*** Nearest Road: A.44 Cowley House is a delightful 17th-century Cotswold stone house set in a 3/4-acre garden, situated just off Broadways village green in a central but secluded position. It has beautiful antiques, and a wealth of charm & character with exposed stone walls, stone-flagged floors & ceiling beams. Bedrooms have private facilities & hairdryers. Complementary beverages are available. Ample car parking. Children over 5. **E-mail: kemp@cowleyhouse.fsnet.co.uk** ***Mr & Mrs Kemp Cowley House Church Street Broadway WR12 7AE Worcestershire Tel: (01386) 853262 Open: ALL YEAR Map Ref No. 12***
£28.00 to £45.00 ***see PHOTO over p. 232*** VISA: M'CARD: AMEX:	Y	N	Y	***Leasow House*** Nearest Road: A.44 Leasow is a charming 17th-century Cotswold stone farmhouse. Recently renovated, it offers 7 delightful spacious bedrooms, with shower/bath en-suite, T.V. & tea/coffee-making facilities. Set in the peaceful tranquillity of the open countryside, it is only 2 1/2 miles from Broadway village. The house has wonderful panoramic views of the Cotswold escarpment. Ideally situated for touring the Cotswolds & the Vale of Evesham. A warm welcome from the friendly hosts is assured. **E-mail: leasow@clara.net** ***Mrs Barbara Meekings Leasow House Laverton Meadows Broadway WR12 7NA Worcestershire Tel: (01386) 584526 Fax 01386 584596 Open: ALL YEAR Map Ref No. 13***
£30.00 to £30.00	Y	Y	N	***Salford Farm House*** Nearest Road: A.46 Salford Farm House dates back to the 19th century & has many original features including beams, flagstones & fireplaces. It is traditionally decorated with antiques. The outstanding en-suite bedrooms have large beds, T.V.s & tea/coffee facilities. Delicious Aga cooked dinners are available & include fresh local produce when in season. Situated on the outskirts of the Vale of Evesham, it is ideally placed for visiting Stratford-upon-Avon & the Cotswolds & many historical attractions. **E-mail: salford@wside.globalnet.co.uk** ***R. Beach & J.Gibson Salford Farm House School Road Salford Priors Evesham WR11 5SG Worcs. Tel: (01386) 870000 Open: ALL YEAR (Excl. Xmas & New Year) Map Ref No. 14***

Leasow House. Broadway.

Worcestershire

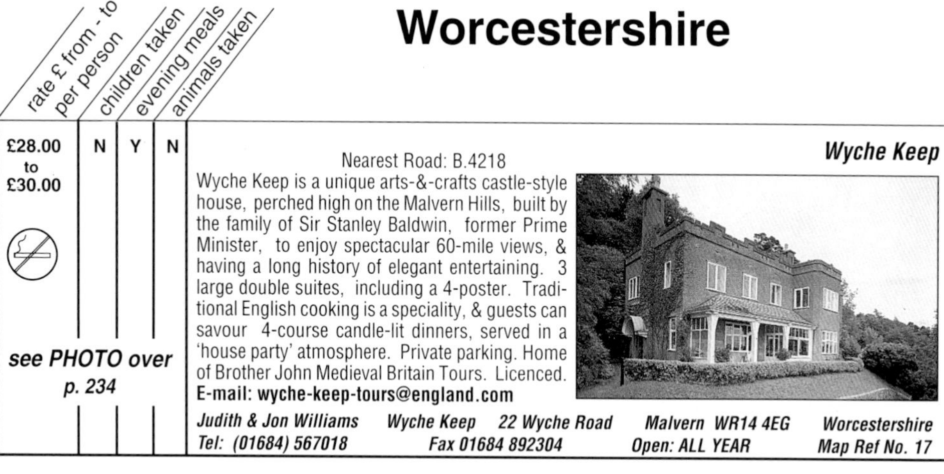

rate £ from - to per person	children taken	evening meals	animals taken	
£28.00 to £30.00	N	Y	N	***Wyche Keep*** Nearest Road: B.4218 Wyche Keep is a unique arts-&-crafts castle-style house, perched high on the Malvern Hills, built by the family of Sir Stanley Baldwin, former Prime Minister, to enjoy spectacular 60-mile views, & having a long history of elegant entertaining. 3 large double suites, including a 4-poster. Traditional English cooking is a speciality, & guests can savour 4-course candle-lit dinners, served in a 'house party' atmosphere. Private parking. Home of Brother John Medieval Britain Tours. Licenced. **E-mail: wyche-keep-tours@england.com**
see PHOTO over p. 234				*Judith & Jon Williams Wyche Keep 22 Wyche Road Malvern WR14 4EG Worcestershire* *Tel: (01684) 567018 Fax 01684 892304 Open: ALL YEAR Map Ref No. 17*

All the establishments mentioned in this guide are members of The Worldwide Bed & Breakfast Association

When booking your accommodation please mention The Best Bed & Breakfast

Wyche Keep. Malvern.

Kent

Kent
(South East)

Kent is best known as "the garden of England". At its heart is a tranquil landscape of apple & cherry orchards, hop-fields & oast-houses, but there are also empty downs, chalk sea-cliffs, rich marshlands, sea ports, castles & the glory of Canterbury Cathedral.

The dramatic chalk ridgeway of the North Downs links the White Cliffs of Dover with the north of the county which extends into the edge of London. It was a trade route in ancient times following the high downs above the Weald, dense forest in those days. It can be followed today & it offers broad views of the now agricultural Weald.

The pilgrims who flocked to Canterbury in the 12th-15th centuries, (colourfully portrayed in Chaucer's Canterbury Tales), probably used the path of the Roman Watling Street rather than the high ridgeway.

Canterbury was the cradle of Christianity in southern England & is by tradition the seat of the Primate of All England. This site, on the River Stour, has been settled since the earliest times & became a Saxon stonghold under King Ethelbert of Kent. He established a church here, but it was in Norman times that the first great building work was carried out, to be continued in stages until the 15th century. The result is a blending of styles with early Norman work, a later Norman choir, a vaulted nave in Gothic style & a great tower of Tudor design. Thomas Becket was murdered on the steps of the Cathedral in 1170. The town retains much of its mediaeval character with half-timbered weavers' cottages, old churches & the twin towers of the west gate.

Two main styles of building give the villages of Kent their special character. The Kentish yeoman's house was the home of the wealthier farmers & is found throughout the county. It is a timber-frame building with white lath & plaster walls & a hipped roof of red tiles. Rather more modest in style is a small weatherboard house, usually painted white or cream. Rolvenden & Groombridge have the typical charm of a Kentish village whilst Tunbridge Wells is an attractive town, with a paved parade known as the Pantiles & excellent antique shops.

There are grand houses & castles throughout the county. Leeds Castle stands in a lake & dates back to the 9th century. It has beautifully landscaped parkland. Knowle House is an impressive Jacobean & Tudor Manor House with rough ragstone walls, & acres of deer-park & woodland.

Kent is easily accessible from the Channel Ports, Gatwick Airport & London.

Leeds Castle.

Kent

Kent Gazeteer

Areas of outstanding natural beauty.
Kent Downs.

Historic Houses & Castles

Aylesford, The Friars - Nr. Maidstone
13th century Friary & shrine of Our Lady, (much restored), 14th century cloisters - original.

Allington Castle -Nr. Maidstone
13th century. One time home of Tudor poet Thomas Wyatt. Restored early 20th century. Icons & Renaissance paintings.

Black Charles - Nr. Sevenoaks
14th century Hall house - Tudor fireplaces, beautiful panelling.

Boughton Monchelsea Place - Nr. Maidstone
Elizabethan Manor House - grey stone battlements - 18th century landscaped park, wonderful views of Weald of Kent.

Chartwell - Westerham
Home of Sir Winston Churchill.
Chiddingstone Castle - Nr. Edenbridge
18th century Gothic revival building encasing old remains of original Manor House - Royal Stuart & Jacobite collection.
Ancient Egyptian collection - Japanese netsuke, etc.

Eyehorne Manor - Hollingbourne
15th century Manor house with 17th century additions.

Cobham Hall - Cobham
16th century house - Gothic & Renaissance - Wyatt interior. Now school for girls.

Fairfield - Eastry, Sandwich
13th-14th centuries - moated castle. Was home of Anne Boleyn. Beautiful gardens with unique collection of classical statuary.

Knole - Sevenoaks
15th century - splendid Jacobean interior - 17th & 18th century furniture. One of the largest private houses in England.

Leeds Castle- Nr. Maidstone
Built in middle of the lake, it was the home of the mediaeval Queens of England.

Lullingstone Castle - Eynsford
14th century mansion house - frequented by Henry VIII & Queen Anne.
Still occupied by descendants of the original owners

Long Barn - Sevenoaks
14th century house - said to be home of William Caxton. Restored by Edwin Lutyens; 16th century barn added to enlarge house. Galleried hall - fine beaming & fireplaces. Lovely gardens created by Sir Harold Nicholson & his wife Vita Sackville-West.

Owletts - Cobham
Carolean house of red brick with plasterwork ceiling & fine staircase.

Owl House - Lamberhurst
16th century cottage, tile hung; said to be home of wool smuggler. Charming gardens.

Penshurst Place - Tonbridge
14th century house with mediaeval Great Hall perfectly preserved.English Gothic. Birthplace of Elizabethan poet, Sir Philip Sidney
Fine staterooms, splendid picture gallery, famous toy museum. Tudor gardens & orchards.

Saltwood Castle - Nr. Hythe
Mediaeval - very fine castle & is privately occupied. Was lived in by Sir Ralph de Broc, murderer of Thomas a Becket.

Squerreys Court - Westerham
Manor house of William & Mary period, with furniture, paintings & tapestries of time. Connections with General Wolfe.

Stoneacre - Otham
15th century yeoman's half-timbered house.

Cathedrals & Churches

Brook (St. Mary)
11th century paintings in this unaltered early Norman church.

Brookland (St. Augustine)
13th century & some later part. Crown-post roofs, detached wooden belfry with conical cap. 12th century lead font.

Canterbury Cathedral
12th century wall paintings, 12th & 13th century stained glass. Very fine Norman crypt. Early perpendicular nave & cloisters which have heraldic bosses. Wonderful central tower.

Charing (St. Peter & St. Paul)
13th & 15th century interior with 15th century tower. 17th century restoration.

Kent

Cobham (St. Mary)
16th century carved & painted tombs - unequalled collection of brasses in county.
Elham (St. Mary the Virgin)
Norman wall with 13th century arcades, perpendicular clerestory. Restored by Eden.
Lullingstone (St. Botolph)
14th century mainly - 16th century wood screen. Painted glass monuments.
Newington-on-the-Street (St. Mary the Virgin)
13th & 14th century - fine tower. 13th century tomb. Wall paintings.
Rochester Cathedral
Norman facade & nave, otherwise early English.
12th century west door. 14th century doorway to Chapter room.
Stone (St. Mary)
13th century - decorated - paintings, 15th century brass, 16th century tomb.
Woodchurch (All Saints)
13th century, having late Norman font & priest's brass of 1320. Arcades alternating octagonal & rounded columns. Triple lancets with banded marble shafting at east end.

Museums & Galleries

Royal Museums - Canterbury
Archaeological, geological, mineralogical exhibits, natural history, pottery & porcelain. Engravings, prints & pictures.
Westgate - Canterbury
Museum of armour, etc. in 14th century gatehouse of city.
Dartford District Museum - Dartford
Roman, Saxon & natural history.
Deal Museum - Deal
Prehistoric & historic antiquities.
Dicken's House Museum - Broadstairs
Personalia of Dickens; prints, costume & Victoriana.
Down House - Downe
The home of Charles Darwin for 40 years, now his memorial & museum.
Dover Museum - Dover
Roman pottery, ceramics, coins, zoology, geology, local history, etc.
Faversham Heritage Society - Faversham
1000 years of history & heritage.
Folkestone Museum & Art Gallery - Folkestone
Archeology, local history & sciences.
Herne Bay Museum - Herne Bay
Stone, Bronze & Early Iron Age specimens. Roman material from Reculver excavations. Items of local & Kentish interest.
Museum & Art Gallery - Maidstone
16th century manor house exhibiting natural history & archaeolgical collections. Costume Gallery, bygones, ceramics, 17th century works by Dutch & Italian painters. Regimental museum

Historic Monuments

Eynsford Castle - Eynsford
12th century castle remains.
Rochester Castle - Rochester
Storied keep - 1126-39
Roman Fort & Anglo-Saxon Church - Reculver
Excavated remains of 3rd century fort & Saxon church.
Little Kit's Coty House - Aylesford
Ruins of burial chambers from 2 long barrows.
Lullingstone Roman Villa - Lullingstone
Roman farmstead excavations.
Roman Fort & Town - Richborough
Roman 'Rutupiae' & fort
Tonbridge Castle - Tonbridge
12th century curtain walls, shell of keep & 14th century gatehouse.
Dover Castle - Dover
Keep built by Henry II in 1180. Outer curtain built 13th century.

Gardens

Chilham Castle Gardens - Nr. Canterbury
25 acre gardens of Jacobean house, laid out by Tradescant.
Lake garden, fine trees & birds of prey. Jousting & mediaeval banquets.
Great Comp Gardens - Nr. Borough Green
Outstanding 7 acre garden with old brick walls.
Owl House Gardens - Lamberhurst
16th century smugglers cottage with beautiful gardens of roses, daffodils & rhododendrons.
S**issinghurst Castl**e Gardens - Sissinghurst
Famous gardens created by Vita Sackville-West around the remains of an Elizabethan mansion.

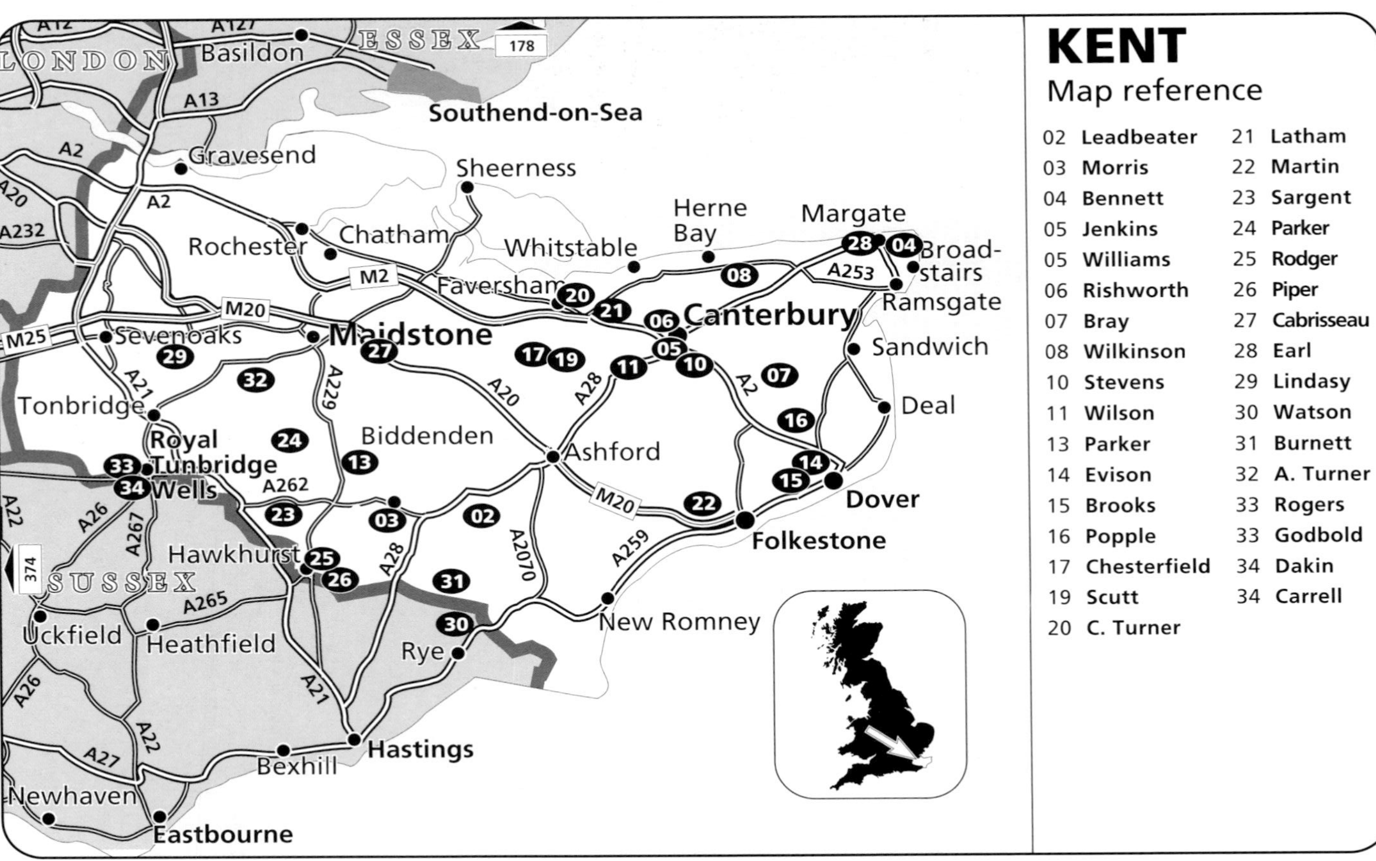
KENT
Map reference
02 Leadbeater
03 Morris
04 Bennett
05 Jenkins
05 Williams
06 Rishworth
07 Bray
08 Wilkinson
10 Stevens
11 Wilson
13 Parker
14 Evison
15 Brooks
16 Popple
17 Chesterfield
19 Scutt
20 C. Turner
21 Latham
22 Martin
23 Sargent
24 Parker
25 Rodger
26 Piper
27 Cabrisseau
28 Earl
29 Lindasy
30 Watson
31 Burnett
32 A. Turner
33 Rogers
33 Godbold
34 Dakin
34 Carrell
LONDON
ESSEX
178
Basildon
Southend-on-Sea
Gravesend
Sheerness
Rochester
Chatham
Whitstable
Herne Bay
Margate
Broad-stairs
Ramsgate
Faversham
Canterbury
Sandwich
Deal
Maidstone
Sevenoaks
Tonbridge
Royal Tunbridge Wells
Biddenden
Ashford
Dover
Folkestone
Hawkhurst
SUSSEX
374
Uckfield
Heathfield
Rye
New Romney
Hastings
Bexhill
Newhaven
Eastbourne
A12
A127
A13
A2
A20
A232
M25
M20
M2
A21
A229
A28
A253
A262
A26
A267
A22
A265
A2070
A259
A27

Kent

rate £ from - to per person	children taken	evening meals	animals taken
£23.50 to £25.00	Y	N	N

VISA: M'CARD:

Shirkoak Farm

Nearest Road: A.28

Lovingly restored 18th-century Georgian farmhouse in 2 acres of beautiful gardens with tennis court. 3 en-suite bedrooms, (2 queen-size doubles & 1 twin). All with T.V. & tea/coffee tray. Elegant dining-room overlooking small lake, drawing-room with oak beams & an inglenook fireplace. Furnished throughout with antiques. Situated in quiet rural setting ideal for Kentish Weald, Sissinghurst Castle, Tenterden, Canterbury & Dover. (M.20 at Ashford only 10 mins' drive.) Children over 10.

E-mail: ShirkoakFarm@aol.com

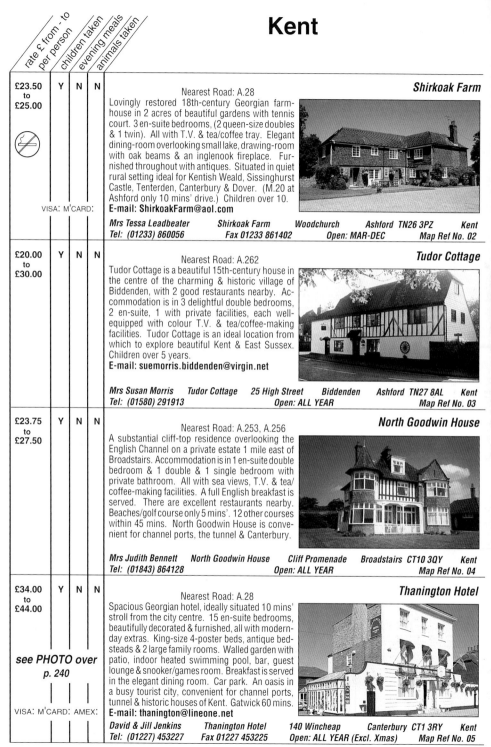

Mrs Tessa Leadbeater *Shirkoak Farm* *Woodchurch* *Ashford TN26 3PZ* *Kent*
Tel: (01233) 860056 *Fax 01233 861402* *Open: MAR-DEC* *Map Ref No. 02*

rate £ from - to per person	children taken	evening meals	animals taken
£20.00 to £30.00	Y	N	N

Tudor Cottage

Nearest Road: A.262

Tudor Cottage is a beautiful 15th-century house in the centre of the charming & historic village of Biddenden, with 2 good restaurants nearby. Accommodation is in 3 delightful double bedrooms, 2 en-suite, 1 with private facilities, each well-equipped with colour T.V. & tea/coffee-making facilities. Tudor Cottage is an ideal location from which to explore beautiful Kent & East Sussex. Children over 5 years.

E-mail: suemorris.biddenden@virgin.net

Mrs Susan Morris *Tudor Cottage* *25 High Street* *Biddenden* *Ashford TN27 8AL* *Kent*
Tel: (01580) 291913 *Open: ALL YEAR* *Map Ref No. 03*

rate £ from - to per person	children taken	evening meals	animals taken
£23.75 to £27.50	Y	N	N

North Goodwin House

Nearest Road: A.253, A.256

A substantial cliff-top residence overlooking the English Channel on a private estate 1 mile east of Broadstairs. Accommodation is in 1 en-suite double bedroom & 1 double & 1 single bedroom with private bathroom. All with sea views, T.V. & tea/coffee-making facilities. A full English breakfast is served. There are excellent restaurants nearby. Beaches/golf course only 5 mins'. 12 other courses within 45 mins. North Goodwin House is convenient for channel ports, the tunnel & Canterbury.

Mrs Judith Bennett *North Goodwin House* *Cliff Promenade* *Broadstairs CT10 3QY* *Kent*
Tel: (01843) 864128 *Open: ALL YEAR* *Map Ref No. 04*

rate £ from - to per person	children taken	evening meals	animals taken
£34.00 to £44.00	Y	N	N

see PHOTO over p. 240

VISA: M'CARD: AMEX:

Thanington Hotel

Nearest Road: A.28

Spacious Georgian hotel, ideally situated 10 mins' stroll from the city centre. 15 en-suite bedrooms, beautifully decorated & furnished, all with modern-day extras. King-size 4-poster beds, antique bedsteads & 2 large family rooms. Walled garden with patio, indoor heated swimming pool, bar, guest lounge & snooker/games room. Breakfast is served in the elegant dining room. Car park. An oasis in a busy tourist city, convenient for channel ports, tunnel & historic houses of Kent. Gatwick 60 mins.

E-mail: thanington@lineone.net

David & Jill Jenkins *Thanington Hotel* *140 Wincheap* *Canterbury CT1 3RY* *Kent*
Tel: (01227) 453227 *Fax 01227 453225* *Open: ALL YEAR (Excl. Xmas)* *Map Ref No. 05*

Thanington Hotel. Canterbury.

Kent

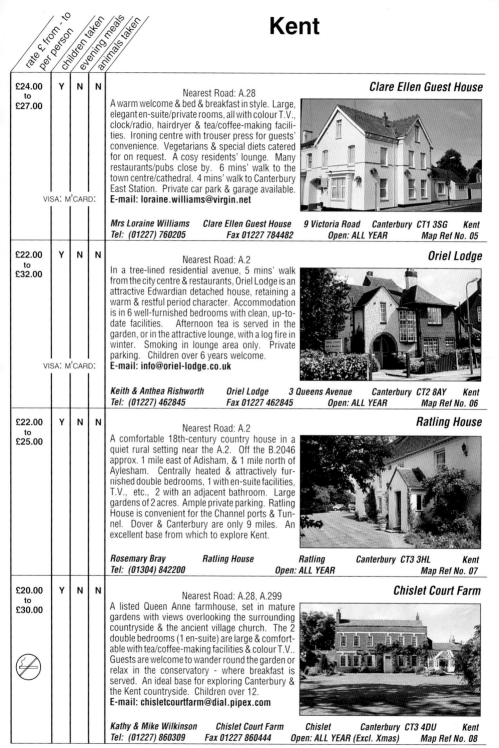

rate £ from - to per person	children taken	evening meals	animals taken
£24.00 to £27.00	Y	N	N

Clare Ellen Guest House

Nearest Road: A.28

A warm welcome & bed & breakfast in style. Large, elegant en-suite/private rooms, all with colour T.V., clock/radio, hairdryer & tea/coffee-making facilities. Ironing centre with trouser press for guests' convenience. Vegetarians & special diets catered for on request. A cosy residents' lounge. Many restaurants/pubs close by. 6 mins' walk to the town centre/cathedral. 4 mins' walk to Canterbury East Station. Private car park & garage available.

E-mail: loraine.williams@virgin.net

VISA: M'CARD:

Mrs Loraine Williams Clare Ellen Guest House 9 Victoria Road Canterbury CT1 3SG Kent
Tel: (01227) 760205 Fax 01227 784482 Open: ALL YEAR Map Ref No. 05

rate £ from - to per person	children taken	evening meals	animals taken
£22.00 to £32.00	Y	N	N

Oriel Lodge

Nearest Road: A.2

In a tree-lined residential avenue, 5 mins' walk from the city centre & restaurants, Oriel Lodge is an attractive Edwardian detached house, retaining a warm & restful period character. Accommodation is in 6 well-furnished bedrooms with clean, up-to-date facilities. Afternoon tea is served in the garden, or in the attractive lounge, with a log fire in winter. Smoking in lounge area only. Private parking. Children over 6 years welcome.

E-mail: info@oriel-lodge.co.uk

VISA: M'CARD:

Keith & Anthea Rishworth Oriel Lodge 3 Queens Avenue Canterbury CT2 8AY Kent
Tel: (01227) 462845 Fax 01227 462845 Open: ALL YEAR Map Ref No. 06

rate £ from - to per person	children taken	evening meals	animals taken
£22.00 to £25.00	Y	N	N

Ratling House

Nearest Road: A.2

A comfortable 18th-century country house in a quiet rural setting near the A.2. Off the B.2046 approx. 1 mile east of Adisham, & 1 mile north of Aylesham. Centrally heated & attractively furnished double bedrooms, 1 with en-suite facilities, T.V., etc., 2 with an adjacent bathroom. Large gardens of 2 acres. Ample private parking. Ratling House is convenient for the Channel ports & Tunnel. Dover & Canterbury are only 9 miles. An excellent base from which to explore Kent.

Rosemary Bray Ratling House Ratling Canterbury CT3 3HL Kent
Tel: (01304) 842200 Open: ALL YEAR Map Ref No. 07

rate £ from - to per person	children taken	evening meals	animals taken
£20.00 to £30.00	Y	N	N

Chislet Court Farm

Nearest Road: A.28, A.299

A listed Queen Anne farmhouse, set in mature gardens with views overlooking the surrounding countryside & the ancient village church. The 2 double bedrooms (1 en-suite) are large & comfortable with tea/coffee-making facilities & colour T.V.. Guests are welcome to wander round the garden or relax in the conservatory - where breakfast is served. An ideal base for exploring Canterbury & the Kent countryside. Children over 12.

E-mail: chisletcourtfarm@dial.pipex.com

Kathy & Mike Wilkinson Chislet Court Farm Chislet Canterbury CT3 4DU Kent
Tel: (01227) 860309 Fax 01227 860444 Open: ALL YEAR (Excl. Xmas) Map Ref No. 08

Iffin Farmhouse. Canterbury.

rate £ from - to per person	children taken	evening meals	animals taken
£25.00 to £30.00	Y	N	N

Iffin Farmhouse

Nearest Road: A.2

A warm welcome awaits you in this old 18th-century farmhouse, renovated to a very high standard. 3 double bedrooms, each with views to the garden & orchards, T.V., tea/coffee-making facilities & an en-suite/private bathroom. Enjoy a full English breakfast, served in a lovely dining room. Set in 10 acres of gardens, paddocks & orchards, Iffin Farmhouse (only 6 mins' drive from Canterbury) is perfect for touring Kent. Children over 5 years. Evening meals available Nov - Mar.

E-mail: iffinfarmhouse@btinternet.com

see PHOTO over p. 242

Rosemary Stevens Iffin Farmhouse Iffin Lane Canterbury CT4 7BE Kent
Tel: (01227) 462776 Fax 01227 462776 Open: ALL YEAR Map Ref No. 10

rate £ from - to per person	children taken	evening meals	animals taken
£23.00 to £35.00	Y	N	N

Stour Farm

Nearest Road: A.28

Jane & Jeremy Wilson welcome you to their delightful barn conversion overlooking the River Stour on the edge of Chartham village, 3 miles from Canterbury. 2 double en-suite bedrooms with T.V. & tea/coffee-making facilities. Breakfast is served in the dining room or, weather permitting, on the sun terrace overlooking the river. Good restaurants & pubs nearby. Parking. Convenient for the ferry & channel tunnel ports. Many gardens, walks & golf courses within easy reach. Children over 12.

E-mail: info@stourfarm.co.uk

VISA: M'CARD:

Jeremy & Jane Wilson Stour Farm Riverside Chartham Canterbury CT4 7NX Kent
Tel: (01227) 731977 Fax 01227 731977 Open: MAR - NOV Map Ref No. 11

rate £ from - to per person	children taken	evening meals	animals taken
£38.00 to £38.00	N	Y	N

Maplehurst Mill

Nearest Road: A.228

Maplehurst Mill is a beautiful water mill, attached to a medieval mill house & standing in 11 acres of landscaped gardens. Offering 5 attractively furnished guest rooms (incl. 1 4-poster), with en-suite bathroom, T.V., etc.. Each has views over the water & the surrounding countryside. A breakfast & candlelit dinner are served in the medieval miller's house, in the beamed dining room with inglenook, antiques & silver. A delightful home, where a warm welcome awaits you. Children over 12.

E-mail: maplehurst@clara.net

VISA: M'CARD:

Heather & Kenneth Parker Maplehurst Mill Mill Lane Frittenden Cranbrook TN17 2DT Kent
Tel: (01580) 852203 Fax 01580 852117 Open: ALL YEAR Map Ref No. 13

rate £ from - to per person	children taken	evening meals	animals taken
£32.50 to £40.00	Y	N	N

The Old Vicarage

Nearest Road: A.20

Many guests are totally surprised by the peaceful atmosphere & commanding position of this house, given its closeness to Dover. This is a beautiful country house built around 1870 & now totally restored, yet retaining many original features. It is elegantly furnished with antiques & provides everything for your stay to the very highest standards, 2 en-suite bedrooms & 1 with private bathroom. Excellent base for touring east Kent. 2 miles ferry ports/9 miles Channel Tunnel. Parking.

E-mail: vicarage@csi.com

see PHOTO over p. 244

VISA: M'CARD:

Mrs Judith P. Evison The Old Vicarage Chilverton Elms Hougham Dover CT15 7AS Kent
Tel: (01304) 210668 Fax 01304 225118 Open: ALL YEAR Map Ref No. 14

The Old Vicarage. Chilverton Elms.

Kent

rate £ from - to per person | children taken | evening meals | animals taken

rate £ from - to per person	children taken	evening meals	animals taken
£25.00 to £28.00	Y	N	N

Rose Hill Farm

Nearest Road: A.20

A sympathetically restored 17th-century farmhouse in peaceful, unspoilt countryside. 1 1/2 acres of beautiful gardens, croquet lawn, swimming pool - a joy for garden lovers & an excellent centre for touring, walking, sailing, golf & visiting the numerous castles, historic houses & gardens of Kent. Only 10 mins' drive to Dover/Channel Tunnel. Accommodation is in 2 comfortable en-suite bedrooms with colour T.V. & tea/coffee-making facilities. A charming home.

Diana Brooks Rose Hill Farm Mill Lane West Hougham Dover CT15 7BD Kent
Tel: (01304) 240609 Fax 01304 240609 Open: ALL YEAR Map Ref No. 15

rate £ from - to per person	children taken	evening meals	animals taken
£22.00 to £25.00	Y	Y	N

VISA: M'CARD:

Sunshine Cottage

Nearest Road: A.2

A 17th-century, Grade II listed cottage, overlooking Shepherdswell village green, with a wealth of beams, an inglenook fireplace & 2 lounges. Tastefully furnished, & with a homely atmosphere. 6 attractive bedrooms. A pretty garden & courtyard are available to guests. Good home-cooking & home-made preserves. Good food also available at a nearby pub. Shepherdswell is situated halfway between Canterbury & Dover, 25 mins' from the Channel Tunnel. BR station 5 mins' walk away.

E-mail: sunshinecottage@shepherdswell.fsnet.co.uk

Barry & Lyn Popple Sunshine Cottage The Green Shepherdswell Dover CT15 7LQ Kent
Tel: (01304) 831359 Open: ALL YEAR Map Ref No. 16

rate £ from - to per person	children taken	evening meals	animals taken
£28.00 to £32.00	Y	Y	N

see PHOTO over *p. 246*

Frith Farm House

Nearest Road: A.20, A.2

This lovingly restored Georgian farmhouse with orchards, gardens & indoor swimming pool is situated on the North Downs. Extremely peaceful & well-positioned for visiting the historic houses, castles & cathedrals of Kent. Accommodation in beautifully furnished en-suite rooms together with breakfasts that include homemade bread & preserves. 3 nights or more - 10% discount. Self-catering cottage available. A warm welcome awaits all to this delightful home. Children over 10.

E-mail: markham@frith.force9.co.uk

Markham & Susan Chesterfield Frith Farm House Otterden Faversham ME13 0DD Kent
Tel: (01795) 890701 Fax 01795 890009 Open: ALL YEAR Map Ref No. 17

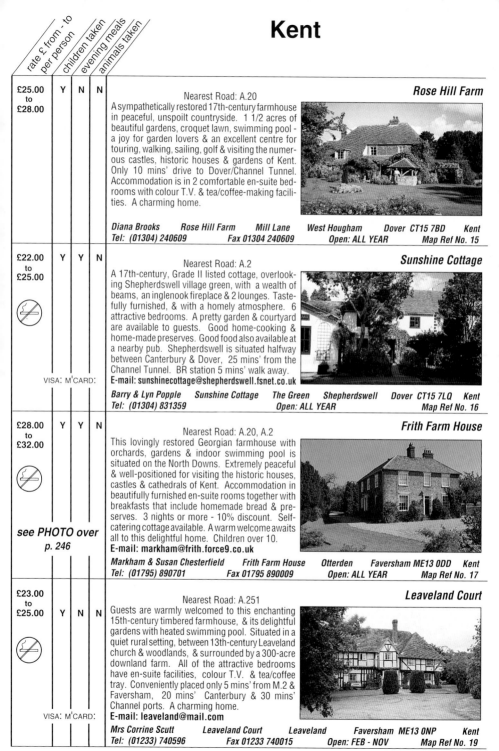

rate £ from - to per person	children taken	evening meals	animals taken
£23.00 to £25.00	Y	N	N

VISA: M'CARD:

Leaveland Court

Nearest Road: A.251

Guests are warmly welcomed to this enchanting 15th-century timbered farmhouse, & its delightful gardens with heated swimming pool. Situated in a quiet rural setting, between 13th-century Leaveland church & woodlands, & surrounded by a 300-acre downland farm. All of the attractive bedrooms have en-suite facilities, colour T.V. & tea/coffee tray. Conveniently placed only 5 mins' from M.2 & Faversham, 20 mins' Canterbury & 30 mins' Channel ports. A charming home.

E-mail: leaveland@mail.com

Mrs Corrine Scutt Leaveland Court Leaveland Faversham ME13 0NP Kent
Tel: (01233) 740596 Fax 01233 740015 Open: FEB - NOV Map Ref No. 19

Frith Farm House. Otterden.

rate £ from - to per person	children taken	evening meals	animals taken

Preston Lea

£25.00 to £30.00	Y	N	N

Nearest Road: A.2

A warm welcome & tea on arrival are guaranteed in this beautiful, elegant private house, set in secluded gardens on the edge of Faversham. Spacious en-suite bedrooms, sunny, with garden views, antique furniture & offering every comfort. The lovely drawing-rooms, pannelled dining-room & gardens are available to guests. Help & advice is on hand from your caring hosts. Delicious breakfasts. Good restaurants nearby, beautiful countryside, beaches & places of interest to visit.

E-mail: preston.lea@which.net

VISA: M'CARD:

Alan & Catherine Turner Preston Lea Canterbury Road Faversham ME13 8XA Kent
Tel: (01795) 535266 Fax 01795 533388 Open: ALL YEAR Map Ref No. 20

Tenterden House

£20.00 to £30.00	Y	N	N

Nearest Road: A.2, M.2

Stay in one of the en-suite bedrooms (1 double, 1 twin) in this delightful gardener's cottage & stroll through the shrubbery to the 16th-century dining room in the main house, for a traditional English breakfast, beneath the dragon beam. Close to Canterbury, Whitstable & the Channel Ports, it makes an ideal base for exploring Kent, then walk to one of the historic inns in the village for your evening meal. Tea/coffee-making facilities are provided as well as secure off-road parking.

Prudence Latham Tenterden House 209 The Street Boughton Faversham ME13 9BL Kent
Tel: (01227) 751593 Open: ALL YEAR Map Ref No. 21

Pigeonwood House

£22.00 to £28.00	Y	N	N

Nearest Road: A.260

Pigeonwood House is the original, 18th-century farmhouse of the surrounding area, positioned in rural tranquillity in chalk downland. The 2 attractive guest bedrooms have beautiful panoramic views over the surrounding countryside & many guests return for the homely, relaxing atmosphere. Pigeonwood House is ideally situated for touring historic Kent as well as having the channel tunnel & ports close by. Children over 5 years.

E-mail: samandmary@aol.com

Mrs Mary Martin Pigeonwood House Grove Farm Arpinge Folkestone CT18 8AQ Kent
Tel: (01303) 891111 Fax 01303 891019 Open: ALL YEAR Map Ref No. 22

Mount House

£25.00 to £25.00	Y	N	N

Nearest Road: A.262

Mount House is an 18th-century Grade II listed country house, which is surrounded by 2 acres of gardens. The house has been sympathetically restored & is tastefully decorated in keeping with its period character. It is set in unspoilt countryside within the designated High Weald conservation area. 2 elegant guest bedrooms, each with an en-suite/private bathroom, T.V. & tea/coffee-making facilities. Sissinghurst, Scotney & Great Dixter gardens are within easy reach. Children over 10.

E-mail: davidmargaretsargent@compuserve.com

David & Margaret Sargent Mount House Ranters Lane Goudhurst TN17 1HN Kent
Tel: (01580) 211230 Open: APR - SEPT Map Ref No. 23

Conghurst Farm. Hawkhurst.

rate £ from - to per person	children taken	evening meals	animals taken
£25.00 to £35.00	Y	N	Y

West Winchet

Nearest Road: A.262

West Winchet is the west wing of a Victorian mansion surrounded by parkland in a secluded & peaceful setting. 2 beautifully decorated rooms, 1 double with private bathroom & 1 twin with en-suite shower. Each with T.V. & tea/coffee, etc. Both rooms are on the ground floor, & the twin-bedded room has French windows onto the terrace & into the garden. A magnificent drawing room. Ideal for touring Kent & East Sussex. 2 1/2 miles mainline station (London 55 mins). Children over 5.

E-mail: annieparker@jpa-ltd.co.uk

Jeremy & Annie Parker West Winchet Winchet Hill Goudhurst TN17 1JX Kent
Tel: (01580) 212024 Fax 01580 212250 Open: ALL YEAR Map Ref No. 24

rate £ from - to per person	children taken	evening meals	animals taken
£27.50 to £27.50	Y	N	N

The Wren's Nest

Nearest Road: A.21

Built in traditional Kentish style, with oak beams & vaulted ceilings, The Wren's Nest suites have been designed specifically for the comfort & pleasure of guests. The suites are spacious & beautifully furnished & are well-equipped with T.V., tea/coffee-making facilities, tourist information literature, etc. & en-suite bathrooms. The suites are entered via their own front door allowing absolute privacy. Full English breakfasts are served in the main house. An idyllic rural setting & well-placed for touring, walking & birdwatching. Children over 10.

Mrs Lynne Rodger The Wren's Nest Hastings Road Hawkhurst TN18 4RT Kent
Tel: (01580) 754919 Fax 01580 754919 Open: ALL YEAR Map Ref No. 25

rate £ from - to per person	children taken	evening meals	animals taken
£25.00 to £28.00	N	Y	N

see PHOTO over p. 248

VISA: M'CARD:

Conghurst Farm

Nearest Road: A.268

Set in peaceful, totally unspoilt countryside, Conghurst Farm offers a perfect spot for a restful holiday. Within easy reach of all the marvellous houses & gardens that this part of the country has to offer. Accommodation is in 3 very comfortable bedrooms, all with en-suite/private bathrooms. There is a drawing room, a separate T.V. room &, in the summer, a delightful garden for guests to enjoy. An ideal base from which to explore Kent.

E-mail: rosa@conghurst.co.uk

Mrs Rosemary Piper Conghurst Farm Hawkhurst TN18 4RW Kent
Tel: (01580) 753331 Fax 01580 754579 Open: FEB - NOV Map Ref No. 26

rate £ from - to per person	children taken	evening meals	animals taken
£30.00 to £35.00	N	Y	N

VISA: M'CARD: AMEX:

Willington Court

Nearest Road: A.20

Willington Court is a Grade II listed Waldean/Tudor building offering elegant accommodation, fine food & congenial hosts. There are 8 bedrooms, all are en-suite & are well-equipped with comfort in mind. Meals are prepared using only the best ingredients (organic when possible). Dinner is complemented by wine from the reputed cellar. Easy access to London, Dover & the Channel Tunnel. Conducted tours in luxury of London, Calais, Lille & Paris are available. Children over 12.

E-mail: willington@maidstone.prestel.co.uk

Sylvette Cabrisseau Willington Court Willington Street Maidstone ME15 8JW Kent
Tel: (01622) 738885 Fax 01622 631790 Open: ALL YEAR Map Ref No. 27

Jordans. Plaxtol.

Kent

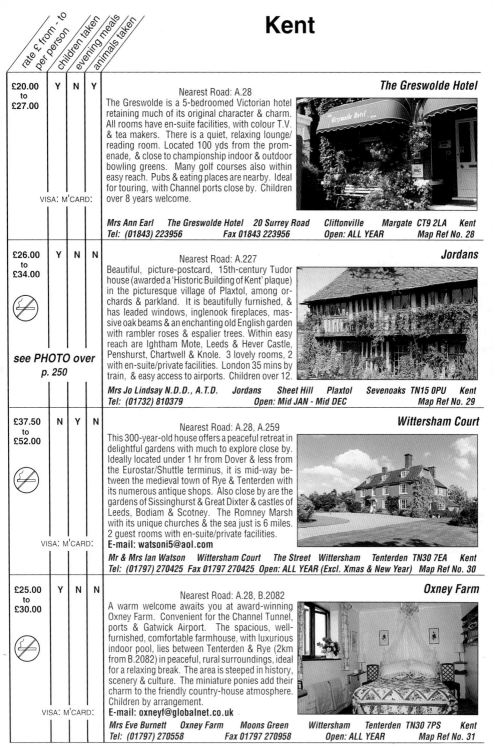

rate £ from - to per person	children taken	evening meals	animals taken
£20.00 to £27.00	Y	N	Y

VISA: M'CARD:

The Greswolde Hotel

Nearest Road: A.28

The Greswolde is a 5-bedroomed Victorian hotel retaining much of its original character & charm. All rooms have en-suite facilities, with colour T.V. & tea makers. There is a quiet, relaxing lounge/ reading room. Located 100 yds from the promenade, & close to championship indoor & outdoor bowling greens. Many golf courses also within easy reach. Pubs & eating places are nearby. Ideal for touring, with Channel ports close by. Children over 8 years welcome.

Mrs Ann Earl The Greswolde Hotel 20 Surrey Road Cliftonville Margate CT9 2LA Kent
Tel: (01843) 223956 Fax 01843 223956 Open: ALL YEAR Map Ref No. 28

rate £ from - to per person	children taken	evening meals	animals taken
£26.00 to £34.00	Y	N	N

see PHOTO over p. 250

Jordans

Nearest Road: A.227

Beautiful, picture-postcard, 15th-century Tudor house (awarded a 'Historic Building of Kent' plaque) in the picturesque village of Plaxtol, among orchards & parkland. It is beautifully furnished, & has leaded windows, inglenook fireplaces, massive oak beams & an enchanting old English garden with rambler roses & espalier trees. Within easy reach are Ightham Mote, Leeds & Hever Castle, Penshurst, Chartwell & Knole. 3 lovely rooms, 2 with en-suite/private facilities. London 35 mins by train, & easy access to airports. Children over 12.

Mrs Jo Lindsay N.D.D., A.T.D. Jordans Sheet Hill Plaxtol Sevenoaks TN15 0PU Kent
Tel: (01732) 810379 Open: Mid JAN - Mid DEC Map Ref No. 29

rate £ from - to per person	children taken	evening meals	animals taken
£37.50 to £52.00	N	Y	N

VISA: M'CARD:

Wittersham Court

Nearest Road: A.28, A.259

This 300-year-old house offers a peaceful retreat in delightful gardens with much to explore close by. Ideally located under 1 hr from Dover & less from the Eurostar/Shuttle terminus, it is mid-way between the medieval town of Rye & Tenterden with its numerous antique shops. Also close by are the gardens of Sissinghurst & Great Dixter & castles of Leeds, Bodiam & Scotney. The Romney Marsh with its unique churches & the sea just is 6 miles. 2 guest rooms with en-suite/private facilities.

E-mail: watsoni5@aol.com

Mr & Mrs Ian Watson Wittersham Court The Street Wittersham Tenterden TN30 7EA Kent
Tel: (01797) 270425 Fax 01797 270425 Open: ALL YEAR (Excl. Xmas & New Year) Map Ref No. 30

rate £ from - to per person	children taken	evening meals	animals taken
£25.00 to £30.00	Y	N	N

VISA: M'CARD:

Oxney Farm

Nearest Road: A.28, B.2082

A warm welcome awaits you at award-winning Oxney Farm. Convenient for the Channel Tunnel, ports & Gatwick Airport. The spacious, well-furnished, comfortable farmhouse, with luxurious indoor pool, lies between Tenterden & Rye (2km from B.2082) in peaceful, rural surroundings, ideal for a relaxing break. The area is steeped in history, scenery & culture. The miniature ponies add their charm to the friendly country-house atmosphere. Children by arrangement.

E-mail: oxneyf@globalnet.co.uk

Mrs Eve Burnett Oxney Farm Moons Green Wittersham Tenterden TN30 7PS Kent
Tel: (01797) 270558 Fax 01797 270958 Open: ALL YEAR Map Ref No. 31

The Old Parsonage. Frant.

rate £ from - to per person	children taken	evening meals	animals taken
£27.50 to £31.00	N	N	N

Nearest Road: A.26

A warm, friendly welcome & imaginative cooking is to be found in this beautiful 19th-century oast. An en-suite bedroom in the barn & 2 roundel bedrooms provide very comfortable accommodation. The house is furnished with interesting antiques, & the lovely garden overlooks open country. Excellent communications make it an ideal base for visiting many historic houses & gardens. London 40 mins by rail. Children over 12 years welcome. Evening meals by arrangement.

E-mail: denis@leavers-oast.freeserve.co.uk

Mrs Anne G. Turner Leavers Oast Stanford Lane Hadlow Tonbridge TN11 0JN Kent
Tel: (01732) 850924 Fax 01732 850924 Open: ALL YEAR Map Ref No. 32

Ash Tree Cottage

rate £ from - to per person	children taken	evening meals	animals taken
£23.50 to £27.00	Y	N	N

Nearest Road: A.21

Ashtree Cottage is situated in a quiet private road just above the famous Pantiles, & within a few minutes' walk of the high street & station. There are 2 charming & attractively furnished bedrooms with en-suite bathrooms, radio, T.V., tea/coffee-making facilities & plenty of tourist information. There is an excellent choice of restaurants & country pubs nearby, & many places of interest are within easy reach. Children over 8 years.

E-mail: rogersashtree@excite.co.uk

Richard & Sue Rogers Ash Tree Cottage 7 Eden Road Tunbridge Wells TN1 1TS Kent
Tel: (01892) 541317 Fax 01892 616770 Open: ALL YEAR (Excl. Xmas & New Year) Map Ref No. 33

The Old Parsonage

rate £ from - to per person	children taken	evening meals	animals taken
£33.00 to £38.00	Y	N	Y

see PHOTO over p. 252

VISA: M'CARD:

Nearest Road: A.267

This award-winning country house is peacefully situated by the church in pretty Frant village with its 2 pubs & restaurant nearby. Overlooking Lord Abergavenny's deer park on one side & the church on the other, this Georgian house provides superb accommodation including en-suite bedrooms, antique-furnished reception rooms & a flower-filled conservatory. Short drive to 15 historic houses & gardens. Gatwick 40 mins. Heathrow 70 mins. London 45 mins by train. Children over 7 years.

E-mail: oldparson@aol.com

Mary & Tony Dakin The Old Parsonage Church Lane Frant Tunbridge Wells TN3 9DX Kent
Tel: (01892) 750773 Fax 01892 750773 Open: ALL YEAR Map Ref No. 34

Rowden House Farm

rate £ from - to per person	children taken	evening meals	animals taken
£24.00 to £28.00	Y	N	N

Nearest Road: A.267

A delightful Elizabethan house, listed as of architectural interest, standing in 20 acres, with sheep, horses, dogs & chickens. Surrounded by the beautiful, rolling, wooded countryside of Sussex, it is perfectly placed for visiting the stately homes & towns of Kent & Sussex. There is 1 twin-bedded room, with private bathroom, & 2 singles with washbasins. All have tea/coffee-making facilities. An attractive drawing room, with T.V.. Gatwick 1 hour, London 1 1/4 hours. Children over 10.

Carolyn Carrell Rowden House Farm Frant Tunbridge Wells TN3 9HS Kent
Tel: (01892) 750259 Open: APR - OCT Map Ref No. 34

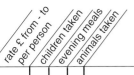

Kent

Danehurst House	rate £ from - to per person	children taken	evening meals	animals taken
Nearest Road: A.264 Danehurst is a charming gabled house in a village setting in the heart of Kent. The tastefully furnished bedrooms afford excellent accommodation, & a delicious breakfast is served in the Victorian conservatory. Angela & Michael are delighted to welcome you to their home & will ensure that your stay is relaxing & enjoyable. Private parking available. Children over 8 years. (Please note Danehurst is closed the last week in August.) **E-mail: danehurst@zoom.co.uk**	£25.00 to £60.00	Y	N	N
	see PHOTO over p. 255			
Mr & Mrs M. Godbold Danehurst House 41 Lower Green Road Rusthall Tunbridge Wells TN4 8TW *Tel: (01892) 527739 Fax 01892 514804 Open: ALL YEAR (Excl. Xmas) Map Ref No. 33*	VISA:	M'CARD:	AMEX:	

All the establishments mentioned in this guide are members of The Worldwide Bed & Breakfast Association

When booking your accommodation please mention The Best Bed & Breakfast

Danehurst. Rustall.

Leicestershire, Nottinghamshire & Rutland

Leicestershire (East Midlands)

Rural Leicestershire is rich in grazing land, a peaceful, undramatic landscape broken up by the waterways that flow through in the south of the county.

The River Avon passes on its way to Stratford, running by 17th century Stanford Hall & its motorcycle museum. The Leicester section of the Grand Union Canal was once very important for the transportation of goods from the factories of the Midlands to London Docks. It passes through a fascinating series of multiple locks at Foxton. The decorative barges, the 'narrow boats' are pleasure craft these days rather than the lifeblood of the closed community of boat people who lived & worked out their lives on the canals.

Rutland was formerly England's smallest county, but was absorbed into East Leicestershire in the 1970's. Recently, once again, it has become a county in its' own right. Rutland Water, is one of Europe's largest reservoirs & an attractive setting for sailing, fishing or enjoying a trip on the pleasure cruiser. There is also the Rutland Theatre at Tolethorpe Hall, where a summer season of Shakespeare's plays is presented in the open air.

Melton Mowbray is famous for its pork pies & it is also the centre of Stilton cheese country. The "King of Cheeses" is made mainly in the Vale of Belvoir where Leicestershire meets Nottinghamshire, & the battlements & turrets of Belvoir Castle overlook the scene from its hill-top.

To the north-west the Charnwood Forest area is pleasantly wooded & the deer park at Bradgate surrounding the ruined home of Lady Jane Grey, England's nine-day queen, is a popular attraction.

Nottinghamshire (East Midlands)

Nottinghamshire has a diversity of landscape from forest to farmland, from coal mines to industrial areas.

The north of the county is dominated by the expanse of Sherwood Forest, smaller now than in the time of legendary Robin Hood & his Merry Men, but still a lovely old woodland of Oak & Birch.

The Dukeries are so called because of the numerous ducal houses built in the area & there is beautiful parkland on these great estates that can be visited. Clumber Park, for instance has a huge lake & a double avenue of Limes.

Newstead Abbey was a mediaeval priory converted into the Byron family home in the 16th century. It houses the poet Byron's manuscripts & possessions & is set in wonderful gardens.

More modest is the terraced house in Eastwood, where D.H. Lawrence was born into the mining community on which his novels are based.

Nottingham was recorded in the Domesday Book as a thriving community & that tradition continues. It was here that Arkwright perfected his cotton-spinning machinery & went on to develop steam as a power source for industry.

Textiles, shoes, bicycles & tobacco are all famous Nottingham products, & the story of Nottingham Lace can be discovered at the Lace Hall, housed in a former church.

Nottingham Castle, high on Castle Rock, was built & destroyed & rebuilt many times during its history. It now houses the city's Art Gallery & Museum. The Castle towers over the ancient 'Trip to Jerusalem' Inn, said to be so named because crusaders stopped there for a drink on their way to fight in the Holy Land.

Leicestershire, Nottinghamshire & Rutland

Leicestershire Gazeteer

Areas of outstanding natural beauty.
Charnwood Forest, Rutland Water.

Historic Houses & Castles

Belvoir Castle - Nr. Grantham
Overlooking the Vale of Belvoir, castle rebuilt in 1816, with many special events including jousting tournaments. Home of the Duke of Rutland since Henry VIII. Paintings, furniture, historic armoury, military museums, magnificent stateroom.

Belvoir Castle

Belgrave Hall - Leicester
18th century Queen Anne house - furnishing of 18th & 19th centuries.
Langton Hall - Nr. Market Harborough
Privately occupied - perfect English country house from mediaeval times - drawing rooms have 18th century Venetian lace.
Oakham Castle - Oakham
Norman banqueting hall of late 12th C.
Stanford Hall - Nr Lutterworth
17th century William & Mary house - collection of Stuart relics & pictures, antiques & costumes of family from Elizabeth I onward. Motor cycle museum.
Stapleford Park - Nr. Melton Mowbray
Old wing dated 1500, restored 1663. Extended to mansion in 1670. Collection of pictures, tapestries, furniture & Balston's Staffordshire portrait figures of Victorian age.

Cathedrals & Churches

Breedon-on-the-Hill (St. Mary & St. Hardulph)
Norman & 13th century. Jacobean canopied pew, 18th century carvings.
Empingham (St. Peter)
14th century west tower, front & crocketed spire. Early English interior - double piscina, triple sedilla.
Lyddington (St. Andrew)
Perpendicular in the main - mediaeval wall paintings & brasses.
Staunton Harol (Holy Trinity)
17th century - quite unique Cromwellian church - painted ceilings.

Museums & Galleries

Bosworth Battlefield Visitor Centre - Nr Market Bosworth
Exhibitions, models, battlefield trails at site of 1485 Battle of Bosworth where Richard III lost his life & crown to Henry.
Leicestershire Museum of Technology - Leicester
Beam engines, steam shovel, knitting machinery & other aspects of the county's industrial past.
Leicester Museum & Art Gallery - Leicester
Painting collection.
18th & 19th century, watercolours & drawings, 20th century French paintings, Old Master & modern prints.
English silver & ceramics, special exhibitions.
Jewry Wall Museum & Site - Leicester
Roman wall & baths site adjoining museum of archaeology.

Leicestershire, Nottinghamshire & Rutland

Melton Carnegie Museum-Melton Mowbray
Displays of Stilton cheese, pork pies & other aspects of the past & present life of the area.
Rutland County Museum - Oakham
Domestic & agricultural life of Rutland, England's smallest county.
Donnington Collection of Single-Seater Racing Cars - Castle Donington
Large collection of grand prix racing cars & racing motorcycles, adjoining Donington Park racing circuit..
Wygson's House Museum of Costume - Leicestershire
Costume, accessories & shop settings in late mediaeval buildings.
The Bellfoundry Museum - Loughborough
Moulding, casting, tuning & fitting of bells, with conducted tours of bellfoundry.

Historic Monuments

The Castle - Ashby-de-la-Zouch
14th century with tower added in 15th century.
Kirby Muxloe Castle - Kirby Muxloe
15th century fortified manor house with moat ruins.

Other things to see & do

Rutland Farm Park - Oakham
Rare & commercial breeds of livestock in 18 acres of park & woodland, with early 19th century farm buildings.
Stoughton Farm Park - Nr. Leicester
Shire horses, rare breeds, small animals & modern 140 dairy herd. Milking demonstrations, farm museum, woodland walks. Adventure playground.
Twycross Zoo - Nr. Atherstone
Gorillas, orang-utans, chimpanzees, gibbons, elephants, giraffes, lions & many other animals.
The Battlefield Line Nr. Market Bosworth
Steam railway & collection of railway relics, adjoining Bosworth Battlefield.
Great Central Railway - Loughborough
Steam railway over 5-mile route in Charnwood Forest area, with steam & diesel museum.
Rutland Railway Museum - Nr. Oakham
Industrial steam & diesel locomotives.

Nottinghamshire Gazeteer

Historic Houses & Castles

Holme Pierrepont Hall - Nr. Nottingham
Outstanding red brick Tudor manor, in continuous family ownership, with 19th century courtyard garden.
Newark Castle - Newark
Dramatic castle ruins on riverside site, once one of the most important castles of the north.
Newstead Abbey - Nr. Mansfield
Priory converted to country mansion, home of poet Lord Byron with many of his possessions & manuscripts on display. Beautiful parkland, lakes & gardens.
Nottingham Castle - Nottingham
17th century residence on site of mediaeval castle.
Fine collections of ceramics, silver, Nottingham alabaster carvings, local historical displays. Art gallery. Special exhibitions & events.
Wollaton Hall - Nottingham
Elizabethan mansion now housing natural history exhibits. Stands in deer park, with Industrial Museum in former stables, illustrating the city's bicycle, hosiery, lace, pharmaceutical & other industries.

Cathedrals & Churches

Egmanton (St. Mary)
Magnificent interior by Comper. Norman doorway & font. Canopied rood screen, 17th century altar.
Newark (St. Mary Magdalene)
15th century. 2 painted panels of "Dance of Death". Reredos by Comper.
Southwell Cathedral
Norman nave, unvaulted, fine early English choir. Decorated pulpitum, 6 canopied stalls, fine misericords. Octagonal chapter house..
Terseval (St. Catherine)
12th century - interior 17th century unrestored.

Museums & Galleries

Castlegate Museum - Nottingham
Row of Georgian terraced houses showing costume & textile collection.
Lace making equipment & lace collection.

Leicestershire, Nottinghamshire & Rutland

Nottingham Castle Museum - Nottingham
Collections of ceramics, glass & silver. Alabaster carvings.

D.H. Lawrence Birthplace - Eastwood
Home of the novelist & poet, as it would have been at time of his birth, 1885.

Millgate Museum of Social & Folk Life - Newark
Local social & folk life, with craft workshops.

Brewhouse Yard Museum - Nottingham
Daily life in Nottingham, displayed in 17th century cottages & rock-cut cellars.

The Lace Hall - Nottingham
The story of Nottingham Lace audio-visual display & exhibition with lace shops, in fine converted church.

Museum of Costume & Textiles - Nottingham
Costumes, lace & textiles on display in fine Georgian buildings.

Bassetlaw Museum - Retford
Local history of north Nottinghamshire.

Canal Museum - Nottinghamshire
History of the River Trent & canal history, in former canal warehouse.

Ruddington Framework Knitters' Museum - Ruddington
Unique complex of early 19th-century framework knitters' buildings with over 20 hand frames in restored workshop.

Other things to see & do

The Tales of Robin Hood - Nottingham
A 'flight to adventure' from mediaeval Nottingham to Sherwood Forest through the tales of the world's most famous outlaw.

Clumber Park - Nr. Worksop
Landscaped parkland, with double avenue of limes, lake, chapel. One of the Dukeries' estates, though the house no longer remains.

Rufford - Nr. Ollerton
Parkland, lake & gallery with fine crafts, around ruin of Cistercian abbey.

Sherwood Forest Visitor Centre - Nr. Edwinstowe
Robin Hood exhibition.
450 acres of ancient oak woodland associated with the outlaw & his merry men.

Sherwood Forest Farm Park - Nr. Edwinstowe
Rare breeds of cattle, sheep, pigs & goats. Lake with wildfowl.

White Post Farm Centre - Farnsfield, Nr Newark
Working modern farm with crops & many animals, including cows, sheep, pigs, hens, geese, ducks, llamas, horses. Indoor displays & exhibits.

Newark Castle.

LEICESTERSHIRE, NOTTINGHAMSHIRE & RUTLAND

Map reference

01 **White**
02 **Goodwin**
03 **Shipside**
04 **Hinchley**
05 **Ibbotson**
06 **Spratt**
07 **Kay**
08 **Kinder**
09 **Hitchen**

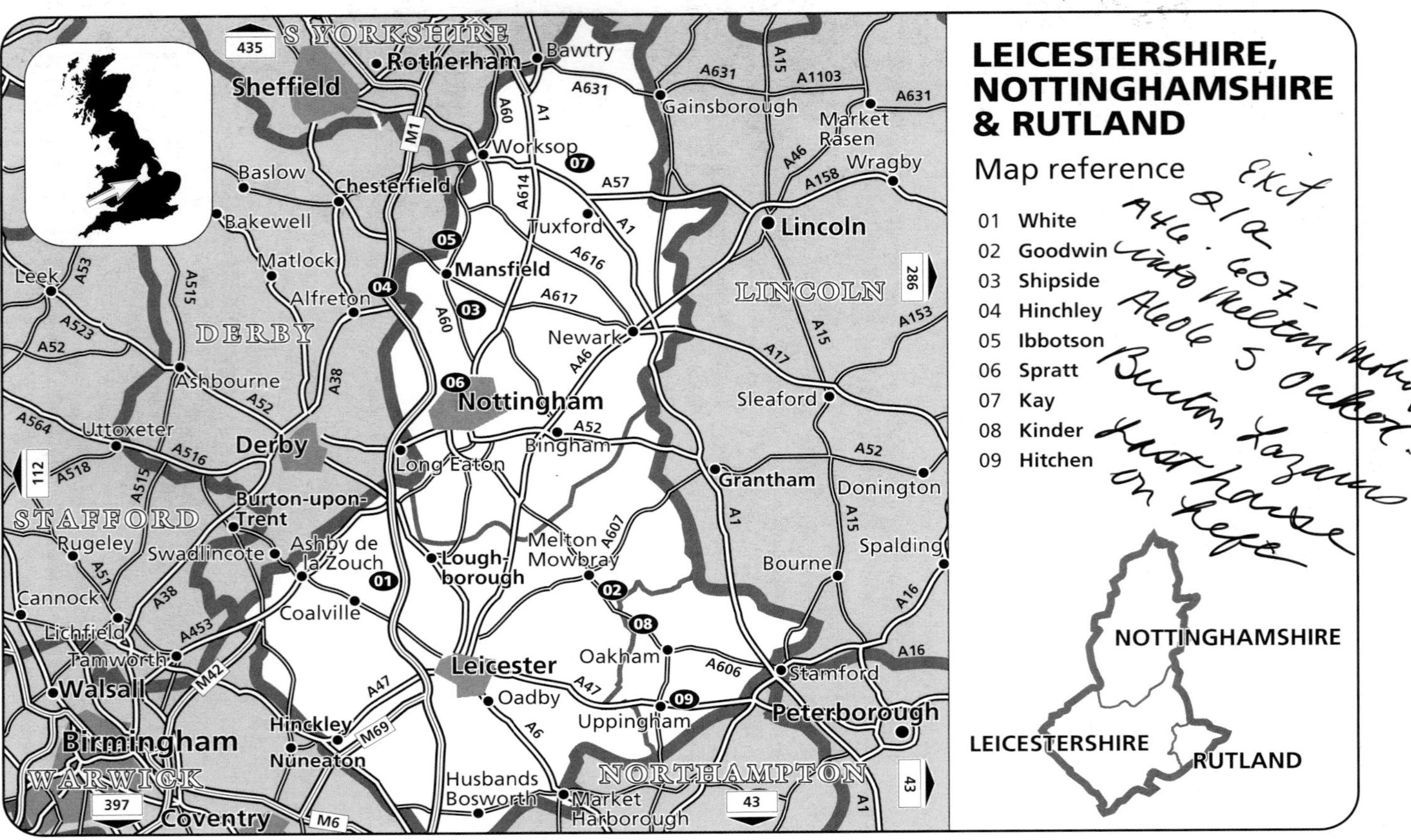

Leicestershire & Nottinghamshire

rate £ from - to per person	children taken	evening meals	animals taken
£30.00 to £60.00	Y	Y	Y

Abbots Oak Country House

Nearest Road: A.511, M.1

A Grade II listed building with a wealth of oak panelling, & including the staircase reputedly from Nell Gwynn's town house. Set in mature gardens & woodland, with natural granite outcrops. 4 delightful rooms, all with en-suite/private bathroom. Open fires create a warm & welcoming atmosphere, & Carolyn's superb dinners are served in the candlelit dining room. Stratford, Belvoir Castle & Rutland Water can all be reached within the hour. Tennis court, billiard room. Children over 6.

Mr & Mrs White Abbots Oak Country House Warren Hills Rd Greenhill Coalville LE67 4UY Leics.
Tel: (01530) 832328 Fax 01530 832328 Open: ALL YEAR Map Ref No. 01

rate £ from - to per person	children taken	evening meals	animals taken
£17.50 to £20.00	Y	N	N

Hillside House

Nearest Road: A.606

Charmingly converted farm buildings with superb views over open countryside, in the small village of Burton Lazars. Offering 1 double & 2 twin-bedded rooms with en-suite/private bathrooms. All have tea/coffee facilities & T.V.. A very pleasant garden. Close to Melton Mowbray, famous for its pork pies & Stilton cheese, & with Burghley House, Belvoir Castle & Rutland Water within easy reach. Children over 10. Single supplement.

E-mail: Hillhs27@aol.com

Sue Goodwin Hillside House 27 Melton Road Burton Lazars Melton Mowbray LE14 2UR Leics.
Tel: (01664) 566312 Fax 01664 501819 Open: ALL YEAR Map Ref No. 02

rate £ from - to per person	children taken	evening meals	animals taken
£24.00 to £34.00	Y	N	N

see PHOTO over p. 262

VISA: M'CARD: AMEX:

Holly Lodge

Nearest Road: A.60

Holly Lodge is situated just off the A.60, 10 miles north of Nottingham. This attractive former hunting lodge stands in 15 acres of grounds. The 4 comfortable & attractive, en-suite guest rooms are housed within the converted stables. There are panoramic countryside views on all sides, with woodland walks, tennis, golf & riding nearby. Ideally situated for a peaceful, rural holiday base with a relaxed & friendly atmosphere.

E-mail: hollylodge@excite.co.uk

Mrs Ann Shipside Holly Lodge Ricket Lane Blidworth NG21 0NQ Nottinghamshire
Tel: (01623) 793853 Fax 01623 490977 Open: ALL YEAR Map Ref No. 03

rate £ from - to per person	children taken	evening meals	animals taken
£18.00 to £18.00	Y	N	Y

VISA: M'CARD: AMEX:

Titchfield Guest House

Nearest Road: A.617

This is 2 houses converted into 1 family-run guest house, offering 8 comfortable rooms, a lounge with T.V., a kitchen for guests' use, a bathroom & showers. There is also has an adjoining garage. Near to Mansfield, which is a busy market town. Sherwood Forest & the Peak District are both easily accessible. Titchfield Guest House is a very handy location for touring this lovely area, & for onward travel. A warm & friendly welcome is assured at this charming home.

Mrs B. Hinchley Titchfield Guest House 300/302 Chesterfield Rd North Pleasley Mansfield NG19 7QU Notts. Tel: (01623) 810356/810921 Fax 01623 810356 Open: ALL YEAR Map Ref No. 04

Holly Lodge. Blidworth.

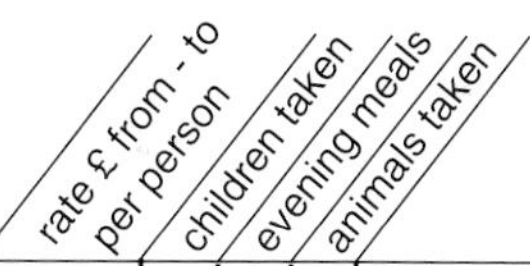

Nottinghamshire & Rutland

Rate £	Children	Evening meals	Animals
£18.00 to £22.00	Y	N	N

Blue Barn Farm

Nearest Road: A.616

An enjoyable visit is guaranteed at this family-run, 250-acre farm, set in tranquil countryside on the edge of Sherwood Forest (Robin Hood country). 3 guest bedrooms, each with modern amenities including tea/coffee-making facilities & a guest bathroom with shower. 1 bedroom is en-suite. A T.V. lounge & garden are also available. Guests are very welcome to walk around the farm. Many interesting places, only a short journey away.

E-mail: ibbotsonbluebarn@netscapeonline.co.uk

June M. Ibbotson Blue Barn Farm Langwith Mansfield NG20 9JD Nottinghamshire
Tel: (01623) 742248 Fax 01623 742248 Open: ALL YEAR (Excl. Xmas) Map Ref No. 05

Rate £	Children	Evening meals	Animals
£28.00 to £35.00	Y	N	Y

VISA: M'CARD:

Greenwood Lodge City Guest House

Nearest Road: A.60

A warm, welcoming Victorian house situated in a quiet cul-de-sac, 1 mile from the city centre. The home of Sheila & Michael Spratt, The Lodge is furnished mainly with antiques, & boasts a fine 4-poster bed. All rooms are en-suite & individually decorated & furnished to a high standard, with T.V., hairdryer & hospitality tray. Evening meals are by prior arrangement. An ideal base from which to explore Nottingham & its many places of interest.

E-mail: coolspratt@aol.com

Mr & Mrs Spratt Greenwood Lodge City Guest House Third Avenue Sherwood Rise Nottingham NG7 6JH Notts. Tel: (0115) 9621206 Fax 0115 9621206 Open: ALL YEAR Map Ref No. 06

Rate £	Children	Evening meals	Animals
£22.00 to £30.00	Y	N	N

VISA: M'CARD:

The Barns Country Guest House

Nearest Road: A.1

A welcoming & pleasant, relaxed atmosphere awaits you at The Barns. This beautifully converted 18th-century barn, furnished in antiques & pine, boasts open fires & oak beams. Prettily decorated bedrooms, including a 4-poster bedroom, are all en-suite with T.V., tea/coffee, etc. Enjoy a delicious Aga cooked breakfast. An interesting base for touring, located at Babworth, home of the Pilgrim Fathers, Robin Hood country & Clumber Park.

E-mail: harry@thebarns.co.uk

Mr & Mrs H. Kay The Barns Country Guest House Morton Farm Babworth Retford DN22 8HA Notts.
Tel: (01777) 706336 Fax 01777 709773 Open: ALL YEAR Map Ref No. 07

Rate £	Children	Evening meals	Animals
£20.00 to £25.00	Y	Y	Y

Torr Lodge

Nearest Road: A.1

Torr Lodge, Barrow is in the heart of scenic Rutland, England's smallest county, but one with the biggest welcome! Oakham, Stamford & Melton Mowbray are within easy access, as is Rutland Water with sailing & fishing. Golf courses nearby. Georgiana has been in the hospitality business for 10 years, & offers tastefully furnished en-suite accommodation, home-cooking on an Aga & hearty breakfasts. Crown Derby & crystal dinner is an optional choice for the evening. Children over 12.

Mrs Georgiana Kinder Torr Lodge Main Street Barrow Oakham LE15 7PE Rutland
Tel: (01572) 813396 Fax 01572 813396 Open: ALL YEAR Map Ref No. 08

Rutland

	rate £ from - to per person	children taken	evening meals	animals taken
Rutland House	£22.00 to £34.00	Y	N	Y

Nearest Road: A.47

Rutland House offers excellent accommodation in 5 delightful guest rooms. All rooms are en-suite, with central heating, colour T.V., radio/alarms & tea/coffee-making facilities. Being a small establishment, the rooms are quiet & homely. Full English or Continental breakfast served. Close to Rutland Water, Burghley House & Geoff Hamiltons' famous gardens. Children over 5 yrs. A lovely home well-placed for touring.

E-mail: rutland.house@virgin.net

VISA: M'CARD:

Mrs Jenny Hitchen ***Rutland House 61 High Street East Uppingham LE15 9PY Rutland***
Tel: (01572) 822497 Fax 01572 820065 Open: ALL YEAR Map Ref No. 09

All the establishments mentioned in this guide are members of The Worldwide Bed & Breakfast Association

When booking your accommodation please mention The Best Bed & Breakfast

Lincolnshire

Lincolnshire (East Midlands)

Lincolnshire is an intriguing mixture of coast & country, of flat fens & gently rising wolds.

There are the popular resorts of Skegness & Mablethorpe as well as quieter coastal regions where flocks of wild birds take food & shelter in the dunes. Gibraltar Point & Saltfleetby are large nature reserves.

Fresh vegetables for much of Britain are produced in the rich soil of the Lincolnshire fens, & windmills punctuate the skyline. There is a unique 8-sailed windmill at Heckington. In spring the fields are ablaze with the red & yellow of tulips. The bulb industry flourishes around Spalding & Holbeach, & in early May tulip flowers in abundance decorate the huge floats of the Spalding Flower Parade.

The city of Lincoln has cobbled streets & ancient buildings & a very beautiful triple-towered Cathedral which shares its hill-top site with the Castle, both dating from the 11th century. There is a 17th century library by Wren in the Cathedral, which has amongst its treasures one of the four original copies of Magna Carta.

Boston has a huge parish church with a distincive octagonal tower which can be seen for miles across the surrounding fenland, & is commonly known as the 'Boston Stump'. The Guildhall Museum displays many aspects of the town's history, including the cells where the early Pilgrim Fathers were imprisioned after their attempt to flee to the Netherlands to find religious freedom. They eventually made the journey & hence to America.

One of England's most outstanding towns is Stamford. It has lovely churches, ancient inns & other fine buildings in a mellow stone.

Sir Isaac Newton was born at Woolsthorpe Manor & educated at nearby Grantham where there is a museum which illustrates his life & work.

The poet Tennyson was born in the village of Somersby, where his father was Rector.

Lincoln Cathedral.

Lincolnshire

Lincolnshire Gazeteer

Areas of outstanding natural beauty.
Lincolnshire Wolds.

Historic Houses & Castles

Auborn House - Nr. Lincoln
16th century house with imposing carved staircase & panelled rooms.
Belton House - Grantham
House built 1684-88 - said to be by Christopher Wren - work by Grinling Gibbons & Wyatt also. Paintings, furniture, porcelain, tapestries, Duke of Windsor mementoes. A great English house with formal gardens & extensive grounds with orangery.
Doddington Hall - Doddington, Nr. Lincoln
16th century Elizabethan mansion with elegant Georgian rooms & gabled Tudor gatehouse. Fine furniture, paintings, porcelain, etc. Formal walled knot gardens, roses & wild gardens.
Burghley House - Stamford
Elizabethan - England's largest & grandest house of the era. Famous for its beautiful painted ceilings, silver fireplaces & art treasures.
Gumby Hall - Burgh-le-Marsh
17th century manor house. Ancient gardens.
Harrington Hall - Spilsby
Mentioned in the Domesday Book - has mediaeval stone base - Carolinean manor house in red brick. Some alterations in 1678 to mullioned windows. Panelling, furnishings of 17th & 18th century.
Marston Hall - Grantham
16th century manor house. Ancient gardens.
The Old Hall - Gainsborough
Fine mediaeval manor house built in 1480's with original kitchen, rebuilt after original hall destroyed during Wars of the Roses. Tower & wings, Great Hall. It was the first meeting place of the "Dissenters", later known as the Pilgrim Fathers.
Woolsthorpe Manor - Grantham
17th century house. Birthplace of Sir Isaac Newton.
Fydell House - Boston
18th century house, now Pilgrim College.
Lincoln Castle - Lincoln
William the Conqueror castle, with complete curtain wall & Norman shell keep. Towers & wall walk. Unique prisoners' chapel.
Tattershall Castle - Tattershall
100 foot high brick keep of 15th century moated castle, with fine views over surrounding country.

Cathedrals & Churches

Addlethorpe (St. Nicholas)
15th century - mediaeval stained glass - original woodwork.
Boston (St. Botolph)
14th century decorated - very large parish church. Beautiful south porch, carved stalls.
Brant Broughton (St. Helens)
13th century arcades - decorated tower & spire - perpendicular clerestory. Exterior decoration.
Ewerby (St. Andrew)
Decorated - splendid example of period - very fine spire. 14th century effigy.
Fleet (St. Mary Magdalene)
14th century - early English arcades - perpendicular windows - detached tower & spire.
Folkingham (St. Andrew)
14th century arcades - 15th century windows - perpendicular tower - early English chancel.
Gedney (St. Mary Magdalene)
Perpendicular spire (unfinished). Early English tower. 13th-14th century monuments, 14th-15th century stained glass.
Grantham (St. Wulfram)
14th century tower & spire - Norman pillars - perpendicular chantry - 14th century vaulted crypt.
Lincoln Cathedral - Lincoln
Magnificent triple-towered Gothic building on fine hill-top site.
Norman west front,
13th century - some 14th century additions. Norman work from 1072.
Angel choir - carved & decorated pulpitum - 13th century chapter house - 17th century library by Wren (containing one of the four original copies of Magna Carta).

Lincolnshire

St. Botolph's Church - Boston
Fine parish church, one of the largest in the country, with 272 foot octagonal tower dominating the surrounding fens.
Long Sutton (St. Mary)
15th century south porch, mediaeval brass lectern, very fine early English spire.
Louth (St. James)
Early 16th century - mediaeval Gothic - wonderful spire.
Scotter (St. Peter)
Saxon to perpendicular - early English nave - 15th century rood screen.
Stow (St. Mary)
Norman - very fine example, particularly west door. Wall painting.
Silk Willoughby (St. Denis)
14th century - tower with spire & flying buttresses. 15th-17th century pulpit.
Stainfield (St. Andrew)
Queen Anne - mediaeval armour & early needlework.
Theddlethorpe (All Saints)
14th century - 15th century & reredos of 15th century, 16th century parcloses, 15th century brasses - some mediaeval glass.
Wrangle (St. Mary the Virgin & St. Nicholas)
Early English - decorated - perpendicular - Elizabethan pulpit. 14th century east window & glass.

Museums & Galleries

Alford Manor House - Alford
Tudor manor house - thatched - folk museum. Nearby windmill.
Boston Guildhall Museum - Boston
15th century building with mayor's parlour, court room & cells where Pilgrim Fathers were imprisoned in 1607. Local exhibits.
Lincoln Cathedral Library - Lincoln
Built by Wren housing early printed books & mediaeval manuscripts.
Lincoln Cathedral Treasury - Lincoln
Diocesan gold & silver plate.
Lincoln City & Country Museum - Lincoln
Prehistoric, Roman & mediaeval antiquities with local associations. Armour & local history.
Museum of Lincolnshire Life - Lincoln
Domestic, agricultural, industrial & social history of the county. Edwardian room settings, shop settings, agricultural machinery.
Usher Gallery - Lincoln
Paintings, watches, miniatures, porcelain, silver, coins & medals. Temporary exhibitions. Tennyson collection. Works of English watercolourist Peter de Wint.
Grantham Museum - Grantham
Archeology, prehistoric, Saxon & Roman. Local history with special display about Sir Isaac Newton, born nearby & educated in Grantham.
Church Farm Museum - Skegness
Farmhouse & buildings with local agricultural collections & temporary exhibitions & special events.
Stamford Museum - Stamford
Local history museum, with temporary special exhibitions.
Battle of Britain Memorial Flight - Coningsby
Lancaster bomber, five Spitfires & two Hurricanes with other Battle of Britain memorabilia.
National Cycle Museum - Lincoln
Development of the cycle.
Stamford Steam Brewery Museum - Stamford
Complete Victorian steam brewery with 19th century equipment.

Other things to see & do

Springfield - Spalding
Show gardens of the British bulb industry, & home of the Spalding Flower Parade each May. Summer bedding plants & roses.
Butlins Funcoast World - Skegness
Funsplash Water World with amusements & entertainments
Castle Leisure Park - Tattershall
Windsurfing, water-skiing, sailing, fishing & other sports & leisure facilities.
Long Sutton Butterfly Park - Long Sutton
Walk-through tropical butterfly house with outdoor wildflower meadows & pets corner.
Skegness Natureland Marine Zoo - Skegness
Seal sanctuary with aquaria, tropical house, pets corner & butterfly house.
Windmills - at Lincoln (Ellis Mill - 4 sails), Boston (Maud Foster - 5 sails), Burgh-le-Marsh (5 sails), Alford (5 sails), Sibsey (6 sails), Heckington (8 sails).

LINCOLNSHIRE

Map reference

01 **Armstrong**
02 **Ramsay**
03 **Honnor**
04 **Pritchard**
04 **Baumber**
05 **Stamp**
06 **Rook**

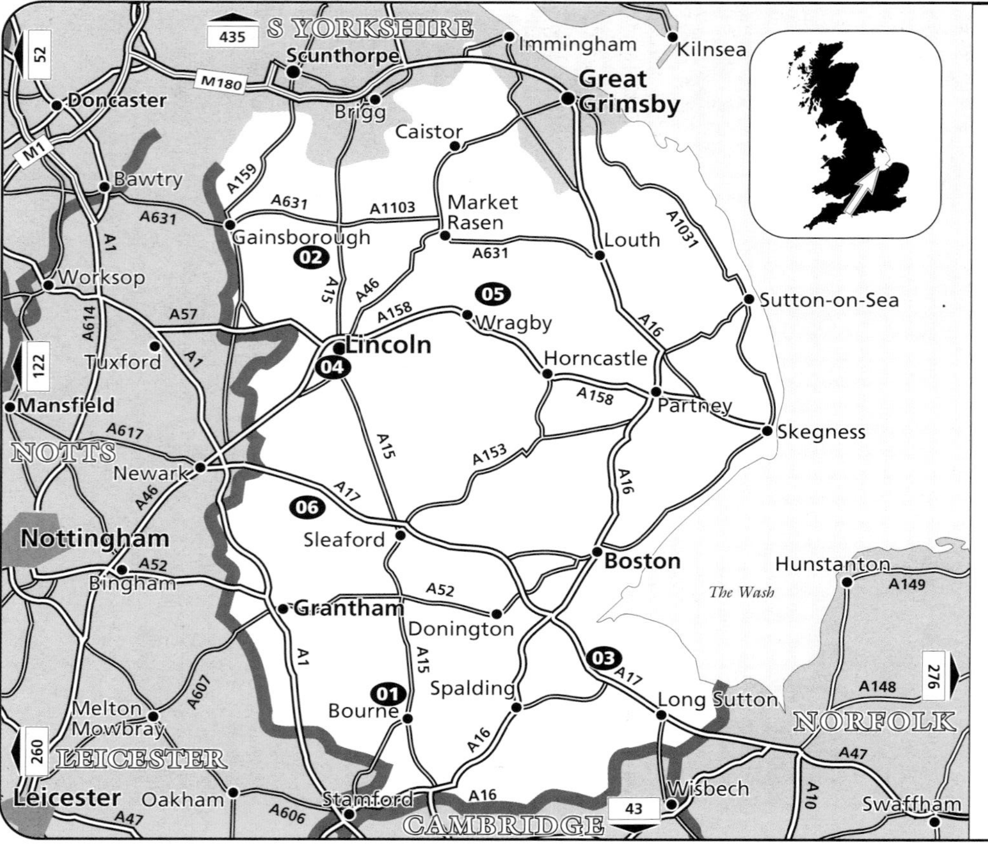

Lincolnshire

rate £ from - to per person	children taken	evening meals	animals taken
£20.00 to £30.00	Y	N	Y

Cawthorpe Hall

Nearest Road: A.15

This fine, old, listed house is surrounded by a large pretty garden & fields of roses supplying the rose distillery with fragrant blooms. The rooms are attractive, bright, spacious & comfortably furnished & have bathrooms en-suite. A delicious full English breakfast will be served in a family country kitchen. Country lovers can enjoy beautiful woodland walks. Horse riding or golf, Grimsthorpe Castle & Park are all within easy reach. Cawthorpe Hall is a charming home.

Mrs Chantal Armstrong Cawthorpe Hall Cawthorpe Bourne PE10 0AB Lincolnshire
Tel: (01778) 423830 Fax 01778 426620 Open: ALL YEAR Map Ref No. 01

rate £ from - to per person	children taken	evening meals	animals taken
£22.50 to £30.00	Y	Y	N

Church Farm

Nearest Road: A.15

Tucked away in unspoilt countryside, the Ramsays guarantee you a friendly welcome. Expect to enjoy good food, conversation, laughter & log fires on chilly evenings. Walk around the beautiful village lake or relax in the garden on sunny days & listen to the birdsong. Hemswell Antique Centre, Lincolnshire Showground, Lincoln & Gainsborough are nearby. Evening meals by arrangement & afternoon teas served. 2 attractive bedrooms with en-suite/private facilities. Children over 5.

E-mail: fillinghambandb@lineone.net

Christine B. Ramsay Church Farm Fillingham Gainsborough DN21 5BS Lincolnshire
Tel: (01427) 668279 Fax 01427 668025 Open: ALL YEAR (Excl. Xmas) Map Ref No. 02

rate £ from - to per person	children taken	evening meals	animals taken
£22.00 to £30.00	N	N	N

Pipwell Manor

see PHOTO over p. 270

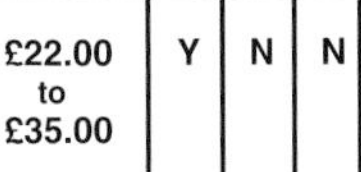

Nearest Road: A.17

Pipwell Manor is a Grade II listed Georgian manor house, built in around 1740, set in paddocks & gardens in a small quiet village in the Lincolnshire Fens, just off the A.17. Beautifully restored & decorated in English-country style, but retaining many original features, Pipwell Manor is a delightful place to stay. 4 comfortably furnished & attractive bedrooms, each with an en-suite/private bathroom & tea/coffee-making facilities. Guests are welcomed with tea & home-made cake. Parking.

Lesley Honnor Pipwell Manor Washway Road Saracens Head Holbeach PE12 8AL Lincolnshire
Tel: (01406) 423119 Fax 01406 423119 Open: ALL YEAR Map Ref No. 03

rate £ from - to per person	children taken	evening meals	animals taken
£22.00 to £35.00	Y	N	N

Carline Guest House

Nearest Road: A.57, A.15

Gill & John Pritchard extend a warm welcome. Excellent accommodation, in 9 attractively furnished bedrooms, each with en-suite facilities, T.V., radio, beverage facilities, hairdryers & trouser press. The Carline is a short, pleasant stroll from the Lawns Tourism & Conference Centre, & from the historic Uphill area of Lincoln. There are several restaurants & public houses nearby for your lunch or evening meal. Ask for recommendations. Children over 2 years welcome.

Gillian & John Pritchard Carline Guest House 1-3 Carline Road Lincoln LN1 1HL Lincolnshire
Tel: (01522) 530422 Fax 01522 530422 Open: ALL YEAR Map Ref No. 04

Pipwell Manor. Saracens Head.

Lincolnshire

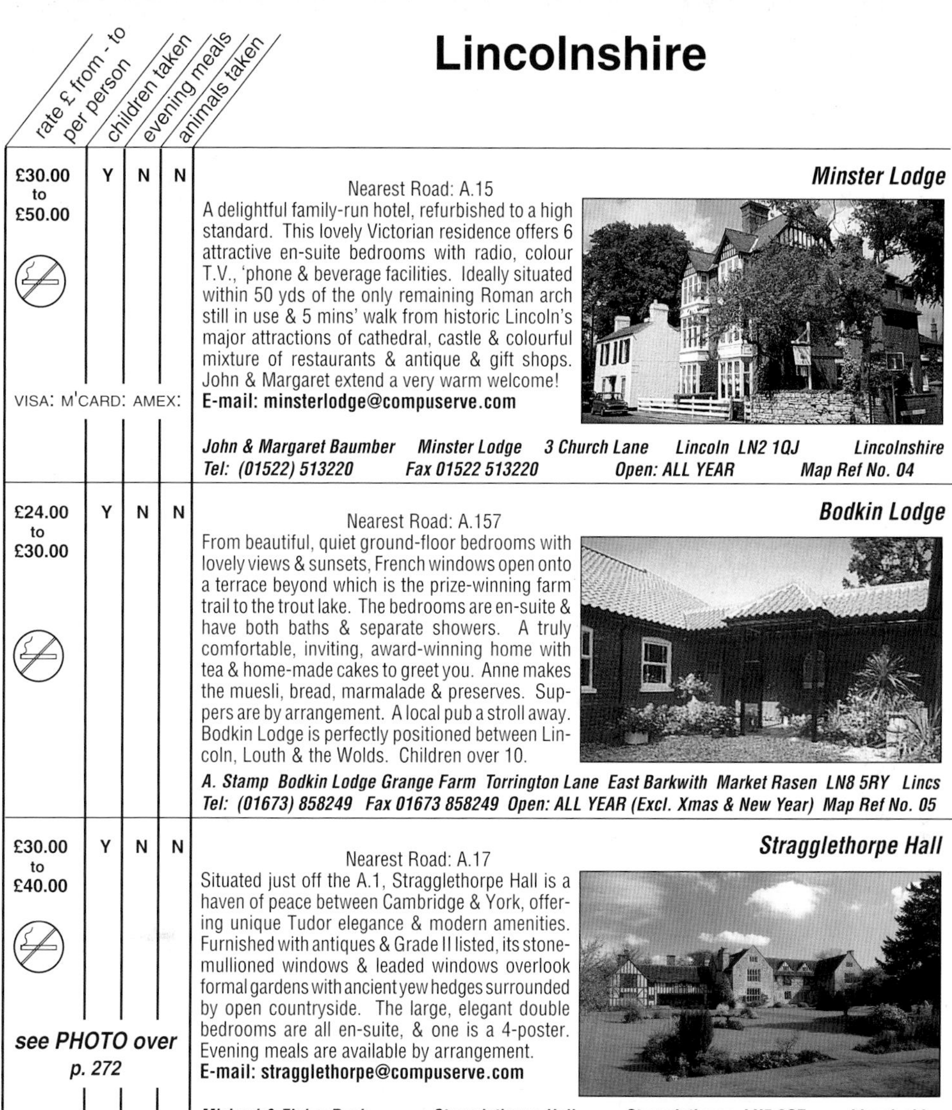

rate £ from - to per person	children taken	evening meals	animals taken
£30.00 to £50.00	Y	N	N

VISA: M'CARD: AMEX:

Minster Lodge

Nearest Road: A.15

A delightful family-run hotel, refurbished to a high standard. This lovely Victorian residence offers 6 attractive en-suite bedrooms with radio, colour T.V., 'phone & beverage facilities. Ideally situated within 50 yds of the only remaining Roman arch still in use & 5 mins' walk from historic Lincoln's major attractions of cathedral, castle & colourful mixture of restaurants & antique & gift shops. John & Margaret extend a very warm welcome!

E-mail: minsterlodge@compuserve.com

John & Margaret Baumber Minster Lodge 3 Church Lane Lincoln LN2 1QJ Lincolnshire
Tel: (01522) 513220 Fax 01522 513220 Open: ALL YEAR Map Ref No. 04

rate £ from - to per person	children taken	evening meals	animals taken
£24.00 to £30.00	Y	N	N

Bodkin Lodge

Nearest Road: A.157

From beautiful, quiet ground-floor bedrooms with lovely views & sunsets, French windows open onto a terrace beyond which is the prize-winning farm trail to the trout lake. The bedrooms are en-suite & have both baths & separate showers. A truly comfortable, inviting, award-winning home with tea & home-made cakes to greet you. Anne makes the muesli, bread, marmalade & preserves. Suppers are by arrangement. A local pub a stroll away. Bodkin Lodge is perfectly positioned between Lincoln, Louth & the Wolds. Children over 10.

A. Stamp Bodkin Lodge Grange Farm Torrington Lane East Barkwith Market Rasen LN8 5RY Lincs
Tel: (01673) 858249 Fax 01673 858249 Open: ALL YEAR (Excl. Xmas & New Year) Map Ref No. 05

rate £ from - to per person	children taken	evening meals	animals taken
£30.00 to £40.00	Y	N	N

see PHOTO over *p. 272*

Stragglethorpe Hall

Nearest Road: A.17

Situated just off the A.1, Stragglethorpe Hall is a haven of peace between Cambridge & York, offering unique Tudor elegance & modern amenities. Furnished with antiques & Grade II listed, its stone-mullioned windows & leaded windows overlook formal gardens with ancient yew hedges surrounded by open countryside. The large, elegant double bedrooms are all en-suite, & one is a 4-poster. Evening meals are available by arrangement.

E-mail: stragglethorpe@compuserve.com

Michael & Elaine Rook Stragglethorpe Hall Stragglethorpe LN5 0QZ Lincolnshire
Tel: (01400) 272308 Fax 01400 273816 Open: ALL YEAR Map Ref No. 06

Stragglethorpe Hall. Stragglethorpe.

Norfolk

Norfolk
(East Anglia)

One of the largest of the old counties, Norfolk is divided by rivers from neighbouring counties & pushes out into the sea on the north & east sides. This is old East Anglia.

Inland there is great concentration on agriculture where fields are hedged with hawthorn which blossoms like snow in summer. A great deal of land drainage is required & the area is crisscrossed by dykes & ditches - some of them dating back to Roman times.

Holkham Hall.

The Norfolk Broads were formed by the flooding of mediaeval peat diggings to form miles & miles of inland waterways, navigable & safe. On a bright summer's day, on a peaceful backwater bounded by reed & sedge, the Broads seem like paradise. Here are hidden treasures like the Bittern, that shyest of birds, the Swallowtail butterfly & the rare Marsh orchid.

Contrasting with the still inland waters is a lively coastline which takes in a host of towns & villages as it arcs around The Wash. Here are the joys of the seaside at its best, miles of safe & sandy golden beaches to delight children, dunes & salt marshes where birdlife flourishes, & busy ports & fishing villages with pink-washed cottages.

Cromer is a little seaside town with a pier & a prom, cream teas & candy floss, where red, white & blue fishing boats are drawn up on the beach.

Hunstanton is more decorous, with a broad green sweeping down to the cliffs. Great Yarmouth is a boisterous resort. It has a beach that runs for miles, with pony rides & almost every amusement imaginable.

It is possible to take a boat into the heart of Norwich, past warehouses, factories & new penthouses, & under stone & iron bridges. Walking along the riverbank you reach Pulls Ferry where a perfectly proportioned grey flint gateway arcs over what was once a canal dug to transport stone to the cathedral site. Norwich Cathedral is magnificent, with a sharply soaring spire, beautiful cloisters & fine 15th century carving preserved in the choir stalls. Cathedral Close is perfectly preserved, as is Elm Hill, a cobbled street from mediaeval times. There are many little shops & narrow alleys going down to the river.

Norfolk is a county much loved by the Royal family & the Queen has a home at Sandringham. It is no castle, but a solid, comfortable family home with red brick turrets & French windows opening onto the terrace.

Norfolk

Norfolk Gazeteer

Areas of outstanding beauty.
Norfolk coast (part)

Historic Houses & Castles

Anna Sewell House - Great Yarmouth
17th century Tudor frontage. Birthplace of writer Anna Sewell.
Blicking Hall - Aylsham
Great Jacobean house. Fine Russian tapestry, long gallery with exceptional ceiling. Formal garden.
Felbrigg Hall - Nr. Cromer
17th century, good Georgian interior. Set in wooded parklands.
Holkham Hall - Wells
Fine Palladian mansion of 1734. Paintings, statuary, tapestries, furnishings & formal garden by Berry.
Houghton Hall - Wells
18th century mansion. Pictures, china & staterooms.
Oxburgh Hall - Swafftham
Late 15th century moated house. Fine gatehouse tower. Needlework by Mary Queen of Scots.
Wolterton Hall - Nr. Norwich
Built in 1741 contains tapestries, porcelain, furniture.
Trinity Hospital - Castle Rising
17th century, nine brick & tile almshouses, court chapel & treasury.

Cathedrals & Churches

Attleborough (St. Mary)
Norman with late 14th century. Fine rood screen & frescoes.
Barton Turf (St. Michael & All Angles)
Magnificent screen with painting of the Nine Orders of Angles.
Beeston-next-Mileham (St. Mary)
14th century. Perpendicular clerestory tower & spire. Hammer Beam roof, parclose screens, benches, front cover. Tracery in nave & chancel windows.
Cawston (St. Agnes)
Tower faced with freestone. Painted screens, wall paintings, tower, screen & gallery. 15th century angel roof.
East Harding (St. Peter & St. Paul)
14th century, some 15th century alterations. Monuments of 15th-17th century. Splendid mediaeval glass.
Erpingham (St. Mary)
14th century military brass to John de Erpingham, 16th century Rhenish glass. Fine tower.
Gunton (St. Andrew)
18th century. Robert Adam - classical interior in dark wood - gilded.
King's Lynn (St. Margaret)
Norman foundation. Two fine 14th century Flemish brasses, 14th century screens, reredos by Bodley, interesting Georgian pulpit with sounding board.
Norwich Cathedral
Romanesque & late Gothic with 15th century spire. Perpendicular lierne vaults in nave, transeptsand presbytery.
Ranworth (St. Helens)
15th century screen, very fine example. Sarum Antiphoner, 14th century illuminated manuscript - East Anglian work.
Salle (St. Peter & St. Paul)
15th century. Highly decorated west tower & porches. Mediaeval glass, pulpit with 15th century panels & Jacobean tester. Stalls, misericords, brasses & monuments, sacrament font.
Terrington (St. Clement)
Detached perpendicular tower. Western front has fire-light window & canopied niches. Georgian panelling west of nave. 17th century painted font cover. Jacobean commandment boards.
Trunch (St. Botolph)
15th century screen with painted panels, mediaeval glass, famous font canopy with fine carving & painting, ringer's gallery, Elizabethan monument.
Wiggenhall (St. Germans)
17th century pulpit, table, clerk's desk & chair, bench ends 15th century.
Wymondham (St. Mary & St. Thomas of Canterbury)
Norman origins including arcades & triforium windows, 13th century font fragments, complete 15th century font. 15th century clerestory & roof. Comper reredos, famous Corporas Case, rare example of 13th century Opus Anglicanum.

Museums & Galleries

Norwich Castle Museum
Art collection, local & natural history,

Norfolk

Strangers Hall - Norwich
Mediaeval mansion furnished as museum of urban domestic life in 16th-19th centuries.

St. Peter Hungate Church Museum - Norwich
15th century church for the exhibition of ecclesiastical art & East Anglican antiquities.

Sainsbury Centre for Visual Arts - University, Norwich
Collection of modern art, ancient, classical & mediaeval art, Art Nouveau, 20th century constructivist art.

Bridewell Museum of Local Industries - Norwich
Crafts, industries & aspects of city life.

Museum of Social History - King's Lynn
Exhibition of domestic life & dress, etc., noted glass collection.

Bishop Bonner's Cottages
Restored cottages with coloured East Anglia pargetting, c. 1502, museum of archaeological discoveries, exhibition of rural crafts.

The Guildhall - Thetford
Duleep Singh Collection of Norfolk & Suffolk portraits.

Shirehall Museum - Walsingham
18th century court room having original fittings, illustrating Walsingham life.

Historic Monuments

Binham Priory & Cross - Binham
12th century ruins of Benedictine foundation.

Caister Castle - Great Yarmouth
15th century moated castle - ruins. Now motor museum.

The Castle - Burgh Castle
3rd century Saxon fort - walls - ruin.

Mannington Hall - Saxthorpe
Saxon church ruin in gardens of 15th century moated house.

Castle Rising - Castle Rising
Splendid Norman keep & earthworks.

Castle Acre Priory & Castle Gate - Swaffham

Other things to see & do

African Violet Centre - Terrington St. Clements.
60 varieties of African Violets. Talks & Tours.

Norfolk Lavender Centre - Heacham
Open to the public in July & August. Demonstrations of harvesting & distilling the oil.

Thetford Forest
Forest walks, rides & picnic places amongst conifers, oak, beech & birch.

The Broads.

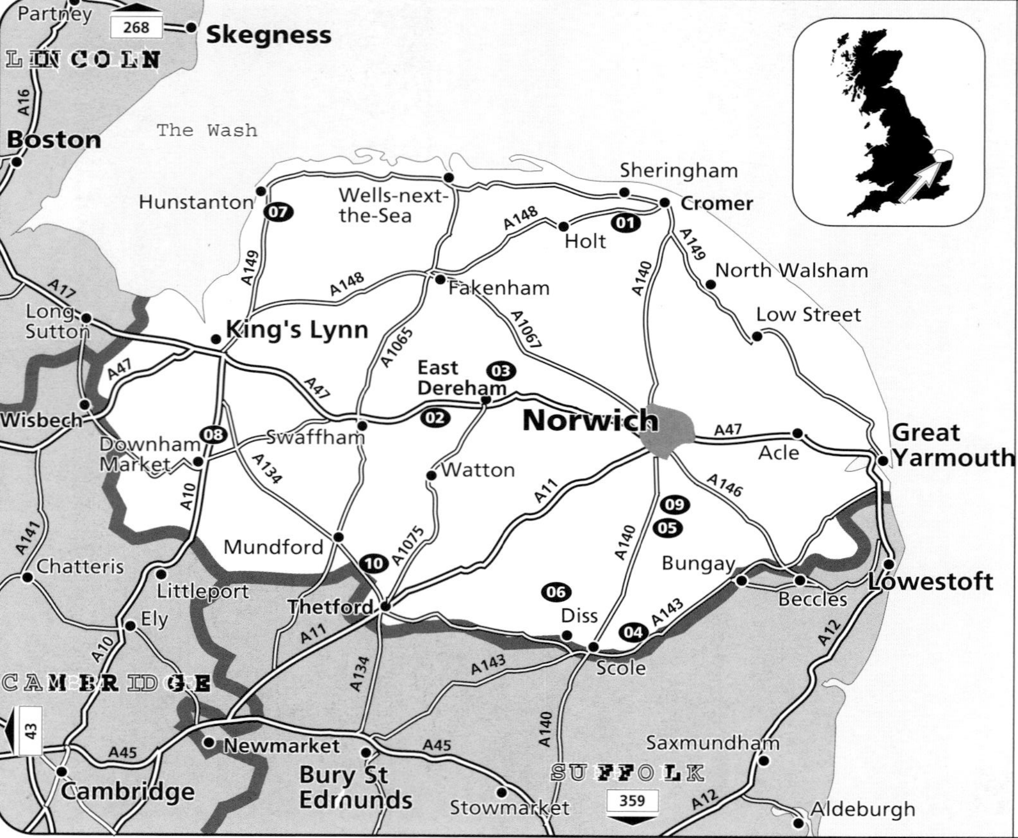

NORFOLK

Map reference

01 **Gillam**
02 **Lock**
03 **Bartlett**
04 **Morrish**
05 **Croft**
06 **Webb**
07 **Tweedy Smith**
08 **Luddington**
09 **Douglas**
10 **Collins**

Felbrigg Lodge. Aylmerton.

Norfolk

	rate £ from - to per person	children taken	evening meals	animals taken
Felbrigg Lodge	£35.00 to £50.00	Y	Y	N
Greenbanks Country Hotel	£32.00 to £48.00	Y	Y	Y
Bartles Lodge	£21.00 to £35.00	N	N	Y
Grove Thorpe	£25.00 to £32.00	N	Y	N

Felbrigg Lodge

Nearest Road: A.148, A.140

Set in beautiful countryside 2 miles from the coast, Felbrigg Lodge is hidden in 8 acres of spectacular woodland gardens. Time has stood still since Edwardian ladies came here in their carriages to take tea & play croquet. Great care has been taken to preserve this atmosphere with comfortable en-suite rooms, luxuriously decorated with every facility. A true haven of peace & tranquillity. A nature lover's paradise. Candlelit dinners & copious breakfast. Indoor heated pool/gym. Children over 10.

E-mail: info@felbrigglodge.co.uk

Jill & Ian Gillam *Felbrigg Lodge* *Aylmerton NR11 8RA* *Norfolk*
Tel: (01263) 837588 *Fax 01263 838012* *Open: ALL YEAR* *Map Ref No. 01*

see PHOTO over p. 277

VISA: M'CARD:

Greenbanks Country Hotel

Nearest Road: A.47

Charming, small, 18th-century hotel, with delightful country restaurant, situated in 9 acres of meadows & lakes. Spectacular gardens. Elegant & attractive en-suite rooms, including 3 ground-floor level access suites, offering peace & comfort. Superb cuisine, with excellent choice from varied menu: special diets catered for. Only 15 mins' from Norwich, & within easy reach of the coast, the Broads & many stately homes. Walking, fishing & golfing breaks available. Pets by arrangement.

E-mail: gb.hotel@talk21.com

Jennie Lock *Greenbanks Country Hotel* *Swaffham Road* *Wendling* *Dereham NR19 2AB* *Norfolk*
Tel: (01362) 687742 *Open: ALL YEAR* *Map Ref No. 02*

see PHOTO over p. 279

VISA: M'CARD:

Bartles Lodge

Nearest Road: A.47, A.1067

Bartles Lodge is in the peaceful, unspoilt village of Elsing, set in 12 acres of landscaped meadows inhabited by plenty of wildlife. The rooms, which are centred around the patio, pond & fountain, are beautifully furnished in country style, & most overlook the Bartletts' own lakes. All of the bedrooms are en-suite with colour T.V.s, etc & are very comfortable. Although Bartles Lodge is licensed, the local village inn is nearby. An ideal base from which to explore Norfolk.

David & Annie Bartlett *Bartles Lodge* *Church Street* *Elsing* *Dereham NR20 3EA* *Norfolk*
Tel: (01362) 637177 *Open: ALL YEAR* *Map Ref No. 03*

VISA: M'CARD:

Grove Thorpe

Nearest Road: A.143

Enjoy this 17th-century Grade II listed country house, nestling in 9 acres of mature, secluded grounds, with private fishing lake, duck pond & horses. Beautifully renovated to a high standard with inglenook fireplaces & oak beamed rooms, full of charm & character. All bedrooms are en-suite with T.V., hospitality tray, robes & hairdryer. Dinners served by arrangement. Local inns nearby. Market town of Diss 5 miles (auctions on Friday). Central for Norwich, Norfolk Broads, Bressingham Gardens & Heritage coast. Children over 12.

Angela & John Morrish *Grove Thorpe* *Grove Road* *Brockdish* *Diss IP21 4JE* *Norfolk*
Tel: (01379) 668305 *Fax 01379 668305* *Open: ALL YEAR* *Map Ref No. 04*

Greenbanks Country Hotel. Wendling.

The Old Bakery. Pulham Market.

Norfolk

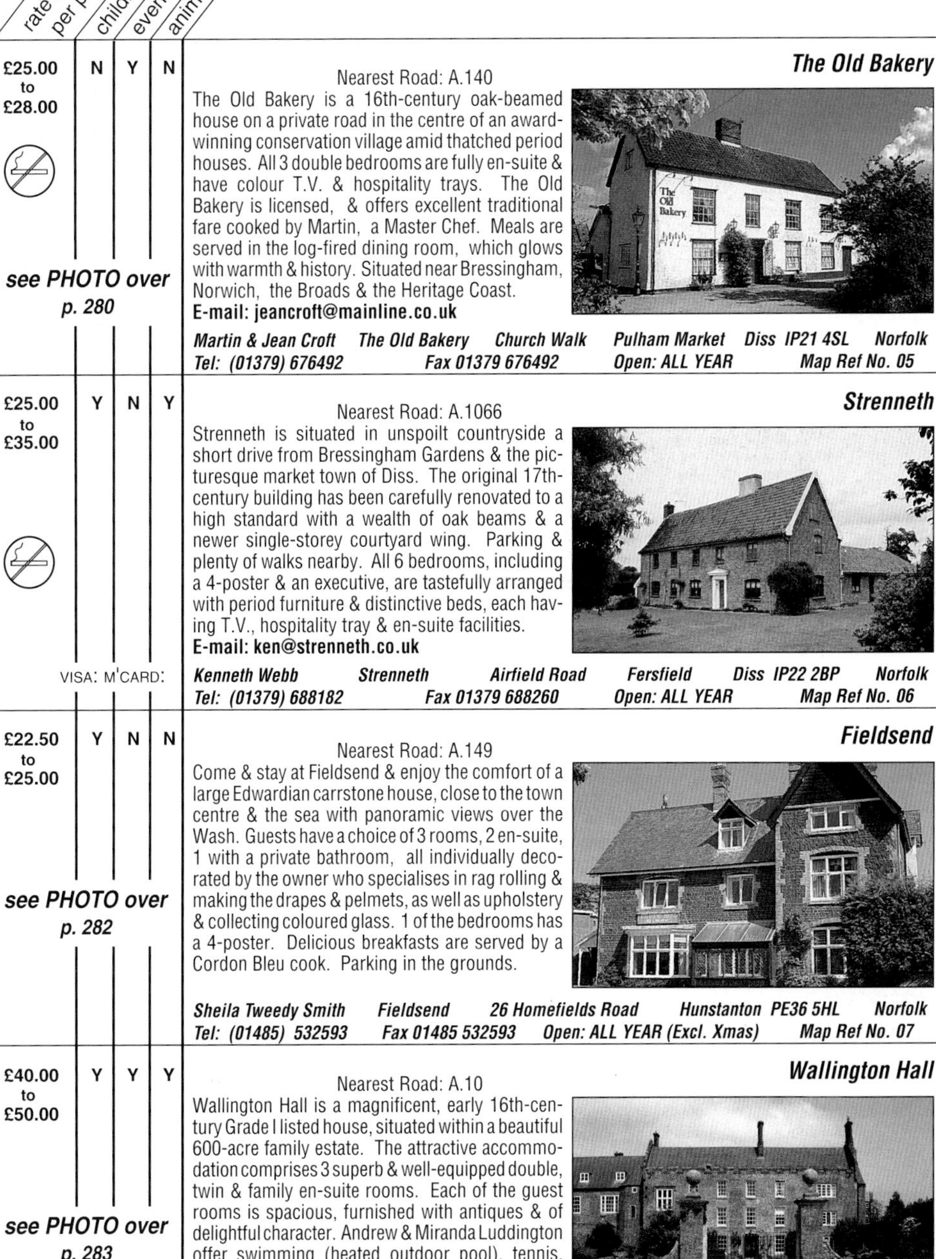

rate £ from - to per person	children taken	evening meals	animals taken
£25.00 to £28.00	N	Y	N

The Old Bakery

Nearest Road: A.140

The Old Bakery is a 16th-century oak-beamed house on a private road in the centre of an award-winning conservation village amid thatched period houses. All 3 double bedrooms are fully en-suite & have colour T.V. & hospitality trays. The Old Bakery is licensed, & offers excellent traditional fare cooked by Martin, a Master Chef. Meals are served in the log-fired dining room, which glows with warmth & history. Situated near Bressingham, Norwich, the Broads & the Heritage Coast.

E-mail: jeancroft@mainline.co.uk

see PHOTO over p. 280

Martin & Jean Croft The Old Bakery Church Walk Pulham Market Diss IP21 4SL Norfolk
Tel: (01379) 676492 Fax 01379 676492 Open: ALL YEAR Map Ref No. 05

rate £ from - to per person	children taken	evening meals	animals taken
£25.00 to £35.00	Y	N	Y

Strenneth

Nearest Road: A.1066

Strenneth is situated in unspoilt countryside a short drive from Bressingham Gardens & the picturesque market town of Diss. The original 17th-century building has been carefully renovated to a high standard with a wealth of oak beams & a newer single-storey courtyard wing. Parking & plenty of walks nearby. All 6 bedrooms, including a 4-poster & an executive, are tastefully arranged with period furniture & distinctive beds, each having T.V., hospitality tray & en-suite facilities.

E-mail: ken@strenneth.co.uk

VISA: M'CARD:

Kenneth Webb Strenneth Airfield Road Fersfield Diss IP22 2BP Norfolk
Tel: (01379) 688182 Fax 01379 688260 Open: ALL YEAR Map Ref No. 06

rate £ from - to per person	children taken	evening meals	animals taken
£22.50 to £25.00	Y	N	N

Fieldsend

Nearest Road: A.149

Come & stay at Fieldsend & enjoy the comfort of a large Edwardian carrstone house, close to the town centre & the sea with panoramic views over the Wash. Guests have a choice of 3 rooms, 2 en-suite, 1 with a private bathroom, all individually decorated by the owner who specialises in rag rolling & making the drapes & pelmets, as well as upholstery & collecting coloured glass. 1 of the bedrooms has a 4-poster. Delicious breakfasts are served by a Cordon Bleu cook. Parking in the grounds.

see PHOTO over p. 282

Sheila Tweedy Smith Fieldsend 26 Homefields Road Hunstanton PE36 5HL Norfolk
Tel: (01485) 532593 Fax 01485 532593 Open: ALL YEAR (Excl. Xmas) Map Ref No. 07

rate £ from - to per person	children taken	evening meals	animals taken
£40.00 to £50.00	Y	Y	Y

Wallington Hall

Nearest Road: A.10

Wallington Hall is a magnificent, early 16th-century Grade I listed house, situated within a beautiful 600-acre family estate. The attractive accommodation comprises 3 superb & well-equipped double, twin & family en-suite rooms. Each of the guest rooms is spacious, furnished with antiques & of delightful character. Andrew & Miranda Luddington offer swimming (heated outdoor pool), tennis, stabling, course fishing & superb walks. Evening meals by arrangement. Wallington Hall is perfect for a relaxing break amid elegant surroundings.

see PHOTO over p. 283

VISA: M'CARD:

Mrs Miranda Luddington Wallington Hall King's Lynn PE33 0EP Norfolk
Tel: (01553) 811567 Fax 01553 810661 Open: ALL YEAR Map Ref No. 08

Fieldsend House. Hunstanton.

Wallington Hall. Kingslynn.

Norfolk

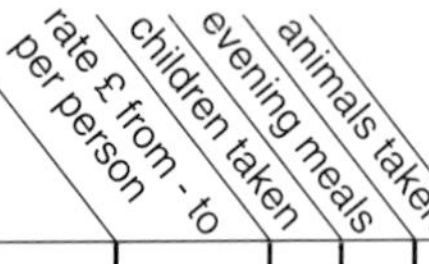

Establishment	rate £ from - to per person	children taken	evening meals	animals taken
Greenacres Farm	£20.00 to £25.00	Y	N	Y
Cedar Lodge	£23.50 to £25.85	Y	Y	N

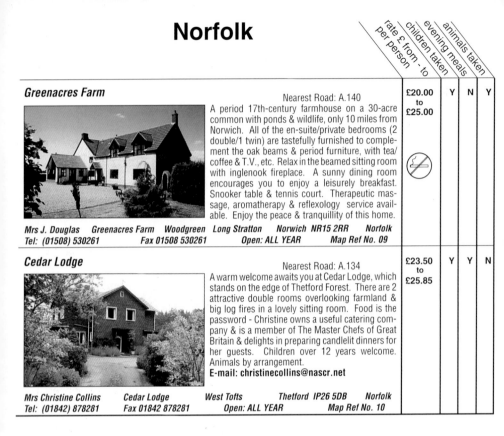

Greenacres Farm

Nearest Road: A.140

A period 17th-century farmhouse on a 30-acre common with ponds & wildlife, only 10 miles from Norwich. All of the en-suite/private bedrooms (2 double/1 twin) are tastefully furnished to complement the oak beams & period furniture, with tea/coffee & T.V., etc. Relax in the beamed sitting room with inglenook fireplace. A sunny dining room encourages you to enjoy a leisurely breakfast. Snooker table & tennis court. Therapeutic massage, aromatherapy & reflexology service available. Enjoy the peace & tranquillity of this home.

Mrs J. Douglas Greenacres Farm Woodgreen Long Stratton Norwich NR15 2RR Norfolk
Tel: (01508) 530261 Fax 01508 530261 Open: ALL YEAR Map Ref No. 09

Cedar Lodge

Nearest Road: A.134

A warm welcome awaits you at Cedar Lodge, which stands on the edge of Thetford Forest. There are 2 attractive double rooms overlooking farmland & big log fires in a lovely sitting room. Food is the password - Christine owns a useful catering company & is a member of The Master Chefs of Great Britain & delights in preparing candlelit dinners for her guests. Children over 12 years welcome. Animals by arrangement.
E-mail: christinecollins@nascr.net

Mrs Christine Collins Cedar Lodge West Tofts Thetford IP26 5DB Norfolk
Tel: (01842) 878281 Fax 01842 878281 Open: ALL YEAR Map Ref No. 10

All the establishments mentioned in this guide are members of The Worldwide Bed & Breakfast Association

When booking your accommodation please mention The Best Bed & Breakfast

Northumbria

Northumbria

Mountains & moors, hills & fells, coast & country are all to be found in this Northern region which embraces four counties - Northumberland, Durham, Cleveland & Tyne & Wear.

Saxons, Celts, Vikings, Romans & Scots all fought to control what was then a great wasteland between the Humber & Scotland.

Northumberland

Northumberland is England's Border country, a land of history, heritage & breathtaking countryside. Hadrian's Wall, stretching across the county from the mouth of the Tyne in the west to the Solway Firth, was built as the Northern frontier of the Roman Empire in 122 AD. Excavations along the Wall have brought many archaeological treasures to light. To walk along the wall is to discover the genius of Roman building & engineering skill. They left a network of roads, used to transport men & equipment in their attempts to maintain discipline among the wild tribes.

Through the following centuries the Border wars with the Scots led to famous battles such as Otterburn in 1388 & Flodden in 1513, & the construction of great castles including Bamburgh & Lindisfarne. Berwick-on-Tweed, the most northerly town, changed hands between England & Scotland 13 times.

Northumberland's superb countryside includes the Cheviot Hills in the Northumberland National Park, the unforgettable heather moorlands of the Northern Pennines to the west, Kielder Water (Western Europe's largest man-made lake), & 40 miles of glorious coastline.

Holy Island, or Lindisfarne, is reached by a narrow causeway that is covered at every incoming tide. Here St. Aidan of Iona founded a monastery in the 7th century, & with St. Cuthbert set out to Christianise the pagan tribes. The site was destroyed by the Danes, but Lindisfarne Priory was built by the monks of Durham in the 11th century to house a Benedictine community. The ruins are hauntingly beautiful.

Durham

County Durham is the land of the Prince Bishops, who with their armies, nobility, courts & coinage controlled the area for centuries. They ruled as a virtually independent State, holding the first line of defence against the Scots.

In Durham City, the impressive Norman Castle standing proudly over the narrow mediaeval streets was the home of the Prince Bishops for 800 years.

Durham Cathedral, on a wooded peninsula high above the River Wear, was built in the early 12th century & is undoubtably one of the world's finest buildings, long a place of Christian pilgrimage.

The region's turbulent history led to the building of forts & castles. Some like Bowes & Barnard Castle are picturesque ruins whilst others, including Raby, Durham & Lumley still stand complete.

The Durham Dales of Weardale, Teesdale & the Derwent Valley cover about one third of the county & are endowed with some of the highest & wildest scenery. Here are High Force, England's highest waterfall, & the Upper Teesdale National Nature Reserve.

The Bowes Museum at Barnard Castle is a magnificent French-style chateau & houses an important art collection.

In contrast is the award-winning museum at Beamish which imaginatively recreates Northern life at the turn of the century.

Northumbria

Cleveland

Cleveland, the smallest 'shire' in England, has long been famous for its steel, chemical & shipbuilding industries but it is also an area of great beauty. The North Yorkshire National Park lies in the south, & includes the cone-shaped summit of Roseberry Topping, "Cleveland's Matterhorn".

Cleveland means 'land of cliffs', & in places along the magnificent coastline, cliffs tower more than 600 feet above the sea, providing important habitat for wild plants & sea-birds.

Pretty villages such as Hart, Elwick & Staithes are full of steep, narrow alleys. Marton was the birthplace of Captain James Cook & the museum there traces the explorer's early life & forms the start of the 'Cook Heritage Trail'.

The Tees estuary is a paradise for birdwatchers, whilst walkers can follow the Cleveland Way or the 38 miles of the Langbaurgh Loop. There is surfing, windsurfing & sailing at Saltburn, & for the less energetic, the scenic Esk Valley Railway runs from Middlesbrough to Whitby.

Tyne & Wear

Tyne & Wear takes its name from the two rivers running through the area, & includes the large & lively city of Newcastle-on-Tyne.

Weardale lies in a beautiful valley surrounded by wild & bleak fells. Peaceful now, it was the setting for a thriving industry mining coal & silver, zinc & lead. Nature trails & recreation areas have been created among the old village & market towns.

The county was the birthplace of George Stephenson, railway engineer, who pioneered the world's first passenger railway on the Stockton to Darlington Line in 1825.

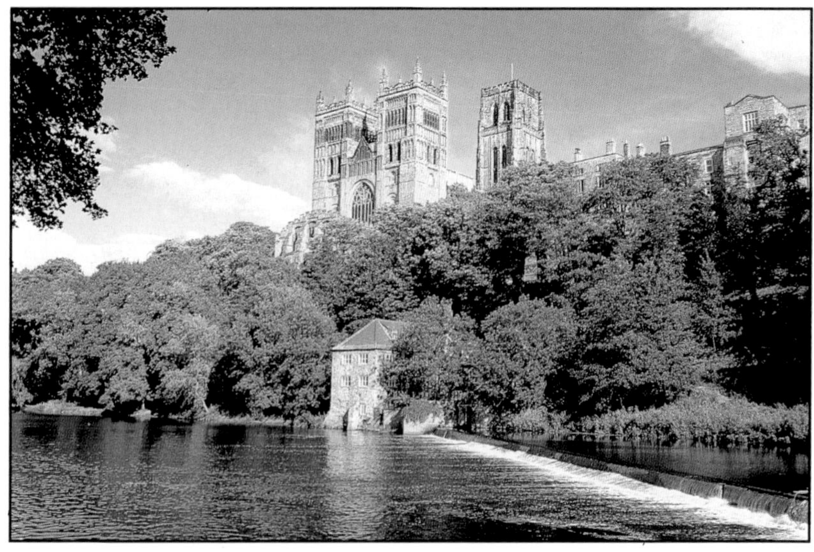

Durham Cathedral.

Northumbria

Northumbria Gazeeter

Areas of Outstanding Natural Beauty
The Heritage Coast, the Cheviot Hills, the North Pennine chain.

Historic Houses & Castles

Alnwick Castle - Alnwick
A superb mediaeval castle of the 12th century.
Bamburgh Castle-Bamburgh
A restored 12th century castle with Norman keep.
Callaly Castle - Whittingham
A 13th century Pele tower with 17th century mansion. Georgian additions.
Durham Castle - Durham
Part of the University of Durham - a Norman castle.
Lindisfarne Castle - Holy Island
An interesting 14th century castle.
Ormesby Hall - Nr. Middlesbrough
A mid 18th century house.
Raby Castle - Staindrop, Darlington
14th century with some later alteration . Fine art & furniture. Large gardens.
Wallington Hall -Combo
A 17th century house with much alteration & addition.
Washington Old Hall-Washington
Jacobean manor house, parts of which date back to 12th century.

Cathedrals & Churches

Brancepeth (St. Brandon)
12th century with superb 17th century woodwork. Part of 2 mediaeval screens. Flemish carved chest.
Durham Cathedral
A superb Norman cathedral. A unique Galilee chapel & early 12th century vaults.
Escombe
An interesting Saxon Church with sundial.
Hartlepool (St. Hilda)
Early English with fine tower & buttresses.
Hexham (St. Andrews)
Remains of a 17th century church with Roman dressing. A unique night staircase & very early stool. Painted screens.
Jarrow (St. Pauls)
Bede worshipped here. Strange in that it was originally 2 churches until 11th century. Mediaeval chair.
Newcastle (St. Nicholas)
14th century with an interesting lantern tower.
Heraldic font. Roundel of 14th century glass.
Morpeth (St. Mary the Virgin)
Fine mediaeval glass in east window - 14th century.
Pittington (St. Lawrence)
Late Norman nave with wall paintings.
Carved tombstone - 13th century.
Skelton (St. Giles)
Early 13th century with notable font, gable crosses, bell-cote & buttresses.
Staindrop (St. Mary)
A fine Saxon window.
Priests dwelling.
Neville tombs & effigies.

Museums & Galleries

Aribea Roman Fort Museum - South Shields
Interesting objects found on site.
Berwick-on-Tweed Museum - Berwick
Special exhibition of interesting local finds.
Bowes Museum - Bernard Castle
European art from mediaeval to 19th century.
Captain Cook Birthplace Museum - Middlesbrough
Cook's life & natural history relating to his travels.
Clayton Collection - Chollerford
A collection of Roman sculpture, weapons & tools from forts.
Corbridge Roman Station - Corbridge
Roman pottery & sculpture.
Dormitory Musuem - Durham Cathedral
Relics of St. Cuthbert.
Mediaeval seats & manuscripts.
Gray Art Gallery - Hartlepool
19th-20th century art & oriental antiquities.
Gulbenkian Museum of Oriental Art - University of Durham
Chinese pottery & porcelain, Chinese jade & stone carvings, Chinese ivories, Chinese textiles, Japenese & Tibetan art. Egyptian & Mesopotamian antiquities.
Jarrow Hall - Jarrow
Excavation finds of Saxon & mediaeval monastery.
Fascinating information room dealing with early Christian sites in England.

Northumbria

Keep Museum - Newcastle-upon-Tyne
Mediaeval collection.
Laing Art Gallery - Newcastle-upon-Tyne
17th-19th century British arts, porcelain, glass & silver.
National Music Hall Museum - Sunderland
19th-20th century costume & artefacts associated with the halls.
Preston Hall Museum - Stockton-on-Tees
Armour & arms, toys, ivory period room
University - New Castle -Upon -Tyne
The Hatton Gallery - housing a fine collection of Italian paintings.
Museum of Antiquities
Prehistoric, Roman & Saxon collection with an interesting reconstruction of a temple.
Beamish North of England Open Air Museum - European Museum of the Year
Chantry Bagpipe Museum - Morpeth
Darlington Museum & Railway Centre.

Historic Monuments

Ariiea Roman Fort - South Shields
Remains which include the gateways & headquarters.
Barnard Castle - Barnard Castle
17th century ruin with interesting keep.
Bowes Castle - Bowes
Roman Fort with Norman keep.
The Castle & Town Walls - Berwick-on-Tweed
12th century remains, reconstructed later.
Dunstanburgh Castle - Alnwick
14th century remains.
Egglestone Abbey - Barnard Castle
Remains of a Poor House.
Finchdale Priory - Durham
13 th century church with much remaining.
Hadrian's Wall - Housesteads
Several miles of the wall including castles & site museum.
Mithramic Temple - Carrawbrough
Mithraic temple dating back to the 3rd century.
Norham Castle - Norham
The partial remains of a 12th century castle.
Prudhoe Castle - Prudhoe
Dating from the 12th century with additions. Bailey & gatehouse well preserved.
The Roman Fort - Chesters
Extensive remains of a Roman bath house.
Tynemouth Priory & Castle - Tynemouth
11th century priory - ruin - with 16th century towers & keep.
Vindolanda - Barton Mill
Roman fort dating from 3rd century.
Warkworth Castle - Warkworth
Dating from the 11th century with additions.
A great keep & gatehouse.
Warkworth Hermitage - Warkworth
An interesting 14th century Hermitage.
Lindisfarne Priory - Holy Island (Lindisfarne)
11th century monastery. Island accessible only at low tide.

Other things to see & do

Botanical Gardens - Durham University
Bird & Seal Colonies - Farne Islands
Conducted tours by boat
Marine Life Centre & Fishing Museum - Seahouses
Museum of sealife, & boat trips to the Farne Islands.
Tower Knowe Visitor Centre - Keilder Water

Saltburn Victorian Festival.

NORTHUMBERLAND, DURHAM & TYNE & WEAR

Map reference

02 **Jackson**
04 **Laverack**
05 **Weightman**
06 **Clyde**
07 **Courage**
08 **Minchin**
09 **Gay**
10 **Reed**
11 **Close**
12 **Booth**

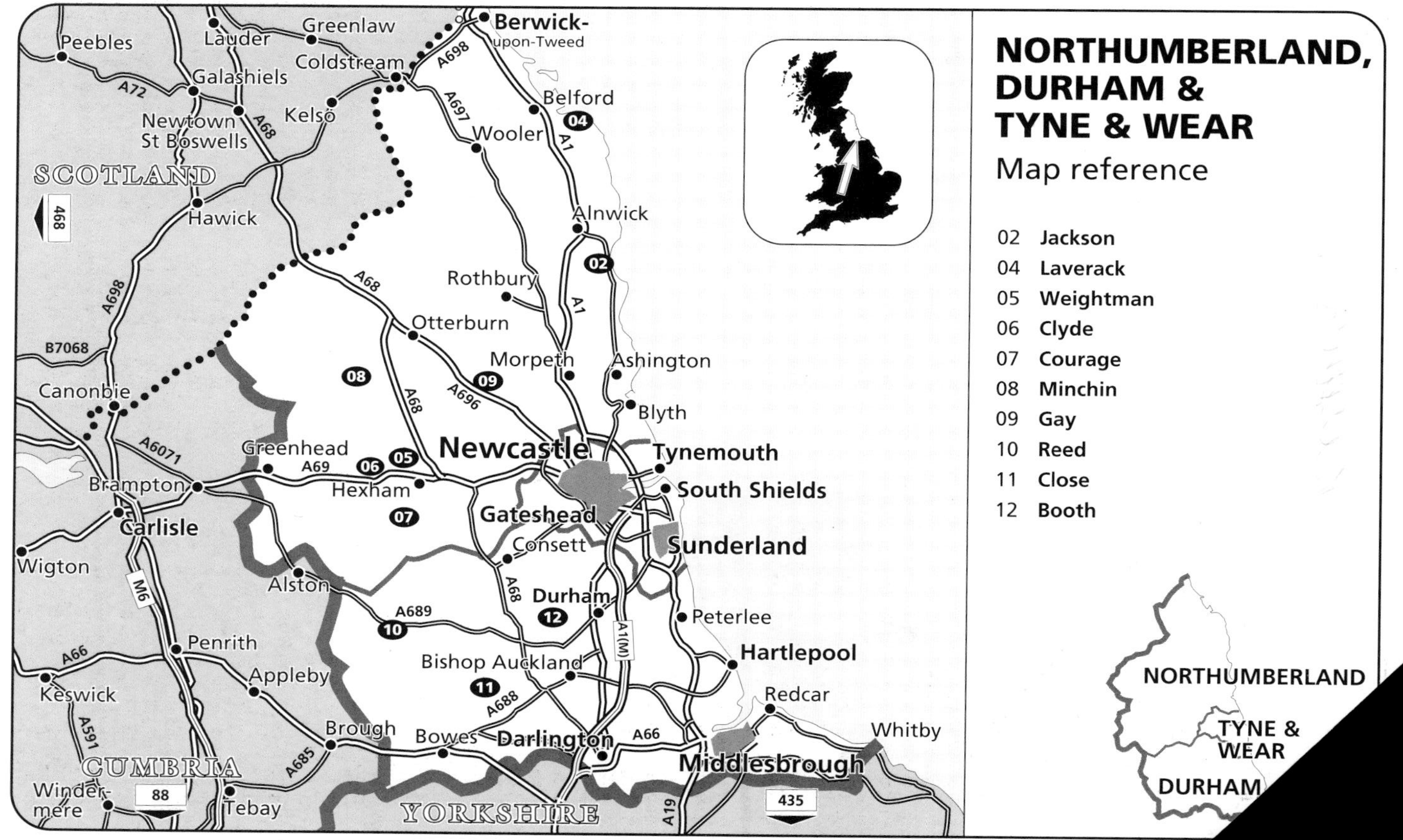

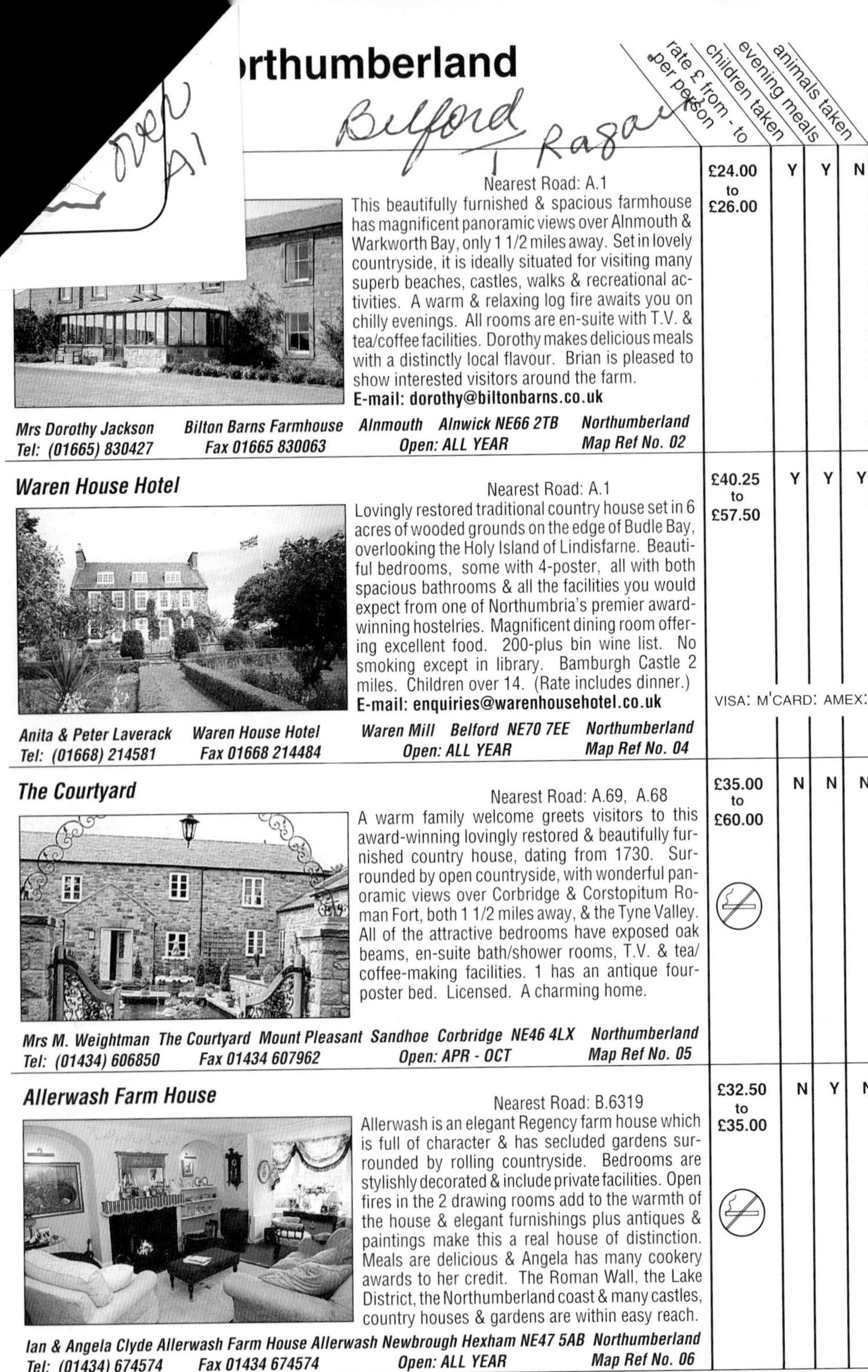

rthumberland

rate £ from - to per person	children taken	evening meals	animals taken
£24.00 to £26.00	Y	Y	N

Nearest Road: A.1

This beautifully furnished & spacious farmhouse has magnificent panoramic views over Alnmouth & Warkworth Bay, only 1 1/2 miles away. Set in lovely countryside, it is ideally situated for visiting many superb beaches, castles, walks & recreational activities. A warm & relaxing log fire awaits you on chilly evenings. All rooms are en-suite with T.V. & tea/coffee facilities. Dorothy makes delicious meals with a distinctly local flavour. Brian is pleased to show interested visitors around the farm.

E-mail: dorothy@biltonbarns.co.uk

Mrs Dorothy Jackson Bilton Barns Farmhouse Alnmouth Alnwick NE66 2TB Northumberland
Tel: (01665) 830427 Fax 01665 830063 Open: ALL YEAR Map Ref No. 02

Waren House Hotel

rate £ from - to per person	children taken	evening meals	animals taken
£40.25 to £57.50	Y	Y	Y

Nearest Road: A.1

Lovingly restored traditional country house set in 6 acres of wooded grounds on the edge of Budle Bay, overlooking the Holy Island of Lindisfarne. Beautiful bedrooms, some with 4-poster, all with both spacious bathrooms & all the facilities you would expect from one of Northumbria's premier award-winning hostelries. Magnificent dining room offering excellent food. 200-plus bin wine list. No smoking except in library. Bamburgh Castle 2 miles. Children over 14. (Rate includes dinner.)

E-mail: enquiries@warenhousehotel.co.uk

VISA: M'CARD: AMEX:

Anita & Peter Laverack Waren House Hotel Waren Mill Belford NE70 7EE Northumberland
Tel: (01668) 214581 Fax 01668 214484 Open: ALL YEAR Map Ref No. 04

The Courtyard

rate £ from - to per person	children taken	evening meals	animals taken
£35.00 to £60.00	N	N	N

Nearest Road: A.69, A.68

A warm family welcome greets visitors to this award-winning lovingly restored & beautifully furnished country house, dating from 1730. Surrounded by open countryside, with wonderful panoramic views over Corbridge & Corstopitum Roman Fort, both 1 1/2 miles away, & the Tyne Valley. All of the attractive bedrooms have exposed oak beams, en-suite bath/shower rooms, T.V. & tea/coffee-making facilities. 1 has an antique four-poster bed. Licensed. A charming home.

Mrs M. Weightman The Courtyard Mount Pleasant Sandhoe Corbridge NE46 4LX Northumberland
Tel: (01434) 606850 Fax 01434 607962 Open: APR - OCT Map Ref No. 05

Allerwash Farm House

rate £ from - to per person	children taken	evening meals	animals taken
£32.50 to £35.00	N	Y	N

Nearest Road: B.6319

Allerwash is an elegant Regency farm house which is full of character & has secluded gardens surrounded by rolling countryside. Bedrooms are stylishly decorated & include private facilities. Open fires in the 2 drawing rooms add to the warmth of the house & elegant furnishings plus antiques & paintings make this a real house of distinction. Meals are delicious & Angela has many cookery awards to her credit. The Roman Wall, the Lake District, the Northumberland coast & many castles, country houses & gardens are within easy reach.

Ian & Angela Clyde Allerwash Farm House Allerwash Newbrough Hexham NE47 5AB Northumberland
Tel: (01434) 674574 Fax 01434 674574 Open: ALL YEAR Map Ref No. 06

Northumberland & Durham

rate £ from - to per person	children taken	evening meals	animals taken
£20.00 to £25.00	Y	Y	Y

VISA: M'CARD:

Rye Hill Farm

Nearest Road: A.68, A.69

Rye Hill Farm dates back some 300 years & is a traditional livestock unit in beautiful countryside just 5 miles south of Hexham. Recently, some of the stone barns adjoining the farmhouse have been converted into superb modern guest accommodation. There are 6 bedrooms, all with private facilities, & all have radio, T.V. & tea/coffee-making facilities. Delicious home-cooked meals. Perfect for a get-away-from-it-all holiday.

E-mail: enquiries@consult-courage.co.uk

Elizabeth Courage Rye Hill Farm Slaley Nr. Hexham NE47 0AH Northumberland
Tel: (01434) 673259 Fax 01434 673259 Open: ALL YEAR Map Ref No. 07

rate £ from - to per person	children taken	evening meals	animals taken
£26.00 to £28.00	Y	Y	Y

VISA: M'CARD:

Westfield Guest House

Nearest Road: A.68

Westfield is a truly hospitable home. Built as an elegant but cosy Victorian gentleman's residence, with nearly an acre of gardens. The 5 bedrooms, including 4 en-suite & a 4-poster, are all totally comfortable, with more than a touch of luxury. Breakfast & dinner are superb, with traditional cooking at its best. Wonderful countryside - ideal touring spot - Roman Wall, castles & National Trust properties, so come & bide awhile & be spoilt. Animals by arrangement.

E-mail: westfield.house@virgin.net

David & June Minchin Westfield Guest House Bellingham Hexham NE48 2DP Northumberland
Tel: (01434) 220340 Fax 01434 220694 Open: ALL YEAR Map Ref No. 08

rate £ from - to per person	children taken	evening meals	animals taken
£23.50 to £28.00	N	Y	N

VISA: M'CARD:

Shieldhall

Nearest Road: A.696

Within acres of well-kept gardens, offering unimpeded views & overlooking the National Trust's Wallington estate, this meticulously restored 18th-century farmhouse is built around a pretty courtyard. All of the 4 bedrooms are beautifully furnished & have en-suite facilities & T.V.. There are very comfortable lounges & an extremely charming inglenooked dining room where home produce is often used for delicious meals which are specially prepared when booked in advance.

E-mail: Robinson.Gay@btinternet.com

Stephen & Celia Gay Shieldhall Wallington by Kirkharle Morpeth NE61 4AQ Northumberland
Tel: (01830) 540387 Fax 01830 540490 Open: MAR - NOV Map Ref No. 09

rate £ from - to per person	children taken	evening meals	animals taken
£22.50 to £27.00	Y	N	N

Lands Farm

Nearest Road: A.689

You will be warmly welcomed to Lands Farm, an old stone-built farmhouse within walking distance of Westgate village. A walled garden with stream meandering by. Accommodation is in centrally heated double & family rooms with luxury en-suite facilities, T.V., tea/coffee-making facilities. Full English breakfast or Continental alternative served in an attractive dining room. This is an ideal base for touring (Durham, Hadrian's Wall, Beamish Museum, etc.) & for walking.

Mrs B. Reed Lands Farm Westgate-in-Weardale Bishop Auckland DL13 1SN Durham
Tel: (01388) 517210 Open: MAR - OCT Map Ref No. 10

Durham

	rate £ from - to per person	children taken	evening meals	animals taken
Grove House	£23.50 to £28.50	Y	Y	N
Ivesley	£33.00 to £40.00	Y	Y	Y

Grove House

Nearest Road: A.68

Grove House, once an aristocrat's shooting lodge, is tastefully furnished throughout, & is situated in an idyllic setting in the middle of Hamsterley Forest. A spacious lounge with log fire gives a warm & comfortable country-house atmosphere. The grandeur of the dining room reminds one of an age gone by. (Take note of the door handles!) 3 bedrooms, all en-suite or with private bathrooms. Helene does all the cooking herself to ensure freshness & quality to her evening meals. Children over 8 years.

E-mail: xov47@dial.pipex.com

Helene Close Grove House Hamsterley Forest Bishop Auckland DL13 3NL Durham
Tel: (01388) 488203 Fax 01388 488174 Open: ALL YEAR (Excl. Xmas & New Year) Map Ref No. 11

Ivesley

Nearest Road: A.68

Ivesley is an elegantly furnished country house set in 220 acres. Each of the 5 attractive bedrooms is decorated to a high standard. 3 of the rooms are en-suite. Ivesley is adjacent to an equestrian centre with first-class facilities. It is an ideal centre for walking, sightseeing & mountain biking. Collection can be arranged from Durham Station & Newcastle Airport. Durham is only 7 miles. Wine cellar. Dogs by arrangement. Children over 8 years.

E-mail: ivesley@msn.com

VISA: M'CARD:

Roger & Pauline Booth Ivesley Waterhouses Durham DH7 9HB Durham
Tel: (0191) 3734324 Fax 0191 3734324 Open: ALL YEAR (Excl. Xmas Day) Map Ref No. 12

All the establishments mentioned in this guide are members of The Worldwide Bed & Breakfast Association

When booking your accommodation please mention The Best Bed & Breakfast

Oxfordshire

Oxfordshire (Thames & Chilterns)

Oxfordshire is a county rich in history & delightful countryside. It has prehistoric sites, early Norman churches, 15th century coaching inns, Regency residences, distinctive cottages of black & white chalk flints & lovely Oxford, the city of dreaming spires.

The countryside ranges from lush meadows with willow-edged river banks scattered with small villages of thatched cottages, to the hills of the Oxfordshire Cotswolds in the west, the wooded Chilterns in the east & the distinctive ridge of the Berkshire Downs in the south. "Old Father Thames" meanders gently across the county to Henley, home of the famous regatta.

The ancient track known as the Great Ridgeway runs across the shire, & a walk along its length reveals barrows, hill forts & stone circles. The 2,000 year old Uffington Horse cut into the chalk of the hillside below an ancient hill fort site, is some 360 feet in length & 160 feet high.

The Romans built villas in the county & the remains of one, including a magnificent mosaic can be seen at North Leigh. In later centuries lovely houses were built. Minster Lovell stands beside the Windrush; Rousham house with its William Kent gardens is situated near Steeple Aston & beside the Thames lies Elizabethan Mapledurham House with its working watermill.

At Woodstock is Blenheim Palace, the largest private house in Britain & birthplace of Sir Winston Churchill. King Alfred's statue stands at Wantage, commemorating his birth there, & Banbury has its cross, made famous in the old nursery rhyme.

Oxford is a town of immense atmosphere with fine college buildings around quiet cloisters, & narrow cobbled lanes. It was during the 12th century that Oxford became a meeting place for scholars & grew into the first established centre of learning, outside the monasteries, in England.

The earliest colleges to be founded were University College, Balliol & Merton. Further colleges were added during the reign of the Tudors, as Oxford became a power in the kingdom. There are now 35 university colleges & many other outstanding historic buildings in the city . Christ Church Chapel is now the Cathedral of Oxford, a magnificent building with a deservedly famous choir.

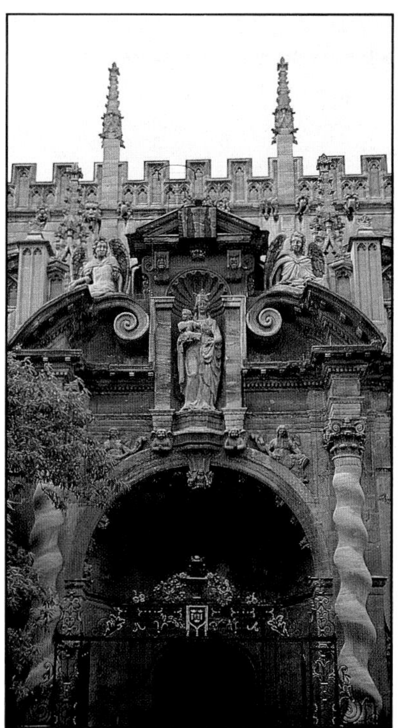

St. Mary's Church.

Oxfordshire

Oxfordshire Gazeteer

Areas of Oustanding Natural Beauty
The North Wessex Downs. The Chiltern Hills. The Cotswolds.

Historic Houses & Castles

Ashdown House - Nr. Lambourn
17th century, built for Elizabeth of Bohemia, now contains portraits associated with her. Mansard roof has cupola with golden ball.
Blenheim Palace - Woodstock
Sir John Vanbrugh's classical masterpiece. Garden designed by Vanbrugh & Henry Wise. Further work done by Capability Brown who created the lake. Collection of pictures & tapestries.
Broughton Castle- Banbury.
14th century mansion with moat - interesting plaster work fine panelling & fire places
Chasleton House-Morton in Marsh
17th century,fine examples of plaster work & panelling.Still has original furniture & tapestries. topiary garden from1700.
Grey Court - Henly-on-Thames
16th century house containing 18th century plasterwork & furniture. Mediaeval ruins. Tudor donkey-wheel for raising water from well.
Mapledurham House - Mapledurham
16th century Elizabethan house. Oak staircase, private chapel, paintings, original moulded ceilings. Watermill nearby.
Milton Manor House - Nr. Abingdon
17th century house designed by Inigo Jones - Georgian wings, walled garden, pleasure grounds.
Rousham House - Steeple Ashton
17th century - contains portraits & miniatures.

University of Oxford Colleges

University college ------------------1249
Balliol---------------------------------1263
Merton---------------------------------1264
Hertford-------------------------------1284
Oriel-----------------------------------1326
New------------------------------------1379
All Souls------------------------------1438
Brasenose----------------------------1509
Christ Church----------------------1546
St. John's---------------------------1555
Pembroke---------------------------1624
Worcester---------------------------1714
Nuffield -----------------------------1937
St. Edmund Hall-------------------1270
Exeter--------------------------------1314
The Queen's-----------------------1340
Lincoln-------------------------------1427
Magdalen ---------------------------1458
Corpus Christi ---------------------1516
Trinity--------------------------------1554
Jesus--------------------------------1571
Wadham-----------------------------1610
Keble--------------------------------1868

Cathedrals & Churches

Abingdon (St. Helen)
14th-16th century perpendicular. Painted roof. Georgian stained & enamelled glass.
Burford (St. John the Baptist)
15th century. Sculptured table tombs in churchyard.
Chislehampton (St. Katherine)
18th century. Unspoilt interior of Georgian period. Bellcote.
Dorchester (St. Peter & St. Paul)
13th century knight in stone effigy. Jesse window.
East Hagbourne (St. Andrew)
14th -15th century. Early glass, wooden roofs, 18th century tombs.
North Moreton (All Saints)
13th century with splendid 14th century chantry chapel - tracery.
Oxford Cathedral
Smallest of our English cathedrals. Stone spire form 1230. Norman arcade has double arches, choir vault.
Ryecote (St. Michael & All Angels)
14th century benches & screen base. 17th century altar-piece & communion rails, old clear glass, good ceiling.
Stanton Harcourt (St. Michael)
Early English - old stone & marble floor. Early screen with painting, monuments of 17th -19th century.
Yarnton (St. Bartholomew)
13th century - late perpendicular additions. Jacobean screen. 15th century alabaster reredos.

Oxfordshire

Museums & Galleries

The Ashmolean Museum of Art & Archaeology - Oxford
British ,European ,Mediterranean, Egyptian & Near Eastern archaeology. Oil paintings of Italian, Dutch, Flemish, French & English schools. Old Master watercolours, prints, drawings, ceramics, silver, bronzes & sculptures. Chinese & Japanese porcelain, lacquer & painting, Tibetan, Islamic & Indian art.

Christ Church Picture Gallery - Oxford
Old Master drawings & paintings.

Museum of Modern Art - Oxford
Exhibitiors of contemporary art.

Museum of Oxford
Many exhibits depicting the history of Oxford & its University.

The Rotunda - Oxford
Privately owned collection of dolls' houses 1700-1900, with contents such as furniture, china, silver, dolls, etc.

Oxford University Museum
Entomological, zoological, geological & mineralogical collections.

Pendon Museum of Miniature Landscape & Transport - Abingdon.
Showing in miniature the countryside & its means of transport in the thirties, with trains & thatched village. Railway relics.

Town Museum - Abingdon
17th century building exhibiting fossil, archaeological items & collection of charters & documents.

Tolsey Museum - Burford
Seals, maces, charters & bygones - replica of Regency room with period furnishings & clothing.

Historic Monuments

Uffington Castle & White Horse - Uffington
White horse cut into the chalk - iron age hill fort.

Rollright Stones - Nr. Chipping Norton
77 stones placed in circle - an isolated King's stone & nearby an ancient burial chamber.

Minster Lovell House - Minster Lovell
15th century mediaeval house - ruins.

Deddington Castle - Deddington

Other things to see & do

Didcot railway centre -a large collection of locomotives etc., from Brunel's Great Western Railway.

Filkins -a working wool mill where rugs & garments are woven in traditional way.

Blenheim Palace. Woodstock.

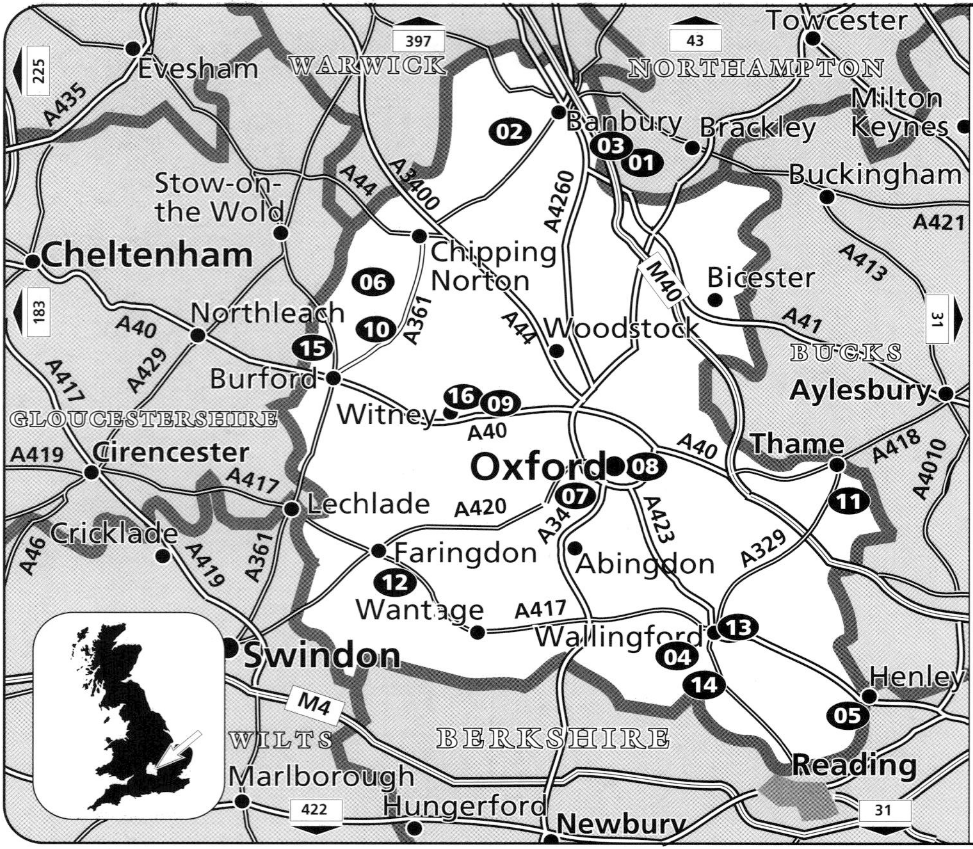

OXFORDSHIRE

Map reference

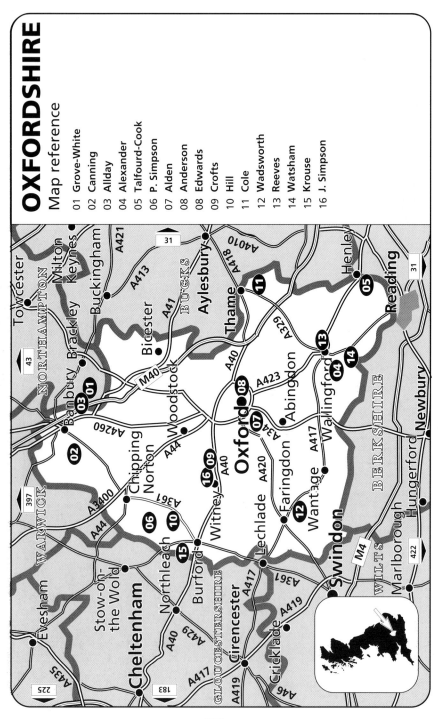

01 **Grove-White**
02 **Canning**
03 **Allday**
04 **Alexander**
05 **Talfourd-Cook**
06 **P. Simpson**
07 **Alden**
08 **Anderson**
08 **Edwards**
09 **Crofts**
10 **Hill**
11 **Cole**
12 **Wadsworth**
13 **Reeves**
14 **Watsham**
15 **Krouse**
16 **J. Simpson**

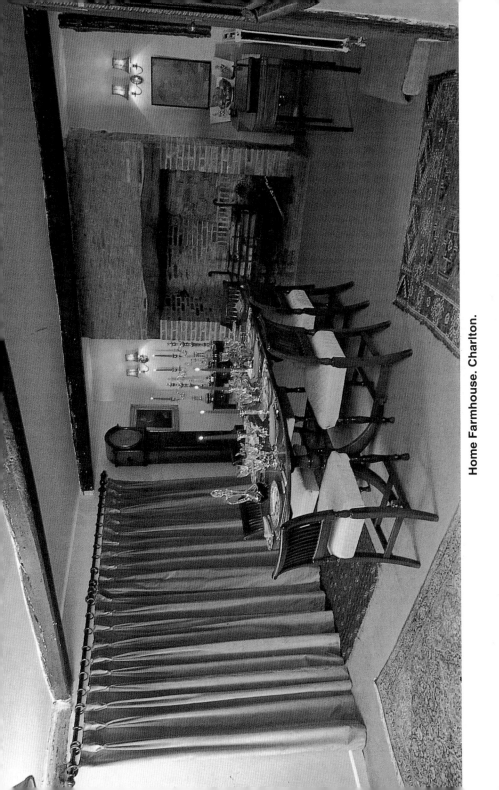

Home Farmhouse. Charlton.

Oxfordshire

	rate £ from - to per person	children taken	evening meals	animals taken

Home Farmhouse

Nearest Road: A.43

This charming, listed stone house dating from 1637, with its attractive, colourful, paved courtyard, provides an excellent base for visiting Oxford, Blenheim, Stratford-upon-Avon, Warwick & the beautiful Cotswold villages. Mrs Grove-White has used her expertise as a professional interior designer to ensure that the 3 double/twin-bedded rooms, with en-suite/private bathroom & colour T.V., are comfortable & elegantly furnished. Evening meals by arrangement only. Children over 12 yrs.

E-mail: grovewhite@lineone.net

Col. & Mrs Grove-White Home Farmhouse Charlton Nr. Banbury OX17 3DR Oxfordshire
Tel: (01295) 811683 Fax 01295 811683 Open: ALL YEAR Map Ref No. 01

rate £ from - to per person	children taken	evening meals	animals taken
£31.00 to £31.00	Y	Y	N

see PHOTO over p. 297

VISA: M'CARD:

La Madonette Country Guest House

Nearest Road: B.4035

A peacefully situated 17th-century millhouse set in rural surroundings, where Patti & Michael offer a warm welcome to their guests. The 5 spacious double en-suite bedrooms are comfortably furnished with full facilities & are attractively decorated throughout. Well located for the Cotswolds, Stratford-upon-Avon, Oxford & Blenheim. Good local pubs & restaurants offering evening meals nearby. An attractive lounge, gardens & swimming pool for guests' use. Licensed.

E-mail: lamadonett@aol.com

P.Ritter & M. Canning La Madonette Country Guest House North Newington Banbury OX15 6AA
Tel: (01295) 730212 Fax 01295 730363 Open: ALL YEAR Map Ref No. 02

rate £ from - to per person	children taken	evening meals	animals taken
£31.00 to £47.50	Y	N	N

VISA: M'CARD:

College Farmhouse

Nearest Road: A.43, M.40

Fine period farmhouse, with lovely views, set in its own secluded grounds, which include a lake, tennis court & organic vegetable garden. Ideally located for visits to Oxford, Warwick, Stratford-upon-Avon & the Cotswolds. Excellent home-produced food - special diets catered for. Stephen & Sara have considerable local knowledge. They enjoy gardening, bridge & racing. You will be sure of a very comfortable & peaceful stay. Evening meals by arrangement.

E-mail: SAllday@compuserve.com

Stephen & Sara Allday College Farmhouse Kings Sutton Banbury OX17 3PS Oxfordshire
Tel: (01295) 811473 Fax 01295 812505 Open: ALL YEAR Map Ref No. 03

rate £ from - to per person	children taken	evening meals	animals taken
£26.00 to £28.00	Y	Y	N

see PHOTO over p. 299

VISA: M'CARD:

The Well Cottage

Nearest Road: A.329

The Well Cottage is situated in a pretty garden, close to the River Thames, the historic town of Wallingford, the Berkshire Downs & the Ridgway. The cottage has been extended & now offers a secluded garden flat with 2 double/twin-bedded rooms, each with an en-suite bathroom, T.V. & tea/coffee-making facilities. Each room has its own private entrance. The Well Cottage is a charming home & is ideal for a relaxing break. Within easy reach of Oxford & Henley-on-Thames.

Joanna Alexander The Well Cottage Caps Lane Cholsey OX10 9HQ Oxfordshire
Tel: (01491) 651959 Mobile 07887 958920 Fax 01491 651675 Open: ALL YEAR Map Ref No. 04

rate £ from - to per person	children taken	evening meals	animals taken
£15.00 to £25.00	Y	N	Y

College Farmhouse. King Sutton.

Holmwood. Binfield Heath.

rate £ from - to per person	children taken	evening meals	animals taken	
£30.00 to £40.00	Y	N	N	**Holmwood** Nearest Road: A.4155 Holmwood is a large elegant Georgian country house, Grade II listed, furnished with antique, period furniture. There is a galleried hall, carved mahogany doors & marble fireplaces (wood fires in winter). All bedrooms are spacious & have en-suite facilities. The beautiful gardens extend to 3 1/2 acres & have extensive views over the Thames Valley. A good base for London & the South East. Heathrow Airport 30 mins', Reading 4 miles, Henley 2 1/2 miles. Children over 12 years. *Mr & Mrs Brian Talfourd-Cook Holmwood Shiplake Row Binfield Heath Henley RG9 4DP* *Tel: (0118) 9478747 Fax 0118 9478637 Open: ALL YEAR (Excl. Xmas) Map Ref No. 05*
see PHOTO over p. 300 VISA: M'CARD:				
£25.00 to £42.00	Y	Y	Y	**The Tollgate Inn & Restaurant** Nearest Road: B.4450 The Tollgate Inn is a charming small hotel & restaurant. There are 9 elegant bedrooms which are individually decorated & naturally, each has it's own bath or shower, T.V. 'phone, etc. The attractive sitting room & bars have a modern feel which sits well with this handsome former Georgian farmhouse. Dinners (available Tues - Sat) are robust & feature, where possible, local fresh produce, the majority from organic farms. Easy access to Burford, Stow-on-the-Wold, Chipping Campden & Broadway. Single supplement. *Penny Simpson The Tollgate Inn & Restaurant Church Street Kingham OX7 6YA Oxfordshire* *Tel: (01608) 658389 Fax 01608 659467 Open: Mid-JAN - DEC Map Ref No. 06*
see PHOTO over p. 302 VISA: M'CARD:				
£30.00 to £40.00	Y	N	N	**Broomhill** Nearest Road: A.34 Broomhill is a large comfortable family house, set in extensive grounds in a secluded lane & enjoying delightful views over the surrounding countryside. It is situated only 5 minutes between the historic town of Oxford & Abingdon-on-Thames. There are 3 double rooms & 1 single room. Each has either an en-suite or private bathroom, T.V. & tea/coffee-making facilities. Only 45 mins' from London & Heathrow Airport. An ideal base from which to explore Oxford. Children over 10. **E-mail: sara@rralden.force9.co.uk** *Richard & Sara Alden Broomhill Lincombe Lane Boars Hill Oxford OX1 5DZ Oxfordshire* *Tel: (01865) 735339 Open: ALL YEAR Map Ref No. 07*
£29.00 to £34.00	Y	N	N	**Sandfield Guest House** Nearest Road: A.40 A family-run guest house offering a high standard of comfort to guests preferring personal service & attention. Quiet & attractive accommodation which is tastefully decorated. Bedrooms are all en-suite or have a private bathroom, T.V. & hospitality tray. Guest lounge & gardens. Convenient for city-centre buses. Easy walking distance to Radcliffe Hospital Complex & Oxford Brookes University. On direct coach routes to London & Heathrow, Gatwick & Stansted Airports. Parking. Children over 6. **E-mail: stay@sandfield-guesthouse.co.uk** *Dr. & Mrs B. Anderson Sandfield Guest House 19 London Road Headington Oxford OX3 7RE* *Tel: (01865) 762406 Fax 01865 762406 Open: ALL YEAR (Excl. Xmas) Map Ref No. 08*
VISA: M'CARD: AMEX:				

Tollgate Inn. Kingham.

Oxfordshire

rate £ from - to per person	children taken	evening meals	animals taken
£24.00 to £40.00	Y	N	N

VISA: M'CARD:

Highfield Guest House

Nearest Road: A.4158

A pleasing & friendly house, with good access to the city centre & ring road. Accommodation is in 7 spacious & comfortable bedrooms, all attractively furnished & with matching decor. 5 with en-suite bathroom. All of the bedrooms have colour T.V. & tea/coffee-making facilities. A short walk brings you to the old attractive village of Iffley. Highfield Guest House is an excellent base for exploring the historic delights of Oxford.

E-mail: highfield.house@tesco.net

Mrs D. Edwards Highfield Guest House 91 Rose Hill Oxford OX4 4HT Oxfordshire
Tel: (01865) 774083 Fax 01865 774083 Open: ALL YEAR (Excl. Xmas) Map Ref No. 08

rate £ from - to per person	children taken	evening meals	animals taken
£20.00 to £30.00	Y	N	N

Crofters Guest House

Nearest Road: A.40

Situated in a lively market town, 10 miles from Oxford, on the edge of the Cotswolds, Blenheim Palace & Burford, & within easy reach of Stratford-upon-Avon. Guests are accommodated in comfortable family, double & twin rooms, all with excellent facilities. En-suite & luxury ground-floor garden rooms available. Your hosts Jean & Peter will make your stay a memorable experience. Arrive as a guest, leave as a friend.

E-mail: crofters.ghouse@virgin.net

Jean A. Crofts Crofters Guest House 29 Oxford Hill Witney Oxford OX8 6JU Oxfordshire
Tel: (01993) 778165 Fax 01993 778165 Open: ALL YEAR Map Ref No. 09

rate £ from - to per person	children taken	evening meals	animals taken
£27.00 to £33.00	Y	N	N

see PHOTO over p. 304

Shipton Grange House

Nearest Road: A.361

A unique conversion of a Georgian coach house & stabling situated in the former grounds of Shipton Court. Secluded in its own walled garden, & approached by a gated archway. There are 3 elegantly furnished guest rooms, each with an en-suite/private bathroom, colour T.V. & beverage facilities. Delicious breakfasts served in the attractive dining room. The friendly hosts are animal lovers & have a number of pet dogs. Shipton Grange is a delightful house, & ideal for visiting Oxford, Blenheim, etc. Children over 12.

Mrs Veronica Hill Shipton Grange House Shipton-under-Wychwood OX7 6DG Oxfordshire
Tel: (01993) 831298 Fax 01993 832082 Open: ALL YEAR (Excl. Xmas) Map Ref No. 10

rate £ from - to per person	children taken	evening meals	animals taken
£41.50 to £59.00	N	N	N

VISA: M'CARD: AMEX:

The Dairy

Nearest Road: A.329

This former milking parlour, set in 4 acres of lawn, provides all that one needs for a beautiful & peaceful stay. All of the bedrooms are bright & airy & include en-suite facilities, hairdryers, fresh flowers, biscuits, comfortable sofas & chairs etc. There is a delightful large open-plan lounge with views of the Chilterns. Evening meals are available at a village pub, only a short walk away. It is convenient for London either by train (50 mins' from local station.), coach or car. Oxford is 20' mins by car.

E-mail: thedairy@freeuk.com

Peter Cole The Dairy Moreton Nr. Thame OX9 2HX Oxfordshire
Tel: (01844) 214075 Fax 01844 214075 Open: ALL YEAR Map Ref No. 11

Shipton Grange House. Shipton-under-Wychwood.

Oxfordshire

rate £ from - to per person	children taken	evening meals	animals taken	
£22.50 to £38.00	Y	Y	N	**The Craven** Nearest Road: A.420 Roses & clematis cover this pretty 17th-century thatched cottage where breakfast is served around the huge pine table in the farmhouse kitchen. The beamed bedrooms have lovely views. One has a 17th-century 4-poster bed with cabbage rose chintz drapes &, as with all bedrooms, hand-embroidered sheets & pillow slips. Daughter, Katie, produces excellent meals using as much local produce as possible. Glorious walks from the doorstep & a shaggy Old English sheepdog. **E-mail: carol@thecraven.co.uk** *Carol A. Wadsworth The Craven Fernham Road Uffington SN7 7RD Oxfordshire* *Tel: (01367) 820449/820351 Open: ALL YEAR Map Ref No. 12*
see PHOTO over p. 306 VISA: M'CARD: AMEX:				
£25.00 to £35.00	Y	N	N	**Little Gables B & B** Nearest Road: A.4130 Little Gables is a detached family home in the outskirts of Wallingford, which is between the regatta town of Henley-on-Thames, Reading & the historic city of Oxford. Each of the 3 bedrooms is well-furnished & has an en-suite/private bathroom, T.V. & tea/coffee-making facilities. Garden seating area for guests. Parking. An excellent selection of pubs within walking distance. Easy access to the Bach Centre, Didcot Railway Centre, the Pendon Museum, M.4, M.40 & Gatwick Bus Link. **E-mail: jfreeves@globalnet.co.uk** *Mrs J Reeves Little Gables B & B 166 Crowmarsh Hill Wallingford OX10 8BG Oxfordshire* *Tel: (01491) 837834 Fax 01491 837834 Open: ALL YEAR Map Ref No. 13*
£25.00 to £45.00	Y	Y	N	**White House** Nearest Road: A.329 White House is an attractive, detached family home in the picturesque Thameside village of Moulsford on the edge of the Berkshire Downs, close to the Ridgeway & Thames Paths. The accommodation is at ground-floor level with its own separate front door, making access easy for disabled guests. Each room is very comfortable. There is a large garden with croquet lawn, which guests are welcome to enjoy. Delicious evening meals are available by prior arrangement. A delightful home. **E-mail: moulsford@whitehouse.com** *Mrs Maria Watsham White House Moulsford On Thames Wallingford OX10 9JD Oxfordshire* *Tel: (01491) 651397 Fax 01491 652560 Open: ALL YEAR (Excl. Xmas & New Year) Map Ref No. 14*
£27.50 to £32.00	N	N	N	**Akeman Cottage** Nearest Road: A.40 A warm welcome awaits you in this outstanding 18th-century cottage with log fires & oak beams. It has been renovated to a very high standard & boasts 3 attractive double bedrooms, each with T.V., tea/coffee-making facilities & an en-suite bathroom. Enjoy a full English breakfast before you start your tour of the Cotswolds, & return to the comfort & warm & friendly atmosphere of Akeman Cottage in the evening. Ramsden is within easy reach of Blenheim Palace, Woodstock & Burford. The historic city of Oxford is 13 miles. *Mr & Mrs Krouse Akeman Cottage Ramsden High Street Ramsden Witney OX7 3AU Oxfordshire* *Tel: (01993) 868383 Open: ALL YEAR (Excl. Xmas) Map Ref No. 15*

The Craven. Uffington.

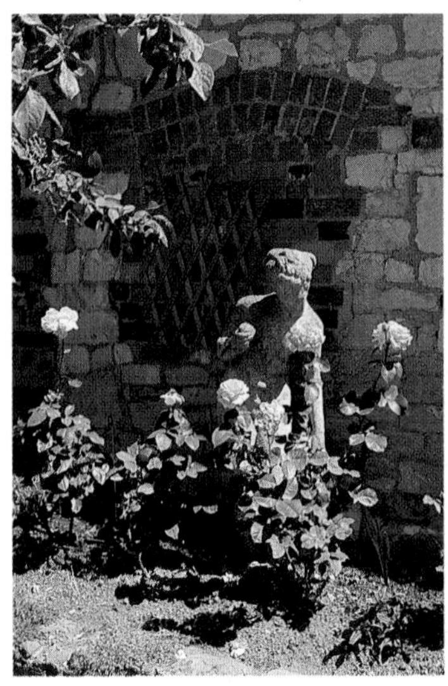

Oxfordshire

rate £ from - to per person	children taken	evening meals	animals taken	
£23.00 to £30.00	N	N	N	***Field View*** Nearest Road: A.40, A.4095 An attractive Cotswold stone house set in 2 acres, situated on picturesque Wood Green, mid-way between Oxford University & the Cotswolds. It is an ideal base for touring & yet is only 8 minutes walk from the centre of this lively Oxfordshire market town. A peaceful setting & a warm, friendly atmosphere await you. The accommodation offered is in 3 comfortable en-suite rooms with all modern amenities, including tea/coffee-making facilities, colour T.V., radio & hairdryer. **E-mail: jsimpson@netcomuk.co.uk** *Liz & John Simpson* *Field View* *Wood Green* *Witney OX8 6DE* *Oxfordshire* *Tel: (01993) 705485* *Mobile 0468 614347* *Open: ALL YEAR* *Map Ref No. 16*

All the establishments mentioned in this guide are members of The Worldwide Bed & Breakfast Association

When booking your accommodation please mention The Best Bed & Breakfast

Shropshire

Shropshire (Heart of England)

Shropshire is a borderland with a very turbulent history. Physically it straddles highlands & lowlands with border mountains to the west, glacial plains, upland, moorlands & fertile valleys & the River Severn cutting through. It has been quarrelled & fought over by rulers & kings from earliest times. The English, the Romans & the Welsh all wanted to hold Shropshire because of its unique situation. The ruined castles & fortifications dotted across the county are all reminders of its troubled life. The most impressive of these defences is Offa's Dyke, an enormous undertaking intended to be a permanent frontier between England & Wales.

Shropshire has great natural beauty, countryside where little has changed with the years. Wenlock Edge & Clun Forest, Carding Mill Valley, the Long Mynd, Caer Caradoc, Stiperstones & the trail along Offa's Dyke itself, are lovely walking areas with magnificent scenery.

Shrewsbury was & is a virtual island, almost completely encircled by the Severn River. The castle was built at the only gap, sealing off the town. In this way all comings & goings were strictly controlled. In the 18th century two bridges, the English bridge & the Welsh bridge, were built to carry the increasing traffic to the town but Shrewsbury still remains England's finest Tudor city.

Massive Ludlow Castle was a Royal residence, home of Kings & Queens through the ages, whilst the town is also noted for its Georgian houses.

As order came out of chaos, the county settled to improving itself & became the cradle of the Industrial Revolution. Here Abraham Darby discovered how to use coke (from the locally mined coal) to smelt iron. There was more iron produced here in the 18th century than in any other county. A variety of great industries sprang up as the county's wealth & ingenuity increased. In 1781 the world's first iron bridge opened to traffic.

There are many fine gardens in the county. At Hodnet Hall near Market Drayton, the grounds cover 60 acres & the landscaping includes lakes & pools, trees, shrubs & flowers in profusion. Weston Park has 1,000 acres of parkland, woodland gardens & lakes landscaped by Capability Brown.

The house is Restoration period & has a splendid collection of pictures, furniture, china & tapestries.

Shrewsbury hosts an annual poetry festival & one of England's best flower shows whilst a Festival of Art, Music & Drama is held each year in Ludlow with Shakespeare performed against the castle ruins.

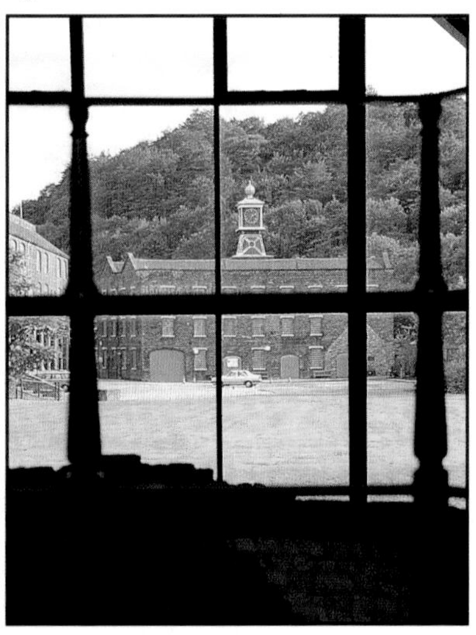

Coalbrookedale Museum.

Shropshire

Shropshire Gazeteer

Areas of Outstanding Natural Beauty
The Shropshire Hills.

Historic Houses & Castles

Stokesay Castle - Craven Arms
13th century fortified manor house. Still occupied - wonderful setting - extremely well preserved. Fine timbered gatehouse.
Weston Park - Nr. Shifnal
17th century - fine example of Restoration period - landscaping by Capability Brown. Superb collection of pictures.
Shrewsbury Castle - Shrewsbury
Built in Norman era - interior decorations - painted boudoir.
Benthall Hall - Much Wenlock
16th century. Stone House - mullioned windows. Fine wooden staircase - splendid plaster ceilings.
Shipton Hall - Much Wenlock
Elizabethan. Manor House - walled garden - mediaeval dovecote.
Upton Cressett Hall - Bridgnorth
Elizabethan. Manor House & Gatehouse. Excellent plaster work. . 14th century great hall.

Cathedrals & Churches

Ludlow (St. Lawrence)
14th century nave & transepts. 15th century pinnacled tower. Restored extensively in 19th century. Carved choir stalls, perpendicular chancel - original glass. Monuments.
Shrewsbury (St. Mary)
14th, 15th, 16th century glass. Norman origins.
Stottesdon (St. Mary)
12th century carvings.Norman font. Fine decorations with columns & tracery.
Lydbury North (St. Michael)
14th century transept, 15th century nave roof, 17th century box pews and altar rails. Norman font.
Longor (St. Mary the Virgin)
13th century having an outer staircase to West gallery.
Cheswardine (St. Swithun)
13th century chapel - largely early English. 19th century glass and old brasses. Fine sculpture.
Tong (St. Mary the Virgin with St. Bartholomew)
15th century. Golden chapel of 1515, stencilled walls, remains of paintings on screens, gilt fan vaulted ceiling. Effigies, fine monuments

Museums & Galleries

Clive House - Shrewsbury
Fine Georgian House - collection of Shropshire ceramics. Regimental museum of 1st Queen's Dragoon Guards.
Rowley's House Museum - Shrewsbury
Roman material from Viroconium and prehistoric collection.
Coleham Pumping Station - Old Coleham
Preserved beam engines
Acton Scott Working Farm Museum - Nr. Church Stretton
Site showing agricultural practice before the advent of mechanization.
Ironbridge Gorge Museum - Telford
Series of industrial sites in the Severn Gorge.
CoalBrookdale Museum & Furnace Site
Showing Abraham Darby's blast furnace history. Ironbridge information centre is next to the world's first iron bridge.
Mortimer Forest Museum - Nr. Ludlow
Forest industries of today and yesterday. Ecology of the forest.
Whitehouse Museum of Buildings & Country life - Aston Munslow
4 houses together in one, drawing from every century 13th to 18th, together with utensils and implements of the time.
The Buttercross Museum - Ludlow
Geology, natural & local history of area.
Reader`s House-Ludlow
Splendid example of a 16th century town house. 3 storied porch.
Much Wenlock Museum.-Much Wenlock
Geology, natural & local history.
Clun Town Museum - Clun
Pre-history earthworks, rights of way, commons & photographs.

Historic Monuments

Acton Burnell Castle - Shrewsbury
13th century fortified manor house - ruins only.

Shropshire

Boscobel House - Shifnal
17th century house.
Bear Steps - Shrewsbury
Half timbered buildings. Mediaeval.
Abbot's House - Shrewsbury
15th century half-timbered.
Buildwas Abbey - Nr. Telford
12th century - Savignac Abbey - ruins. The church is nearly complete with 14 Norman arches.
Haughmond Abbey - Shrewsbury
12th century - remains of house of Augustinian canons.
Wenlock Priory - Much Wenlock
13th century abbey - ruins.
Roman Town - Wroxeter
2nd century - remains of town of Viroconium including public baths and colonnade.
Moreton Corbet Castle - Moreton Corbet
13th century keep, Elizabethan features - gatehouse altered 1519.
Lilleshall Abbey
12th century - completed 13th century, West front has notable doorway.
Bridgnorth Castle - Bridgnorth
Ruins of Norman castle whose angle of incline is greater than Pisa.
Whiteladies Priory - Boscobel
12th century cruciform church - ruins.
Old Oswestry - Oswestry
Iron age hill fort covering 68 acres; five ramparts and having an elaborate western portal.

Other things to see & do

Ludlow Festival of Art and Drama - annual event
Shrewsbury Flower Show - every August
Severn Valley Railway - the longest full guage steam railway in the country

Kings Head Inn. Shrewsbury.

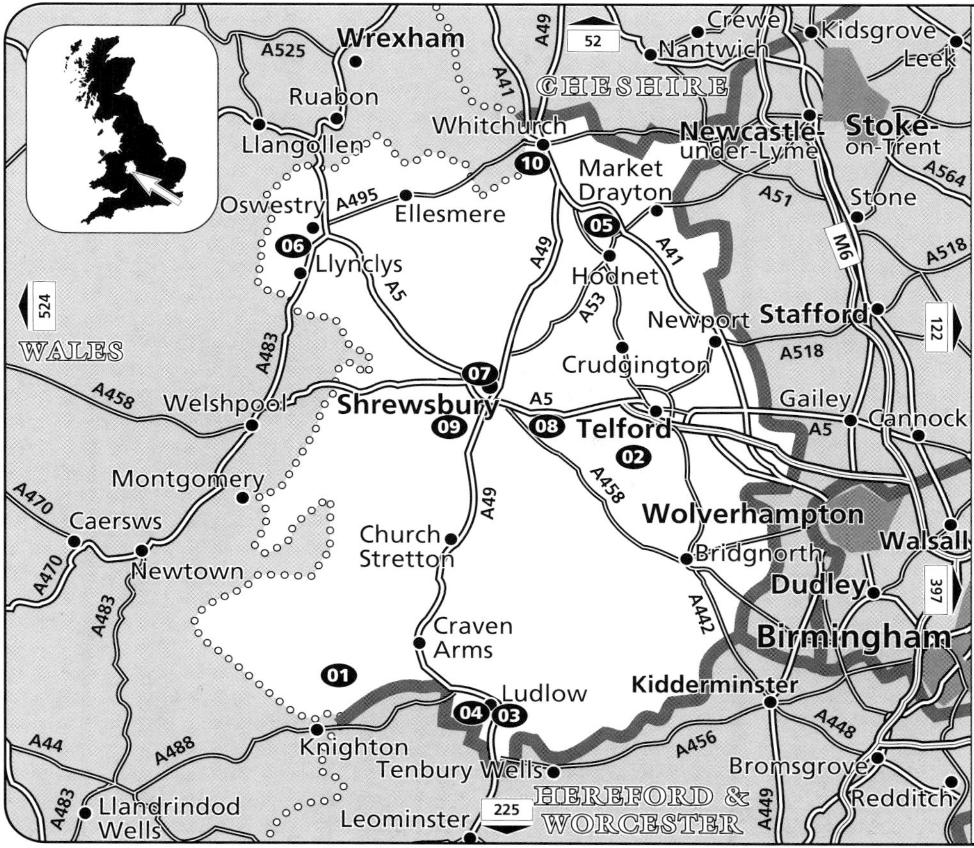

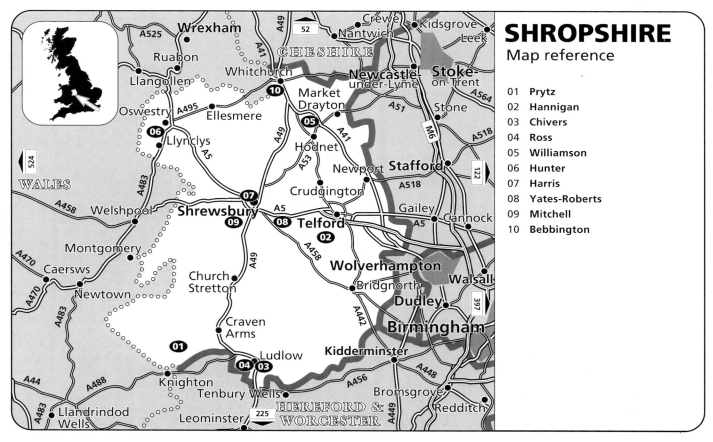

SHROPSHIRE

Map reference

01 **Prytz**
02 **Hannigan**
03 **Chivers**
04 **Ross**
05 **Williamson**
06 **Hunter**
07 **Harris**
08 **Yates-Roberts**
09 **Mitchell**
10 **Bebbington**

Shropshire

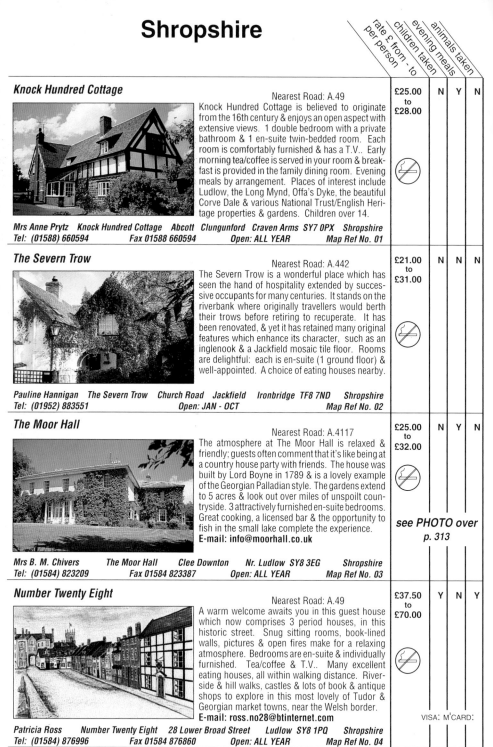

	rate £ from - to per person	children taken	evening meals	animals taken

Knock Hundred Cottage

Nearest Road: A.49

Knock Hundred Cottage is believed to originate from the 16th century & enjoys an open aspect with extensive views. 1 double bedroom with a private bathroom & 1 en-suite twin-bedded room. Each room is comfortably furnished & has a T.V.. Early morning tea/coffee is served in your room & breakfast is provided in the family dining room. Evening meals by arrangement. Places of interest include Ludlow, the Long Mynd, Offa's Dyke, the beautiful Corve Dale & various National Trust/English Heritage properties & gardens. Children over 14.

Mrs Anne Prytz Knock Hundred Cottage Abcott Clungunford Craven Arms SY7 0PX Shropshire
Tel: (01588) 660594 Fax 01588 660594 Open: ALL YEAR Map Ref No. 01

rate £ from - to per person	children taken	evening meals	animals taken
£25.00 to £28.00	N	Y	N

The Severn Trow

Nearest Road: A.442

The Severn Trow is a wonderful place which has seen the hand of hospitality extended by successive occupants for many centuries. It stands on the riverbank where originally travellers would berth their trows before retiring to recuperate. It has been renovated, & yet it has retained many original features which enhance its character, such as an inglenook & a Jackfield mosaic tile floor. Rooms are delightful: each is en-suite (1 ground floor) & well-appointed. A choice of eating houses nearby.

Pauline Hannigan The Severn Trow Church Road Jackfield Ironbridge TF8 7ND Shropshire
Tel: (01952) 883551 Open: JAN - OCT Map Ref No. 02

rate £ from - to per person	children taken	evening meals	animals taken
£21.00 to £31.00	N	N	N

The Moor Hall

Nearest Road: A.4117

The atmosphere at The Moor Hall is relaxed & friendly; guests often comment that it's like being at a country house party with friends. The house was built by Lord Boyne in 1789 & is a lovely example of the Georgian Palladian style. The gardens extend to 5 acres & look out over miles of unspoilt countryside. 3 attractively furnished en-suite bedrooms. Great cooking, a licensed bar & the opportunity to fish in the small lake complete the experience.

E-mail: info@moorhall.co.uk

Mrs B. M. Chivers The Moor Hall Clee Downton Nr. Ludlow SY8 3EG Shropshire
Tel: (01584) 823209 Fax 01584 823387 Open: ALL YEAR Map Ref No. 03

rate £ from - to per person	children taken	evening meals	animals taken
£25.00 to £32.00	N	Y	N

see PHOTO over p. 313

Number Twenty Eight

Nearest Road: A.49

A warm welcome awaits you in this guest house which now comprises 3 period houses, in this historic street. Snug sitting rooms, book-lined walls, pictures & open fires make for a relaxing atmosphere. Bedrooms are en-suite & individually furnished. Tea/coffee & T.V.. Many excellent eating houses, all within walking distance. Riverside & hill walks, castles & lots of book & antique shops to explore in this most lovely of Tudor & Georgian market towns, near the Welsh border.

E-mail: ross.no28@btinternet.com

Patricia Ross Number Twenty Eight 28 Lower Broad Street Ludlow SY8 1PQ Shropshire
Tel: (01584) 876996 Fax 01584 876860 Open: ALL YEAR Map Ref No. 04

rate £ from - to per person	children taken	evening meals	animals taken
£37.50 to £70.00	Y	N	Y

VISA: M'CARD:

The Moor Hall. Ludlow.

Pen-Y-Dyffryn Country Hotel . Rhydycroesau.

rate £ from - to per person	children taken	evening meals	animals taken	
£22.00 to £35.00	N	N	N	**Mickley House** Nearest Road: A.41, A.53 When visiting Ironbridge, Shrewsbury or Chester, your hosts offer peace, quiet & comfort in their tastefully restored farmhouse, retaining many internal Victorian features. The tranquillity of the house spills out into landscaped gardens. Relax or meander through rose-scented pergolas to pools & a trickling waterfall. The restful drawing room beckons after sight-seeing. Restaurants/pubs nearby. En-suite bedrooms of different style/decor, with all facilities. 1 bedroom with authentic Louis XV king-size bed. Also, ground-floor room. *Mrs Pauline Williamson Mickley House Faulsgreen Tern Hill Market Drayton TF9 3QW Shropshire* *Tel: (01630) 638505 Fax 01630 638505 Open: ALL YEAR (Excl. Xmas) Map Ref No. 05*
£36.00 to £48.00 *see PHOTO over p. 314* VISA: M'CARD: AMEX:	Y	Y	Y	**Pen-Y-Dyffryn Country Hotel** Nearest Road: A.5 Set almost a thousand feet up in the peaceful Shropshire/Wales border hills, this silver-stone Georgian rectory has a real 'away from it all' atmosphere. But the medieval towns of Chester & Shrewsbury are only a short drive, so civilisation is close by. High-quality local & increasingly organic food is served in the restaurant, complete with its own log fire. All bedrooms are en-suite, with colour T.V., telephone etc. & some even have their own private patios. Fully licensed. **E-mail: stay@peny.co.uk** *Miles & Audrey Hunter Pen-Y-Dyffryn Country Hotel Rhydycroesau Oswestry SY10 7JD Shropshire* *Tel: (01691) 653700 Fax 01691 650066 Open: ALL YEAR Map Ref No. 06*
£22.00 to £27.00	N	N	N	**Tudor House** Nearest Road: A.5 This Grade II listed building is centrally situated in a quiet medieval street in picturesque & historic Shrewsbury (Brother Cadfael country). Dating from 1450, the house has a wealth of oak beams, & has been tastefully redecorated & refurbished throughout. Some of the bedrooms have en-suite facilities; all have washbasins, colour T.V. & central heating & are very comfortable. Special diets available in non-smoking dining room. Drinks are served in residents' licensed lounge. *Mrs Mair Harris Tudor House 2 Fish Street Shrewsbury SY1 1UR Shropshire* *Tel: (01743) 351735 Open: ALL YEAR Map Ref No. 07*
£35.00 to £50.00 *see PHOTO over p. 316* VISA: M'CARD: AMEX:	N	Y	N	**Upper Brompton Farm** Nearest Road: A.458 Upper Brompton Farm is the quintessence of English country living. Croquet on the lawn, 4-poster beds, a roaring open fire, roast beef & great British puddings. These things together with the personal attention of the hosts has won a prestigious award. Glorious landscapes, perfect walking country together with N. T. properties, Ironbridge (15 mins') & other places of interest are within easy reach. Only 5 mins' from Shrewsbury, it is ideally situated for exploring this "best kept secret", Shropshire. **E-mail: upper-brompton.farm@dial.pipex.com** *Mrs Christine Yates-Roberts Upper Brompton Farm Cross Houses Shrewsbury SY5 6LE Shropshire* *Tel: (01743) 761629 Fax 01743 761679 Open: ALL YEAR Map Ref No. 08*

Upper Brompton Farm. Cross Houses.

Shropshire

rate £ from - to per person	children taken	evening meals	animals taken	
£25.00 to £30.00	N	Y	N	***The White House*** Nearest Road: A.488, A.5 A lovely, 16th-century, black-and-white, half-timbered guest house with nearly 2 acres of gardens & river, 3 miles south-west of medieval Shrewsbury. Ironbridge, Mid-Wales & the Long Mynd within 30 mins' drive. 6 guest rooms, some en-suite, each with tea/coffee, etc. 2 sitting rooms, 1 with T.V.. Parking. The dining room offers a fresh, varied menu supplemented by vegetables and herbs from the garden, and the house hens provide your breakfast eggs! Children over 12. **E-mail: mgm@whitehousehanwood.freeserve.co.uk** *Mike & Gill Mitchell The White House Hanwood Shrewsbury SY5 8LP Shropshire* *Tel: (01743) 860414 Fax 01743 860414 Open: ALL YEAR Map Ref No. 09*
£35.00 to £50.00	N	N	Y	***Dearnford Hall*** Nearest Road: A.41, A.49 'Country House hospitality at its best' at this magnificent family home. Cosy sofas, log fires, music & memorable breakfasts in a relaxed atmosphere. Beautiful en-suite bedrooms & drawing room overlook sweeping lawns & a garden. Paradise for garden enthusiasts, N. T. visitors, antique browsers & lovers of country pursuits, with fly-fishing on the Bebbingtons' own trout lake. Ideal for Chester, Shrewsbury, the Potteries & the Welsh Borders. Children over 12. Animals by arrangement. **E-mail: dearnford_hall@yahoo.com** *Charles & Jane Bebbington Dearnford Hall Whitchurch SY13 3JJ Shropshire* *Tel: (01948) 662319 Fax 01948 666670 Open: ALL YEAR (Excl. Xmas) Map Ref No. 10*

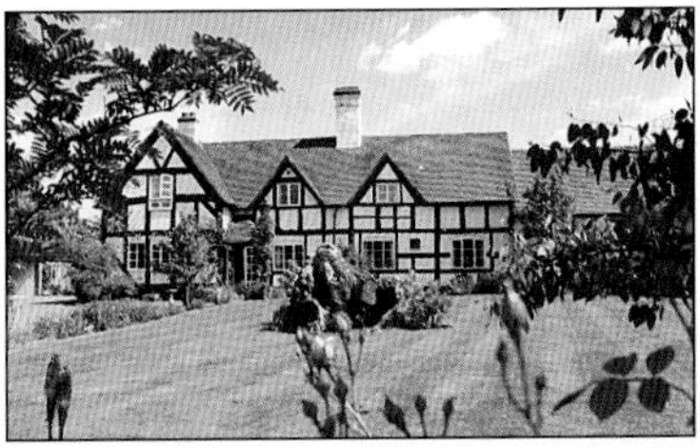

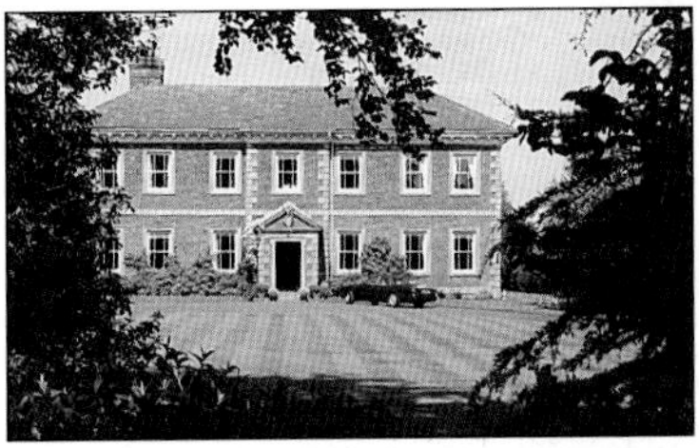

All the establishments mentioned in this guide are members of The Worldwide Bed & Breakfast Association

When booking your accommodation please mention The Best Bed & Breakfast

Somerset, Bath & Bristol

Somerset

(West Country)

Fabulous legends, ancient customs, charming villages, beautiful churches, breathtaking scenery & a glorious cathedral, Somerset has them all, along with a distinctively rich local dialect. The essence of Somerset lies in its history & myth & particularly in the unfolding of the Arthurian tale.

Legend grows from the bringing of the Holy Grail to Glastonbury by Joseph of Arimathea, to King Arthur's castle at Camelot, held by many to be sited at Cadbury, to the image of the dead King's barge moving silently through the mists over the lake to the Isle of Avalon. Archaeological fact lends support to the conjecture that Glastonbury, with its famous Tor, was an island in an ancient lake. Another island story surrounds King Alfred, reputedly sheltering from the Danes on the Isle of Athelney & there burning his cakes.

Historically, Somerset saw the last battle fought on English soil, at Sedgemoor in 1685. The defeat of the Monmouth rebellion resulted in the wrath of James II falling on the West Country in the form of Judge Jeffreys & his "Bloody Assize".

To the west of the county lies part of the Exmoor National Park, with high moorland where deer roam & buzzards soar & a wonderful stretch of cliffs from Minehead to Devon. Dunster is a popular village with its octagonal Yarn market, & its old world cottages, dominated at one end by the castle & at the other by the tower on Conygar Hill.

To the east the woods & moors of the Quantocks are protected as an area of outstanding natural beauty. The Vale of Taunton is famous for its apple orchards & for the golden cider produced from them.

The south of the county is a land of rolling countryside & charming little towns, Chard, Crewkerne, Ilchester & Ilminster amongst others.

To the north the limestone hills of Mendip are honeycombed with spectacular caves & gorges, some with neolithic remains, as at Wookey Hole & Cheddar Gorge.

Wells is nearby, so named because of the multitude of natural springs. Hardly a city, Wells boasts a magnificent cathedral set amongst spacious lawns & trees. The west front is one of the glories of English architecture with its sculptured figures & soaring arches. A spectacular feature is the astronomical clock, the work of 14th century monk Peter Lightfoot. The intricate face tells the hours, minutes, days & phases of the moon. On the hour, four mounted knights charge forth & knock one another from their horses.

Wells Cathedral Choir.

Somerset, Bath & Bristol

Bath is one of the most loved historic cities in England. It owes its existence to the hot springs which bubble up five hundred thousand gallons of water a day at a temperature of some 120' F. According to legend, King Bladud appreciated the healing qualities of the waters & established his capital here, calling it Aquae Sulis. He built an elaborate healing & entertainment centre around the springs including reservoirs, baths & hypercaust rooms.

The Roman Baths, not uncovered until modern times, are on the lowest of three levels. Above them came the mediaeval city & on the top layer at modern street level is the elegant Georgian Pump Room.

Edward was crowned the first King of all England in 973, in the Saxon Abbey which stood on the site of the present fifteenth century abbey. This building, in the graceful perpendicular style with elegant fan vaulting, is sometimes called the "lantern of the West", on account of its vast clerestories & large areas of glass.

During the Middle Ages the town prospered through Royal patronage & the development of the wool industry. Bath became a city of weavers, the leading industrial town in the West of England.

The 18th century gave us the superb Georgian architecture which is the city's glory. John Wood, an ambitious young architect laid out Queen Anne's Square in the grand Palladian style, & went on to produce his masterpiece, the Royal Crescent. His scheme for the city was continued by his son & a number of other fine architects, using the beautiful Bath stone. Bath was a centre of fashion, with Beau Nash the leader of a glittering society.

In 1497 John & Sebastian Cabot sailed from the Bristol quayside to the land they called Ameryke, in honour of the King's agent in Bristol, Richard Ameryke. Bristol's involvement in the colonisation of the New World & the trade in sugar, tobacco & slaves that followed, made her the second city in the kingdom in the 18th century. John Cabot is commemorated by the Cabot Tower on grassy Brandon Hill - a fine vantage point from which to view the city. On the old docks below are the Bristol Industrial Museum & the SS Great Britain, Brunel's famous iron ship. Another achievement of this master engineer, the Clifton Suspension Bridge, spans Bristol's renowned beauty spot, the Clifton Gorge. For a glimpse of Bristol's elegant past, stroll through Clifton with its stately terraces & spacious Downs.

A short walk from the busy city centre & modern shopping area, the visitor in search of history will find cobbled King Street with its merchant seamen's almhouses & The Theatre Royal, the oldest theatre in continuous use in England, & also Llandoger Trow, an ancient inn associated with Treasure Island & Robinson Crusoe.

Bath Abbey.

Somerset, Bath & Bristol

Somerset, Bath & Bristol Gazeteer

Areas of Outstanding Natural Beauty
Mendip Hills. Quantock Hills. National Park - Exmoor. The Cotswolds.

Historic Houses & Castles

Abbot's Fish House - Meare
14th century house.
Barrington Court - Illminster
16th century house & gardens.
Blaise Castle House - Henbury Nr. Bristol
18th century house - now folk museum, extensive woodlands.
Brympton D'Evercy - Nr. Yeovil
Mansion with 17th century front & Tudor west front. Adjacent is 13th century priest's house & church. Formal gardens & vineyard.
Claverton Manor - Nr. Bath
Greek revival house - furnished with 17th, 18th, 19th century American originals.
Clevedon Court - Clevedon
14th century manor house, 13th century hall, 12th century tower. Lovely garden with rare trees & shrubs. This is where Thackerey wrote much of 'Vanity Fair'.
Dyrham Park - Between Bristol & Bath
17th century house - fine panelled rooms, Dutch paintings, furniture.
Dunster Castle - Dunster
13th century castle with fine 17th century staircase & ceilings.
East Lambrook Manor - South Petherton
15th century house with good panelling.
Gaulden Manor - Tolland
12th century manor. Great Hall having unique plaster ceiling & oak screen. Antique furniture.
Halsway Manor - Crowcombe
14th century house with fine panelling.
Hatch Court - Hatch Beauchamp
Georgian house in the Palladian style with China room.
King John's Hunting Lodge - Axbridge
Early Tudor merchant's house.
Lytes Carry - Somerton
14th & 15th century manor house with a chapel & formal garden.
Montacute House - Yeovil
Elizabethan house with fine examples of Heraldic Glass, tapestries, panelling & furniture. Portrait gallery of Elizabethan & Jacobean paintings.
Tintinhull House - Yeovil
17th century house with beautiful gardens.
Priory Park College - Bath
18th century Georgian mansion, now Roman Catholic school.
No. 1 Royal Crescent - Bath
An unaltered Georgian house built 1767.
Red Lodge - Bristol
16th century house - period furniture & panelling.
St. Vincent's Priory - Bristol
Gothic revival house, built over caves which were sanctuary for Christians.
St Catherine's Court - Nr. Bath
Small Tudor house - associations with Henry VIII & Elizabeth I.

Cathedrals & Churches

Axbridge (St. John)
1636 plaster ceiling & panelled roofs.
Backwell (St. Andrew)
12th to 17th century, 15th century tower, repaired 17th century. 15th century tomb & chancel, 16th century screen, 18th century brass chandelier.
Bath Abbey
Perpendicular - monastic church, 15th century foundation. Nave finished 17th century, restorations in 1674.
Bishop's Lydeard (St. Mary)
15th century. Notable tower, rood screen & glass.
Bristol Cathedral
Mediaeval. Eastern halfnave Victorian. Chapterhouse richly ornamented.
Iron screen, 3 fonts, "fairest parish church in all England".
Bristol (St. Mary Radcliffe)
Bristol (St. Stephens')
Perpendicular - monuments, magnificent tower.
Bruton (St. Mary)
Fine 2 towered 15th century church. Georgian chancel, tie beam roof, Georgian reredos. Jacobean screen. 15th century embroidery.
Chewton Mendip (St. Mary Magdalene)
12th century with later additions. 12th century doorway, 15th century bench ends, magnificent 16th century tower & 17th century lecturn.

Somerset, Bath & Bristol

Crewkerne (St. Bartholomew)
Magnificent west front & roofs, 15th & 16th century. South doorway dating from 13th century, wonderful 15th century painted glass & 18th century chandeliers.
East Brent (St. Mary)
Mainly 15th century. Plaster ceiling, painted glass & carved bench ends.
Glastonbury (St. John)
One of the finest examples of perpendicular towers. Tie beam roof, late mediaeval painted glass, mediaeval vestment & early 16th century altar tomb.
High Ham (St. Andrew)
Sumptuous roofs & vaulted rood screen. Carved bench ends. Jacobean lecturn, mediaeval painted glass. Norman font.
Kingsbury Episcopi (St. Martin)
14th-15th century. Good tower with fan vaulting. Late mediaeval painted glass.
Long Sutton (Holy Trinity)
15th century with noble tower & magnificent tie beam roof. 15th century pulpit & rood screen, tower vaulting.
Martock (All Saints)
13th century chancel. Nave with tie beam roof, outstanding of its kind. 17th century paintings of Apostles.
North Cadbury (St. Michael)
painted glass.
Pilton (St. John)
12th century with arcades. 15th century roofs.
Taunton (St. Mary Magdalene)
Highest towers in the county. Five nave roof, fragments of mediaeval painted glass.
Trull (All Saints)
15th century with many mediaeval art treasures & 15th century glass.
Wells Cathedral-Wells
Magnificent west front with carved figures. Splendid tower. Early English arcade of nave & transepts. 60 fine misericords c.1330. Lady chapel with glass & star vault. Chapter House & Bishop's Palace.
Weston Zoyland (St. Mary)
15th century bench ends. 16th century heraldic glass. Jacobean pulpit.
Wrington (All Souls)
15th century aisles & nave; font, stone pulpit, notable screens.

Museums & Galleries

Admiral Blake Museum - Bridgewater
Exhibits relating to Battle of Sedgemoor, archaeology.
American Museum in Britain - Claverton Nr. Bath
American decorative arts 17th to 19th century displayed in series of furnished rooms & galleries of special exhibits. Paintings, furniture, glass wood & metal work, textiles, folk sculpture, etc.
Borough Museum - Hendford Manor Hall, Yeovil
Archaeology, firearms collections & Bailward Costume Collection.
Bristol Industrial Museum - Bristol
Collections of transport items of land, sea & air. Many unique items.
Burdon Manor - Washford
14th century manor house with Saxon fireplace & cockpit.
City of Bristol Art Gallery - Bristol
Permanent & loan collections of paintings, English & Oriental ceramics.
Glastonbury Lake Village Museum - Glastonbury
Late prehistoric antiquities.
Gough's Cave Museum - Cheddar
Upper Paleolithic remains, skeleton, flints, amber & engraved stones.
Holburne of Menstrie Museum - Bath
Old Master paintings, silver, glass, porcelain, furniture & miniatures in 18th century building. Work of 20th century craftworkers.
Hinton Priory - Hinton Charterhouse
13th century - ruins of Carthusian priory.
Kings Weston Roman Villa - Lawrence Weston
3rd & 4th centuries - mosaics of villa - some walls.
Museum of Costume - Bath
Collection of fashion from 17th century to present day.
Roman Baths - Bath
Roman Museum - Bath
Material from remains of extensive Roman baths & other Roman sites.
Stoney Littleton Barrow - Nr. Bath
Neolithic burial chamber - restoration work 1858.
St. Nicholas Church & City Museum - Bristol
Mediaeval antiquities relating to local

Somerset, Bath & Bristol

history, Church plate & vestments. Altarpiece by Hogarth.

Temple Church - Bristol
14th & 15th century ruins.

Victoria Art Gallery - Bath
Paintings, prints, drawings, glass, ceramics, watches, coins, etc. Bygones - permanent & temporary exhibitions. Geology collections.

Wookey Hole Cave Museum - Wookey Hole
Remains from Pliocene period. Relics of Celtic & Roman civilization. Exhibition of handmade paper-making.

Historic Monuments

Cleeve Abbey - Cleeve
Ruined 13th century house, with timber roof & wall paintings.

Farleigh Castle - Farleigh Hungerford
14th century remains - museums in chapel.

Glastonbury Abbey - Glastonbury
12th & 13th century ruins of St. Joseph's chapel & Abbot's kitchen.

Muchelney Abbey - Muchelney
15th century ruins of Benedictine abbey.

Other things to see & do

Black Rock Nature Reserve - Cheddar
Circular walk through plantation woodland, downland grazing.

Cheddar Caves
Show caves at the foot of beautiful Cheddar Gorge.

Clifton Zoological Gardens - Bristol
Flourishing zoo with many exhibits - beautiful gardens.

Clifton Suspension Bridge - Bristol
Designed by Isambard Kingdom Brunel, opened in 1864. Viewpoint & picnic spot Camera Obscura.

Cricket St. Thomas Wildlife Park - Nr. Chard
Wildlife park, heavy horse centre, countryside museum, etc.

The Pump Room - Bath
18th century neo-classical interior. Spa.

Clifton Suspension Bridge. Bristol.

SOMERSET, BATH & BRISTOL

Map reference

00	Youngs
01	Dodd
01	Besley
01	Lanz
01	Poole
01	Ford
01	Beckett
01	Addison
01	Stabbins
01	Huxley
01	King
01	Smith
01	Lanz
01	Gordon-Duff
01	Metcalf
01	Bryan
01	Seymour
01	Thwaites
01	Selby
02	Westlake
03	Riley
04	Priddle
04	Graham
05	Holder
06	Henry
07	Hoose
11	Gallannaugh
12	Tasker
13	Shellard
14	Newman-C.
15	Bale
16	Vicary
17	Redmond
18	Cooper
21	Brewer
22	Dearden
24	Copeland
26	Mitchem
29	Eyre
34	Frost
35	Nowell
36	Thompson
37	Parsons
38	Durbin

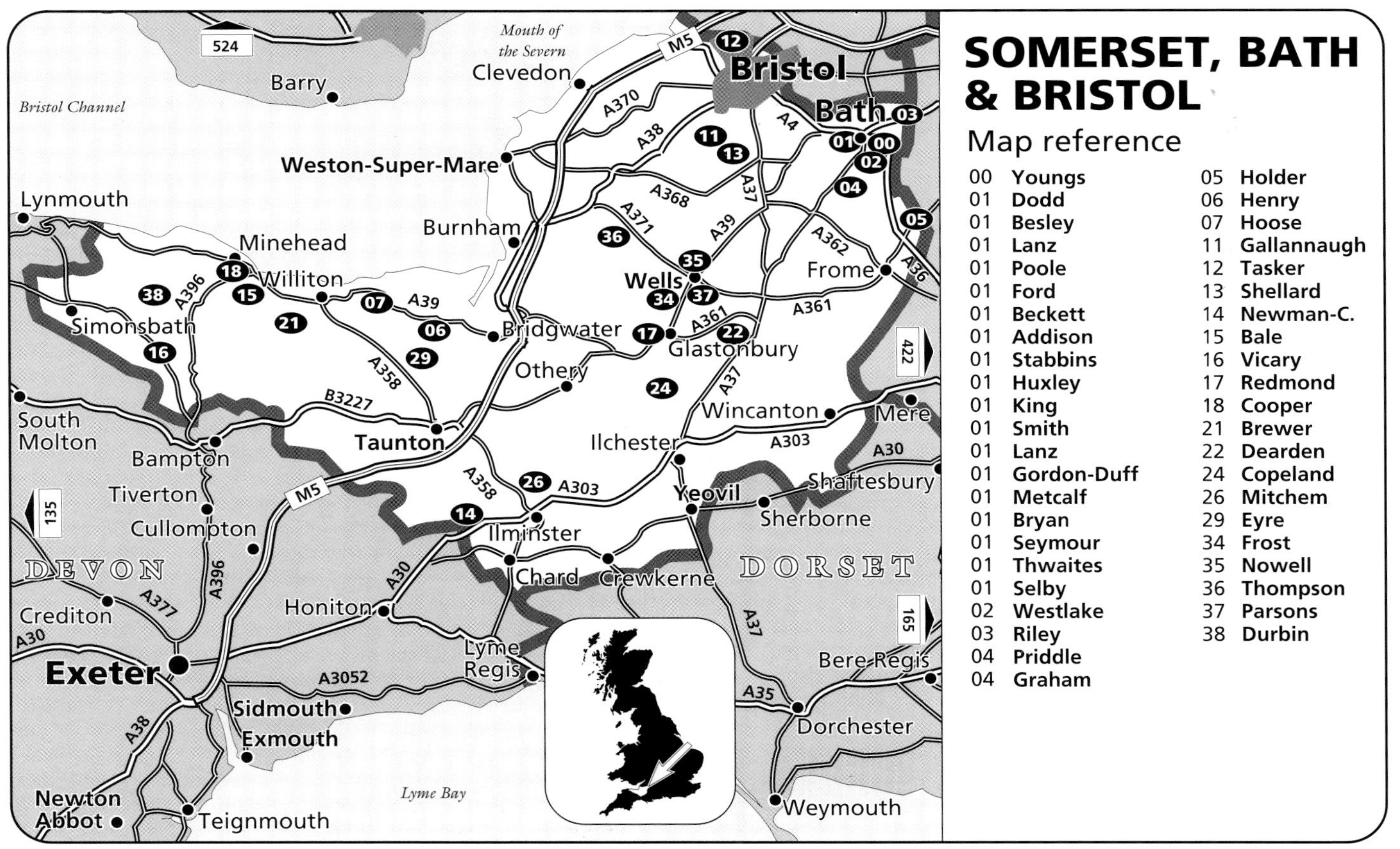

The Old Red House. Bath.

Apsley House Hotel. Bath.

Somerset

rate £ from - to per person	children taken	evening meals	animals taken

Brocks

Nearest Road: A.4

Brocks is a beautiful Georgian town house built in 1765 by John Wood, situated between the Circus and Royal Crescent. Very close to the Roman Baths, Assembly Rooms, etc. This really is a wonderful part of Bath. This historic house has all modern conveniences, & all of the comfortable bedrooms are en-suite. The aim here is to offer guests the highest standards, & personal attention. An ideal base from which to explore beautiful Bath.
E-mail: marion@brocksguesthouse.co.uk

£30.00 to £36.00 | Y | N | N

VISA: M'CARD:

Marion Dodd *Brocks* *32 Brock Street* *Bath BA1 2LN* *Somerset*
Tel: (01225) 338374 *Fax (01225) 334245* *Open: ALL YEAR* *Map Ref No. 01*

The Old Red House

Nearest Road: A.4

This charming Victorian Gingerbread House is colourful, comfortable & warm; full of unexpected touches & intriguing little curiosities. Its leaded & stained glass windows are now double-glazed to ensure a peaceful stay. The extensive breakfast menu, a delight in itself, is served in an attractive & sunny conservatory. Car parking. Special rates for 3 or more nights. Dinner is available at a local riverside pub. A brochure on request. Children over 4 years welcome.

£22.00 to £45.00 | Y | N | Y

see PHOTO over p. 324

VISA: M'CARD: AMEX:

Mrs Chrissie Besley *The Old Red House* *37 Newbridge Road* *Bath BA1 3HE* *Somerset*
Tel: (01225) 330464 *Fax 01225 331661* *Open: MAR - NOV* *Map Ref No. 01*

Apsley House Hotel

Nearest Road: A.341

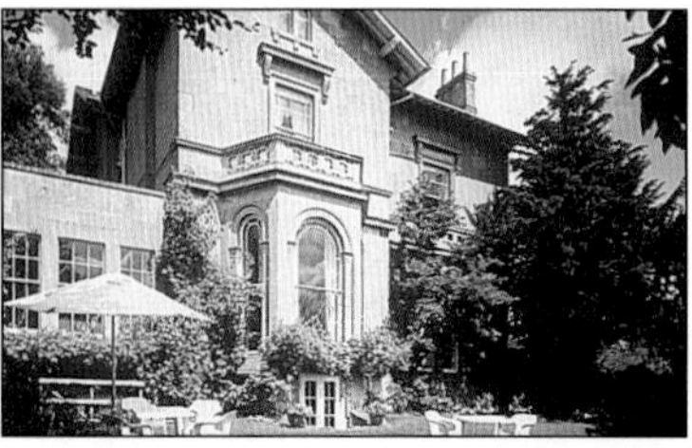

An elegant Georgian country house built for the Duke of Wellington in 1830, situated just over 1 mile from the city centre with private parking. A small privately-run hotel, guests are offered a warm welcome & personal care. The interior includes many period features, the house is furnished with fine antiques & oil paintings. A sumptuous breakfast is served in the delightful dining room. Children over 5 years welcome.
E-mail: info@apsley-house.co.uk

£32.50 to £55.00 | Y | N | N

see PHOTO over p. 325

VISA: M'CARD: AMEX:

David & Annie Lanz *Apsley House Hotel* *Newbridge Hill* *Bath BA1 3PT* *Somerset*
Tel: (01225) 336966 *Fax 01225 425462* *Open: ALL YEAR (Excl. Xmas)* *Map Ref No. 01*

Cranleigh

Nearest Road: A.431

Situated in a quiet residential area, this comfortable Victorian house has great character, with exceptionally spacious, stylish en-suite bedrooms. Most have lovely views across the Avon Valley. You are welcome to relax in the garden. Breakfast includes such choices as fresh-fruit salad & scrambled eggs with smoked salmon. Easy access to the heart of Bath. Parking. The Pooles have a wealth of information to help you make the most of your stay in Bath. Children over 5 years.
E-mail: cranleigh@btinternet.com

£33.00 to £££ | Y | N | N

see PHOTO over p. 327

VISA: M'CARD:

Tony & Jan Poole *Cranleigh* *159 Newbridge Hill* *Bath BA1 3PX* *Somerset*
Tel: (01225) 310197 *Fax 01225 423143* *Open: ALL YEAR* *Map Ref No. 01*

Cranleigh. Bath.

Gainsborough Hotel. Bath.

rate £ from - to per person	children taken	evening meals	animals taken

The Gainsborough

£30.00 to £46.00	Y	N	N

see PHOTO over p. 328

VISA: M'CARD: AMEX:

Nearest Road: A.4

The Gainsborough is a large country-house hotel, comfortably furnished & set in its own grounds near the Botanical Gardens & Victoria Park. Offering 17 attractive en-suite bedrooms, each with colour T.V., direct-dial telephone, tea/coffee-making facilities & hairdryer. The dining room & small cocktail bar overlook the lawns, where guests often relax during the summer on the sun terrace. Private parking available.

E-mail: gainsborough_hotel@compuserve.com

Mrs Anna Ford The Gainsborough Weston Lane Bath BA1 4AB Somerset
Tel: (01225) 311380 Fax 01225 447411 Open: ALL YEAR Map Ref No. 01

Cedar Lodge

£27.50 to £35.00	Y	N	N

Nearest Road: A.4, A.46

Within easy level walk to the historic city centre, this beautiful, detached Georgian house offers period elegance with modern amenities. There are 3 lovely bedrooms (1 with 4-poster, 1 half-tester, 1 twin), all with en-suite/private bathrooms. Delightful gardens & comfortable drawing room, with fire, to relax in. Ideally situated for excursions to Avebury, Stonehenge, Salisbury, Longleat, Wells, Cotswolds, Wales & many other attractions. Secure private parking. Children over 10 years.

Derek & Maria Beckett Cedar Lodge 13 Lambridge Bath BA1 6BJ Somerset
Tel: (01225) 423468 Open: ALL YEAR Map Ref No. 01

Dolphin House

£25.00 to £35.00	N	Y	N

Nearest Road: A.4

Dolphin House is a detached Georgian Grade II listed house with a mature terraced walled garden. Centrally heated & with period furnishings. There is a private suite consisting of a twin-bedded room, lounge & a large bathroom. Also, a large double bedroom with a private bathroom. T.V. & tea/coffee-making facilities in each room. All meals are served in the privacy of your own room or on the terrace. The historic city of Bath is only 2 1/2 miles. Children over 12 years.

Mr & Mrs G. Riley Dolphin House 8 Northend Batheaston Bath BA1 7EH Somerset
Tel: (01225) 858915 Fax 01225 858915 Open: ALL YEAR Map Ref No. 03

Bailbrook Lodge Hotel

£30.00 to £40.00	Y	Y	N

see PHOTO over p. 330

VISA: M'CARD: AMEX:

Nearest Road: A.46

Bailbrook Lodge is an imposing Grade II listed Georgian house located 1 mile east of Bath. There is a choice of 12 elegantly furnished en-suite bedrooms (some 4-posters), all with T.V. & hospitality tray. Evening meals with traditional English cuisine are provided. The lounge bar & dining room overlook the garden. Bailbrook Lodge is an ideal base for exploring Bath & touring the beautiful surrounding countryside. Ample car-parking.

E-mail: hotel@bailbrooklodge.demon.co.uk

Mr & Mrs R.N. Addison Bailbrook Lodge Hotel 35/37 London Road West Bath BA1 7HZ Somerset
Tel: (01225) 859090 Fax 01225 852299 Open: ALL YEAR Map Ref No. 01

Bailbrook Lodge. Bath.

rate £ from - to per person	children taken	evening meals	animals taken
£24.00 to £30.00	Y	N	N

The Hollies

Nearest Road: A.367

The Hollies is a lovely old Victorian, Grade II listed house situated within walking distance of the city. With just 3 pretty guest rooms, personal attention and hospitality are assured. Each room has en-suite or private facilities, colour T.V., beverage-making facilities, hairdryer & radio/alarm clock. A wide breakfast menu is served. Private parking is available. Rooms overlook the secluded garden of apple trees, herbs & roses. A charming home, ideal for exploring Bath. Children over 5.

VISA: M'CARD:

Mrs N. Stabbins ***The Hollies*** ***Hatfield Road*** ***Bath BA2 2BD*** ***Somerset***
Tel: (01225) 313366 ***Fax 01225 313366*** ***Open: Mid JAN - DEC (Excl. Xmas)*** ***Map Ref No. 01***

rate £ from - to per person	children taken	evening meals	animals taken
£32.50 to £52.00	Y	N	N

Lavender House

Nearest Road: A.367

Set in a quiet conservation area, within easy reach of Bath city centre. Lavender House is an Edwardian house which affords 5 lovely guest rooms. Each is individually designed & has a large, luxurious bathroom, T.V. & hospitality tray. In addition to serving a traditional English breakfast, using free-range & fresh local produce, there are special Vegetarian Cordon Vert options. Evening meals by arrangement. Lavender House is a special place to unwind, relax & be spoiled. Parking.

E-mail: Lavenderhouse@btinternet.com

see PHOTO over p. 332

VISA: M'CARD:

Carol & Bill Huxley ***Lavender House*** ***17 Bloomfield Park*** ***Bath BA2 2BY*** ***Somerset***
Tel: (01225) 314500 ***Fax 01225 448564*** ***Open: ALL YEAR*** ***Map Ref No. 01***

rate £ from - to per person	children taken	evening meals	animals taken
£30.00 to £36.00	N	N	N

Oakleigh Guest House

Nearest Road: A.367

Your comfort is assured at Oakleigh House, quietly situated only 10 mins from the city centre. Oakleigh combines Victorian elegance with today's comforts to make your stay that extra bit special. All of the 3 bedrooms are comfortable, attractively furnished & have an en-suite bath/shower & W.C., hairdryers, colour T.V., clock radios & tea/coffee-making facilities. A private car park. Oakleigh is an ideal base for beautiful Bath and beyond.

E-mail: oakleigh@which.net

VISA: M'CARD: AMEX:

David & Jenny King ***Oakleigh Guest House*** ***19 Upper Oldfield Park*** ***Bath BA2 3JX*** ***Somerset***
Tel: (01225) 315698 ***Fax 01225 448223*** ***Open: ALL YEAR*** ***Map Ref No. 01***

rate £ from - to per person	children taken	evening meals	animals taken
£25.00 to £28.00	N	N	N

Apartment 1

Nearest Road: A.4

An elegant, 2-storey, garden apartment within a Grade I listed Georgian house, situated in one of Bath's most desirable streets. Brian & Chan Loo Smith, who have for many years lived abroad, offer friendly hospitality in their charming home. There is 1 attractive bedroom (which can be arranged as a double, twin or family room) with an en-suite bathroom. Breakfast can be taken (weather permitting) on the pretty courtyard surrounded by potted herbs, flowers & shrubs. Overseas guests are especially welcome.

Mrs C. L. Smith ***Apartment 1*** ***60, Great Pulteney Street*** ***Bath BA2 4DN*** ***Somerset***
Tel: (01225) 464134 ***Fax 01225 483663*** ***Open: ALL YEAR*** ***Map Ref No. 01***

Lavender House. Bath.

Ravenscroft. Bath.

Somerset

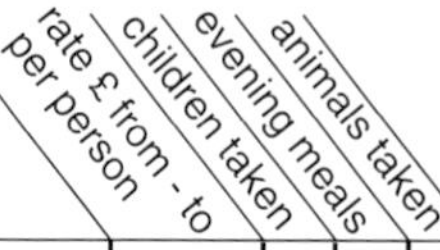

Paradise House

Nearest Road: A.367

Paradise House was built in the 1720s, on the ancient Roman Fosse Way. The Fosse Way, now a cul-de-sac, is one of the quietest streets in Bath & provides easy access to the city centre. (The Roman Baths are only 7 mins' walk away.) 11 attractively furnished & well-appointed bedrooms, each with an en-suite bathroom, etc.. The house enjoys fine views over the Georgian city & has over 1/2 an acre of walled gardens which compete with the golden splendour of the city below.

E-mail: info@paradise-house.co.uk

David & Annie Lanz   Paradise House   88 Holloway   Bath BA2 4PX   Somerset
Tel: (01225) 317723   Fax 01225 482005   Open: ALL YEAR (Excl. Xmas)   Map Ref No. 01

rate £ from - to per person	children taken	evening meals	animals taken
£35.00 to £65.00	Y	N	N

VISA: M'CARD: AMEX:

Blantyre House

Nearest Road: A.36

Set in an elevated position in its own grounds, with magnificent views over Bath to the north. Blantyre House, Georgian in style, is luxuriously appointed & furnished with antiques & family paintings. Each comfortable & attractive bedroom has en-suite/ private facilities, T.V. & tea/coffee. Within easy walking distance of the city centre, close to the university, Blantyre House makes an ideal base for exploring Bath & the surrounding countryside. Private parking. Children over 12.

E-mail: blantyrebath@aol.com

Philippa & Andrew Gordon-Duff   Blantyre House   Widcombe Hill   Bath BA2 6AE   Somerset
Tel: (01225) 480682 Fax 01225 789543 Open: MAR - DEC & New Year (Excl. Xmas) Map Ref No. 01

rate £ from - to per person	children taken	evening meals	animals taken
£32.50 to £32.50	Y	N	N

Northwick House

Nearest Road: A.36

With outstanding views over Bath & the surrounding countryside, this comfortable & unusual Grade II listed Georgian house was built in 1821 on the upper slopes of Bathwick Hill, renowned for its Italianate villas. 5 mins' to city centre, near a regular bus route & also the university. Wonderful walks in National Trust woodland for those weary of Bath's architectural delights! 3 attractively furnished bedrooms, each with T.V., radio/alarm, hairdryer & tea/coffee facilities. Children over 12.

E-mail: northwickhouse@aol.com

Veronica Metcalfe   Northwick House   North Road   Bathwick   Bath BA2 6HD   Somerset
Tel: (01225) 420963   Fax 01225 420963   Open: ALL YEAR   Map Ref No. 01

rate £ from - to per person	children taken	evening meals	animals taken
£25.00 to £28.00	Y	N	Y

Ravenscroft

Nearest Road: A.36

Built in 1876, Ravenscroft is an elegant Victorian residence with a wealth of period features. Its elevated position provides spectacular views over the city of Bath & countryside beyond. Only a few minutes from the city centre, it is surrounded by an acre of secluded, mature gardens which offer guests peace & tranquillity. There are 4 lovely bedrooms with colour T.V., tea/coffee & hair-drying facilities. Private parking. Children over 12.

E-mail: ravenscroft@compuserve.com

Patrick & Hilary Bryan   Ravenscroft   North Road   Bathwick   Bath BA2 6HZ   Somerset
Tel: (01225) 461919   Fax 01225 461919   Open: ALL YEAR   Map Ref No. 01

rate £ from - to per person	children taken	evening meals	animals taken
£30.00 to £35.00	Y	N	N

see PHOTO over p. 333

Somerset House. Bath.

Villa Magdala. Bath.

Somerset

rate £ from - to per person	children taken	evening meals	animals taken
£29.00 to £52.50	Y	N	Y

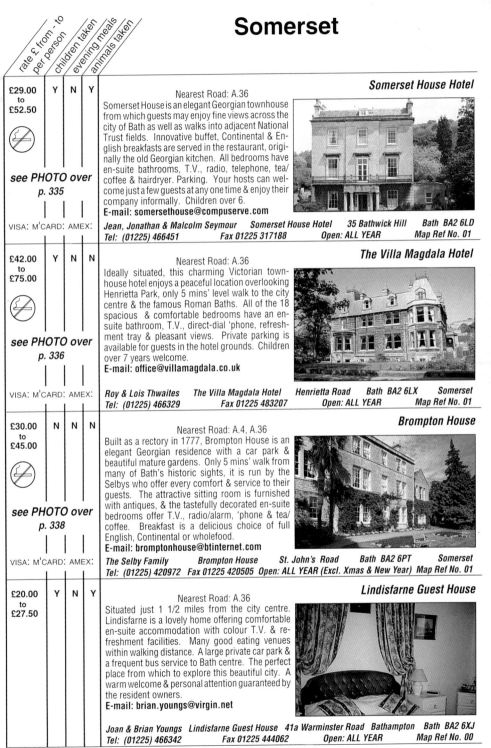

see PHOTO over p. 335

VISA: M'CARD: AMEX:

Somerset House Hotel

Nearest Road: A.36

Somerset House is an elegant Georgian townhouse from which guests may enjoy fine views across the city of Bath as well as walks into adjacent National Trust fields. Innovative buffet, Continental & English breakfasts are served in the restaurant, originally the old Georgian kitchen. All bedrooms have en-suite bathrooms, T.V., radio, telephone, tea/coffee & hairdryer. Parking. Your hosts can welcome just a few guests at any one time & enjoy their company informally. Children over 6.

E-mail: somersethouse@compuserve.com

Jean, Jonathan & Malcolm Seymour Somerset House Hotel 35 Bathwick Hill Bath BA2 6LD
Tel: (01225) 466451 Fax 01225 317188 Open: ALL YEAR Map Ref No. 01

rate £ from - to per person	children taken	evening meals	animals taken
£42.00 to £75.00	Y	N	N

see PHOTO over p. 336

VISA: M'CARD: AMEX:

The Villa Magdala Hotel

Nearest Road: A.36

Ideally situated, this charming Victorian townhouse hotel enjoys a peaceful location overlooking Henrietta Park, only 5 mins' level walk to the city centre & the famous Roman Baths. All of the 18 spacious & comfortable bedrooms have an en-suite bathroom, T.V., direct-dial 'phone, refreshment tray & pleasant views. Private parking is available for guests in the hotel grounds. Children over 7 years welcome.

E-mail: office@villamagdala.co.uk

Roy & Lois Thwaites The Villa Magdala Hotel Henrietta Road Bath BA2 6LX Somerset
Tel: (01225) 466329 Fax 01225 483207 Open: ALL YEAR Map Ref No. 01

rate £ from - to per person	children taken	evening meals	animals taken
£30.00 to £45.00	N	N	N

see PHOTO over p. 338

VISA: M'CARD: AMEX:

Brompton House

Nearest Road: A.4, A.36

Built as a rectory in 1777, Brompton House is an elegant Georgian residence with a car park & beautiful mature gardens. Only 5 mins' walk from many of Bath's historic sights, it is run by the Selbys who offer every comfort & service to their guests. The attractive sitting room is furnished with antiques, & the tastefully decorated en-suite bedrooms offer T.V., radio/alarm, 'phone & tea/coffee. Breakfast is a delicious choice of full English, Continental or wholefood.

E-mail: bromptonhouse@btinternet.com

The Selby Family Brompton House St. John's Road Bath BA2 6PT Somerset
Tel: (01225) 420972 Fax 01225 420505 Open: ALL YEAR (Excl. Xmas & New Year) Map Ref No. 01

rate £ from - to per person	children taken	evening meals	animals taken
£20.00 to £27.50	Y	N	Y

Lindisfarne Guest House

Nearest Road: A.36

Situated just 1 1/2 miles from the city centre. Lindisfarne is a lovely home offering comfortable en-suite accommodation with colour T.V. & refreshment facilities. Many good eating venues within walking distance. A large private car park & a frequent bus service to Bath centre. The perfect place from which to explore this beautiful city. A warm welcome & personal attention guaranteed by the resident owners.

E-mail: brian.youngs@virgin.net

Joan & Brian Youngs Lindisfarne Guest House 41a Warminster Road Bathampton Bath BA2 6XJ
Tel: (01225) 466342 Fax 01225 444062 Open: ALL YEAR Map Ref No. 00

Brompton House. Bath.

Monkshill. Monkton Combe.

Somerset

rate £ from - to per person	children taken	evening meals	animals taken

se

Nearest Road: A.36

This distinguished Edwardian house is set in its own beautiful gardens, on an English-country hill-top commanding spectacular countryside views, & yet lies only 5 mins from the centre of Bath. Stroll through the small medieval village of Monkton Combe, at the valley's base, & return to tea amid the elegant antiques, fireplace & grand piano that complement the drawing room. The bedrooms are elegant, with flowing drapes, brass beds, bath/ shower & views over the gardens & valley below.

E-mail: monks.hill@virgin.net

Mrs C. Westlake Monkshill Guest House Shaft Road Monkton Combe Bath BA2 7HL Somerset
Tel: (01225) 833028 Fax 01225 833028 Open: ALL YEAR Map Ref No. 02

rate £ from - to per person	children taken	evening meals	animals taken
£32.50 to £40.00	Y	N	Y

see PHOTO over p. 339

VISA: M'CARD:

Monmouth Lodge

Nearest Road: A.36

Set in an acre of attractive garden, looking on to the Somerset Hills surrounding this historic village. There are 3 attractively furnished ground-floor en-suite bedrooms, with T.V., tea/coffee-making facilities, king-size beds & own patio doors, which offer space & comfort. In the charming sitting room & stylish dining room, there is the same attention to detail & quality, where a good choice of excellent breakfast is served. Ideally situated for Bath, Wells, Stonehenge etc. Private parking. Famous 13th-century pub nearby. Children over 5.

Leslie & Traudle Graham Monmouth Lodge Norton St. Philip Bath BA3 6LH Somerset
Tel: (01373) 834367 Open: FEB - DEC Map Ref No. 04

rate £ from - to per person	children taken	evening meals	animals taken
£30.00 to £35.00	Y	N	N

VISA: M'CARD:

The Plaine

Nearest Road: A.366

The Plaine is a delightful listed building, dating from the 16th century & situated in the heart of an historic conservation village. There are 3 beautiful en-suite rooms, all with 4-poster beds. Opposite is the famous George Inn - one of the oldest hostelries in England. Delicious breakfasts are prepared with local produce and free-range eggs. A convenient location for Bath, Wells, Longleat and the Cotswolds. Parking. Children over 3.

E-mail: theplaine@easynet.co.uk

Sarah Priddle & John Webster The Plaine Bell Hill Norton St. Philip Bath BA3 6LT Somerset
Tel: (01373) 834723 Fax 01373 834101 Open: ALL YEAR Map Ref No. 04

rate £ from - to per person	children taken	evening meals	animals taken
£29.00 to £35.00	Y	N	N

see PHOTO over p. 341

VISA: M'CARD:

Irondale House

Nearest Road: A.36

A warm welcome awaits you at this elegant 18th-century Georgian home, set in a quiet village 10 mins' drive from Bath. The house is decorated to the highest standard. Bedrooms are en-suite with T.V., etc. & king-size beds. Breakfasts are delicious. The family room is a suite with a sitting room which leads into the lovely walled garden from a patio door. The drawing room which overlooks the garden has amazing views. Ideal for visiting Bath, Wells, Longleat, Lacock & Stonehenge.

E-mail: holder@irondalebnb.freeserve.co.uk

Mrs Jayne Holder Irondale House 67 High Street Rode Bath BA3 6PB Somerset
Tel: (01373) 830730 Fax 01373 830730 Open: ALL YEAR Map Ref No. 05

rate £ from - to per person	children taken	evening meals	animals taken
£32.50 to £60.00	Y	N	N

see PHOTO over p. 342

VISA: M'CARD:

The Plaine. Norton St. Philip.

Irondale House. Rode.

rate £ from - to per person	children taken	evening meals	animals taken	
£25.00 to £30.00	N	N	N	**Brook House** Nearest Road: A.39 A warm welcome awaits the discerning visitor at Brook House, an elegant & lovingly restored Georgian house, situated in the centre of this beautiful historic village at the foot of the Quantocks where Coleridge once lived. Hearty breakfasts & tastefully furnished en-suite rooms with colour T.V. & tea/coffee-making facilities. Good local pubs within walking distance. Wonderful coastal & hill walks in an Area of Outstanding Natural Beauty. (M.5 8 miles Junction 23.) *Mr & Mrs Michael Henry Brook House 2 Castle Street Nether Stowey Bridgwater TA5 1LN* *Tel: (01278) 732881 Open: ALL YEAR (Excl. Xmas & New Year) Map Ref No. 06*
£22.00 to £29.00 *see PHOTO over p. 344*	N	N	N	**Honeymead** Nearest Road: A.39 Warm & welcoming Honeymead, an arts-&-crafts-style house nestles at the foot of the Quantock Hills. Walk in the footsteps of Coleridge & Wordsworth, through moorland & secluded combes, on cliff paths with views of the Welsh coast. Beautiful & tranquil rooms with en-suite facilities, a selection of refreshments; T.V., radio, books & maps. Guest conservatory & beautiful gardens. 10% off bookings of 3 nights & over. **E-mail: Lucille.Hoose@nationwideisp.net** *Mrs Lucille Hoose Honeymead Holford Bridgwater TA5 1RZ Somerset* *Tel: (01278) 741668 Fax 01278 741668 Open: ALL YEAR (Excl. Xmas) Map Ref No. 07*
£20.00 to £25.00	Y	N	N	**Spring Farm** Nearest Road: A.38 A cosy informal farmhouse set in a peaceful garden, Spring Farm has views across fields to the Mendip Hills. Offering 2 comfortable double-bedded rooms, each with an en-suite/private bathroom & tea/coffee facilities. The guest sitting/breakfast room has an open fire in winter. A good choice of pubs for dinner. Within easy reach by car are Chew Magna, Bristol, Bath & Wells. An ideal base for exploring north Somerset & fishing on the renowned Chew & Blagdon lakes. Children over 2. **E-mail: bookings@springfarm.swest.co.uk** *Mrs Judy Gallannaugh Spring Farm The Street Regil Bristol BS40 8BB Somerset* *Tel: (01275) 472735 Open: ALL YEAR (Excl. Xmas) Map Ref No. 11*
£29.50 to £33.00 VISA: M'CARD: AMEX:	Y	N	N	**Downs Edge** Nearest Road: A.4018 Downs Edge is situated in a superb position on the very edge of Bristol's famous Downs - an open park of some 450 acres. Furnished with fine period furniture, the house is set in magnificent gardens close to the spectacular Avon Gorge & its breathtaking views. This uniquely peaceful location is ideally situated for the city centre, Clifton & the university. Downs Edge is served by an excellent public transport system with easy access to the motorway network. Children over 6 years. **E-mail: downsedge@sbishop99.freeserve.co.uk** *Mrs Philippa Tasker Downs Edge Saville Road Stoke Bishop Bristol BS9 1JD Somerset* *Tel: (0117) 9683264 Fax 0117 9683264 Open: ALL YEAR (Excl. Xmas & New Year) Map Ref No. 12*

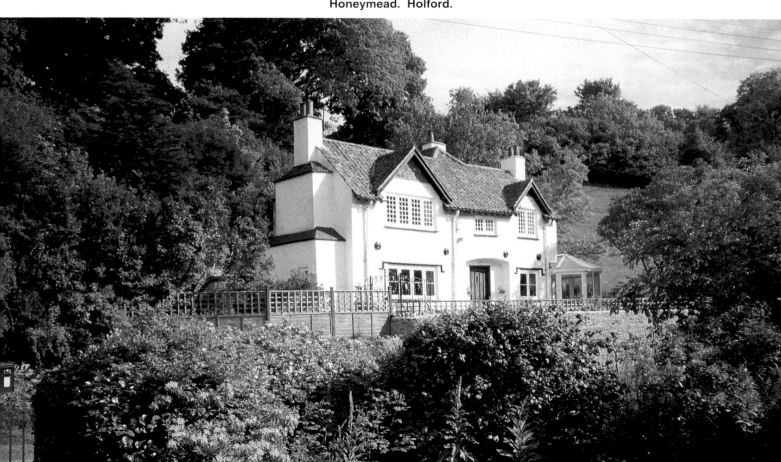

Honeymead. Holford.

Somerset

rate £ from - to per person | children taken | evening meals | animals taken

Overbrook

rate £ from - to per person	children taken	evening meals	animals taken
£20.00 to £22.00	Y	N	N

Nearest Road: A.368

Overbrook is a charming wisteria-clad house, tastefully furnished, with a lovely garden by a brook. Situated in rural seclusion in a quiet & peaceful lane, with a little ford by the front gate. Breakfast is taken in the conservatory overlooking the garden. There are 2 beautifully furnished bedrooms, each with en-suite/private facilities. Overbrook is only 1/2 mile from the village & close to the beautiful Chew Valley Lake. Cheddar Gorge, Bath, Wells & Bristol are within easy reach.

Ruth Shellard Overbrook Stowey Bottom Bishop Sutton Nr. Bristol BS39 5TN Somerset
Tel: (01275) 332648 Fax 01275 332648 Open: APR - OCT Map Ref No. 13

Hawthorne House

rate £ from - to per person	children taken	evening meals	animals taken
£20.00 to £20.00	Y	Y	Y

Nearest Road: A.303

Hawthorne House is a cosy 19th-century stone house set in the Blackdown Hills, an Area of Outstanding Natural Beauty. It is ideally situated for an overnight stay en-route to Cornwall, & for visiting N.T. properties & the many other attractions in Somerset & Devon. Each of the 3 comfortable bedrooms has an en-suite/private bathroom & tea/coffee-making facilities. The attractive dining room has panoramic views over the extensive gardens & surrounding hills. Children over 12.

E-mail: roger-sarah@supanet.com

Roger & Sarah Newman-Coburn Hawthorne House Bishopswood Chard TA20 3RS Somerset
Tel: (01460) 234482 Fax 01460 234482 Open: ALL YEAR Map Ref No. 14

Conygar House

rate £ from - to per person	children taken	evening meals	animals taken
£22.00 to £25.00	Y	N	N

Nearest Road: A.39

Conygar House is situated in a quiet road just off the main street of medieval Dunster village. Restaurants, bars & shops are all within 1 mins' walking distance. Wonderful views of castle & moors. A delightful sunny garden & patio for guests' use. Ideal for exploring Exmoor & coast. All rooms decorated & furnished to a high standard. Personal service & your comfort is guaranteed. Dunster Beach is 1 1/2 miles away, Minehead 2 1/2 miles & Porlock 8 miles.

E-mail: bale.dunster@virgin.net

Mrs B. Bale Conygar House 2A The Ball Dunster TA24 6SD Somerset
Tel: (01643) 821872 Fax 01643 821872 Open: FEB - OCT Map Ref No. 15

Larcombe Foot

rate £ from - to per person	children taken	evening meals	animals taken
£23.00 to £23.00	Y	Y	Y

Nearest Road: A.358

Larcombe Foot, a comfortable old country house set in the beautiful & tranquil Upper Exe Valley, is an ideal base for walking, riding, fishing & touring Exmoor. Guests' comfort is paramount. Accommodation is in 3 bedrooms, 2 with private bathroom, & tea/coffee makers in all rooms. A comfortable sitting room with log fire & T.V., plus a pretty garden to relax in. Evening meals by prior arrangement. Winsford is considered one of the prettiest villages on the moor. Children over 8.

Mrs V. Vicary Larcombe Foot Winsford Exmoor National Park TA24 7HS Somerset
Tel: (01643) 851306 Fax 01643 851306 Open: APR - OCT Map Ref No. 16

Number Three Hotel.Glastonbury.

rate £ from - to per person	children taken	evening meals	animals taken	
£37.50 to £47.50	Y	N	N	**Number Three Hotel** Nearest Road: M.5 Ex. 23, A.39 Number Three is a beautiful, listed town house offering secluded & peaceful accommodation. There are 5 individually designed rooms all with en-suite bathrooms, T.V., telephone & tea/coffee-making facilities. Number Three stands beside Glastonbury Abbey, surrounded by a large walled garden, wonderful mature trees, floodlit at night. Cars can be parked here behind security gates. Single supplement. Pat Redmond is here to make your stay as enjoyable as possible. *Mrs Pat Redmond Number Three Hotel 3 Magdalene Street Glastonbury BA6 9EW Somerset* *Tel: (01458) 832129 Fax 01458 834227 Open: ALL YEAR (Excl. Xmas) Map Ref No. 17*
see PHOTO over p. 346 VISA: M'CARD: AMEX:				
£27.50 to £30.00	N	N	N	**Dollons House** Nearest Road: A.39 17th-century Dollons House nestles beneath the castle in this delightful medieval village in the Exmoor National Park. There are 3 attractive & very comfortable en-suite bedrooms, each with its own character & special decor. 100 years ago, the local pharmacist had his shop in Dollons, & in the back he made marmalade for the Houses of Parliament. A delightful home. Dunster is an ideal base for touring. Pull up outside the front door to unload & get instructions for parking. **E-mail: mc2@lineone.net** *Mr & Mrs M.Cooper Dollons House 10-12 Church Street Dunster Minehead TA24 6SH Somerset* *Tel: (01643) 821880 Fax 01643 822016 Open: ALL YEAR Map Ref No. 18*
see PHOTO over p. 348 VISA: M'CARD:				
£28.00 to £35.00	Y	N	N	**Pennard House** Nearest Road: A.37 Pennard House is a beautiful Grade II listed Georgian house situated on the last south-facing slope of the Mendip Hills, in secluded gardens & surrounded by meadows, woodlands & cider orchards. Furnished throughout with antiques, it offers 4 attractive bedrooms, 3 with en-suite/private facilities. Tennis court & Victorian spring fed swimming pool. Ideally situated for visiting Glastonbury, Wells, Bath & historic houses & gardens of Stourhead, Longleat, Montacute & many others. **E-mail: m.dearden@ukonline.co.uk** *Mr & Mrs M. Dearden Pennard House East Pennard Shepton Mallet BA4 6TP Somerset* *Tel: (01749) 860266 Fax 01749 860266 Open: ALL YEAR Map Ref No. 22*
VISA: M'CARD: AMEX:				

Dollons House. Dunster.

The Lynch Country House Hotel.   Somerton.

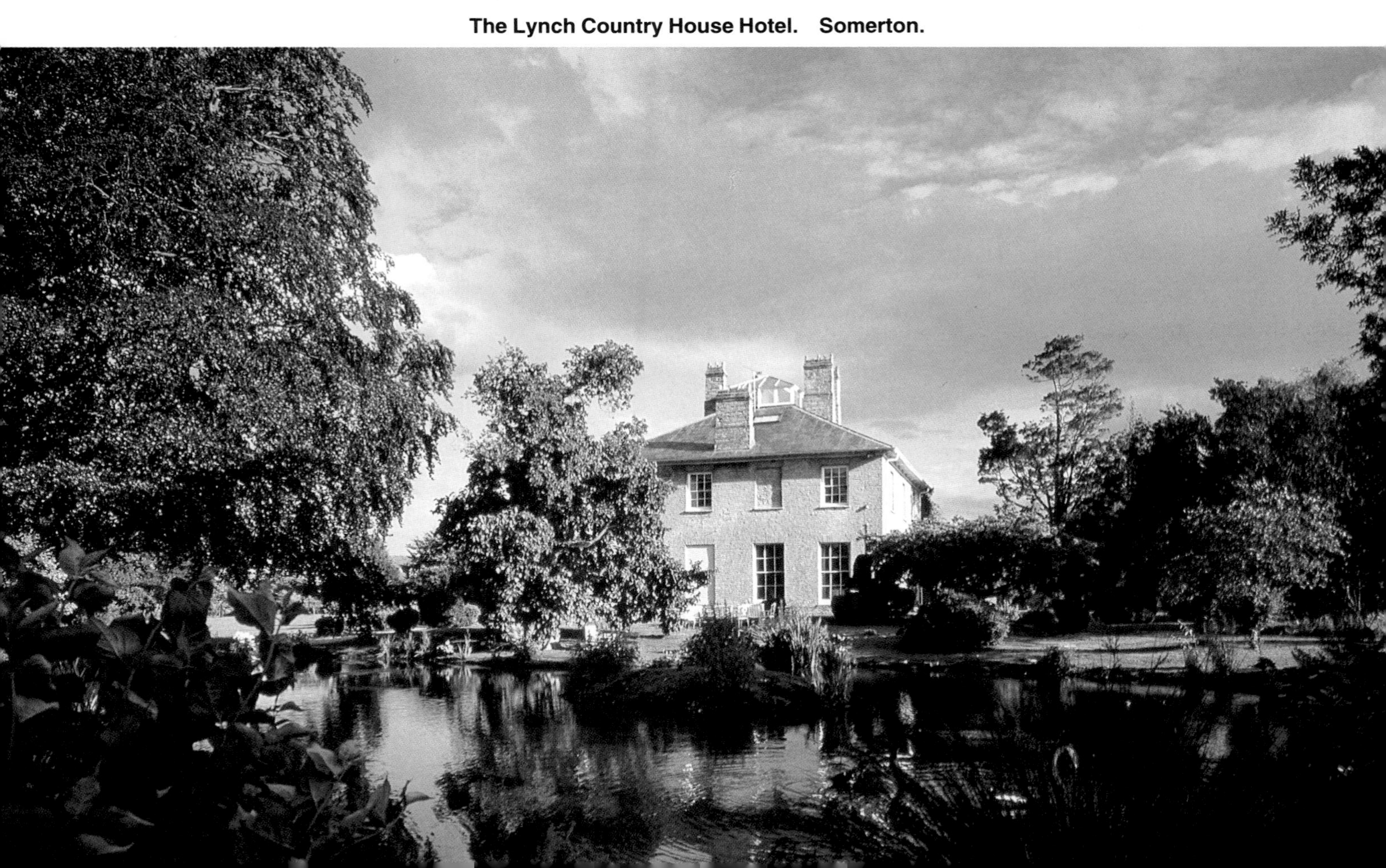

	rate £ from - to per person	children taken	evening meals	animals taken
The Lynch Country House	£24.50 to £37.50	N	N	Y
Whittles Farm	£24.00 to £30.00	N	Y	N
Higher House	£26.00 to £28.00	Y	Y	N
Southway Farm	£22.50 to £25.00	Y	N	N

The Lynch Country House

Nearest Road: A.372

The Lynch is a charming small hotel, standing in acres of carefully tended, wonderfully mature grounds. Beautifully refurbished & decorated to retain all its Georgian style & elegance, it now offers 5 attractively presented rooms, some with 4-posters, others with Victorian bedsteads, all with thoughtful extras including bathrobes & magazines. Each room has en-suite facilities, 'phone, radio, T.V. & tea/coffee. The elegant dining room overlooks the lawns & lake. Single supplement.
E-mail: the_lynch@talk21.com

see PHOTO over p. 349

VISA: M'CARD: AMEX:

Roy Copeland The Lynch Country House 4 Behind Berry Somerton TA11 7PD Somerset
Tel: (01458) 272316 Fax 01458 272590 Open: ALL YEAR (Excl. Xmas) Map Ref No. 24

Whittles Farm

Nearest Road: A.358

Guests at Whittles Farm can be sure of a high standard of accommodation & service. A superior 16th-century farmhouse set in 200 acres of pastureland, it is luxuriously carpeted & furnished in traditional style. Inglenook fireplaces & log-burners. 2 en-suite bedrooms, individually furnished, with T.V. & tea/coffee-making facilities. Super farmhouse food, using own meat, eggs & vegetables, & local Cheddar cheese & butter. Evening meals by prior arrangement. Table licence.
E-mail: dj.CM.MITCHEM@themail.co.uk

Mrs Claire Mitchem Whittles Farm Beercrocombe Taunton TA3 6AH Somerset
Tel: (01823) 480301 Fax 01823 480301 Open: FEB - NOV Map Ref No. 26

Higher House

Nearest Road: A.358

Higher House is set 650 feet up on the southern slopes of the Quantock Hills. The views from the house & gardens are exceptional. The principal part of the house is 17th century, built around 2 courtyards, 1 with a heated pool. Each bedroom has its own bathroom, 'phone, T.V., tea/coffee facilities, books, magazines. There is a beautifully presented drawing room. A tennis court together with 2 well-appointed cottages, are also available. Evening meals by prior arrangement.
E-mail: eyre@bagborough.u-net.com

see PHOTO over p. 351

Martin & Marise Eyre Higher House West Bagborough Taunton TA4 3EF Somerset
Tel: (01823) 432996 Fax 01823 433568 Open: ALL YEAR Map Ref No. 29

Southway Farm

Nearest Road: A.39

Southway Farm is a Grade II listed Georgian farmhouse situated halfway between Glastonbury & Wells. Accommodation is in 3 comfortable & attractively furnished bedrooms, 1 en-suite & 2 with a private bathroom. A delicious full English breakfast is served, although vegetarians are also catered for. Guests may relax in the cosy lounge, with colour T.V., or in the pretty, tranquil garden. An ideal location for a restful holiday, or for touring the glorious West Country.

Anita Frost Southway Farm Polsham Wells BA5 1RW Somerset
Tel: (01749) 673396 Fax 01749 670373 Open: MAR - OCT Map Ref No. 34

Higher House. West Bagborough.

Beryl. Wells.

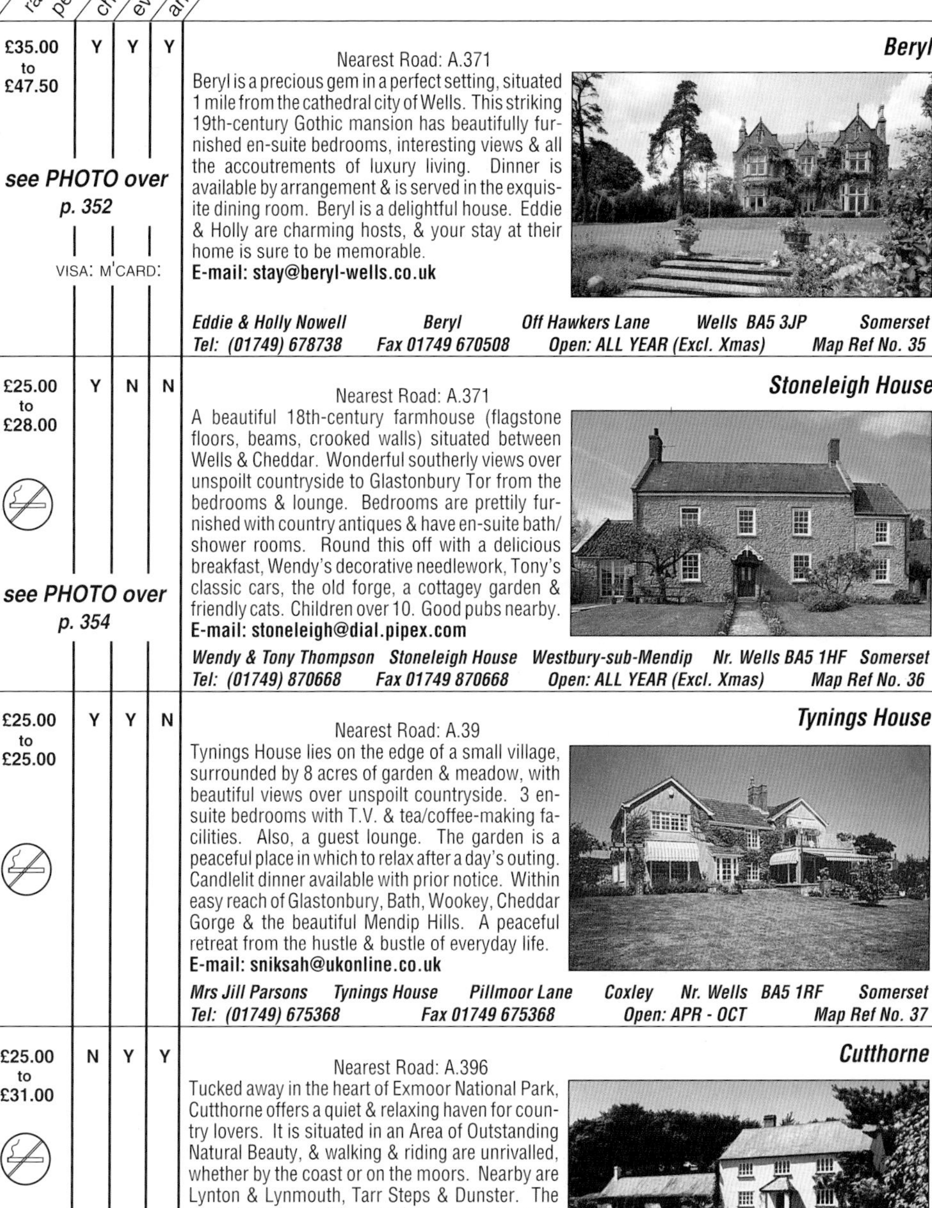

rate £ from - to per person	children taken	evening meals	animals taken
£35.00 to £47.50	Y	Y	Y

see PHOTO over p. 352

VISA: M'CARD:

Beryl

Nearest Road: A.371

Beryl is a precious gem in a perfect setting, situated 1 mile from the cathedral city of Wells. This striking 19th-century Gothic mansion has beautifully furnished en-suite bedrooms, interesting views & all the accoutrements of luxury living. Dinner is available by arrangement & is served in the exquisite dining room. Beryl is a delightful house. Eddie & Holly are charming hosts, & your stay at their home is sure to be memorable.

E-mail: stay@beryl-wells.co.uk

Eddie & Holly Nowell   Beryl   Off Hawkers Lane   Wells BA5 3JP   Somerset
Tel: (01749) 678738   Fax 01749 670508   Open: ALL YEAR (Excl. Xmas)   Map Ref No. 35

rate £ from - to per person	children taken	evening meals	animals taken
£25.00 to £28.00	Y	N	N

see PHOTO over p. 354

Stoneleigh House

Nearest Road: A.371

A beautiful 18th-century farmhouse (flagstone floors, beams, crooked walls) situated between Wells & Cheddar. Wonderful southerly views over unspoilt countryside to Glastonbury Tor from the bedrooms & lounge. Bedrooms are prettily furnished with country antiques & have en-suite bath/shower rooms. Round this off with a delicious breakfast, Wendy's decorative needlework, Tony's classic cars, the old forge, a cottagey garden & friendly cats. Children over 10. Good pubs nearby.

E-mail: stoneleigh@dial.pipex.com

Wendy & Tony Thompson   Stoneleigh House   Westbury-sub-Mendip   Nr. Wells BA5 1HF   Somerset
Tel: (01749) 870668   Fax 01749 870668   Open: ALL YEAR (Excl. Xmas)   Map Ref No. 36

rate £ from - to per person	children taken	evening meals	animals taken
£25.00 to £25.00	Y	Y	N

Tynings House

Nearest Road: A.39

Tynings House lies on the edge of a small village, surrounded by 8 acres of garden & meadow, with beautiful views over unspoilt countryside. 3 en-suite bedrooms with T.V. & tea/coffee-making facilities. Also, a guest lounge. The garden is a peaceful place in which to relax after a day's outing. Candlelit dinner available with prior notice. Within easy reach of Glastonbury, Bath, Wookey, Cheddar Gorge & the beautiful Mendip Hills. A peaceful retreat from the hustle & bustle of everyday life.

E-mail: sniksah@ukonline.co.uk

Mrs Jill Parsons   Tynings House   Pillmoor Lane   Coxley   Nr. Wells   BA5 1RF   Somerset
Tel: (01749) 675368   Fax 01749 675368   Open: APR - OCT   Map Ref No. 37

rate £ from - to per person	children taken	evening meals	animals taken
£25.00 to £31.00	N	Y	Y

see PHOTO over p. 355

Cutthorne

Nearest Road: A.396

Tucked away in the heart of Exmoor National Park, Cutthorne offers a quiet & relaxing haven for country lovers. It is situated in an Area of Outstanding Natural Beauty, & walking & riding are unrivalled, whether by the coast or on the moors. Nearby are Lynton & Lynmouth, Tarr Steps & Dunster. The pretty bedrooms all have bathrooms & 1 has a 4-poster bed. The cuisine is traditional or vegetarian, using the finest local meat & organic vegetables.

E-mail: durbin@cutthorne.co.uk

Ann Durbin   Cutthorne   Luckwell Bridge   Wheddon Cross   TA24 7EW   Somerset
Tel: (01643) 831255   Fax 01643 831255   Open: ALL YEAR   Map Ref No. 38

Stoneleigh House. Westbury- sub- Mendip.

Cutthorne. Luckwell Bridge.

Suffolk

Suffolk

(East Anglia)

In July, the lower reaches of the River Orwell hold the essence of Suffolk. Broad fields of green and gold with wooded horizons sweep down to the quiet water. Orwell Bridge spans the wide river where yachts and tan-sailed barges share the water with ocean-going container ships out of Ipswich. Downstream the saltmarshes echo to the cry of the Curlew. The small towns and villages of Suffolk are typical of an area with long seafairing traditions. This is the county of men of vision; like Constable and Gainsborough, Admiral Lord Nelson and Benjamin Britten.

The land is green and fertile and highly productive. The hedgerows shelter some of our prettiest wild flowers, & the narrow country lanes are a pure delight. Most memorable is the ever-changing sky, appearing higher and wider here than elsewhere in England. There is a great deal of heathland, probably the best known being Newmarket where horses have been trained and raced for some hundreds of years. Gorse-covered heath meets sandy cliffs on Suffolks Heritage Coast. Here are bird reserves and the remains of the great mediaeval city of Dunwich, sliding into the sea.

West Suffolk was famous for its wool trade in the Middle Ages, & the merchants gave thanks for their good fortune by building magnificent "Wool Churches". Much-photographed Lavenham has the most perfect black & white timbered houses in Britain, built by the merchants of Tudor times. Ipswich was granted the first charter by King John in 1200, but had long been a trading community of seafarers. Its history can be read from the names of the streets - Buttermarket, Friars Street, Cornhill, Dial Lane & Tavern Street. The latter holds the Great White Horse Hotel mentioned by Charles Dickens in Pickwick Papers. Sadly not many ancient buildings remain, but the mediaeval street pattern and the churches make an interesting trail to follow. The Market town of Bury St. Edmunds is charming, with much of its architectural heritage still surviving, from the Norman Cornhill to a fine Queen Anne House. The great Abbey, now in ruins, was the meeting place of the Barons of England for the creation of the Magna Carta, enshrining the principals of individual freedom, parliamentary democracy and the supremacy of the law. Suffolk has some very fine churches, notably at Mildenhall, Lakenheath, Framlingham, Lavenham & Stoke-by-Nayland, & also a large number of wonderful houses & great halls, evidence of the county's prosperity.

Lavenham.

Suffolk

Suffolk Gazeteer

Areas of Outstanding Natural Beauty
Suffolk Coast. Heathlands. Dedham Vale.

Historic Houses & Castles

Euston Hall - Thetford
18th century house with fine collection of pictures. Gardens & 17th century Parish Church nearby.

Christchurch Mansion - Ipswich
16th century mansion built on site of 12th century Augustinian Priory. Gables & dormers added in 17th century & other alteration & additions made in 17th & 18th centuries.

Gainsborough's House - Sudbury
Birthplace of Gainsborough, well furnished, collection of paintings.

The Guildhall - Hadleigh
15th century.

Glemham Hall - Nr Woodbridge
Elizabethan house of red brick - 18th century alterations. Fine stair, panelled rooms with Queen Anne furniture.

Haughley Park - Nr. Stowmarket
Jacobean manor house.

Heveningham Hall - Nr. Halesworth
Georgian mansion - English Palladian - Interior in Neo-Classical style. Garden by Capability Brown.

Ickworth - Nr. Bury St. Edmunds
Mixed architectural styles - late Regency & 18th century. French furniture, pictures & superb silver. Gardens with orangery.

Kentwell Hall - Long Melford
Elizabethan mansion in red brick, built in E plan, surrounded by moat.

Little Hall - Lavenham
15th century hall house, collection of furniture, pictures, china, etc.

Melford Hall - Nr. Sudbury
16th century - fine pictures, Chinese porcelain, furniture. Garden with gazebo.

Somerleyton Hall - Nr. Lowestoft
Dating from 16th century - additional work in 19th century. Carving by Grinling Gibbons. Tapestries, library, pictures.

Cathedrals & Churches

Bury St. Edmunds (St. Mary)
15th century. Hammer Beam roof in nave, wagon roof in chancel. Boret monument 1467.

Bramfield (St. Andrew)
Early circular tower. Fine screen & vaulting. Renaissance effigy.

Bacton (St. Mary)
15th century timbered roof. East Anglian stone & flintwork.

Dennington (St. Mary)
15th century alabaster monuments & bench ends. Aisle & Parclose screens with lofts & parapets.

Earl Stonhay (St. Mary)
14th century - rebuilt with fine hammer roof & 17th century pulpit with four hour-glasses.

Euston (St. Genevieve)
17th century. Fine panelling, reredos may be Grinling Gibbons.

Framlingham (St. Michael)
15th century nave & west tower, hammer beam roof in false vaulting. Chancel was rebuilt in 16th century for the tombs of the Howard family, monumental art treasures. Thamar organ. 1674.

Fressingfield (St. Peter & St. Paul)
15th century woodwork - very fine.

Lavenham (St. Peter & St. Paul)
15th century. Perpendicular. Fine towers. 14th century chancel screen. 17th century monument in alabaster.

Long Melford (Holy Trinity)
15th century Lady Chapel, splendid brasses. 15th century glass of note. Chantry chapel with fine roof. Like cathedral in proportions.

Stoke-by-Nayland (St. Mary)
16th-17th century library, great tower. Fine nave & arcades. Good brasses & monuments.

Ufford (St. Mary)
Mediaeval font cover - glorious.

Museums & Galleries

Christchurch Mansion - Ipswich
Country house, collection of furniture, pictures, bygones, ceramics of 18th century. Paintings by Gainsborough, Constable & modern artists.

Ipswich Museum - Ipswich
Natural History; prehistory, geology & archaeology to mediaeval period.

Suffolk

Moyse's Hall Musuem - Bury St. Edmunds
12th century dwelling house with local antiquities & natural history.
Abbot's Hall Museum of Rural Life - Stowmarket
Collections describing agriculture, crafts & domestic utensils.
Gershom-Parkington Collection - Bury St. Edmunds
Queen Anne House containing collection of watches & clocks.
Dunwich Musuem - Dunwich
Flora & fauna; local history.

Historic Monuments

The Abbey - Bury St. Edmunds
Only west end now standing.
Framlingham Castle
12th & 13th centuries - Tudor almshouses.
Bungay Castle - Bungay
12th century. Restored 13th century drawbridge & gatehouse.
Burgh Castle Roman Fort - Burgh
Coastal defences - 3rd century.
Herringfleet Priory - Herringfleet
13th century - remains of small Augustinian priory.
Leiston Abbey - Leiston
14th century - remains of cloisters, choir & trancepts.
Orford Castle - Orford
12th century - 18-sided keep - three towers.

The House in the Clouds. Thorpeness.

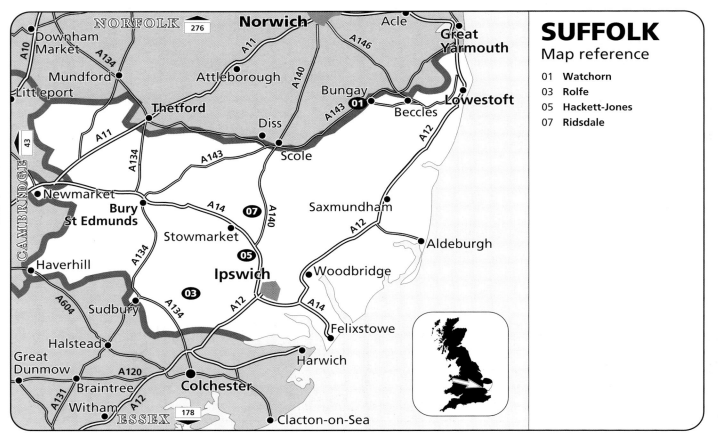

SUFFOLK

Map reference

01 **Watchorn**
03 **Rolfe**
05 **Hackett-Jones**
07 **Ridsdale**

Edgehill Hotel. Hadleigh.

Suffolk

rate £ from - to per person	children taken	evening meals	animals taken
£22.00 to £34.00	Y	N	Y

VISA: M'CARD:

Earsham Park Farm

Nearest Road: A.143

A Victorian farmhouse set on a hill overlooking the Waveney Valley, with superb views. Park Farm offers 3 really delightful guest rooms, all furnished to a high standard. Each is en-suite, & well-equipped with T.V., radio/alarm & tea/coffee-making facilities. 1 room has a 4-poster bed. Breakfast is served in the lovely dining room. Within easy reach of Norwich, Lowestoft & Southwold. A wonderful home, where comfort & a relaxed atmosphere prevail.

E-mail: WATCHORN_S@Freenet.co.uk

Mrs Bobbie Watchorn Earsham Park Farm Harleston Road Earsham Bungay NR35 2AQ Suffolk
Tel: (01986) 892180 Fax 01986 894796 Open: ALL YEAR Map Ref No. 01

rate £ from - to per person	children taken	evening meals	animals taken
£25.00 to £45.00	Y	Y	Y

see PHOTO over p. 360

Edge Hall

Nearest Road: A.12, A.14

Edge Hall is a family-run Georgian house in central Hadleigh. Beautifully restored & tastefully modernised, the hotel offers the ultimate in accommodation with 9 attractive bedrooms. Particular attention is paid to friendly service & traditional home cooking with organic vegetables. Situated in the most picturesque part of Suffolk, it is a good base from which to visit the surrounding towns & the many pretty villages of East Anglia.

Angela Rolfe Edge Hall 2 High Street Hadleigh IP7 5AP Suffolk
Tel: (01473) 822458 Fax 01473 827751 Open: ALL YEAR Map Ref No. 03

rate £ from - to per person	children taken	evening meals	animals taken
£27.50 to £44.50	Y	Y	N

see PHOTO over p. 362

VISA: M'CARD:

Pipps Ford

Nearest Road: A.14

A beautiful, Grade II listed Tudor, beamed guest house in a pretty, old-fashioned garden by the Gipping river. 6 attractive bedrooms, with private bathrooms & tea/coffee-making facilities. A very extensive breakfast menu & delicious 4-course evening meals, served in the delightful conservatory. Licensed. Tennis court. Winner of The Best Bed & Breakfast award for East Anglia. A good central position for touring all of East Anglia. Children over 5 years. Animals by arrangement.

E-mail: b&b@pippsford.co.uk

Mrs Raewyn Hackett-Jones Pipps Ford Needham Market IP6 8LJ Suffolk
Tel: (01449) 760208 Fax 01449 760561 Open: Mid JAN - Mid DEC Map Ref No. 05

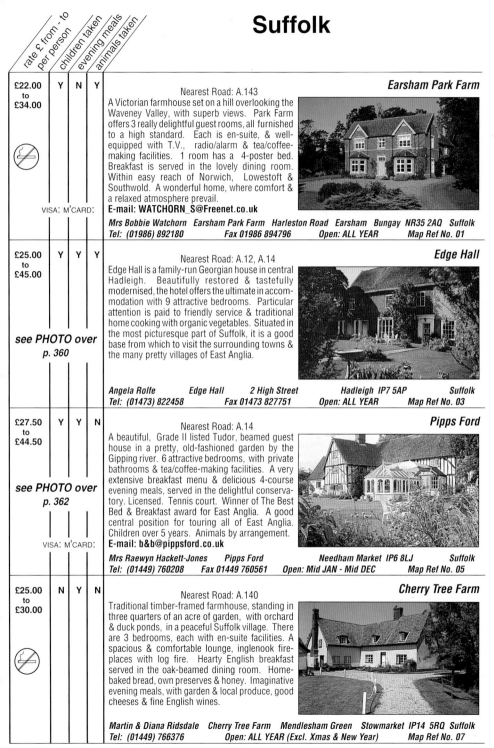

rate £ from - to per person	children taken	evening meals	animals taken
£25.00 to £30.00	N	Y	N

Cherry Tree Farm

Nearest Road: A.140

Traditional timber-framed farmhouse, standing in three quarters of an acre of garden, with orchard & duck ponds, in a peaceful Suffolk village. There are 3 bedrooms, each with en-suite facilities. A spacious & comfortable lounge, inglenook fire-places with log fire. Hearty English breakfast served in the oak-beamed dining room. Home-baked bread, own preserves & honey. Imaginative evening meals, with garden & local produce, good cheeses & fine English wines.

Martin & Diana Ridsdale Cherry Tree Farm Mendlesham Green Stowmarket IP14 5RQ Suffolk
Tel: (01449) 766376 Open: ALL YEAR (Excl. Xmas & New Year) Map Ref No. 07

Pipps Ford. Needham Market.

Surrey

Surrey (South East)

One of the Home Counties, Surrey includes a large area of London, south of the Thames. Communications are good in all directions so it is easy to stay in Surrey & travel either into central London or out to enjoy the lovely countryside which, despite urban development, survives thanks to the 'Green Belt' policy. The county is also very accessible from Gatwick Airport.

The land geographically, is chalk sandwiched in clay, & probably the lack of handy building material was responsible for the area remaining largely uninhabited for centuries. The North Downs were a considerable barrier to cross, but gradually settlements grew along the rivers which were the main routes through. The Romans used the gap created by the River Mole to build Stane Street between London & Chichester, this encouraged the development of small towns. The gap cut by the passage of the River Wey allows the Pilgrims Way to cross the foot of the Downs. Dorking, Reigate & Farnham are small towns along this route, all with attracitve main streets & interesting shops & buildings.

Polesden Lacey.

Surrey has very little mention in the Domesday Book, &, although the patronage of the church & of wealthy families established manors which developed over the years, little happened to disturb the rural tranquility of the region. As a county it made little history but rather reflected passing times, although Magna Carta was signed at Egham in 1215.

The heathlands of Surrey were a Royal playground for centuries. The Norman Kings hunted here & horses became part of the landscape & life of the people, as they are today on Epsom Downs.

Nearness to London & Royal patronage began to influence the area, & the buildings of the Tudor period reflect this. Royal palaces were built at Hampton Court & Richmond, & great houses such as Loseley near Guildford often using stone from the monasteries emptied during the Reformation. Huge deer parks were enclosed & stocked. Richmond, described as the "finest village in the British Dominions", is now beset by 20th century traffic but still has a wonderful park with deer, lakes & woodland that was enclosed by Charles I. The terraces & gardens of such buildings as Trumpeters House & Asgill House on the slopes of Richmond overlooking the Thames, have an air of spaciousness & elegance & there are lovely & interesting riverside walks at Richmond.

Surrey

Surrey Gazeteer

Historic Houses & Castles

Albury Park - Albury, Nr. Guildford
A delightful country mansion designed by Pugin.

Clandon Park - Guildford
A fine house in the Palladian style by Leoni. A good collection of furniture & pictures. The house boasts some fine plasterwork.

Claremont - Esher
A superb Palladian house with interesting interior.

Detillens - Limpsfield
A fine 15th century house with inglenook fireplaces & mediaeval furniture. A large, pleasant garden.

Greathed Manor- Lingfield
An imposing Victorian manor house.

Hatchlands - East Clandon
A National Trust property of the 18th century with a fine Adam interior

Loseley House - Guildford
A very fine Elizabethan mansion with superb panelling, furniture & paintings.

Polesden Lacy - Dorking
A Regency villa housing the Grevill collection of tapestries, pictures & furnishings. Extensive gardens.

Cathedrals & Churches

Compton (St. Nicholas)
The only surviving 2-storey sanctuary in the country. A fine 17th century pulpit.

Esher (St. George)
A fine altar-piece & marble monument.

Hascombe (St. Peter)
A rich interior with much gilding & painted reredos & roofs.

Lingfield (St. Peter & St. Paul)
15th century. Holding a chained bible.

Ockham (St. Mary & All Saints)
Early church with 13th century east window.

Stoke D'Abernon (St. Mary)
Dating back to Pre-conquest time with additions from the 12th-15th centuries. A fine 13th century painting. Early brasses.

Museums & Galleries

Charterhouse School Museum - Godalming
Peruvian pottery, Greek pottery, archaeology & natural history.

Chertsey Museum - Chertsey
18th-19th century costume & furnishing displayed & local history.

Guildford House - Guildford
The house is 17th century & of architectural interest housing monthly exhibitions.

Guildford Museum - Guildford
A fine needlework collection & plenty on local history.

Old Kiln Agricultural - Tilford
A very interesting collection of old farm implements.

Watermill Museum - Haxted
A restored 17th century mill with working water wheels & machinery.

Weybridge Museum - Weybridge
Good archaeological exhibition plus costume & local history.

The Gardens. Wisley

SURREY

Map reference

01	**McCarthy**
03	**Hill**
04	**Wallis**
08	**Dale**
09	**Grinsted**
10	**Franklin-Adams**
11	**Carmichael**
12	**Lees**
13	**Wolf**
14	**Warren**
15	**Leeper**
16	**Rowse**
17	**Carey**

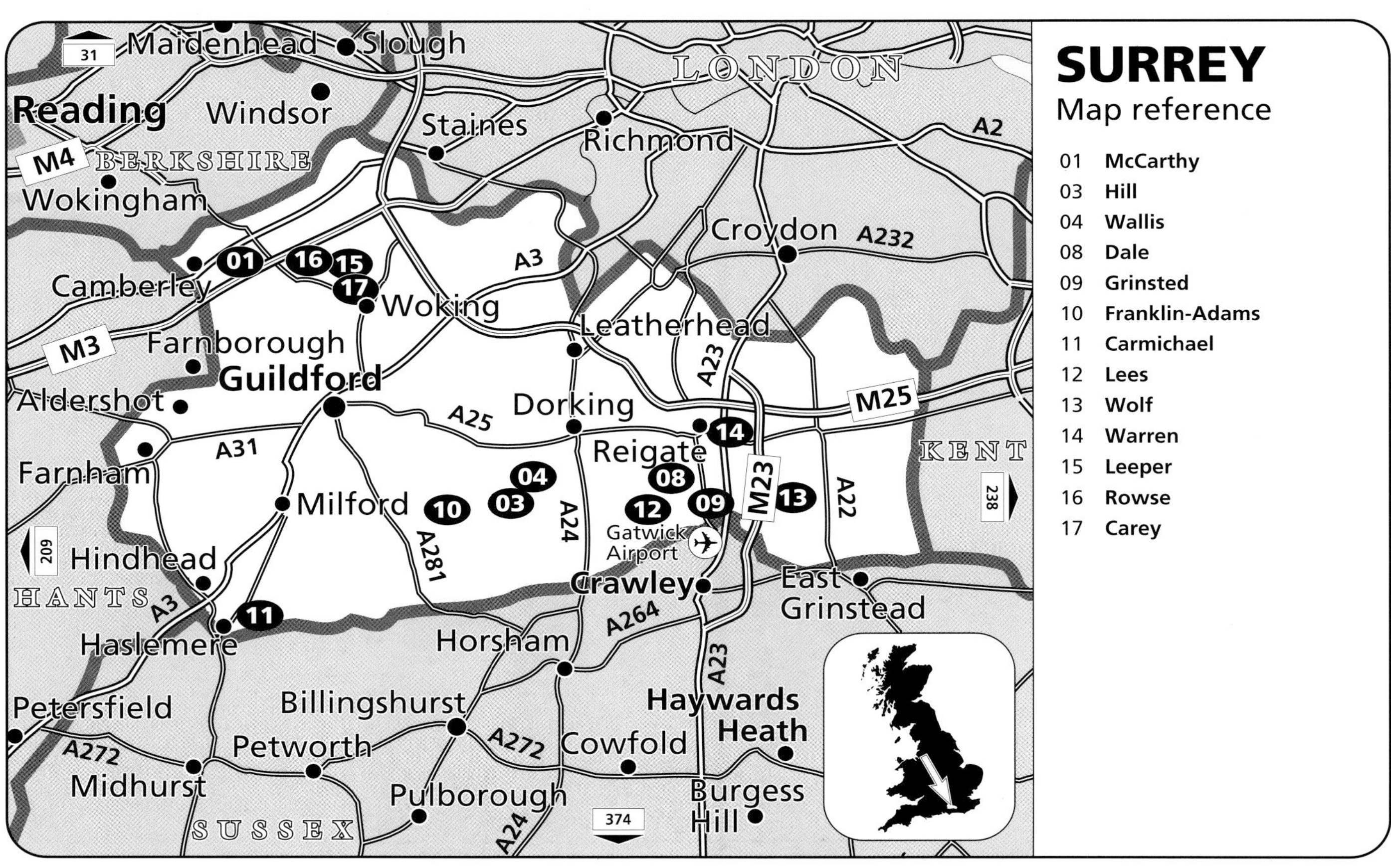

Surrey

Pineleigh

Nearest Road: A.325

Pineleigh is a spacious Edwardian house, built in 1906 & set in half an acre of mature garden in a very quiet area. Accommodation is in 4 comfortable & pleasantly decorated guest rooms, all with en-suite facilities, & including telephone, T.V. & hospitality tray. Attractively furnished in Victorian style with many old prints & pictures. A delicious full English breakfast is served, evening meals are by arrangement. A charming home, Pineleigh is conveniently located for Heathrow Airport & London.

rate £ from - to per person	children taken	evening meals	animals taken
£30.00 to £45.00	N	N	N

VISA: M'CARD: AMEX:

Tommy & Ann McCarthy Pineleigh 10 Castle Road Waverley Drive Camberley GU15 2DS Surrey
Tel: (01276) 64787 Fax 01276 64787 Open: ALL YEAR Map Ref No. 01

Bulmer Farm

Nearest Road: A.25

Enjoy a warm welcome at this delightful 17th-century farmhouse, complete with many beams & an inglenook fireplace. Offering 3 charming rooms, all with h/c & tea/coffee-making facilities. Adjoining the house around a courtyard are 5 attractive barn-conversion en-suite bedrooms for non-smokers. Farm produce & home-made preserves are provided. Situated in a picturesque village, it is convenient for London airports. Children over 12 years. Animals by arrangement.

rate £ from - to per person	children taken	evening meals	animals taken
£22.00 to £36.00	Y	N	Y

Gill Hill Bulmer Farm Pasturewood Road Holmbury St. Mary Dorking RH5 6LG Surrey
Tel: (01306) 730210 Open: ALL YEAR Map Ref No. 03

Park House Farm

Nearest Road: A.25

A delightful large family home, tastefully furnished with many antiques. Accommodation is very comfortable with en-suite/private facilities, satellite T.V., tea/coffee etc.. It is set in 25 acres in an Area of Outstanding Natural Beauty within easy reach of Heathrow & Gatwick Airports, many gardens & National Trust properties. Good train service to London. Ideal walking country, with many village pubs for food. Children over 12.
E-mail: Peterwallis@msn.com

rate £ from - to per person	children taken	evening meals	animals taken
£22.50 to £30.00	Y	N	N

Ann & Peter Wallis Park House Farm Hollow Lane Abinger Common Dorking RH5 6LW Surrey
Tel: (01306) 730101 Fax 01306 730643 Open: ALL YEAR Map Ref No. 04

Herons Head Farm

Nearest Road: A.217

A charming, quintessentially British Grade II listed beamed farmhouse set in 5 acres of gardens & paddocks, with a small lake surrounded by pastureland. The house boasts many original features: antique furnishings, a farmhouse kitchen, inglenook & log fires, & a conservatory overlooking the lake. Bedrooms have a four-poster & a king-size bed with whirlpool. Close to Dorking & Reigate, Leigh is a picturesque village with inns/restaurants. Gatwick Airport 10 mins. London 33 mins.
E-mail: heronshead@hotmail.com

rate £ from - to per person	children taken	evening meals	animals taken
£27.50 to £50.00	Y	N	N

Ann & David Dale Herons Head Farm Mynthurst Leigh Nr. Gatwick RH2 8QD Surrey
Tel: (01293) 862475 Fax 01293 863350 Open: ALL YEAR Map Ref No. 08

Surrey

The Lawn Guest House

rate £ from - to per person	children taken	evening meals	animals taken
£17.00 to £25.00	Y	N	Y

VISA: M'CARD: AMEX:

Nearest Road: A.23

A well-appointed Victorian house only 5 mins' from Gatwick Airport & 25 miles to London or Brighton. Very useful as a base for travelling, it is close to the rail station & town centre. 12 bedrooms, all with en-suite facilities & very comfortable & well decorated, with T.V., hairdryer, 'phone & tea/coffee-making facilities, etc. A full English breakfast, or a healthy alternative including fruit, yoghurt & muesli, is served in the dining room. Also, a garden for guests' use. Single supplement. Parking.

E-mail: info@lawnguesthouse.co.uk

Mr & Mrs A. Grinsted The Lawn Guest House 30 Massetts Road Horley Gatwick RH6 7DE Surrey
Tel: (01293) 775751 Fax 01293 821803 Open: ALL YEAR Map Ref No. 09

High Edser

rate £ from - to per person	children taken	evening meals	animals taken
£25.00 to £30.00	Y	N	N

Nearest Road: A.25

A large, handsome Grade II listed home, the earliest part built in the 16th century, situated in an Area of Outstanding Natural Beauty. There are three attractively furnished bedrooms available: two doubles and one twin. (1 bedroom has en-suite facilities.) Residents' lounge and T.V.. Tennis court in grounds, and golf nearby. Only 35 minutes to Gatwick and London Airports. Approximately an hour's drive to London. High Edser is a delightful home & is perfect for a relaxing break.

Carol Franklin-Adams High Edser Shere Road Ewhurst Cranleigh Guildford GU6 7PQ Surrey
Tel: (01483) 278214 Fax 01483 278200 Open: ALL YEAR Map Ref No. 10

Deerfell

rate £ from - to per person	children taken	evening meals	animals taken
£23.00 to £28.00	Y	Y	N

Nearest Road: A.286

A warm welcome at a spacious & comfortable stone-built home set in downland countryside, with breathtaking views to the hills & valleys of Surrey/Sussex. 2 pretty en-suite rooms which are very comfortable & have tea/coffee-making facilities & T.V.. Wonderful walks right on doorstep. Close by - Haslemere station, (4 miles), London (45 mins'), Guildford/Chichester (20 miles), Heathrow/Gatwick Airports 1 hour. Children over 6 years. Evening meals by arrangement.

E-mail: deerfell@tesco.net

Mrs Elizabeth Carmichael Deerfell Blackdown Park Fernden Lane Haslemere GU27 3LA Surrey
Tel: (01428) 653409 Fax 01428 656106 Open: Mid JAN - Mid DEC Map Ref No. 11

Latchetts Cottage

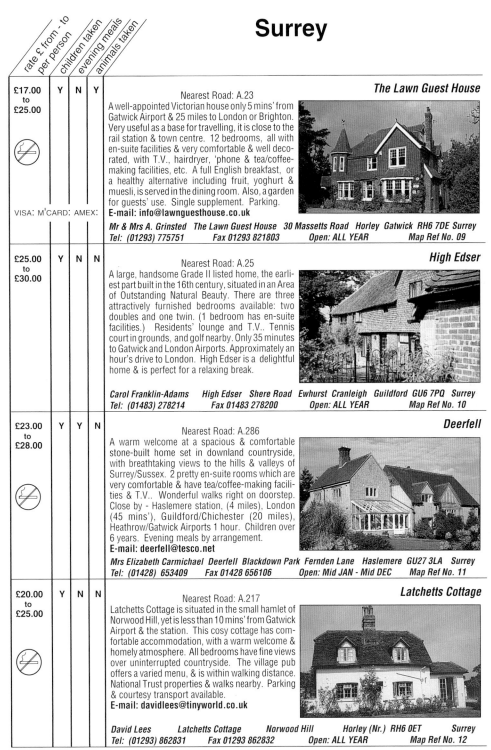

rate £ from - to per person	children taken	evening meals	animals taken
£20.00 to £25.00	Y	N	N

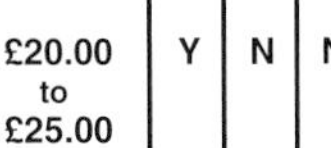

Nearest Road: A.217

Latchetts Cottage is situated in the small hamlet of Norwood Hill, yet is less than 10 mins' from Gatwick Airport & the station. This cosy cottage has comfortable accommodation, with a warm welcome & homely atmosphere. All bedrooms have fine views over uninterrupted countryside. The village pub offers a varied menu, & is within walking distance. National Trust properties & walks nearby. Parking & courtesy transport available.

E-mail: davidlees@tinyworld.co.uk

David Lees Latchetts Cottage Norwood Hill Horley (Nr.) RH6 0ET Surrey
Tel: (01293) 862831 Fax 01293 862832 Open: ALL YEAR Map Ref No. 12

Surrey

rate £ from - to per person	children taken	evening meals	animals taken

The Old Farmhouse

Nearest Road: A.25

An early 15th-century medieval 4-bay hall house, which is little altered & retains many original features, including the diamond mullions for the hall window & fine panelling. It also has one of the longest unsupported crossing beams in Surrey. 2 of the attractively furnished bedrooms have brass bedsteads, & 1 has an original oak 4-poster bed. A delightful home. The Old Farmhouse is perfect for exploring the south-east of England & many places of historic interest. Children over 10.

E-mail: philip@theoldfarmhouse.demon.co.uk

Philip & Judie Wolf The Old Farmhouse Wasp Green Lane Outwood Nr. Redhill RH1 5QE Surrey
Tel: (01342) 842313 Fax 01342 844744 Open: ALL YEAR (Excl. Xmas) Map Ref No. 13

rate £ from - to per person	children taken	evening meals	animals taken
£25.00 to £25.00	Y	Y	N

Ashleigh House Hotel

Nearest Road: A.25

An Edwardian merchant's house situated within 600 yds of Redhill centre, with rail links to Gatwick (15 mins') & London (30 mins') & 4 miles from M.25 motorway with many historic houses within easy reach. The house is comfortably furnished & offers 8 bedrooms, 6 en-suite. The breakfast room overlooks an English garden. Jill & Michael extend a very hospitable welcome to all their guests from around the world. Parking available.

Mr & Mrs Warren Ashleigh House Hotel 39 Redstone Hill Redhill RH1 4BG Surrey
Tel: (01737) 764763 Fax 01737 780308 Open: ALL YEAR (Excl. Xmas) Map Ref No. 14

rate £ from - to per person	children taken	evening meals	animals taken
£34.50 to £50.00	Y	N	N

VISA: M'CARD:

Knaphill Manor

Nearest Road: M.25 Jt. 11

A delightful, large family home, dating back to the 1700s, set in 6 acres of grounds, with a tennis court & croquet lawn. Located in a farming area, the house is quiet & secluded, yet Heathrow & Gatwick are only a 35-mins'. drive away. Accommodation is very comfortable, with en-suite facilities plus T.V. & tea/coffee makers. A guests' colour-T.V. lounge is also available. Early-morning arrivals are welcome. London 25 mins'. Ascot, Windsor & Oxford are also easily reached. Children over 8 yrs.

Kevin & Teresa Leeper Knaphill Manor Carthouse Lane Woking GU21 4XT Surrey
Tel: (01276) 857962 Fax 01276 855503 Open: ALL YEAR (Excl. Xmas & Easter) Map Ref No. 15

rate £ from - to per person	children taken	evening meals	animals taken
£37.50 to £50.00	Y	N	N

see PHOTO over p. 369

VISA: M'CARD:

Pankhurst

Nearest Road: A.319

Pankhurst is an attractive & historic Grade II listed country house, set in a walled garden amid 8 acres of gardens & woods. Situated close to the picturesque village of Chobham, Pankhurst offers 3 beautiful guest rooms, each equipped with T.V., radio & tea/coffee-making facilities, etc. There is also a tennis court & heated outdoor swimming pool. It is ideally situated cose to Heathrow & Gatwick Airports, Ascot, Windsor, Sunningdale & Wentworth. 3 miles M.3., 7 miles M.25.

Tony & Susie Rowse Pankhurst Bagshot Road West End Woking GU24 9QR Surrey
Tel: (01276) 858149 Fax 01276 858149 Open: ALL YEAR Map Ref No. 16

rate £ from - to per person	children taken	evening meals	animals taken
£32.50 to £45.00	N	N	N

Knaphill Manor. Knaphill.

Swallow Barn	rate £ from - to per person	children taken	evening meals	animals taken
Swallow Barn Nearest Road: A.3046 Situated in quiet, secluded surroundings on the edge of Chobham, attractively converted outbuildings & stables with outdoor swimming pool. 3 bedrooms with en-suite/private bathrooms, T.V. & tea/coffee. Ideal for Sunningdale, Wentworth & Foxhills golf courses. Also, Wisley & Savill Gardens are within easy reach. Convenient for M.3, M.25, Heathrow Airport, Windsor, Ascot & Hampton Court. Woking station 2 miles - London 25 mins' by train. Single supplement. Children over 8. **E-mail: swallowbarn@compuserve.com** *Joan & David Carey Swallow Barn Milford Green Chobham Nr. Woking GU24 8AU Tel: (01276) 856030 Fax 01276 856030 Open: ALL YEAR Map Ref No. 17*	**£32.50 to £45.00**	Y	N	N

All the establishments mentioned in this guide are members of The Worldwide Bed & Breakfast Association

When booking your accommodation please mention The Best Bed & Breakfast

Sussex

Sussex

(South East)

The South Downs of Sussex stretch along the coast, reflecting the expanse of the North Downs of Kent, over the vast stretches of the Weald.

The South Downs extend from dramatic Beachy Head along the coast to Chichester & like the North Downs, they are crossed by an ancient trackway. There is much evidence of prehistoric settlement on the Downs. Mount Caburn, near Lewes, is crowned by an iron age fort, & Cissbury Ring is one of the most important archaeological sites in England. This large earthwork covers 80 acres & must have held a strategic defensive position. Hollingbury Fort carved into the hillside above Brighton, & the Trundle (meaning circle) date from 300-250 B.C., & were constructed on an existing neolithic settlement. The Long Man of Wilmington stands 226 feet high & is believed to be Nordic, possibly representing Woden, the God of War.

Only two towns are located on the Downs but both are of considerable interest. Lewes retains much of its mediaeval past & there is a folk museum in Ann of Cleves' house, which itself is partly 16th century. Arundel has a fascinating mixture of architectural styles, a castle & a superb park with a lake, magnificent beech trees & an unrivalled view of the Arun valley.

The landscape of the inland Weald ranges from bracken-covered heathlands where deer roam, to the deep woodland stretches of the Ashdown Forest, eventually giving way to soft undulating hills & valleys, patterned with hop-fields, meadows, oast houses, windmills & fruit orchards. Originally the whole Weald was dense with forest. Villages like Midhurst & Wadhurst hold the Saxon suffix "hurst" which means wood. As the forests were cleared for agriculture the names of the villages changed & we find Bosham & Stedham whose suffix "ham" means homestead or farm.

Battle, above Hastings, is the site of the famous Norman victory & 16th century Bodiam Castle, built as defence against the French in later times, has a beautiful setting encircled by a lily-covered moat.

Sussex has an extensive coastline, with cliffs near Eastbourne at Beachy Head, & at Hastings. Further east, the great flat Romney Marshes stretch out to sea, & there is considerable variety in the coastal towns.

Chichester has a magnificent cathedral & a harbour reaching deep into the coastal plain that is rich in archaeological remains. The creeks & mudflats make it an excellent place for bird watching.

Brighton is the most famous of the Sussex resorts with its Pier, the Promenade above the beaches, the oriental folly of George IV's Royal Pavilion & its Regency architecture. "The Lanes" are a maze of alleys & small squares full of fascinating shops, a thriving antique trade, & many good pubs & eating places. Hastings to the east preserves its "Old Town" where timbered houses nestle beneath the cliffs & the fishing boats are drawn up on the shingle whilst the nets are hung up to dry in curious tall, thin net stores. Winchelsea stands on a hill where it was rebuilt in the 13th century by Edward I when the original town was engulfed by the sea. It is a beautiful town with a fine Norman church, an excellent museum in the Town Hall, & many pretty houses. Across the Romney Marshes on the next hill stands Rye, its profile dominated by its church. It is a fascinating town with timbered houses & cobbled streets.

Sussex

Sussex Gazeteer

Areas of Outstanding Natural Beauty
The Sussex Downs. Chichester Harbour.

Historic Houses & Castles

Arundel Castle - Arundel
18th century rebuilding of ancient castle, fine portraits, 15th century furniture.
Cuckfield Park - Cuckfield
Elizabethan manor house, gatehouse. Very fine panelling & ceilings.
Danny - Hurstpierpoint
16th century - Elizabethan .
Goodwood House - Chichester
18th century - Jacobean house - Fine Sussex flintwork, paintings by Van Dyck, Canaletto & Stubbs, English & French furniture, tapestries & porcelain.
Newtimber Place - Newtimber
Moated house - Etruscan style wall paintings.
Purham - Pulborough
Elizabethan house containing important collection of Elizabethan, Jacobean & Georgian portraits, also fine furniture.
Petworth House - Petworth
17th century - landscaped by Capability Brown - important paintings - 14th century chapel.
St. Mary's - Bramber
15th century timber framed house - rare panelling.
Tanyard - Sharpthorne
Mediaeval tannery - 16th & 17th century additions.
The Thatched Cottage - Lindfield
Close-studded weald house - reputedly Henry VII hunting lodge.
Uppark - Petersfield
17th century - 18th century interior decorations remain unaltered.
Alfriston Clergy House - Nr. Seaford
14th century parish priest's house - pre-reformation.
Battle Abbey - Battle
Founded by William the Conqueror.
Charleston Manor - Westdean
Norman, Tudor & Georgian architectural styles - Romanesque window in the Norman wing.
Bull House - Lewes
15th century half-timbered house - was home of Tom Paine.
Bateman's - Burwash
17th century - watermill - home of Rudyard Kipling.
Bodiam Castle - Nr. Hawkshurst
14th century - noted example of mediaeval moated military architecture.
Great Dixter - Northiam
15th century half-timbered manor house - great hall - Lutyens gardens
Glynde Place - Nr. Lewes
16th century flint & brick - built around courtyard-collection of paintings by Rubens, Hoppner, Kneller, Lely, Zoffany.
Michelham Priory - Upper Dicker, Nr. Hailsham
13th century Augustinian Priory - became Tudor farmhouse - working watermill, ancient stained glass, etc., enclosed by moat.
Royal Pavilion - Brighton
Built for Prince Regent by Nash upon classical villa by Holland. Exotic Building - has superb original works of art lent by H.M. The Queen. Collections of Regency furniture also Art Nouveau & Art Deco in the Art Gallery & Museum.
Sheffield Park - Nr. Uckfield
Beautiful Tudor House - 18th century alterations - splendid staircase.

Cathedrals & Churches

Alfriston (St. Andrew)
14th century - transition from decorated style to perpendicular, Easter sepulchre.
Boxgrove (St. Mary & St. Blaise)
13th century choir with 16th century painted decoration on vaulting. Relic of Benedictine priory. 16th century chantry. Much decoration.
Chichester Cathedral
Norman & earliest Gothic. Large Romanesque relief sculptures in south choir aisle.
Etchingham (St. Mary & St. Nicholas)
14th century. Old glass, brasses, screen, carved stalls.
Hardham (St. Botolph)
11th century - 12th century wall paintings.
Rotherfield (St. Denys)
16th century font cover, 17th century canopied pulpit, glass by Burne-Jones, wall paintings, Georgian Royal Arms.

Sussex

Sompting (St. Mary)
11th century Saxon tower - Rhenish Helm Spire - quite unique.
Worth (St. Nicholas)
10th century - chancel arch is the largest Saxon arch in England. German carved pulpit c.1500 together with altar rails.
Winchelsea (St. Thomas the Apostle)
14th century - choir & aisles only. Canopied sedilia & piscina.

Museums & Galleries

Barbican House Museum - Lewes
Collection relating to pre-historic, Romano-British & , mediaeval antiquities of the area. Prints & water colours of the area.
Battle Museum-Battle
Remains from archeological sites in area. Diorama of Battle of Hastings.
Bignor Roman Villa Collection - Bignor
4th century mosaics, Samian pottery, hypocaust, etc.
Brighton Museum & Art Gallery - Brighton
Old Master Paintings, watercolours, ceramics, furniture. Surrealist paintings, Art Nouveau & Art Deco applied art, musical instruments & many other exhibits.
Marlipins Museum - Shoreham
12th century building housing collections of ship models, photographs, old maps, geological specimens, etc.
Royal National Lifeboat Institution Museum - Eastbourne
Lifeboats of all types used from earliest times to present.
Tower 73 - Eastbourne
Martello tower restored to display the history of these forts. Exhibition of equipment, uniforms & weapons of the times.
The Toy Museum - Rottingdean, Brighton
Toys & playthings from many countries - children's delight.

Other things to see & do

Bewl Water - Nr. Wadhurst
Boat trips, walks, adventure playground
Chichester Festival Theatre - Chichester
Summer season of plays from May to September.
Goodwood Racecourse

The Royal Pavilion. Brighton.

SUSSEX

Map reference

01	**Fuente**	23	**Gittoes**
02	**Richards**	24	**Hedley- C.**
03	**Earlam**	25	**Cox**
04	**Hansell**	26	**Skinner**
07	**Davis**	27	**Walters**
08	**Field**	28	**Mulcare**
08	**Waller**	29	**Costaras**
08	**Reeves**	30	**Field**
11	**Dridge**	31	**Francis**
12	**Skriczka**	32	**Steele**
15	**Pyemont**	33	**Apperly**
17	**Cooper**	33	**Brinkhurst**
18	**Kent**	33	**Hadfield**
19	**Pontifex**	34	**Warton**
20	**Birchell**	35	**Salmon**
21	**Fowler**	36	**Woods**
22	**Kerridge**	37	**Carver**

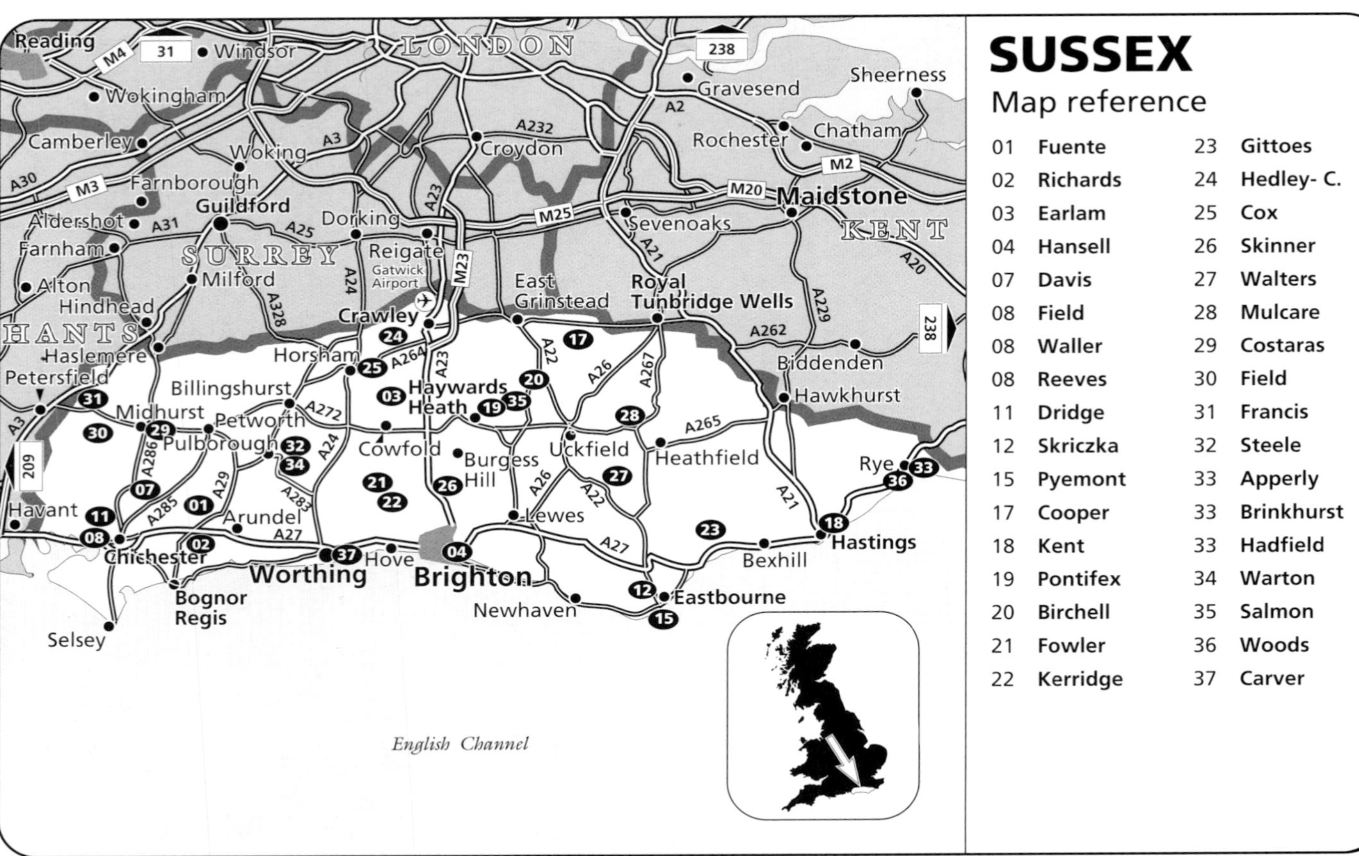

Sussex

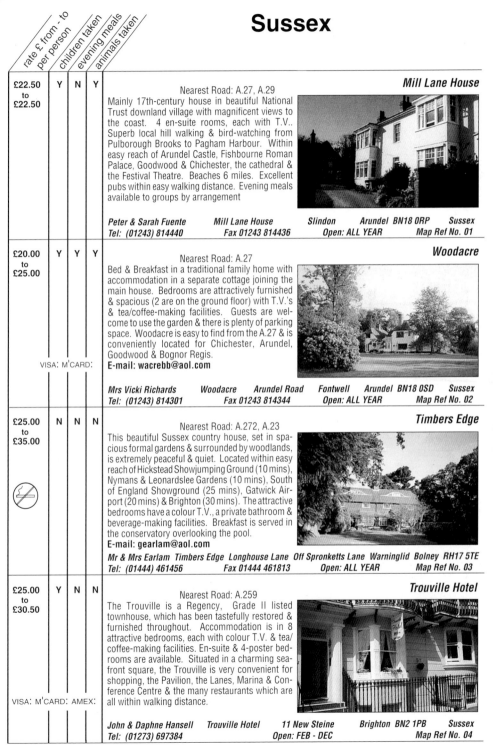

rate £ from - to per person	children taken	evening meals	animals taken
£22.50 to £22.50	Y	N	Y

Mill Lane House

Nearest Road: A.27, A.29

Mainly 17th-century house in beautiful National Trust downland village with magnificent views to the coast. 4 en-suite rooms, each with T.V.. Superb local hill walking & bird-watching from Pulborough Brooks to Pagham Harbour. Within easy reach of Arundel Castle, Fishbourne Roman Palace, Goodwood & Chichester, the cathedral & the Festival Theatre. Beaches 6 miles. Excellent pubs within easy walking distance. Evening meals available to groups by arrangement

Peter & Sarah Fuente Mill Lane House Slindon Arundel BN18 0RP Sussex
Tel: (01243) 814440 Fax 01243 814436 Open: ALL YEAR Map Ref No. 01

rate £ from - to per person	children taken	evening meals	animals taken
£20.00 to £25.00	Y	Y	Y

VISA: M'CARD:

Woodacre

Nearest Road: A.27

Bed & Breakfast in a traditional family home with accommodation in a separate cottage joining the main house. Bedrooms are attractively furnished & spacious (2 are on the ground floor) with T.V.'s & tea/coffee-making facilities. Guests are welcome to use the garden & there is plenty of parking space. Woodacre is easy to find from the A.27 & is conveniently located for Chichester, Arundel, Goodwood & Bognor Regis.

E-mail: wacrebb@aol.com

Mrs Vicki Richards Woodacre Arundel Road Fontwell Arundel BN18 0SD Sussex
Tel: (01243) 814301 Fax 01243 814344 Open: ALL YEAR Map Ref No. 02

rate £ from - to per person	children taken	evening meals	animals taken
£25.00 to £35.00	N	N	N

Timbers Edge

Nearest Road: A.272, A.23

This beautiful Sussex country house, set in spacious formal gardens & surrounded by woodlands, is extremely peaceful & quiet. Located within easy reach of Hickstead Showjumping Ground (10 mins), Nymans & Leonardslee Gardens (10 mins), South of England Showground (25 mins), Gatwick Airport (20 mins) & Brighton (30 mins). The attractive bedrooms have a colour T.V., a private bathroom & beverage-making facilities. Breakfast is served in the conservatory overlooking the pool.

E-mail: gearlam@aol.com

Mr & Mrs Earlam Timbers Edge Longhouse Lane Off Spronketts Lane Warninglid Bolney RH17 5TE
Tel: (01444) 461456 Fax 01444 461813 Open: ALL YEAR Map Ref No. 03

rate £ from - to per person	children taken	evening meals	animals taken
£25.00 to £30.50	Y	N	N

VISA: M'CARD: AMEX:

Trouville Hotel

Nearest Road: A.259

The Trouville is a Regency, Grade II listed townhouse, which has been tastefully restored & furnished throughout. Accommodation is in 8 attractive bedrooms, each with colour T.V. & tea/coffee-making facilities. En-suite & 4-poster bedrooms are available. Situated in a charming seafront square, the Trouville is very convenient for shopping, the Pavilion, the Lanes, Marina & Conference Centre & the many restaurants which are all within walking distance.

John & Daphne Hansell Trouville Hotel 11 New Steine Brighton BN2 1PB Sussex
Tel: (01273) 697384 Open: FEB - DEC Map Ref No. 04

Critchfield House. Bosham.

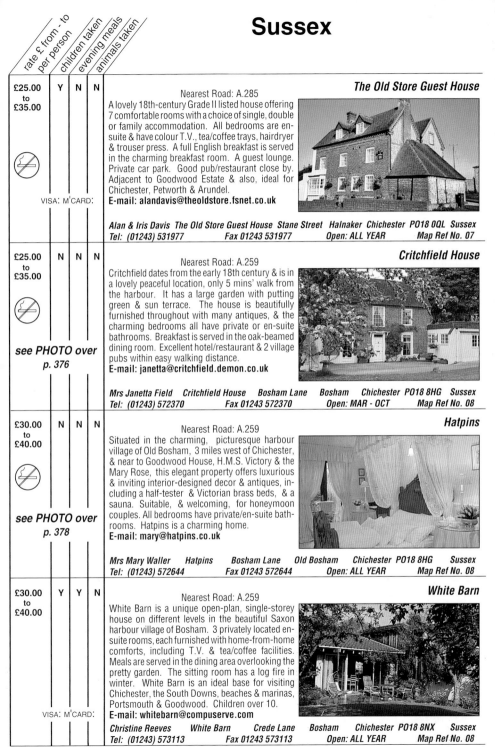

rate £ from - to per person	children taken	evening meals	animals taken	
£25.00 to £35.00	Y	N	N	**The Old Store Guest House** Nearest Road: A.285 A lovely 18th-century Grade II listed house offering 7 comfortable rooms with a choice of single, double or family accommodation. All bedrooms are en-suite & have colour T.V., tea/coffee trays, hairdryer & trouser press. A full English breakfast is served in the charming breakfast room. A guest lounge. Private car park. Good pub/restaurant close by. Adjacent to Goodwood Estate & also, ideal for Chichester, Petworth & Arundel. **E-mail: alandavis@theoldstore.fsnet.co.uk** *Alan & Iris Davis The Old Store Guest House Stane Street Halnaker Chichester PO18 0QL Sussex* *Tel: (01243) 531977 Fax 01243 531977 Open: ALL YEAR Map Ref No. 07*
VISA: M'CARD:				
£25.00 to £35.00	N	N	N	**Critchfield House** Nearest Road: A.259 Critchfield dates from the early 18th century & is in a lovely peaceful location, only 5 mins' walk from the harbour. It has a large garden with putting green & sun terrace. The house is beautifully furnished throughout with many antiques, & the charming bedrooms all have private or en-suite bathrooms. Breakfast is served in the oak-beamed dining room. Excellent hotel/restaurant & 2 village pubs within easy walking distance. **E-mail: janetta@critchfield.demon.co.uk** *Mrs Janetta Field Critchfield House Bosham Lane Bosham Chichester PO18 8HG Sussex* *Tel: (01243) 572370 Fax 01243 572370 Open: MAR - OCT Map Ref No. 08*
see PHOTO over p. 376				
£30.00 to £40.00	N	N	N	**Hatpins** Nearest Road: A.259 Situated in the charming, picturesque harbour village of Old Bosham, 3 miles west of Chichester, & near to Goodwood House, H.M.S. Victory & the Mary Rose, this elegant property offers luxurious & inviting interior-designed decor & antiques, including a half-tester & Victorian brass beds, & a sauna. Suitable, & welcoming, for honeymoon couples. All bedrooms have private/en-suite bathrooms. Hatpins is a charming home. **E-mail: mary@hatpins.co.uk** *Mrs Mary Waller Hatpins Bosham Lane Old Bosham Chichester PO18 8HG Sussex* *Tel: (01243) 572644 Fax 01243 572644 Open: ALL YEAR Map Ref No. 08*
see PHOTO over p. 378				
£30.00 to £40.00	Y	Y	N	**White Barn** Nearest Road: A.259 White Barn is a unique open-plan, single-storey house on different levels in the beautiful Saxon harbour village of Bosham. 3 privately located en-suite rooms, each furnished with home-from-home comforts, including T.V. & tea/coffee facilities. Meals are served in the dining area overlooking the pretty garden. The sitting room has a log fire in winter. White Barn is an ideal base for visiting Chichester, the South Downs, beaches & marinas, Portsmouth & Goodwood. Children over 10. **E-mail: whitebarn@compuserve.com** *Christine Reeves White Barn Crede Lane Bosham Chichester PO18 8NX Sussex* *Tel: (01243) 573113 Fax 01243 573113 Open: ALL YEAR Map Ref No. 08*
VISA: M'CARD:				

Hatpins. Old Bosham.

Pinnacle Point. Meads Village.

rate £ from - to per person	children taken	evening meals	animals taken

Chichester Lodge

Nearest Road: B.2178

A picturesque, Grade II listed 1840s Gothic Lodge set in very quiet country surroundings, yet only 4 mins' drive from the city centre and the Festival Theatre. Accommodation is in comfortable & 2 tastefully furnished bedrooms with 4-poster beds & en-suite bathrooms. An adjoining garden room, in which guests may choose to relax, has tea-making facilities & a cosy log-burning fire. You are assured of a warm and friendly welcome from your hosts at this charming home.

rate £ from - to per person	children taken	evening meals	animals taken
£25.00 to £35.00	N	N	N

Jeannette Dridge Chichester Lodge Oakwood Chichester PO18 9AL Sussex
Tel: (01243) 786560 Fax 01243 784525 Open: ALL YEAR Map Ref No. 11

Southcroft Hotel

Nearest Road: A.259, A.22

Situated in a quiet location, Southcroft is only minutes from the theatres, seas, Devonshire Park, the town centre & the South Downs Way. All 6 en-suite bedrooms are tastefully furnished & well-equipped. Home cooking a speciality. Meals are served in the dining room overlooking a pretty patio garden where Kiwi fruit trees flourish. Patchwork & quilting workshops are held. Direct train service from London & Gatwick. Ideally placed for exploring Eastbourne & the beautiful Sussex countryside.
E-mail: southcroft@eastbourne34.freeserve.co.uk

rate £ from - to per person	children taken	evening meals	animals taken
£25.00 to £26.00	Y	Y	N

Milly & Dick Skriczka Southcroft Hotel 15 South Cliff Avenue Eastbourne BN20 7AH Sussex
Tel: (01323) 729071 Open: ALL YEAR Map Ref No. 12

Pinnacle Point

Nearest Road: A.22

Pinnacle Point is a secluded house with unrivalled views over the English Channel. It is very special & occupies an idyllic & unique position on the cliffs near the foot of the South Downs in Eastbourne. A number of showbusiness & international sports stars regularly use the house. It is very modern with 3 designer-decorated en-suite bedrooms. Close to all the facilities in Eastbourne. The host encourages guests to take early morning Downland walks with him before breakfast! A must for bird lovers. Children over 10. Dinner by arrangement.

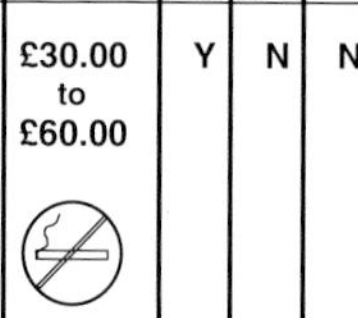

rate £ from - to per person	children taken	evening meals	animals taken
£30.00 to £60.00	Y	N	N

see PHOTO over p. 379

VISA:

Mr & Mrs P. Pyemont Pinnacle Point Foyle Way Upper Duke's Drive Meads Eastbourne BN20 7XL
Tel: (01323) 726666 Fax 01323 643946 Open: ALL YEAR Map Ref No. 15

Bolebroke Mill

Nearest Road: A.264

A magical watermill, first recorded in 1086 A.D., & an Elizabethan miller's barn offer 5 en-suite rooms of genuine, unspoilt rustic charm, set amid woodland, water & pasture, & used as the idyllic setting for the film 'Carrington'. The mill is complete with machinery, trap doors & very steep stairs. The barn has low doors & beamed ceilings, & includes the honeymooners' hayloft with a 4-poster bed. Light supper trays available, & award-winning breakfasts are served in the mill-house. Children over 8.
E-mail: b+b@bolebrokemill.demon.co.uk

rate £ from - to per person	children taken	evening meals	animals taken
£32.50 to £39.00	N	N	N

see PHOTO over p. 381

VISA: M'CARD: AMEX:

Mr D. J. Cooper Bolebroke Mill Perry Hill Edenbridge Road Hartfield TN7 4JP Sussex
Tel: (01892) 770425 Fax 01892 770425 Open: Mid FEB - Mid DEC Map Ref No. 17

Bolebroke Watermill. Hartfield.

rate £ from - to per person	children taken	evening meals	animals taken

Parkside House

Nearest Road: A.21

Located in a quiet residential conservation area, & set in an elevated position opposite a beautiful park. This elegant Victorian house retains all its original features, but with every modern facility. High standards of hospitality, comfort & good home-cooking are provided, creating an informal, friendly & welcoming atmosphere. Bedrooms are en-suite & offer every luxury. The 'Apricot' room has an antique French bed. A quiet location only 15 mins' walk from the town centre & sea front.

rate £ from - to per person	children taken	evening meals	animals taken
£25.00 to £27.00	Y	N	N

VISA: M'CARD:

B. W. Kent Parkside House 59 Lower Park Road Hastings TN34 2LD Sussex
Tel: (01424) 433096 Fax 01424 421431 Open: ALL YEAR Map Ref No. 18

The Pilstyes

Nearest Road: A.272, A.22, A.23

Romantic Elizabethan cottage in enviable location on the heart of what is reputed to be the prettiest village in Sussex, yet with easy access to Gatwick Airport, London & Brighton. Roy & Carol live in the adjoining cottage. There is a suite of 2 attractive bedrooms, 1 has a four-poster bed with crisp linen bedding & 1 has twin beds. A comfortable sitting room with log fire. A 'bucks fizz' breakfast is available for that special occasion!
E-mail: bnbuk@pavilion.co.uk

rate £ from - to per person	children taken	evening meals	animals taken
£27.50 to £37.50	N	N	N

VISA: M'CARD: AMEX:

Roy & Carol Pontifex The Pilstyes 106 & 108 High Street Lindfield Haywards Heath RH16 2HS
Tel: (01444) 484101 Fax 01444 484100 Open: ALL YEAR Map Ref No. 19

Holly House

Nearest Road: A.275

Holly House, an early-Victorian forest farmhouse with character, offers a warm, friendly welcome to visitors. A 1-acre garden with long views. Situated in an Ashdown Forest village & ideal for touring Sussex, with many N.T. properties nearby. A comfortable lounge is available, & breakfast is taken in the conservatory overlooking the garden. The 5 pleasant rooms, 3 en-suite, have tea-making facilities & T.V.. A small swimming pool heated during the summer. Animals welcome.
E-mail:db@hollyhousebnb.demon.co.uk

rate £ from - to per person	children taken	evening meals	animals taken
£23.00 to £35.00	Y	Y	Y

Mrs D. A. Birchell Holly House Beaconsfield Road Chelwood Gate Haywards Heath RH17 7LF
Tel: (01825) 740484 Fax 01825 740172 Open: ALL YEAR Map Ref No. 20

Frylands

Nearest Road: A.272

Frylands is a timber-framed Tudor farmhouse in a quiet setting of farmland, woods & river. There are 3 lovely bedrooms, 1 with private facilities, & all with colour T.V., radio & tea/coffee tray with home-made biscuits. A traditional breakfast, cooked to order, is served with a selection of home-made preserves & local honey. A large garden with heated swimming pool. Good pubs & food nearby. Only 20 mins Gatwick & Brighton.
E-mail: fowler@pavilion.co.uk

rate £ from - to per person	children taken	evening meals	animals taken
£20.00 to £25.00	Y	N	N

Mrs Sylvia Fowler Frylands Frylands Lane Henfield BN5 9BP Sussex
Tel: (01403) 710214 Fax 01403 711449 Open: ALL YEAR (Excl. Xmas & New Year) Map Ref No. 21

Wartling Place. Wartling.

	rate £ from - to per person	children taken	evening meals	animals taken
Yeomans Hall	£23.00 to £26.00	N	N	N
Wartling Place	£34.00 to £45.00	Y	Y	N
The Willows	£25.00 to £35.00	Y	N	N
Glebe End	£20.00 to £30.00	Y	N	Y

Yeomans Hall

Nearest Road: A.281

Yeomans Hall is a listed 15th-century hall house situated in a conservation area in a farming hamlet. It is attractively decorated & boasts country-style furnishings with beams & inglenook fireplaces. The 2 en-suite bedrooms combine old charm with modern day comforts. It is situated within easy reach of the A.23, Brighton, fast trains to London & is also convenient for National Trust properties, Ardingly Showground, Hickstead & Glyndebourne. Excellent walks & pubs nearby. Parking.

E-mail: stay@yeomanshall.fsnet.co.uk

Alan Kerridge Yeomans Hall Blackstone Nr. Henfield BN5 9TB Sussex
Tel: (01273) 494224 Fax 01273 494224 Open: ALL YEAR (Excl. Xmas & New Year) Map Ref No. 22

Wartling Place

Nearest Road: A.271, A.27

A superb Grade II listed Georgian country house set in 2 acres of mature secluded gardens. Beautifully restored with period furnishings offering 3 luxurious, individual bedrooms & romantic 4-posters for that special occasion. Each room is en-suite with bath & shower, T.V. & courtesy tray. Ideal for visiting the many National Trust houses, castles & gardens of Sussex & Kent. Private parking. Self-catering lodge cottage available. Evening meals available by prior arrangement.

E-mail: accom@wartlingplace.prestel.co.uk

see PHOTO over p. 383

VISA: M'CARD: AMEX:

Rowena Ann Gittoes Wartling Place Wartling Herstmonceux BN27 1RY Sussex
Tel: (01323) 832590 Fax 01323 831558 Open: ALL YEAR Map Ref No. 23

The Willows

Nearest Road: A.264

The Willows has a beautifully converted barn separate from the main house. The views are idyllic with a patio garden & lily pond for guest's enjoyment. The barn consists of twin, king-size double & single en-suite rooms with T.V. & tea/coffee trays. All bathrooms are luxuriously appointed. There is a conservatory/dining room leading to a beamed lounge, which is charmingly furnished & has patio doors opening into the garden. The Willows is 8 miles from Gatwick Airport & is near Horsham. Parking by arrangement.

Mrs C. M. Hedley-Coates The Willows Wimlands Lane Faygate Nr. Horsham RH12 4SP Sussex
Tel: (01293) 851030 Fax 01293 852466 Open: ALL YEAR Map Ref No. 24

Glebe End

Nearest Road: A.24

Glebe End is a fascinating medieval house, with a secluded, sunny, walled garden, set in the heart of Warnham village. It retains many original features, including heavy flagstones, curving ships' timbers & an inglenook fireplace. 4 single, twin or king-sized en-suite rooms, charmingly furnished with antiques & each with T.V. & hot-drink trays. Mrs Cox is an excellent cook, & meals (by arrangement) are delicious & include home-grown produce. Tennis & golf nearby. 20 mins to Gatwick Airport. Animals by arrangement.

Elizabeth Cox Glebe End Church Street Warnham Horsham RH12 3QW Sussex
Tel: (01403) 261711 Fax 01403 257572 Open: ALL YEAR Map Ref No. 25

Shortgate Manor Farm. Halland.

Sussex

	rate £ from - to per person	children taken	evening meals	animals taken
Clayton Wickham Farmhouse	£35.00 to £45.00	Y	Y	Y
Shortgate Manor Farm	£25.00 to £30.00	Y	N	N
Huggetts Furnace Farm	£27.50 to £37.50	Y	Y	N
Amberfold	£25.00 to £££	N	N	N

Clayton Wickham Farmhouse

Nearest Road: A.23

A delightful, secluded 16th-century farmhouse with lovely views, set amidst the beautiful Sussex countryside. The friendly hosts have refurbished their home to a high standard, yet have retained many original features, hence there are a wealth of beams & a huge inglenook fireplace in the drawing room. A variety of tastefully furnished & well-appointed bedrooms, including a super 4-poster en-suite. Excellent 4-course candlelit dinner by arrangement, & lovely 3-acre grounds with tennis court. Ample parking. Animals by arrangement.

Mike & Susie Skinner *Clayton Wickham Farmhouse* *Belmont Lane* *Hurstpierpoint BN6 9EP*
Tel: (01273) 845698 *Fax 01273 841970* *Open: ALL YEAR* *Map Ref No. 26*

Shortgate Manor Farm

Nearest Road: A.22

Shortgate Manor Farm is an enchanting 18th-century farmhouse set in 8 acres approached by an avenue of poplars festooned with rambling roses. The 3 charming bedrooms all offer en-suite/private facilities, T.V.'s, courtesy trays, with bathrobes provided for your comfort. The house is surrounded by 2 acres of landscaped gardens which are open under the National Gardens Scheme every June. Glyndebourne 4 miles. A charming home from which to explore Sussex. Children over 10.
E-mail: ewalt@shortgate.co.uk

see PHOTO over p. 385

David & Ethel Walters *Shortgate Manor Farm* *Halland* *Lewes BN8 6PS* *Sussex*
Tel: (01825) 840320 *Fax 01825 840320* *Open: ALL YEAR* *Map Ref No. 27*

Huggetts Furnace Farm

Nearest Road: A.272

A beautiful medieval farmhouse (Grade II listed) set well off the beaten track in tranquil countryside. 3 attractive bedrooms, all with en-suite/private facilities, radio & tea/coffee trays. The oak-beamed guests' room has an inglenook fireplace & a T.V.. Super dinners & breakfasts using home-grown & local produce. Heated outdoor swimming pool, & 120 acres of grounds. Self-catering cottage (non-smokers). Gatwick 45 mins. 30 mins coast. Nearby, many N. T. properties. Children over 7.
E-mail: huggettsfurnacefarm@freenet.co.uk

see PHOTO over p. 387

Gillian & John Mulcare *Huggetts Furnace Farm* *Stonehurst Lane Five Ashes* *Mayfield TN20 6LL*
Tel: (01825) 830220 *Fax 01825 830722* *Open: ALL YEAR (Excl. Xmas)* *Map Ref No. 28*

Amberfold

Nearest Road: A.286

Amberfold is a charming 17th-century listed cottage, situated in quiet, idyllic countryside yet only 5 mins' drive from Midhurst. 2 self-contained annexes with access all day. 1 is situated on the ground floor. Each annex is comfortably furnished & has private facilities, T.V., clock/radio, fridge, etc. To allow you complete freedom & privacy, a large Continental breakfast is self-service & is taken in your room. An attractive garden in which to relax. Parking. An ideal base from which to explore Goodwood, Singleton, Chichester & the coast.

Annabelle & Alexander Costaras *Amberfold* *Heyshott* *Midhurst GU29 0DA* *Sussex*
Tel: (01730) 812385 *Open: ALL YEAR* *Map Ref No. 29*

Huggetts Furnace Farm. Five Ashes.

Sussex

Mill Farm

rate £ from - to per person	children taken	evening meals	animals taken
£17.50 to £25.00	Y	N	N

Nearest Road: A.272

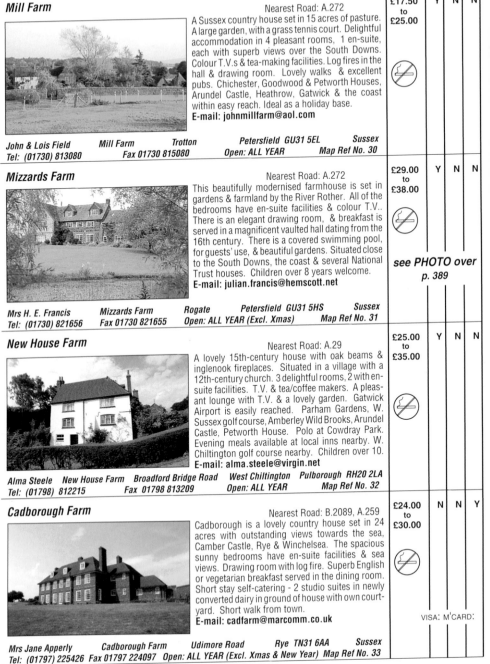

A Sussex country house set in 15 acres of pasture. A large garden, with a grass tennis court. Delightful accommodation in 4 pleasant rooms, 1 en-suite, each with superb views over the South Downs. Colour T.V.s & tea-making facilities. Log fires in the hall & drawing room. Lovely walks & excellent pubs. Chichester, Goodwood & Petworth Houses, Arundel Castle, Heathrow, Gatwick & the coast within easy reach. Ideal as a holiday base.

E-mail: johnmillfarm@aol.com

John & Lois Field *Mill Farm* *Trotton* *Petersfield GU31 5EL* *Sussex*
Tel: (01730) 813080 *Fax 01730 815080* *Open: ALL YEAR* *Map Ref No. 30*

Mizzards Farm

rate £ from - to per person	children taken	evening meals	animals taken
£29.00 to £38.00	Y	N	N

Nearest Road: A.272

This beautifully modernised farmhouse is set in gardens & farmland by the River Rother. All of the bedrooms have en-suite facilities & colour T.V.. There is an elegant drawing room, & breakfast is served in a magnificent vaulted hall dating from the 16th century. There is a covered swimming pool, for guests' use, & beautiful gardens. Situated close to the South Downs, the coast & several National Trust houses. Children over 8 years welcome.

E-mail: julian.francis@hemscott.net

see PHOTO over p. 389

Mrs H. E. Francis *Mizzards Farm* *Rogate* *Petersfield GU31 5HS* *Sussex*
Tel: (01730) 821656 *Fax 01730 821655* *Open: ALL YEAR (Excl. Xmas)* *Map Ref No. 31*

New House Farm

rate £ from - to per person	children taken	evening meals	animals taken
£25.00 to £35.00	Y	N	N

Nearest Road: A.29

A lovely 15th-century house with oak beams & inglenook fireplaces. Situated in a village with a 12th-century church. 3 delightful rooms, 2 with en-suite facilities. T.V. & tea/coffee makers. A pleasant lounge with T.V. & a lovely garden. Gatwick Airport is easily reached. Parham Gardens, W. Sussex golf course, Amberley Wild Brooks, Arundel Castle, Petworth House. Polo at Cowdray Park. Evening meals available at local inns nearby. W. Chiltington golf course nearby. Children over 10.

E-mail: alma.steele@virgin.net

Alma Steele *New House Farm* *Broadford Bridge Road* *West Chiltington* *Pulborough RH20 2LA*
Tel: (01798) 812215 *Fax 01798 813209* *Open: ALL YEAR* *Map Ref No. 32*

Cadborough Farm

rate £ from - to per person	children taken	evening meals	animals taken
£24.00 to £30.00	N	N	Y

Nearest Road: B.2089, A.259

Cadborough is a lovely country house set in 24 acres with outstanding views towards the sea, Camber Castle, Rye & Winchelsea. The spacious sunny bedrooms have en-suite facilities & sea views. Drawing room with log fire. Superb English or vegetarian breakfast served in the dining room. Short stay self-catering - 2 studio suites in newly converted dairy in ground of house with own courtyard. Short walk from town.

E-mail: cadfarm@marcomm.co.uk

VISA: M'CARD:

Mrs Jane Apperly *Cadborough Farm* *Udimore Road* *Rye TN31 6AA* *Sussex*
Tel: (01797) 225426 *Fax 01797 224097* *Open: ALL YEAR (Excl. Xmas & New Year)* *Map Ref No. 33*

Mizzards Farm. Rogate.

Jeake's House. Rye.

1 Lime Chase. Storrington.

	rate £ from - to per person	children taken	evening meals	animals taken
Little Orchard House	£32.00 to £45.00	Y	N	N
Jeake's House	£27.50 to £46.50	Y	N	Y
No. 1 Lime Chase	£32.50 to £40.00	Y	N	N
Sliders Farm	£22.00 to £40.00	Y	N	N

Little Orchard House

Nearest Road: A.259, A.268

This charming Georgian townhouse, with traditional walled garden & Smuggler's Watchtower, is at the heart of ancient Rye. Whilst a perfect touring base, it retains many original features. Open fires, antique furnishings & books ensure a peaceful, relaxed atmosphere. Generous country breakfasts feature organic & free-range local products. 2 lovely en-suite bedrooms - 1 with 4-poster - have T.V. & hot-drinks tray. A romantic suite with kitchen facilities in the detached Tower offers real seclusion. Children over 12.

VISA: M'CARD:

Sara Brinkhurst Little Orchard House West Street Rye TN31 7ES Sussex
Tel: (01797) 223831 Fax 01797 223831 Open: ALL YEAR Map Ref No. 33

Jeake's House

Nearest Road: A.259

Jeakes House is an outstanding 17th-century listed building. Retaining many original features, oak beams & wood panelling, & decorated throughout with antiques. 12 bedrooms overlook the gardens, en-suite/private facilities, T.V., etc. 4-poster available. Dine in the galleried former Baptist chapel, where full English, wholefood vegetarian or Continental breakfasta are served. Located in one of Britain's most picturesque medieval streets. Parking. Children over 11. Animals by arrangement.
E-mail: jeakeshouse@btinternet.com

see PHOTO over p. 390

VISA: M'CARD:

Jenny Hadfield Jeake's House Mermaid Street Rye TN31 7ET Sussex
Tel: (01797) 222828 Fax 01797 222623 Open: ALL YEAR Map Ref No. 33

No. 1 Lime Chase

Nearest Road: A.283

This multiple award-winning home offers quiet, secluded village location within the South Downs, an Area of Outstanding Natural Beauty. Elegant twin & double/family rooms with antiques, T.V., etc. & luxury bathrooms, some en-suite. Enjoy afternoon tea in the conservatory or by the log fire. Traditional English breakfast with home-made bread. Good restaurants close by. Ideal location: Arundel, Goodwood, Petworth, Chichester, Gatwick 35 mins & Heathrow 75 mins. Children over 12.
E-mail: fionawarton@limechase.co.uk

see PHOTO over p. 391

Mrs Fiona Warton No. 1 Lime Chase Storrington RH20 4LX Sussex
Tel: (01903) 740437 Fax 01903 740437 Open: ALL YEAR Map Ref No. 34

Sliders Farm

Nearest Road: A.275

A listed 16th-century farmhouse, with a wealth of oak beams & inglenook fireplaces, in a secluded setting on the Sussex Weald. All rooms are en-suite, with T.V., etc. Home-grown produce & home-cooking. Dining room & lounge with inglenooks & billiard table. An outdoor pool, tennis court & private trout fishing. Convenient for Ardingly Showground, Sheffield Park Gardens, the Bluebell Railway & N. T. properties & gardens. Coast & Gatwick 30 mins (car). London 45 mins (train).
E-mail: jean&davidsalmon@freeserve.co.uk

see PHOTO over p. 393

David & Jean Salmon Sliders Farm Furners Green Danehill Uckfield TN22 3RT Sussex
Tel: (01825) 790258 Fax 01825 790258 Open: ALL YEAR (Excl. Xmas) Map Ref No. 35

Sliders Farm. Furners Green.

	rate £ from - to per person	children taken	evening meals	animals taken
The Strand House	£23.00 to £33.00	Y	N	N
Bonchurch House	£23.00 to £26.00	Y	N	N

The Strand House

Nearest Road: A.259

Nestling at the foot of the cliffs beneath the 13th-century Strand Gate lies The Strand House, full of atmosphere with oak beams & inglenook fireplaces. Without a level floor or wall, the bedrooms have their own individual charm. (4-poster available.) A traditional English breakfast, using local fresh produce, is served in the heavily beamed dining room. Cosy log fires in season. Pretty gardens. Children over 2 years welcome.

E-mail: strandhouse@winchelsea98.fsnet.co.uk

VISA: M'CARD:

Geoff & Gillian Woods The Strand House Tanyard's Lane Winchelsea TN36 4JT Sussex
Tel: (01797) 226276 Fax 01797 224806 Open: ALL YEAR Map Ref No. 36

Bonchurch House

Nearest Road: A.259

Bonchurch is a home-from-home guest house where a warm welcome is extended to all guests by John & Doreen Carver, resident proprietors for 26 years. There are 6 bedrooms, all well-equipped with shaver points & an en-suite/private shower/bathroom, T.V., easy chairs & tea/coffee-making facilities. Home cooking is a speciality. Ideally situated in a picturesque setting, yet close to the sea front, shops & entertainment. Children over 3.

E-mail: bonchurch@enta.net

VISA: M'CARD:

John & Doreen Carver Bonchurch House 1 Winchester Road Worthing BN11 4DJ Sussex
Tel: (01903) 202492 Fax 01903 202492 Open: FEB - DEC Map Ref No. 37

All the establishments mentioned in this guide are members of The Worldwide Bed & Breakfast Association

When booking your accommodation please mention The Best Bed & Breakfast

Warwickshire

Warwickshire (Heart of England)

Warwickshire contains much that is thought of as traditional rural England, but it is a county of contradictions. Rural tranquillity surrounds industrial towns, working canals run along with meandering rivers, the mediaeval splendour of Warwick Castle vies with the handsome Regency grace of Leamington Spa.

Of course, Warwickshire is Shakespeare's county, with his birthplace, Stratford-upon-Avon standing at the northern edge of the Cotswolds. You can visit any of half a dozen houses with Shakespearian associations, see his tomb in the lovely Parish church or enjoy a performance by the world famous Royal Shakespeare Company in their theatre on the banks of the River Avon.

Warwickshire was created as the Kingdom of Mercia after the departure of the Romans. King Offa of Mercia left us his own particular mark - a coin which bore the imprint of his likeness known as his "pen" & this became our penny. Lady Godiva was the wife of an Earl of Mercia who pleaded with her husband to lessen the taxation burden on his people. He challenged her to ride naked through the streets of Coventry as the price of her request. She did this knowing that her long hair would cover her nakedness, & the people, who loved her, stayed indoors out of respect. Only Peeping Tom found the temptation irresistible.

The 15th, 16th, & 17th centuries were the heyday of fine building in the county, when many gracious homes were built. Exceptional Compton Wynyates has rosy pink bricks, twisted chimney stacks, battlements & moats & presents an unforgettably romantic picture of a perfect Tudor House.

Coventry has long enjoyed the reputation of a thriving city, noted for its weaving of silks and ribbons, learned from the refugee Huguenots. When progress brought industry, watches, bicycles & cars became the mainstay of the city. Coventry suffered grievously from aerial bombardment in the war & innumerable ancient & treasured buildings were lost.

A magnificent new Cathedral stands besides the shell of the old. Mystery plays enacting the life of Christ are performed in the haunting ruin.

Warwick Castle.

Fulready Manor. Fulready

Warwickshire

rate £ from - to per person	children taken	evening meals	animals taken
£25.00 to £25.00	Y	N	Y

Little Knighton Farm

Nearest Road: A.442

Standing in 15 acres on the Warwickshire/ Worcestershire borders, Little Knighton Farm is a Grade II listed farmhouse in a charming rural setting. Accommodation offers 1 twin room en-suite & 1 double room with private bathroom. Each bedroom has colour T.V., radio/alarm & tea/coffee-making facilities. A comfortable guests lounge. Ideal central location for Stratford, Warwick & Worcester area. Animals by arrangement. Children over 10 years welcome.

E-mail: b-b@littleknighton.co.uk

Clive & Sue May Little Knighton Farm Knighton Alcester B49 5LT Warwickshire
Tel: (01386) 793650 Fax 01386 793833 Open: ALL YEAR (Excl. Xmas) Map Ref No. 00

rate £ from - to per person	children taken	evening meals	animals taken
£37.50 to £55.00	N	N	N

see PHOTO over p. 398

Fulready Manor

Nearest Road: A.422

Michael & Maureen Spencer invite you to experience their unique home, Fulready Manor, set in 120 acres overlooking its own lake, in the beautiful south Warwickshire countryside. It is on the doorstep of the Cotswolds & is only 7 miles from historic Stratford-upon-Avon. Fulready Manor boasts sumptuously furnished, individually designed four-poster bedrooms, all with dramatic views & en-suite bathrooms. All of the rooms have been skilfully created by an interior designer.

E-mail: reservations@fulreadymanor.co.uk

Mrs M. V. Spencer Fulready Manor Fulready Ettington CV37 7PE Warwickshire
Tel: (01789) 740152 Open: ALL YEAR (Excl. Xmas) Map Ref No. 01

rate £ from - to per person	children taken	evening meals	animals taken
£20.00 to £26.00	Y	N	N

Ferndale Guest House

Nearest Road: A.452

You are assured of a warm welcome in this family-run, spacious Victorian house situated in a quiet tree-lined avenue only 5 mins' walk from the town centre. All 7 bedrooms are en-suite & tastefully decorated & include colour T.V. & coffee/tea-making facilities. A guests' T.V. lounge is available throughout the day. Ideally located for Warwick, Coventry, Leamington Spa, the N.E.C., Stoneleigh Agricultural Centre & Warwick University.

E-mail: derekwilson1@compuserve.com

Mrs J. Wilson Ferndale Guest House 45 Priory Road Kenilworth CV8 1LL Warwickshire
Tel: (01926) 853214 Fax 01926 858336 Open: ALL YEAR Map Ref No. 02

rate £ from - to per person	children taken	evening meals	animals taken
£32.00 to £35.00	Y	N	N

see PHOTO over p. 400

VISA: M'CARD:

Comber House

Nearest Road: A.445, M.40

Built in the early 1800s Comber House has been lovingly converted into a welcoming guest house, catering both for the tired executive & the inquisitive tourist. You can relax in the spacious lounge, walk in the private garden or try your hand in the billiards room. All of the 5 attractive bedrooms have en-suite facilities & offer an overall feeling of luxury & individuality. Children over 12 years. Guide dogs welcome.

E-mail: b-b@comberhouse.freeserve.co.uk

David, Brian & Roma Shorthouse Comber House 2, Union Road Leamington Spa CV32 5LT Warks.
Tel: (01926) 421332 Fax 01926 313930 Open: Mid JAN - Mid DEC Map Ref No. 03

Comber House. Leamington Spa.

8 Clarendon Crescent. Leamington Spa.

Warwickshire

	rate £ from - to per person	children taken	evening meals	animals taken

8 Clarendon Crescent

Nearest Road: A.452

A Grade II listed Regency house overlooking a private dell. Situated in a quiet backwater of Leamington. Elegantly furnished with antiques, & offering accommodation in 5 comfortable & tastefully furnished bedrooms, 4 with en-suite facilities. A delicious full English breakfast is served. Only 5 mins' walk from the town centre. Very convenient for Warwick, Stratford, Stoneleigh Agricultural Centre, Warwick University & the N.E.C.. Children over 4 years welcome.

rate £ from - to per person	children taken	evening meals	animals taken
£27.50 to £35.00	Y	N	N

see PHOTO over p. 401

Christine & David Lawson 8 Clarendon Crescent Leamington Spa CV32 5NR Warwickshire
Tel: (01926) 429840 Fax 01926 429190 *Open: ALL YEAR Map Ref No. 04*

Crandon House

Nearest Road: M.40, A.423

Crandon House offers an especially warm welcome & exceptionally high standard of accommodation & comfort. Set in 20 acres of beautiful countryside. There are 5 pretty bedrooms (1 ground-floor) with en-suite/private bathroom, T.V. & tea/coffee. Log fire. Extensive breakfast menu. A tranquil rural retreat, yet within easy reach of Stratford, Warwick, Oxford & the Cotswolds. Located between the M.40 Jts 11 & 12 (4 miles). Animals by arrangement. Children over 8yrs. Special winter breaks.
E-mail: crandonhouse@talk21.com

rate £ from - to per person	children taken	evening meals	animals taken
£20.00 to £30.00	Y	N	Y

VISA: M'CARD:

Deborah Lea Crandon House Avon Dassett Leamington Spa CV47 2AA Warwickshire
Tel: (01295) 770652 Fax 01295 770632 *Open: ALL YEAR (Excl. Xmas) Map Ref No. 05*

The Old Rectory

Nearest Road: A.425

This Victorian rectory is situated in a peaceful village in 1/2 an acre of walled garden. Offering a relaxed & friendly atmosphere with spacious public areas. Bright tastefully furnished bedrooms (non-smoking) with all amenities & views over the surrounding countryside. Breakfast can be served on the patio. Conveniently placed for touring the Cotswolds & Shakespeare country with easy access to motorway links, including the N.E.C. at Birmingham. Good local pubs. Children over 10.
E-mail: oldrectory@cwcom.net

rate £ from - to per person	children taken	evening meals	animals taken
£25.00 to £35.00	Y	N	Y

Mr & Mrs E. Parkinnen The Old Rectory Main Street Harborough Magna Rugby CV23 0HS Warks,
Tel: (01788) 833151 Fax 01788 833151 *Open: ALL YEAR (Excl. Xmas) Map Ref No. 07*

Tibbits

Nearest Road: A.45, A.425

Retreat along the pretty country lanes on the border of Warwickshire & Northamptonshire to the haven of this totally secluded 17th-century house, beautifully furnished with antiques, where superb accommodation is offered. The spacious & pretty bedrooms have books, tea/coffee-making facilities, T.V. & en-suite bathroom. Idyllically situated within acres of rolling countryside, providing an ideal base for exploring an area rich in places of historical, scenic & cultural interest.

rate £ from - to per person	children taken	evening meals	animals taken
£25.00 to £30.00	Y	N	N

C. A. Mills Tibbits Nethercote Rugby CV23 8AS Warwickshire
Tel: (01788) 890239 *Open: ALL YEAR Map Ref No. 08*

Warwickshire

rate £ from - to per person	children taken	evening meals	animals taken

Lawford Hill Farm

£20.00 to £28.00 | Y | N | Y

VISA: M'CARD:

Nearest Road: A.428, A.45

Gardens surround this Grade II listed Georgian farmhouse in an acre of formal lawns, herbaceous borders, shrubberies & a traditional walled vegetable & herb garden. The bedrooms, 3 in the main house & 3 in the converted stables are charmingly decorated & comfortably furnished. Mostly en-suite, colour T.V. & all with tea/coffee tray. Perfectly placed for touring Stratford-upon-Avon, Warwick & the lovely Cotswolds.

E-mail: lawford.hill@talk21.com

Don & Susan Moses Lawford Hill Farm Lawford Heath Lane Rugby CV23 9HG Warwickshire
Tel: (01788) 542001 Fax 01788 537880 Open: ALL YEAR (Excl. Xmas & New Year) Map Ref No. 09

Lower Farm

£22.50 to £30.00 | Y | N | N

Nearest Road: A.429

On the edge of the Cotswolds, just off the Fosse Way in the pretty, unspoilt hamlet of Darlingscott stands this fine, 18th-century, listed farmhouse. The guest accommodation comprises 2 attractive double rooms & 1 twin-bedded room, each with an en-suite bathroom, T.V. & tea-making facilities. A perfect location from which to visit Chipping Campden. The magnificent gardens of Hidcote & Kiftsgate are just 5 miles away, & Stratford-upon-Avon only 9 miles. Children over 12 yrs.

E-mail: lowerfarmbb@beeb.net

Jackie Smith Lower Farm Darlingscott Shipston-on-Stour CV36 4PN Warwickshire
Tel: (01608) 682750 Fax 01608 682750 Open: ALL YEAR Map Ref No. 10

Lower Farm Barn

£20.00 to £25.00 | Y | N | N

Nearest Road: A.3400, A.44

This lovely, 100-year-old, converted barn stands in the small, peaceful Warwickshire village of Great Wolford. The property retains much of its original form, including exposed beams & ancient stone work. Now tastefully modernised, it makes a very comfortable home. Accommodation is in 2 comfortable & beautifully furnished double rooms, each with en-suite facilities. A delightful base from which to explore this fascinating area, & within easy reach of Stratford-upon-Avon.

Rebecca Mawle Lower Farm Barn Great Wolford Shipston-on-Stour CV36 5NQ Warwickshire
Tel: (01608) 674435 Open: ALL YEAR Map Ref No. 11

Burton Farm

£25.00 to £35.00 | Y | N | N

see PHOTO over p. 404

Nearest Road: A.46

Burton Farm is a 140-acre working farm only 1 1/2 miles from Stratford-upon-Avon. The farmhouse & barns date from Tudor times & are steeped in the character for which the area is world famous. The accommodation, all of which has en-suite/private facilities, is quietly situated & enjoys an environment of colourful gardens & pools which support wildlife & a collection of rare birds & plants. The friendly atmosphere & quiet retreat will ensure a pleasant stay. A charming home.

E-mail: tony.crook@ukonline.co.uk

Eileen Crook Burton Farm Bishopton Stratford-upon-Avon CV37 0RW Warwickshire
Tel: (01789) 293338 Fax 01789 262877 Open: ALL YEAR Map Ref No. 14

Burton Farm. Bishopston.

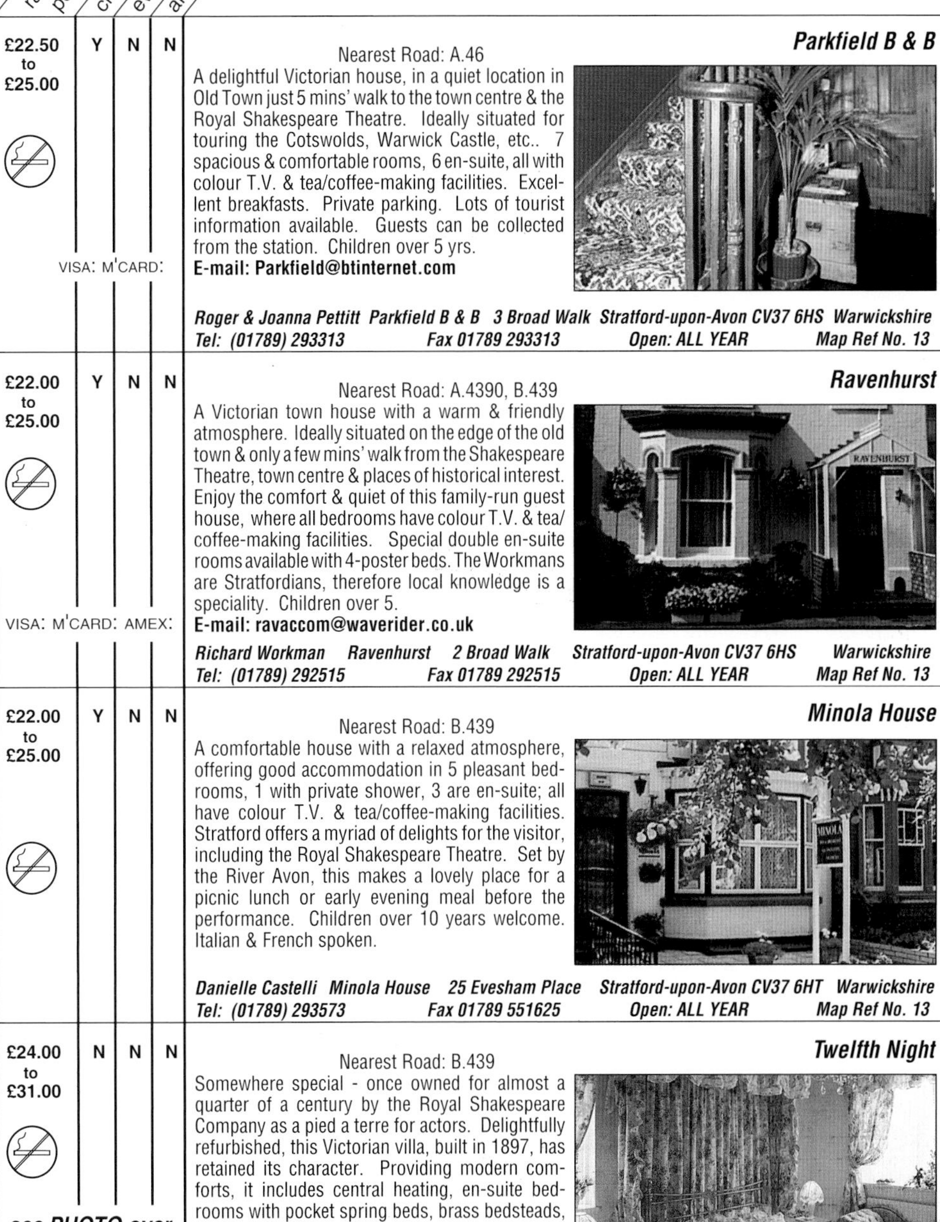

rate £ from - to per person	children taken	evening meals	animals taken
£22.50 to £25.00	Y	N	N

Parkfield B & B

Nearest Road: A.46

A delightful Victorian house, in a quiet location in Old Town just 5 mins' walk to the town centre & the Royal Shakespeare Theatre. Ideally situated for touring the Cotswolds, Warwick Castle, etc.. 7 spacious & comfortable rooms, 6 en-suite, all with colour T.V. & tea/coffee-making facilities. Excellent breakfasts. Private parking. Lots of tourist information available. Guests can be collected from the station. Children over 5 yrs.

E-mail: Parkfield@btinternet.com

VISA: M'CARD:

Roger & Joanna Pettitt Parkfield B & B 3 Broad Walk Stratford-upon-Avon CV37 6HS Warwickshire
Tel: (01789) 293313 Fax 01789 293313 Open: ALL YEAR Map Ref No. 13

rate £ from - to per person	children taken	evening meals	animals taken
£22.00 to £25.00	Y	N	N

Ravenhurst

Nearest Road: A.4390, B.439

A Victorian town house with a warm & friendly atmosphere. Ideally situated on the edge of the old town & only a few mins' walk from the Shakespeare Theatre, town centre & places of historical interest. Enjoy the comfort & quiet of this family-run guest house, where all bedrooms have colour T.V. & tea/coffee-making facilities. Special double en-suite rooms available with 4-poster beds. The Workmans are Stratfordians, therefore local knowledge is a speciality. Children over 5.

E-mail: ravaccom@waverider.co.uk

VISA: M'CARD: AMEX:

Richard Workman Ravenhurst 2 Broad Walk Stratford-upon-Avon CV37 6HS Warwickshire
Tel: (01789) 292515 Fax 01789 292515 Open: ALL YEAR Map Ref No. 13

rate £ from - to per person	children taken	evening meals	animals taken
£22.00 to £25.00	Y	N	N

Minola House

Nearest Road: B.439

A comfortable house with a relaxed atmosphere, offering good accommodation in 5 pleasant bedrooms, 1 with private shower, 3 are en-suite; all have colour T.V. & tea/coffee-making facilities. Stratford offers a myriad of delights for the visitor, including the Royal Shakespeare Theatre. Set by the River Avon, this makes a lovely place for a picnic lunch or early evening meal before the performance. Children over 10 years welcome. Italian & French spoken.

Danielle Castelli Minola House 25 Evesham Place Stratford-upon-Avon CV37 6HT Warwickshire
Tel: (01789) 293573 Fax 01789 551625 Open: ALL YEAR Map Ref No. 13

rate £ from - to per person	children taken	evening meals	animals taken
£24.00 to £31.00	N	N	N

Twelfth Night

Nearest Road: B.439

Somewhere special - once owned for almost a quarter of a century by the Royal Shakespeare Company as a pied a terre for actors. Delightfully refurbished, this Victorian villa, built in 1897, has retained its character. Providing modern comforts, it includes central heating, en-suite bedrooms with pocket spring beds, brass bedsteads, canopies & half testers plus many other personal touches. Centrally placed with private parking. A non-smoking establishment.

E-mail: twelfth.night@ntlworld.com

see PHOTO over p. 406

VISA:

Margaret Harvard Twelfth Night Evesham Place Stratford-upon-Avon CV37 6HT Warwickshire
Tel: (01789) 414595 Fax 01789 414595 Open: ALL YEAR Map Ref No. 13

Twelfth Night. Stratford-upon-Avon.

Kawartha House. Stratford-upon-Avon.

Stretton House. Stratford-upon-Avon.

Warwickshire

rate £ from - to per person	children taken	evening meals	animals taken
£15.00 to £28.00	Y	N	Y

see PHOTO over p. 407

VISA: M'CARD:

Kawartha House

Nearest Road: A.439

Kawartha House is a well-appointed town house with a friendly atmosphere, overlooking the 'old town' park. It is located just a few mins' walk from the town centre & is ideal for visiting the places of historic interest. Private parking is available. With pretty en-suite/private bedrooms & quality food, these are the ingredients for a memorable stay. This is a delightful base from which to explore Warwickshire, & is within easy reach of the Cotswolds with its many attractive villages.

E-mail: mavis@kawarthahouse.freeserve.co.uk

Mrs M. Evans Kawartha House 39 Grove Road Stratford-upon-Avon CV37 6PB Warwickshire
Tel: (01789) 204469 Fax 01789 292837 Open: ALL YEAR Map Ref No. 13

---

rate £ from - to per person	children taken	evening meals	animals taken
£15.00 to £28.00	Y	N	Y

see PHOTO over p. 408

Stretton House

Nearest Road: A.439

Stretton House is a 'home from home' where a warm & friendly welcome awaits you. Very comfortable accommodation at reasonable prices. Pretty, en-suite bedrooms & standard rooms, all having T.V. & tea/coffee-making facilities. Excellent full English breakfast, vegetarians catered for. Limited car parking. Situated opposite lovely Fir Park, within easy reach of the country, yet only 3 mins' walk from the town centre. Children over 8.

E-mail: skyblues@strettonhouse.co.uk

Mr & Mrs M. Machin Stretton House 38 Grove Road Stratford-upon-Avon CV37 6PB Warwickshire
Tel: (01789) 268647 Fax 01789 268647 Open: ALL YEAR Map Ref No. 13

---

rate £ from - to per person	children taken	evening meals	animals taken
£21.00 to £29.00	Y	N	N

see PHOTO over p. 410

VISA: M'CARD: AMEX:

Hardwick House

Nearest Road: A.439

Hardwick House is situated in a quiet, residential area of Stratford-upon-Avon, away from main roads yet only a 5-min. walk into the town. All 14 bedrooms are non-smoking, clean & comfortable, with tea/coffee-making facilities & T.V.. Resident proprietors ensure a warm welcome & attention to detail. There is an on-site car park. Directions from M.40: on the A.439, take the first right turn past the 30-mph sign into St. Gregory's Road, & Hardwick House is 200 yds on the right.

E-mail: hardwick@waverider.co.uk

Mr & Mrs S. Wootton Hardwick House 1 Avenue Road Stratford-upon-Avon CV37 6UY Warwickshire
Tel: (01789) 204307 Fax 01789 296760 Open: ALL YEAR Map Ref No. 13

---

rate £ from - to per person	children taken	evening meals	animals taken
£30.00 to £40.00	Y	N	N

see PHOTO over p. 411

VISA: M'CARD:

Eastnor House Hotel

Nearest Road: A.3400

By the River Avon, 125 metres from Clopton Bridge, with private parking & just a stroll from theatres & birthplace. This large Victorian townhouse, built for a wealthy draper, offers excellent accommodation, with oak panelling, central open staircase, a pleasant breakfast room & an elegant lounge in which to relax. 9 spacious, tastefully furnished bedrooms with private bathrooms, T.V. & welcome tray. Breakfast is individually prepared, completing a comfortable & restful stay.

E-mail: eastnor.house@tesco.net

Margaret Everitt Eastnor House Hotel 33 Shipston Road Stratford-upon-Avon CV37 7LN Warks.
Tel: (01789) 268115 Fax 01789 266516 Open: ALL YEAR Map Ref No. 13

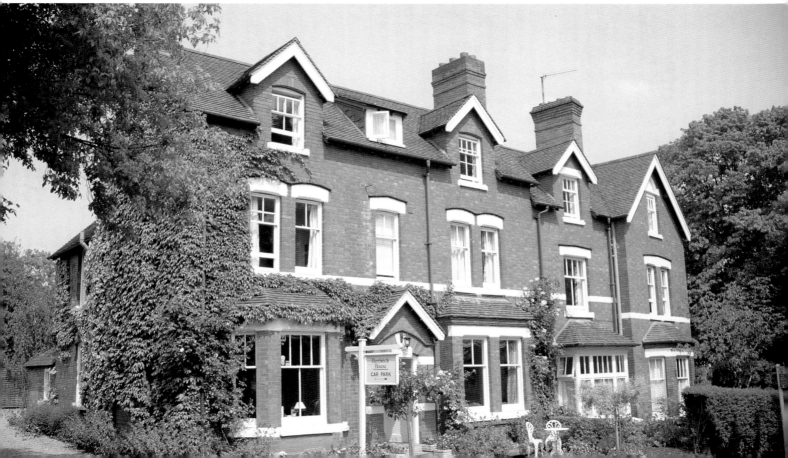

Hardwick House. Stratford-upon-Avon.

Eastnor House Hotel. Stratford-upon-Avon.

Melita Hotel. Stratford-upon-Avon.

Warwickshire

rate £ from - to per person	children taken	evening meals	animals taken

Melita Private Hotel

£32.00 to £40.00	Y	N	Y

see PHOTO over p. 412

VISA: M'CARD: AMEX:

Nearest Road: A.3400

An extremely friendly family-run hotel. Offering pleasant service, good food & accommodation in 12 excellent bedrooms, with en-suite/private facilities, T.V., tea/coffee & 'phones. A comfortable lounge/bar & pretty, award-winning garden for guests' use. Parking is available. A pleasant 5-min. walk to Shakespearian properties/theatres, shopping centre & riverside gardens. Superbly situated for Warwick Castle, Coventry & the Cotswolds.

E-mail: Melita37@email.msn.com

Patricia Anne Andrews Melita Private Hotel 37 Shipston Road Stratford-upon-Avon CV37 7LN
Tel: (01789) 292432 Fax 01789 204867 Open: ALL YEAR (Excl. Xmas) Map Ref No. 13

Sequoia House

£34.50 to £59.00	Y	N	N

see PHOTO over p. 414

VISA: M'CARD: AMEX:

Nearest Road: A.3400

A beautifully appointed private hotel situated across the River Avon from the Royal Shakespeare Theatre. 26 bedrooms (mostly en-suite), a cocktail bar, a cottage annex & a fully air-conditioned dining room. The hotel is comfortably furnished, & decorated in a warm & restful style, with many extra thoughtful touches. The garden overlooks the town cricket ground & the old tramway. Pleasant walks along the banks of the River Avon opposite the Theatre & Holy Trinity Church. Children over 5.

E-mail: info@sequoiahotel.co.uk

Philip & Jean Evans Sequoia House 51-53 Shipston Road Stratford-upon-Avon CV37 7LN
Tel: (01789) 268852 Fax 01789 414559 Open: ALL YEAR (Excl. Xmas) Map Ref No. 13

Victoria Spa Lodge

£30.00 to £35.00	Y	N	N

see PHOTO over p. 415

VISA: M'CARD: AMEX:

Nearest Road: A.3400, A.422

Large 19th-century house in country setting, overlooking Stratford canal, with ample parking. A royal coat of arms was built into the gables (with the permission of Queen Victoria) of this Grade II listed building. 7 attractive & comfortable en-suite bedrooms, each having a hostess tray, T.V., radio/alarm & hairdryer. 1 1/2 miles from the centre of town. An excellent base for the Cotswolds & Shakespearian properties. Pleasant walks along the tow path to Stratford & Wilmcote.

E-mail: PTOZER@VICTORIASPALODGE.DEMON.CO.UK

Paul & Dreen Tozer Victoria Spa Lodge Bishopton Lane Bishopton Stratford-upon-Avon CV37 9QY
Tel: (01789) 267985 Fax 01789 204728 Open: ALL YEAR Map Ref No. 13

Pear Tree Cottage

£26.00 to £28.00	N	N	N

see PHOTO over p. 416

Nearest Road: A.3400

A delightful half-timbered 16th-century house located in the Shakespeare village of Wilmcote. It retains all its original charm & character, with oak beams, flagstone floors, inglenook fireplaces, thick stone walls with deep-set windows & antiques. Offering 7 very comfortable en-suite rooms, all with tea/coffee-making facilities & colour T.V.. A delicious breakfast is served each morning in the dining room. A comfortable lounge is also provided. A lovely base from which to tour this region.

E-mail: mander@peartreecot.co.uk

Mrs Margaret Mander Pear Tree Cottage 7, Church Road Wilmcote Stratford-upon-Avon CV37 9UX
Tel: (01789) 205889 Fax 01789 262862 Open: ALL YEAR (Excl. Xmas & New Year) Map Ref No. 13

Sequoia House. Stratford-upon-Avon.

Victoria Spa Lodge. Stratford-upon-Avon.

Pear Tree Cottage. Wilmcote.

rate £ from - to per person	children taken	evening meals	animals taken	
£25.00 to £32.00	Y	N	N	**Forth House**
£20.00 to £25.00	N	N	N	**Flowerdale**
£20.00 to £25.00	Y	N	N	**Redlands Farm**
£20.00 to £26.00	Y	Y	N	**Nolands Farm & Country Restaurant**

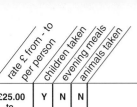

Forth House

Nearest Road: A.429

This rambling Georgian family home in the centre of Warwick provides 2 peaceful guest suites hidden away at the back. 1 family-sized ground-floor suite with en-suite bathroom, sitting room (with T.V.), fridge & drink facilities opens onto the garden, whilst the other room, also en-suite, overlooks the garden. Ideally situated for holidays or business. Junction 15 (M.40), 2 miles away, brings Oxford, Birmingham (Airport & N.E.C.), Stratford & the Cotswolds within easy reach.

E-mail: info@forthhouseuk.co.uk

Mrs Elizabeth Draisey Forth House 44 High Street Warwick CV34 4AX Warwickshire
Tel: (01926) 401512 Fax 01926 490809 Open: ALL YEAR Map Ref No. 15

Flowerdale

Nearest Road: A.429

Flowerdale is a modern house on the main Coventry Road (A.429, 1/4 mile from the centre of Warwick. Of the 2 letting bedrooms, 1 has an en-suite bathroom & the other a large private bathroom. Both have T.V., radios, hairdryer & tea/coffee trays. Car parking available. A lovely south-facing garden where guests may sit in the summer. There is also a conservatory sitting room. Ideally located for Warwick Castle, Stratford-upon-Avon, Warwick University, the N.A.C. & the N.E.C. A warm welcome is assured.

VISA: M'CARD:

Bill & Barbara Powell Flowerdale 29a Coventry Road Warwick CV34 5HN Warwickshire
Tel: (01926) 496393 Open: ALL YEAR Map Ref No. 16

Redlands Farm

Nearest Road: B.4100

A lovely 16th-century farmhouse in 2 acres of garden, with a swimming pool. A quiet location, with delightful views over open countryside. The large, beamed bedrooms are tastefully decorated throughout, 1 is en-suite & has a Victorian brass bed. All centrally heated, with tea/coffee-making facilities. There is a comfortable guests' lounge with T.V., log fires & homely atmosphere. Ideal for Warwick, Stratford-upon-Avon, Cotswolds & Motor Heritage Museum. Parking.

Mrs Judith Stanton Redlands Farm Banbury Road Lighthorne Warwick CV35 0AH Warwickshire
Tel: (01926) 651241 Fax 01926 651241 Open: APR - OCT Map Ref No. 17

Nolands Farm & Country Restaurant

Nearest Road: A.422

A working farm situated in a tranquil valley 8 miles from Stratford-upon-Avon. All bedrooms are annexed, some on the ground floor, overlooking either the old stableyard or fields. A selection of 4-posters, king-size doubles, twins, family & single rooms are available. All en-suite with T.V., tea tray, hairdryers, clock/radios & much more. Large gardens. Your hosts also offer clay pigeon shooting, fishing & bicyles. Horse riding nearby. Ample parking. Dinner by arrangement. Children over 12.

E-mail: inthecountry@nolandsfarm.co.uk

see PHOTO over p. 418

VISA: M'CARD:

Sue Hutsby Nolands Farm & Country Restaurant Oxhill Warwick CV35 0RJ Warwickshire
Tel: (01926) 640309 Fax 01926 641662 Open: ALL YEAR Map Ref No. 18

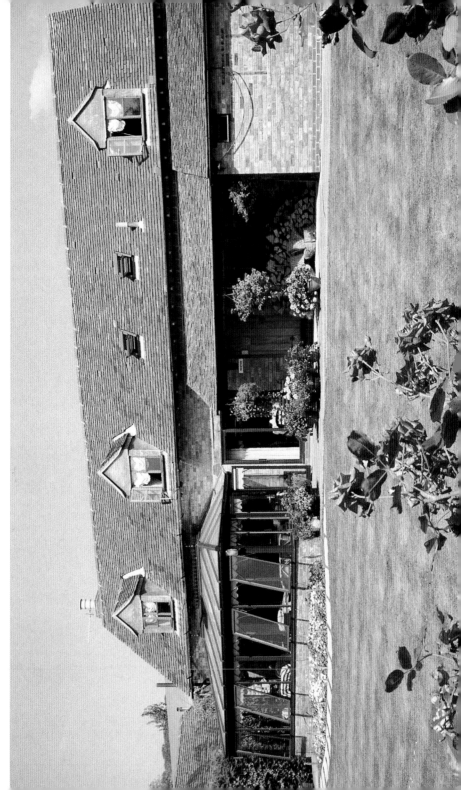

Nolands Farm. Oxhill.

Wiltshire

Wiltshire (West Country)

Wiltshire is a county of rolling chalk downs, small towns, delightful villages, fine churches & great country houses. The expanse of Salisbury Plain is divided by the beautiful valleys of Nadder, Wylye, Ebble & Avon. In a county of open landscapes, Savernake Forest, with its stately avenues of trees strikes a note of contrast. In the north west the Cotswolds spill over into Wiltshire from neighbouring Gloucestershire.

No other county is so rich in archaeological sites. Long barrows and ancient hill forts stand on the skylines as evidence of the early habitation of the chalk uplands. Many of these prehistoric sites are at once magnificent and mysterious. The massive stone arches and monoliths of Stonehenge were built over a period of 500 years with stones transported over great distances. At Avebury the small village is completely encircled by standing stones and a massive bank and ditch earthwork. Silbury Hill is a huge, enigmatic man-made mound. England's largest chambered tomb is West Kennet Long Barrow and at Bush Barrow, finds have included fine bronze and gold daggers and a stone sceptre-head similar to one found at Mycenae in Greece.

Some of England's greatest historic houses are in Wiltshire. Longleat is an Elizabethan mansion with priceless collections of paintings, books & furniture. The surrounding park was landscaped by Capability Brown and its great fame in recent years has been its Safari Park, particularly the lions which roam freely around the visiting cars. Stourhead has celebrated 18th century landscaped gardens which are exceptional in spring when rhododendrons bloom.

Two delightful villages are Castle Combe, nestling in a Cotswold valley, & Lacock where the twisting streets hold examples of buildings ranging from mediaeval half-timbered, to Tudor & Georgian. 13th century Lacock Abbey, converted to a house in the 16th century, was the home of Fox Talbot, pioneer of photography.

There are many notable churches in Wiltshire. In Bradford-on-Avon, a fascinating old town, is the church of St. Lawrence, a rare example of an almost perfect Saxon church from around 900. Farley has an unusual brick church thought to have been designed by Sir Christopher Wren, & there is stained glass by William Morris in the church at Rodbourne.

Devizes Castle

Salisbury stands where three rivers join, on a plain of luxuriant water-meadows, where the focal point of the landscape is the soaring spire of the Cathedral; at 404 feet, it is the tallest in England. The 13th century cathedral has a marvellous & rare visual unity. The body of the building was completed in just 38 years, although the spire was added in the next century. Salisbury, or "New Sarum" was founded in 1220 when the Bishop abandoned the original cathedral at Old Sarum, to start the present edifice two miles to the south. At Old Sarum you can see the foundation of the old city including the outline of the first cathedral.

Wiltshire

Wiltshire Gazeteer

Area of Outstanding Natural Beauty
The Costwolds & the North Wessex Downs.

Historic Houses & Castles

Corsham Court - Chippenham
16th & 17th centuries from Elizabethan & Georgian periods. 18th century furniture, British, Flemish & Italian Old Masters. Gardens by Capability Brown.

Great Chalfield Manor - Melksham
15th century manor house - moated.

Church House - Salisbury
15th century house.

Chalcot House - Westbury
17th century small house in Palladian manner.

Lacock Abbey - Nr. Chippenham
13th century abbey. In 1540 converted into house - 18th century alterations. Mediaeval cloisters & brewery.

Longleat House - Warminster
16th century - early Renaissance, alterations in early 1800's. Italian Renaissance decorations. Splendid state rooms, pictures, books, furniture. Victorian kitchens. Game reserve.

Littlecote - Nr. Hungerford
15th century Tudor manor. Panelled rooms, moulded plaster ceilings.

Luckington Court - Luckington
Queen Anne for the most part - fine ancient buildings.

Malmesbury House - Salisbury
Queen Anne house - part 14th century. Rococo plasterwork.

Newhouse - Redlynch
17th century brick Jacobean trinity house - two Georgian wings,

Philips House - Dinton
1816 Classical house.

Sheldon Manor - Chippenham
13th century porch & 15th century chapel in this Plantagenet manor.

Stourhead - Stourton
18th century Palladian house with framed landscape gardens.

Westwood Manor - Bradford-on-Avon
15th century manor house - alterations in 16th & 17th centuries.

Wardour Castle - Tisbury
18th century house in Palladian manner.

Wilton House - Salisbury
17th century - work of Inigo Jones & later of James Wyatt in 1810. Paintings, Kent & Chippendale furniture.

Avebury Manor - Nr Malborough
Elizabethan manor house - beautiful plasterwork, panelling & furniture. Gardens with topiary.

Bowood - Calne
18th century - work of several famous architects. Gardens by Capability Brown - famous beechwoods.

Mompesson House - Salisbury
Queen Anne town house - Georgian plasterwork.

Cathedrals & Churches

Salisbury Cathedral
13th century - decorated tower with stone spire. Part of original stone pulpitum is preserved. Beautiful large decorated cloister. Exterior mostly early English.

Salisbury (St. Thomas of Canterbury)
15th century rebuilding - 12th century font, 14th & 15th century glass, 17th century monuments. 'Doom' painting over chancel & murals in south chapel

Amesbury (St. Mary & St. Melor)
13th century - refashioned 15th & restored in 19th century. Splendid timber roofs, stone vaulting over chapel of north transept, mediaeval painted glass, 15th century screen, Norman font.

Bishops Cannings (St. Mary the Virgin)
13th-15th centuries. Fine arcading in transept - fine porch doorway.
17th century almsbox, Jacobean Holy table.

Bradford-on-Avon (St. Lawrence)
Best known of all Saxon churches in England.

Cricklade (St. Sampson)
12th -16th century. Tudor central tower vault, 15th century chapel.

Inglesham (St. John the Baptist)
Mediaeval wall paintings, high pews, clear glass, remains of painted screens.

Malmesbury (St. Mary)
Norman - 12th century arcades, refashioning in 14th century with clerestory, 15th century stone pulpitum added. Fine sculpture.

Wiltshire

Tisbury (St. John the Baptist)
14th-15th centuries. 15th-17th century roofing to nave & aisles. Two storeyed porch & chancel.
Potterne (St. Mary)
13th,14th,15th centuries. Inscribed Norman tub font. Wooden pulpit.

Museums & Galleries

Salisbury & South Wiltshire Museum - Salisbury
Collections showing history of the area in all periods. Models of Stonehenge & Old Sarum - archaeologically important collection.
Devizes Museum - Devizes
Unique archaeological & geological collections, including Sir Richard Colt-Hoare's Stourhead collection of prehistoric material.
Alexander Keiller Museum - Avebury
Collection of items from the Neolithic & Bronze ages & from excavations in district.
Athelstan Museum - Malmesbury
Collection of articles referring to the town - household, coin, etc.
Bedwyn Stone Museum - Great Bedwyn
Open-air museum showing where Stonehenge was carved.
Lydiard Park - Lydiard Tregoze
Parish church of St. Mary & a splendid Georgian mansion standing in park & also permanent & travelling exhibitions.
Borough of Thamesdown Museum & Art Gallery - Swindon
Natural History & Geology of Wiltshire, Bygones, coins, etc. 20th century British art & ceramic collection.
Great Western Railway Museum - Swindon
Historic locomotives.

Historic Monuments

Stonehenge - Nr. Amesbury
Prehistoric monument - encircling bank & ditch & Augrey holes are Neolithic. Stone circles possibly early Bronze age.
Avebury
Relics of enormous circular gathering place B.C. 2700-1700.
Old Sarum - Nr. Salisbury
Possibly first Iron Age camp, later Roman area, then Norman castle.
Silbury Hill - Nr. Avebury
Mound - conical in shape - probably a memorial c.3000-2000 B.C.
Windmill Hill - Nr. Avebury
Causewayed camp c.3000-2300 B.C.
Bratton Camp & White Horse - Bratton
Hill fort standing above White Horse.
West Kennet Long Barrow
Burial place c.4000-2500 B.C.
Ludgershall Castle - Lugershall
Motte & bailey of Norman castle, earthworks, also flint walling from later castle.

Castle Combe.

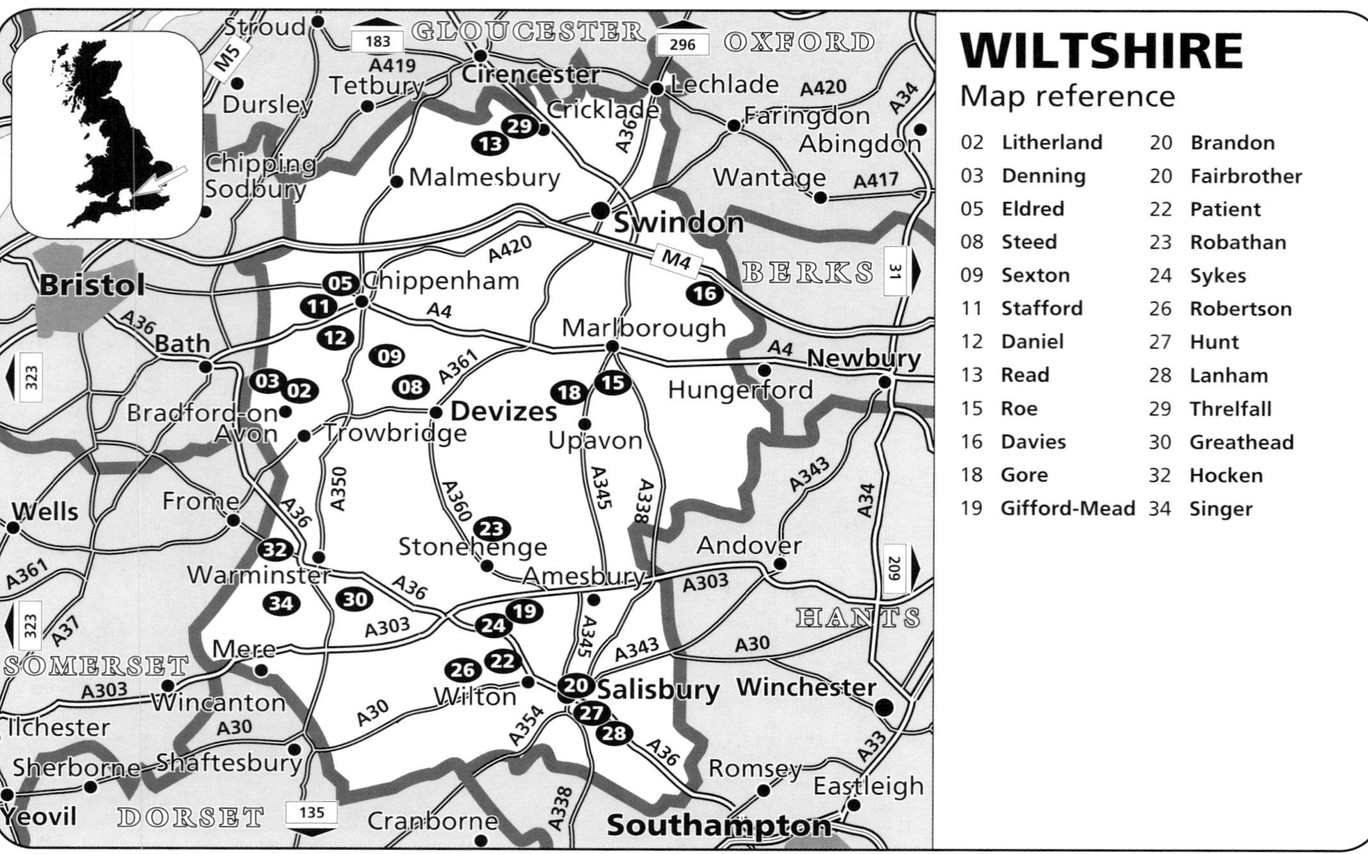

WILTSHIRE

Map reference

02 **Litherland**
03 **Denning**
05 **Eldred**
08 **Steed**
09 **Sexton**
11 **Stafford**
12 **Daniel**
13 **Read**
15 **Roe**
16 **Davies**
18 **Gore**
19 **Gifford-Mead**
20 **Brandon**
20 **Fairbrother**
22 **Patient**
23 **Robathan**
24 **Sykes**
26 **Robertson**
27 **Hunt**
28 **Lanham**
29 **Threlfall**
30 **Greathead**
32 **Hocken**
34 **Singer**

Wiltshire

rate £ from - to per person	children taken	evening meals	animals taken	
£26.50 to £30.00	Y	N	N	**Hillcrest**

Nearest Road: A.36

Only 6 miles from Bath & 2 miles from Bradford-on-Avon at the southern edge of the Cotswold Hills, Hillcrest is surrounded by old dry stone walls with magnificent views across the Avon Valley. Both bedrooms are fully en-suite. Your hosts pride themselves on the quality of their food. The a la carte breakfast menu offers an excellent choice. A quaint 17th-century village pub serving excellent food is only 10 mins' walk. Children over 7 years.

E-mail: enquiries@hillcrestwinsley.free-online.co.uk

VISA: M'CARD:

Barbara & Rob Litherland Hillcrest Bradford Road Winsley Bradford-on-Avon BA15 2HN Wiltshire
Tel: (01225) 868677 Fax 01225 868655 Open: ALL YEAR Map Ref No. 02

rate £ from - to per person	children taken	evening meals	animals taken	
£42.50 to £45.00	Y	N	N	**Burghope Manor**

Nearest Road: A.36

This historic 13th-century family home is set in beautiful countryside on the edge of the village of Winsley - overlooking the Avon Valley - 5 miles from Bath & 1 1/2 miles from Bradford-on-Avon. Although steeped in history, Burghope Manor is first & foremost a family home, has been carefully modernised so that the wealth of historical features may complement the present-day comforts. A village pub & restaurant nearby. Dinner for groups only. Children over 10. Single supplement.

E-mail: burghope.manor@virgin.net

see PHOTO over p. 424

VISA: M'CARD: AMEX:

Elizabeth & John Denning Burghope Manor Winsley Bradford-on-Avon BA15 2LA Wiltshire
Tel: (01225) 723557 Fax 01225 723113 Open: ALL YEAR (Excl. Xmas & New Year) Map Ref No. 03

rate £ from - to per person	children taken	evening meals	animals taken	
£34.00 to £££	Y	N	Y	**The Old Rectory**

Nearest Road: A.423

A Regency country house situated in an Area of Outstanding Natural Beauty on the Avon, here just a brook. The house stands in 10 acres with a large garden, stables, tennis court & swimming pool & is peacefully situated at the end of a long private drive. The comfortable en-suite bedrooms, 1 double, 1 twin, overlook beautiful countryside. The delightful reception rooms are furnished with antiques. Nearby is an excellent choice of pubs & restaurants. Children over 10 years welcome. Animals by arrangement.

Mr & Mrs J. Eldred The Old Rectory Luckington Chippenham SN14 6PH Wiltshire
Tel: (01666) 840556 Fax 01666 840989 Open: ALL YEAR Map Ref No. 05

rate £ from - to per person	children taken	evening meals	animals taken	
£22.50 to £25.00	Y	N	N	**The Cottage**

Nearest Road: A.342, A.3102

This delightful cottage is reputed to have been a coaching inn, & dates back to 1450. There are 3 charming bedrooms, all with private shower, T.V. & tea/coffee makers, in a beautifully converted barn. Also, many exposed beams that were once ships' timbers. Breakfast is served in the old beamed dining room. A lovely garden & paddock for guests' use. An ideal centre for visiting Bath, Bristol, Devizes, Marlborough, Avebury, Stonehenge, Longleat, Castle Combe & Lacock.

E-mail: RJSteed@cottage16.freeserve.co.uk

Richard & Gloria Steed The Cottage Westbrook Bromham Chippenham SN15 2EE Wiltshire
Tel: (01380) 850255 Open: ALL YEAR Map Ref No. 08

Burghope Manor. Bradford-upon-Avon.

rate £ from - to per person	children taken	evening meals	animals taken	
£25.00 to £30.00	Y	N	Y	**The Old Rectory** Nearest Road: A.350 Situated in the medieval village of Lacock, The Old Rectory, built in 1866, is a fine example of Victorian Gothic architecture, with creeper-clad walls & mullioned windows. It stands in 12 acres of its own carefully tended grounds, which include a tennis court & a croquet lawn. The Old Rectory offers 3 very attractive bedrooms, all with en-suite facilities. This is an excellent base from which to explore the glorious West Country. **E-mail: elaine@oldrectorylacock.co.uk** *Paul & Elaine Sexton The Old Rectory Cantax Hill Lacock Chippenham SN15 2JZ Wiltshire* *Tel: (01249) 730335 Fax 01249 730166 Open: ALL YEAR Map Ref No. 09*
see PHOTO over p. 426				
£22.50 to £30.00	Y	N	N	**Pickwick Lodge Farm** Nearest Road: A.4 A delightful 17th-century Cotswold stone farmhouse, set in peaceful surroundings. 3 well-appointed, tastefully furnished bedrooms, each with an en-suite/private bathroom, radio, T.V. & tea/coffee-making facilities. Hearty & delicious breakfasts are served. Ideally situated for visiting many sites of historical interest, such as the Wiltshire White Horses, Avebury & Stonehenge; many stately homes & National Trust properties within easy reach. Parking. Children by arrangement. **E-mail: BandB@pickwickfarm.freeserve.co.uk** *Mrs Gill Stafford Pickwick Lodge Farm Guyers Lane Corsham SN13 0PS Wiltshire* *Tel: (01249) 712207 Fax 01249 701904 Open: ALL YEAR (Excl. Xmas & New Year) Map Ref No. 11*
£22.00 to £25.00	Y	N	N	**Heatherly Cottage** Nearest Road: A.4 Heatherly Cottage was built in the 17th century & has a large garden with plenty of parking space & beautiful views towards the Westbury White Horse. Each of the 3 attractive bedrooms is well-equipped & has a T.V., tea/coffee-making facilities & an en-suite bathroom. In nearby Lacock & Gastard, there are traditional English pubs which serve excellent lunches & evening meals. The hosts aim to ensure that you enjoy your stay, & are happy to advise of local attractions, walks, etc. Children over 10. **E-mail: ladbrook1@aol.com** *Peter & Jenny Daniel Heatherly Cottage Ladbrook Lane Gastard Corsham SN13 9PE Wiltshire* *Tel: (01249) 701402 Fax 01249 701412 Open: ALL YEAR Map Ref No. 12*
£30.00 to £35.00	Y	Y	N	**Leighfield Lodge Farm** Nearest Road: A.419 Leighfield Lodge is a lovely old farmhouse in a secluded & rural setting. It is built on the site of a former Royal hunting lodge. Discover en-suite rooms with comfortable beds, crisp cotton bed linen, power showers, T.V. & tea/coffee-making facilities. A guests' sitting room. Well situated for Oxford, Bath, Stonehenge, Avebury, the Thames Path & the Cotswolds. Brochure on request. Evening meals by prior arrangement. Single supplement. Your hosts look forward to welcoming you. **E-mail: claireread@leighfieldlodge.fsnet.co.uk** *Mrs Claire Read Leighfield Lodge Farm Malmesbury Road Leigh Cricklade SN6 6RH Wiltshire* *Tel: (01666) 860241 Fax 01666 860241 Open: ALL YEAR Map Ref No. 13*
VISA: M'CARD:				

Old Rectory. Lacock.

Wiltshire

rate £ from - to per person	children taken	evening meals	animals taken
£25.00 to £35.00	Y	Y	Y

Clench Farmhouse

Nearest Road: A.345, A.346

A warm & friendly atmosphere awaits guests when they arrive at this attractive 18th-century farmhouse, which is set in its own grounds & surrounded by lovely countryside. There are 2 comfortable double bedrooms & 1 twin bedroom, each with either an en-suite or private bathroom. All well decorated & furnished. Delicious dinners are also served. There is a tennis court & outdoor heated swimming pool. Well situated for Bath, Stonehenge & Salisbury. Ample parking.

Clarissa Roe Clench Farmhouse Clench Nr. Marlborough SN8 4NT Wiltshire
Tel: (01672) 810264 Fax 01672 811458 Open: ALL YEAR Map Ref No. 15

rate £ from - to per person	children taken	evening meals	animals taken
£20.00 to £24.00	Y	N	Y

VISA: M'CARD:

Marridge Hill House

Nearest Road: M.4, B.4192

The house originated in 1750 & is set in glorious countryside, only 1 hrs. drive from Heathrow Airport. You will be warmly welcomed into the relaxed, informal atmosphere of this family home, with its pleasant sitting & dining rooms, books galore & an acre of garden. 3 attractive twin bedrooms (1 en-suite). Both bathrooms have power showers. An ideal base for visiting Avebury, Salisbury, Bath, Oxford & the Cotswolds. Good pubs & restaurants nearby. Children over 5.

E-mail: dando@impedaci.demon.co.uk

Mrs Judy Davies Marridge Hill House Ramsbury Marlborough SN8 2HG Wiltshire
Tel: (01672) 520237 Fax 01672 520053 Open: ALL YEAR Map Ref No. 16

rate £ from - to per person	children taken	evening meals	animals taken
£25.00 to £27.50	Y	Y	Y

St. Cross

Nearest Road: A.4

St. Cross is a 17th-century thatched cottage in a quiet village close to the Downs & Kennet & Avon Canal. Also, Salisbury, Bath & Devizes are all close by. The cottage is decorated to a high standard throughout & has a very friendly atmosphere. 2 comfortable bedrooms, each with tea/coffee-making facilities. All food is fresh, the breakfast is delicious & dinner can be arranged. Also, some good pubs in the village serving food. An ideal base for exploring this beautiful county. Dogs are welcome. Children over 5.

Mrs Serena Gore St. Cross Woodborough Pewsey SN9 5PL Wiltshire
Tel: (01672) 851346 Fax 01672 851346 Open: ALL YEAR (Excl. Xmas) Map Ref No. 18

rate £ from - to per person	children taken	evening meals	animals taken
£25.00 to £30.00	Y	N	N

see PHOTO over p. 428

The Mill House

Nearest Road: A.36, A.303

Stonehenge is only 3 miles away. Diana welcomes you to the Mill House set in acres of nature reserve abounding in wild flowers & infinite peace. An island paradise with the River Till running through the working mill & gardens. Diana's old fashioned roses long to see you as do the lovely walks, antiquities & houses. Built by the miller in 1785, the bedrooms all have tea/coffee facilities & T.V.. Fishing in the mill pool. Golf & riding nearby. Attention to healthy & organic food. Sample superb cuisine at the Boot Inn. Children over 5.

Diana Gifford Mead The Mill House Berwick St. James Nr. Salisbury SP3 4TS Wiltshire
Tel: (01722) 790331 Open: ALL YEAR Map Ref No. 19

The Mill House. Berwick St. James

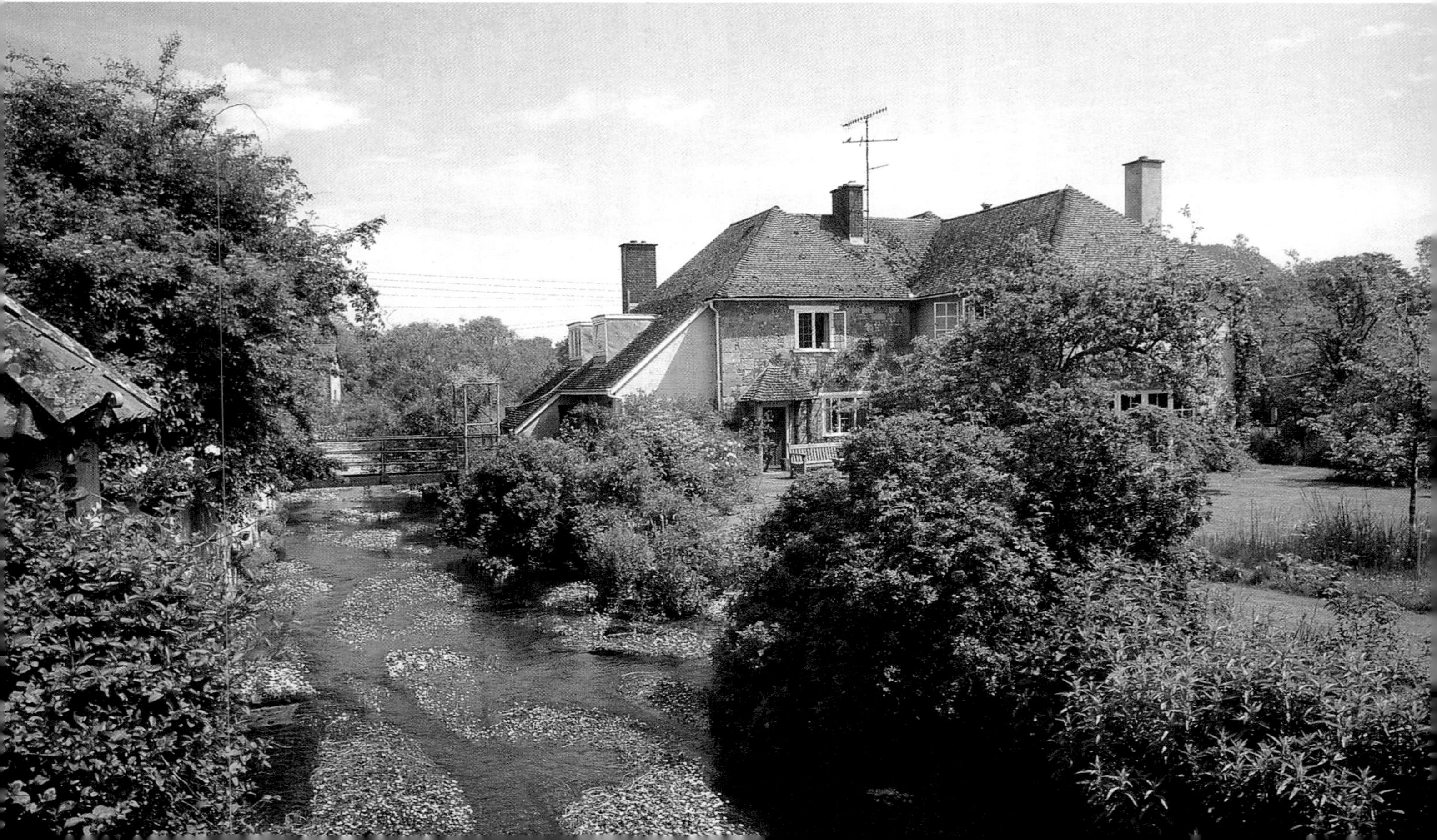

Wiltshire

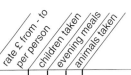

rate £ from - to per person	children taken	evening meals	animals taken	
£19.00 to £22.00	N	N	N	***Griffin Cottage*** Nearest Road: A.36, A.30 Within 3 mins' of the market square. The house was built 300/500 years ago. Central heating & a real fire greet you in winter. Organic home-produced food where possible, including the bread. Antique furniture mixed with modern comforts to give a warm & informal welcome. The 2 guest rooms have recently been refurbished with comfortable beds, a must when staying away from home. Single supplement. (Hosts can also be contacted on Mobile 0467 395898.) **E-mail: mark@brandonasoc.demon.co.uk** *Mrs Sue Brandon Griffin Cottage 10 St. Edmunds Church Street Salisbury SP1 1EF Wiltshire* *Tel: (01722) 328259 Fax 01722 416928 Open: ALL YEAR (Excl. Xmas) Map Ref No. 20*
£31.00 to £44.00 VISA: M'CARD: AMEX:	Y	N	Y	***Glen Lyn House*** Nearest Road: A.36 Situated in a quiet tree-lined lane, 5 mins' walk from the city centre, Glen Lyn is an elegant Victorian house offering 7 individually appointed bedrooms, 4 en-suite & all with colour T.V.. Enjoy a great English breakfast & superb home-produced dinner, then relax in the lounge or listen to birdsong in the beautiful garden. The ideal tranquil base for visiting the cathedral & Stonehenge, & for exploring the New Forest. Ample parking. Children over 12. Evening meals by prior arrangement. **E-mail: glen.lyn@btinternet.com** *Patrick Fairbrother & Felicity Watts Glen Lyn House 6 Bellamy Lane Milford Hill Salisbury SP1 2SP* *Tel: (01722) 327880 Fax 01722 327880 Open: ALL YEAR Map Ref No. 20*
£22.00 to £27.50	Y	N	Y	***The Old Post House*** Nearest Road: A.36 A warm welcome awaits you in this beautiful 17th-century home, situated in the quiet & peaceful village of Great Wishford. Well away from the hustle & bustle, yet only 5 mins' from Salisbury & Stonehenge & 40 mins' from Bath. 3 comfortable en-suite bedrooms with T.V. & tea/coffee-making facilities. Good local pubs offering evening meals. The perfect base for visiting Stonehenge, Avebury, Stourhead, Winchester & Bath, & for exploring the beautiful Wiltshire & Dorset countryside. **E-mail: bookings@greatwishford.freeserve.co.uk** *Paulene Patient The Old Post House South Street Great Wishford Salisbury SP2 0NN Wiltshire* *Tel: (01722) 790211 Open: ALL YEAR (Excl. Xmas & New Year) Map Ref No. 22*
£22.50 to £25.00	Y	N	N	***Maddington House*** Nearest Road: A.360 Maddington House is the family home of Dick & Joan Robathan. It is an elegant 17th-century Grade II listed house in the centre of the pretty village of Shrewton - about 2 1/2 miles from Stonehenge & 11 miles from Salisbury. Accommodation is in 3 attractive guest rooms, 2 with en-suite facilities. The village has 4 good pubs, all within easy walking distance. Maddington House is a delightful home, & the perfect base for a relaxing break. **E-mail: rsrobathan@Freenet.co.uk** *Dick & Joan Robathan Maddington House Maddington Street Shrewton Salisbury SP3 4JD* *Tel: (01980) 620406 Fax 01980 620406 Open: ALL YEAR Map Ref No. 23*

	rate £ from - to per person	children taken	evening meals	animals taken
Elm Tree Cottage	£25.00 to £25.00	Y	N	Y
Wyndham Cottage	£25.00 to £30.00	Y	N	N
Bridge Farm	£23.00 to £25.00	Y	N	N
Newton Farmhouse	£20.00 to £30.00	Y	Y	N

Elm Tree Cottage

Nearest Road: A.36

Elm Tree Cottage is a 17th-century character cottage with inglenook & beams & a lower garden to relax in. The bedrooms, each with an en-suite/ private bathroom, are light & airy, are attractively decorated & have T.V. & tea/coffee-making facilities. The atmosphere is relaxed & warm, & breakfast is served as required. Situated in a picturesque village, there are views across various valleys, & it is a good centre for Salisbury, Wilton, Longleat, Stonehenge, Avebury, etc.

Mrs Christine Sykes Elm Tree Cottage Chain Hill Stapleford Salisbury SP3 4LH Wiltshire
Tel: (01722) 790507 Open: ALL YEAR Map Ref No. 24

Wyndham Cottage

Nearest Road: A.36, A.303

A charming 18th-century thatched stone cottage, lovingly restored & set in magnificent National Trust countryside on the edge of a picturesque village. Bluebells, lambs & calves in Spring, delightful walks with marvellous views of the surrounding area. The cottage garden has many interesting plants. Good pubs nearby. Ideally situated for several days sight-seeing: Stonehenge, Avebury, Salisbury, Bath, Wells, Wilton House, Stourhead & Longleat. 2 double en-suite bedrooms with tea/coffee & T.V.. Children over 12.

Ian & Rosie Robertson Wyndham Cottage St. Mary's Road Dinton Salisbury SP3 5HH Wiltshire
Tel: (01722) 716343 Mobile 0776 9911660 Open: MAR - OCT Map Ref No. 26

Bridge Farm

Nearest Road: A.338

A warm welcome & a hearty English breakfast are assured at this charming 18th-century farmhouse on a working farm on the southern edge of Salisbury. Accommodation is in 2 double & 1 twin en-suite rooms which are spacious & individually & tastefully furnished. Within easy walking distance of the cathedral, & has famous views of the spire along the River Avon that flows alongside the beautiful gardens. Single supplement.

E-mail: mail@bridgefarmbb.co.uk

Mrs Norma Hunt Bridge Farm Lower Road Britford Salisbury SP4 5DY Wiltshire
Tel: (01722) 332376 Fax 01722 332376 Open: ALL YEAR Map Ref No. 27

Newton Farmhouse

Nearest Road: A.36

This historic listed 16th-century farmhouse, on the borders of the New Forest, was formerly part of the Trafalgar Estate & is situated 8 miles south of Salisbury, convenient for Stonehenge, Romsey, Winchester, Portsmouth. All rooms are en-suite, 3 with genuine period 4-poster beds. The beamed dining room houses a collection of Nelson memorabilia & antiques & has an inglenook fireplace. Breakfast includes home-made breads & preserves. (Dinner by arrangement.) Swimming pool.

E-mail: reservations@newtonfarmhouse.co.uk

Suzi & John Lanham Newton Farmhouse Southampton Road Whiteparish Salisbury SP5 2QL
Tel: (01794) 884416 Fax 01794 884416 Open: ALL YEAR Map Ref No. 28

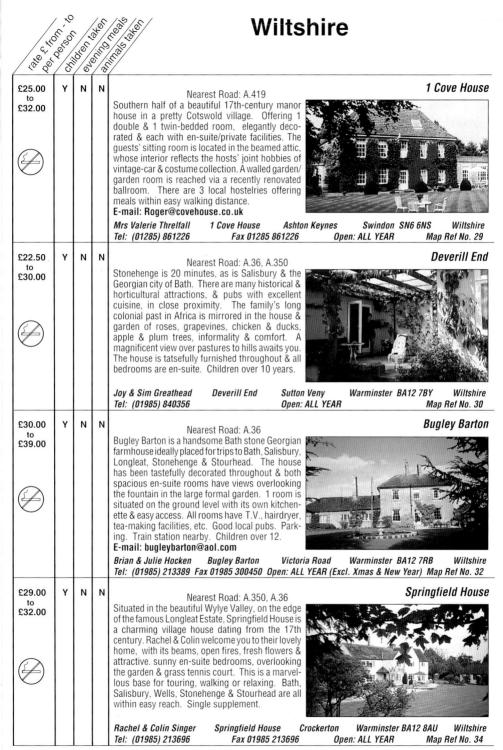

rate £ from - to per person	children taken	evening meals	animals taken	
£25.00 to £32.00	Y	N	N	**1 Cove House** Nearest Road: A.419 Southern half of a beautiful 17th-century manor house in a pretty Cotswold village. Offering 1 double & 1 twin-bedded room, elegantly decorated & each with en-suite/private facilities. The guests' sitting room is located in the beamed attic, whose interior reflects the hosts' joint hobbies of vintage-car & costume collection. A walled garden/garden room is reached via a recently renovated ballroom. There are 3 local hostelries offering meals within easy walking distance. **E-mail: Roger@covehouse.co.uk** *Mrs Valerie Threlfall 1 Cove House Ashton Keynes Swindon SN6 6NS Wiltshire* *Tel: (01285) 861226 Fax 01285 861226 Open: ALL YEAR Map Ref No. 29*
£22.50 to £30.00	Y	N	N	**Deverill End** Nearest Road: A.36, A.350 Stonehenge is 20 minutes, as is Salisbury & the Georgian city of Bath. There are many historical & horticultural attractions, & pubs with excellent cuisine, in close proximity. The family's long colonial past in Africa is mirrored in the house & garden of roses, grapevines, chicken & ducks, apple & plum trees, informality & comfort. A magnificent view over pastures to hills awaits you. The house is tatsefully furnished throughout & all bedrooms are en-suite. Children over 10 years. *Joy & Sim Greathead Deverill End Sutton Veny Warminster BA12 7BY Wiltshire* *Tel: (01985) 840356 Open: ALL YEAR Map Ref No. 30*
£30.00 to £39.00	Y	N	N	**Bugley Barton** Nearest Road: A.36 Bugley Barton is a handsome Bath stone Georgian farmhouse ideally placed for trips to Bath, Salisbury, Longleat, Stonehenge & Stourhead. The house has been tastefully decorated throughout & both spacious en-suite rooms have views overlooking the fountain in the large formal garden. 1 room is situated on the ground level with its own kitchenette & easy access. All rooms have T.V., hairdryer, tea-making facilities, etc. Good local pubs. Parking. Train station nearby. Children over 12. **E-mail: bugleybarton@aol.com** *Brian & Julie Hocken Bugley Barton Victoria Road Warminster BA12 7RB Wiltshire* *Tel: (01985) 213389 Fax 01985 300450 Open: ALL YEAR (Excl. Xmas & New Year) Map Ref No. 32*
£29.00 to £32.00	Y	N	N	**Springfield House** Nearest Road: A.350, A.36 Situated in the beautiful Wylye Valley, on the edge of the famous Longleat Estate, Springfield House is a charming village house dating from the 17th century. Rachel & Colin welcome you to their lovely home, with its beams, open fires, fresh flowers & attractive. sunny en-suite bedrooms, overlooking the garden & grass tennis court. This is a marvellous base for touring, walking or relaxing. Bath, Salisbury, Wells, Stonehenge & Stourhead are all within easy reach. Single supplement. *Rachel & Colin Singer Springfield House Crockerton Warminster BA12 8AU Wiltshire* *Tel: (01985) 213696 Fax 01985 213696 Open: ALL YEAR Map Ref No. 34*

Yorkshire

Whitby Abbey - Whitby (St. Hilda)
7th century superb ruin - venue of Synod of 664. Destroyed by Vikings, restored 1078 - magnificent north transept.
Halifax (St. John the Baptist)
12th century origins, showing work from each succeeding century - heraldic ceilings. Cromwell glass.
Beverley Minster - Beverley
14th century. Fine Gothic Minster - remarkable mediaeval effigies of musicians playing instruments. Founded as monastery in 700.
Bolton Priory - Nr. Skipton
Nave of Augustinian Priory, now Bolton's Parish Church, amidst ruins of choir & transepts, in beautiful riverside setting.
Selby Abbey - Selby
11th century Benedictine abbey of which the huge church remains. Roof & furnishings are modern after a fire of 1906, but the stonework is intact.

Museums & Galleries

Aldborough Roman Museum - Boroughbridge
Remnants of Roman period of the town - coins, glass, pottery, etc.
Great Ayton
Home of Captain Cook, explorer & seaman. Exhibits of maps, etc.
Art Gallery - City of York
Modern paintings, Old Masters, watercolours, prints, ceramics.
Lotherton Hall - Nr. Leeds
Museum with furniture, paintings, silver, works of art from the Leeds collection & oriental art gallery.
National Railway Museum - York
Devoted to railway engineering & its development.
York Castle Museum
The Kirk Collection of bygones including cobbled streets, shops, costumes, toys, household & farm equipment - fascinating collection.
Cannon Hall Art Gallery - Barnsley
18th century house with fine furniture & glass, etc. Flemish & Dutch paintings. Also houses museum of the 13/18 Royal Hussars.
Mappin Art Gallery - Sheffield
Works from 18th,19th & 20th century.
Graves Art gallery-Sheffield.
British portraiture. European works, & examples of Asian & African art. Loan exhibitions are held there.
Royal Pump Room Museum - Harrogate
Original sulphur well used in the Victorian Spa. Local history costume & pottery.
Bolling Hall - Bradford
A period house with mixture of styles - collections of 17th century oak furniture, domestic utensils, toys & bygones.
Georgian Theatre - Richmond
Oldest theatre in the country - interesting theatrical memorabilia.
Jorvik Viking Centre - York
Recently excavated site in the centre of York showing hundreds of artifacts dating from the Viking period. One of the most important archaeological discoveries this century.
Abbey House Museum - Kirkstall, Leeds
Illustrated past 300 years of Yorkshire life. Shows 3 full streets from 19th century with houses, shops & workplaces.
Piece Hall - Halifax
Remarkable building - constructed around huge quadrangle - now Textile Industrial Museum, Art Gallery & has craft & antique shops.
National Museum of Photography, Film & Television - Bradford
Displays look at art & science of photography, film & T.V. Britain's only IMAX arena.
The Colour Museum - Bradford
Award-winning interactive museum,which allows visitors to explore the world of colour & discover the story of dyeing & textile printing.
Calderdale Industrial Museum - Halifax
Social & industrial Museum of the year 1987
Shibden Hall & Folk Museum of Halifax
Half-timbered house with folk museum, farmland, miniature train & boating lake.
Leeds City Art Gallery & Henry Moore Sculpture Gallery
Yorkshire Sculpture Park - Wakefield
Yorkshire Museum of Farming - Murton
Award-winning museum of farming & the countryside.

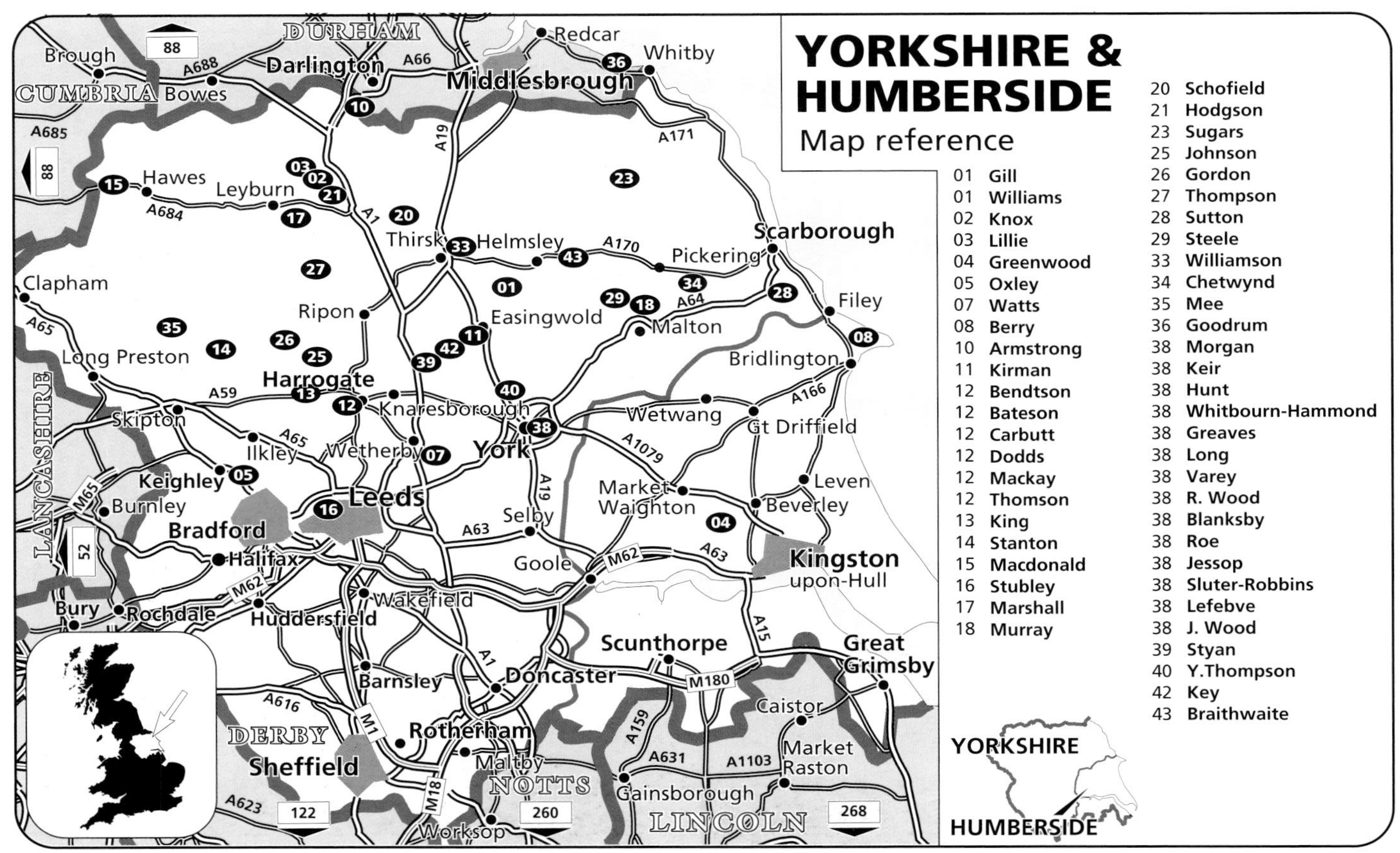

YORKSHIRE & HUMBERSIDE

Map reference

01 Gill
01 Williams
02 Knox
03 Lillie
04 Greenwood
05 Oxley
07 Watts
08 Berry
10 Armstrong
11 Kirman
12 Bendtson
12 Bateson
12 Carbutt
12 Dodds
12 Mackay
12 Thomson
13 King
14 Stanton
15 Macdonald
16 Stubley
17 Marshall
18 Murray
20 Schofield
21 Hodgson
23 Sugars
25 Johnson
26 Gordon
27 Thompson
28 Sutton
29 Steele
33 Williamson
34 Chetwynd
35 Mee
36 Goodrum
38 Morgan
38 Keir
38 Hunt
38 Whitbourn-Hammond
38 Greaves
38 Long
38 Varey
38 R. Wood
38 Blanksby
38 Roe
38 Jessop
38 Sluter-Robbins
38 Lefebve
38 J. Wood
39 Styan
40 Y.Thompson
42 Key
43 Braithwaite

	rate £ from - to per person	children taken	evening meals	animals taken
Daleside	£26.00 to £29.50	Y	Y	N
Shallowdale House	£32.00 to £40.00	Y	Y	N
Mill Close Farm	£20.00 to £28.00	N	N	Y
Elmfield Country House	£25.00 to £27.50	Y	Y	N

Daleside

Nearest Road: A.170, A.19

Daleside is listed, the oldest house in this charming stone village, with 400 year old cruck beams & oak panelling. The house has been sympathetically restored, with the 2 en-suite guests' rooms (1 twin, 1 double with half-tester bed) overlooking the garden. Dinner is available some evenings, if booked in advance. There are 2 inns in the village & other good restaurants nearby. Ampleforth is on the edge of the North York Moors National Park with excellent walks all around. Children from 12.

VISA: M'CARD:

Paul & Pat Williams Daleside East End Ampleforth YO62 4DA Yorkshire
Tel: (01439) 788266 Open: End MAR - End OCT Map Ref No. 01

Shallowdale House

Nearest Road: A.170

This is an outstanding modern country house, with 2 acres of hillside garden, on the southern edge of the North York Moors National Park. All of the spacious rooms enjoy stunning views of unspoilt countryside & are furnished with style & attention to detail. There are 3 guest bedrooms (with bath & shower) & 2 sitting rooms. Meals are imaginatively prepared from fresh seasonal ingredients & there is a drinks licence. A perfect place to unwind when exploring Herriot country & York. Children over 12.

VISA: M'CARD:

Phillip Gill & Anton Van Der Horst Shallowdale House West End Ampleforth YO62 4DY Yorkshire
Tel: (01439) 788325 Fax 01439 788885 Open: ALL YEAR (Excl. Xmas & New Year) Map Ref No. 01

Mill Close Farm

Nearest Road: A.684

A 17th-century working farm surrounded by beautiful rolling countryside at the foothills of the Yorkshire Dales & Herriot country. Exceptional views yet only 3 miles from A1(M). Lovely en-suite bedrooms with many extras - jacuzzi, super king-size bed, toiletries, hairdryers, T.V. with choice of videos. Highland cattle, sheep & calves roam the grounds amongst wild flowers. Enchanting walled garden with pond & waterfall. Sumptuous breakfasts. Excellent local pubs. Ideal stopover for Scotland. Animals by arrangement.

Mrs Patricia Knox Mill Close Farm Patrick Brompton Bedale DL8 1JY Yorkshire
Tel: (01677) 450257 Fax 01677 450585 Open: MAR - NOV Map Ref No. 02

Elmfield Country House

Nearest Road: A.684

Located in its own grounds in the country. Enjoy a relaxed, friendly atmosphere in spacious surroundings, with a high standard of furnishings. 9 en-suite bedrooms comprising twin-bedded, double & family rooms. 2 rooms have been adapted for disabled guests & another has a 4-poster bed. All rooms have satellite T.V., 'phone, radio/alarm & tea/coffee makers. A games room & solarium are also available. Excellent farmhouse cooking. Residential licence. A delightful home. Single supplement.
E-mail: bed@elmfieldhouse.freeserve.co.uk

see PHOTO over p. 437

VISA: M'CARD:

Jim & Edith Lillie Elmfield Country House Arrathorne Bedale DL8 1NE Yorkshire
Tel: (01677) 450558 Fax 01677 450557 Open: ALL YEAR Map Ref No. 03

Elmfield Country House. Arrathorne.

	rate £ from - to per person	children taken	evening meals	animals taken
Rudstone Walk	£29.50 to £45.00	Y	Y	Y
Five Rise Locks Hotel	£28.00 to £30.00	Y	Y	Y
Four Gables	£25.00 to £28.00	Y	N	N
The Manor House	£32.00 to £39.50	Y	Y	N

Rudstone Walk

Nearest Road: A.1034

Rudstone Walk is renowned for its hospitality & good food. Accommodation is in the very tastefully converted farm buildings, adjacent to the main farmhouse where meals are served. The attractive bedrooms have excellent en-suite facilities, T.V., 'phone, hairdryer & more. Rudstone provides a peaceful retreat after a tiring day. It is ideal for a relaxing break, & is within easy reach of York & many other attractions. Animals by arrangement.

E-mail: office@rudstone-walk.co.uk

VISA: M'CARD: AMEX:

Charles & Laura Greenwood Rudstone Walk South Cave Beverley HU15 2AH Yorkshire
Tel: (01430) 422230 Fax 01430 424552 Open: ALL YEAR Map Ref No. 04

Five Rise Locks Hotel

Nearest Road: A.650

A Victorian manor house standing in mature terraced gardens overlooking the Aire Valley, minutes walk from Bingley & the Five Rise Locks. Each of the 9 en-suite bedrooms has been individually designed & furnished with antique stripped pine. The Bistro restaurant is open for lunch & dinner & offers imaginative meals complemented by a selection of wines. Five Rise Locks is the perfect spot from which to visit Haworth, Saltaire, steam trains, York, Leeds, Mill shopping, Skipton & the Dales.

E-mail: 101731.2134@compuserve.com

VISA: M'CARD:

Mrs P. Oxley Five Rise Locks Hotel Beck Lane Bingley BD16 4DD Yorkshire
Tel: (01274) 565296 Fax 01274 568828 Open: ALL YEAR Map Ref No. 05

Four Gables

Nearest Road: A.659

Visitors will love this special Art-and-Craft movement house with its wealth of original features, stripped oak & terracotta floors, fireplaces & beautiful ceilings & gardens of over 1/2 acre which contain many interesting plants & a croquet lawn. Enjoy the peaceful setting, down a private lane, yet only 3 mins' walk from the bussling Georgian stone village of Boston Spa with all its facilities, shops & restaurants, etc. 3 attractive en-suite bedrooms. Log fires in winter. Children over 2.

E-mail: info@fourgables.co.uk

David Watts Four Gables Oaks Lane Boston Spa LS23 6DS Yorkshire
Tel: (01937) 849031/845592 Open: ALL YEAR Map Ref No. 07

The Manor House

Nearest Road: A.165, A.166

A manor of Flamborough is recorded in the Domesday Book. The current Georgian house is a handsomely proportioned family home offering spacious & comfortable accommodation in well-appointed rooms. Historic Flamborough Head is designated a Heritage Coast, with many interesting walks & a nearby bird reserve. Ideally placed for exploration of North & East Yorkshire. Dinner, by prior arrangement, features local seafood when available. Children over 8 years welcome.

E-mail: manorhouse@clara.co.uk

VISA: M'CARD: AMEX:

Lesley Berry & Geoffrey Miller The Manor House Flamborough Bridlington YO15 1PD Yorkshire
Tel: (01262) 850943 Fax 01262 850943 Open: ALL YEAR (Excl. Xmas) Map Ref No. 08

Clow-beck House. Croft-on-Tees.

Yorkshire

	rate £ from - to per person	children taken	evening meals	animals taken
Clow Beck House	£37.50 to £47.50	Y	Y	N
The Old Vicarage	£25.00 to £40.00	Y	N	N
Ashwood House	£27.50 to £33.00	Y	N	N
Acacia Lodge	£29.00 to £34.00	Y	N	N

Clow Beck House

Nearest Road: A.1, A.167

Clow Beck House is decorated with some flamboyance - chandeliers, antiques & Adam-style panels. This award-winning country house exudes warmth, friendliness & relaxation with a tinge of luxury. 14 beautiful, individually styled rooms with en-suite/private facilities & many extras. Excellent for Herriot country, York & the Dales - route planning is your hosts' speciality. Facilities are available for families & those with impaired mobility. Be pampered with old-fashioned hospitality & service.

E-mail: david@clowbeckhouse.co.uk

see PHOTO over p. 439

VISA: M'CARD: AMEX:

David & Heather Armstrong Clow Beck House Monk End Farm Croft-on-Tees Darlington DL2 2SW
Tel: (01325) 721075 Fax 01325 720419 Open: ALL YEAR Map Ref No. 10

The Old Vicarage

Nearest Road: A.19

A listed property of immense character built in the 18th century & thoughtfully brought up to modern standards, & yet still retaining many delightful features. Now offering 4 en-suite rooms with T.V. & tea/coffee makers. Standing in extensive lawned gardens, overlooking the market square, & with a croquet lawn & a walled rose garden, it is an ideal touring centre for York, the Dales, the Yorkshire Moors & 'Herriot' countryside. Parking.

E-mail: kirman@oldvic-easingwold.freeserve.co.uk

see PHOTO over p. 441

VISA: M'CARD:

Christine & John Kirman The Old Vicarage Market Place Easingwold YO61 3AL Yorkshire
Tel: (01347) 821015 Fax 01347 823465 Open: FEB - NOV Map Ref No. 11

Ashwood House

Nearest Road: A.61

A charming 9-bedroomed Edwardian house retaining many of its original features. Situated in a quiet, residential cul-de-sac mins' from the town centre. The attractive en-suite bedrooms are spacious, some with 4-poster beds, all with hospitality tray, T.V., hairdryer & toiletries. A delicious breakfast is served from lovely Royal Copenhagen china in the elegant dining room. A high standard of service & a warm welcome is assured. Scandinavian languages spoken. Children over 7 years.

E-mail: ashwoodhouse@aol.com

Gill & Kristian Bendtson Ashwood House 7 Spring Grove Harrogate HG1 2HS Yorkshire
Tel: (01423) 560081 Fax 01423 527928 Open: ALL YEAR (Excl. Xmas & New Year) Map Ref No. 12

Acacia Lodge

Nearest Road: A.61

Acacia Lodge is a warm, lovingly restored & charming, small family-run hotel with pretty gardens in a select central conservation area just a short stroll from Harrogate's fashionable shops, many restaurants & attractions. It retains all its original character with fine furnishings, antiques & old paintings. Bedrooms are en-suite & well-furnished with every comfort. Award-winning breakfasts served in the oak-furnished dining room, & guests can relax in the lounge with open fire & library of books. Private floodlit car park. Children over 10 years.

Peter & Dee Bateson Acacia Lodge 21 Ripon Road Harrogate HG1 2JL Yorkshire
Tel: (01423) 560752 Fax 01423 503725 Open: ALL YEAR Map Ref No. 12

The Old Vicarage. Easingwold.

rate £ from - to per person	children taken	evening meals	animals taken

Daryl House

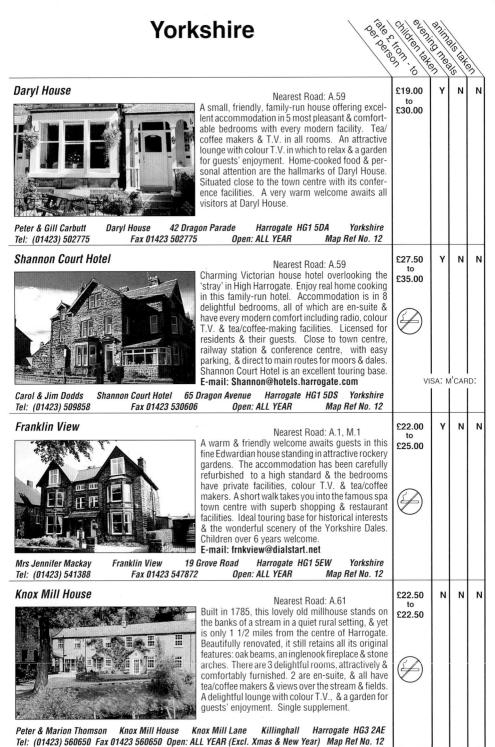

Nearest Road: A.59

A small, friendly, family-run house offering excellent accommodation in 5 most pleasant & comfortable bedrooms with every modern facility. Tea/coffee makers & T.V. in all rooms. An attractive lounge with colour T.V. in which to relax & a garden for guests' enjoyment. Home-cooked food & personal attention are the hallmarks of Daryl House. Situated close to the town centre with its conference facilities. A very warm welcome awaits all visitors at Daryl House.

Peter & Gill Carbutt   Daryl House   42 Dragon Parade   Harrogate HG1 5DA   Yorkshire
Tel: (01423) 502775   Fax 01423 502775   Open: ALL YEAR   Map Ref No. 12

rate £ from - to per person	children taken	evening meals	animals taken
£19.00 to £30.00	Y	N	N

Shannon Court Hotel

Nearest Road: A.59

Charming Victorian house hotel overlooking the 'stray' in High Harrogate. Enjoy real home cooking in this family-run hotel. Accommodation is in 8 delightful bedrooms, all of which are en-suite & have every modern comfort including radio, colour T.V. & tea/coffee-making facilities. Licensed for residents & their guests. Close to town centre, railway station & conference centre, with easy parking, & direct to main routes for moors & dales. Shannon Court Hotel is an excellent touring base.

E-mail: Shannon@hotels.harrogate.com

Carol & Jim Dodds   Shannon Court Hotel   65 Dragon Avenue   Harrogate HG1 5DS   Yorkshire
Tel: (01423) 509858   Fax 01423 530606   Open: ALL YEAR   Map Ref No. 12

rate £ from - to per person	children taken	evening meals	animals taken
£27.50 to £35.00	Y	N	N

VISA: M'CARD:

Franklin View

Nearest Road: A.1, M.1

A warm & friendly welcome awaits guests in this fine Edwardian house standing in attractive rockery gardens. The accommodation has been carefully refurbished to a high standard & the bedrooms have private facilities, colour T.V. & tea/coffee makers. A short walk takes you into the famous spa town centre with superb shopping & restaurant facilities. Ideal touring base for historical interests & the wonderful scenery of the Yorkshire Dales. Children over 6 years welcome.

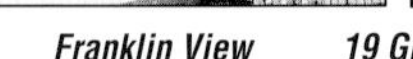

E-mail: frnkview@dialstart.net

Mrs Jennifer Mackay   Franklin View   19 Grove Road   Harrogate HG1 5EW   Yorkshire
Tel: (01423) 541388   Fax 01423 547872   Open: ALL YEAR   Map Ref No. 12

rate £ from - to per person	children taken	evening meals	animals taken
£22.00 to £25.00	Y	N	N

Knox Mill House

Nearest Road: A.61

Built in 1785, this lovely old millhouse stands on the banks of a stream in a quiet rural setting, & yet is only 1 1/2 miles from the centre of Harrogate. Beautifully renovated, it still retains all its original features: oak beams, an inglenook fireplace & stone arches. There are 3 delightful rooms, attractively & comfortably furnished. 2 are en-suite, & all have tea/coffee makers & views over the stream & fields. A delightful lounge with colour T.V., & a garden for guests' enjoyment. Single supplement.

Peter & Marion Thomson   Knox Mill House   Knox Mill Lane   Killinghall   Harrogate HG3 2AE
Tel: (01423) 560650 Fax 01423 560650 Open: ALL YEAR (Excl. Xmas & New Year) Map Ref No. 12

rate £ from - to per person	children taken	evening meals	animals taken
£22.50 to £22.50	N	N	N

rate £ from - to per person	children taken	evening meals	animals taken
£28.00 to £40.00	N	Y	Y

Knottside Farm

Nearest Road: A.59

Knottside Farm, a beautiful 17th-century farmhouse, is in Nidderdale, an Area of Outstanding Natural Beauty. It is ideal for walking, fishing, pony trekking & bird-watching or visiting the Moors, Dales, Harrogate & historic York. The guest's rooms are delightfully furnished to a very high standard & have wonderful views over this peaceful dale. Nigel creates mouth-watering Cordon Bleu dinners which include local lamb & trout. Knottside Farm is a charming home.

Mr & Mrs E. Stanton   Knottside Farm   The Knott   Pateley Bridge   Harrogate   HG3 5DQ   Yorkshire
Tel: (01423) 712927   Fax 01423 712927   Open: ALL YEAR   Map Ref No. 14

rate £ from - to per person	children taken	evening meals	animals taken
£21.50 to £28.00	Y	Y	N

see PHOTO over p. 444

High Winsley Cottage

Nearest Road: A.61

Traditional Dales cottage in Nidderdale, situated well off the road in peaceful countryside, with lovely views all around, & ideally placed for both town & country. Accommodation is in 2 twin & 2 double rooms, well-appointed & all with en-suite facilities. There are 2 large sitting rooms, with guide books, games, T.V., etc. Imaginative home cooking using produce from the extensive kitchen garden, complemented by wines from an interesting list. Children over 11 years.

Clive & Gill King   High Winsley Cottage   Burnt Yates   Nr. Harrogate   HG3 3EP   Yorkshire
Tel: (01423) 770662   Open: MAR - NOV   Map Ref No. 13

rate £ from - to per person	children taken	evening meals	animals taken
£19.00 to £20.00	N	Y	Y

Brandymires Guest House

Nearest Road: A.684

A warm welcome awaits you in this comfortable mid-19th-century stone house in a tranquil rural setting. Every room has a splendid view over the fells. There are 4 spacious & attractive double bedrooms, 2 with 4-poster beds, full central heating. Good home cooking, including home-made bread, is an important feature, & dinner is available with prior notice, except on Thursdays. Brandymires is an ideal centre for exploring both the glorious countryside of the Yorkshire Dales & the historic surrounding towns. No T.V.. Ample parking.

Gail Ainley & Ann Macdonald   Brandymires Guest House   Muker Road   Hawes   DL8 3PR   Yorkshire
Tel: (01969) 667482   Open: Mid FEB - OCT   Map Ref No. 15

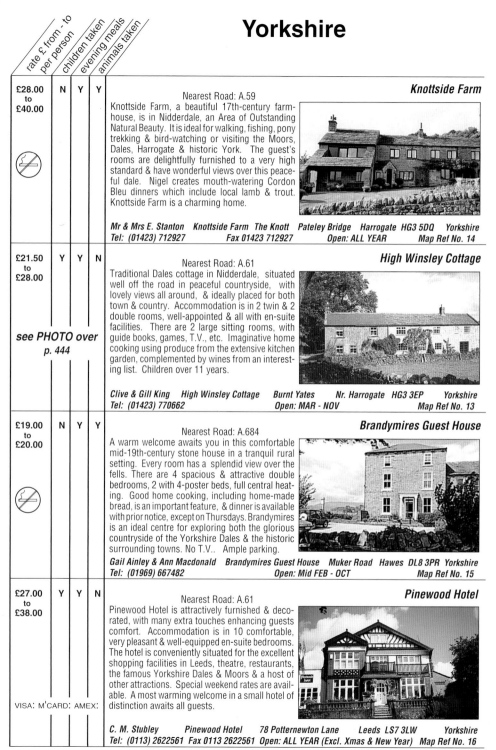

rate £ from - to per person	children taken	evening meals	animals taken
£27.00 to £38.00	Y	Y	N

VISA: M'CARD: AMEX:

Pinewood Hotel

Nearest Road: A.61

Pinewood Hotel is attractively furnished & decorated, with many extra touches enhancing guests comfort. Accommodation is in 10 comfortable, very pleasant & well-equipped en-suite bedrooms. The hotel is conveniently situated for the excellent shopping facilities in Leeds, theatre, restaurants, the famous Yorkshire Dales & Moors & a host of other attractions. Special weekend rates are available. A most warming welcome in a small hotel of distinction awaits all guests.

C. M. Stubley   Pinewood Hotel   78 Potternewton Lane   Leeds   LS7 3LW   Yorkshire
Tel: (0113) 2622561   Fax 0113 2622561   Open: ALL YEAR (Excl. Xmas & New Year)   Map Ref No. 16

High Winsley Cottage. Burnt Yates.

Yorkshire

rate £ from - to per person	children taken	evening meals	animals taken
£27.50 to £32.50	Y	Y	N

Park Gate House

Nearest Road: A.684

A warm welcome awaits all guests at this lovely 18th-century house, situated in Lower Wensleydale, an Area of Outstanding Natural Beauty & historical interest. Park Gate House retains its charm with low oak beams, inglenook log fire & cottage gardens. Bedrooms are decorated in country-style old pine furniture, T.V. & private facilities & echo comfort & style. Breakfast is a delight & very high quality. Evening meals are available by prior arrangement. Single supplement. Children over 12.

E-mail: parkgatehouse@freenet.co.uk

VISA: M'CARD:

Terry & Linda Marshall Park Gate House Constable Burton Leyburn DL8 5RG Yorkshire
Tel: (01677) 450466 Fax 01677 450466 Open: ALL YEAR Map Ref No. 17

rate £ from - to per person	children taken	evening meals	animals taken
£24.00 to £££	Y	Y	Y

Manor Farm

Nearest Road: A.169

A charming Georgian manor house set in spacious grounds with hard tennis court, croquet lawn & views to the Howardian Hills. Accommodation is in 3 comfortable & attractively furnished bedrooms, with either an en-suite or a private bathroom. Excellent cooking caters for all tastes. Manor Farm is within easy reach of York, Scarborough, the Moors, Castle Howard & Flamingoland. Dogs & children are most welcome.

E-mail: cphmurray@compuserve.com

Mrs Judith M. Murray Manor Farm Little Barugh Malton YO17 6UY Yorkshire
Tel: (01653) 668262 Fax 01653 668600 Open: ALL YEAR Map Ref No. 18

rate £ from - to per person	children taken	evening meals	animals taken
£25.00 to £30.00	Y	N	N

Elmscott

Nearest Road: A.684

Elmscott is a charming cottage-style property which is set in a delightful landscaped garden. Yet, it is situated close to the centre of Northallerton, a thriving market town. Your charming hosts offer 2 attractively furnished bedrooms, each with an en-suite bathroom, tea/coffee-making facilities & T.V.. A delicious breakfast is served. Elmscott is located mid-way between the North York Moors & the beautiful Yorkshire Dales National Parks, with their famous 'Herriott' connections. A lovely home, perfect for a relaxing break.

Mike & Pauline Schofield Elmscott 10 Hatfield Road Northallerton DL7 8QX Yorkshire
Tel: (01609) 760575 Open: ALL YEAR Map Ref No. 20

rate £ from - to per person	children taken	evening meals	animals taken
£22.50 to £25.00	Y	Y	N

Little Holtby

Nearest Road: A.1

With one foot in the past, but with present day comforts, Little Holtby is the 'somewhere special' in which to relax & unwind. Antiques, beams, polished wood floors & cosy log fires all add to the ambience of a period farmhouse. Each of the 3 comfortable guest rooms has wonderful views over rolling countryside to the Dales. En-suite or private facilities are available. Facilities for golf, tennis, riding, fishing & walking are all close by. (Children over 12.) Come & spoil yourself - other guests do again & again.

Dorothy Hodgson Little Holtby Leeming Bar Northallerton DL7 9LH Yorkshire
Tel: (01609) 748762 Fax 01609 748822 Open: ALL YEAR (Excl. Xmas) Map Ref No. 21

Sevenford House. Rosedale Abbey.

Yorkshire

rate £ from - to per person	children taken	evening meals	animals taken
£22.50 to £££	Y	N	N

Sevenford House

Nearest Road: A.170

Originally a vicarage, & built from the stones of Rosedale Abbey, Sevenford House stands in 4 acres of lovely gardens in the heart of the beautiful Yorkshire Moors National Park. 3 tastefully furnished, en-suite bedrooms, with T.V., radio & tea/coffee, etc., offering wonderful views overlooking valley & moorland. A lounge/library. An ideal base for exploring the region. Riding & golf locally. Also, ruined abbeys, Roman roads, steam railways, the beautiful coastline & pretty fishing towns.
E-mail: sevenford@aol.com

see PHOTO over p. 446

Linda Sugars Sevenford House Rosedale Abbey Nr. Pickering YO18 8SE Yorkshire
Tel: (01751) 417283 Fax 01751 417505 Open: ALL YEAR Map Ref No. 23

rate £ from - to per person	children taken	evening meals	animals taken
£25.00 to £30.00	N	N	N

Mallard Grange

Nearest Road: B.6265

Rambling 16th-century farmhouse full of character & charm in glorious countryside near Fountains Abbey. Offering superb quality & comfort, spacious rooms furnished with care & some lovely antique pieces. En-suite bedrooms have large comfortable beds, warm towels, colour T.V., hairdryer & refreshments tray. Delicious breakfasts with homemade preserves. Pretty walled garden tended by enthusiastic amateur. Safe parking. Excellent evening meals locally.

Mrs Maggie Johnson Mallard Grange Aldfield Nr. Fountains Abbey Ripon HG4 3BE Yorkshire
Tel: (01765) 620242 Open: ALL YEAR (Excl. Xmas) Map Ref No. 25

rate £ from - to per person	children taken	evening meals	animals taken
£23.50 to £25.00	Y	N	Y

St. George's Court

Nearest Road: A.1

St. George's Court is beautifully situated in peaceful countryside & provides comfortable ground-floor rooms in renovated farm buildings. All modern facilities whilst retaining much charm & character. Delicious breakfasts are served in the conservatory dining room, with views, in the delightful listed farmhouse. Peace & tranquillity is the password here. St. George's Court is near Fountains Abbey & Brimham Rocks. Ripon, Harrogate & York are all within easy reach. Children over 2.

see PHOTO over p. 448

VISA: M'CARD:

Mrs Sandra Gordon St. George's Court Old Home Farm Grantley Ripon HG4 3EU Yorkshire
Tel: (01765) 620618 Fax 01765 620618 Open: ALL YEAR Map Ref No. 26

rate £ from - to per person	children taken	evening meals	animals taken
£20.00 to £27.50	Y	Y	N

Bank Villa

Nearest Road: A.6108, A.1

Set in half an acre of terraced garden, this welcoming Grade II listed home has recently been renovated & refurbished to a high standard. It offers guests 2 delightful lounges in which to relax & 6 double bedrooms, 4 with en-suite or private facilities, 2 with private shower. Bank Villa is an excellent spot for a relaxing break & is an ideal base from which to explore the glorious Yorkshire Dales, tour around, walk, horse-ride or fish. Children over 5 years welcome. A warm welcome awaits you.

Bobby & Lucy Thomson Bank Villa The Avenue Masham Ripon HG4 4DB Yorkshire
Tel: (01765) 689605 Fax 01765 689605 Open: ALL YEAR (Excl. Xmas) Map Ref No. 27

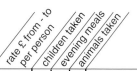

St. Georges Court. Grantley.

Yorkshire

rate £ from - to per person	children taken	evening meals	animals taken
£22.50 to £25.00	Y	Y	N

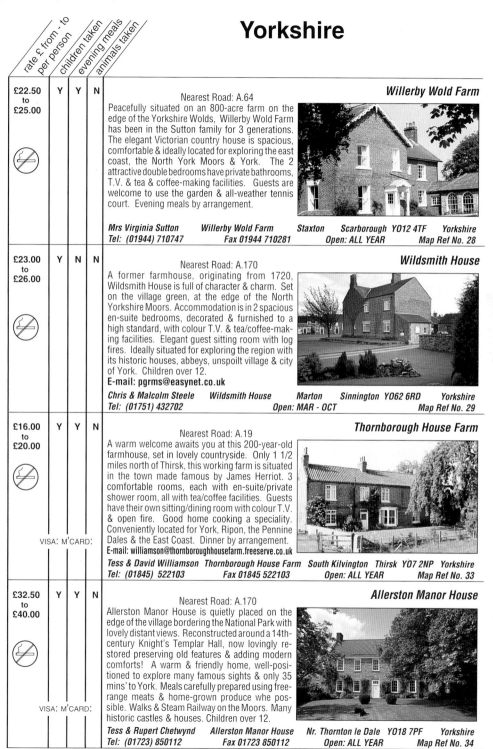

Willerby Wold Farm

Nearest Road: A.64

Peacefully situated on an 800-acre farm on the edge of the Yorkshire Wolds, Willerby Wold Farm has been in the Sutton family for 3 generations. The elegant Victorian country house is spacious, comfortable & ideally located for exploring the east coast, the North York Moors & York. The 2 attractive double bedrooms have private bathrooms, T.V. & tea & coffee-making facilities. Guests are welcome to use the garden & all-weather tennis court. Evening meals by arrangement.

Mrs Virginia Sutton *Willerby Wold Farm* *Staxton* *Scarborough* *YO12 4TF* *Yorkshire*
Tel: (01944) 710747 *Fax 01944 710281* *Open: ALL YEAR* *Map Ref No. 28*

rate £ from - to per person	children taken	evening meals	animals taken
£23.00 to £26.00	Y	N	N

Wildsmith House

Nearest Road: A.170

A former farmhouse, originating from 1720, Wildsmith House is full of character & charm. Set on the village green, at the edge of the North Yorkshire Moors. Accommodation is in 2 spacious en-suite bedrooms, decorated & furnished to a high standard, with colour T.V. & tea/coffee-making facilities. Elegant guest sitting room with log fires. Ideally situated for exploring the region with its historic houses, abbeys, unspoilt village & city of York. Children over 12.

E-mail: pgrms@easynet.co.uk

Chris & Malcolm Steele *Wildsmith House* *Marton* *Sinnington* *YO62 6RD* *Yorkshire*
Tel: (01751) 432702 *Open: MAR - OCT* *Map Ref No. 29*

rate £ from - to per person	children taken	evening meals	animals taken
£16.00 to £20.00	Y	Y	N

VISA: M'CARD:

Thornborough House Farm

Nearest Road: A.19

A warm welcome awaits you at this 200-year-old farmhouse, set in lovely countryside. Only 1 1/2 miles north of Thirsk, this working farm is situated in the town made famous by James Herriot. 3 comfortable rooms, each with en-suite/private shower room, all with tea/coffee facilities. Guests have their own sitting/dining room with colour T.V. & open fire. Good home cooking a speciality. Conveniently located for York, Ripon, the Pennine Dales & the East Coast. Dinner by arrangement.

E-mail: williamson@thornboroughhousefarm.freeserve.co.uk

Tess & David Williamson *Thornborough House Farm* *South Kilvington* *Thirsk* *YO7 2NP* *Yorkshire*
Tel: (01845) 522103 *Fax 01845 522103* *Open: ALL YEAR* *Map Ref No. 33*

rate £ from - to per person	children taken	evening meals	animals taken
£32.50 to £40.00	Y	Y	N

VISA: M'CARD:

Allerston Manor House

Nearest Road: A.170

Allerston Manor House is quietly placed on the edge of the village bordering the National Park with lovely distant views. Reconstructed around a 14th-century Knight's Templar Hall, now lovingly restored preserving old features & adding modern comforts! A warm & friendly home, well-positioned to explore many famous sights & only 35 mins' to York. Meals carefully prepared using free-range meats & home-grown produce whe possible. Walks & Steam Railway on the Moors. Many historic castles & houses. Children over 12.

Tess & Rupert Chetwynd *Allerston Manor House* *Nr. Thornton le Dale* *YO18 7PF* *Yorkshire*
Tel: (01723) 850112 *Fax 01723 850112* *Open: ALL YEAR* *Map Ref No. 34*

Barbican House. York.

Yorkshire

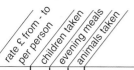

rate £ from - to per person	children taken	evening meals	animals taken
£30.00 to £30.00	Y	N	Y

High Fold

Nearest Road: A.59

High Fold is a converted 18th-century barn in the Dales village of Kettlewell. It is in an ideal position for touring, walking or cycling. This pretty village boasts 3 pubs with a host of other culinary delights in other villages. The accommodation is eclectically elegant & is enhanced by beamed ceilings, stone features & antiques. 3 en-suite bedrooms. Enjoy a delicious breakfast, including fresh local produce, in the dining room overlooking the Dalesway. Single supplement. Children over 12.

E-mail: deborah@highfold.fsnet.co.uk

Mrs Deborah Mee High Fold Kettlewell Upper Wharfedale BD23 5RJ Yorkshire
Tel: (01756) 760390 Fax 01756 760390 Open: ALL YEAR Map Ref No. 35

rate £ from - to per person	children taken	evening meals	animals taken
£30.00 to £45.00	Y	Y	Y

VISA: M'CARD:

Cliffemount Hotel

Nearest Road: A.174

As the name implies, this privately-run hotel is situated on a clifftop with panoramic views over Runswick Bay. Built in the 1920s with later additions, the hotel is tastefully decorated throughout. 12 of the 13 comfortably furnished bedrooms are en-suite, & the majority have spectacular sea views. Cliffemount, with its warm & friendly atmosphere, also enjoys a good reputation for its high standard of food. Fully licensed. Log fires in winter.

E-mail: cliffemount@runswickbay.fsnet.co.uk

Mrs Ashley Goodrum Cliffemount Hotel Bank Top Lane Runswick Bay Whitby TS13 5HU
Tel: (01947) 840103 Fax 01947 841025 Open: ALL YEAR (Excl. Xmas) Map Ref No. 36

rate £ from - to per person	children taken	evening meals	animals taken
£26.00 to £30.00	Y	N	N

see PHOTO over p. 450

VISA: M'CARD:

Barbican House

Nearest Road: A.19

The Barbican House is a Victorian residence of individual charm & character, overlooking the medieval city walls. Leave your car in the floodlit car park & enjoy a 10 minute walk to all the citys attractions. Bedrooms have en-suite/private facilities & are attractively furnished with T.V., 'phone, tea/coffee & hairdryer etc. Enjoy a traditional English breakfast & more, in the dining room. A friendly Yorkshire welcome is assured. Arrive as guests, leave as friends. Children over 12.

E-mail: info@barbicanhouse.com

Michael & Juliet Morgan Barbican House 20 Barbican Road York YO10 5AA Yorkshire
Tel: (01904) 627617 Fax 01904 647140 Open: ALL YEAR (Excl. Xmas & New Year) Map Ref No. 38

rate £ from - to per person	children taken	evening meals	animals taken
£25.50 to £38.00	Y	N	N

see PHOTO over p. 452

Easton's

Nearest Road: A.64, A.1036

Award-winning accommodation at a sympathetically & beautifully restored Victorian wine-merchant's residence, centrally situated just 300 yds from the medieval city walls. The period furniture, William Morris decor, open fires & fully equipped bedrooms are in accord with the character of the building, & with the standard of excellence that the owners strive for. The Victorian sideboard breakfast menu follows the same theme of quality, & includes a selection of traditional & vegetarian dishes. Children over 5 yrs.

Lynn M. Keir Easton's 88-90 Bishopthorpe Road York YO23 1JS Yorkshire
Tel: (01904) 626646 Fax 01904 626165 Open: ALL YEAR (Excl. Xmas) Map Ref No. 38

Easton's. York.

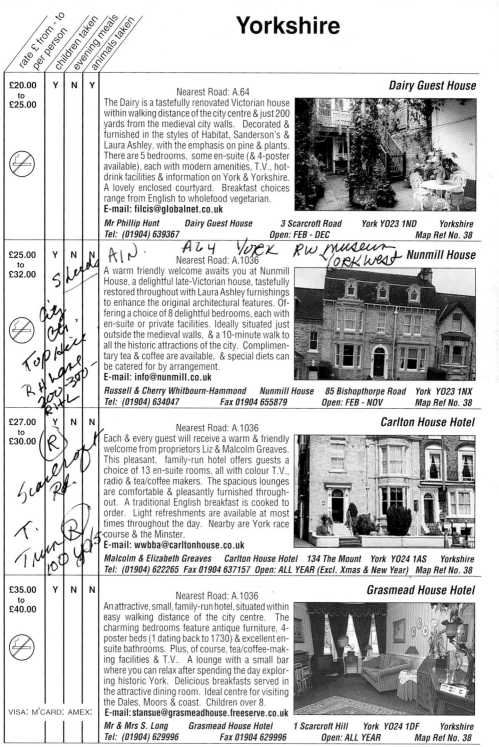

Yorkshire

rate £ from - to per person	children taken	evening meals	animals taken
£20.00 to £25.00	Y	N	Y

Dairy Guest House

Nearest Road: A.64

The Dairy is a tastefully renovated Victorian house within walking distance of the city centre & just 200 yards from the medieval city walls. Decorated & furnished in the styles of Habitat, Sanderson's & Laura Ashley, with the emphasis on pine & plants. There are 5 bedrooms, some en-suite (& 4-poster available), each with modern amenities, T.V., hot-drink facilities & information on York & Yorkshire. A lovely enclosed courtyard. Breakfast choices range from English to wholefood vegetarian.

E-mail: filcis@globalnet.co.uk

Mr Phillip Hunt Dairy Guest House 3 Scarcroft Road York YO23 1ND Yorkshire
Tel: (01904) 639367 Open: FEB - DEC Map Ref No. 38

rate £ from - to per person	children taken	evening meals	animals taken
£25.00 to £32.00	Y	N	N

Nunmill House

Nearest Road: A.1036

A warm friendly welcome awaits you at Nunmill House, a delightful late-Victorian house, tastefully restored throughout with Laura Ashley furnishings to enhance the original architectural features. Offering a choice of 8 delightful bedrooms, each with en-suite or private facilities. Ideally situated just outside the medieval walls, & a 10-minute walk to all the historic attractions of the city. Complimentary tea & coffee are available, & special diets can be catered for by arrangement.

E-mail: info@nunmill.co.uk

Russell & Cherry Whitbourn-Hammond Nunmill House 85 Bishopthorpe Road York YO23 1NX
Tel: (01904) 634047 Fax 01904 655879 Open: FEB - NOV Map Ref No. 38

rate £ from - to per person	children taken	evening meals	animals taken
£27.00 to £30.00	Y	N	N

Carlton House Hotel

Nearest Road: A.1036

Each & every guest will receive a warm & friendly welcome from proprietors Liz & Malcolm Greaves. This pleasant, family-run hotel offers guests a choice of 13 en-suite rooms, all with colour T.V., radio & tea/coffee makers. The spacious lounges are comfortable & pleasantly furnished throughout. A traditional English breakfast is cooked to order. Light refreshments are available at most times throughout the day. Nearby are York race course & the Minster.

E-mail: wwbba@carltonhouse.co.uk

Malcolm & Elizabeth Greaves Carlton House Hotel 134 The Mount York YO24 1AS Yorkshire
Tel: (01904) 622265 Fax 01904 637157 Open: ALL YEAR (Excl. Xmas & New Year) Map Ref No. 38

rate £ from - to per person	children taken	evening meals	animals taken
£35.00 to £40.00	Y	N	N

Grasmead House Hotel

Nearest Road: A.1036

An attractive, small, family-run hotel, situated within easy walking distance of the city centre. The charming bedrooms feature antique furniture, 4-poster beds (1 dating back to 1730) & excellent en-suite bathrooms. Plus, of course, tea/coffee-making facilities & T.V.. A lounge with a small bar where you can relax after spending the day exploring historic York. Delicious breakfasts served in the attractive dining room. Ideal centre for visiting the Dales, Moors & coast. Children over 8.

VISA: M'CARD: AMEX:

E-mail: stansue@grasmeadhouse.freeserve.co.uk

Mr & Mrs S. Long Grasmead House Hotel 1 Scarcroft Hill York YO24 1DF Yorkshire
Tel: (01904) 629996 Fax 01904 629996 Open: ALL YEAR Map Ref No. 38

Arndale Hotel. York

rate £ from - to per person	children taken	evening meals	animals taken
			N

VISA: M'CARD:

Arndale Hotel

...oad: A.64

...directly overlooking ..., with beautiful en...g a country-house at... There is a spacious, ...e with antiques, fresh ...all bar. The 12 outstand...pped bedrooms are all en...s are Victorian in style, with modern whirlpool baths. Antique half-tester/4-poster beds. Delicious quality breakfasts. Friendly, attentive service. Large enclosed gated car park.

Mrs M. Varey Arndale Hotel 290 Tadcaster Road York YO24 1ET Yorkshire
Tel: (01904) 702424 Fax 01904 709800 Open: ALL YEAR (Excl. Xmas & New Year) Map Ref No. 38

---

rate £ from - to per person	children taken	evening meals	animals taken
£27.50 to £37.50	Y	N	N

VISA: M'CARD:

Curzon Lodge & Stable Cottages

Nearest Road: A.1036

A charming 17th-century Grade II listed house & oak-beamed stables within city conservation area overlooking the racecourse. Once a home of renowned York chocolate makers, guests are now invited to share the unique atmosphere in 10 delightful & fully-equipped en-suite rooms. Some 4-poster & brass beds. Country antiques, old prints, books, maps, fresh flowers & sherry in the cosy sitting room lend traditional ambience. Warm & informal. Delicious English breakfasts. Parking. Restaurants within 1-min walk. Children over 7.

Mr & Mrs R. Wood Curzon Lodge & Stable Cottages 23 Tadcaster Road Dringhouses York YO24 1QG
Tel: (01904) 703157 Fax 01904 703157 Open: ALL YEAR (Excl. Xmas) Map Ref No. 38

---

rate £ from - to per person	children taken	evening meals	animals taken
£30.00 to £45.00	Y	N	N

see PHOTO over p. 456

VISA: M'CARD: AMEX:

Holmwood House Hotel

Nearest Road: A.59

The conversion of 2 listed, early-Victorian town houses has created an elegant hotel that offers guests a feeling of home with a touch of luxury. All rooms, of course, have en-suite facilities but are very different in both size & decoration. There are 3 honeymoon rooms (2 with 4-poster beds) & 1 with a spa bath. 3 family suites are available. The guest sitting room, with an open fire, is on the ground floor. Children over 8 welcome.

E-mail: holmwood.house@dial.pipex.com

Rosie Blanksby & Bill Pitts Holmwood House Hotel 114 Holgate Road York YO24 4BB Yorkshire
Tel: (01904) 626183 Fax 01904 670899 Open: ALL YEAR Map Ref No. 38

---

rate £ from - to per person	children taken	evening meals	animals taken
£20.00 to £23.00	Y	N	N

VISA: M'CARD:

Brentwood Cottage

Nearest Road: A.19

A warm & friendly welcome awaits all guests at Brentwood Cottage. Located 5 miles outside the historic city of York, it offers guests a choice of 5 very pleasant (non-smoking) bedrooms, 2 with en-suite/private facilities & amenities, & each with tea/coffee makers. There is also a comfortable residents' lounge & garden available. Brentwood Cottage makes a good base for touring York & the surrounding countryside. A large car park.

E-mail: yvonne@yorkcity.co.uk

Yvonne Thompson Brentwood Cottage Main Street Shipton-by-Beningbrough York YO30 1AB
Tel: (01904) 470111 Fax 01904 426384 Open: ALL YEAR Map Ref No. 40

Holmwood House Hotel. York.

Four Seasons Hotel. York.

Bloomsbury Hotel. York.

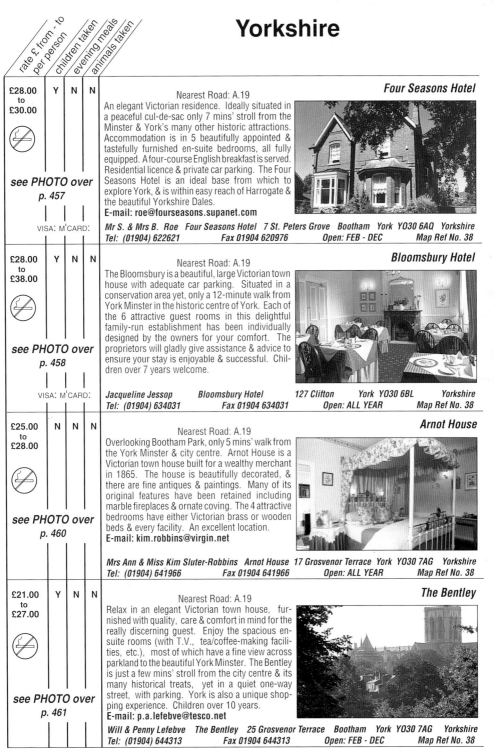

rate £ from - to per person	children taken	evening meals	animals taken
£28.00 to £30.00	Y	N	N

see PHOTO over p. 457

VISA: M'CARD:

Four Seasons Hotel

Nearest Road: A.19

An elegant Victorian residence. Ideally situated in a peaceful cul-de-sac only 7 mins' stroll from the Minster & York's many other historic attractions. Accommodation is in 5 beautifully appointed & tastefully furnished en-suite bedrooms, all fully equipped. A four-course English breakfast is served. Residential licence & private car parking. The Four Seasons Hotel is an ideal base from which to explore York, & is within easy reach of Harrogate & the beautiful Yorkshire Dales.

E-mail: roe@fourseasons.supanet.com

Mr S. & Mrs B. Roe Four Seasons Hotel 7 St. Peters Grove Bootham York YO30 6AQ Yorkshire
Tel: (01904) 622621 Fax 01904 620976 Open: FEB - DEC Map Ref No. 38

rate £ from - to per person	children taken	evening meals	animals taken
£28.00 to £38.00	Y	N	N

see PHOTO over p. 458

VISA: M'CARD:

Bloomsbury Hotel

Nearest Road: A.19

The Bloomsbury is a beautiful, large Victorian town house with adequate car parking. Situated in a conservation area yet, only a 12-minute walk from York Minster in the historic centre of York. Each of the 6 attractive guest rooms in this delightful family-run establishment has been individually designed by the owners for your comfort. The proprietors will gladly give assistance & advice to ensure your stay is enjoyable & successful. Children over 7 years welcome.

Jacqueline Jessop Bloomsbury Hotel 127 Clifton York YO30 6BL Yorkshire
Tel: (01904) 634031 Fax 01904 634031 Open: ALL YEAR Map Ref No. 38

rate £ from - to per person	children taken	evening meals	animals taken
£25.00 to £28.00	N	N	N

see PHOTO over p. 460

Arnot House

Nearest Road: A.19

Overlooking Bootham Park, only 5 mins' walk from the York Minster & city centre. Arnot House is a Victorian town house built for a wealthy merchant in 1865. The house is beautifully decorated, & there are fine antiques & paintings. Many of its original features have been retained including marble fireplaces & ornate coving. The 4 attractive bedrooms have either Victorian brass or wooden beds & every facility. An excellent location.

E-mail: kim.robbins@virgin.net

Mrs Ann & Miss Kim Sluter-Robbins Arnot House 17 Grosvenor Terrace York YO30 7AG Yorkshire
Tel: (01904) 641966 Fax 01904 641966 Open: ALL YEAR Map Ref No. 38

rate £ from - to per person	children taken	evening meals	animals taken
£21.00 to £27.00	Y	N	N

see PHOTO over p. 461

The Bentley

Nearest Road: A.19

Relax in an elegant Victorian town house, furnished with quality, care & comfort in mind for the really discerning guest. Enjoy the spacious en-suite rooms (with T.V., tea/coffee-making facilities, etc.), most of which have a fine view across parkland to the beautiful York Minster. The Bentley is just a few mins' stroll from the city centre & its many historical treats, yet in a quiet one-way street, with parking. York is also a unique shopping experience. Children over 10 years.

E-mail: p.a.lefebve@tesco.net

Will & Penny Lefebve The Bentley 25 Grosvenor Terrace Bootham York YO30 7AG Yorkshire
Tel: (01904) 644313 Fax 01904 644313 Open: FEB - DEC Map Ref No. 38

Arnot House. Bootham.

The Bentley. York.

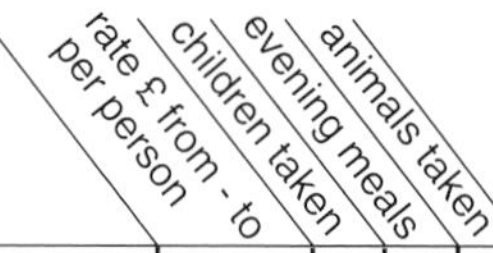

Ascot House

Nearest Road: A.1036

Ascot House is a family-run Victorian villa built in 1869. There are 15 en-suite rooms of character, many having four-poster or canopy beds. Each is well-equipped with T.V., tea/coffee-making facilities, etc. Delicious traditional English or vegetarian breakfasts are served in the dining room. Ascot House is only 15 mins' walk to the city centre with its ancient narrow streets, medieval churches, Roman, Viking & National Railway Museums & the York Minster. Licensed. Sauna available. Car park.

E-mail: J+K@ascot-house-york.demon.co.uk

June & Keith Wood *Ascot House* *80 East Parade* *York YO31 7YH* *Yorkshire*
Tel: (01904) 426826 *Fax 01904 431077* *Open: ALL YEAR (Excl. Xmas)* *Map Ref No. 38*

rate £ from - to per person	children taken	evening meals	animals taken
£20.00 to £25.00	Y	N	Y

VISA: M'CARD:

Primrose Cottage

Nearest Road: A.1 M.

A warm friendly welcome awaits you at Primrose Cottage, in a quiet picturesque village 1 mile east of the A.1. Comfortable bedrooms with washbasins & tea/coffee-making facilities. 2 bath/shower rooms. Spacious T.V. lounge, & sheltered patio garden with barbecue for guests' use. 2 local inns serving excellent food. Ideally situated 15 mins' north of York. Ripon, Harrogate & Yorkshire Dales within easy distance.

E-mail: primrosecottage@btinternet.com

Tony & Tricia Styan *Primrose Cottage* *Lime Bar Lane* *Grafton* *York YO51 9QJ* *Yorkshire*
Tel: (01423) 322835/322711 *Fax 01423 323985* *Open: ALL YEAR* *Map Ref No. 39*

rate £ from - to per person	children taken	evening meals	animals taken
£19.00 to £25.00	Y	N	Y

Laurel Manor Farm

Nearest Road: A.1, A.19

Hidden up a lane, beside the village church, is Laurel Manor Farm, its 28 acres running down to the River Swale. The recently refurbished bedrooms have en-suite/private bathrooms & are furnished with antiques, a 4-poster, family portraits, beams & open fireplaces. Dine with your hosts or walk 2 mins' to one of 4 inns. The Keys have a tennis court, croquet lawn & river walks, & are licensed. Laurel Manor Farm is situated only 4 miles from the A.1M. 12 miles York/Harrogate.

E-mail: laurelmf@aol.com

Sam & Annie Key *Laurel Manor Farm* *Brafferton - Helperby* *York YO61 2NZ* *Yorkshire*
Tel: (01423) 360436 *Fax 01423 360437* *Open: ALL YEAR* *Map Ref No. 42*

rate £ from - to per person	children taken	evening meals	animals taken
£27.00 to £30.00	Y	Y	Y

see PHOTO over p. 463

Plumpton Court

Nearest Road: A.170

Plumpton Court is a family-run 17th-century guest house set in the foothills of the North Yorkshire Moors, & is ideally situated for York & exploring the east coast. Offering 7 en-suite, comfortable & well-appointed bedrooms, many with bath & shower, all with clock/radio, tea/coffee-making facilities & colour T.V.. A comfortable lounge in which guests may relax, with real fire, small bar & T.V.. Delicious evening meals served using fresh local produce. Secure, gated car park & garden. Children over 12.

E-mail: plumptoncourt@ukgateway.net

Chris & Sarah Braithwaite *Plumpton Court* *High Street* *Nawton* *Nr. Helmsley* *York YO62 7TT*
Tel: (01439) 771223 *Fax 01439 771223* *Open: ALL YEAR* *Map Ref No. 43*

rate £ from - to per person	children taken	evening meals	animals taken
£21.00 to £25.00	Y	Y	N

Laurel Farm. Brafferton

Scotland

Scotland

Scotland's culture & traditions, history & literature, languages & accents, its landscape & architecture, even its wildlife set it apart from the rest of Britain. Much of Scotland's history is concerned with the struggle to retain independence from England.

The Romans never conquered the Scottish tribes, but preferred to keep them at bay with Hadrian's Wall, stretching across the Border country from Tynemouth to the Solway Firth.

Time lends glamour to events, but from the massacre of Glencoe to the Highland Clearances, much of Scotland's fate has been a harsh one. Robert the Bruce did rout the English enemy at Bannockburn after scaling the heights of Edinburgh Castle to take the city, but in later years Mary, Queen of Scots was to spend much of her life imprisoned by her sister Elizabeth I of England. Bonnie Prince Charlie (Charles Edward Stuart) led the Jacobite rebellion which ended in defeat at Culloden.

These events are recorded in the folklore & songs of Scotland. The Border & Highland Gatherings & the Common Ridings are more than a chance to wear the Tartan, they are reminders of national pride.

Highland Games are held throughout the country where local & national champions compete in events like tossing the caber & in piping contests. There are sword dances & Highland flings, the speciality of young men & boys wearing the full dress tartan of their clan.

Scotland's landscape is rich in variety from the lush green lowlands to the handsome splendour of the mountainous Highlands, from the rounded hills of the Borders to the far-flung islands of the Hebrides, Orkney & Shetland where the sea is ever-present. There are glens & beautiful lochs deep in the mountains, a spectacular coastline of high cliffs & white sandy beaches, expanses of purple heather moorland where the sparkling water in the burns runs brown with peat, & huge skies bright with cloud & gorgeous sunsets.

Argyll & The Islands

This area has ocean & sea lochs, forests & mountains, 3000 miles of coastline, about 30 inhabited islands, the warming influence of the Gulf Stream & the tallest tree in Britain (in Strone Gardens, near Loch Fyne).

Sites both historic & prehistoric are to be found in plenty. There is a hilltop fort at Dunadd, near Crinan with curious cup-&-ring carvings, & numerous ancient sites surround Kilmartin, from burial cairns to grave slabs.

Kilchurn Castle is a magnificent ruin in contrast to the opulence of Inveraray. Both are associated with the once-powerful Clan Campbell. There are remains of fortresses built by the Lords of the Isles, the proud chieftains who ruled the west after driving out the Norse invaders in the 12th century.

Oban is a small harbour town accessible by road & rail & the point of departure for many of the islands including Mull.

Tobermory. Isle of Mull.

Scotland

Mull is a peaceful island with rugged seascapes, lovely walks & villages, a miniature railway & the famous Mull Little Theatre. It is a short hop from here to the tiny island of Iona & St. Columba's Abbey, cradle of Christianity in Scotland.

Coll & Tiree have lovely beaches & fields of waving barley. The grain grown here was once supplied to the Lords of the Isles but today most goes to Islay & into the whisky. Tiree has superb windsurfing.

Jura is a wilder island famous for its red deer. The Isles of Colonsay & Oronsay are joined at low water.

Gigha, 'God's Isle', is a fertile area of gardens with rare & semitropical plants.The Island of Staffa has Fingal's Cave.

The Borders, Dumfries & Galloway

The borderland with England is a landscape of subtle colours & contours from the round foothills of the Cheviots, purple with heather, to the dark green valley of the Tweed.

The Lammermuir Hills sweep eastwards to a coastline of small harbours & the spectacular cliffs at St. Abbs Head where colonies of seabirds thrive.

The Border towns, set in fine countryside, have distinctive personalities. Hawick, Galashiels, Selkirk & Melrose all played their parts in the various Border skirmishes of this historically turbulent region & then prospered with a textile industry which survives today. They celebrate their traditions in the Common Riding ceremonies.

The years of destructive border warfare have left towers & castles throughout the country. Roxburgh was once a Royal castle & James II was killed here during a seige. Now there are only the shattered remains of the massive stone walls. Hermitage Castle is set amid wild scenery near Hawick & impressive Floors Castle stands above Kelso.

At Jedburgh the Augustine abbey is remarkably complete, & a visitors centre here tells the story of the four great Border Abbeys; Jedburgh itself, Kelso, Dryburgh & Melrose.

The lovely estate of Abbotsford where Sir Walter Scott lived & worked is near Melrose. A prolific poet & novelist, his most famous works are the Waverley novels written around 1800. His house holds many of his possessions, including a collection of armour. Scott's View is one of the best vantage points in the borderlands with a prospect of the silvery Tweed & the three distinctive summits of the Eildon Hills.

Eildon Hills.

There are many gracious stately homes. Manderston is a classical house of great luxury, & Mellerstain is the work of the Adam family. Traquair was originally a Royal hunting lodge. Its main gates were locked in 1745 after a visit from Bonnie Prince Charlie, never to be opened until a Stuart King takes the throne.

Dumfries & Galloway to the southwest is an area of rolling hills with a fine coastline.

Plants flourish in the mild air here & there are palm trees at Ardwell House & the Logan Botanic Garden.

Scotland

The gardens at Castle Kennedy have rhododendrons, azaleas & magnolias & Threave Gardens near Castle Douglas are the National Trust for Scotland's School of gardening.

The Galloway Forest Park covers a vast area of lochs & hills & has views across to offshore Ailsa Craig. At Caerlaveroch Castle, an early Renaissance building near the coast of Dumfries, there is a national nature reserve.

The first church in Scotland was built by St. Ninian at Whithorn in 400 on a site now occupied by the 13th century priory. The spread of Christianity is marked by early memorial stones like the Latinus stone at Whithorn, & the abbeys of Dundrennan, Crossraguel, Glenluce & Sweetheart, named after its founder who carried her husband's heart in a casket & is buried with it in the abbey.

At Dumfries is the poet Burns' house, his mausoleum & the Burns Heritage Centre overlooking the River Nith.

In Upper Nithsdale the Mennock Pass leads to Wanlockhead & Leadhills, once centres of the lead-mining industry. There is a fascinating museum here & the opportunity of an underground trip.

Lowland

The Frith of Clyde & Glascow in the west, & the Firth of Forth with Edinburgh in the east are both areas of rich history, tradition & culture.

Edinburgh is the capital of Scotland & amongst the most visually exciting cities in the world. The New Town is a treasure trove of inspired neo-classical architecture, & below Edinburgh Castle high on the Rock, is the Old Town, a network of courts, closes, wynds & gaunt tenements around the Royal Mile.

The Palace of Holyrood House, home of Mary, Queen of Scots for several years overlooks Holyrood Park & nearby Arthur's Seat, is a popular landmark.

The City's varied art galleries include The Royal Scottish Academy, The National Gallery, Portrait Gallery, Gallery of Modern Art & many other civic & private collections.

The Royal Museum of Scotland displays superb historical & scientific material. The Royal Botanic Gardens are world famous.

Cultural life in Edinburgh peaks at Festival time in August. The official Festival, the Fringe, the Book Festival, Jazz Festival & Film Festival bring together artistes of international reputation.

The gentle hills around the city offer many opportunities for walking. The Pentland Hills are easily reached, with the Lammermuir Hills a little further south. There are fine beaches at Gullane, Yellowcraigs, North Berwick & at Dunbar.

Inverary Castle.

Tantallon Castle, a 14th century stronghold, stands on the rocky Firth of Forth, & 17th century Hopetoun House, on the outskirts of the city is only one of a number of great houses in the area.

North of Edinburgh across the Firth of Forth lies the ancient Kingdom of Fife. Here is St. Andrews, a pleasant town on the seafront, an old university

Scotland

town & Scotland's ecclesiastical capital, but famous primarily for golf.

Glasgow is the industrial & business capital of Scotland. John Betjeman called it the 'finest Victorian city in Britain' & many buildings are remarkable examples of Victorian splendour, notably the City Chambers.

Many buildings are associated with the architect Charles Rennie MacKintosh; the Glasgow School of Art is one of them. Glasgow Cathedral is a perfect example of pre-Reformation Gothic architecture.

Glasgow is Scotland's largest city with the greatest number of parks & fine Botanic Garden. It is home to both the Scottish Opera & the Scottish Ballet, & has a strong & diverse cultural tradition from theatre to jazz. Its museums include the matchless Burrell Collection, & the Kelvingrove Museum & Art Gallery, which houses one of the best civic collections of paintings in Britain, as well as reflecting the city's engineering & shipbuilding heritage.

The coastal waters of the Clyde are world famous for cruising & sailing, with many harbours & marinas. The long coastline offers many opportunities for sea-angling from Largs to Troon & Prestwick, & right around to Luce Bay on the Solway.

There are many places for birdwatching on the Estuary, whilst the Clyde Valley is famous for its garden centres & nurseries.

Paisley has a mediaeval abbey, an observatory & a museum with a fine display of the famous 'Paisley' pattern shawls.

Further south, Ayr is a large seaside resort with sandy beach, safe bathing & a racecourse. In the Ayrshire valleys there is traditional weaving & lace & bonnet making, & Sorn, in the rolling countryside boasts its 'Best Kept Village' award.

Culzean Castle is one of the finest Adam houses in Scotland & stands in spacious grounds on the Ayrshire cliffs.

Robert Burns is Scotland's best loved poet, & 'Burns night' is widely celebrated. The region of Strathclyde shares with Dumfries & Galloway the title of 'Burns Country' . The son of a peasant farmer, Burns lived in poverty for much of his life. The simple house where he was born is in the village of Alloway. In the town of Ayr is the Auld Kirk where he was baptised & the footbridge of 'The Brigs of Ayr' is still in use. The Tam O'Shanter Inn is now a Burns museum & retains its thatched roof & simple fittings. The Burns Trail leads on to Mauchline where Possie Nansie's Inn remains. At Tarbolton the National Trust now care for the old house where Burns founded the 'Batchelors Club' debating society.

Perthshire, Loch Lomond & The Trossachs

By a happy accident of geology, the Highland Boundary fault which separates the Highlands from the Lowlands runs through Loch Lomond, close to the Trossachs & on through Perthshire, giving rise to marvellous scenery.

In former times Highlanders & Lowlanders raided & fought here. Great castles like Stirling, Huntingtower & Doune were built to protect the routes between the two different cultures.

Stirling was once the seat of Scotland's monarchs & the great Royal castle is set high on a basalt rock. The Guildhall & the Kirk of the Holy Rude are also interesting buildings in the town, with Cambuskenneth Abbey & the Bannockburn Heritage Centre close by.

Perth 'fair city' on the River Tay,

Scotland

has excellent shops & its own repertory theatre. Close by are the Black Watch Museum at Balhousie Castle, & the Branklyn Gardens, which are superb in May & June.

Scone Palace, to the north of Perth was home to the Stone or Scone of Destiny for nearly 500 years until its removal to Westminster. 40 kings of Scotland were crowned here.

Pitlochry sits amid beautiful Highland scenery with forest & hill walks, two nearby distilleries, the famous Festival theatre, Loch Faskally & the Dam Visitor Centre & Fish Ladder.

In the Pass of Killiecrankie, a short drive away, a simple stone marks the spot where the Highlanders charged barefoot to overwhelm the redcoat soldiers of General MacKay.

Queens View.

Famous Queen's View overlooks Loch Tummel beyond Pitlochry with the graceful peak of Schiehallion completing a perfect picture.

Other lochs are picturesque too; Loch Earn, Loch Katrine & bonnie Loch Lomond itself, & they can be enjoyed from a boat on the water. Ospreys nest at the Loch of the Lowes near Dunkeld.

Mountain trails lead through Ben Lawers & the 'Arrocher Alps' beyond Loch Lomond. The Ochils & the Campsie Fells have grassy slopes for walking. Near Callander are the Bracklinn Falls, the Callander Crags & the Falls of Leny.

Wooded areas include the Queen Elizabeth Forest Park & the Black Wood of Rannoch which is a fragment of an ancient Caledonian forest. There are some very tall old trees around Killiecrankie, & the world's tallest beech hedge - 26 metres high - grows at Meikleour near Blairgowrie.

Creiff & Blairgowrie have excellent golf courses set in magnificent scenery.

The Grampians, Highlands & Islands

This is spacious countryside with glacier-scarred mountains & deep glens cut through by tumbling rivers. The Grampian Highlands make for fine mountaineering & walking.

There is excellent skiing at Glenshee, & a centre at the Lecht for the less experienced, whilst the broad tops of the giant mountains are ideal for cross-country skiing. The chair-lift at Glenshee is worth a visit at any season.

The Dee, The Spey & The Don flow down to the coastal plain from the heights. Some of the world's finest trout & salmon beats are on these rivers.

Speyside is dotted with famous distilleries from Grantown-on-Spey to Aberdeen, & the unique Malt Whisky Trail can be followed.

Royal Deeside & Donside hold a number of notable castles. Balmoral is the present Royal family's holiday home, & Kildrummy is a romantic ruin in a lovely garden. Fyvie Castle has five dramatic towers & stands in peaceful parkland. Nearby Haddo House, by contrast, is an elegant Georgian home.

There is a 17th century castle at Braemar, but more famous here is the Royal Highland Gathering. There are wonderful walks in the vicinity -

Scotland

Morrone Hill, Glen Quoich & the Linn O'Dee are just a few.

The city of Aberdeen is famed for its sparkling granite buildings, its university, its harbour & fish market & for North Sea Oil. It also has long sandy beaches & lovely year-round flower displays, of roses in particular.

Around the coast are fishing towns & villages. Crovie & Pennan sit below impressive cliffs. Buckie is a typical small port along the picturesque coastline of the Moray Firth.

The Auld Kirk at Cullen has fine architectural features & elegant Elgin has beautiful cathedral ruins. Pluscarden Abbey, Spynie Palace & Duffus Castle are all nearby.

Dunnottar Castle.

Nairn has a long stretch of sandy beach & a golf course with an international reputation. Inland are Cawdor Castle & Culloden Battlefield.

The Northern Highlands are divided from the rest of Scotland by the dramatic valley of the Great Glen. From Fort William to Inverness, sea lochs, canals & the depths of Loch Ness form a chain of waterways linking both coasts.

Here are some of the wildest & most beautiful landscapes in Britain. Far Western Knoydart, the Glens of Cannich & Affric, the mysterious lochs, including Loch Morar, deeper than the North Sea, & the marvellous coastline; all are exceptional.

The glens were once the home of crofting communities, & of the clansmen who supported the Jacobite cause. The wild scenery of Glencoe is a favourite with walkers & climbers, but it has a tragic history. Its name means 'the glen of weeping' & refers to the massacre of the MacDonald clan in 1692, when the Royal troops who had been received as guests treacherously attacked their hosts at dawn.

The valleys are empty today largely as a result of the infamous Highland Clearances in the 19th century when the landowners turned the tenant crofters off the land in order to introduce the more profitable Cheviot sheep. The emigration of many Scots to the U.S.A. & the British Colonies resulted from these events.

South of Inverness lie the majestic Cairngorms. The Aviemore centre provides both summer & winter sports facilities here.

To the north of Loch Ness are the remains of the ancient Caledonian forest where red deer & stags are a common sight on the hills. Rarer are sightings of the Peregrine Falcon, the osprey, the Golden Eagle & the Scottish wildcat. Kincraig has excellent wildlife parks.

Inverness is the last large town in the north, & a natural gateway to the Highlands & to Moray, the Black Isle & the north-east.

The east coast is characterised by the Firths of Moray, Cromarty & Dornoch & by its changing scenery from gentle pastureland, wooded hillsides to sweeping coastal cliffs.

On the Black Isle, which is not a true island but has a causeway & bridge links with the mainland, Fortrose & Rosemarkie in particular have lovely beaches, caves & coastal walks. There is golf on the headland at Rosemarkie & a 13th century cathedral of rosy pink sandstone stands in Fortrose.

Hazlehurst Lodge

Nearest Road: A.93

Hazlehurst, once the coachman's lodge to Aboyne Castle, is set in a wooded old-world garden. Now, the interior is an expression of the best of Scottish design & art. Scottish music, also from traditional roots is played. Art from the Strachan's own collection with sculptures & works of invited artists are shown throughout the 5 attractive en-suite bedrooms. Anne is an outstanding chef, serving seriously good food, best wines & unusual whiskies at friendly prices.

E-mail: as@scotlandbedandbreakfast.co.uk

Anne & Eddie Strachan *Hazlehurst Lodge* *Ballater Road* *Aboyne AB34 5HY* *Aberdeenshire*
Tel: (013398) 86921 *Fax 013398 86660* *Open: ALL YEAR* *Map Ref No. 00*

rate £ from - to per person	children taken	evening meals	animals taken
£27.00 to £40.00	Y	Y	Y

VISA: M'CARD: AMEX:

Lys-Na-Greyne House

Nearest Road: A.93

Lys-Na-Greyne is a beautiful Edwardian mansion situated in idyllic surroundings on the banks of the River Dee on the outskirts of Aboyne in Royal Deeside, set in grounds of 3 acres. This is a perfect place for exploring the surrounding countryside where there are many castles & places of historic interest. Golf, riding, fishing, hillwalking & tennis available locally. Shooting, stalking available by arrangement. All rooms with en-suite/private bathroom & breathtaking views over the garden or river.

E-mail: dwhite7301@aol.com

David & Meg White *Lys-Na-Greyne House* *Rhu-Na-Haven Road* *Aboyne AB34 5JD* *Aberdeenshire*
Tel: (013398) 87397 *Fax 013398 86441* *Open: ALL YEAR* *Map Ref No. 00*

rate £ from - to per person	children taken	evening meals	animals taken
£27.00 to £40.00	Y	Y	Y

see PHOTO over p. 475

Lochside Cottage

Nearest Road: A.828

Total peace on the shore of Loch Baile Mhic Chailen, in an idyllic glen of outstanding beauty. There are many walks from the cottage garden; or, visit Fort William, Glencoe & Oban, from where you can board a steamer to explore the Western Isles. At the end of the day, a warm welcome awaits you at Lochside Cottage: delicious home-cooked dinner, a log fire & the certainty of a perfect night's sleep in one of 3 attractive en-suite bedrooms. An ideal spot for a relaxing break.

Earle & Stella Broadbent *Lochside Cottage* *Fasnacloich* *Appin PA38 4BJ* *Argyll*
Tel: (01631) 730216 *Fax 01631 730216* *Open: ALL YEAR* *Map Ref No. 01*

rate £ from - to per person	children taken	evening meals	animals taken
£22.00 to £30.00	Y	Y	Y

Allt-na-Craig

Nearest Road: A.83

The McKays warmly welcome all their guests to Allt-na-Craig, a lovely old Victorian mansion set in picturesque grounds overlooking Loch Fyne. Accommodation in 6 comfortable en-suite bedrooms with tea/coffee makers. A guests' lounge with open fire & dining room is also available. This is a perfect base for outdoor activities, like hill-walking, fishing, golf, riding & windsurfing, or for visiting the islands. Delicious evening meals are available by arrangement. A charming home.

Margaret McKay *Allt-na-Craig* *Tarbert Road* *Ardrishaig PA30 8EP* *Argyll*
Tel: (01546) 603245 *Open: ALL YEAR (Excl. Xmas & New Year)* *Map Ref No. 02*

rate £ from - to per person	children taken	evening meals	animals taken
£32.00 to £35.00	Y	Y	Y

Lys Na Greyne. Aboyne

rate £ from - to per person	children taken	evening meals	animals taken

Abbot's Brae Hotel

Nearest Road: A.815

Abbot's Brae is an award-winning family-run country house hotel, set in its own secluded woodland garden with breathtaking views of the sea & hills. Accommodation is in 7 spacious en-suite bedrooms including Four-poster, king-size double & twin rooms. All are well-equipped & attractively furnished throughout. The welcoming, homely atmosphere & appetising menus ensure a memorable stay. An ideal base for exploring Argyll & the Western Highlands. 1 hour from Glasgow Airport.
E-mail: enquiry@abbotsbrae.co.uk

Helen & Gavin Dick *Abbot's Brae Hotel* *West Bay* *Dunoon PA23 7QJ* *Argyll*
Tel: (01369) 705021 *Fax 01369 701191* *Open: ALL YEAR* *Map Ref No. 03*

£30.00 to £42.00	Y	Y	Y

see PHOTO over p. 477

VISA: M'CARD:

Ardsheal Home Farm

Nearest Road: A.828

A charming Scottish hill farm of 1,000 acres, surrounded by breathtaking scenery on the shores of Loch Linnhe, overlooking the Morvern Hills. A warm welcome is assured from the friendly hosts. 3 attractive bedrooms, comfortable & well-furnished, with tea/coffee-making facilities, electric blankets, etc. Seafood & other eating places nearby. Convenient for touring & sailing to the inner Isles. An idyllic holiday retreat, there is even 1 mile of private beach. Riding nearby. Single supplement.

Flavia J. MacArthur *Ardsheal Home Farm* *Kentallen* *Duror in Appin PA38 4BZ* *Argyll*
Tel: (01631) 740229 *Fax 01631 740229* *Open: APR - OCT* *Map Ref No. 04*

£18.00 to £19.00	Y	Y	N

The House of Keil

Nearest Road: A.828

A family home set on the shores of Loch Linnhie, with 1 mile of private foreshore. 2 bedrooms overlook the loch & have stunning views to the Morven hills. Pony trekking, boat hire/fishing & the historic & picturesque Castle Stalker are within 5 miles; Glencoe is within 10 miles. An old Stewart house with many unusual features, it is situated close to the burial ground, where James Stewart is reputed to be buried. An ideal base from which to explore the magnificent west coast scenery.
E-mail: houseofkeil@hotmail.com

Ronald W. Rice-Garwood *The House of Keil* *Duror of Appin PA38 4BW* *Argyll*
Tel: (01631) 740255 *Fax 01631 740365* *Open: ALL YEAR* *Map Ref No. 04*

£20.00 to £25.00	Y	Y	Y

VISA: M'CARD:

Kilmeny Country Guest House

Nearest Road: A.846

Islay is well-known for its abundant & wonderful wildlife & its many malt-whisky distilleries. Kilmeny Country Guest House, in the heart of a 300-acre beef farm, commands magnificent views of the surrounding hills & glen. This family-run business places emphasis on quality & personal service. The exquisite en-suite bedrooms, with country views, are elegantly furnished. The public rooms are charming, with a country-house influence. A 4-course dinner menu is available. Children over 5.
E-mail: info@kilmeny.co.uk

Mrs Margaret Rozga *Kilmeny Country Guest House* *Ballygrant* *Isle of Islay PA45 7QW* *Argyll*
Tel: (01496) 840668 *Fax 01496 840668* *Open: ALL YEAR* *Map Ref No. 05*

£36.00 to £36.00	Y	Y	Y

Abbot's Brae. Dunoon.

Scotland
Argyll & Ayrshire

	rate £ from - to per person	children taken	evening meals	animals taken
Red Bay Cottage	£16.50 to £16.50	Y	Y	Y
Ardsheal House	£45.00 to £45.00	Y	Y	Y
Thistle House	£23.50 to £27.00	Y	N	N
The Crescent	£25.00 to £35.00	Y	N	N

Red Bay Cottage

Nearest Road: A.849

A really warm welcome awaits the visitor to this charming modern house, offering 3 very comfortable rooms with modern facilities. Situated only 20 metres from the sea, & overlooking Iona Sound & the white sandy beaches on the Isle of Iona, this surely must be the ideal base for a relaxing & peaceful holiday. Mr Wagstaff offers superb food. Eleanor is a qualified, practising silversmith, so why not enjoy a winter break on their residential silversmithing course?

John & Eleanor Wagstaff Red Bay Cottage Deargphort Fionnphort Isle of Mull PA66 6BP Argyll
Tel: (01681) 700396 Open: ALL YEAR Map Ref No. 06

Ardsheal House

Nearest Road: A.828

Ardsheal House is spectacularly situated on the shores of Loch Linnhe, in 800 acres of woodlands, fields & gardens. It is a wonderful place for a relaxing holiday. This historic mansion is elegantly furnished throughout with family antiques & pictures, & offers 8 en-suite bedrooms which are attractive & well-appointed. The food at Ardsheal is excellent. It delights the eye & pleases the palate, & includes local fresh produce & home-made bread & preserves. A delightful home.
E-mail: info@ardsheal.co.uk

see PHOTO over p. 479

VISA: M'CARD: AMEX:

Neil & Philippa Sutherland Ardsheal House Kentallen of Appin PA38 4BX Argyll
Tel: (01631) 740227 Fax 01631 740342 Open: FEB - NOV Map Ref No. 04

Thistle House

Nearest Road: A.815

Superbly situated Victorian country house retaining many original features. Surrounded by 2 acres of mature garden, commanding spectacular views of Loch Fyne & sitting directly across the Loch from Inverary & its famous castle. Accommodation is in 4 en-suite bedrooms with tea/coffee-making facilities & colour T.V.. Lounge with open fire. Good eating place in village & other restaurants nearby for evening meals. The Cowal Peninsula is well located for exploring Argyll & the Loch Lomond area. 1 hr's drive from Glasgow Airport.

VISA: M'CARD:

Mrs Sandra Cameron Thistle House St. Catherines PA25 8AZ Argyll
Tel: (01499) 302209 Fax 01499 302531 Open: APR - OCT Map Ref No. 07

The Crescent

Nearest Road: B.7024

Elegant Victorian terraced house set in the heart of Ayr. All rooms are very comfortable & individually styled including 1 with 4-poster bed. Each of the bedrooms has a private bathroom. Within 5 minutes walk, guests can enjoy a leisurely stroll along the promenade or a relaxing drink in one of Ayr's cosy pubs. Ideal location for golf, Burns Heritage, Culzean Castle & the Galloway Forest. Children over 8 years welcome.
E-mail: carrie@26crescent.freeserve.co.uk

VISA: M'CARD:

Mrs Caroline McDonald The Crescent 26 Bellevue Crescent Ayr KA7 2DR Ayrshire
Tel: (01292) 287329 Fax 01292 286779 Open: FEB - NOV Map Ref No. 08

Ardsheal House. Kentallen of Appin.

	rate £ from - to per person	children taken	evening meals	animals taken
Brenalder Lodge	£25.00 to £30.00	Y	N	Y
Dunduff House	£22.00 to £35.00	N	N	N
Cosses Country House	£32.00 to £46.00	Y	Y	Y
Balkissock Lodge	£24.00 to £28.00	Y	Y	N

Brenalder Lodge

Nearest Road: A.719

A warm welcome is assured at Brenalder Lodge. Located on the coastal route yet only 2 miles from Ayr town centre & 1 1/2 miles from the A.77. Set in the heart of Burns country, a perfect base for Turnberry, Troon & Prestwick golf courses & nearby Culzean Castle. All rooms are en-suite with T.V. & tea/coffee makers. After a day touring, relax & unwind in the comfort of the spacious lounge & enjoy breakfast in the conservatory style dining room. An excellent location for a relaxing break. Children over 8 years welcome.

Helen Martin Brenalder Lodge 39 Dunure Road Doonfoot Ayr KA7 4HR Ayrshire
Tel: (01292) 443939 Open: ALL YEAR Map Ref No. 09

Dunduff House

Nearest Road: A.719

A warm friendly welcome awaits you at Dunduff House. Situated just south of Ayr at the coastal village of Dunure, this family-run beef & sheep unit of some 600 acres, is only 15 mins from the shore. Excellent accommodation, yet homely & comfortable. Bedrooms have panoramic coastal views over Arran, the Holy Isle, Mull of Kintyre & Ailsa Craig. Each is well-equipped an en-suite or private bathroom. Ideal for south-west Scotland, Culzean Castle, Robert Burns' Cottage & the Heritage Trail.
E-mail: gemmelldunduff@aol.com

VISA: M'CARD:

Mrs Agnes Gemmell Dunduff House Dunure Ayr KA7 4LH Ayrshire
Tel: (01292) 500225 Fax 01292 500222 Open: FEB - NOV Map Ref No. 10

Cosses Country House

Nearest Road: A.77

A former shooting lodge (1800s) & home farm (1900s), set in a secluded valley of garden & woodland. Superb accommodation, en-suite facilities, T.V., a hospitality tray & a roaring log fire on chilly evenings. The kitchen & herb garden supplement local produce for you to enjoy the 'Taste of Scotland' dinners. Many castles (incl. Culzean), gardens, Burns' birthplace, golf, fishing, walks & cycling within easy reach. Irish ferry terminals 30 mins' drive. Children over 6.
E-mail: cosses@compuserve.com

see PHOTO over p. 481

VISA: M'CARD:

Susan & Robin Crosthwaite Cosses Country House Ballantrae KA26 0LR Ayrshire
Tel: (01465) 831363 Fax 01465 831598 Open: MAR - OCT Map Ref No. 11

Balkissock Lodge

Nearest Road: A.77

Janet offers bed & breakfast in her lovely Georgian home, quietly situated amid superb countryside. Comfortable beds, full en-suite facilities & a choice of delicious breakfasts. Peace & quiet combine to make a stay at the lodge memorable. Balkissock Lodge is ideally situated for touring Burns country, Culzean Castle & the Irish ferries. There are numerous golf courses within easy reach. An ideal base for a relaxing break.
E-mail: bookings@greenarrow.demon.co.uk

VISA: M'CARD:

Janet Beale Balkissock Lodge Balkissock by Ballantrae Girvan KA26 0LP Ayrshire
Tel: (01465) 831588 Fax 01465 831537 Open: ALL YEAR Map Ref No. 11

Cosses. Ballantrae.

Scotland

Ayrshire, Berwickshire, Clackmannanshire

rate £ from - to per person | children taken | evening meals | animals taken

Hawkhill Farm

Nearest Road: A.77

Hawkhill Farm offers superior farmhouse hospitality in a spacious 17th-century former coaching inn, where the emphasis is on comfort & good food. 2 delightfully furnished bedrooms with en-suite/private facilities, T.V., etc. Relax in the warm atmosphere of the Adam inspired lounge. Hawkhill Farm is in a peaceful setting, & is perfect for exploring south-west Scotland, Culzean Castle, the Robert Burns Centre, golf, pony-trekking, walking, cycling (hire one here) & gardens. Brochure available.

E-mail: hawkhill@infinnet.co.uk

Mrs Isobel Kyle   Hawkhill Farm   Old Daily   Girvan KA26 9RD   Ayrshire
Tel: (01465) 871232   Open: MAR - OCT   Map Ref No. 12

rate £ from - to per person	children taken	evening meals	animals taken
£20.00 to £26.00	Y	N	Y

Nether Underwood Country House

Nearest Road: A.77

Nether Underwood is a delightful country house set in 15 acres of garden, fields & woodland. Tucked into Ayrshire's rolling farmland, it promises superb accommodation & wonderful food. All bedrooms have en-suite or private bathrooms, T.V. & early morning tea. A log fire in the drawing room, where afternoon tea & pre-dinner drinks can be enjoyed. Very well placed for golf courses, Burn's birthplace & Glasgow's museums, galleries, & first-class shopping & eating places. Children over 16.

E-mail: netherund@aol.com

Felicity Thomson   Nether Underwood Country House   By Symington   Kilmarnock KA1 5NG   Ayrshire
Tel: (01563) 830666   Fax 01563 830777   Open: ALL YEAR   Map Ref No. 13

rate £ from - to per person	children taken	evening meals	animals taken
£40.00 to £50.00	N	Y	N

see PHOTO over p. 483

VISA: M'CARD:

Kirkside House

Nearest Road: A.1

Kirkside House is an early-Victorian former manse, situated in a peaceful rural location. The spacious & attractively decorated bedrooms have lovely views to the hills & are well-equipped. Guests are welcome to relax in the charming walled garden with its herbaceous borders, old roses & ornamental pond. Kirkside House is ideally located for exploring the Borders area, & wonderful hill & coastal walks. Edinburgh is approx. 1 hr. Children over 12 years welcome. A charming home.

Martin & Libby Taylor   Kirkside House   Bonkyl   Duns TD11 3RJ   Berwickshire
Tel: (01361) 884340   Fax 01361 884340   Open: APR - OCT   Map Ref No. 14

rate £ from - to per person	children taken	evening meals	animals taken
£23.00 to £25.00	Y	Y	N

Westbourne House B & B

Nearest Road: A.91

A Victorian mill-owner's mansion set in wooded grounds beneath Ochil Hills, in excellent walking country with numerous golf courses. Warm, friendly atmosphere, delicious home-cooking including vegetarian dishes. Log fires, croquet lawn, T.V., radio & tea/coffee-making facilities in all rooms (en-suite is on the ground floor). Centrally situated for Edinburgh, Glasgow, Perth & Stirling, home of 'Braveheart'. Secure off-street parking.

E-mail: odellwestbourne@compuserve.com

Mrs O'Dell   Westbourne House B & B   10 Dollar Rd   Tillicoultry   Stirling FK13 6PA   Clackmannanshire
Tel: (01259) 750314   Fax 01259 750642   Open: ALL YEAR   Map Ref No. 15

rate £ from - to per person	children taken	evening meals	animals taken
£21.00 to £26.00	Y	N	Y

Nether Underwood. By Symington.

Cavens House. Kirkbean-by-Dumfries.

rate £ from - to per person	children taken	evening meals	animals taken

Cavens Country House Hotel

£30.00 to £40.00	Y	Y	Y

see PHOTO over p. 484

VISA: M'CARD:

Nearest Road: A.710

Formerly an old mansion with a strong American historical connection, Cavens, now a charming small country house hotel, offers 8 comfortable en-suite bedrooms. 2 lounges with open fires add to the ambience of the house. Standing in 11 acres of gardens & woodland, it is ideal for those wishing to explore the joys of the Solway Coast, with its beautiful scenery & beaches. Sailing, walking, golfing, shooting, fishing & riding by arrangement. Animals by arrangement. Excellent cuisine.

E-mail: enquiries@cavens.com

Angus & Jane Fordyce Cavens Country House Hotel Kirkbean Dumfries DG2 8AA Dumfriesshire
Tel: (01387) 880234 Fax 01387 880467 Open: ALL YEAR Map Ref No. 16

Applegarth House

£32.00 to £37.00	Y	Y	Y

VISA: M'CARD:

Nearest Road: A.74 (M.)

Applegarth House is a delightful former manse in a peaceful situation overlooking the River Annan, yet only 3 miles from Lockerbie & Jt. 17 on the M.74. A perfect centre from which to explore the beautiful Border country, or an ideal overnight stop. Shooting, fishing & wildfowling can be arranged locally. Jane is an excellent cook, & you are assured a warm welcome in their relaxed home with its sunny & spacious rooms. Children over 10. 'Phone for directions. Animals by arrangement.

E-mail: frank@applegarthtown.demon.co.uk

Mrs Jane Pearson Applegarth House Lockerbie DG11 1SX Dumfriesshire
Tel: (01387) 810270 Fax 01387 811701 Open: ALL YEAR Map Ref No. 17

Hartfell House

£23.00 to £25.00	Y	Y	Y

Nearest Road: A.701

Hartfell House is a splendid Victorian manor house located in a rural setting overlooking the hills, yet only a few mins' walk from the town. A listed building known locally for its fine interior woodwork. Accommodation is in 8 spacious & tastefully furnished bedrooms, 7 with en-suite facilities. Standing in landscaped gardens of approximately 2 acres of lawns & trees, & providing an atmosphere of peaceful relaxation.

E-mail: robert.white@virgin.net

Margaret White Hartfell House Hartfell Crescent Moffat DG10 9AL Dumfriesshire
Tel: (01683) 220153 Open: ALL YEAR (Excl. Xmas & New Year) Map Ref No. 18

Kirkton House

£30.50 to £45.00	Y	Y	Y

see PHOTO over p. 486

VISA: M'CARD: AMEX:

Nearest Road: A.814

Experience a blend of "olde worlde" charm, modern amenities & superb views at this converted 18/19th-century farmhouse, set in a tranquil location & yet handy for Glasgow Airport (20/25 mins'), Loch Lomond, The Trossachs & most West Highland routes. En-suite bedrooms. A roaring fire on chilly evenings. Enjoy home-cooked food & good wine at dinner by oil lamplight. The dining room has original stone walls & a fireplace, with the old swee from which the cooking pots were hung.

E-mail: bbiw@kirktonhouse.co.uk

Stewart H. Macdonald Kirkton House Darleith Road Cardross Dumbarton G82 5EZ Dunbartonshire
Tel: (01389) 841951 Fax (01389) 841868 Open: FEB - NOV Map Ref No. 20

Kirkton House. Cardross.

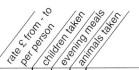

rate £ from - to per person	children taken	evening meals	animals taken	
£23.00 to £27.00	Y	N	N	**Arisaig**
£30.00 to £45.00	N	N	N	**Sandeman House**
£30.00 to £40.00 VISA: M'CARD:	Y	N	N	**Ashgrove House**
£35.00 to £40.00 VISA: M'CARD:	Y	N	Y	**The Avenue Hotel**

Arisaig

Nearest Road: M.8, M.9, A.720

A warm Scottish welcome awaits you here at this luxury detached bungalow, situated only 3 miles from the city centre. Accommodation is in 2 beautiful bedrooms, all with modern amenities, & all kept to a very high standard. Tea/coffee-making & en-suite facilities available. Parking. Excellent bus service. An ideal base from which to explore Edinburgh. Children over 12 years welcome. Brochure available on request.

E-mail: helen_baird@hotmail.com

Helen Baird Arisaig 64 Glasgow Road Corstorphine EH12 8LN Edinburgh
Tel: (0131) 3342610 Fax 0131 3341800 Open: APR - OCT Map Ref No. 19

Sandeman House

Nearest Road: A.702

Built in 1860, Sandeman House is a charming family home which has been sympathetically restored by Neil & Joyce Sandeman. The 3 bedrooms are individually furnished & are bright & tastefully decorated to a very high standard. Each has an en-suite/private bathroom, T.V., tea/coffee-making facilities, hairdryer etc. A full traditional Scottish breakfast is served including home-made preserves. Shops, bars & restaurants close by. Within easy reach of most of the city's attractions.

E-mail: joycesandeman@freezone.co.uk

Joyce Sandeman Sandeman House 33 Colinton Road Edinburgh EH10 5DR Edinburgh
Tel: (0131) 4478080 Fax 0131 4478080 Open: ALL YEAR Map Ref No. 19

Ashgrove House

Nearest Road: A.8

Heather & Magid warmly invite you to their recently refurbished Victorian guest house. Most of the comfortable bedrooms are en-suite. Ashgrove House is only 1 mile from the heart of Edinburgh. There is a car park, & it is conveniently situated on the A.8 near Murrayfield & the Edinburgh International Conference Centre. An ideal base for exploring historic Edinburgh & its many attractions & the surrounding countryside.

E-mail: info@theashgrovehouse.com

Mr & Mrs M. El-Ghamri Ashgrove House 12 Osborne Terrace Edinburgh EH12 5HG Edinburgh
Tel: (0131) 3375014 Fax 0131 3135043 Open: ALL YEAR Map Ref No. 19

The Avenue Hotel

Nearest Road: A.8

The Avenue Hotel is a Victorian terraced villa situated in a quiet tree-lined avenue, west of & only minutes from the city centre. It is ideal for both the business traveller & the tourist, with easy access to the airport, city bypass & motorway links to the north & west of Scotland. Fully refurbished it offers tasteful accommodation in 9 en-suite rooms. Each of the rooms has T.V., radio, 'phone & hospitality tray. Ample free parking. Adrian & Jackie Hayes look forward to welcoming you.

E-mail: avenue.hotel@virgin.net

Adrian & Jackie Hayes The Avenue Hotel 4 Murrayfield Avenue Edinburgh EH12 6AX Edinburgh
Tel: (0131) 3467270 Fax 0131 3379733 Open: ALL YEAR Map Ref No. 19

Kingsburgh House. Edinburgh.

rate £ from - to per person	children taken	evening meals	animals taken
£40.00 to £70.00	Y	N	N

see PHOTO over p. 488

VISA: M'CARD:

Kingsburgh House

Nearest Road: A.8

Kingsburgh House is a detached Victorian villa situated in Murrayfield, one of Edinburgh's most desirable areas. This is a charming guest house 1 1/2 miles from Edinburgh's city centre. If you enjoy comfort in delightful surroundings make this your base from which to explore Edinburghs' many attractions. Bedrooms are all en-suite with T.V. & hospitality tray. Start your day with a delicious breakfast served from the extensive menu. Children over 10 years welcome.

E-mail: brian@THEKINGSBURGH.COM

Brian & Fiona Femister Kingsburgh House 2 Corstorphine Road Murrayfield Edinburgh EH12 6HN
Tel: (0131) 3131679 Fax 0131 3460554 Open: ALL YEAR Map Ref No. 19

rate £ from - to per person	children taken	evening meals	animals taken
£25.00 to £35.00	Y	N	N

VISA: M'CARD:

Tudorbank Lodge

Nearest Road: A.8

An enchanting Tudor-style house (Historic Scotland listed building) set in private gardens with parking. Come & enjoy the warmth of Scottish hospitality. Superb breakfasts are freshly cooked to order with an ample choice for vegetarians. Colour T.V., tea/coffee-making facilities, washbasins in all bedrooms, some are en-suite. Ideal for touring, business, golf & especially the Festival, Fringe & Tattoo. Easy access to city centre, zoo, Murrayfield, airport & motorways.

E-mail: tudorbank@cwcom.net

William Clark Tudorbank Lodge 18 St. John's Road Corstorphine Edinburgh EH12 6NY
Tel: (0131) 3347845 Fax 0131 3345386 Open: ALL YEAR Map Ref No. 19

rate £ from - to per person	children taken	evening meals	animals taken
£25.00 to £35.00	Y	N	Y

VISA: M'CARD:

Cairn Lodge Guest House

Nearest Road: A.8

Cairn Lodge is an elegant Victorian house, conveniently situated for Murrayfield, the airport, motorways & the city. A warm, friendly Scottish welcome awaits you in this charming house, which has been lovingly restored. Excellent bedrooms with marble fireplaces & original cornices, en-suite facilities, colour T.V. & hospitality trays in all rooms. Superb breakfasts. Private parking & an excellent bus service. An ideal base for exploring Edinburgh.

E-mail: janice@cairnlodge.demon.co.uk

Mrs J. Cairns-Winson Cairn Lodge Guest House 2 Downie Terrace Murrayfield Edinburgh EH12 7AU
Tel: (0131) 5392117 Fax 0131 5398117 Open: ALL YEAR Map Ref No. 19

rate £ from - to per person	children taken	evening meals	animals taken
£20.00 to £ 30.00	Y	N	N

VISA: M'CARD:

Camus Guest House

Nearest Road: A.1

A Victorian, terraced villa overlooking the Firth of Forth, Camus House enjoys the peace of the seaside, along with an excellent bus service to the city centre, with its cultural, historical and leisure interests. The 5 guest rooms are attractive & comfortably furnished, and have wash basins, colour T.V., radio alarms & tea/coffee-making facilities. Four of the bedrooms are en-suite. A genuine and friendly welcome is assured at Camus House.

E-mail: rowan@camus.ndo.co.uk

Debbie Rowan Camus Guest House 4 Seaview Terrace Joppa Edinburgh EH15 2HD Edinburgh
Tel: (0131) 6572003 Fax 0131 6572003 Open: ALL YEAR Map Ref No. 19

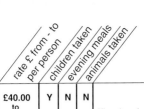

Kildonan Lodge Hotel. Edinburgh.

Scotland
Edinburgh

rate £ from - to per person	children taken	evening meals	animals taken
£32.00 to £49.00	Y	Y	N

VISA: M'CARD:

Salisbury View Hotel

Nearest Road: A.7

Small Georgian hotel situated within an historic conservation area opposite Holyrood Park & the Commonwealth swimming pool with easy access to the Royal Mile & Princes Street. The building has retained many original features while being tastefully prepared for the 21st century. There are 8 elegantly furnished en-suite bedrooms with all facilities. The hotel boasts a highly acclaimed restaurant & award-winning chef. The charming lounge is the perfect spot for pre-dinner drinks.

E-mail: enquiries@salisburyviewhotel.co.uk

Robert & Alex Pelling Salisbury View Hotel 64 Dalkeith Road Edinburgh EH16 5AE Edinburgh
Tel: (0131) 6671133 Fax 0131 6671133 Open: ALL YEAR (Excl. Xmas) Map Ref No. 19

rate £ from - to per person	children taken	evening meals	animals taken
£26.00 to £30.00	Y	N	N

VISA: M'CARD:

Kenvie Guest House

Nearest Road: A.7, A.68, A.1

Kenvie Guest House is charming, comfortable, warm, friendly & inviting. This small Victorian town house is situated in a quiet residential street, 1 small block from the main road, leading to the city centre (an excellent bus service) & the bypass to all routes. Offering, for your comfort, lots of caring touches, including complimentary tea/coffee, colour T.V. & no-smoking rooms. Private facilities available. A warm welcome awaits you..

E-mail: dorothy@kenvie.co.uk

Mrs Dorothy Vidler Kenvie Guest House 16 Kilmaurs Road Edinburgh EH16 5DA Edinburgh
Tel: (0131) 6681964 Fax 0131 6681926 Open: ALL YEAR Map Ref No.19

rate £ from - to per person	children taken	evening meals	animals taken
£35.00 to £49.00	Y	N	N

see PHOTO over p. 490

VISA: M'CARD: AMEX:

Kildonan Lodge Hotel

Nearest Road: A.701

Ideally situated in central Edinburgh, Kildonan Lodge is an outstanding example of Victorian elegance providing the perfect setting for your visit to Scotland's capital. Relax & enjoy a 'dram' at the Honesty bar. Each of the well-appointed non-smoking en-suite bedrooms have colour T.V., 'phone, radio/alarm & welcome trays. Spa bath & 4-poster beds available in selected rooms. Car park. Delicious wholesome Scottish breakfasts are served. A warm friendly welcome awaits you.

E-mail: kildonanlodge@compuserve.com

Maggie Urquhart Kildonan Lodge Hotel 27 Craigmillar Park Edinburgh EH16 5PE Edinburgh
Tel: (0131) 6672793 Fax 0131 6679777 Open: ALL YEAR Map Ref No. 19

rate £ from - to per person	children taken	evening meals	animals taken
£18.00 to £35.00	Y	N	N

Kingsley Guest House

Nearest Road: A.701

A warm, friendly welcome awaits you at this Victorian terraced villa. Offering 5 comfortably furnished bedrooms, each with either en-suite or private facilities, T.V. & tea/coffee-making facilities. A full English or Continental breakfast is served. Kingsley Guest House is conveniently situated in the south of the city with an excellent bus service at the door to & from the city centre with its many tourist attractions. Private parking.

E-mail: lynredmayne@kingsleyguesthouse.co.uk

Lyn Redmayne Kingsley Guest House 30 Craigmillar Park Newington Edinburgh EH16 5PS
Tel: (0131) 6673177 Tel/Fax 0131 6678439 Open: ALL YEAR Map Ref No. 19

Southdown Guest House.   Edinburgh.

rate £ from - to per person	children taken	evening meals	animals taken
£18.00 to £40.00	Y	N	N

see PHOTO over p. 492

VISA: M'CARD:

Southdown Guest House

Nearest Road: A.701

Good value accommodation is offered at this friendly guest house which is situated on the south side of Edinburgh. John & Muriel are welcoming hosts who enjoy caring for their guests. There is a comfortable lounge with books & board games in which guests may choose to relax after a day's sight-seeing. A hearty Scottish breakfast is served. There are 6 comfortable bedrooms, each with T.V. & tea/coffee-making facilities. Car parking. An ideal spot from which to explore historic Edinburgh.

E-mail: haml20@aol.com

John & Muriel Hamilton   Southdown Guest House   20 Craigmillar Park   Edinburgh EH16 5PS
Tel: (0131) 6672410   Fax 0131 6676056   Open: FEB - NOV (& New Year)   Map Ref No. 19

rate £ from - to per person	children taken	evening meals	animals taken
£18.00 to £36.00	Y	N	N

Tiree Guest House

Nearest Road: A.701

Situated on the south side of Edinburgh, about 1 1/2 miles from the city centre. Offering accommodation in 6 pleasantly furnished comfortable bedrooms, all with en-suite facilities. All rooms have colour T.V. & tea/coffee makers. Tiree Guest House is conveniently located for Edinburgh University, Holyrood Palace & the shopping centre. Children are very welcome here, & are given reduced rates. (Min. age 6 years.) A delicious full Scottish breakfast is served.

Norah Alexander   Tiree Guest House   26 Craigmillar Park   Edinburgh EH16 5PS   Edinburgh
Tel: (0131) 667 7477   Fax 0131 662 1608   Open: ALL YEAR   Map Ref No. 19

rate £ from - to per person	children taken	evening meals	animals taken
£25.00 to £45.00	Y	N	N

VISA: M'CARD: AMEX:

Frederick House Hotel

Nearest Road: A.7

Frederick House Hotel is perfectly situated in the very heart of Edinburgh's city centre, a stones' throw from Princes Street. All of the 44 newly refurbished & tastefully decorated bedrooms feature en-suite bathrooms (with bath & shower); breakfast is served in your room. Your hosts' aim is to make your stay as comfortable & relaxing as possible, with all modern conveniences combined together with an 'olde worlde' atmosphere.

E-mail: frederickhouse@ednet.co.uk

Emily Walton   Frederick House Hotel   42 Frederick Street   Edinburgh EH2 1EX   Edinburgh
Tel: (0131) 2261999   Fax 0131 6247064   Open: ALL YEAR   Map Ref No. 19

rate £ from - to per person	children taken	evening meals	animals taken
£29.50 to £39.50	N	N	N

see PHOTO over p. 494

Geralds Place

Nearest Road: A.1

Your host Gerald, welcomes you to his delightful home full of character, colour & comforts. The accommodation includes 2 double bedrooms (each with one king-size bed or 2 3ft beds of supreme quality & comfort) with 2 private bathrooms (each with power shower & bath tub). It is the ideal place for 2 couples travelling together. The delicious full Scottish breakfast is a feast Abercromby Place is very central, only 6 mins' walk from Waverley station. One of the finest streets in Edinburgh.

E-mail: gerald@geraldsplace.com

Gerald Della-Porta   Geralds Place   21B Abercromby Place   Edinburgh EH3 6QE   Edinburgh
Tel: (0131) 5587017   Fax 0131 5587014   Open: ALL YEAR   Map Ref No. 19

Gerald's Place. Edinburgh.

Ellesmere Guest House. Edinburgh.

Scotland
Edinburgh

rate £ from - to per person | children taken | evening meals | animals taken

Ellesmere Guest House

Nearest Road: A.702

Guests are made welcome at this very elegant tastefully restored Victorian town house, quietly situated overlooking golf links in the centre of Edinburgh. Bedrooms are all en-suite & decorated to a very high standard & are well-equipped with every comfort in mind. Delicious breakfasts are served in the pleasant dining room. 'A home away from home.' Convenient for the castle, Princes Street, Royal Mile, International Conference Centre, theatres & restaurants.
E-mail: celia@edinburghbandb.co.uk

Mrs Cecilia Leishman Ellesmere Guest House 11 Glengyle Terrace Edinburgh EH3 9LN Edinburgh
Tel: (0131) 229 4823 Fax 0131 229 5285 Open: ALL YEAR Map Ref No. 19

£25.00 to **£36.00** | N | N | N

see PHOTO over p. 495

Elmview

Nearest Road: A.702

Marny Hill's luxurious bed & breakfast is situated in the heart of Edinburgh within easy walking distance of Edinburgh Castle & Princes Street (1 km). Elmview is a wonderful base from which to enjoy your stay in Edinburgh. Each bedroom has been elegantly furnished throughout & all have en-suite facilities. Direct-dial 'phones, fridges, beautiful fresh flowers are but a few of the thoughtful extras in each bedroom. A delightful home.
E-mail: marny@elmview.co.uk.

Marny Hill Elmview 15 Glengyle Terrace Edinburgh EH3 9LN Edinburgh
Tel: (0131) 228 1973 Fax 0131 229 7296 Open: ALL YEAR Map Ref No. 19

£40.00 to **£47.50** | N | N | N

see PHOTO over p. 497

VISA: M'CARD:

The Stuarts

Nearest Road: A.702

Quietly situated overlooking a park, Stuarts is warm, comfortable & spacious, with a friendly atmosphere. There are 3 attractive rooms, all with colour T.V. & tea/coffee-making facilities & an en-suite bathroom. Jon & Gloria will welcome you, & help you with where to go, what to do & where to eat. Bookings of 3 nights or more taken in advance. Centrally located & within easy reach of the Castle, Princes St., shops, theatres & restaurants.
E-mail: best@the-stuarts.com

Jon & Gloria Stuart The Stuarts 17 Glengyle Terrace Edinburgh EH3 9LN Edinburgh
Tel: (0131) 2299559 Fax 0131 2292226 Open: ALL YEAR Map Ref No. 19

£35.00 to **£45.00** | Y | N | N

VISA: M'CARD: AMEX:

The Town House

Nearest Road: A.702

Attractive Victorian town house, located in the city centre. Theatres & restaurants are only minutes walk away. The Town House has been fully restored & tastefully decorated, retaining many original architectural features. The bedrooms are tastefully furnished & individually decorated, all have en-suite bath or shower & w.c., radio/alarm, colour T.V., hairdryer & tea/coffee tray. Parking is situated at the rear of the house. Self-catering apartment also available. Children over 10.
E-mail: SUSAN@thetownhouse.com

Susan Virtue The Town House 65 Gilmore Place Edinburgh EH3 9NU Edinburgh
Tel: (0131) 2291985 Open: ALL YEAR Map Ref No. 19

£25.00 to **£38.00** | Y | N | N

Elmview. Edinburgh.

Scotland
Edinburgh

	rate £ from - to per person	children taken	evening meals	animals taken

Crannoch But & Ben

Nearest Road: A.90

A warm Scottish welcome at this delightful private house. Offering 2 tastefully furnished ground-floor bedrooms, each with en-suite facilities & tea/coffee makers. The comfortable guest lounge has T.V. & information packs on Edinburgh & the surrounding area. There is on-site private parking. Easy access to the airport & an excellent bus service to the city centre (just 3 miles journey) & all that Edinburgh has to offer. A charming home.

E-mail: moiraconway@crannoch467.freeserve.co.uk

Mrs Moira Conway Crannoch But & Ben 467 Queensferry Road Edinburgh EH4 7ND Edinburgh
Tel: (0131) 3365688 Fax 0131 3365688 Open: ALL YEAR Map Ref No. 19

rate £ from - to per person	children taken	evening meals	animals taken
£26.00 to £28.00	Y	N	N

Ravensdown Guest House

Nearest Road: A.1

Built at the beginning of the 1900s, Ravensdown offers unsurpassed panoramic views of the Edinburgh skyline. 6 spacious, individually decorated rooms with T.V. & coffee/tea facilities & an en-suite or private bathroom. Guests may socialise in the lounge, with a bar service on the premises. Your friendly hosts are on hand to give advice about local attractions & tours. A delicious breakfast sets you up for a busy day of sightseeing. An excellent bus service means you can leave the car in the car park & commute the 2 miles to the centre.

Mr Leonard Welch Ravensdown Guest House 248 Ferry Road Edinburgh EH5 3AN Edinburgh
Tel: (0131) 5525438 Fax 0131 5527559 Open: ALL YEAR Map Ref No. 19

rate £ from - to per person	children taken	evening meals	animals taken
£22.50 to £35.00	Y	N	N

Ben Cruachan

Nearest Road: A.1

Guests are assured of a warm welcome & a friendly atmosphere at this attractive house, situated 1 km from Princes Street. Offering comfortable en-suite bedrooms, well-equipped with every comfort in mind & serving an excellent breakfast. Centrally situated within easy reach of the castle, Royal Mile, Holyrood Palace, shops, theatres & restaurants this is an ideal base from which to explore Edinburgh. Unrestricted parking & on all main bus routes. Children over 10 years welcome.

Mrs A. Stark Ben Cruachan 17 McDonald Road Edinburgh EH7 4LX Edinburgh
Tel: (0131) 5563709 Open: APR - OCT Map Ref No. 19

rate £ from - to per person	children taken	evening meals	animals taken
£25.00 to £35.00	Y	N	N

Greenside Hotel

Nearest Road: A.1

Built in 1820, the Greenside Hotel is an elegant Georgian town-house hotel situated in the city centre & surrounded by peaceful garden settings in one of Edinburgh's most prestigious terraces. A few mins' walk from Waverly Station, Princes St., tourist attractions, local restaurants & theatre. There are 16 tastefully decorated rooms with all facilities. Large family rooms also available. Full Scottish Breakfast is served each morning.

E-mail: greensidehotel@ednet.co.uk

Mr Alan Maguire Greenside Hotel 9 Royal Terrace Edinburgh EH7 5AB Edinburgh
Tel: (0131) 5570022/5570121 Fax 0131 5570022 Open: ALL YEAR Map Ref No. 19

rate £ from - to per person	children taken	evening meals	animals taken
£22.50 to £37.50	Y	Y	N

VISA: M'CARD: AMEX:

rate £ from - to per person	children taken	evening meals	animals taken	
£22.50 to £37.50 VISA: M'CARD: AMEX:	Y	Y	N	**Ailsa Craig Hotel** Nearest Road: A.1 Ailsa Craig Hotel is situated in the heart of Edinburgh near the city centre in one of the most prestigious terraces. This elegant Georgian town house hotel is situated only 10 mins' walk from Princes Street, Waverly Station & many attractions. 18 tastefully furnished & decorated bedrooms, 15 with en-suite facilities, & all with 'phone, hairdryer, colour T.V. & tea/coffee-making facilities. A delicious breakfast & good evening meals are served. A perfect base for exploring Edinburgh. **E-mail: ailsacraighotel@ednet.co.uk** *Cathie Hamilton Ailsa Craig Hotel 24 Royal Terrace Edinburgh EH7 5AH Edinburgh* *Tel: (0131) 5566055/5561022 Fax 0131 5566055 Open: ALL YEAR Map Ref No. 19*
£20.00 to £34.00	Y	Y	N	**Barony House** Nearest Road: A.7 A fine detached Victorian house situated in a select residential area just off the main road. Queens Crescent lies between the A.7/A.701 & A.68 main roads coming into the city from the south, but is only 1 1/2 miles from the city centre. Parking. Breakfast is a wonderful buffet experience! Also, super 3-course evening meals using local produce. All tastes & special requirements can be catered for. 8 bedrooms (4 en-suite) with 'phones, refreshment facilities, hairdryers & a complimentary sherry. **E-mail: baronyhouse@cableinet.co.uk** *Susie Berkengoff Barony House 4 Queens Crescent Edinburgh EH9 2AZ Edinburgh* *Tel: (0131) 6675806 Fax 0131 6676833 Open: ALL YEAR (Excl. Xmas) Map Ref No. 19*
£20.00 to £35.00	Y	N	N	**Parklands Guest House** Nearest Road: A.701 Parklands is an attractive Victorian terraced house conveniently located 1 1/2 miles from Princes Street & all the main tourist attractions. Accommodation is in 6 bedrooms, each is furnished to a high standard & is fully equipped with en-suite/ private facilities, colour T.V. & tea/coffee makers. A full Scottish breakfast is served. Nearby are many excellent restaurants. Parklands is family-run with a friendly atmosphere. You are assured of a warm & friendly welcome. **E-mail: parklands_guesthouse@yahoo.com** *Alan Drummond Parklands Guest House 20 Mayfield Gardens Edinburgh EH9 2BZ Edinburgh* *Tel: (0131) 6677184 Fax 0131 6672011 Open: ALL YEAR Map Ref No. 19*
£21.00 to £35.00	Y	N	N	**Ard-Thor** Nearest Road: A.701 A charming, 19th-century Victorian guest house situated only 10 mins from the city centre, castle & Princes Street by a good local bus service. The Ard-Thor is quiet & friendly, & your comfort is ensured by the personal attention of your host. Guests are offered a choice of 3 rooms, all with T.V. & tea/coffee-making facilities. Queens Park & Commonwealth Pool are nearby. This is an ideal place from which to explore Edinburgh. Children over 12 years welcome. *Mrs A. Helen Telfer Ard-Thor 10 Mentone Terrace Newington Edinburgh EH9 2DG Edinburgh* *Tel: (0131) 6671647 Open: ALL YEAR Map Ref No. 19*

Scotland
Edinburgh & Fifeshire

	rate £ from - to per person	children taken	evening meals	animals taken
Rowan Guest House	£23.00 to £33.00	Y	N	N
Roselea House	£30.00 to £50.00	Y	N	N
Beaumont Lodge Guest House	£25.00 to £30.00	Y	Y	N
The Spindrift	£26.50 to £32.50	N	N	N

Rowan Guest House

Nearest Road: A.701

Elegant Victorian home in one of the city's loveliest areas with free parking & only a 10-min. bus ride to the centre. The castle, Royal Mile, restaurants & other amenities easily reached. The charmingly decorated bedrooms are comfortably & tastefully furnished with complimentary tea/coffee & biscuits. Breakfast, including traditional porridge & freshly baked scones, will keep you going until dinner! Attentive, welcoming & friendly hosts. Partially non-smoking.

E-mail: rowanhouse@hotmail.com

VISA: M'CARD:

Alan & Angela Vidler Rowan Guest House 13 Glenorchy Terrace Edinburgh EH9 2DQ Edinburgh
Tel: (0131) 6672463 Fax 0131 6672463 Open: ALL YEAR Map Ref No. 19

Roselea House

Nearest Road: A.701

Always a warm welcome from Maureen & Adolfo at their elegant Victorian house. They have tastefully restored & refurbished their home to a high standard; whilst still retaining the original features. Each room has T.V., tea/coffee-making facilities &, of course, an en-suite or private bathroom. Whether on business or on holiday, this is an ideal oasis to return to & relax in. A delightful home, with easy access to the many attractions & places of historic interest that Edinburgh has to offer. Parking.

E-mail: roselea@aol.com

VISA: M'CARD:

Maureen & Adolfo Invernizzi Roselea House 11 Mayfield Road Edinburgh EH9 2NG Edinburgh
Tel: (0131) 6676115 Fax 0131 6673556 Open: ALL YEAR Map Ref No. 19

Beaumont Lodge Guest House

Nearest Road: A.917

Only 1 hr's drive from Edinburgh Airport & 9 miles from St. Andrews, this family-run guest house offers excellent accommodation & a cosy dining room where food of a high standard is served. The spacious & comfortable en-suite/private bedrooms have many extras which you would only find in the best of hotels. Enjoy true Scottish hospitality in this charming home. Private parking available. Children over 10 years welcome.

E-mail: reservations@beau-lodge.demon.co.uk

see PHOTO over p. 501

VISA: M'CARD:

Julia Anderson Beaumont Lodge Guest House 43 Pittenweem Road Anstruther KY10 3DT Fifeshire
Tel: (01333) 310315 Fax 01333 310315 Open: ALL YEAR Map Ref No. 23

The Spindrift

Nearest Road: A.917

Set in the picturesque fishing village of Anstruther, The Spindrift is an imposing, stone-built Victorian home with many original features carefully restored. 6 individually & tastefully furnished bedrooms with en-suite/private bathrooms, colour T.V., 'phone, hospitality tray & much more. Delicious evening meals are served. The Spindrift is only 10 mins' from St. Andrews with its world famous golf courses & excellent beaches. An ideal base for exploring the splendours of central Scotland.

E-mail: INFO@thespindrift.co.uk

VISA: M'CARD:

Eric & Moyra McFarlane The Spindrift Pittenweem Road Anstruther KY10 3DT Fifeshire
Tel: (01333) 310573 Fax 01333 310573 Open: ALL YEAR Map Ref No. 23

Beaumont Lodge Guest House. Anstruther.

Scotland
Fifeshire & Glasgow

	rate £ from - to per person	children taken	evening meals	animals taken
Ardchoille Farmhouse	£25.00 to £35.00	N	Y	N
Pitlethie Farm	£25.00 to £25.00	Y	Y	N
Cambo House	£38.00 to £42.00	Y	Y	N
Glenmiln House	£30.00 to £40.00	Y	Y	Y

Ardchoille Farmhouse

Nearest Road: A.91, B.936

Relax & enjoy the warm comfort, delicious Taste of Scotland food & the excellent hospitality at Ardchoille Farmhouse. 3 tastefully furnished twin-bedded rooms, each with an en-suite/private bathroom, colour T.V. & tea/coffee trays offering home-made butter shortbread. Large comfortable lounge, & elegant dining room with fine china & crystal. Dinner by arrangement. Close by the Royal Palace of Falkland, home of Mary Queen of Scots. 20 mins from St. Andrews, & 1 hr Edinburgh. Ideal base for golfing & touring. Children over 12.

VISA: M'CARD:

Mr & Mrs D. Steven Ardchoille Farmhouse Dunshalt Nr. Auchtermuchty KY14 7EY Fifeshire
Tel: (01337) 828414 Fax 01337 828414 Open: ALL YEAR Map Ref No. 24

Pitlethie Farm

Nearest Road: A.919

Pitlethie, a comfortable family farmhouse is situated in quiet countryside with views over prime farmland to Tentsmuir Forest which which skirts miles of unspoilt sandy beach. The accommodation (2 bedrooms) is ideal for up to 4 people travelling together. Private facilities. The house is artistically decorated, chintz, tapestries & patchwork prevail to make this a comfortable & convenient plaçe to stay whilst enjoying historic St. Andrews & the surrounding area. Dinner by arrangement (local & home produce).

VISA: M'CARD:

Mrs Gillian Black Pitlethie Farm Leuchars St. Andrews KY16 0DP Fifeshire
Tel: (01334) 838649 Fax 01334 839281 Open: ALL YEAR Map Ref No. 25

Cambo House

Nearest Road: A. 917

There is a unique quality about Cambo, the Erskine family home since 1688. This impressive Victorian mansion house, built in 1881, lies at the heart of a 1200 acre estate in one of the most unspoilt areas of Scotland. Offering 2 comfortable & elegantly furnished bedrooms (1 with 4-poster) with en-suite/private facilities. The family welcome you to share the comfort of their home, enjoy the beautiful gardens & woodland walks & unwind in the restful atmosphere. Evening meals by prior arrangement.
E-mail: cambohouse@compuserve.com

VISA: M'CARD:

Peter Erskine Cambo House Nr. St. Andrews KY16 8QD Fifeshire
Tel: (01333) 450054 Fax 01333 450987 Open: ALL YEAR (Excl. Xmas & New Year) Map Ref No. 26

Glenmiln House

Nearest Road: A.891

Glenmiln House is a quiet, spacious Victorian country house, standing in 2 acres of garden with views to Lennox Forest & the Campsie Fells. It is ideally located for Glasgow (Burrell Collection, Charles Rennie Mackintosh Trail etc.), Loch Lomond, Stirling & Argyll. Here, guests are treated as friends; open wood fires, Scottish breakfasts, bedrooms with en-suite/private facilities, etc. Dinner & animals by arrangement. Children over 8. (Restricted smoking.) Edinburgh 1 hour, Glasgow Airport 30 mins'.
E-mail: glenmiln@aol.com

VISA: M'CARD:

Gerard & Sally Henry Glenmiln House Campsie Glen By Glasgow G65 7AP Glasgow
Tel: (01360) 311322 Fax 01360 310501 Open: ALL YEAR (Excl. Xmas & New Year) Map Ref No. 27

Scotland
Glasgow & Inverness-shire

rate £ from - to per person | children taken | evening meals | animals taken

New Borland

£24.00 to £25.00 | N | N | N

Nearest Road: A.77, A.726

Near the picturesque village of Eaglesham, yet only 9 miles from Glasgow, a warm Scottish welcome is assured at this converted barn. 2 twin rooms (en-suite) & 2 single rooms sharing a bathroom. All rooms have T.V., radio/alarm & hostess tray, & are furnished to a high standard. Lounge (log fire) & games room. Hearty Scottish breakfasts are served. Convenient for Glasgow, M.74, Loch Lomond, The Trossachs, Burns Country & the Burrell. Golf & fishing nearby. Parking. Children over 12.

E-mail: newborland@dial.pipex.com

Mrs Fiona Allison New Borland Glasgow Road Eaglesham Glasgow G76 0DN Glasgow
Tel: (01355) 302051 Fax 01355 302051 Open: ALL YEAR Map Ref No. 28

The Grange

£38.00 to £46.00 | N | N | N

see PHOTO over p. 504

VISA: M'CARD:

Nearest Road: A.82

Set in quiet gardens overlooking Loch Linnhe, yet only 10 mins from the town centre. The Grange offers superb accommodation in 4 en-suite rooms, each well-equipped & enhanced by a very relaxed atmosphere. The area is charming & the house is well-situated, only 1 1/2 hrs from Oban, Inverness & the Isles. An ideal base for touring the Highlands, & returning to a comfortable lounge log fire for chilly evenings. Vegetarians catered for.

E-mail: joan@thegrange-lochaber.co.uk

Mrs Joan Campbell The Grange Grange Road Fort William PH33 6JF Inverness-shire
Tel: (01397) 705516 Fax 01397 701595 Open: MAR - NOV Map Ref No. 29

Cabana House

£26.00 to £28.00 | N | N | N

Nearest Road: A.82

This elegant Victorian house has been renovated to an exceptional standard. Accommodation is in 3 attractive designer-decorated bedrooms, 2 with en-suite facilities, 1 with private bathroom. Cabana House is situated in a prime position only 5 mins from the town centre, with private parking & a garden. It is an ideal holiday base for touring the spectacular Highlands & islands. Special interest courses in curtain design & paint effects are held during spring & autumn.

Vera G. Waugh Cabana House Union Road Fort William PH33 6RB Inverness-shire
Tel: (01397) 705991 Fax 01397 705991 Open: ALL YEAR Map Ref No. 29

Ashburn House

£30.00 to £45.00 | Y | N | N

see PHOTO over p. 505

VISA: M'CARD: AMEX:

Nearest Road: A.82

Ashburn is a splendid Victorian house personally run by Highland hosts. Quietly situated by the shores of Loch Linnhe only 600 yards from the town centre & among others the renowned Crannog Seafood Restaurant. An excellent base for touring the Highlands. Sample an imaginative Highland breakfast, served at your own individual table, complemented with freshly baked scones from the aga. 7 en-suite bedrooms, 4 with super-king-size beds. Parking. Brochure & weekly rates available.

E-mail: ashburn.house@tinyworld.co.uk

B. B. Henderson Ashburn House 1 Ashburn Lane Fort William PH33 6RQ Inverness-shire
Tel: (01397) 706000 Fax 01397 702024 Open: FEB - DEC Map Ref No. 29

The Grange. Fort William.

Ashburn House. Fort William.

Scotland
Inverness-shire

	rate £ from - to per person	children taken	evening meals	animals taken
The Inn at Ardgour	£30.00 to £45.00	Y	Y	Y
The Old Royal Guest House	£20.00 to £28.00	Y	N	N
Ballindarroch House	£20.00 to £30.00	Y	N	Y
Glenashdale	£22.00 to £25.00	Y	N	N

The Inn at Ardgour

Nearest Road: A.861

This family-run inn at the entrance to the Great Glen enjoys spectacular sea views from all bedrooms. For centuries, travellers have enjoyed the famous West Highland Welcome here. A menu featuring fresh local produce & a local bar well-stocked with malts complement modern en-suite bedrooms. Ardgour is the gateway to the Ardnamurchan peninsula, the most westerly part of Britain. It is ideal for walking, fishing & touring the West Highlands. Also, daytrips to the islands of Mull, Iona & Skye.

E-mail: reception@ardgour.com

VISA: M'CARD:

Graham M. Marshall The Inn at Ardgour Ardgour Fort William PH33 7AA Inverness-shire
Tel: (01855) 841225 Fax 01855 841214 Open: MAR - NOV (& Xmas & New Year) Map Ref No. 30

The Old Royal Guest House

Nearest Road: A.9

Personally managed by the resident proprietor Jane Ozmus, The Old Royal is conveniently situated in the centre of town, opposite the railway station. Accommodation is in 12 comfortable guest bedrooms, 5 with en-suite facilities. All have colour T.V. & tea/coffee makers. The Old Royal has a home-from-home atmosphere, & provides visitors with a comfortable holiday base from which to tour the locality. Children over 3 yrs.

E-mail: info@old-royal.co.uk

VISA: M'CARD:

Jane Ozmus The Old Royal Guest House 10 Union Street Inverness IV1 1PL Inverness-shire
Tel: (01463) 230551 Fax 01463 711916 Open: ALL YEAR Map Ref No. 31

Ballindarroch House

Nearest Road: A.9, B.862

Ballindarroch was originally built as a shooting lodge around 1870, & stands in 10 acres of woodland gardens above the Caledonian Canal. Decorated with hand-painted wallpaper & furnished with antiques & an eclectic selection of family pieces, the house offers a totally relaxing & peaceful environment only 10 mins' from Inverness. The generous breakfast includes local specialities, home-made bread & preserves Lovely river & woodland walks. French, Italian, Spanish & German spoken.

E-mail: alison@ballindarroch.freeserve.co.uk

Alison Parsons & Philip Alvy Ballindarroch House Aldourie Inverness IV12 6EL Inverness-shire
Tel: (01463) 751348 Fax 01463 751372 Open: ALL YEAR Map Ref No. 31

Glenashdale

Nearest Road: A.9

Glenashdale is a modern country house situated 7 miles south of Inverness in quiet countryside, with lovely views. The 2 comfortable bedrooms have en-suite facilities, T.V., radio & tea/coffee tray. Joe & Babs Kinnear invite you to escape the hustle & bustle of everyday living & join them in the beauty of the Scottish Highlands, where making all guests feel welcome is a top priority. Babs is a qualified massage therapist & treatments are available to guests. Children over 6 years.

E-mail: glenashdale@jkinnear.freeserve.co.uk

Barbara Kinnear Glenashdale Daviot East Inverness IV2 5XQ Inverness-shire
Tel: (01463) 772221 Fax 01463 772131 Open: ALL YEAR Map Ref No. 31

Scotland
Inverness-shire & Isle of Skye

rate £ from - to per person	children taken	evening meals	animals taken	
£19.00 to £22.00	Y	N	Y	**Easter Dalziel Farmhouse** Nearest Road: A.96, B.9039 This Scottish farming family offer the visitor a friendly Highland welcome on their 200-acre stock/ arable farm. 3 charming bedrooms are available in the delightful early-Victorian farmhouse. The lounge has log fire & colour T.V.. Delicious home cooking & baking served, including a choice of breakfasts. Evening meals available summer only. Ideal base for exploring the scenic Highlands. Local attractions are Cawdor Castle, Culloden, Fort George, Loch Ness & nearby Castle Stuart. *Mrs Margaret Pottie Easter Dalziel Farmhouse Dalcross Inverness IV2 7JL Inverness-shire* *Tel: (01667) 462213 Fax 01667 462213 Open: ALL YEAR (Excl. Xmas & New Year) Map Ref No. 32*
VISA: M'CARD:				
£22.00 to £23.00	Y	N	N	**Invergloy House** Nearest Road: A.82 A really interesting Scottish coach house, dating back 120 years, offering 3 charming, comfortable twin-bedded rooms, with modern facilities, 2 with en-suite shower rooms & 1 with an en-suite bathroom. 5 miles north of the village of Spean Bridge towards Inverness, (signposted on the left, along a wooded drive). Guest sitting room, overlooking Loch Lochy in 50 acres of woodland of rhododendron & azaleas. Fishing from the private beach & rowing boats. Hard tennis court. Children over 8. **E-mail: cairns@invergloy-house.co.uk** *Mrs Margaret Cairns Invergloy House Spean Bridge PH34 4DY Inverness-shire* *Tel: (01397) 712681 Fax 01397 712681 Open: ALL YEAR Map Ref No. 33*
£25.00 to £30.00	Y	Y	Y	**Corry Lodge** Nearest Road: A.87 Corry Lodge, on the Isle of Skye, is a most attractive period house dating from the late 18th century. It has a fine open outlook over Broadford Bay, but with a sheltered location, & approximately 1,150 metres of unspoilt sea frontage. There are 4 comfortable & tastefully furnished bedrooms, each with en-suite bathroom, radio, colour T.V. & tea/ coffee-making facilities. Corry Lodge forms an ideal base from which to tour the island either by car or bicycle, or on foot. **E-mail: jane@corrylodge.co.uk** *Jane & Anthony Wilcken Corry Lodge Broadford IV49 9AA Isle of Skye* *Tel: (01471) 822235 Fax 01471 822318 Open: APR - OCT Map Ref No. 34*
VISA: M'CARD:				
£35.00 to £40.00	N	N	N	**Lyndale House** Nearest Road: A.850 Lyndale is an elegant house in a wonderfully secluded position overlooking the sea. The spacious rooms are tastefully & comfortably furnished to the highest standard. Hidden at the end of a long wooded driveway, Lyndale House has been painstakingly restored to is original 18th-century style. It is now a beautiful family home & offers tranquillity & seclusion with magnificent views & stunning sunsets. Ideally situated for exploring the rest of the island. A non-smoking house. **E-mail: linda@lyndale.free-online.co.uk** *Marcus & Linda Ridsdill Smith Lyndale House Edinbane IV51 9PX Isle of Skye* *Tel: (01470) 582329 Open: ALL YEAR (Excl. Xmas & New Year) Map Ref No. 35*

	rate £ from - to per person	children taken	evening meals	animals taken
Glenview Inn & Restaurant	£25.00 to £35.00	Y	Y	Y
Talisker House	£43.00 to £43.00	Y	Y	N
The Glebe House	£30.00 to £35.00	Y	N	N
Ashcroft Farm Guest House	£28.00 to £50.00	Y	N	N

Glenview Inn & Restaurant

Nearest Road: A.855

A traditional island house lying between Trotternish Ridge & the sea & ideally situated for exploring North Skye. All the bedrooms have private facilities & are individually decorated, warm & comfortable, with tea/coffee-making facilities. Glenview offers a relaxed & friendly atmosphere & the best of Scotland's varied larder. Only fresh food is used to create a menu including traditional, ethnic & vegetarian specialities. Glenview is an excellent base for a relaxing break.

E-mail: valtos@lineone.net

VISA: M'CARD:

Paul & Cathie Booth *Glenview Inn & Restaurant* *Culnacnoc Staffin IV51 9JH* *Isle of Skye*
Tel: (01470) 562248 *Fax 01470 562211* *Open: MAR - OCT* *Map Ref No. 36*

Talisker House

Nearest Road: A.863

Set on Skye's ruggedly beautiful west coast, Talisker House welcomes visitors today as it welcomed Johnson & Boswell during their historic Hebridean tour of 1773. With its fine trees & garden, it offers superb views to the sea & currently accommodates up to 4 couples in spacious & elegantly appointed comfort of a high standard. Meals feature the very best of local produce, & are complemented by carefully selected wines.

E-mail: jon_and_ros.wathen@virgin.net

VISA: M'CARD:

Jon & Ros Wathen *Talisker House* *Talisker IV47 8SF* *Isle of Skye*
Tel: (01478) 640245 *Fax 01478 640214* *Open: Mid MAR - OCT* *Map Ref No. 37*

The Glebe House

Nearest Road: A.198

A beautiful listed Georgian manse built in 1780, situated in secluded grounds yet in the centre of historic North Berwick. It is elegantly furnished with many fine original features. The attractive en-suite bedrooms are all decorated to the highest standard (1 with four-poster bed). Edinburgh is 30 mins' by car, or there is a train service into the city. Castles, museums & a distillery nearby & 18 golf courses within easy reach. A haven for golfers yet a perfect base for exploring Edinburgh.

E-mail: J.A.Scott@tesco.net

Jake & Gwen Scott *The Glebe House* *Law Road* *North Berwick* *East Lothian EH39 4PL* *Lothian*
Tel: (01620) 892608 *Fax 01620 892608* *Open: ALL YEAR (Excl. Xmas & New Year)* *Map Ref No. 38*

Ashcroft Farm Guest House

Nearest Road: A.71

New farmhouse set in beautifully landscaped gardens, enjoying lovely views of the surrounding farmland. 10 miles from Edinburgh, 5 miles from the airport, city bypass, M.8/M.9, Ingliston & Livingston. Parking. Bedrooms, including a 4-poster, are attractively furnished in pine with co-ordinating fabrics. Good bus/train service to city centre (20 mins). Choice of breakfasts with home-made sausage, smoked salmon, kippers, local produce & even whisky marmalade. Children over 5.

E-mail: elizabethscott7@aol.com

VISA: M'CARD: AMEX:

Derek & Elizabeth Scott *Ashcroft Farm Guest House* *East Calder* *Nr. Edinburgh* *EH53 0ET* *Lothian*
Tel: (01506) 881810 *Fax 01506 881810* *Open: ALL YEAR* *Map Ref No. 39*

Scotland
Morayshire & Nairnshire

Blervie

rate £ from - to per person	children taken	evening meals	animals taken
£30.00 to £30.00	Y	Y	Y

VISA: M'CARD:

Nearest Road: A.96

Built in 1776 from the stone of the ruined Blervie castle, the Grade 'A' listed house is only 20 mins' from Inverness Airport. Within an easy day's driving are Strathspey, the Monaliadhs & the West Highlands. Fiona & Paddy enjoy acquainting their guests with the local features & culture, & making them feel at home among attractive furnishings & antiques. Dinner features game dishes & fresh local produce. Castles, museums, Findhorn Gorge & golf courses within easy reach. Children over 10.

E-mail: meiklejohn@btinternet.com

Lt. Cdr. & Mrs I. P. F. Meiklejohn Blervie Forres IV36 2RH Morayshire
Tel: (01309) 672358 Fax 01309 672358 Open: ALL YEAR Map Ref No. 40

The Pines

rate £ from - to per person	children taken	evening meals	animals taken
£26.00 to £35.00	Y	Y	Y

VISA: M'CARD:

Nearest Road: A.9, A.95

The Pines has a timeless atmosphere of peaceful tranquillity & backs directly onto beautiful woodlands. Antiques, water colours & oil paintings increase the sense of heritage in this fine 19th-century country house. Bedrooms have en-suite or private facilities & their own distinctive style & furnishings. The dining room creates a warm ambience for the candlelit dinners which are a fascinating blend of traditional & modern Scottish cooking. A charming home. Children over 12.

E-mail: enquiry@pinesgrantown.freeserve.co.uk

Gwen Stewart The Pines Woodside Avenue Grantown-on-Spey PH26 3JR Morayshire
Tel: (01479) 872092 Fax 01479 872092 Open: APR - OCT (& by arrangement) Map Ref No. 41

Ardconnel House

rate £ from - to per person	children taken	evening meals	animals taken
£26.00 to £35.00	Y	Y	N

see PHOTO over p. 510

VISA: M'CARD:

Nearest Road: A.95

Built in 1890, during the Victorian era of elegance, Ardconnel House stands in its own spacious grounds overlooking a glorious pine forest, Lochan & Cromdale Hills. 6 bedrooms are en-suite, with quality beds, colour T.V., hairdryer & welcome tray, & are charmingly decorated. A superb 4-poster bedroom. Excellent home cooking is complemented by a well-selected, modestly priced wine list. Taste of Scotland selected member. Children over 8 years welcome.

E-mail: ardconnel.grantown@virgin.net

Mr & Mrs Bouchard Ardconnel House Woodlands Terrace Grantown-on-Spey PH26 3JU Morayshire
Tel: (01479) 872104 Fax 01479 872104 Open: APR - OCT Map Ref No. 41

Geddes House

rate £ from - to per person	children taken	evening meals	animals taken
£35.00 to £££	Y	Y	Y

VISA:

Nearest Road: A.9

Geddes, a lovely old Georgian family home situated on the southern side of the Moray Firth, offers a chance to enjoy all the pleasures of a Highland estate. Nearby is Nairn, a seaside town with superb sandy beaches & a championship golf course & many other places of interest to explore are within easy reach. The house offers a warm welcome to guests & meals feature the best of local produce with fruit & veg grown in the beautiful garden. There are 2 tastefully furnished en-suite rooms.

E-mail: elizabeth@geddes55.freeserve.co.uk

Mrs E. Mackintosh-Walker Geddes House Nairn IV12 5QY Nairnshire
Tel: (01667) 452241 Fax 01667 456707 Open: APR - OCT Map Ref No. 42

Ardconnel House. Grantown-on-Spey.

Scotland
Perthshire

rate £ from - to per person | children taken | evening meals | animals taken

rate £ from - to per person	children taken	evening meals	animals taken
£45.00 to £££	Y	Y	N

see PHOTO over p. 512

VISA: M'CARD:

Leny House

Nearest Road: A.84

Award-winning Leny House is a spacious country mansion, set in acres of farmland in the Leny Hills. This magnificent house was originally built as a fortalice in 1513 & featured heavily in much of the local history, particularly during the Jacobite rebellion. Now, it has been sympathetically restored & is elegantly furnished throughout. The attractive guest bedrooms offer every modern-day comfort. Dinner is available at the inn on the estate. A perfect location for a relaxing break. Children over 12.

E-mail: res@lenyestate.com

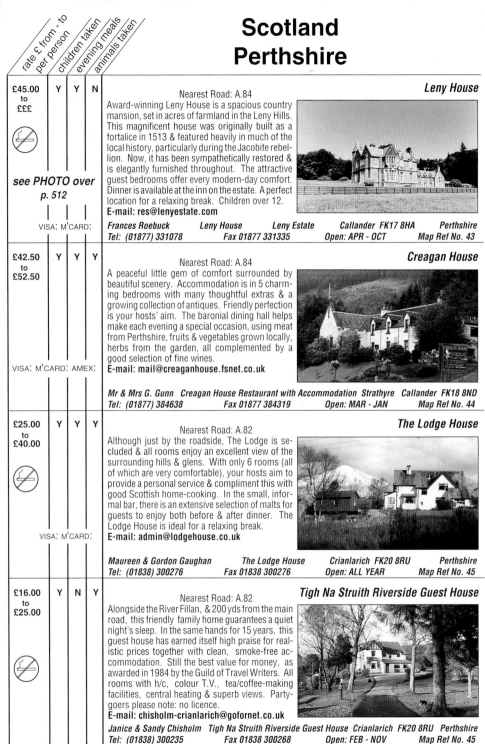

Frances Roebuck Leny House Leny Estate Callander FK17 8HA Perthshire
Tel: (01877) 331078 Fax 01877 331335 Open: APR - OCT Map Ref No. 43

rate £ from - to per person	children taken	evening meals	animals taken
£42.50 to £52.50	Y	Y	Y

VISA: M'CARD: AMEX:

Creagan House

Nearest Road: A.84

A peaceful little gem of comfort surrounded by beautiful scenery. Accommodation is in 5 charming bedrooms with many thoughtful extras & a growing collection of antiques. Friendly perfection is your hosts' aim. The baronial dining hall helps make each evening a special occasion, using meat from Perthshire, fruits & vegetables grown locally, herbs from the garden, all complemented by a good selection of fine wines.

E-mail: mail@creaganhouse.fsnet.co.uk

Mr & Mrs G. Gunn Creagan House Restaurant with Accommodation Strathyre Callander FK18 8ND
Tel: (01877) 384638 Fax 01877 384319 Open: MAR - JAN Map Ref No. 44

rate £ from - to per person	children taken	evening meals	animals taken
£25.00 to £40.00	Y	Y	Y

VISA: M'CARD:

The Lodge House

Nearest Road: A.82

Although just by the roadside, The Lodge is secluded & all rooms enjoy an excellent view of the surrounding hills & glens. With only 6 rooms (all of which are very comfortable), your hosts aim to provide a personal service & compliment this with good Scottish home-cooking. In the small, informal bar, there is an extensive selection of malts for guests to enjoy both before & after dinner. The Lodge House is ideal for a relaxing break.

E-mail: admin@lodgehouse.co.uk

Maureen & Gordon Gaughan The Lodge House Crianlarich FK20 8RU Perthshire
Tel: (01838) 300276 Fax 01838 300276 Open: ALL YEAR Map Ref No. 45

rate £ from - to per person	children taken	evening meals	animals taken
£16.00 to £25.00	Y	N	Y

Tigh Na Struith Riverside Guest House

Nearest Road: A.82

Alongside the River Fillan, & 200 yds from the main road, this friendly family home guarantees a quiet night's sleep. In the same hands for 15 years, this guest house has earned itself high praise for realistic prices together with clean, smoke-free accommodation. Still the best value for money, as awarded in 1984 by the Guild of Travel Writers. All rooms with h/c, colour T.V., tea/coffee-making facilities, central heating & superb views. Party-goers please note: no licence.

E-mail: chisholm-crianlarich@gofornet.co.uk

Janice & Sandy Chisholm Tigh Na Struith Riverside Guest House Crianlarich FK20 8RU Perthshire
Tel: (01838) 300235 Fax 01838 300268 Open: FEB - NOV Map Ref No. 45

Leny House. Callander.

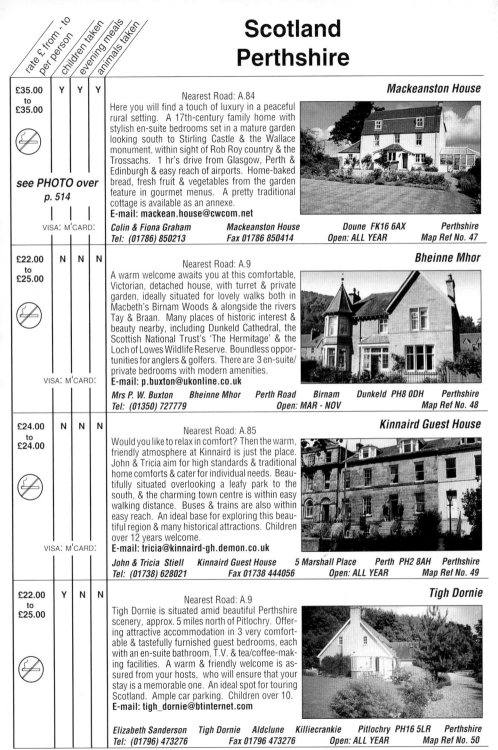

Scotland
Perthshire

rate £ from - to per person | children taken | evening meals | animals taken

---

£35.00 to £35.00 | Y | Y | Y

see PHOTO over p. 514

VISA: M'CARD:

Mackeanston House

Nearest Road: A.84

Here you will find a touch of luxury in a peaceful rural setting. A 17th-century family home with stylish en-suite bedrooms set in a mature garden looking south to Stirling Castle & the Wallace monument, within sight of Rob Roy country & the Trossachs. 1 hr's drive from Glasgow, Perth & Edinburgh & easy reach of airports. Home-baked bread, fresh fruit & vegetables from the garden feature in gourmet menus. A pretty traditional cottage is available as an annexe.

E-mail: mackean.house@cwcom.net

Colin & Fiona Graham *Mackeanston House* *Doune FK16 6AX* *Perthshire*
Tel: (01786) 850213 *Fax 01786 850414* *Open: ALL YEAR* *Map Ref No. 47*

£22.00 to £25.00 | N | N | N

VISA: M'CARD:

Bheinne Mhor

Nearest Road: A.9

A warm welcome awaits you at this comfortable, Victorian, detached house, with turret & private garden, ideally situated for lovely walks both in Macbeth's Birnam Woods & alongside the rivers Tay & Braan. Many places of historic interest & beauty nearby, including Dunkeld Cathedral, the Scottish National Trust's 'The Hermitage' & the Loch of Lowes Wildlife Reserve. Boundless opportunities for anglers & golfers. There are 3 en-suite/private bedrooms with modern amenities.

E-mail: p.buxton@ukonline.co.uk

Mrs P. W. Buxton *Bheinne Mhor* *Perth Road* *Birnam* *Dunkeld PH8 0DH* *Perthshire*
Tel: (01350) 727779 *Open: MAR - NOV* *Map Ref No. 48*

£24.00 to £24.00 | N | N | N

VISA: M'CARD:

Kinnaird Guest House

Nearest Road: A.85

Would you like to relax in comfort? Then the warm, friendly atmosphere at Kinnaird is just the place. John & Tricia aim for high standards & traditional home comforts & cater for individual needs. Beautifully situated overlooking a leafy park to the south, & the charming town centre is within easy walking distance. Buses & trains are also within easy reach. An ideal base for exploring this beautiful region & many historical attractions. Children over 12 years welcome.

E-mail: tricia@kinnaird-gh.demon.co.uk

John & Tricia Stiell *Kinnaird Guest House* *5 Marshall Place* *Perth PH2 8AH* *Perthshire*
Tel: (01738) 628021 *Fax 01738 444056* *Open: ALL YEAR* *Map Ref No. 49*

£22.00 to £25.00 | Y | N | N

Tigh Dornie

Nearest Road: A.9

Tigh Dornie is situated amid beautiful Perthshire scenery, approx. 5 miles north of Pitlochry. Offering attractive accommodation in 3 very comfortable & tastefully furnished guest bedrooms, each with an en-suite bathroom, T.V. & tea/coffee-making facilities. A warm & friendly welcome is assured from your hosts, who will ensure that your stay is a memorable one. An ideal spot for touring Scotland. Ample car parking. Children over 10.

E-mail: tigh_dornie@btinternet.com

Elizabeth Sanderson *Tigh Dornie* *Aldclune* *Killiecrankie* *Pitlochry PH16 5LR* *Perthshire*
Tel: (01796) 473276 *Fax 01796 473276* *Open: ALL YEAR* *Map Ref No. 50*

Mackeanston House. Doune .

Perthshire, Renfrewshire, Ross-shire & Roxburghshire

rate £ from - to per person	children taken	evening meals	animals taken
£28.00 to £28.00	N	N	N

Easter Dunfallandy Country House B & B

see PHOTO over p. 516

Nearest Road: A.9

A delightful Victorian country house quietly situated 2 miles south of Pitlochry, off the road to Logierait with wonderful views. 3 twin/double rooms with en-suite bath/shower, T.V. & complimentary toiletries. Each room is individually decorated & furnished. Breakfast includes porridge made from local stoneground oats, fresh cream & heather honey & scrambled free-range eggs with cream & smoked salmon - delicious! An elegant home, perfectly situated for a relaxing break.

E-mail: sue@dunfallandy.co.uk

Andrew & Sue Mathieson Easter Dunfallandy Country House B & B Pitlochry PH16 5NA Perthshire
Tel: (01796) 474128 Fax 01796 473994 Open: MAR - NOV Map Ref No. 50

rate £ from - to per person	children taken	evening meals	animals taken
£35.00 to £35.00	Y	Y	Y

East Lochhead

Nearest Road: A.760

East Lochhead is a large 100-year-old Scottish farmhouse commanding beautiful views to the south east over Barr Loch & the Renfrewshire hills. 2 beautifully furnished bedrooms with panoramic views, an en-suite/private bathroom, T.V. & tea/coffee facilities. Janet is an enthusiastic cook & the breakfast & dinner are delicious. (Vegetarian & special diets catered for.) An ideal base for visiting Glasgow & touring Ayrshire, the Clyde coast, the Trossachs (Rob Roy country) & Loch Lomond.

E-mail: winnoch@aol.com

VISA: M'CARD: AMEX:

Janet Anderson East Lochhead Largs Road Lochwinnoch PA12 4DX Renfrewshire
Tel: (01505) 842610 Fax 01505 842610 Open: ALL YEAR Map Ref No. 51

rate £ from - to per person	children taken	evening meals	animals taken
£20.00 to £30.00	Y	N	Y

The Manse

Nearest Road: A.87

Situated in the picturesque village of Plockton, called 'the Jewel of the Highlands'. The T.V. series 'Hamish Macbeth' was filmed in & around the village. The Manse was converted from the Free Church of Scotland Manse, & it now offers a range of accommodation - a large Victorian suite with bathroom & antiques/Chesterfield etc., a modern 4-poster room with en-suite shower room, & 2 smaller rooms with handbasins, tea/coffee & T.V.. All rooms have a view of Loch Carron.

E-mail: JFran97271@aol.com

John & Ariana Franchi The Manse Innes Street Plockton IV52 8TW Ross-shire
Tel: (01599) 544442 Fax 01599 544442 Open: ALL YEAR Map Ref No. 52

rate £ from - to per person	children taken	evening meals	animals taken
£18.00 to £20.00	Y	N	N

Froylehurst

Nearest Road: A.68

An attractive Grade 'B' listed late-Victorian sandstone townhouse retaining most original features, offering 4 comfortable guest bedrooms & residents lounge. All rooms have washbasins with h & c, tea/coffee-making facilities, colour T.V. & radio/alarms. Two shared bathrooms & toilets. Situated in a large garden overlooking the town in a quiet residential area but within 2 mins' walking distance of many good pubs & restaurants. Ample parking. Children over 5 welcome. An ideal base from which to explore this region.

H. H. Irvine Froylehurst Friars Jedburgh TD8 6BN Roxburghshire
Tel: (01835) 862477 Fax 01835 862477 Open: MAR - NOV Map Ref No. 53

Easter Dunfallandy Country House. Pitlochry.

Scotland

Roxburghshire, Stirlingshire & Tayside

rate £ from - to per person	children taken	evening meals	animals taken
£22.00 to £23.00	Y	Y	Y

Whitehill Farm

Nearest Road: A.6089

A comfortable & peaceful farmhouse with a large garden standing on a 455-acre, mixed farm 4 miles from Kelso. 4 attractive bedrooms - 2 single & 2 twin, 1 with en-suite shower room - have superb views over rolling countryside. All have central heating & washbasins. A pleasant sitting room with log fire is available to guests. An ideal base for touring this glorious region; maps available. Good home cooking. Dinner by prior arrangement. (Smoking is restricted.)

E-mail: besmith@whitehillfarm.freeserve.co.uk

Mrs Betty Smith Whitehill Farm Nenthorn Kelso TD5 7RZ Roxburghshire
Tel: (01573) 470203 Fax 01573 470203 Open: ALL YEAR (Excl. Xmas & New Year) Map Ref No. 54

rate £ from - to per person	children taken	evening meals	animals taken
£38.00 to £75.00	Y	Y	Y

see PHOTO over p. 518

VISA: M'CARD: AMEX:

Culcreuch Castle & Country Park

Nearest Road: A.811

Retreat to 700 years of history at magical Culcreuch, the ancestral fortalice & clan castle of the Galbraiths, home of the Barons of Culcreuch, & now a country house hotel where the Laird and his family extend an hospitable welcome. Set in 1,600 spectacular acres, yet only 19 miles from central Glasgow & 17 miles from Stirling. 8 well-appointed bedrooms with en-suite/private facilities, 4-poster bedroom supplement. Elegant period-style decor, antiques & log fires. Animals by arrangement.

E-mail: reservations@culcreuch.com

Laird Andrew Haslam Culcreuch Castle & Country Park Fintry G63 0LW Stirlingshire
Tel: (01360) 860555 Fax 01360 860556 Open: ALL YEAR Map Ref No. 55

rate £ from - to per person	children taken	evening meals	animals taken
£20.00 to £££	Y	N	Y

Redwood Guest House

Nearest Road: A.930

Redwood is a delightful guest house situated in a conservation area with superb views over the silvery River Tay. It has been elegantly furnished throughout & now offers 3 attractive bedrooms with en-suite/private bathroom, colour T.V. & tea/coffee-making facilities. Explore the quaint fishing villages nearby & the many country parks. After a day's sight-seeing, relax in the residents lounge with real log fire or in the pretty secluded garden. The town of Broughty Ferry is 1/2 mile away with many excellent restaurants, pubs & shops.

Mrs Rogerson Redwood Guest House 89 Monifieth Road Broughty Ferry Dundee DD5 2SB Tayside
Tel: (01382) 736550 Open: ALL YEAR Map Ref No. 56

Visit our website at:
http://www.bestbandb.co.uk

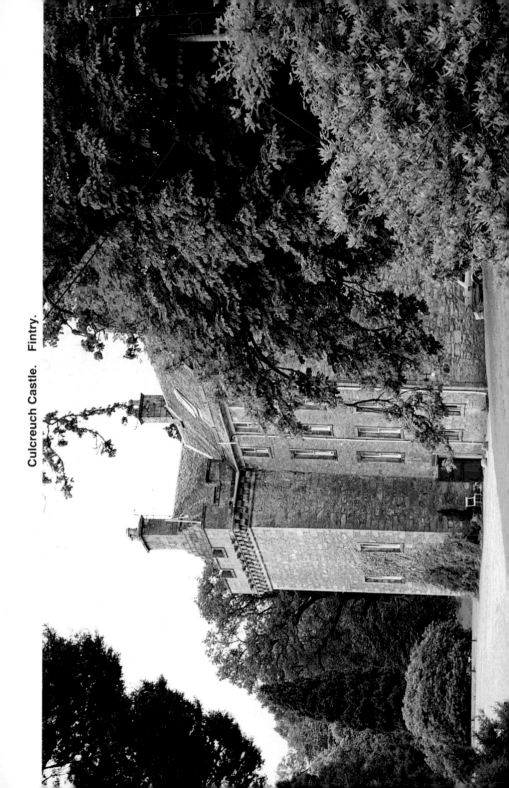

Culcreuch Castle. Fintry.

Wales

Wales

Wales is a small country with landscapes of intense beauty. In the north are the massive mountains of the Snowdonia National Park, split by chasms & narrow passes, & bounded by quiet vales & moorland. The Lleyn peninsula & the Isle of Anglesey have lovely remote coastlines.

Forests, hills & lakeland form the scenery of Mid Wales, with the great arc of Cardigan Bay in the west.

To the south there is fertile farming land in the Vale of Glamorgan, mountains & high plateaux in the Brecon Beacons, & also the industrial valleys. The coastline forms two peninsulas, around Pembroke & the Gower.

Welsh, the oldest living language of Europe is spoken & used, most obviously in the north, & is enjoying a resurgence in the number of its speakers.

From Taliesin, the 6th century Celtic poet, to Dylan Thomas, Wales has inspired poetry & song. Every August, at the Royal National Eisteddfod, thousands gather to compete as singers, musicians & poets, or to listen & learn. In the small town of Llangollen, there is an International Music Eisteddfod for a week every July

North Wales.

North Wales is chiefly renowned for the 850 miles of the Snowdonia National Park. It is a land of mountains & lakes, rivers & waterfalls & deep glacier valleys. The scenery is justly popular with walkers & pony-trekkers, but the Snowdon Mountain Railway provides easy access to the summit of the highest mountain in the range with views over the "roof of Wales".

The Snowdon Mountain Railway.

Within miles of this wild highland landscape is a coastline of smooth beaches & little fishing villages.

Barmouth has mountain scenery on its doorstep & miles of golden sands & estuary walks. Bangor & Llandudno are popular resort towns.

The Lleyn peninsula reaches west & is an area of great charm. Abersoch is a dinghy & windsurfing centre with safe sandy beaches. In the Middle Ages pilgrims would come to visit Bardsey, the Isle of 20,000 saints, just off Aberdaron, at the tip of the peninsula.

The Isle of Anglesey is linked to the mainland by the handsome Menai Straits Suspension Bridge. Beaumaris has a 13th century castle & many other fine buildings in its historic town centre.

Historically North Wales is a fiercely independent land where powerful local lords resisted first the Romans & later the armies of the English Kings.

The coastline is studded with 13th century castles. Dramatically sited Harlech Castle, famed in fable & song, commands the town, & wide sweep of the coastline.

The great citadel of Edward I at Caernarfon comprises the castle & the encircling town walls. In 1969 it was the scene of the investiture of His Royal Highness Prince Charles as Prince of Wales.

There are elegant stately homes like Plas Newydd in Anglesey & Eriddig House near Wrexham, but it is the variety of domestic architecture that is most charming. The timber-frame buildings of the Border country are seen at their best in historic Ruthin set in the beautiful Vale of Clwyd. Further west, the stone cottages of Snowdonia are built of large stones & roofed with the distinctive blue & green local slate. The low, snow-white cottages of Anglesey & the Lleyn Peninsula are typical of the "Atlantic Coast" architecture that can be found on all the western coasts of Europe. The houses are constructed of huge boulders with tiny windows & doors.

By contrast there is the marvellous fantasy of Portmeirion village. On a wooded peninsula between Harlech & Porthmadog, Sir Clough Williams Ellis created a perfect Italianate village with pastel coloured buildings, a town hall & luxury hotel.

Mid Wales

Mid Wales is farming country where people are outnumbered three to one by sheep. A flock of ewes, a lone shepherd & a Border Collie are a common sight on these green hills. Country towns like Old Radnor, Knighton & Montgomery with its castle ruin, have a timeless quality. The market towns of Rhyader, Lampeter & Dolgellau have their weekly livestock sales & annual agricultural festivals, the largest of which is the Royal Welsh Show at Builth Wells in July.

This is the background to the craft of weaving practised here for centuries. In the valley of the River Tefi & on an upper tributary of the Wye & the Irfon, there are tiny riverbank mills which produce the colourful Welsh plaid cloth.

Towards the Snowdonia National Park in the North, the land rises to the scale of true mountains. Mighty Cader Idris & the expanses of Plynlimon, once inaccessible to all but the shepherd & the mountaineer, are now popular centres for walking & pony trekking with well-signposted trails.

The line of the border with England is followed by a huge earth work of bank & ditch. This is Offa's Dyke, built by the King of Mercia around 750 A.D. to deter the Welsh from their incessant raids into his kingdom. Later the border was guarded by the castles at Hay-on-Wye, Builth Wells, Welshpool, & Chirk which date from mediaeval times.

North from Rhayader, lies the Dovey estuary & the historic town of Machynlleth. This is where Owain Glyndwr's parliament is thought to have met in 1404, & there is an exhibition about the Welsh leader in the building, believed to have been Parliament House.

Wales lost many fine religious houses during the Dissolution of the Monasteries under Henry VIII. The ruins at Cymer near Dolgellau & at Strata Florida were abbeys of the Cistercian order. However, many remote Parish Churches show evidence of the skills of mediaeval craftsmen with soaring columns & fine rood screens.

The Cambrian Coast (Cardigan Bay) has sand dunes to the north & cliffs to the south with sandy coves & miles of cliff walks.

Llangrannog Headland.

Aberystwyth is the main town of the region with two beaches & a yachting harbour, a Camera Obscura on the cliff top & some fine walks in the area.

Water-skiing, windsurfing &

Wales

sailing are popular at Aberdovey, Aberaeron, New Quay, Tywyn & Barmouth & there are delightful little beaches further south at Aberporth, Tresaith or Llangrannog.

South Wales

South Wales is a region of scenic variety. The Pembrokeshire coastline has sheer cliffs, little coves & lovely beaches. Most of the area is National Park with an 80 mile foot path running along its length, passing pretty harbour villages like Solva & Broad Haven.

A great circle of Norman Castles stands guard over South Pembrokeshire, Roch, Haverfordwest, Tenby, Carew, Pembroke & Manorbier.

The northern headland of Saint Brides Bay is the most westerly point in the country & at the centre of a tiny village stands the Cathedral of Saint David, the Patron Saint of Wales. At Bosherton near Saint Govans Head, there is a tiny chapel hidden in a cleft in the massive limestone cliffs.

Tenby.

The Preseli Hills hold the vast prehistoric burial chambers of Pentre Ifan, & the same mountains provided the great blue stones used at faraway Stonehenge.

Laugharne is the village where Dylan Thomas lived & worked in what was a boat-house & is now a museum.

In the valleys, towns like Merthyr Tydfil, Ebbw Vale & Treorchy were in the forefront of the boom years of the Industrial Revolution. Now the heavy industries are fast declining & the ravages of the indiscriminate mining & belching smoke of the blast furnaces are disappearing. The famous Male Voice Choirs & the love of rugby football survives.

The Vale of Glamorgan is a rural area with pretty villages. Beyond here the land rises steeply to the high wild moorlands & hill farms of the Brecon Beacons National Park & the Black Mountains, lovely areas for walking & pony trekking.

The Wye Valley leads down to Chepstow & here set amidst the beautiful woodlands is the ruin of the Great Abbey of Tintern, founded in 1131 by the Cistercian Order.

Swansea has a strong sea-faring tradition maintained by its new Marine Quarter - marina, waterfront village, restaurants, art gallery & theatre.

Cardiff, the capital of Wales, is a pleasant city with acres of parkland, the lovely River Taff, & a great castle, as well as a new civic centre, two theatres & the ultra-modern St. David's Concert Hall. It is the home of the Welsh National Opera & here also is the National Stadium where the singing of the rugby crowd on a Saturday afternoon is a treat.

Pony Trekking

Wales

Wales Gazeteer

Areas of Outstanding Natural Beauty
The Pembrokeshire Coast. The Brecon Beacons. Snowdonia. Gower.'

Historic Houses & Castles

Cardiff Castle - Cardiff
Built on a Roman site in the 11th century.
Caerphilly Castle - Caerphilly
13th century fortress.
Chirk Castle - Nr. Wrexham
14th century Border Castle. Lovely gardens.
Coity Castle - Coity
Mediaeval stronghold - three storied round tower.
Gwydir Castle - Nr. Lanrwst
Royal residence in past days - wonderful Tudor furnishings. Gardens with peacocks.
Penrhyn Castle - Bangor
Neo-Norman architecture 19th century - large grounds with museum & exhibitions. Victorian garden.
Picton Castle - Haverfordwest
12th century - lived in by the same family continuously. Fine gardens.
Caernarfon Castle - Caernarfon
13th century - castle of great importance to Edward I.
Conway Castle - Conwy
13th century - one of Edward I's chain of castles.
Powis Castle - Welshpool
14th century - reconstruction work in 17th century.
Murals, furnishings, tapestries & paintings, terraced gardens.
Pembroke Castle - Pembroke
12th century Norman castle with huge keep & immense walls.
Birthplace of Henry VII.
Plas Newydd - Isle of Anglesey
18th century Gothic style house.
Home of the Marquis of Anglesey.
Stands on the edge of the Menai Strait looking across to the Snowdonia Range.
Famous for the Rex Whistler murals.
The Tudor Merchant's House - Tenby
Built in 15th century.
Tretower Court & Castle - Crickhowell
Mediaeval - finest example in Wales.

Cathedrals & Churches

St. Asaph Cathedral
13th century - 19th century restoration.
Smallest of Cathedrals in England & Wales.
Holywell (St. Winifred)
15th century well chapel & chamber - fine example.
St. Davids (St. David)
12th century Cathedral - splendid tower - oak roof to nave.
Gwent (St. Woolos)
Norman Cathedral - Gothic additions - 19th century restoration.
Abergavenny (St. Mary)
14th century church of 12th century Benedictine priory.
Llanengan (St. Engan)
Mediaeval church - very large with original roof & stalls 16th century tower.
Esyronen
17th century chapel, much original interior remaining.
Llangdegley (St. Tegla)
18th century Quaker meeting house - thatched roof - simple structure divided into schoolroom & meeting room.
Llandaff Cathedral (St. Peter & St. Paul)
Founded in 6th century - present building began in 12th century. Great damage suffered in bombing during war, restored with Epstein's famous figure of Christ.

Museums & Galleries

National Museum of Wales - Cardiff (also Turner House)
Geology, archaeology, zoology, botany, industry, & art exhibitions.
Welsh Folk Museum - St. Fagans Castle - Cardiff
13th century walls curtaining a 16th century house - now a most interesting & comprehensive folk museum.
County Museum - Carmarthen
Roman jewellery, gold, etc. Romano-British & Stone Age relics.
National Library of Wales - Aberystwyth
Records of Wales & Celtic areas. Great historical interest.
University College of Wales Gallery - AberystwythTravelling exhibitions of painting & sculpture.

Wales

Museum & Art Gallery - Newport
Specialist collection of English watercolours - natural history, Roman remains, etc.
Legionary Museum - Caerleon
Roman relics found on the site of legionary fortress at Risca.
Nelson Museum - Monmouth
Interesting relics of Admiral Lord Nelson & Lady Hamilton.
Bangor Art Gallery - Bangor
Exhibitions of contemporary paintings & sculpture.
Bangor Museum of Welsh Antiquities - Bangor
History of North Wales is shown. Splendid exhibits of furniture, clothing, domestic objects, etc. Also Roman antiquities.
Narrow Gauge Railway Museum - Tywyn
Rolling stock & exhibitions of narrow gauge railways of U.K.
Museum of Childhood - Menai Bridge
Charming museum of dolls & toys & children's things.
Brecknock Museum - Brecon
Natural history, archaeology, agriculture, local history, etc.
Glynn Vivian Art Gallery & Museum - Swansea
Ceramics, old & contemporary, British paintings & drawings, sculpture, loan exhibitions.
Stone Museum - Margam
Carved stones & crosses from pre-historic times.
Plas Mawr - Conwy
A beautiful Elizabethan town mansion house in its original condition. Now holds the Royal Cambrain Academy of Art.

Historic Monuments

Rhuddlan Castle - Rhuddlan
13th century castle - interesting diamond plan.
Valle Crucis Abbey - Llangollen
13th century Cistercian Abbey Church.

Cader Idris.

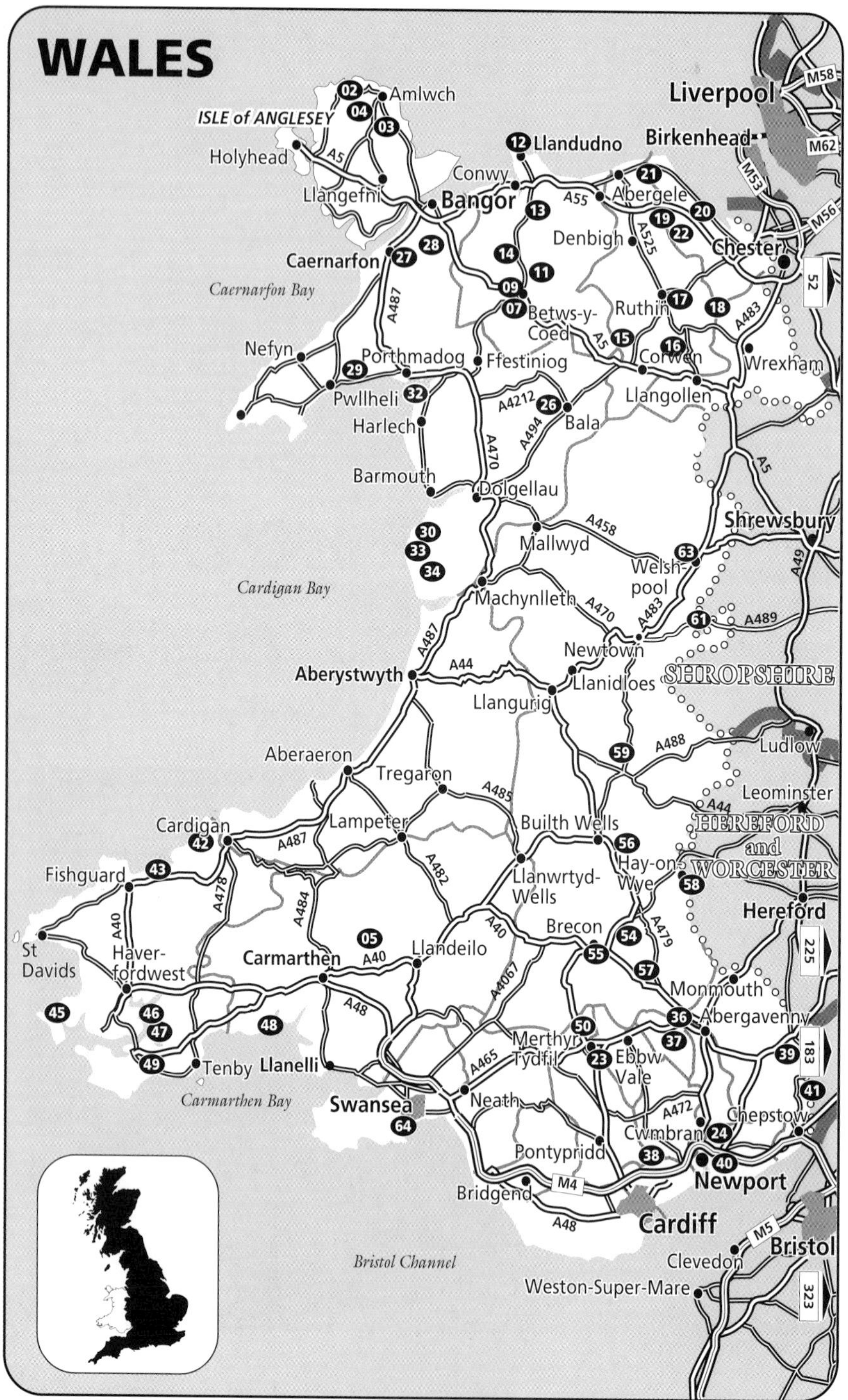
WALES
ISLE of ANGLESEY
Amlwch
Holyhead
Llangefni
Bangor
Conwy
Llandudno
Liverpool
Birkenhead
Abergele
Denbigh
Chester
Caernarfon
Caernarfon Bay
Betws-y-Coed
Ruthin
Corwen
Wrexham
Nefyn
Porthmadog
Ffestiniog
Pwllheli
Harlech
Bala
Llangollen
Barmouth
Dolgellau
Mallwyd
Shrewsbury
Welshpool
Cardigan Bay
Machynlleth
Newtown
Aberystwyth
Llanidloes
Llangurig
SHROPSHIRE
Ludlow
Aberaeron
Tregaron
Leominster
Cardigan
Lampeter
Builth Wells
HEREFORD and WORCESTER
Fishguard
Hay-on-Wye
Llanwrtyd-Wells
Hereford
St Davids
Haverfordwest
Carmarthen
Llandeilo
Brecon
Monmouth
Abergavenny
Merthyr Tydfil
Ebbw Vale
Tenby
Llanelli
Carmarthen Bay
Swansea
Neath
Chepstow
Cwmbran
Pontypridd
Newport
Bridgend
Cardiff
Bristol
Clevedon
Bristol Channel
Weston-Super-Mare
52
225
183
323

WALES

Map references

02 **Hirst**
03 **Brown**
04 **Hughes**
05 **Dent**
07 **Betteney**
09 **Howard**
09 **K. Jones**
11 **Pitman**
12 **Saunders**
13 **Marrow**
14 **Nichols**
15 **Hart**
16 **Harman**
17 **J. Spencer**
18 **Parry**
19 **A. Roberts**
20 **M. Jones**
21 **Steele-Mortimer**
22 **T. Spencer**
23 **M. Hurley**
24 **B. Watkins**
26 **Cunningham**
27 **Bayles**
28 **Kettle**
29 **Murray**
30 **Smyth**
32 **Williams**
33 **Sylvester**
34 **Tregarthen**
36 **Harris**
37 **Weatherill**
38 **Price**
39 **Harmston**
40 **C. Park**
41 **Stubbs**
42 **Phillips**
43 **Cooper**
45 **Webber**
46 **Lort-Phillips**
47 **Moonie**
48 **S. Evans**
49 **McHugh**
50 **K. Hurley**
54 **Cole**
55 **P. Jackson**
56 **N. Jones**
57 **C. Jackson**
58 **Roberts**
59 **Millan**
61 **Bright**
63 **S. Jones**
64 **Maybery**

Llwydiarth Fawr Farm. Anglesey.

Wales
Isle of Anglesey & Carmarthenshire

Hafod Country House

rate £ from - to per person	children taken	evening meals	animals taken
£21.00 to £23.00	Y	N	N

Nearest Road: A.5025

A spacious Edwardian house set in an acre of beautiful gardens with wildlife pond, superb sea & mountain views. Peacefully situated on the outskirts of Cemaes with its picturesque harbour & sandy beach. 3 fully equipped en-suite bedrooms. A drawing room with antiques & a dining room where a superb breakfast is served & includes homemade preserves & fresh apple/pear juice when in season. Good local pubs. Nearby bird sanctuary, lake/sea fishing, golf & superb headland walks.

E-mail: hirst.hafod@tesco.net

Gina Hirst Hafod Country House Cemaes Bay Isle of Anglesey LL67 0DS Anglesey
Tel: (01407) 710500 Fax 01407 710055 Open: Easter - SEPT Map Ref No. 02

Drws Y Coed

rate £ from - to per person	children taken	evening meals	animals taken
£22.50 to £24.50	Y	N	N

Nearest Road: A.5025, A.5

Enjoy wonderful panoramic views of Snowdonia & countryside at this beautifully appointed farmhouse on a 550-acre working beef, sheep & arable farm. It's situated in peaceful, wooded countryside in the centre of Anglesey. An ideal base to explore the island. Tastefully decorated & furnished, superb en-suite bedrooms with all facilities. An inviting spacious lounge with antiques & log fire. Excellent breakfasts. Historic farmstead. Lovely private walks. 25 mins' to Holyhead Port. A warm Welsh welcome is assured.

VISA: M'CARD:

Mrs Jane Bown Drws Y Coed Llannerch-Y-Medd Isle of Anglesey LL71 8AD Anglesey
Tel: (01248) 470473 Fax 01248 470473 Open: ALL YEAR Map Ref No. 03

Llwydiarth Fawr Farm

rate £ from - to per person	children taken	evening meals	animals taken
£25.00 to £25.00	Y	N	N

see PHOTO over p. 526

Nearest Road: A.5

Secluded Georgian mansion set in 800 acres of woodland & farmland, with lovely open views. Ideal touring base for the island's coastline, Snowdonia & North Wales coast. 5 delightfully furnished bedrooms with en-suite facilities & T.V., & 2 cottage suites. Full central heating, log fires. Enjoy a taste of Wales with delicious country cooking using farm & local produce. Personal attention & a warm Welsh welcome to guests, who will enjoy the scenic walks & private fishing. Convenient for Holyhead-to-Ireland crossings.

VISA: M'CARD:

Margaret Hughes Llwydiarth Fawr Farm Llanerchymedd Isle of Anglesey LL71 8DF Anglesey
Tel: (01248) 470321/470540 Open: ALL YEAR (Excl. Xmas) Map Ref No. 04

Plas Alltyferin

rate £ from - to per person	children taken	evening meals	animals taken
£25.00 to £25.00	Y	N	Y

Nearest Road: A.40

A classic Georgian country house lying in the hills above the beautiful Towy Valley, overlooking a Norman hillfort & the River Cothi - famous for salmon & sea trout. There are 2 spacious twin bedrooms, each with an en-suite bathroom & stunning views, for guests who are welcomed as friends of the family. Antique furniture & log fires. Excellent local pubs & restaurants. Totally peaceful. Marvellous touring country for castles, beaches & rural Wales. Just 5 miles from the new National Botanic Garden of Wales. Children over 10.

E-mail: dent@alltyferin.fsnet.co.uk

Mr & Mrs G. Dent Plas Alltyferin Pontargothi Nantgaredig Carmarthen SA32 7PF Carmarthenshire
Tel: (01267) 290662 Fax 01267 290662 Open: ALL YEAR (Excl. Xmas) Map Ref No. 05

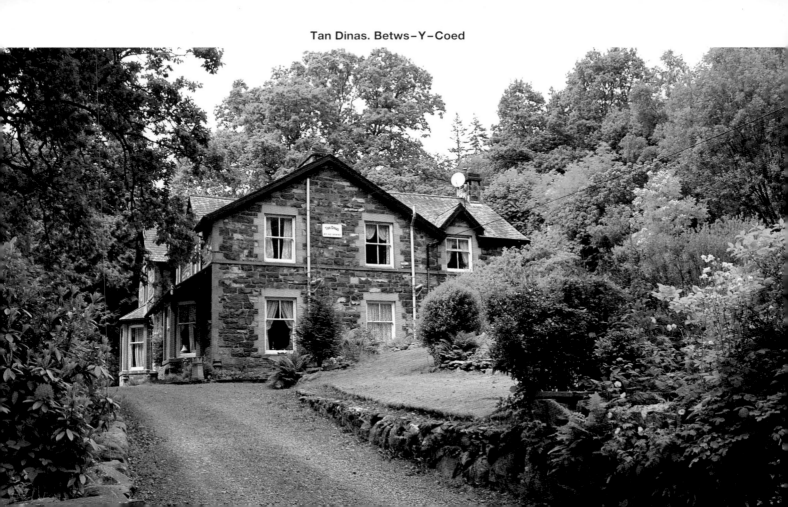

Tan Dinas. Betws-Y-Coed

Wales
Conwy

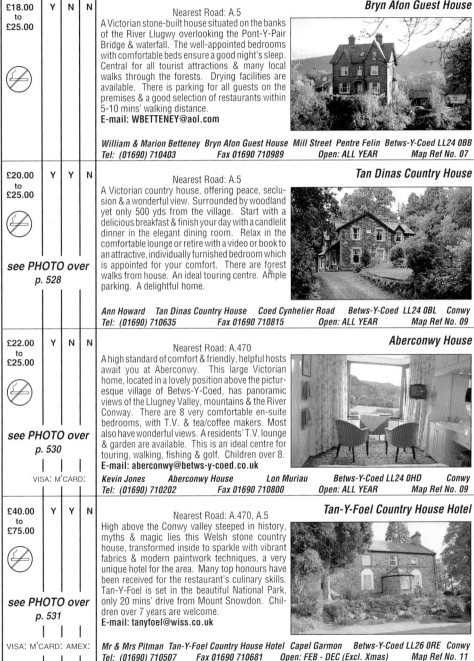

rate £ from - to per person	children taken	evening meals	animals taken
£18.00 to £25.00	Y	N	N

Bryn Afon Guest House

Nearest Road: A.5

A Victorian stone-built house situated on the banks of the River Llugwy overlooking the Pont-Y-Pair Bridge & waterfall. The well-appointed bedrooms with comfortable beds ensure a good night's sleep. Central for all tourist attractions & many local walks through the forests. Drying facilities are available. There is parking for all guests on the premises & a good selection of restaurants within 5-10 mins' walking distance.

E-mail: WBETTENEY@aol.com

William & Marion Betteney Bryn Afon Guest House Mill Street Pentre Felin Betws-Y-Coed LL24 0BB
Tel: (01690) 710403 Fax 01690 710989 Open: ALL YEAR Map Ref No. 07

rate £ from - to per person	children taken	evening meals	animals taken
£20.00 to £25.00	Y	Y	N

see PHOTO over p. 528

Tan Dinas Country House

Nearest Road: A.5

A Victorian country house, offering peace, seclusion & a wonderful view. Surrounded by woodland yet only 500 yds from the village. Start with a delicious breakfast & finish your day with a candlelit dinner in the elegant dining room. Relax in the comfortable lounge or retire with a video or book to an attractive, individually furnished bedroom which is appointed for your comfort. There are forest walks from house. An ideal touring centre. Ample parking. A delightful home.

Ann Howard Tan Dinas Country House Coed Cynhelier Road Betws-Y-Coed LL24 0BL Conwy
Tel: (01690) 710635 Fax 01690 710815 Open: ALL YEAR Map Ref No. 09

rate £ from - to per person	children taken	evening meals	animals taken
£22.00 to £25.00	Y	N	N

see PHOTO over p. 530

VISA: M'CARD:

Aberconwy House

Nearest Road: A.470

A high standard of comfort & friendly, helpful hosts await you at Aberconwy. This large Victorian home, located in a lovely position above the picturesque village of Betws-Y-Coed, has panoramic views of the Llugney Valley, mountains & the River Conway. There are 8 very comfortable en-suite bedrooms, with T.V. & tea/coffee makers. Most also have wonderful views. A residents' T.V. lounge & garden are available. This is an ideal centre for touring, walking, fishing & golf. Children over 8.

E-mail: aberconwy@betws-y-coed.co.uk

Kevin Jones Aberconwy House Lon Muriau Betws-Y-Coed LL24 0HD Conwy
Tel: (01690) 710202 Fax 01690 710800 Open: ALL YEAR Map Ref No. 09

rate £ from - to per person	children taken	evening meals	animals taken
£40.00 to £75.00	Y	Y	N

see PHOTO over p. 531

VISA: M'CARD: AMEX:

Tan-Y-Foel Country House Hotel

Nearest Road: A.470, A.5

High above the Conwy valley steeped in history, myths & magic lies this Welsh stone country house, transformed inside to sparkle with vibrant fabrics & modern paintwork techniques, a very unique hotel for the area. Many top honours have been received for the restaurant's culinary skills. Tan-Y-Foel is set in the beautiful National Park, only 20 mins' drive from Mount Snowdon. Children over 7 years are welcome.

E-mail: tanyfoel@wiss.co.uk

Mr & Mrs Pitman Tan-Y-Foel Country House Hotel Capel Garmon Betws-Y-Coed LL26 0RE Conwy
Tel: (01690) 710507 Fax 01690 710681 Open: FEB - DEC (Excl. Xmas) Map Ref No. 11

Aberconwy House. Betws-Y-Coed.

Tan-Y-Foel. Capel Garmon.

Wales
Conwy & Denbighshire

	rate £ from - to per person	children taken	evening meals	animals taken
Tan Lan Hotel	£21.00 to £37.00	Y	Y	Y

Nearest Road: A.55

Tan Lan is a warm, welcoming hotel on the edge of town, close to the sea. Service is attentive & is combined with a friendly atmosphere in which you can feel genuinely at home. The hotel is renowned for its excellent food. There are 17 comfortably furnished & well-equipped en-suite rooms, 2 non-smoking, together with a restaurant & cosy lounge bar. Ideal base to explore castles, Snowdonia & also experience a classic Victorian seaside resort.

E-mail: info@tanlanhotel.co.uk

VISA: M'CARD:

Peter & Kerry Saunders Tan Lan Hotel Great Ormes Road Llandudno LL30 2AR Conwy
Tel: (01492) 860221 Fax 01492 870219 Open: FEB - NOV Map Ref No. 12

	rate £ from - to per person	children taken	evening meals	animals taken
Firs Cottage	£17.00 to £21.00	Y	N	Y

Nearest Road: A.470

A 17th-century Welsh cottage & comfortable family home, situated in the beautiful Conway Valley, with excellent views to the hills. Firs Cottage offers 3 very comfortable & attractively furnished bedrooms, as well as a beautiful garden in which to relax & plan visits to the many North Wales attractions, which are all within easy reach. Good food & a warm Welsh welcome will make for a memorable holiday at this charming home. The perfect spot for a relaxing break.

Mary & Jack Marrow Firs Cottage Maenan Llanrwst LL26 0YR Conwy
Tel: (01492) 660244 Open: ALL YEAR (Excl. Xmas) Map Ref No. 13

	rate £ from - to per person	children taken	evening meals	animals taken
Hafod Country Hotel	£30.50 to £40.50	Y	Y	Y

Nearest Road: A.470

Set in the lovely Conwy Valley, on the edge of Snowdonia, Yr Hafod (The Summer Dwelling) is a former 17th-century farmhouse, extensively furnished with antiques. The bedrooms each offer a highly individual sense of style. Warm hospitality at this award-winning hotel is complimented by outstanding food, while drinks can be enjoyed in the oak-panelled bar or in front of a log fire. Children over 11 years welcome.

E-mail: hafod@breathemail.net

VISA: M'CARD: AMEX:

Christopher & Rosina Nichols Hafod Country Hotel Trefriw LL27 0RQ Conwy
Tel: (01492) 640029 Fax 01492 641351 Open: Mid FEB - JAN Map Ref No. 14

	rate £ from - to per person	children taken	evening meals	animals taken
Delfryn (The Old Rectory)	£28.00 to £33.00	Y	Y	N

Nearest Road: A.5

Small country rectory dating from 1714, situated on the edge of Snowdonia in a beautiful, quiet, hilly setting. There is a private walled garden with views. Bedroom with balcony overlooking the pond. Meals are amongst some of the finest anywhere & are cooked to individual tastes & served with guests own wine. No corkage. Home-baked breads, biscuits & preserves. Homely atmosphere, log fires, small panelled dining room. Books, guides, classical music, grand piano. No T.V.s anywhere.

Mr & Mrs F. Hart Delfryn (The Old Rectory) Bettws Gwerfyl Goch Corwen LL21 9PU Denbighshire
Tel: (01490) 460387 Open: MAR - JAN Map Ref No. 15

Wales
Denbighshire

rate £ from - to per person	children taken	evening meals	animals taken
£20.00 to £23.00	Y	N	Y

Dee Farm

Nearest Road: A.5

Dee Farm is set high in the hamlet of Rhewl, with the River Dee running just below the garden. This charming old stone farmhouse was once a slate-miners inn & now offers attractive & comfortable accommodation. 2 twin-bedded rooms, with en-suite/private bathrooms. (1 of the rooms has high beams & was the original hayloft, the other has a wonderful view over the river & the hills beyond.) Evening meals (by arrangement) include fresh vegetables & herbs from the garden when possible. An ideal base for the attractions of Llangollen.

Mrs Mary Harman Dee Farm Rhewl Llangollen LL20 7YT Denbighshire
Tel: (01978) 861598 Fax 01978 861598 Open: MAR - NOV Map Ref No. 16

rate £ from - to per person	children taken	evening meals	animals taken
£23.00 to £25.00	Y	Y	Y

see PHOTO over p. 534

VISA: M'CARD:

Eyarth Station

Nearest Road: A.525

A warm & friendly reception awaits the visitor to Eyarth Station. A super, converted, former railway station located in the beautiful countryside of the Vale of Clwyd. 6 en-suite bedrooms. A comfortable T.V. lounge, & guests are welcome to use the garden, sun patio & outdoor heated pool. Conveniently located for the many historic towns in the region including Conwy, Caernarfon & Ruthin & their castles, with medieval banquet 2 minutes drive away. Chester is also within driving distance. 1987 winner of Best Bed & Breakfast Award.

Jen & Bert Spencer Eyarth Station Llanfair D. C. Ruthin LL15 2EE Denbighshire
Tel: (01824) 703643 Fax 01824 707464 Open: ALL YEAR Map Ref No. 17

rate £ from - to per person	children taken	evening meals	animals taken
£17.00 to £19.00	Y	Y	N

Llainwen Ucha

Nearest Road: A.525

A working farm set in 130 acres overlooking the very beautiful Vale of Clwyd. Offering 3 pleasantly decorated rooms with modern amenities, & accommodating up to 6 persons. All rooms are centrally heated. Good home cooking made with fresh local produce; vegetarian meals on request. Conveniently situated for visiting Chester, Llangollen, Snowdonia & the coast. Offa's Dyke & fishing nearby. Medieval banquets are held at Ruthin Castle throughout the year.

E-mail: brynparry@farming.co.uk

Elizabeth A. Parry Llainwen Ucha Pentre Celyn Ruthin LL15 2HL Denbighshire
Tel: (01978) 790253 Open: ALL YEAR Map Ref No. 18

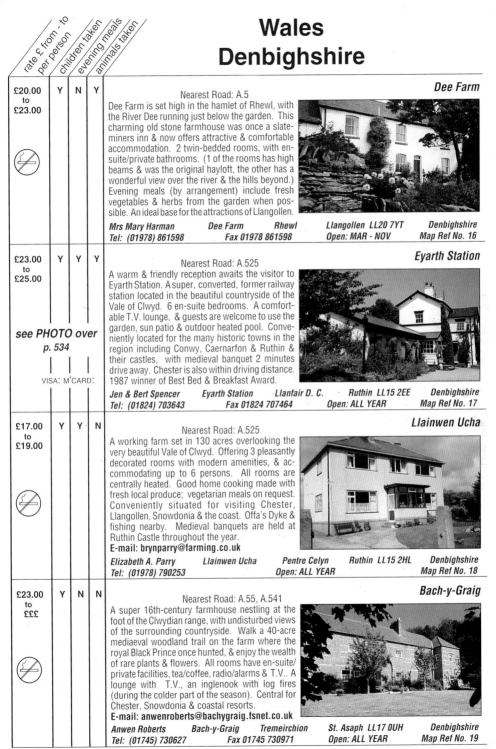

rate £ from - to per person	children taken	evening meals	animals taken
£23.00 to £££	Y	N	N

Bach-y-Graig

Nearest Road: A.55, A.541

A super 16th-century farmhouse nestling at the foot of the Clwydian range, with undisturbed views of the surrounding countryside. Walk a 40-acre mediaeval woodland trail on the farm where the royal Black Prince once hunted, & enjoy the wealth of rare plants & flowers. All rooms have en-suite/private facilities, tea/coffee, radio/alarms & T.V.. A lounge with T.V., an inglenook with log fires (during the colder part of the season). Central for Chester, Snowdonia & coastal resorts.

E-mail: anwenroberts@bachygraig.fsnet.co.uk

Anwen Roberts Bach-y-Graig Tremeirchion St. Asaph LL17 0UH Denbighshire
Tel: (01745) 730627 Fax 01745 730971 Open: ALL YEAR Map Ref No. 19

Eyarth Station. Llanfair D.C.

Golden Grove. Llanasa.

rate £ from - to per person | children taken | evening meals | animals taken

Greenhill Farm

Nearest Road: A.55

A 16th-century working dairy farm, overlooking the Dee Estuary, which retains its old-world charm, with a beamed & panelled interior. Bedrooms are tastefully furnished, some having bathroom/shower en-suite. Relax & enjoy typical farmhouse food in the attractive dining room. (Dinner by prior arrangement.) Children's play area & utility/games room also available. A lovely home, within easy reach of both the coastal & mountain areas of North Wales.

E-mail: mary@greenhillfarm.fsnet.co.uk

Mrs Mary Jones *Greenhill Farm* *Bryn Celyn* *Holywell CH8 7QF* *Flintshire*
Tel: (01352) 713270 *Open: MAR - NOV* *Map Ref No. 20*

rate £ from - to per person	children taken	evening meals	animals taken
£18.50 to £20.50	Y	Y	N

Golden Grove

Nearest Road: A.5151

Beautiful Elizabethan manor house set in 1,000 acres, close to Chester, Bodnant Gardens & Snowdonia, & en route to Holyhead. The Steele-Mortimer brothers & wives, having returned to the family home from Canada & Ireland, provide a warm welcome for their guests. The menu features home produce, including lamb & game, together with interesting wines & home baking. The atmosphere is friendly & informal. No smoking upstairs. Children over 12 yrs. Licensed.

E-mail: golden.grove@lineone.net

N. & M. Steele-Mortimer *Golden Grove* *Llanasa* *Nr. Holywell CH8 9NA* *Flintshire*
Tel: (01745) 854452 *Fax 01745 854547* *Open: FEB - NOV* *Map Ref No. 21*

rate £ from - to per person	children taken	evening meals	animals taken
£37.00 to £47.00	Y	Y	N

see PHOTO over p. 535

VISA: M'CARD:

Pentre Cerrig Mawr

Nearest Road: A.494

Pheasants & badgers visit the gardens of this peaceful 17th-century country house. Convenient for Chester, Snowdonia, the coast, Holyhead & 50 mins' to Manchester or Liverpool. The principal rooms have beams & open fires. Bedrooms are en-suite with T.V., hospitality tray & magical views across the valley. Country pubs, walks, riding, golf & the theatre all nearby. The atmosphere is friendly & welcoming. Home-baking & local organic produce. Animals by arrangement. Children over 12.

E-mail: pentre.cerrig@virgin.net

Ted & Charmian Spencer *Pentre Cerrig Mawr* *Maeshafn* *Nr. Mold CH7 5LU* *Flintshire*
Tel: (01352) 810607 *Fax 01352 810607* *Open: ALL YEAR* *Map Ref No. 22*

rate £ from - to per person	children taken	evening meals	animals taken
£35.00 to £45.00	Y	Y	Y

see PHOTO over p. 537

VISA: M'CARD:

Tregenna Hotel

Nearest Road: A.470, A.465

Family-run hotel with high level of comfort & class. 24 bedrooms with bathroom, 7 of which are designated for tourists & family use at special rates (50% reduction for children sharing). Telephone, tea/coffee service tray & colour T.V. in all rooms. Lunch, afternoon tea & dinner served 7 days a week. Brecon Beacons National Park 8 mins' drive. Only 45 mins' Cardiff/Wales Airport, 2 1/4 hours London Heathrow Airport.

E-mail: reception@tregenna.co.uk

Michael Hurley *Tregenna Hotel* *Park Terrace* *Merthyr Tydfil CF47 8RF* *Glamorgan*
Tel: (01685) 723627 *Fax 01685 721951* *Open: ALL YEAR* *Map Ref No. 23*

rate £ from - to per person	children taken	evening meals	animals taken
£30.00 to £45.00	Y	Y	Y

VISA: M'CARD: AMEX:

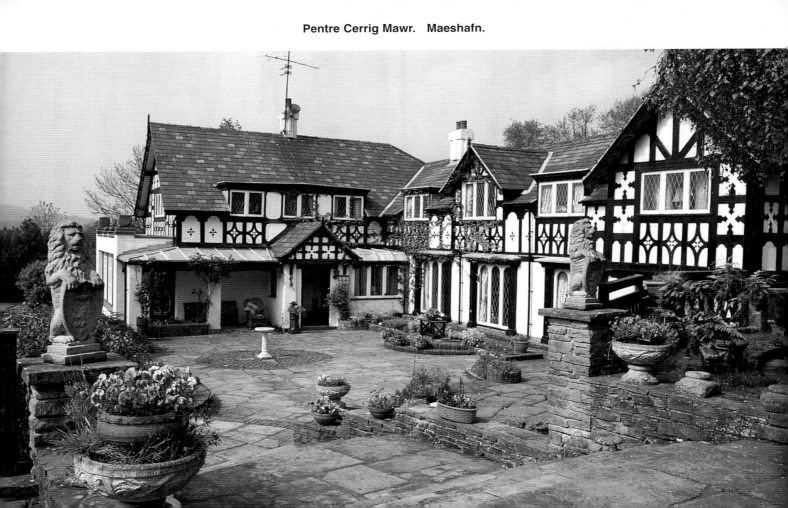

Pentre Cerrig Mawr. Maeshafn.

Wales
Gwent & Gwynedd

	rate £ from - to per person	children taken	evening meals	animals taken
The Glebe	£19.00 to £22.00	Y	N	N
Abercelyn Country House	£22.50 to £26.50	Y	N	N
The White House	£19.50 to £21.50	Y	N	Y
Ty'n Rhos	£60.00 to £98.00	Y	Y	N

The Glebe

Nearest Road: A.4042, M.4

The Glebe, overlooking this lovely part of rural Wales, is an ideal spot from which to explore this historic region with its numerous castles & abbeys & the book shops of Hay-on-Wye. Your friendly & helpful host is only too happy to help you plan if need be. Cardiff, capital of Wales, is 20 mins', London Heathrow Airport 2 1/2 hrs. The tastefully decorated bedrooms are centrally heated & have a hospitality tray. Breakfast menu. In the evening good pub fare is a pleasant country stroll away. Very convenient M.4 & M.5.

Mrs Beryl Watkins The Glebe Croes-Y-Ceiliog Cwmbran Newport NP44 2DE Gwent
Tel: (01633) 450251/450242 Open: ALL YEAR Map Ref No. 24

Abercelyn Country House

Nearest Road: A.494

Set in landscaped gardens with its own mountain stream running alongside, this former rectory dates back to before 1721. Situated in the Snowdonia National Park, it is ideally located for walking or touring amongst the spectacular scenery. Bright & spacious en-suite bedrooms with views over Bala Lake, evenings relaxing before open log fires, & informal conversation over traditional breakfasts with home-baked bread, preserves & fresh coffee.
E-mail: abercelyn@celtrail.com

see PHOTO over p. 539

VISA: M'CARD:

Mrs Judith Cunningham Abercelyn Country House Llanycil Bala LL23 7YF Gwynedd
Tel: (01678) 521109 Fax 01678 520556 Open: ALL YEAR (Excl. Xmas) Map Ref No. 26

The White House

Nearest Road: A.487

The White House is a large detached house set in its own grounds, overlooking Foryd Bay, & with the Snowdonia mountains behind. Accommodation is in 4 tastefully decorated bedrooms, all with bath or shower, tea/coffee-making facilities & colour T.V.. Guests are welcome to use the residents' lounge, outdoor pool & gardens. Ideally situated for birdwatching, walking, windsurfing, golf & visiting the historic Welsh castles.
E-mail: RWBAYLES@SJMS.CO.UK

Richard W. Bayles The White House Llanfaglan Caernarfon LL54 5RA Gwynedd
Tel: (01286) 673003 Fax 01286 673003 Open: MAR - NOV Map Ref No. 27

Ty'n Rhos

Nearest Road: B.4366

Tyn Rhos is a special place, set in a splendid location on the wide-open plain running between Snowdonia & the sea. Once a working farmhouse, it has now been transformed into a country house of great charm & comfort. Each individually designed bedroom is furnished to a high standard. 5 ground floor bedrooms have patio doors opening onto the garden. Award-winning Ty'n Rhos serves super meals. Quality & exceptional value are the keynotes here. Children over 6.
E-mail: Enquiries@tynrhos.co.uk

VISA: M'CARD: AMEX:

Lynda Kettle Ty'n Rhos Seion Llanddeiniolen Caernarfon LL55 3AE Gwynedd
Tel: (01248) 670489 Fax 01248 670079 Open: ALL YEAR (Excl. Xmas) Map Ref No. 28

Abercelyn. Llanycil.

Pentre Bach. Llwyngwril.

rate £ from - to per person | children taken | evening meals | animals taken

Wales
Gwynedd

Min-Y-Gaer Hotel

rate £ from - to per person	children taken	evening meals	animals taken
£22.00 to £25.00	Y	N	Y

VISA: M'CARD: AMEX:

Nearest Road: A.497

A pleasant, licensed house in a quiet residential area, offering very good accommodation in 10 comfortable rooms, all of which have a bathroom en-suite. All rooms are non-smoking & have colour T.V. & tea/coffee-making facilities. The hotel enjoys commanding views of Criccieth Castle & the scenic Cardigan Bay coastline, & is only 2 mins' walk from the safe, sandy beach. Car parking. An ideal base for touring Snowdonia.

E-mail: info@minygaerhotel.co.uk

Mrs Rita Murray Min-Y-Gaer Hotel Porthmadog Road Criccieth LL52 0HP Gwynedd
Tel: (01766) 522151 Fax 01766 523540 Open: APR- OCT Map Ref No. 29

Pentre Bach

rate £ from - to per person	children taken	evening meals	animals taken
£25.00 to £30.00	N	Y	N

see PHOTO over p. 540

VISA: M'CARD:

Nearest Road: A.493

Large, warm, peaceful, award-winning farmhouse in pretty coastal village in Snowdonia National Park, with BR station. Delicious food prepared by Mid-Wales Cook of the Year 1994, including free-range eggs, organic produce & herbs. Accommodation is in 3 attractive en-suite guest rooms, each with T.V. & easy chairs. Nick Smyth offers Land Rover tours through history in the adjacent mountains. Close to the sea, beaches, forests, rivers, steam railways, castles & pony trekking.

Email: bbb@pentrebach.com

Mrs Margaret Smyth Pentre Bach Llwyngwril Nr. Dolgellau LL37 2JU Gwynedd
Tel: (01341) 250294 Fax 01341 250885 Open: FEB - NOV Map Ref No. 30

Gwrach Ynys Country Guest House

rate £ from - to per person	children taken	evening meals	animals taken
£22.00 to £28.00	Y	Y	N

Nearest Road: A.496

A warm Welsh welcome awaits you at Gwrach Ynys, a 7 bedroom Edwardian country house set in 1 acre of garden, nestled between the sea & the mountains in beautiful Snowdonia National Park. En-suite bedrooms, individually decorated & furnished to a high standard. 2 comfortable guest lounges & a separate dining room. Ideally located for exploring North Wales. Superb area for walkers, birdwatchers & golfers. Children over 3.

E-mail: gwynfor@talk21.com

Deborah Williams Gwrach Ynys Country Guest House Talsarnall Harlech LL47 6TS Gwynedd
Tel: (01766) 780742 Fax 01766 781199 Open: MAR - OCT Map Ref No. 32

Cefn Coch Country Guest House

rate £ from - to per person	children taken	evening meals	animals taken
£22.00 to £24.00	N	Y	N

Nearest Road: A.493

Cefn Coch is an old coaching inn on the edge of the Snowdonia National Park & is surrounded by over an acre of gardens & paddock. It has been tastefully renovated throughout & now provides quality accommodation. There are 2 attractively furnished bedrooms, each with an en-suite bathroom & tea/coffee-making facilities. Delicious evening meals are served. Guests can enjoy the extensive views of the local countryside. The beautiful Cardigan Bay coast is nearby. A delightful home.

E-mail: david@cefncoch.force9.co.uk

David & Anne Sylvester Cefn Coch Country Guest House Llanegryn Tywyn LL36 9SD Gwynedd
Tel: (01654) 712193 Fax 01654 712193 Open: FEB - OCT Map Ref No. 33

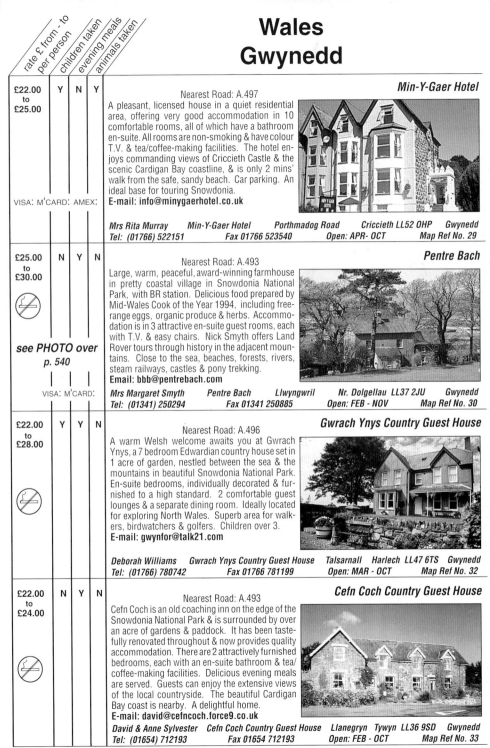

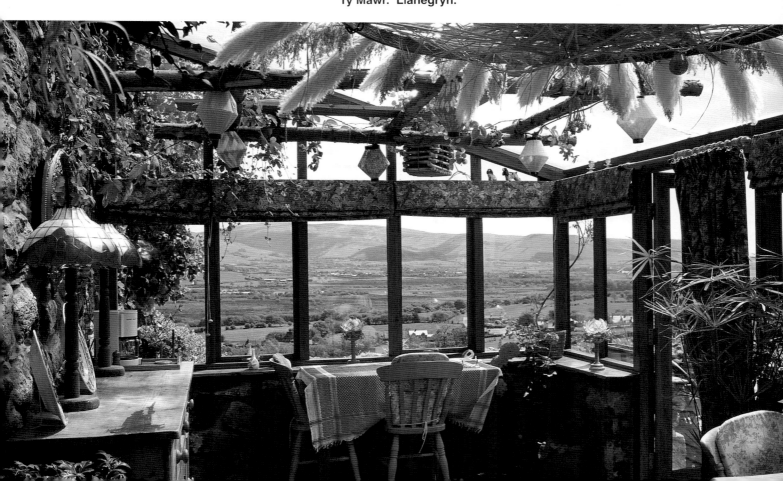

Ty Mawr. Llanegryn.

The Wenallt. Gilwern.

Wales
Gwynedd & Monmouthshire

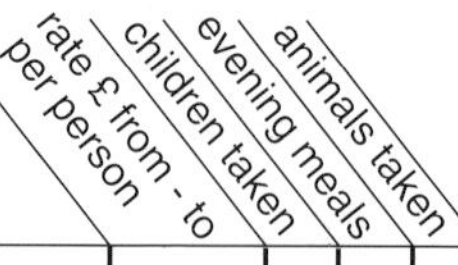

Ty Mawr

Nearest Road: A.493

With mountains to the east & sea to the west, Ty Mawr snugs into the south-facing slope of the Dysnni Valley. Total peace & quiet. There are private entrances to each ground-floor, en-suite bedroom, which are very comfortable & also have tea/coffee-making facilities. Enjoy meals in the conservatory overlooking the garden & valley. Numerous venues of interest, & local heritage. Links golf at Aberdovey. Children over 10 years welcome. Animals by arrangement.

Richard & Elizabeth Tregarthen *Ty Mawr* *Llanegryn* *Tywyn LL36 9SY* *Gwynedd*
Tel: (01654) 710507 *Fax 01654 710507* *Open: ALL YEAR* *Map Ref No. 34*

rate £ from - to per person	children taken	evening meals	animals taken
£22.50 to £££	Y	N	Y

see PHOTO over p. 542

The Wenallt

Nearest Road: A.465

A 16th-century Welsh longhouse set in 50 acres of farmland in the beautiful Brecon Beacons National Park & commanding magnificent views over the Usk Valley. Retaining all its old charm, with oak beams & an inglenook fireplace, yet offering a high standard of accommodation throughout, with comfortable en-suite bedrooms, good food & a very warm welcome. The Wenallt is an ideal base from which to see glorious Wales & the surrounding areas & attractions. Licensed.

B. L. Harris *The Wenallt* *Abergavenny NP7 0HP* *Monmouthshire*
Tel: (01873) 830694 *Fax 01873 830694* *Open: ALL YEAR* *Map Ref No. 36*

rate £ from - to per person	children taken	evening meals	animals taken
£19.50 to £28.00	Y	Y	Y

see PHOTO over p. 543

Llanwenarth House

Nearest Road: A.465

A truly delightful 16th-century manor house, standing in its own beautiful grounds & surrounded by the tranquil scenic hills of the Brecon Beacons National Park. Elegantly furnished, tastefully decorated & with superb views, this house is a real pleasure to visit. Dinner, prepared by Amanda, a Cordon Bleu cook, is a delight. It is served by candlelight in the lovely dining room. 4 en-suite bedrooms. Fishing, golf, climbing, walking & shooting nearby. No smoking in dining room or bedrooms. Single supplement. Children over 10.

Mrs Amanda Weatherill *Llanwenarth House* *Govilon* *Abergavenny NP7 9SF* *Monmouthshire*
Tel: (01873) 830289 *Fax 01873 832199* *Open: Late FEB - Mid JAN* *Map Ref No. 37*

rate £ from - to per person	children taken	evening meals	animals taken
£40.00 to £44.00	Y	Y	Y

see PHOTO over p. 545

Great House

Nearest Road: B.4596

Great House is an attractive 16th-century Grade II listed house located on the banks of the River Usk. Retaining much of its original character with beams & inglenook fireplaces, it offers 3 bedrooms (1 en-suite) with T.V. & tea/coffee facilities. A drawing room with woodburner. Within easy reach of golf, fishing & forest trails. Caerleon is very near with its amphitheatre, museums & Roman Baths. Good pubs. Ideal as a stop-over for those on the way through Wales or onto Ireland. Children over 10.
E-mail: price.greathouse@tesco.net

Dinah Price *Great House* *Isca Road* *Old Village* *Caerleon NP18 1QG* *Monmouthshire*
Tel: (01633) 420216 *Open: ALL YEAR* *Map Ref No. 38*

rate £ from - to per person	children taken	evening meals	animals taken
£25.00 to £30.00	Y	N	N

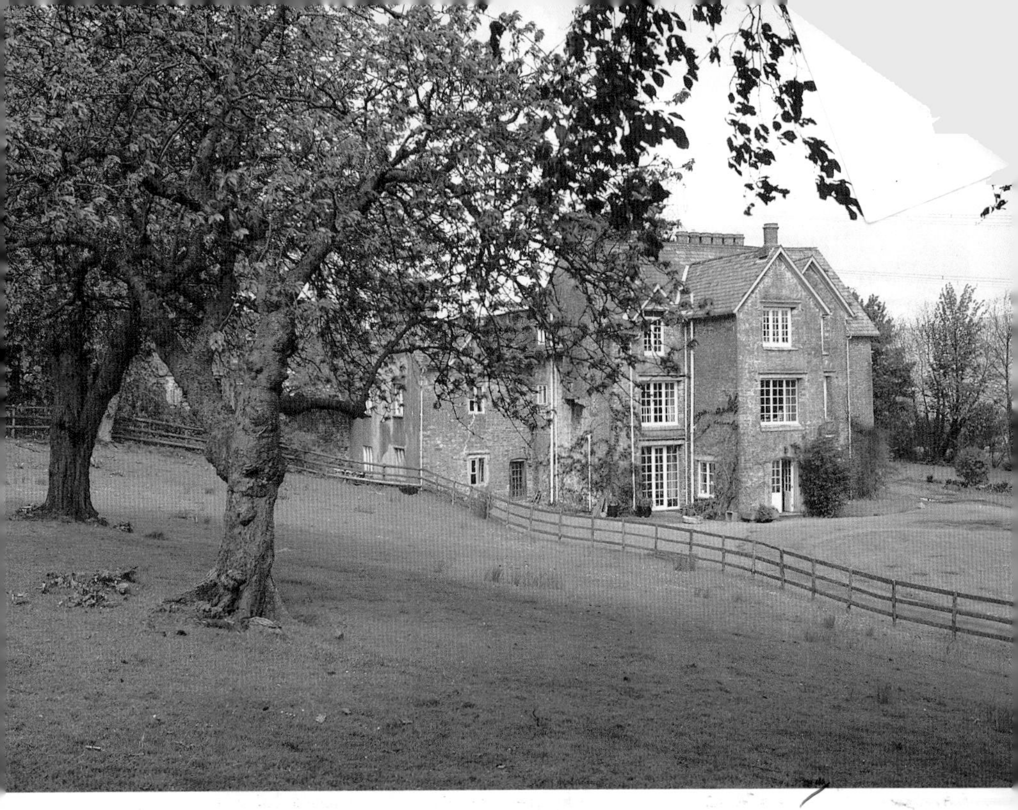

Llanwenarth House. Govilon.

Wales
Monmouthshire & Pembrokeshire

	rate £ from - to per person	children taken	evening meals	animals taken
Llanishen House	£25.00 to £35.00	Y	N	N
Brick House Country Guest House	£25.00 to £25.00	Y	Y	N
Parva Farmhouse Hotel & Restaurant	£34.00 to £38.00	Y	Y	Y
The Old Vicarage	£25.00 to £28.00	N	Y	N

Llanishen House

Nearest Road: A.466

17th-century country house set in 5 acres, in a beautiful, elevated position. Equidistant between Usk, Chepstow, Tintern & Monmouth. Twin-bedded en-suite room in tranquil converted stables with own sitting room & courtyard. Double-bedded room & private bathroom with stunning views over Usk Valley. Ideal touring centre for Wales & the West Country. 15 mins' from Severn Bridge. A walker's paradise. Light meals available by arrangement. Children over 10.

E-mail: dharmston@llewellin7.freeserve.co.uk

Mrs Jane Harmston Llanishen House Llanishen Chepstow NP16 6QS Monmouthshire
Tel: (01600) 860700 Fax 01600 860700 Open: ALL YEAR Map Ref No. 39

Brick House Country Guest House

Nearest Road: M.4 Jt. 23A

Brick House is a Grade II listed Georgian country house dating from about 1765, but with up-to-date conveniences. All double bedrooms have an en-suite bathroom. A pleasant T.V. lounge, dining room & bar. Full central heating. There is also a delightful garden where guests may take cream teas, weather permitting. Brick House is ideally situated for touring South Wales & the Wye Valley, or as a stopping-off point just over the Severn Bridge. Single supplement. Children over 10.

E-mail: brickhouse@compuserve.com

Mrs C. Park Brick House North Row Redwick Magor Newport NP26 3DX Monmouthshire
Tel: (01633) 880230 Fax 01633 882441 Open: ALL YEAR Map Ref No. 40

Parva Farmhouse Hotel & Restaurant

Nearest Road: A.466

A delightful 17th-century stone farmhouse situated 50 yards from the River Wye. The quaint en-suite bedrooms, with their designer fabrics, are gorgeous, & some offer breathtaking views over the River Wye & woodland. The beamed lounge, with log fires, leather Chesterfields & 'Honesty Bar', is a tranquil haven in which to unwind. Mouth-watering dishes, served in the intimate, candlelit Inglenook Restaurant, reflect the owner's love of cooking. A super home, perfect for a relaxing break or for exploring beautiful Wales.

see PHOTO over p. 547

VISA: M'CARD: AMEX:

Dereck & Vickie Stubbs Parva Farmhouse Hotel & Restaurant Tintern NP16 6SQ Monmouthshire
Tel: (01291) 689411 Fax 01291 689557 Open: ALL YEAR Map Ref No. 41

The Old Vicarage

Nearest Road: A.487

Patricia & David welcome you to their elegant Edwardian home set in an elevated position with large lawned gardens & glorious views to the sea. Offering 3 comfortably furnished en-suite bedrooms with tea/coffee-making facilities. Situated in Britain's only coastal National Park, 1 mile from one of the most dramatic sections of the Pembrokeshire Coast Path at Ceibwr Bay, with the Preseli Hills & Teifi Valley nearby. Enjoy the timeless & leisurely tranquillity of north Pembrokeshire. Croeso!

E-mail: stay@old-vic.co.uk

Patricia & David Phillips The Old Vicarage Moylegrove Cardigan SA43 3BN Pembrokeshire
Tel: (01239) 881231 Fax 01239 881341 Open: MAR - OCT Map Ref No. 42

Parva Farmhouse and Restaurant. Tintern.

	rate £ from - to per person	children taken	evening meals	animals taken
Cnapan	£30.00 to £37.00	Y	Y	N
Allenbrook	£25.00 to £25.00	N	N	N
Knowles Farm	£17.00 to £25.00	Y	Y	Y
The Peacock Tea Garden	£24.50 to £26.50	N	Y	N

Cnapan

Nearest Road: A.487

Cnapan is a Grade II listed house in the heart of historic Newport. It is beautifully furnished throughout & blessed with character. Bedrooms are spacious, comfortable & individually decorated. (All are en-suite with T.V. & tea/coffee-making facilities.) Meals are superb, from the hearty breakfasts to the mouth-watering dishes served at dinner. Many varied interests & activities are on the doorstep. Parrog Beach & Newport Sands are within a short walk, also the spectacular coastal path.

E-mail: cnapan@online-holidays.net

VISA: M'CARD:

Mr & Mrs Cooper & Mr & Mrs Lloyd Cnapan East Street Newport Fishguard SA42 0SY
Tel: (01239) 820575 Fax 01239 820878 Open: MAR - DEC Map Ref No. 43

Allenbrook

Nearest Road: A.40

Allenbrook is a charming country house set in its own grounds. It is adjacent to the beach & situated in the Pembrokeshire National Park on the coastal path. The house is very comfortable with spacious bedrooms fully-equipped with T.V. & tea/coffee-making facilities. All the bedrooms have en-suite or private bathrooms, & there is a large, comfortable guests' sitting room. A delightful home & an ideal spot for a relaxing short break or holiday.

E-mail: allenbrook@talk21.com

Mrs E. A. Webber Allenbrook Dale Haverfordwest SA62 3RN Pembrokeshire
Tel: (01646) 636254 Fax 01646 636954 Open: ALL YEAR Map Ref No. 45

Knowles Farm

Nearest Road: A.4075

Relax, unwind & prepare to be pampered in this lovely south-facing family home overlooking the Milford Haven Estuary. Knowles Farm has access to farmland & ancient woodland & is within 15 mins' of the glorious Pembrokeshire coast. There are castles, ancient monuments & theme parks surrounding Knowles Farm, & lovely walks are on the doorstep. Riding, fishing, bird-watching & boating within minutes. After a day out, a special meal (with notice) in the lovely dining room.

E-mail: ginilp@lawrenny.org.uk

Mrs Virginia Lort Phillips Knowles Farm Lawrenny SA68 0PX Pembrokeshire
Tel: (01834) 891221 Fax 01834 891344 Open: EASTER - OCT Map Ref No. 46

The Peacock Tea Garden

Nearest Road: A.40, A.477

Set in its own grounds in the heart of the Pembrokeshire countryside. The Peacock Tea Garden offers attractive accommodation in 2 pretty bedrooms. 1 double en-suite & 1 twin with private bathroom, each with T.V. & tea/coffee. Excellent breakfasts. Delicious traditional afternoon & cream teas served in the tea garden & conservatory. A lovely base for exploring the glorious Welsh countryside & many attractions. Evening meals by arrangement. Licensed. Children over 12.

E-mail: Peacock@jpmarketing.co.uk

Ros & Joe Mooney The Peacock Tea Garden Hoarstone House Martletwy Narberth SA67 8AZ
Tel: (01834) 891707 Fax 01834 891707 Open: APR - OCT Map Ref No. 47

Wales
Pembrokeshire & Powys

rate £ from - to per person	children taken	evening meals	animals taken	
£22.50 to £22.50	Y	N	N	**Merrifields** Nearest Road: A.477 Merrifields is a modern Scandinavian-style bungalow in an elevated position overlooking Carmarthen Bay. Attractive gardens, with patios & ample parking, give splendid isolation yet easy access to the many tourist attractions of the area. There are 2 attractive bedrooms, each with an en-suite/private bathroom. Situated on the outskirts of Amroth offering unrivalled views over Carmarthen Bay to the popular resorts of Tenby & Saundersfoot. Merrifields is the ideal place to unwind. *Mrs Suzanne Evans Merrifields Amroth Narberth SA67 8NW Pembrokeshire* *Tel: (01834) 813005 Open: ALL YEAR Map Ref No. 48*
£22.50 to £25.00	Y	N	N	**The Old Vicarage** Nearest Road: A.4139 Situated in the coastal village of Manorbier with its beautiful beaches & castle, The Old Vicarage offers gracious accommodation with glimpses of Barafundle Bay. The en-suite bedrooms are furnished with antiques & have tea/coffee facilities. Guests may enjoy the mature gardens or sit by a log fire in the drawing room. For the more energetic, the Pembrokeshire Coastal Path passes through the village. Beaches a 5-min. walk. Irish ferries from Pembroke (20 mins') & Fishguard (50 mins'). **E-mail: Oldvic@manorbier-tenby.fsnet.co.uk** *Mrs Jill McHugh The Old Vicarage Manorbier Tenby SA70 7TN Pembrokeshire* *Tel: (01834) 871452 Fax 01834 871452 Open: ALL YEAR Map Ref No. 49*
£35.00 to £45.00 VISA: M'CARD: AMEX:	Y	Y	N	**Penrhadw Farm** Nearest Road: A.470 A wonderful opportunity for you to base yourself deep in the National Park, yet benefit from the high level of service typically afforded of a top grade hotel. Penrhadw Farm has been specially designed to cater for guests wishing to explore the surrounding countryside. The farm allows easy access straight out onto the Beacons. It is popular with artists, photographers, hangliders, pony trekkers & bird watchers. A pair of Red Kites & Peregrine Falcons regularly visit the surrounding farmland. **E-mail: reception@tregenna.co.uk** *Mrs Kathleen Hurley Penrhadw Farm Pontsticill Brecon CF48 2TU Powys* *Tel: (01685) 723481 Fax 01685 721951 Open: ALL YEAR Map Ref No. 50*
£20.00 to £20.00	Y	N	Y	**Dolycoed** Nearest Road: A.40 Dolycoed, built at the turn of the century, retains many of its interesting original features. Standing in a sheltered position in the Brecon Beacons National Park, it offers a warm, friendly, homely welcome to all. Accommodation is in 2 comfortably furnished guest bedrooms, with radio & tea/coffee makers, & a guests' lounge with colour T.V.. There are many outdoor activities nearby including pony trekking, riding, fishing, watersports & walking. Dolycoed is ideal for a relaxing break. *Mrs H. M. Cole Dolycoed Talyllyn Brecon LD3 7SY Powys* *Tel: (01874) 658666 Open: ALL YEAR Map Ref No. 54*

Glangrwyney Court. Crickhowell.

York House. Cusop.

Wales
Powys

	rate £ from - to per person	children taken	evening meals	animals taken
The Beacons	£19.00 to £32.50	Y	Y	Y
Ty-Isaf Farm	£15.00 to £16.00	Y	N	Y
Glangrwyney Court	£27.50 to £30.00	Y	N	Y
York House	£25.00 to £27.00	Y	Y	Y

The Beacons

Nearest Road: A.40

Recently restored 17th/18th-century house retaining many of its original features. Well-appointed standard, en-suite & luxury period rooms. Enjoy a drink in the original meat cellar (complete with hooks) or relax in a comfortable armchair in front of the fire. The award-winning chef will spoil you with outstanding cuisine freshly cooked to your order. The Beacons is a delightful home & an excellent base for a relaxing break.

E-mail: beacons@brecon.co.uk

VISA: M'CARD:

Peter & Barbara Jackson *The Beacons* *16 Bridge Street* *Brecon LD3 8AH* *Powys*
Tel: (01874) 623339 *Fax 01874 623339* *Open: ALL YEAR* *Map Ref No. 55*

Ty-Isaf Farm

Nearest Road: A.470

Ty-Isaf Farm, situated in the attractive village of Erwood, offers charming accommodation in 3 attractive & comfortably furnished rooms with modern amenities & tea/coffee-making facilities. Plentiful English or Continental breakfasts are served. Special diets & packed lunches are provided by arrangement. Guests may chose to relax in the cosy lounge, with T.V. throughout the day. An ideal base for a relaxing break or for exploring this lovely part of Wales & its many attractions.

Nancy M. Jones *Ty-Isaf Farm* *Erwood* *Builth Wells LD2 3SZ* *Powys*
Tel: (01982) 560607 *Open: ALL YEAR* *Map Ref No. 56*

Glangrwyney Court

Nearest Road: A.40

Glangrwyney Court is a Georgian mansion set in 4 acres of established gardens & surrounded by parkland. All rooms are comfortably furnished with antiques & fine porcelain & paintings, & there is a welcoming & homely atmosphere. Accommodation is in 5 attractive & well-appointed bedrooms, each with a private or en-suite bathroom. During the winter, log fires burn in all the sitting rooms, & in the summer guests are able to relax with a drink in the gardens. Evening meals by arrangement.

E-mail: glangrwyne@aol.com

see PHOTO over p. 550

Mrs C. R. Jackson *Glangrwyney Court* *Crickhowell NP8 1ES* *Powys*
Tel: (01873) 811288 *Fax 01873 810317* *Open: ALL YEAR* *Map Ref No. 57*

York House

Nearest Road: A.438

Peter and Olwen Roberts welcome you to their traditional Victorian guest house quietly situated in beautiful gardens on the edge of Hay. Sunny mountain views are enjoyed by all the well-appointed en-suite rooms. Ideal for a relaxing holiday spent browsing in the world-famous bookshops, exploring the National Park and Kilvert country, or just enjoying the freshly prepared home cooking. Evening meals by arrangement. Private parking. Children over 8 years welcome.

see PHOTO over p. 551

VISA: M'CARD: AMEX:

Peter & Olwen Roberts *York House* *Hardwicke Road* *Cusop* *Hay-on-Wye HR3 5QX* *Powys*
Tel: (01497) 820705 *Fax 01497 820705* *Open: ALL YEAR* *Map Ref No. 58*

Guidfa House. Llandrindod Wells.

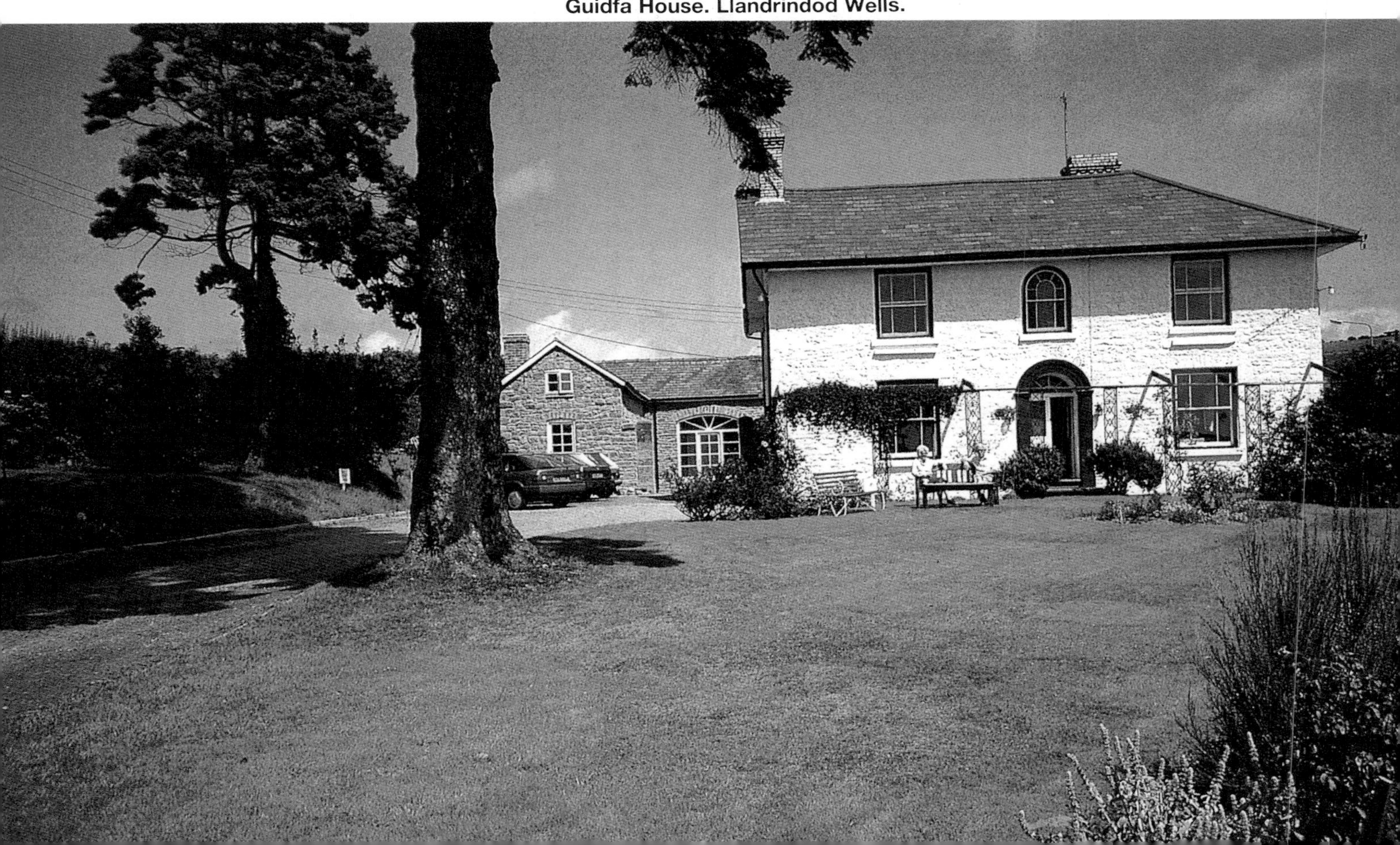

Wales
Powys & Swansea

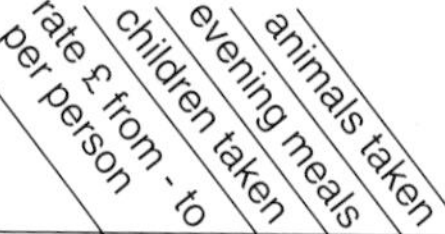

Guidfa House

Nearest Road: A.483, A.44

Licensed Georgian guest house, situated in an ideal location for touring lakes, mountains, national parks & the coast. The bedrooms are all comfortable, non-smoking & spacious, most en-suite, all with colour T.V. & tea/coffee-making facilities. A ground-floor room is also available. Meals are prepared by Anne, who is Cordon-Bleu-trained. Dinner is a set menu, but special diets/requests can always be catered for with prior notice. Children over 10.
E-mail: guidfa@globalnet.co.uk

rate £ from - to per person	children taken	evening meals	animals taken
£26.50 to £26.50	Y	Y	N

see PHOTO over p. 553

VISA: M'CARD:

Anne & Tony Millan — *Guidfa House* — *Crossgates* — *Llandrindod Wells LD1 6RF* — *Powys*
Tel: (01597) 851241 — *Fax 01597 851875* — *Open: ALL YEAR* — *Map Ref No. 59*

Little Brompton Farm

Nearest Road: B.4385, A.489

Robert & Gaynor welcome you to this charming 17th-century farmhouse, situated on this working farm. The house has much original character, with beautiful old oak beams. Pretty en-suite bedrooms enhanced by quality antiques. T.V.. Home-cooking is a speciality, although evening meals are by arrangement. Offa's Dyke runs through the farm. Situated on the B.4385, 2 miles east of the Georgian town of Montgomery. Relax in peaceful, stress-free countryside. Animals by arrangement.
E-mail: gaynor.brompton@virgin.net

rate £ from - to per person	children taken	evening meals	animals taken
£21.00 to £23.00	Y	Y	Y

Robert & Gaynor Bright — *Little Brompton Farm* — *Montgomery SY15 6HY* — *Powys*
Tel: (01686) 668371 — *Fax 01686 668371* — *Open: ALL YEAR* — *Map Ref No. 61*

Lower Trelydan

Nearest Road: A.490

Graham & Sue welcome you to their wonderful, award-winning black-&-white farmhouse, set on their working farm & listed for its history & beauty. Bedrooms are en-suite, tastefully furnished & have T.V.. An oak-beamed lounge, & a dining room where evening meals are served most nights. Home cooking a speciality. Licensed bar. Powis Castle & many beauty spots are nearby, as well as leisure activities & walks. Capture the atmosphere of 4 centuries of history in this outstanding house.
E-mail: stay@lowertrelydan.com

rate £ from - to per person	children taken	evening meals	animals taken
£24.00 to £25.00	Y	Y	N

see PHOTO over p. 555

Mrs Sue Jones — *Lower Trelydan* — *Guilsfield* — *Welshpool SY21 9PH* — *Powys*
Tel: (01938) 553105 — *Fax 01938 553105* — *Open: ALL YEAR* — *Map Ref No. 63*

Tides Reach

Nearest Road: A.40367

The warmest of welcomes awaits you at Tides Reach, where you will find a lovingly restored early Victorian town house elegantly furnished with antiques. There are 6 attractive bedrooms, each with private facilities. Well situated on the seafront in the delightful village of Mumbles (the gateway to Gower), only 4 miles from the city centre. An ideal base for business or pleasure & convenient as a stop on your way to Ireland.
E-mail: mayberyantiques@hemscott.net

rate £ from - to per person	children taken	evening meals	animals taken
£25.00 to £30.00	N	N	Y

Mrs Jan Maybery — *Tides Reach* — *388 Mumbles Road* — *Mumbles* — *Swansea SA3 5TN* — *Swansea*
Tel: (01792) 404877 — *Fax 01792 404775* — *Open: FEB - NOV* — *Map Ref No. 64*

Lower Trelydan Farm. Guilsfield.

Towns & Counties Index

Town	County	Country
Abergavenny	Monmouthshire	Wales
Aboyne	Aberdeenshire	Scotland
Alcester	Warwickshire	England
Alnwick	Northumberland	England
Alresford	Hampshire	England
Altrincham	Cheshire	England
Ambleside	Cumbria	England
Ampleforth	Yorkshire	England
Andover	Hampshire	England
Anstruther	Fifeshire	Scotland
Appin	Argyll	Scotland
Ardrishaig	Argyll	Scotland
Arundel	Sussex	England
Ashbourne	Derbyshire	England
Ashford	Kent	England
Auchtermuchty	Fifeshire	Scotland
Aylmerton	Norfolk	England
Ayr	Ayrshire	Scotland
Bala	Gwynedd	Wales
Ballantrae	Ayrshire	Scotland
Banbury	Oxfordshire	England
Barnstaple	Devon	England
Bath	Somerset	England
Bedale	Yorkshire	England
Bedford	Bedfordshire	England
Belford	Northumberland	England
Belper	Derbyshire	England
Berkhamsted	Hertfordshire	England
Betws-Y-Coed	Conwy	Wales
Beverley	Yorkshire	England
Bideford	Devon	England
Bingley	Yorkshire	England
Bishop Auckland	Durham	England
Bishop's Stortford	Essex	England
Blidworth	Nottinghamshire	England
Bolney	Sussex	England
Bordon	Hampshire	England
Boscastle	Cornwall	England
Boston Spa	Yorkshire	England
Bourne	Lincolnshire	England
Bournemouth	Dorset	England
Bourton-on-the-Water	Gloucestershire	England
Bovey Tracey	Devon	England
Bowness-on-Windermere	Cumbria	England
Bradford-on-Avon	Wiltshire	England
Brampton	Cumbria	England
Braunton	Devon	England
Brecon	Powys	Wales
Bridgwater	Somerset	England
Bridlington	Yorkshire	England
Bridport	Dorset	England
Brighton	Sussex	England
Bristol	Gloucestershire	England
Bristol	Somerset	England
Broadford	Isle of Skye	Scotland
Broadstairs	Kent	England
Broadway	Worcestershire	England
Broadway	Gloucestershire	England
Builth Wells	Powys	Wales
Bungay	Suffolk	England
Burnley	Lancashire	England
Buttermere	Cumbria	England
Buxton	Derbyshire	England
Caerleon	Monmouthshire	Wales
Caernarfon	Gwynedd	Wales
Callander	Perthshire	Scotland
Camberley	Surrey	England
Cambridge	Cambridgeshire	England
Canterbury	Kent	England
Cardigan	Pembrokeshire	Wales
Carlisle	Cumbria	England
Carmarthen	Carmarthenshire	Wales
Carnforth	Lancashire	England
Chagford	Devon	England
Chard	Somerset	England
Chelmsford	Essex	England
Cheltenham	Gloucestershire	England
Chepstow	Monmouthshire	Wales
Chester	Cheshire	England
Chichester	Sussex	England
Chippenham	Wiltshire	England
Chipping Campden	Gloucestershire	England
Cholsey	Oxfordshire	England
Christchurch	Hampshire	England
Cirencester	Gloucestershire	England
Clitheroe	Lancashire	England
Coalville	Leicestershire	England
Cockermouth	Cumbria	England
Colchester	Essex	England
Corbridge	Northumberland	England
Corfe Castle	Dorset	England
Corsham	Wiltshire	England
Corstorphine	Edinburgh	Scotland
Corwen	Denbighshire	Wales
Crackington Haven	Cornwall	England
Cranbrook	Kent	England
Craven Arms	Shropshire	England
Crediton	Devon	England
Crianlarich	Perthshire	Scotland
Criccieth	Gwynedd	Wales
Crickhowell	Powys	Wales
Cricklade	Wiltshire	England
Darlington	Yorkshire	England
Dartmouth	Devon	England
Dereham	Norfolk	England
Didmarton	Gloucestershire	England
Diss	Norfolk	England
Dolgellau	Gwynedd	Wales
Dorchester	Dorset	England
Dorking	Surrey	England
Doune	Perthshire	Scotland
Dover	Kent	England
Dumbarton	Dunbartonshire	Scotland
Dumfries	Dumfriesshire	Scotland
Dundee	Tayside	Scotland
Dunkeld	Perthshire	Scotland
Dunoon	Argyll	Scotland
Duns	Berwickshire	Scotland
Dunster	Somerset	England
Durham	Durham	England
Duror in Appin	Argyll	Scotland
Easingwold	Yorkshire	England
East Lothian	Lothian	Scotland
Eastbourne	Sussex	England
Edinbane	Isle of Skye	Scotland
Edinburgh	Edinburgh	Scotland
Ely	Cambridgeshire	England
Ettington	Warwickshire	England
Evesham	Worcestershire	England
Exeter	Devon	England
Exmoor National Park	Somerset	England
Eyam	Derbyshire	England

Towns & Counties Index

Town	County	Country
Falmouth	Cornwall	England
Farnham	Hampshire	England
Faversham	Kent	England
Fintry	Stirlingshire	Scotland
Fishguard	Pembrokeshire	Wales
Folkestone	Kent	England
Fordham	Cambridgeshire	England
Fordingbridge	Hampshire	England
Forres	Morayshire	Scotland
Fort William	Inverness-shire	Scotland
Gainsborough	Lincolnshire	England
Garway	Herefordshire	England
Gatwick	Surrey	England
Girvan	Ayrshire	Scotland
Glasgow	Glasgow	Scotland
Glastonbury	Somerset	England
Goudhurst	Kent	England
Grange-over-Sands	Cumbria	England
Grantown-on-Spey	Morayshire	Scotland
Grasmere	Cumbria	England
Guildford	Surrey	England
Hadleigh	Suffolk	England
Harlech	Gwynedd	Wales
Harrogate	Yorkshire	England
Hartfield	Sussex	England
Haslemere	Surrey	England
Hastings	Sussex	England
Haverfordwest	Pembrokeshire	Wales
Hawes	Yorkshire	England
Hawkhurst	Kent	England
Hay-on-Wye	Powys	Wales
Haywards Heath	Sussex	England
Helston	Cornwall	England
Henfield	Sussex	England
Henley	Oxfordshire	England
Henley-on-Thames	Buckinghamshire	England
Hereford	Herefordshire	England
Herstmonceux	Sussex	England
Hexham	Northumberland	England
Hillesden Hamlet	Buckinghamshire	England
Holbeach	Lincolnshire	England
Holywell	Flintshire	Wales
Honiton	Devon	England
Hope Valley	Derbyshire	England
Horley	Surrey	England
Horsham	Sussex	England
Hungerford	Berkshire	England
Hunstanton	Norfolk	England
Hurstpierpoint	Sussex	England
Inverness	Inverness-shire	Scotland
Ironbridge	Shropshire	England
Isle of Anglesey	Anglesey	Wales
Isle of Islay	Argyll	Scotland
Isle of Mull	Argyll	Scotland
Isle of Wight	Hampshire	England
Jedburgh	Roxburghshire	Scotland
Kelso	Roxburghshire	Scotland
Kendal	Cumbria	England
Kenilworth	Warwickshire	England
Kentallen of Appin	Argyll	Scotland
Keswick	Cumbria	England
Kettering	Northamptonshire	England
Kilmarnock	Ayrshire	Scotland
King's Lynn	Norfolk	England
Kingham	Oxfordshire	England
Kingsbridge	Devon	England
Kington	Herefordshire	England
Kirkby Lonsdale	Cumbria	England
Knebworth	Hertfordshire	England
Knutsford	Cheshire	England
Launceston	Cornwall	England
Lawrenny	Pembrokeshire	Wales
Leamington Spa	Warwickshire	England
Leeds	Yorkshire	England
Leek	Staffordshire	England
Leigh	Gloucestershire	England
Leighton Buzzard	Bedfordshire	England
Leominster	Herefordshire	England
Lewes	Sussex	England
Leyburn	Yorkshire	England
Lincoln	Lincolnshire	England
Liskeard	Cornwall	England
Lizard	Cornwall	England
Llandrindod	Powys	Wales
Llandudno	Conwy	Wales
Llangollen	Denbighshire	Wales
Llanrwst	Conwy	Wales
Lochwinnoch	Renfrewshire	Scotland
Lockerbie	Dumfriesshire	Scotland
London	London	England
Longhope	Gloucestershire	England
Looe	Cornwall	England
Lorton	Cumbria	England
Ludlow	Shropshire	England
Lydney	Gloucestershire	England
Lyme Regis	Dorset	England
Lymington	Hampshire	England
Lyndhurst	Hampshire	England
Lynton	Devon	England
Macclesfield	Cheshire	England
Maidenhead	Berkshire	England
Maidstone	Kent	England
Malton	Yorkshire	England
Malvern	Worcestershire	England
Mansfield	Nottinghamshire	England
Margate	Kent	England
Market Drayton	Shropshire	England
Market Rasen	Lincolnshire	England
Marlborough	Wiltshire	England
Matlock	Derbyshire	England
Mayfield	Sussex	England
Melton Mowbray	Leicestershire	England
Merthyr Tydfil	Glamorgan	Wales
Midhurst	Sussex	England
Minchinhampton	Gloucestershire	England
Minehead	Somerset	England
Mitcheldean	Gloucestershire	England
Moffat	Dumfriesshire	Scotland
Mold	Flintshire	Wales
Montgomery	Powys	Wales
Morchard Bishop	Devon	England
Moreton-in-Marsh	Gloucestershire	England
Moretonhampstead	Devon	England
Morpeth	Northumberland	England
Nairn	Nairnshire	Scotland
Narberth	Pembrokeshire	Wales
Needham Market	Suffolk	England
New Forest	Hampshire	England
Newbury	Berkshire	England
Newport	Monmouthshire	Wales
Newport	Gwent	Wales
Newquay	Cornwall	England

Towns & Counties Index

Complaint 2001

Thank you for taking the trouble to supply this information .
We value your comments & will take appropriate action where necessary.
We regret that we are unable to reply to you individually.

Proprietors____

House Name______________________________________

Address____

____

Please be specific about your complaint. State exactly what was wrong with your stay e.g. the room, food, house keeping etc.

*Date of stay*____

____

____

____

____

____

____

____

Your Name_______________________________________

Address____

____

Reply to:W.W.B.B.A. P.O. Box 2070,
London. W12 8QW

Recommendation 2001

Thank you for taking the trouble to supply this information .
We value your comments & will take appropriate action where necessary.
We regret that we are unable to reply to you individually.

Proprietors ____

House Name ____

Address ____

Please give some general information about your stay, the house, rooms, food & hosts etc.

Date of stay ____

Your Name ____

Address ____

Reply to: W.W.B.B.A. P.O. Box 2070.
London. W12 8QW